ATLAS OF THE EASTERN FRONT 1941–45

'ROADS TO MOSCOW', BY AL STEWART

They crossed over the border the hour before dawn
moving in lines through the day
Most of our planes were destroyed on the ground where they lay
Waiting for orders we held in the wood
Word from the front never came
By evening the sound of the gunfire was miles away
I softly move through the shadows, slip away through the trees
Crossing their lines in the mist in the fields on our hands and our knees

And all that I ever
Was able to see
The fire in the air, glowing red
Silhouetting the smoke on the breeze

All summer they drove us back through the Ukraine
Smolensk and Viazma soon fell
By autumn we stood with our backs to the town of Orel
Closer and closer to Moscow they come
Riding the wind like a bell
General Guderian stands at the crest of the hill
Winter brought with it the rains, oceans of mud filled the roads
Gluing the tracks of their tanks to the ground, while the skies filled
with snow

And all that I ever
Was able to see
The fire in the air, glowing red
Silhouetting the snow on the breeze

In the footsteps of Napoleon, the shadow figures stagger through the
winter
Falling back before the gates of Moscow, standing in the wings like an
avenger
And far away behind their lines, the partisans are stirring in the forest
Coming unexpectedly upon their outpost, growing like a promise
You'll never know, you'll never know, which way to turn, which way to
look, you'll never see us
As we steal into the blackness of the night you'll never know, you'll

never hear us
And evening sings in a voice of amber, the dawn is surely coming
The morning road leads to Stalingrad, and the sky is softly humming

Two broken Tigers on fire in the night
Flicker their souls to the wind
We wait in the lines for the final approach to begin
It's been almost four years that I've carried a gun
At home, it will almost be spring
The flames of the Tigers are lighting the road to Berlin
I quickly move through the ruins that bow to the ground
The old men and children they send out to face us, they can't slow us
down

And all that I ever
Was able to see
The eyes of the city are opening
Now it's the end of a dream

I'm coming home, I'm coming home , now you can taste it in the wind
the war is over
And I listen to the clicking of the train wheels as we roll across the
border
And now they ask about the time that I was caught behind their lines
and taken prisoner
They only held me for a day, a lucky break I say
They turn and listen closer
I'll never know, I'll never know, why I was taken from the line with all
the others
to board a special train and journey deep into the heart of holy Russia

And it's cold and damp in the transit camp and the air is still and sullen
and the pale sun of October whispers the snow will soon be coming
And I wonder when, I'll be home again and the morning answers 'never'
And the evening sighs and the steely Russian skies go on,
forever ...

Used by permission.

ATLAS OF THE
EASTERN
FRONT
1941–45

ROBERT KIRCHUBEL

with GARY KOMAR

OSPREY
PUBLISHING

OSPREY PUBLISHING
Bloomsbury Publishing Plc

Kemp House, Chawley Park, Cumnor Hill, Oxford OX2 9PH, UK
1385 Broadway, 5th Floor, New York, NY 10018, USA
29 Earlsfort Terrace, Dublin 2, Ireland
Email: info@ospreypublishing.com

OSPREY is a trademark of Osprey Publishing, a division of Bloomsbury Publishing Plc

First published in Great Britain in 2016

A CIP catalogue record for this book is available from the British Library

Robert Kirchubel has asserted his right under the Copyright, Designs and Patents Act, 1988, to be identified as the Author of this Work.

ISBN: 978 1 4728 0774 8

Maps by bounford.com
Typeset in Adobe Garamond Pro and Trajan Pro
Originated by PDQ Media, Bungay, UK
Printed and bound in India by Replika Press Private Ltd.

21 22 23 24 25   10 9 8 7 6 5 4

The Woodland Trust
Osprey Publishing supports the Woodland Trust, the UK's leading woodland conservation charity.

www.ospreypublishing.com
To find out more about our authors and books visit our website. Here you will find extracts, author interviews, details of forthcoming events and the option to sign-up for our newsletter.

AUTHOR'S NOTES

This book is written to the glory of God. I want to thank the usual suspects, especially Linda, Gary and Joe. More than once while preparing this atlas I had many other demands on my time, so had to lean particularly hard on Gary to do basic research. He came through like a hero, so therefore I gladly and thankfully share the title page with him. Also, thanks to Cheryl at Purdue University Library Interlibrary Loan, who managed to track down 99 per cent of my obscure requests. Compared to my other Osprey books, this atlas was a massive undertaking, and I'm very appreciative for Marcus' patience and understanding. Russell managed to juggle the project's numerous and complex parts with skill and equanimity.

Of course I've always known there is much more to the Nazi-Soviet War besides Operation *Barbarossa*. This atlas gave me the opportunity to study and write about the other 90 per cent of that war, plus attempt to redress the Campaign Series' emphasis on operations *Barbarossa*, *Blau*, *Zitadelle* and the German point of view in general, while giving the Red Army and Soviet operations their due.

More than half of the maps here are new and unique to this atlas. Of the remaining maps, many were almost completely redone while others needed only minor corrections or updates. Pre-existing Osprey maps or birds'-eye view graphics came from my own *Barbarossa* (2013) and the following Campaign Series volumes: *Bagration 1944* (CAM 42), *Berlin 1945* (CAM 159), *Demyansk 1942–43* (CAM 245), *Kharkov 1942* (CAM 254), *Kursk 1943* (CAM 16), *Leningrad 1941–44* (CAM 215), *Moscow 1941* (CAM 167), *Sevastopol 1942* (CAM 189), *Stalingrad 1942* (CAM 184), and *Warsaw 1944* (CAM 205). I also used maps from Osprey's hardbound *Battleground Prussia*, *Between Giants* and *Where the Iron Crosses Grow*.

I recall sitting in my California home as a young man in the mid-1970s, listening to rock'n'roll music on KZAP-FM and reading military history, probably something by Paul Carell. A song played in the background, but when I first heard the words 'Smolensk and Viazma soon fell', my ears perked up. The line 'General Guderian stands at the crest of the hill' soon followed and I really began to pay attention. As soon as the song finished I phoned the radio station to ask what the song was! It was Al Stewart's 'Roads to Moscow'. A couple of years later in 1977 I saw Al Stewart in concert at the University of California, Davis where I was as an undergraduate. He performed 'Roads to Moscow' complete with a slideshow of Nazi-Soviet War images. It was very cool and the high point of the evening. So far as I know it remains the only song, popular or otherwise, about that war from *Barbarossatag* to VE Day (and even beyond!).

The usual caveat for the study of all history, and it seems especially for the study of the Nazi-Soviet War, applies: no two sources completely agree and something by David Glantz usually had to serve as tiebreaker. Some notes on orders of battle and unit designations: all armies adjust their organization during operations as conditions dictate, but during World War II the Germans did this with great frequency. Therefore while a unit may belong to one headquarters at the beginning of an operation it could be shifted to different headquarters a week later and then back after another month. It is impractical to note all these changes on the maps or in the short texts explaining any given map. The German Army also changed the titles of its formations in the course of the war. For example, I have noted the change from 'panzer group' to 'panzer army', 'motorized infantry' to 'panzer grenadier' and 'light infantry' to 'Jäger'. However, I have employed 'panzer corps' throughout instead of using 'army corps (motorized)' before mid-1942 and then panzer corps afterwards. I use the following convention for numbering Wehrmacht organizations: Arabic for divisions and armies, Roman numerals for corps. Red Army units are always referred to by Arabic numerals except for named fronts. 'Infantry' and 'panzer' always refer to German units, while 'rifle' and 'tank' always refer to Red Army formations.

CONTENTS

CHAPTER 3, OPERATION *BLAU*, 1942   94

CHAPTER 4, SOVIET WINTER COUNTEROFFENSIVES, 1942–43   122

CHAPTER 5, SUMMER AND AUTUMN 1943   152

CHAPTER 6, SOVIET OFFENSIVES, 1944   180

CHAPTER 7, CENTRAL EUROPE AND GERMANY, 1945   224

APPENDICES   254

BIBLIOGRAPHY   270

LEGEND TO MAPS

←———	Advance (German)
←-----	Retreat (Soviet)
←.........	Movement (German)
↙	Screen (German)
------	Encirclement (Soviet)
⊓⊔⊓⊔⊓	Defensive line (German)
✿	Strongpoint (German)
⊕	Airfield

—··—··—	National border
++++++++++	Railway
	Marsh
═══════	Road
———————	River

———xxxxx———	Army Group boundary (German)
———xxxx———	Army boundary (Soviet)
———xxx———	Corps boundary (German)
———xx———	Division boundary (Soviet)

Army Group		⊠ (Mountain symbol)	Mountain
Army		⊠⚓	Navy
Corps		⊠	Commando
Division		⊡	Motorized
Brigade		⊓	Engineer
Regiment		•	Artillery
Battalion		••	Motorcycle
Company		⌣	Airborne
Infantry ⊠		Air defence	
Tank ⊜		▽ Parachute	
Cavalry ⊠		☐ Scattered units/remnants/outposts	

National forces are represented by the following colours. The darker shade is used to indicate initial positions and the lighter shade indicates later positions. Dates for these positions are usually indicated in the key on individual maps.

German	Italian
Soviet	Finnish
Romanian	Hungarian
Spanish	Slovakian
Polish	

To save space on the detailed maps in this book, the abbreviations below are often used alongside the unit symbols:

Soviet

Gd	Guard
LOG	Luga Operational Group
NKVD	People's Commissariat for Internal Affairs
NOG	Novgorod Operational Group

German

AH (SS)	Leibstandarte Adolf Hitler
D (SS)	Deutschland
Det	Corps Detachment
DF (SS)	Der Führer
DR (SS)	Das Reich
F (GD)	Fusilier
FBB (GD)	Führer Begleit Battalion
FG (SS)	Florian Geyer
FHH	Feldherrenhalle
FP	Fretter-Pico
G (GD)	Grenadier
GD	Grossdeutschland
H (SS)	Hohenstaufen
HG	Heeresgruppe
HG (LW)	Herman Göring
HJ (SS)	Hitler Jugend
Jäg	Jäger
KG	Kampfgruppe
Lt	Liecht (Light)
LW	Luftwaffe
MT (SS)	Maria Theresa
N (SS)	Nord
Ne (SS)	Nederland
No (SS)	Nordland
P (SS)	Polizei
Sec	Security
T (SS)	Totenkopf
V	Volksgrenadier
W (SS)	Wiking

Italian

C	Celere
Co	Cosseria
Cu	Cuneense
J	Julia
P	Pasubio
T	Torino
Tr	Tridentina
S	Szforesca
R	Ravenna
V	Vincenza

FINLAND

Helsinki

Lake
Onega

Lake
Ladoga

Leningrad

Tallinn

ESTONIA

Luga

Narva

Volkhov

Svir

Pskov

Staraya Russa

LATVIA

Riga

Daugavpils

Dvina

Vitebsk

Dnepr

Smolensk

Yelnia

Rzhev

Viazma

Kalinin

Moscow

Yaroslavl

Volga

Volga

Gorky

LITHUANIA

Kaunas

Königsberg

Vilnius

Minsk

Nemen

Ryazan

Danzig

Bryansk

Gomel

Orel

Berezina

Pripiat

Desna

Kursk

Voronezh

Rokitno Marshes

Warsaw

Brest

POLAND

Western Bug

SOVIET UNION

Rossosh

Krakow

Zithomir

Kiev

Kharkov

Przsmyzl

L'vov

Cherkassy

Poltava

Donets

Don

CZECHOSLOVAKIA

Uman

Dnepr

Millerovo

Southern Bug

Dnepropetrovsk

Voroshilovgrad

Stalingrad

HUNGARY

Dnestr

Krivoi Rog

Zaporozhe

Stalino

Budapest

Kishinev

Don

Kotelnikovo

Cluj

Rostov

Salsk

ROMANIA

Odessa

Cherson

Elista

Bucharest

Sevastopol

Krasnodar

Novorossisk

Maikop

YUGOSLAVIA

Tuapse

Piatigorsk

BULGARIA

Grozny

Sofia

Black Sea

Front line June 1941: pre war
Front line November 1941
Front line November 1942
Front line June 1943
Front line December 1943
Front line June 1944
Front line December 1944

0   200 miles
0   200km

OVERVIEW

The Nazi-Soviet War, the so-called Eastern Front, is the critical theatre of World War II. The titanic struggle between German Führer Adolf Hitler and Soviet Premier Josef Stalin and their despicable dictatorships has no equal. It is probably not an exaggeration to say that it is hard to imagine two nations, millions of combatants and tens of thousands of artillery pieces, armoured fighting vehicles and aircraft facing off along a single frontier at a single moment ever again. Other theatres of World War II exceeded the Nazi-Soviet War in some ways: the Battle for the Atlantic lasted longer, the Pacific theatre covered more square miles, and the Japanese war in China might have had every bit as much criminal behaviour. The Nazi-Soviet War went on continuously for nearly four years across varied terrain, with only minor pauses. It spanned Europe's highest peak and the desert-like steppe. Fighting took place in cities of millions, isolated outposts, nameless settlements, marshes and forests stretching from the Arctic Circle to the Black Sea. It spared neither combatants, nor wounded, nor civilians. Headline grabbing mechanized formations, huge infantry armies and irregular forces far from the fighting fronts killed and were killed with equal ferocity. Three German fighter aces combined to shoot down nearly 1,000 enemy aircraft, more planes than possessed by all but the world's very largest modern (in 2015) air forces. In short, the Nazi-Soviet War mirrored the toxic personalities of Hitler and Stalin on a continental scale.

At least as early as 1923, when writing *Mein Kampf*, Hitler considered domination of 'the east' as a German birthright. As his vision expanded, he saw Russia's human and natural resources as the perfect adjunct for his planned war of global domination against American-British maritime powers. For two years following the temporary and mutually beneficial Molotov-Ribbentrop treaty, Hitler consolidated power and tidied up the Third Reich's immediate vicinity, largely at the expense of France and Britain. During the same period Stalin was not idle, purging his officer corps, building up his military

and invading neighbours. The Red Army's performance until October 1942, however, reveals time poorly spent.

No responsible historian can write of Germany's involvement in World War II, especially in the east, without discussing Hitler's genocide. His anti-Semitic and anti-Slavic racial hatred pre-dates World War II by at least two decades. However, Operation *Barbarossa* is the intersection of Nazism's two main trajectories: aggressive war and eliminationist racism. There is no proof that Hitler told his subordinates to slaughter Jews and central and eastern Europeans; he did not have to, as they knew his intent. With the German military as willing accomplices, various Nazi organs came up with schemes such as *Generalplan Ost* (General Plan East) to exploit and exterminate their way east. Amateurs and the uninformed often ask, 'Why did Hitler waste so much potential anti-Soviet goodwill with his brutal occupation of the east?' or 'Why did Hitler waste so many resources – manpower, rail capacity, etc – on killing Jews and others in the region?' The answer is simple: to him racial murder was not some arbitrary or nonsensical afterthought, distraction or policy footnote tacked on to military conquest, but a main objective. The two goals were absolutely equal as the main foreign policy bookends of the Third Reich, and I urge the reader not to forget that fact while reading this volume.

***

When Hitler launched Operation *Barbarossa* on 22 June 1941, few people besides American President Franklin D. Roosevelt gave the USSR a chance; even Stalin required a few weeks to get over the shock of the invasion (Chapter 1). Consistent with centuries of doctrinal development, the Germans accepted huge risks in attacking the USSR and achieved strategic, operational and tactical surprise. To the Soviets' amazement, the Germans attacked simultaneously with apparent equal violence on northern, central and southern axes. The Red Army's forward defence, mandated by Stalin's personality and desire to hold on to his eastern European plunder, played to the Germans' strengths.

With panzer groups far to the fore, the Wehrmacht rent massive gaps in the defenders' lines and encircled pockets numbering tens and even hundreds of thousands of Soviet troops. As had happened to France a year before, the blitzkrieg shattered the defensive Soviets' system.[1] Unfortunately for the Germans, dissonance at the peak of their leadership, the relatively small size of their forces and sanguine logistical planning from the war's beginning minimized their advantages. Distance, weather and the defenders' constant counterattacks likewise took their toll on the Germans, but few contemporaries comprehended the damage done or understood its implications. By late August Hitler asserted himself over wilful German generals, keeping the Wehrmacht oriented on destroying the Red Army and seemingly back on track.

In September and October 1941, the Germans executed encirclement battles at Kiev and Viazma–Bryansk that netted two-thirds of a million Soviet POWs each. The road to Moscow looked open to them, as the blitzkrieg presented the Wehrmacht's leadership with numerous opportunities. At the gates of Moscow, with the battle they had wanted for the entire campaign before them, the German generals could not successfully pull the trigger. As Stalin resolved to remain in his capital, Red Army defences stiffened, while the Germans could now add strategic overstretch to their list of woes. After five months of constant manoeuvre, the entire German military machine was an overstressed organization.[2] The Wehrmacht threw its last ounce of strength against Leningrad, Moscow and Rostov as the Soviets patiently husbanded their reserves.

In late November and early December, the USSR threw these fresh forces against the Germans' eastern army with success along most of the front, forcing the Wehrmacht to give back hard-won gains (Chapter 2). At the same time Hitler, his megalomania and ignorance of the wider world in full bloom, ill-advisedly declared war on the United States. His war was truly global. Now it was Hitler's turn to purge his top leadership, and by January 1942 he had replaced the army commander-in-chief, all three field marshals commanding army groups and numerous subordinate generals. Stalin's winter counteroffensives permanently put Moscow out of danger and also guaranteed there would be no deep encirclement of Leningrad via a German–Finnish union on the Svir River. These critical tasks accomplished, in mid-spring the Soviets turned to the eastern Ukraine. Attacks around Kharkov and in the Crimea foundered when they unexpectedly hit and were repulsed by large German units preparing for the summer 1942 campaigns. The relatively inexperienced Stavka leadership is generally criticized for trying to do too much with too little that winter.

Nazi Germany's small size and lack of resources became apparent with Operation *Blau*, when in 1942 it could attack only on the southern half of the front (Chapter 3). Always (correctly) concerned about his oil

supplies, Hitler's objective that June was the Baku–Maikop region. As he had the year before, Stalin obliged by giving his forces 'not one step back' orders in the face of more mobile Wehrmacht armies. However, after only a couple of weeks, also as in the year before, a trio of German limitations made themselves felt: unclear goal setting, underestimating the enemy, and careless logistics. Soon Stalingrad exerted a pull on both tyrants, seemingly merely by the power of its name. Before the summer ran out, the city began first to attract and then to consume divisions and corps of both sides. Again, as in the year before, the Germans stood exhausted, isolated and undersupplied while the Red Army prepared to counterattack. Three differences from 1941 must be noted, however: 1) any slack or surplus that existed earlier in the German system had vanished, 2) flanks of the exposed German salient were manned by Romanian, Hungarian and Italian armies of dubious ability, and 3) the Soviets prudently limited their counteroffensive to obtainable objectives.

Operation *Uranus* that November encircled Wehrmacht units in Stalingrad, obliterated allied Axis formations guarding its flanks, and initiated the second phase of the war (Chapter 4). The Germans could neither free nor adequately resupply their entrapped comrades, while sister forces still fighting toward Baku–Maikop barely escaped the subsequent Operation *Little Saturn*. Unanticipated stiff Wehrmacht resistance within the pocket put the Soviets behind schedule, but there could be only one outcome to that battle. By mid-winter, Operations *Gallup* and *Star* carried the Red Army over the Don River and back into eastern Ukraine. With their backs to the mighty Dnepr River, the Germans tried to regain their equilibrium. By March they had managed a limited operational victory culminating in the fourth battle of Kharkov. Seasonal weather and Soviet overstretch plus exhaustion on both sides brought the fighting to a halt. The thawing snow revealed the previous winter's dead and the front stabilized, leaving a bulging salient centred on the city of Kursk. For months the pace of Soviet operations prevented the Wehrmacht from creating a viable defensive system; all it could do was reflexively plug holes.

The summer 1943 offensive displayed Germany's continued weakness for the entire world to see (Chapter 5). It could muster only enough force to attack on the southern flank of the Kursk bulge in any strength. Operation *Zitadelle*'s 'success' against stout Red Army defences amounted to a few days and a couple of dozen miles. Following the collapse of the offensive, the Wehrmacht's last of any size in the east, Soviet reserves launched a devastating counterattack that began with the final battle of Kharkov. Meanwhile, Hitler became distracted by fighting in Italy and the growing prospect of an invasion of north-west France. Generally pivoting on Smolensk, key Red Army assaults moved clockwise through the Ukraine, while fighting in the north remained basically static along existing front lines. However, within two months Operation *Rumiantsev* had liberated most of the left bank of the Dnepr and had even crossed the river in numerous places, including at Kiev, the USSR's third city. With no coherent defensive plan and few natural barriers between the Dnepr and the Carpathian Mountains, the Germans surrendered huge tracts of land.

The winter of 1943–44 marked the beginning of the third and final stage of the war (Chapter 6). Far from being transitional, the second

---

1   'Blitzkrieg' is a controversial word. Omer Bartov has described it as a 'heroic, fast, dangerous, exhilarating, glorious and sensuous' alternative to the trench warfare of World War I. As described in my *Hitler's Panzer Armies on the Eastern Front*, the word refers to the combination of 'flexible command structure, combined-arms tactics, the internal combustion engine, radios and aircraft' used by Germany from 1939–41 and later adapted and customized by armies of other nations under various indigenous names.

2   As used here, 'manoeuvre' is a US Army doctrinal word meaning combat plus movement.

phase had seen the rise of Soviet abilities – doctrinal, material and skill. Once Hitler had surrendered the strategic initiative at Stalingrad, he would never recapture it. From then on the rare German successes would be small and transitory, usually relegating an unmitigated disaster to the status of 'only' a defeat. Neither defender nor weather slowed the attackers any longer. By April 1944, the isolated Crimea had been all but overrun and the southern battlefields were littered with encircled pockets of German troops, at times numbering many corps. In the south, Red Army forces stood on the frontiers of Hitler's shaky Hungarian and Romanian allies and German-occupied Poland. In the north they lifted the 900-day siege of Leningrad and approached the Baltic States. Only in the centre, between Smolensk and Minsk, did German defences manage to hold a sizeable eastward bulge.

The Soviets' answer to Kiev and Viazma–Bryansk came that June in the form of Operation *Bagration*, timed to coincide with both the Western Allied invasion of Normandy and *Barbarossa*'s third anniversary. Within weeks, the bulk of an entire German army group ceased to exist. The new generation of generals now directing Red Army operations adroitly shifted their assaults from central to northern to southern theatres, and by September all of the USSR had been liberated and swept clean of Germans. As Soviet units approached the gates of Warsaw, the Wehrmacht could not mount a credible defence anywhere along the front. Although German industry now produced more armoured vehicles than at any point in the war, these were never employed en masse as intended. Romania switched sides and Hungary wavered. By October 1944, vengeful Red Army troops had entered the Third Reich proper in East Prussia. With the attacking Soviets drained after four months of continuous operations and aided by the Vistula River and Carpathian Mountains, the Germans temporarily caught their breath. As had been the case since the dark days of Stalingrad, any German defensive successes were very limited.

Through January 1945, the Red Army planned and prepared for its final offensives against the Nazi Reich (Chapter 7). Despite the failure of Operation *Wacht am Rhein* (Battle of the Bulge) and the arrival of Western Allied armies in western Germany, the Wehrmacht still sent its best units to the east. However, these accomplished little in the face of absolutely overwhelming Soviet force. East Prussia, Pomerania and Silesia fell, as did Belgrade and Budapest. By mid-April final arrangements for the assault on Berlin were complete. Wehrmacht defenders – fanatic SS, fatalistic soldiers, old men and boys, plus armed factory workers (their useless workplaces long since bombed out or starved of resources) – waited for the end that must surely come soon. Red Army attackers – likewise fatigued and suffering from massive losses – increasingly undisciplined and also looking forward to the war's end, were driven by competitive marshals whose zeal for personal glory was fuelled by Stalin and bordered on negligence. With Hitler dead and his capital pounded into rubble, the last days of the Nazi-Soviet War slid toward the inevitable.

As one anecdote has it, the Soviet Union prevailed because it had the better dictator. Saying it had better allies is equally correct. With detached hindsight, it is incredible that the army of a medium-sized country like Germany could have made it to Stalingrad and beyond against the globe's largest army and country. In 1941 Hitler's generals followed their Führer east with barely a complaint, but when Plan A failed they could not devise a suitable Plan B. Conversely, while the Red Army barely survived the mistakes of the war's first 16 months, the Soviet state did not falter. It threw countless freshly-mobilized armies in *Barbarossa*'s way; recreated its industrial might, whether from scratch or from the ruins of the old; sustained partisan warfare that hounded the Germans' every step; learned from past mistakes; and, above all, kept the country fighting. More than once the USSR teetered on the brink of destruction, but after surviving the initial shock, Stalin put his faith in the new crop of talented generals that ultimately led his country to success. In the face of serious manpower problems, they perfected their own version of mobile warfare based on an adaptable command structure, combined arms tactics, mechanization and close air support (CAS).[3] In the summer of 1945, with all of Germany in ruins, it took the victors just a couple of months to construct a memorial in the shadows of the Brandenburg Gate and Reichstag; they had earned it.

---

3   Purists chafe at referring to this variety of mobile warfare as a blitzkrieg.

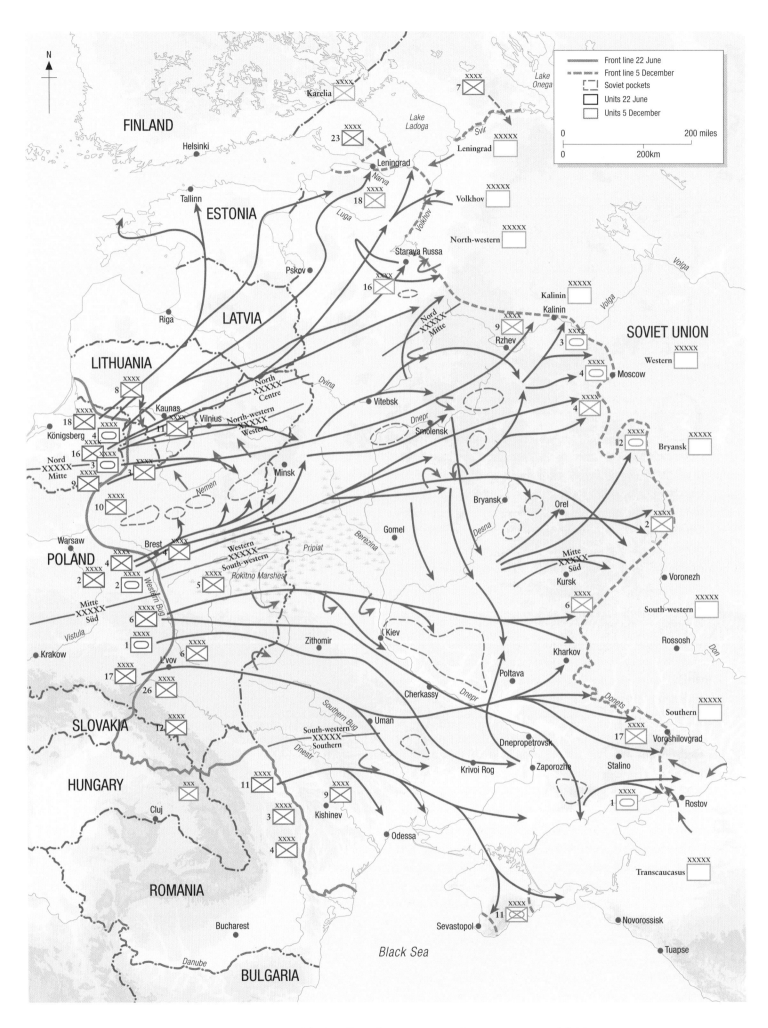

N

FINLAND

Helsinki

Karelia

Lake Onega

7

Lake Ladoga

Svir

23

Leningrad

Leningrad

ESTONIA

Tallinn

18

Narva

Volkhov

Volkhov

Luga

North-western

Pskov

Staraya Russa

LATVIA

Riga

16

Nord XXXXX Mitte

Volga

Kalinin

Kalinin

9

Rzhev

3

SOVIET UNION

Western

Dvina

North XXXXX Centre

Vitebsk

Dnepr

4

Moscow

LITHUANIA

8

Kaunas

Vilnius

North-western XXXXX Western

Smolensk

4

18

11

2

Bryansk

Königsberg

4

Minsk

Nemen

16

Nord XXXXX Mitte

3

9

Bryansk

Orel

2

10

Berezina

Gomel

Desna

Mitte XXXXX Süd

Voronezh

Warsaw

Brest

4

Western XXXXX South-western

Pripiat

Kursk

6

POLAND

4

Rokitno Marshes

5

Kiev

South-western

2

2

Vistula

Western Bug

Mitte XXXXX Süd

6

Kharkov

Rossosh

Don

1

Zithomir

Krakow

L'vov

6

Poltava

17

Cherkassy

Dnepr

26

Donets

Southern

SLOVAKIA

T2

Southern Bug

Uman

17

Voroshilovgrad

HUNGARY

11

South-western XXXXX Southern

Dnestr

Dnepropetrovsk

Stalino

1

Cluj

3

Kishinev

9

Krivoi Rog

Zaporozhe

Rostov

4

Odessa

Transcaucasus

ROMANIA

11

Sevastopol

Novorossisk

Bucharest

Black Sea

Tuapse

Danube

BULGARIA

Front line 22 June
Front line 5 December
Soviet pockets
Units 22 June
Units 5 December

0   200 miles
0   200km

CHAPTER 1:
OPERATION *BARBAROSSA*, 1941

O n the last day of July 1940, Hitler called Germany's top military leaders to his mountain retreat outside Berchtesgaden and officially informed them of his intention to invade the 'Jewish-Bolshevik' USSR. He did not have much enthusiasm for the ongoing Battle of Britain, reflecting his corresponding lack of interest in the finer points in aerial, naval or commerce warfare. He brushed aside any early token objections from generals and admirals in attendance and within weeks had two rival plans from his two principal and competing Oberkommando des Heeres (OKH) and Oberkommando der Wehrmacht (OKW) headquarters. Both plans assumed the destruction of the Red Army west of the Dvina–Dnepr line and aimed the *Schwerpunkt* (main effort) for Moscow. Further, both assumed a relatively easy victory within approximately two months. Building on the successful model demonstrated in France, large panzer forces would lead the way while marching infantry followed. Throughout the autumn of 1940, operations staffs fine-tuned and further developed the plan, although critically minimizing logistical problems. Adjustments included taking into account Hitler's insistent emphasis on the twin objectives of securing the flanks of any thrust on Moscow as well as capturing natural resource areas, mainly in the Soviet Union's south. Meanwhile Stalin and his staffs made their own plans. Mirroring the turmoil common under his regime, Red Army planners could not settle on key priorities such as offensive or defensive strategy, northern or southern orientation, forward or in-depth positions, marching or mechanized armies. The unexpectedly rapid fall of France did not decide these questions, but did give Soviet planners new urgency. Hoping war would not come before 1942, they began mobilizing additional cohorts and started an ambitious reorganization. Also critically, in early 1941 Stalin named General G. K. Zhukov – destined to become the scourge of Hitler – Red Army Chief of Staff and Supreme Command Staff member.

Battle-tested German forces were divided into three army groups (Heeresgruppen Nord, Mitte, and Süd) made up of seven field armies (4., 6., 9., 11., 16., 17. and 18. Armeen) and four panzer groups (1., 2., 3. and 4. Panzergruppen), augmented by the Third and Fourth Romanian Armies and later Italian, Hungarian, Slovak, Spanish and other foreign formations. One German 'Norway', and one Finnish 'Karelian' army manned the distant far north. By far the majority of all Axis forces consisted of marching infantry supported by horse-drawn artillery and logistics. Hitler employed more than three million soldiers, approximately 7,000 artillery pieces and 3,000 each of armoured vehicles and aircraft.

In the main sector, raw Red Army forces deployed in four fronts (North-western, Western, South-western and Southern) consisting of 13 field armies (3rd, 4th, 5th, 6th, 8th, 9th Independent, 10th, 11th, 12th, 13th, 18th, 26th and 27th) backed up by 18 mechanized, three cavalry and four airborne corps. Along the Finnish border stood the Northern Front with three armies (7th Independent, 14th and 23rd) plus one mechanized corps under its command. More than three million men, 30,000 indirect-fire weapons, 11,000 armoured vehicles and 7,000 aircraft held the USSR's defences. The Germans initially held back one army (2. Armee), but since this deployed within days of *Barbarossatag*, 22 June, it cannot be properly considered a true reserve. On the other hand the Soviets had six armies in close, immediate reserve (16th, 19th, 20th, 21st, 22nd and 24th), with a great many more arriving in the coming months.

Lavishly resourced Heeresgruppe Mitte under Generalfeldmarschall Fedor von Bock served as *Barbarossa*'s *Schwerpunkt*. Facing it stood General Colonel D. G. Pavlov's Western Front in the fatally exposed Bialystok salient. Outclassed by every measure, from day one Pavlov's men largely gave way. Two panzer groups working in tandem routinely made daily advances of 30–40 miles. It took them only four days to close the first of many *Kessel* (cauldron) battles and just one more day to slam shut another subsequent trap at Minsk. Barely waiting for the marching infantry divisions to catch up and properly seal the pockets, the panzer groups sped on toward Smolensk. The job of digesting the encirclements and tidying up the battlefield fell largely but not exclusively on the infantry. While most Red Army soldiers fought to the death or surrendered, others evaded capture, melting into the countryside to join comrades, civilians and eventually, communist cadres in order to keep on fighting in partisan bands. On 15 July the two panzer groups closed the next massive *Kessel* at Smolensk, bagging another third of a million POWs. Not only was fighting ferocious in the vicinity of the pocket, but the Soviet Stavka (main staff) directed Marshal S. K. Timoshenko to lead a series of counteroffensives against Heeresgruppe Mitte's entire front. Individually insignificant from a strategic standpoint, taken together these mini-offensives signal the informal beginning of Stalin's defensive tactic of contesting every yard of Soviet soil.

Fighting along *Barbarossa*'s flanks took its own unique courses. Generalfeldmarschall Wilhelm *Ritter* von Leeb's Heeresgruppe Nord, the smallest of the three, probably had the most spectacular start. In just four days his panzer group had captured a bridgehead over the Dvina River, a key terrain feature in both Wehrmacht and Red Army plans. However, Leeb's timidity plus unfavourable terrain conspired to stall the drive temporarily. The Soviets' dangerously split operational defences barely contributed to the slowdown and were unable to capitalize on the delay. Soon, another burst by the panzer group captured bridges over the Luga River on 14 July. This represented Leningrad's last natural barrier just a few dozen miles from the great city. Fortunately for the Soviets, Leeb once again failed to exploit a hard-won achievement, although in this case Red Army forces deserved some tribute. At the opposite end of the front, Stalin's best operational commander, General Lieutenant M. P. Kirponos, and its strongest

front, the South-western, put up a stiff fight in the western Ukraine against Heeresgruppe Süd under Generalfeldmarschall Gerd von Rundstedt. Slashing manoeuvres and huge *Kesseln* would have to wait weeks until the defenders had been bludgeoned into numerical and positional inferiority. Neither a panzer group reaching the gates of Kiev on 10 July nor Romania opening a new front along the Black Sea a week earlier seriously undermined Kirponos. It took nearly a month for Rundstedt's men to earn true operational freedom and until 3 August to achieve their first *Kessel* at Uman.

Late July and early August coincided with a serious impasse among the top German leadership. From *Barbarossa*'s earliest planning stages Hitler had not attached much importance to Moscow and had often told his generals so. Many of them disagreed, top among them Army Chief of Staff Generaloberst Franz Halder,[4] who believed the USSR's capital to be the intuitively obvious choice for the invasion's main objective. He had worked overtly and covertly to orient the eastern army on the city. Individually Hitler and Halder each considered the argument closed in his own favour, but the issue remained in doubt. A series of directives (with supplements) from Hitler's headquarters in July and August failed to clear up the matter. In the resulting power vacuum, German generals took sides, or more often, just did what they thought best in accordance with existing guidance. A mini-mutiny orchestrated by Halder fizzled, largely as a result of numerous defections to Hitler's way of thinking. Only on 22 August did Hitler really assert himself, take control and reorient *Barbarossa* away from Moscow and toward destroying Red Army forces massed east of Kiev.

Coincidentally, the command crisis unfolded at roughly the same time as the Germans' anticipated 'logistics pause', which had been planned to allow rearward services and supply elements to catch up with the fighting front. However, in reality the slowdown represented just one more in a long line of German staff failures. Stalin was in no mood to give his mortal enemy the luxury of a 'pause' with which to catch his breath. (Additionally, defensive fighting consumes just about the same amount of materiel as being on the attack, just in different commodities.) With the campaign once again supposedly on a steady course, the Wehrmacht opened massive battles on the two flanks. Already in progress were Leeb's attempts to overthrow the Luga River line shielding Leningrad. With the help of panzer corps on loan from Heeresgruppe Mitte and the VIII Flieger-Korps (CAS) experts, his men levered the defenders off the fortified river and back toward what Hitler considered the 'birthplace of Bolshevism'. By 8 September German troops had captured Shlisselburg on Lake Ladoga, effectively cutting overland communication to the city for 900 days. They began their last assault on Leningrad's defences on the 11th, but it ground to a halt a dozen days later still far from the heart of the city. For reasons of

---

4   Halder, a career enemy of Hitler – his opposition continued for decades after the dictator's death – had been brought into the exalted chief of staff position in September 1938 specifically to lead the anti-Nazi resistance. The proximate cause for this open rebellion among the military was to be the Western Allies' expected reaction to Hitler's pending attack on Czechoslovakia. Fear and trembling gripped Halder while he sat at his desk, crying as he waited for the fateful phone call that never came announcing the British and French declarations of war. Instead, Mussolini invited Chamberlain and Deladier to meet Hitler in Munich.

national strategy, the Finnish Karelian Army halted its own attacks near the pre-1940 border, quite a distance from Leningrad. Over the next year the Germans would try again to take the city, but would not get significantly closer.

With Uman, Kirponos' luck in the Ukraine had run out. During late August and early September Rundstedt's army group closed in on Kiev and the length of the lower Dnepr. Part of the new arrangements now demanded by Hitler consisted of halting the drive on Moscow and turning Heeresgruppe Mitte's panzer groups north toward Leningrad (mentioned above) and south toward Kiev, temporarily pausing the drive on Moscow. As a result, Bock's infantry had the nasty job of attempting to hold the line at Yelnia against determined attacks. Together with the panzers working their way southward behind the Rokitno Marshes, Heeresgruppe Süd's panzer group would cross the Dnepr and push north to a rendezvous. All that remained was for the Red Army defenders to hold fast until the Germans' armoured jaws slammed shut. This is exactly what Stalin demanded, and on 14 September the two panzer spearheads met at Lokhvitsa. In history's largest encirclement battle, two-thirds of a million soldiers disappeared from the Red Army's order of battle, leaving a massive gap in the defensive lines. Eschewing the direct attack on Moscow, while consistent with German military technique from the days of Frederick the Great, has nonetheless been controversial ever since. In a typical misreading of cause and consequence, many assume that because the Kiev decision did not win the war for Germany, attacking Moscow naturally would have. Critics of the Kiev operation describe Moscow as the administrative, industrial and transportation centrepiece of the USSR, a veritable magic 'key to the kingdom'. Likewise, they describe the encirclement manoeuvre against the Kiev grouping as a clueless dilettante grasping for the low-hanging fruit or a shiny bauble. In point of fact, even though the Nazi-Soviet War would be nearly impossible for Germany to win, attacking Kiev was the correct decision.

Rundstedt attempted to exploit the disrupted Soviet defence, but once again the distances involved and his own manpower and logistical woes, plus the fact that he had lost numerous mechanized formations to Bock, limited his success. His men made significant gains in the Crimea and toward Rostov, but as we shall see, could not hold on to them. East of Leningrad, Leeb sought a union with Finnish units arriving on the Svir River, but likewise could not. The Wehrmacht's *Schwerpunkt* that autumn was clearly Operation *Typhoon*, directed against Moscow. Bock's attacking force, three armies and an equal number of panzer armies (as the panzer groups were being renamed) faced 13 Soviet armies, largely co-ordinated by Zhukov, newly arrived from rescuing Leningrad. Between 30 September and 2 October, German forces moved out and had soon created two new *Kesseln* near Viazma and Bryansk. An additional two-thirds of a million troops were struck from the Soviet rolls and another tremendous gap appeared, again bereft of defenders and now barely 50 miles from Moscow. However, tenacious resistance and fragile logistics limited *Typhoon* almost as soon as it began, then a week later the rains came.

Most movement came to a halt until freezing weather arrived in early November. Zhukov used the slowdown to buttress Moscow's defences as the Soviet state poured new men and units into the front lines. At the far extremities of the main front, at Tikhvin and Volkhov south of Lake Ladoga and at Rostov, counterattacks threw the Germans back, their first reverses since Yelnia. Stalin and Zhukov awaited Bock's final push against Moscow with confidence. For every German disadvantage, the Soviets seemed to have the corresponding advantage. Between 15 November and 3 December, the Germans made their first, and best, attempt to reach Moscow, driving toward the city from the north-west. The corresponding attack from the south of the city ran from 18 November until the end of the month. The last assault, supposedly the *Schwerpunkt*, but ineptly led by Generalfeldmarschall Günther von Kluge, came in the middle sector, starting only on 1 December. It quickly faded after only a couple of days. In the end all three came up short, ending in the futile and well-known *Flucht nach vorn* (flight forward) toward the capital. The Wehrmacht's dazed and vermin-eaten remnant, frozen to the bone and a shadow of the magnificent army that had stepped out on 22 June, weakly lapped against the rocks that represented Moscow's defences.

MAP 3: OPPOSING PLANS

In early June 1940, with operations in France clearly heading toward German success, Hitler started dropping hints to his senior military leaders that his next target would be the USSR. Less than a month after the French surrender, army commander Generalfeldmarschall Walther von Brauchitsch and Chief of Staff Halder instructed their staffs to begin planning. The initial task went to Generalmajor Erich Marcks at Headquarters, 18. Armee.[5] His original plan called for the German *Schwerpunkt* to aim for the Ukraine, but Halder redirected the invasion's main effort toward Moscow – as he would continue to do overtly and covertly for the next year. Hitler made official his decision to invade the Soviet Union on 31 July and Marcks' edited plan or *Operationsentwurf Ost* (Operational Draft East) came out a week later. Just days before the Berghof meeting, Hitler instructed General der Artillerie Alfred Jodl and his OKW staff to draw up its own plan. This chore fell on Oberstleutnant Bernhard von Lossberg[6] who completed his initial *Aufbau Ost* (Build-up East) and subsequent *Operationsstudie Ost* (Operational Study East) by mid-September. Fatally for *Barbarossa*, both plans used the same flawed military intelligence estimate of the USSR and Red Army provided by *Fremde Heere Ost* (FHO, Foreign Armies East) as their weak foundation, with national-strategic intelligence input – also wildly inaccurate – from the Gestapo.

The OKH operations section under newly appointed Generalleutnant Friedrich Paulus completed a preliminary comparison of the OKH and OKW plans in just two weeks and a more thorough study a month later. In another glaring weakness, Paulus admitted after the war that he looked at *Barbarossa* 'from the purely military point of view', absolutely ignoring the culminating point of the Soviet Union: the strength of the ruthless Stalinist state. In late November and early December Paulus's staff war-gamed *Barbarossa*, but these simulations merely confirmed the Wehrmacht's pre-existing notions, such as the wisdom of emphasizing Moscow. At the conclusion of the war games Brauchitsch and Halder briefed Hitler, only to be told that the Führer

considered the city 'not so very important'. Hitler and Halder would clash over this issue until late August of the following year. By mid-December Luftwaffe and logistical plans were complete and on the 18th Hitler approved the Lossberg-authored Führer Directive 21, his strategic overview. The OKH operational guidance, *Aufmarschanweisung Ost* (Deployment Directive East) came out at the end of January 1941, and, very significantly, placed capturing Moscow *after* breaking 'Russian' resistance on the battlefield.

Meanwhile, Stalin had not been idle. Quite correctly, much is made of the premier's failure to anticipate *Barbarossa*, but Soviet spies told him of Hitler's Berghof meeting within days and Red Army planning would generally run parallel to the Wehrmacht's. In mid-October 1940, the Soviets published Mobilization Plan 1941 (MP 41), heavily oriented toward defending the resource-rich Ukraine and counterattacking into German-occupied Poland. Planning conferences and war games at the Kremlin that December and January had three effects: they firstly called into question the wisdom of a Soviet counteroffensive, secondly showcased Zhukov's skill in front of the entire Red Army leadership and thirdly initiated a new Defensive Plan 1941 (DP 41), which kept many of MP 41's weaknesses such as the (too far) forward defensive deployment and fanciful attacks (red arrows, opposite) toward Germany. Largely because of Zhukov's insistence, in the months prior to *Barbarossa* Stalin mobilized 500,000 reservists.

The map opposite shows the Marcks (blue) and Lossberg (green) plans. Both acknowledged that the Rokitno Marshes would divide the campaign into two unequal parts, with the *Schwerpunkt* to the north. In Phase I, both plans show almost parallel axes aiming for Leningrad and Smolensk, plus the destruction of Red Army forces west of the Dvina–Dnepr River line. In the south, while Marcks indicated a major effort toward Kiev, Lossberg headed for the Dnepr River bend. The two plans diverge in Phases II and III. Both men considered that Red Army forces east of the marshes would require attention from the central and Ukrainian axes – basically the historical Kiev pocket operation. Marcks continues to make straight for Moscow, but we see Lossberg bleed off forces toward Leningrad and the Donbas. Under the Lossberg plan, these forces previously diverted eventually return to attack Moscow from the north and south, again consistent with the historical Operation *Typhoon*. It is possible to see therefore that both Hitler and historical events favoured Lossberg's OKW plan.

---

5   Marcks was the son of a famous German historian by the same name. In the Weimar Republic he mainly held political posts, what we would call a press secretary today. During that time he was a close confederate of General Kurt von Schleicher, but managed to survive that relationship. He lost his left leg commanding a division in combat just four days into *Barbarossa* and died three years later commanding the LXXXIV Armee-Korps in Normandy.

6   Lossberg also came from a highly politicized background. His father, a general, had been an anti-republican putschist in 1918 and 1919.

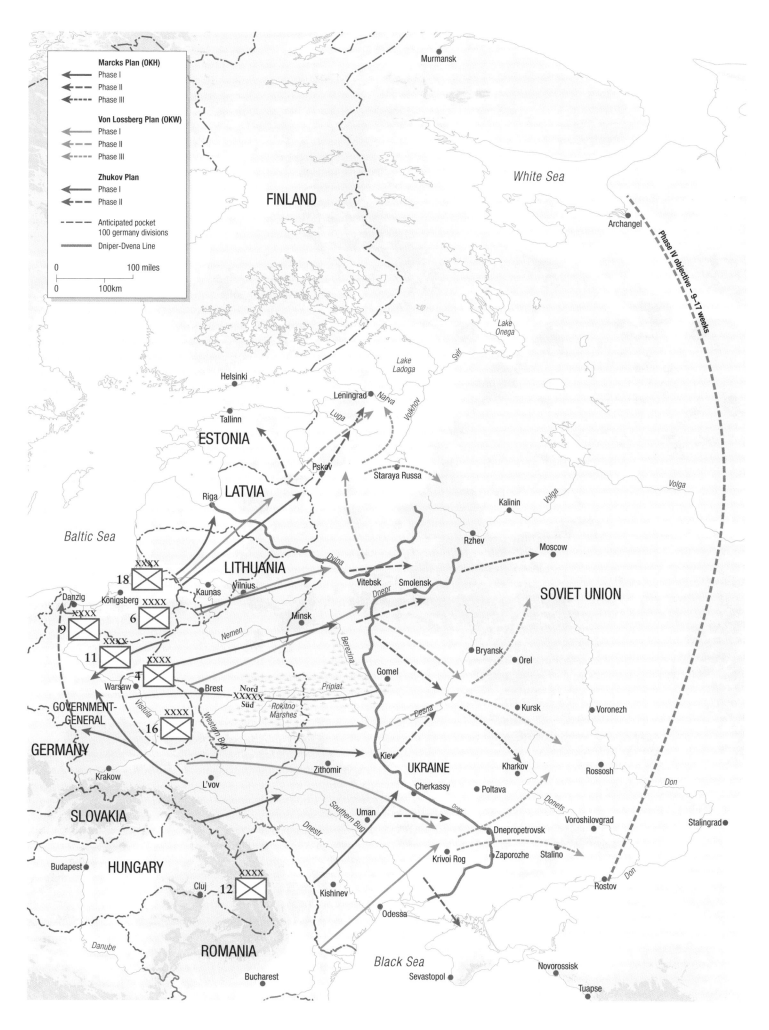

MAP 4: FRONTIER BATTLES NORTH 22–30 JUNE, 1941

With his OKH staff myopically and self-admittedly concentrating only on 'purely military' issues, political/strategic matters fell to Hitler. Leeb's men had perhaps the most politically-oriented objectives of all three army groups. Besides destroying Red Army forces in the theatre, they would 1) capture Leningrad, 2) capture or neutralize Soviet naval bases, thereby depriving the Baltic Fleet of any ports and 3) link up with the Finns. With the 16. and 18. Armeen, 4. Panzergruppe and a small Luftwaffe contingent under command, Heeresgruppe Nord would thrust along the Dünaburg–Opochka–Leningrad axis while maintaining contact with Bock to its right. Throughout *Barbarossa*, and indeed the entire Nazi-Soviet War, Wehrmacht efforts in the north would be severely under-resourced, almost guaranteeing failure. Soviet plans addressed defences in the north only belatedly. The pre-war Baltic Special Military District [7] (which would become the North-western Front once war broke out) intended to fight along the frontier and then fall back to the Dvina River. In the event that the Germans levered the defenders off that position, they would execute a fighting withdrawal through the forested and marshy terrain that dominated Leningrad's approaches. The Soviet 11th, 18th and 26th Armies were unequal to the task, as was front commander General Colonel F. I. Kuznetsov.

Barbarossa's funnel-shaped front repeated itself in a smaller scale in the Heersgruppe Nord sector. Leeb's formations were crammed into starting positions in the Memelland and northern East Prussia. When they attacked at 0500 on *Barbarossatag* it had already been light for hours. Defending usually with one regiment forward and two back, Kuznetsov's men were quickly overrun and soon gave way as German infantry divisions measured advances that day in many 10-mile increments. Generaloberst Erich Hoepner's panzer troops made even more spectacular advances along the attack's leading edge. The 8. Panzer-Division captured the Ariogala Bridge over the Dubysa River, a key intermediate objective on the road to Dünaburg.

On the war's second day, General Lieutenant P. P. Sobeninkov, commanding 8th Army, organized a counterattack by two mechanized corps against the panzer spearheads. The XLI Panzer-Korps under General der Panzertruppen Georg-Hans Reinhardt was dangerously extended, with 1. and 6. Panzer-Divisionen not within supporting distance of each other. The 3rd and 12th Mechanized Corps attacked and overwhelmed isolated Wehrmacht advanced detachments around Raseiniai and Tytuvenai respectively. Soviet KV-1/2 and T-34 tanks manhandled the much smaller panzers and inadequate anti-tank guns stalling the advance. It took the Germans, who had to resort to expedients, over three days to master the situation. Finally, by 25 June the two mechanized corps had been encircled, with their armoured divisions losing many hundreds of tanks each, often representing more than 90 per cent of their original establishments.

With Reinhardt absorbing so much of the defenders' attention, General der Infanterie Erich von Manstein's LVI Panzer-Korps made almost unimpeded progress on Hoepner's right. From the Ariogala Bridge he sped along the one decent road to Dünaburg in a race against the 27th Army and the attached 21st Mechanized Corps. In the early morning of 26 June his men, augmented by Brandenburger commandos and special pioneer detachments – some riding captured Soviet vehicles – won the competition and captured two bridges over the broad Dvina River. For the next three days the stranded LVI Panzer-Korps held back determined ground and air attacks as German infantry marched as fast as they could to help. Luftwaffe CAS provided expert assistance from above until first Reinhardt pulled alongside downriver at Jekolpils and then 16. Armee *Landsers*[8] finally arrived. Meanwhile Leeb's two infantry armies made slow but steady progress on either side of Hoepner. On the far left, the 18. Armee cleared the Baltic coast and captured Riga on the last day of June. To the right, the 16. Armee advanced through eastern Lithuania. Its task was made easier by Kuznetsov's poor leadership; his 11th Army, being simultaneously pummelled by 3. Panzergruppe (Map 9), slipped east, rather than north with the rest of the North-western Front, thereby opening a massive break with neighbouring Western Front.

Leadership at the top was weak on both sides of the Northern Front. Stalin replaced Kuznetsov one week into *Barbarossa* and promoted Sobeninkov in his place. Leeb squandered the Dünaburg bridgehead by halting Hoepner for six critical days. Even with Hitler telling anyone who would listen to get 4. Panzergruppe attacking toward Leningrad, the overly cautious Bavarian would not budge.

---

7   The word 'Special' in the three main front-line military districts meant that they could accomplish their assigned missions without substantial reinforcement, an unrealistic expectation.

8   German colloquialism for infantrymen, literally those of the land.

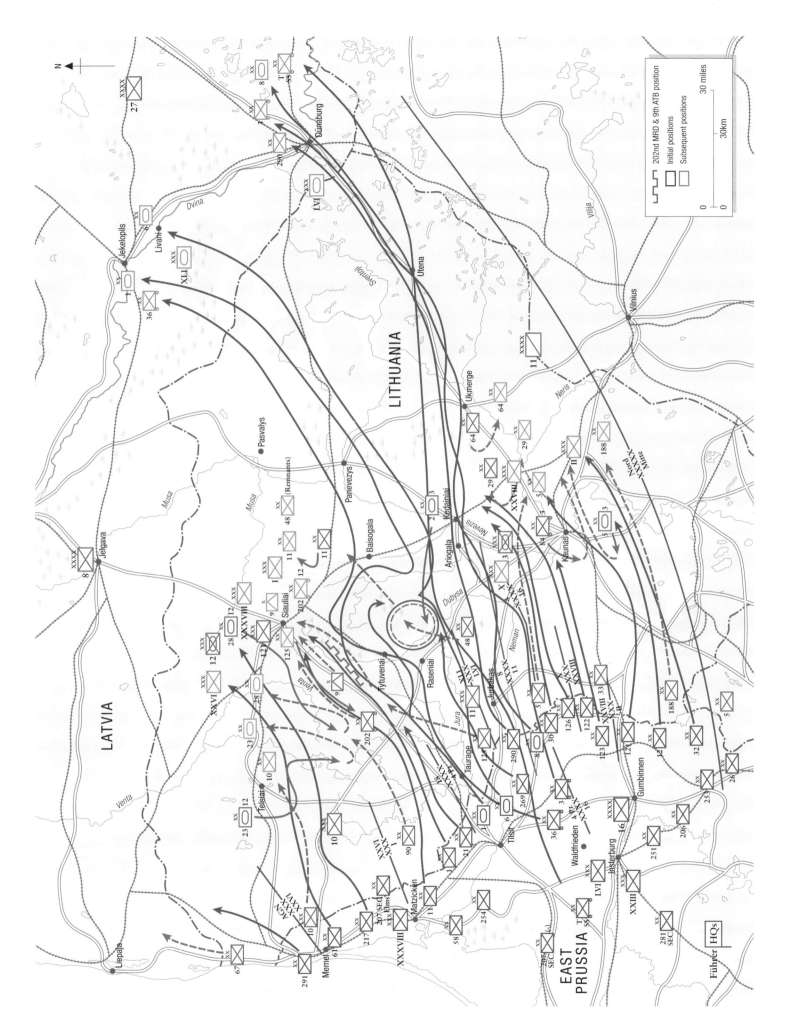

21

MAP 5: BATTLE FOR THE LUGA RIVER AND APPROACHES TO LENINGRAD 9 JULY TO 18 SEPTEMBER, 1941

Nowhere in *Barbarossa* were the disparities between the Wehrmacht's two armies, one mechanized and the other marching, more noticeable than in Heersgruppe Nord. There are many reasons for this: its position as the campaign's tertiary effort, lack of a clear idea how to subdue a massive city like Leningrad, Leeb's inexperience with the blitzkrieg, plus unfavourable climate and terrain, just to name the most obvious. After manoeuvring 650 miles in less than a month, XLI Panzer-Korps sat on the Luga River and waited for Leeb to bring up the remainder of the army group and develop a plan for covering the last 90-odd miles to the USSR's second city. Meanwhile Stalin and Red Army leaders had to decide how best to defend the birthplace of Bolshevism, protect the main base of the Red Banner Baltic Fleet and keep the Germans and Finns separated. With incompetents like Kuznetsov and Marshal K. E. Voroshilov leading the operational defence, the tactical responsibility for holding the 250-mile-long river line fell on General K. P. Piadyshev, in charge of the Luga Operational Group (LOG).

Piadyshev, just assigned on 9 July, did not last long in command and within two weeks was arrested for dereliction of duty. With his departure the Stavka divided the LOG into three parts: Kingisepp, Luga (town) and Eastern.[9] The Kingisepp sector had responsibility for restraining the XLI Panzer-Korps' bridgeheads (reinforced by the 8. Panzer-Division and 36. Infanterie-Division (Mot.)), and stiff fighting took place there during the second week of August. Manstein joined the battle against the Luga defensive sector on 10 August. Supported by 16. Armee infantry and Luftwaffe CAS, by 12–13 August Reinhardt drove the Red Army troops from their hastily fortified positions. The German exploitation plan called for the bulk of the XLI Panzer-Korps to drive on Leningrad while 8. Panzer-Division would veer to the right to rendezvous with the L Armee-Korps advancing from Luga; by the end of August this latter manoeuvre had entrapped 20,000 Soviet POWs near Krasnogvardeisk. At this point the German effort in the north suffered from two self-inflicted wounds: command indecision at Rastenburg and an over-reaction to a tactical threat south of Lake Il'men. The disproportionate response to the Staraya Russa attacks

'merely' ruined Heeresgruppe Nord's third opportunity to rush Leningrad (Map 6) while the crisis at Hitler's headquarters hamstrung the entire *Barbarossa* campaign.

By 21 August the Germans had solved both distractions and on 4 September the Führer, Brauchitsch and Generalfeldmarschall Wilhelm Keitel arrived at Leeb's headquarters to discuss arrangements for the final assault on Leningrad, which, significantly, no longer included actually capturing the city. Heeresgruppe Nord's twin objectives were to create close and deep encirclements of Leningrad, at Shlisselburg and the Svir River respectively, while it would have use of its high-powered reinforcements, including VIII Flieger-Korps, for another 11 days. Meanwhile, during the second half of August and early September, Leeb's men had been pushing toward the once and future St Petersburg. Against them stood a ring of 452,000 defenders under the operational command of General Lieutenant M. M. Popov, arranged from east to west: General Major I. G. Lazarev's 55th Army, General Major V. I. Shcherbakov's 42nd Army and General Lieutenant F. S. Ivanov's 8th Army. Heeresgruppe Nord launched its offensive over the last few miles to Leningrad on 8 September. On loan from Generaloberst Hermann Hoth, General der Panzertruppen Rudolf Schmidt's XXXIX Panzer-Korps led the way in the eastern sector, slogging through Chudovo while keeping a wary eye open for any potential Red Army relief efforts coming from the right. Operations in this sector culminated on 8 September with the capture of Shlisselburg, which cut off Leningrad from direct overland communication for the next 900 days.

The more direct threat to Leningrad came from Reinhardt to the south-west. With Generaloberst Wolfram Freiherr von Richthofen's Stukas flying overhead, 1. Panzer-Division and 36. Infanterie-Division (Mot.) captured Dudergof Heights on 11 September, while 6. Panzer-Division and elements of 1. Panzer-Division took Krasnoye Selo a day later. On the 13th, Reinhardt created a four-division *Schwerpunkt* at Uritsk while reinforcing Schmidt with 8. Panzer-Division. With the Leningrad skyline in sight, on 18 September Heeresgruppe Nord troops captured both Pushkin and Slutsk. Unfortunately for Reinhardt, nine days earlier Zhukov had arrived to take over control of the defence from Voroshilov, and against Stalin's best general Leeb's men would not get much closer to the city.

---

9   Commanded by General Majors V. V. Semashko, A. N. Astanin and F. N. Starikov respectively.

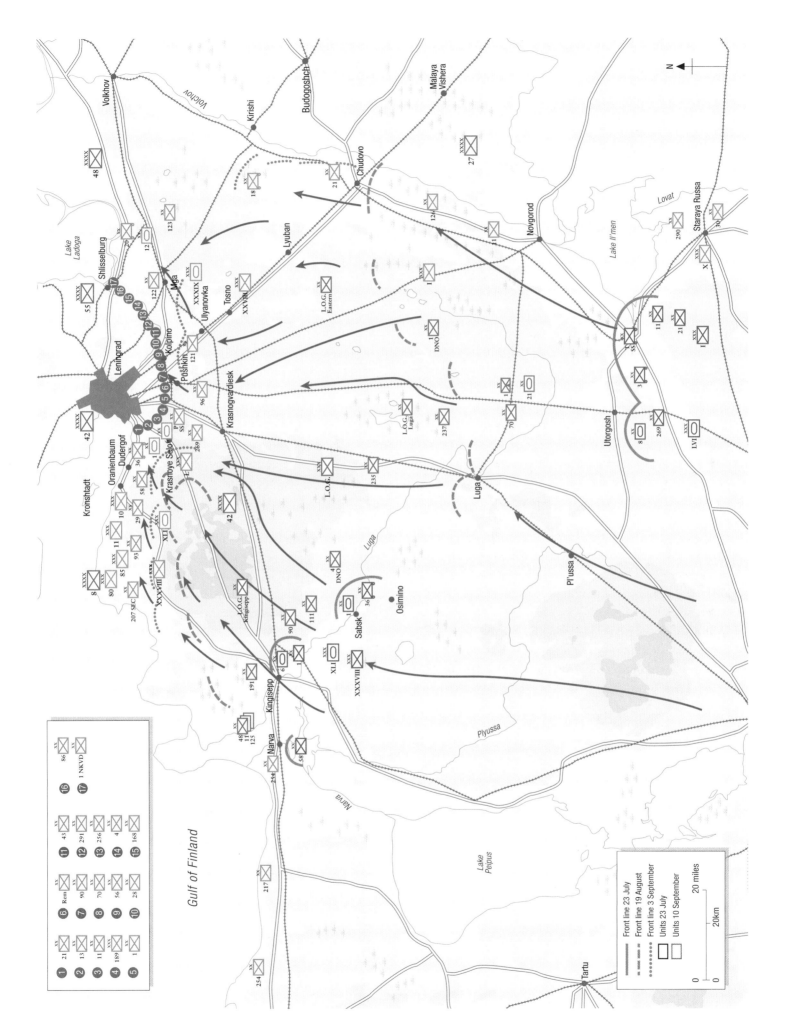

MAP 6: SOVIET ATTACKS AROUND STARAYA RUSSA – 12–23 AUGUST, 1941

Boundaries between two headquarters are common problem areas in military operations, and that dividing Heeresgruppen Nord and Mitte only proves the point. With one command heading north-east toward Leningrad and the other advancing slightly north of due east on Moscow, the seam between them grew with every mile covered. Along with their numerous other missions, the better part of three Wehrmacht armies shared responsibility for securing communications in this sector: Leeb's 16. Armee and Bock's 9. Armee and 3. Panzergruppe. However, with high-value prestige targets like Leningrad and Moscow in front of them, flank security slipped down the priority list.

Considering the leadership vacuum at the top of the North-western Front, the job of exploiting this German liability fell to chief of staff General Lieutenant N. F. Vatutin, who arrived in early July with orders to stabilize the situation at all costs. He spent the next month assembling an assault force and perfecting his plan. During that time Leeb's army group had closed in along the length of the Luga defensive positions. At the same time its right flank had become more exposed and its connection to Heeresgruppe Mitte more tenuous. Vatutin had remnants of the 11th and 27th Armies, in action since 22 June, plus the fresh 34th and 48th Armies (the 48th was north of lake Il'men), which the Stavka also placed at his disposal. His initial plan called for attacks both north and south of Lake Il'men, but higher headquarters downgraded the assault to south of the lake only, a more reasonable 'limited mission'. Leading the way was the 34th Army (12 divisions) under General Major K. M. Kachanov, plus 11th Army in support with a mission of splitting Generaloberst Ernst Busch's X and II Armee-Korps. (These formations had boundary problems of their own, as light screening forces were all that held a 40-mile gap.) The new 48th Army would cover the main effort's north, while the 27th Army covered its southern flank. For a number of reasons, the original 3–4 August start dates were pushed back to 12 August.

Surprise was complete and the 34th Army shoved back the three divisions of X Corps. In two days it penetrated the weakly-held German front to a depth of 24 miles and cut the critical Dno–Staraya Russa rail line on 14 August before command confusion plus bad terrain and weather slowed its advance. Vatutin reinforced success with four additional divisions. On 14 August, Leeb ordered the SS Division Totenkopf toward the threatened area, and a day later pulled Manstein's LVI Panzer-Korps (corps headquarters and 3. Infanterie-Division (Mot.)) out of the Luga River fight and sent it toward Dno. He also redirected significant Luftwaffe assets from the Luga area toward the rupture. On 16 August, the three divisions of the 21st Rifle Corps levered the 30. Infanterie-Division out of Staraya Russa. Vatutin's high water mark came on the same day when the 245th Rifle and 163rd Motorized Rifle Divisions reached Gorki. But the 16th also saw Totenkopf move out against the left flank of this threat.

After secretly moving 150 miles at night, Manstein was ready to attack. Beginning on 19 August, he co-ordinated 3. Infanterie-Division (Mot.) (on right) and Totenkopf (left) against the leading elements of the 34th Army. This time Kachanov was surprised and when the two German divisions met at Velikoye Selo on 20 August, most of the 202nd, 245th and 262nd Rifle, 163rd Motorized Rifle and 25th Cavalry Divisions – 18,000 men in total – were trapped.[10] At the same time to the south, around Kholm, II Armee-Korps moved from defence to offence and pushed back the 27th Army's lacklustre attack. By 23 August, 30. Infanterie-Division had regained the Lovat River south-east of Lake Il'men and Leeb considered the situation stabilized.

But at what cost to *Barbarossa*? At Staraya Russa, Hitler and Leeb are rightly criticized for weakening either the German assault on Leningrad or their link-up operation with the Finns. By the time of the LVI Panzer-Korps counterattack, Vatutin's own manoeuvres, which Halder called 'irrelevant pinpricks', were close to culmination. Heeresgruppe Nord's assault on the Luga River line lost valuable motorized, command and control and Luftwaffe assets to a secondary effort. This diversion and error was compounded by sending Hoth's LVII Panzer-Korps against Velikie Luki–Kholm–Demyansk–Valdai Hills instead of the Svir River (or even Leningrad, all off the map to the South), objectives of true operational value. As for the Soviets, Vatutin's attacks once again demonstrated their desire to contest every step of the way.

---

10   Kachanov was court-martialled on 27 September and executed two days later.

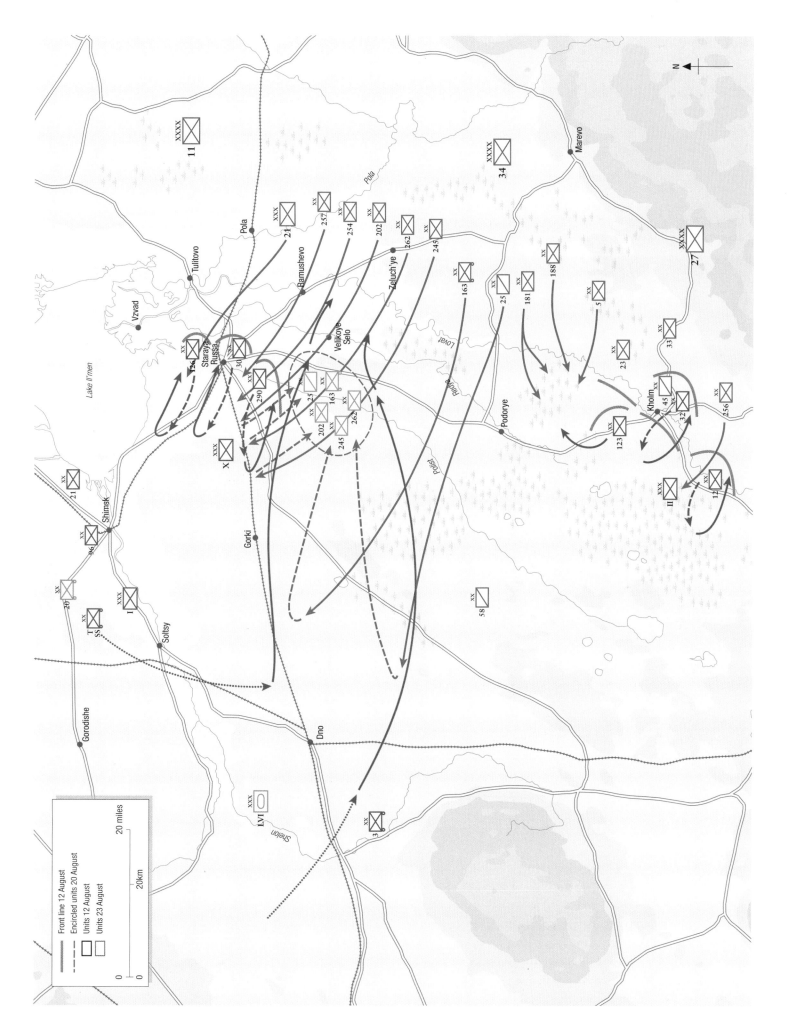

MAP 7: OPERATIONS *BEOWULF* AND *SIEGFRIED* 14 SEPTEMBER TO 22 OCTOBER, 1941

The Wehrmacht was not known for joint operations involving land, sea and air forces, with the 1940 invasion of Norway being the main exception. Anticipating this eventual requirement, however, two months prior to *Barbarossatag* Heeresgruppe Nord planners devised Operation *Beowulf*, an assault against the Estonian islands at the mouth of the Gulf of Riga. At approximately 1,000 square miles Saaremaa was the largest island, joined to tiny Muhu by a 2 ¼-mile causeway, while Hiiumaa measured *c.*500 square miles. General Major A. B. Elisseyev commanded 24,000 Red Army troops, mainly the 3rd Independent Rifle Brigade on Saaremaa and two battalions of the 79th Rifle Regiment on Muhu. Ten coastal and 16 field artillery batteries gave them ample indirect fire support, but Elisseyev had neglected to prepare adequately for the attack he should have known was coming.

The German plan called for General Siegfried Haenicke's 61. Infanterie-Division to conduct an amphibious attack from the Estonian mainland on 14 September 1941, supported by Brandenburger commandos and Kriegsmarine and Luftwaffe elements. German and Finnish naval forces performed shore bombardment the day before: Operation *Südwind* by light cruisers *Leipzig, Köln* and *Emden* plus supporting vessels against the west coast of Saaremaa, and Operation *Nordwind* led by two Finnish 10-inch gun monitors and smaller units against the north of Hiiumaa. Their gunfire was meant to trick the defenders into believing that the attack would come from the sea (as it had during Operation *Albion* in October 1917). At the cost of the Finnish flagship, the monitor *Ilmarinen,* the ruses had the desired effect, as Elisseyev sent his men westward.

The real attack came from the east at 0400 hours the next morning. Using pioneer assault craft intended for river use, 270 boatloads of Haenicke's men crossed the 6-mile-wide sound separating Muhu from the mainland. The Brandenburgers' Sonderkommando Benesch landed by gliders on nearby Kuebassare Peninsula in order to neutralize its coastal guns. After many mishaps mainly involving poor boat handling on the open water, the 151. Infanterie-Regiment, the 161. Aufklärungs Abteilung and one battalion of light mountain artillery had established a beachhead four miles wide. The next day the 151. Infanterie-Regiment successfully fought its way across the causeway; Elisseyev's men were still oriented principally toward the east. Now on the big island of Saaremaa in strength, Haenicke split his forces in two with the 151. and 162. Infanterie-Regiments heading south and the 176. Infanterie and the recon battalion aiming north. By September 17 Red Army defenders had recovered sufficiently at least to create a coherent line across the width of the island, but fell back through successive positions over the next couple of days. By 21 September they had abandoned the capital town of Kuresaare and except for the 1 ¼-mile-wide Sorve Peninsula had given up Saaremaa. On this narrow spit of land Haenicke's two southern regiments had a difficult two-week fight clearing Sorve of 15,000 defenders. Alternating the leading effort, 151. and 162. Infanterie-Regiments worked their way south under Luftwaffe CAS. Resistance ended on 5 October with the capture of 5,000 POWs while 1,500 Soviet troops made good their escape to Hiiumaa.

General Haenicke then turned his attention to Operation *Siegfried* against Hiiumaa, starting again with a naval gunfire feint to the north. Improbably the 176. Infanterie-Regiment achieved surprise when it landed on the east shore of the island at 0500 hours on 12 October. Later that afternoon 161. Aufklärungs Abteilung and 151. Infanterie-Regiment troops (the latter transferred from Sorve) joined the fight to the west. Eventually troops from 217. Infanterie-Division also contributed against about 4,000 Red Army defenders who, once they regained their balance, put up a worthy effort. After a week of heavy combat the Soviets were pinned to the northern tip of Hiiumaa. During the night of 21–22 October, 570 men managed to escape by ship to the mainland. The 61. Infanterie-Division lost 2,850 men taking the Baltic Islands but cleared this obstruction to the Gulf of Riga, taking 15,000 Soviet POWs and over 200 guns. With the exception of the initial hasty Japanese attack on Wake Island, every amphibious landing during World War II succeeded. Operations *Beowulf* and *Siegfried* provided a very good example of German tri-service co-operation at the tactical level.

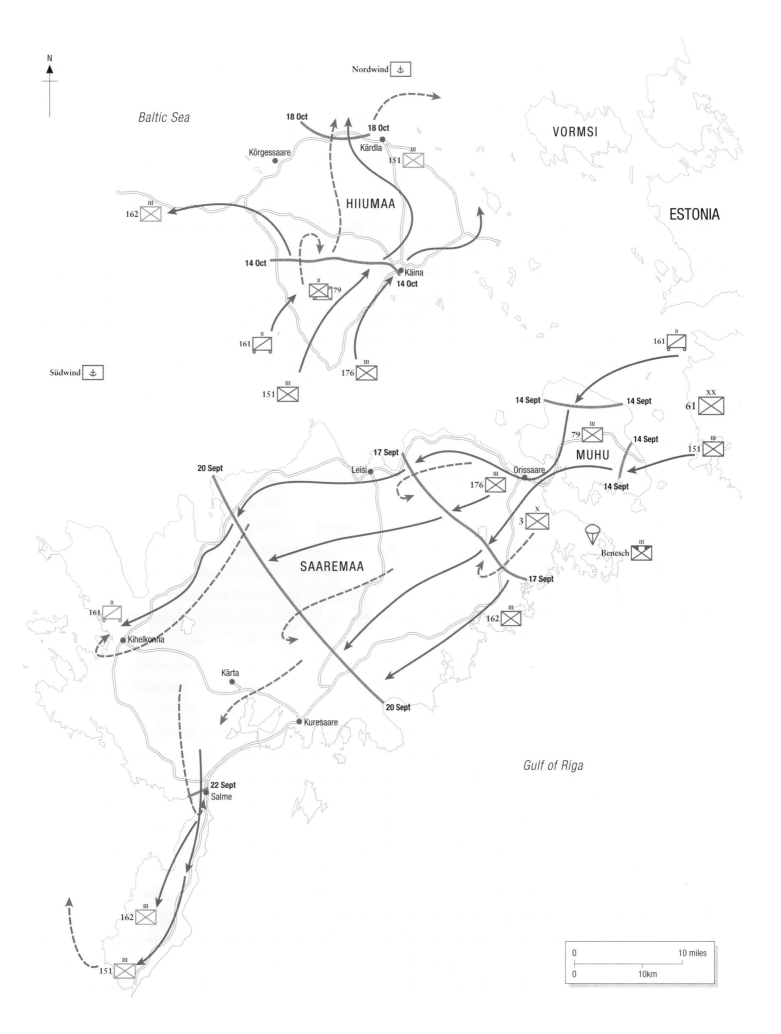

N

Baltic Sea

Nordwind ⚓

18 Oct

18 Oct

Kärdla

Kõrgessaare

HIIUMAA

III
151

ESTONIA

VORMSI

III
162

14 Oct

Käina

14 Oct

Südwind ⚓

II
79

II
161

III
176

III
151

II
161

14 Sept

14 Sept

XX
61

III
79

III
151

14 Sept

14 Sept

MUHU

17 Sept

Leisi

Orissaare

20 Sept

III
176

SAAREMAA

X
3

Benesch

III

II
161

Kihelkonna

Kärta

17 Sept

III
162

Gulf of Riga

20 Sept

Kuresaare

22 Sept
Salme

III
162

III
151

0   10 miles

0   10km

27

MAP 8: THE BATTLES FOR TIKHVIN AND VOLKHOV – 16 OCTOBER TO 7 DECEMBER, 1941

By the last week of September Leeb's final assaults on Leningrad had ground to a halt, victims of Soviet resistance, the Germans' weakness, poor planning and insufficient logistics plus Hitler's halt order. So long as the Wehrmacht held the tenuous Shlisselburg barrier, few gave the surrounded city's three million inhabitants and garrison much chance of surviving. When bombing proved unexpectedly hazardous for the Luftwaffe, the Germans brought in their heavy artillery, but its effects were dissipated by Leningrad's 1,000 square mile hinterland. What he could not conquer outright the Führer would starve into submission. Stalin had other ideas, however. He would keep his outpost supplied and fighting while the Red Army attempted to lift the siege.

At this point Operation *Typhoon* had yet to begin and even in late September the Wehrmacht (plus military experts in much of the world) assumed that the USSR would not survive into 1942. Just to make sure and help its cause, the Germans had three reasons for pushing northeast beyond the existing Shlisselburg–Kirishi–Chudovo–Novgorod line: further to insulate Leningrad, to join up with the Finns on the Svir River and to capture the bauxite mines at Tikhvin. In the north, 18. Armee's I Armee-Korps would attack toward Volkhov, while XXXIX Panzer-Korps under 16. Armee made for Tikhvin. With the UK and USA applying considerable political pressure on Finland to go no farther than the Svir River, the Soviets considered the 7th Independent Army sufficient to hold that sector. In front of Volkhov and Tikhvin the Stavka arrayed 54th, 4th and 52nd Armies, 63,000 men and 475 artillery pieces. Recent reinforcements to each side favoured the Red Army 9:2.

General der Panzertruppen Hans-Jürgen von Arnim attacked on 16 October and got the advantage on Marshal G. I. Kulik, who had been planning his own offensive. Running the seam between 4th and 52nd Armies, XXXIX Panzer made rapid advances past Malaya Vishera and swung northward. Terrain favoured the defender, while the climate alternated between cool and muddy or cold and frozen; German progress suffered or succeeded accordingly. After one week 12. Panzer-Division took Budogoshch, almost halfway to Tihhvin. Along with

18th Infanterie-Division (Mot.), it somehow continued to push ahead, albeit slowly, against the 4th Army charged with holding Tikhvin. The 4th could not accomplish this mission, however, and, with scattered defenders streaming back, it gave up the town on 8 November. The Soviets lost 20,000 POWs and 179 guns. At the same time I Armee-Korps pushed back General Lieutenant I. I. Fedyuninsky's 54th Army guarding Volkhov, coming within four miles of that town. General K. A. Meretskov from the 7th Independent Army replaced the hapless Marshal G. I. Kulik and took measures to stabilize the fighting and if possible re-open the rail line to Leningrad.[11]

Stalin demanded results and, outnumbering the Germans nearly 3:1, Meretskov soon delivered. The 52nd Army, now under General Lieutenant N. K. Klykov, began by attacking against the southern edge of Leeb's bulge on 12 November. Besides drawing off scarce reserves, it achieved little. A week later Meretskov, in personal command of the 4th Army, attacked the tip of the salient on either side of Tikhvin. Within three days Wehrmacht troops were practically cut off in the town with only one division in reserve, the 61. Infanterie-Division. Arnim's men managed to hold out for another two weeks but by early December could do so no longer. Hitler and Leeb then began the back-and-forth telephone negotiations that would punctuate the remainder of the Nazi-Soviet War, with the general requesting permission to withdraw and the dictator telling him 'No'. Finally on 7 December, Leeb authorized the abandonment of Tikhvin, which Hitler approved retroactively early the next morning. Near Volkhov, only 50 miles from the Finns on the Svir River, the 54th Army began operations against I Armee-Korps and soon had it in full retreat. The front came to rest back along the Volkhov River by the middle of December. Heeresgruppe Nord, fighting a poor-man's war throughout *Barbarossa*, had failed to achieve any of its four missions: to create its own huge *Kessel*, link up with the Finns, neutralize Kronshtadt or capture Leningrad.

---

11 After making a hash of the Kerch Peninsula defences in November, Stalin recalled Kulik to Moscow and demoted him to major general; he would spend the rest of the war in low-level leadership positions.

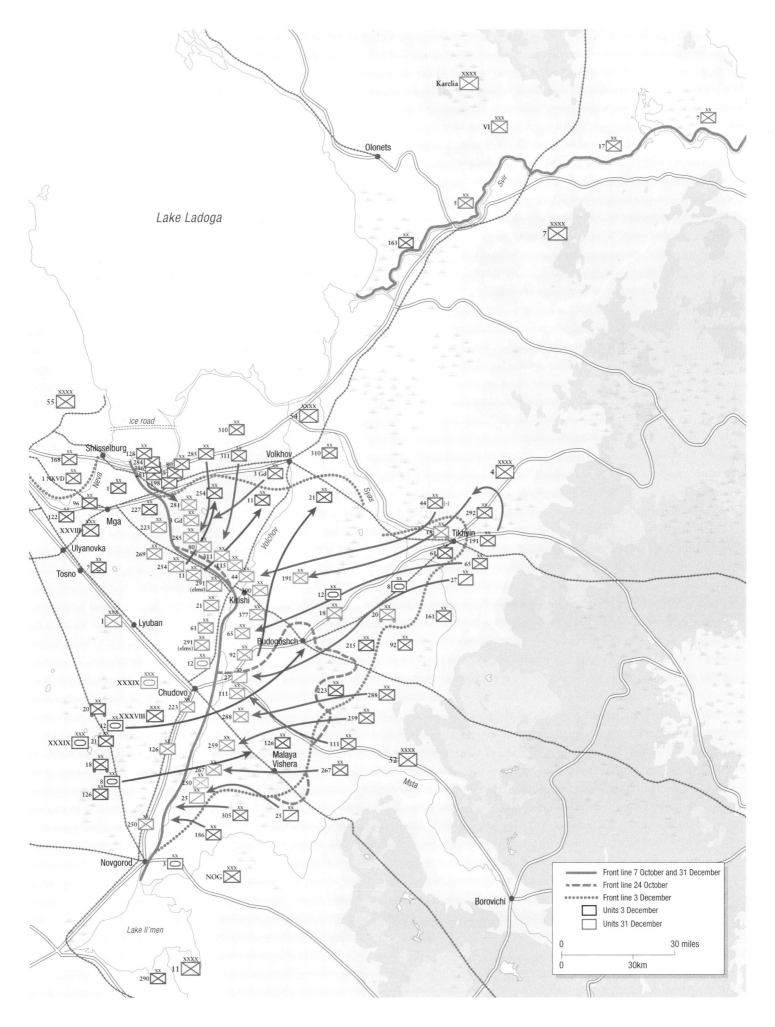

Lake Ladoga

Karelia XXXX

VI XXX

7 XX

Olonets

17 XX

Svir

5 XX

7 XXXX

163 XX

55 XXXX

ice road

54 XXXX

310 XX

Shlisselburg 128 XX

285 XX

311 XX

Volkhov

310 XX

4 XXXX

168 XX

284 XX
286 XX
281 XX

80 XX
5 XX

3 Gd XX

Syas

44 XX (-)

292 XX

1 NKVD

Neva

198 XX

254 XX

11 XX

21 XX

18 XX   Tikhvin

191 XX

1 XX

96 XX

227 XX

281 XX

Volchov

61 XX

122 XX

XXVIII   Mga

223 XX

3 Gd XX

65 XX

27 XX

269 XX

285 XX

80 XX
311 XX

115 XX

44 XX

191 XX

8 XX

Ulyanovka

254 XX

11 XX

12 XX

Tosno   7 XX

291 XX (elms)

20 XX

161 XX

21 XX   Kirishi

377 XX

18 XX

I XX   Lyuban

61 XX

65 XX

Budogoshch

215 XX

92 XX

291 XX (elms)

92 XX

XXXIX

12 XX

27 XX

Chudovo

111 XX

223 XX

288 XX

20 XX   XXXVIII XXX

223 XX

288 XX

259 XX

111 XX

XXXIX   21 XX

12 XX

126 XX

259 XX

126 XX

Malaya Vishera

52 XXXX

18 XX

267 XX

8 XX

250 XX

267 XX

126 XX

25 XX

Msta

250 XX

305 XX

25 XX

186 XX

Novgorod   3 XX

NOG XXX

Borovichi

Lake Il'men

Front line 7 October and 31 December
Front line 24 October
Front line 3 December
Units 3 December
Units 31 December

0   30 miles
0   30km

11 XXXX

290 XX

29

MAP 9: FRONTIER BATTLES CENTRE 22–30 JUNE, 1941

With Moscow as the goal, all eyes – at the time and since – would be on the drive up the centre. Bock's men advanced along the same high ground Napoleon had used. It marked the limit of advance of the last ice age and included the headwaters of the Dvina and Dnepr Rivers. Along the way, *Kesseln* at Minsk and Smolensk represented intermediate objectives; Wehrmacht planners assumed they could destroy the Red Army by this point. Bock commanded 9. and 4. Armeen, plus 3. and 2. Panzergruppen, while the highly specialized and well-trained VIII Flieger-Korps provided CAS. In March 1941 Hitler placed the eastern army's sole strategic reserve, 2. Armee, behind Heeresgruppe Mitte. This formation, assumed to be held ready for tasks of strategic importance – say to provide a body of fresh troops for a critical mission like attacking Moscow – was instead inserted into the campaign at an early stage and by July was soon indistinguishable from any other field army. As mentioned previously, Pavlov's Western Special Military District – later the Western Front (composed of 3rd, 10th and 4th Armies including six mechanized corps) – occupied precarious positions almost surrounded by Bock on three sides. Under DP 41 he lost Soviet defensive main effort status and resourcing suffered accordingly.

Pavlov received permission to alert his troops five minutes before the invasion, but his hands were tied by Stalin's curious concern that the Red Army did not seem to provoke the attacking Germans. Neither the Neman River in the sector's far north nor the Bug in its southern half offered his men any succour. The 3. Panzergruppe in the Suwalki 'beak' and 2. Panzergruppe near Brest began with great positional advantages and made the most of them. By the end of *Barbarossatag*, both had broken into the open field – contributing mightily to unhinging the defence of Pavlov, who at no point had positive control of the situation. A day later the Western Front began to lose contact with its neighbour to the north as Hoth's men in 3. Panzergruppe, despite early fuel shortages, soon reached Vitebsk and Polotsk north-east of Vilnius (off

the map). The 2. Panzergruppe under Generaloberst Heinz Guderian likewise made impressive advances past Baranovichi and on to Bobruisk and Rogachev (both off the map to the east). These two thrusts caused *Barbarossa*'s first *Kessel* to begin to form near Bialystok, a development that caught the eye of Hitler at Rastenburg. The Führer wanted to close the pocket quickly while Brauchitsch, Halder and Bock all wanted to continue eastward. They compromised and did both; the 29. Infanterie-Division (Mot.) closed the pocket three days into the war as the panzer groups probed in the direction of Minsk.

Pavlov's men were not done, however. He organized an attack group led by more than 1,300 tanks under his deputy General Lieutenant I. V. Boldin to attempt to cut off the base of Hoth's penetration near Grodno. Hoth was long gone to the east, so Boldin's assault fell on the infantry of 9. Armee. Fighting was heaviest on 24 June, but with Luftwaffe CAS overhead, the *Landser*s held steady. Condemned by poor leadership, little tactical training or logistical support, the counterattack ground to a halt the next day with severe Red Army losses and practically no effect on Hoth's progress. On the southern edge of the Bialystok salient the fortress of Brest held out against German attempts to reduce it. This difficult task fell on the 45. Infanterie-Division, supported by railway siege guns and Luftwaffe aircraft dropping two-ton ordnance on the old brick structure. An assortment of Soviet organizations defended the locale, which stood astride Bock's southern supply route. They kept fighting for over a week, organized combat ending on the last day of June, although isolated groups continued to resist for weeks.

It took Bock just a few days to destroy the better part of three Soviet armies. The various pockets around Bialystok netted his men 290,000 POWs. By this time the vanguards of his two panzer groups stood more than 200 miles beyond. The Western Front was in a shambles and out of contact with the North-western Front to its left, while Heeresgruppe Mitte stood on the brink of another, larger encirclement.

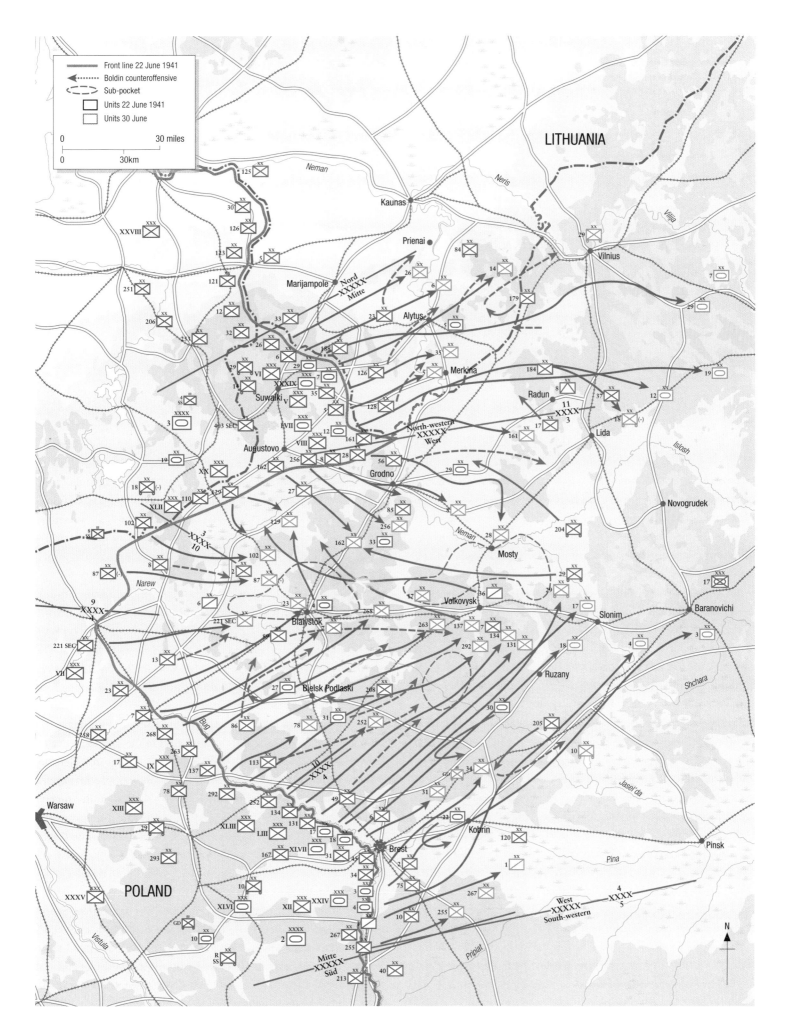

LITHUANIA

Front line 22 June 1941
Boldin counteroffensive
Sub-pocket
Units 22 June 1941
Units 30 June

0   30 miles
0   30km

Neman
Neris
Vilija
Islosh
Shchara
Jasel'da
Pina
Pripiat
Narew
Bug
Vistula

Kaunas
Prienai
Marijampole
Alytus
Merkina
Radun
Vilnius
Novogrudek
Lida
Mosty
Volkovysk
Slonim
Baranovichi
Ruzany
Kobrin
Pinsk
Grodno
Suwalki
Augustovo
Bialystok
Bielsk Podlaski
Brest
Warsaw
POLAND

Nord
XXXXX
Mitte

North-western
XXXXX
West

West
XXXXX
South-western

Mitte
XXXXX
Süd

N

31

MAP 10: MINSK ENCIRCLEMENT 25–30 JUNE, 1941

The Western Front barely survived the first week of *Barbarossa*. Between units destroyed in the border fight and those encircled in the various Bialystok pockets, the vulnerability of the salient was clear and Pavlov had lost half of his command in a matter of days. But the manner in which the Germans either scattered or encircled Red Army units here in 1941 by using movement was entirely different from how the Soviet offensives would obliterate Wehrmacht units with firepower on the same battlefields exactly three years later.

The Bialystok and Novogrudek *Kesseln*, approximately six divisions in each, had been unexpected by-products of Pavlov's exposed positions, but now all German eyes were on Minsk, where *Barbarossa* planners had long anticipated their first major victory. Meanwhile the Stavka [12] cast about for a solution for defending the main route to Moscow. General Hoth's decisive splitting of the boundary between Western and North-western fronts made this task infinitely more difficult. The limited Red Army counterattacks that could be mounted suffered from the usual problems of outclassed command and control, nonexistent combined-arms tactics and weak logistics. Marshal Timoshenko's attempts to manage a coherent defence and withdraw along successive river lines predictably failed when mechanized German units breached the watercourses before marching Soviet formations could even establish themselves. The Stavka settled on ordering the 19th, 20th, 21st and 22nd Armies of Marshal S. M. Budenny's Reserve Front, sitting behind Pavlov, to create defences along the line Nevel–Vitebsk–Orsha–Gomel and then following the middle Dnepr. Within days three more armies, the 16th, 24th and 28th, were added to the defensive effort. Unfortunately for the defenders, the speed of the panzers' advance and the chaos left in their wake precluded organized opposition. Absolutely the wrong man for such a crisis, Budenny owed his position solely to personal acquaintance with Stalin dating back to the Russian Civil War: he was soon overcome by events and cashiered. Back in Moscow Zhukov planned a second position near Yelnia and a third even closer

to the capital stretching from Viazma to Kaluga. Sure enough, some of the key battles on the Moscow axis would be fought along both lines.

Zhukov ordered Pavlov to behave like a commander, get control of the situation and counterattack against Bock however and whenever possible. At the same time, on 27 June Moscow received intelligence indicating that Heeresgruppe Mitte represented *Barbarossa's Schwerpunkt*. Versus such a superior force, Pavlov's last vestiges, for whom avoiding defeat was itself a small victory, would be incapable of launching more than nuisance counterattacks and would be fortunate to remain a viable force on the battlefield for very long. Events would prove that this condition was acceptable to Stalin and the rest of the Soviet high command, who valued Moscow over a body of troops.

The adjacent map shows the next disaster to befall the defence of Moscow. Like two seine fishing boats dragging a net, Hoth's 3. Panzergruppe manoeuvred north of the ridgeline Bialystok–Minsk while Guderian's 2. Panzergruppe advanced to the south. Hoth, always more of a team player, directed his men toward Minsk, while Guderian, prone to prima donna tendencies, veered away. Pavlov's reactions were ineffective, although he did commit the 13th Army to hold the city. Hoth's 12. Panzer-Division did its part when it entered the Belorussian capital on the afternoon of 28 June. Guderian's troops coming from the south, however, were still a way off. It took 18. Panzer-Division another 24 hours to enter Minsk and close the pocket from the south, which included remnants of the 3rd, 10th and 13th Armies, but in the meantime significant Red Army units continued to evade entrapment toward the south-east.

The Wehrmacht claimed 310,000 POWs captured and 2,500 tanks and 1,500 guns destroyed at Minsk. Unfortunately for the Germans, the process of digesting the pockets took more time and resources than anticipated, and Red Army resistance was resolute. At Hitler's headquarters, OKH and Heeresgruppe Mitte, the time had come to decide what to do next. With only vague guidance from above, both Hoth and Guderian simply continued eastward. Stalin finally gave up on Pavlov, relieved him on the last day of June, recalled him to Moscow and had him executed. Stalin's old warhorse, Timoshenko, took charge of defending Moscow's approaches.

---

12 Stalin played a minimal role during *Barbarossa's* first ten days. The Soviet premier withdrew to his dacha and took until 3 July to compose himself and return to the public eye with his famous 'Comrades, citizens, brothers and sisters…' speech.

MAP 11: SMOLENSK ENCIRCLEMENT 1–15 JULY, 1941

Heeresgruppe Mitte had racked up an impressive and, for the USSR, disastrous string of victories between the Bug River and Minsk. The next stop for the Wehrmacht on the road to Moscow would be Smolensk on the portage between the Dvina and Dnepr rivers, sure to be heavily defended by Soviet troops. Following its defeats during *Barbarossa*'s first two weeks, the Red Army planned to make a stand along the Berezina River, scene of the defeat of Napoleon's rearguard in November 1812. Hopes Soviet planners had placed in the Stalin Line defences proved to be unfounded, firstly because they had been basically stripped clean for a year and a half prior to the Germans' arrival, and secondly, and more to the point, because fixed fortifications of this type proved almost useless in World War II.[13] With this in mind, the Stavka ordered Timoshenko to create a viable counter to the two marauding panzer groups, to include launching counterattacks against both. Starting on 4 July, the marshal placed eight rifle divisions and two mechanized corps astride the most threatened portion of the new line, west of Senno, in the centre of the so-called 'river gate' between the upper reaches of the two rivers.

While Guderian ignored any directions other than to drive on Moscow by the most direct route, Hoth had an additional mission beyond keeping a course parallel to Guderian, that of maintaining contact with Heeresgruppe Nord to his left. Not only could Bock's two panzer groups offer each other no mutual support, but, on a smaller scale, Hoth's panzer corps could not act in concert as up to 100 miles separated them.[14] Though Red Army forces in front of both panzer groups were in complete disarray, Guderian had relatively open and rolling terrain, while Hoth operated in the much more forested and constrained environment common in northern Russia. Under these inauspicious conditions between Senno and Vitebsk Timoshenko launched the 5th and 7th Mechanized Corps against Hoth's right-hand outfit, XXXIX Panzer-Korps. Initially the 7. Panzer-Division took the brunt of the 2,000-tank assault, which sent the Germans reeling. Over

the next five days Hoth dispatched three more panzer divisions to stabilize the situation. While the Stavka had correctly identified the panzer groups' vulnerable advanced guards, boundaries and flanks, the disparity between Wehrmacht and Soviet skills meant it could not successfully translate ambitious plans into successful outcomes.

During the second week of July, Bock fully exploited his advantages and the corresponding Red Army deficiencies. Hoth made for crossings over the middle Desna, with some of his units recording advances of over 100 miles per day despite occasional Soviet counterattacks. The operational requirement to maintain communication with Heeresgruppe Nord continued to hamstring Hoth and dissipate the impact of his panzer group, however; at first glance far-flung spearheads to Nevel and Velikie Luki (off the map to the north) might look impressive on a map, but in reality they robbed Hoth of mass. Meanwhile, with difficulty Guderian breached the Dnepr at Bychov and Rogachev; here the Stalin Line still had some teeth. He shifted his *Schwerpunkt* back and forth between bridgeheads to gain some advantage until achieving decisive success near Mogilev on 10–11 July. His panzer troops created a small *Kessel* of 35,000 men in the heavily fortified town while smashing a large hole in Timoshenko's Dnepr position. *Landser*s (with their thousands of horses) marched and marched, averaging 20 miles per day for weeks, trying to maintain pace with the mechanized forces. Along the way they fended off enemy breakout attempts, counterattacks and partisan ambushes – sometimes all three almost simultaneously.

After 11 July, with the Dnepr and Stalin Line behind him and the VIII Flieger-Korps over him, Guderian had broken free and Smolensk's days of holding out were clearly numbered. Although focused on Moscow (witness his dispatching XLVI Panzer-Korps to Yelnia) he did not ignore Smolensk, toward which he directed the XLVII Panzer-Korps. Hoth's XXXIX Panzer-Korps likewise angled south-east and converged with 2. Panzergruppe in order to encircle the ancient city. Soviet countermeasures had little immediate effect and on 15 July men of Hoth and Guderian met and cut off 300,000 Red Army troops, militiamen and communist cadres. Trapped defenders and rescuers sent from outside struggled against the Germans' inner and outer pincers. Ferocious fighting took place all along the pocket. With marching infantry often far to the rear, the very difficult task of sealing off the cordons fell to Hoth's and Guderian's highly-trained panzer specialists. Despite this steep cost, it looked to the world as though Hitler had scored a decisive win and the way to Moscow had been laid open yet again.

---

13 While anecdotes of strongpoints affecting tactical combat certainly abound, from the Atlantic Wall to Mount Suribachi permanent fortifications failed to live up to the hype and consistently had minimal impact on operational or strategic levels, despite much cost and effort.

14 During Barbarossa the Germans learned operational-level blitzkrieg leadership on the fly. To co-ordinate Bock's panzer groups and calm Hitler's nerves, on the night of 2–3 July they created the short-lived and ad hoc 4. Panzer-Armee under Kluge. This plodding and unimaginative general was a terrible choice for a potentially critical position; his headquarters quickly became totally superfluous and was abandoned by the end of the month. Not to be confused with the 4. Panzer-Gruppe's new incarnation in January 1942.

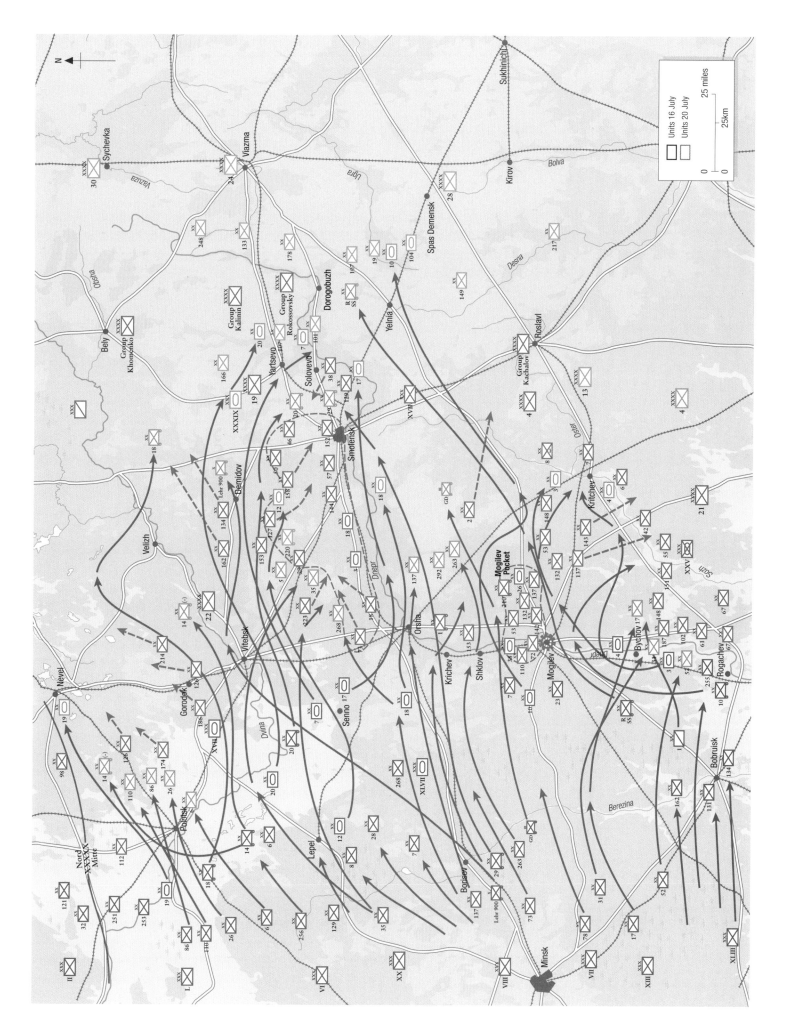

35

MAP 12: TIMOSHENKO COUNTEROFFENSIVES 23–31 JULY, 1941

After the German successes at Bialystok, Minsk and Smolensk, and following the Soviet failures at the Stalin Line and along the Berezina and Dvina–Dnepr rivers, the Stavka needed to assert itself on the Moscow axis. In less than a month of fighting they had lost their first two operational defensive echelons. Although Red Army attempts to halt or at least slow *Barbarossa* did not appear to be having much success at the time, we know now that they caused German losses to rise to debilitating levels while the task of digesting encircled Soviet forces took more time and effort than pre-war Wehrmacht planners had estimated. It seemed that everything associated with the invasion of the USSR was more difficult, consumed more fuel and time, resulted in more casualties and generally had an overall sobering effect on Hitler and his eastern army.

Stalin's headquarters had learned the hard way that Timoshenko's counterattacks on the eve of Smolensk, usually consisting of two or three divisions, spread out and only loosely co-ordinated, had been ineffective in doing any more than causing the army-sized panzer groups to pause for a couple of days. Although the *Kessel* had closed in name only on 15 July and some of Hoth and Guderian's mechanized units had continued eastward, the battle in and immediately outside the pocket raged on for weeks. The door to the trap closed for real only two weeks later, approximately 27–28 July. Bock considered the Smolensk battles officially over on 5 August, but many of his formations, especially the infantry divisions, would be in action in the area for much longer. The Stavka therefore created five armies and ordered Timoshenko to blunt the drive on Moscow and relieve the besieged encirclement starting in the third week of July.

These attacks became known collectively as the Timoshenko Counteroffensives. Group Kachalov, basically the 28th Army under NKVD General Lieutenant V. I. Kachalov, launched first against Guderian's southern flank. Threatening the rear of the XLVI Panzer-Korps, which was heading for Yelnia, between 23 and 27 July, Kachalov's two rifle and one tank divisions advanced over 15 miles from Roslavl in the direction of Pochep. Bock had to counter with Guderian's own XXIV Panzer-Korps plus Kluge's VII and IX Armee-Korps, attacking on 31 July and 1 August. Elements of these three headquarters required the better part of a week to neutralize the threat posed by Kachalov, who died during the fighting.

Next came a two-part effort in the far north of Bock's sector. On 24 July Group Khomenko, NKVD General Major V. A. Khomenko's 30th Army consisting of three rifle divisions, attacked due west over the Vop River. Behind this force stood Group Kalinin, three rifle divisions of the 24th Army under NKVD General Major S. A. Kalinin, which would exploit Khomenko's success. Neither the initial attack nor the subsequent exploitation amounted to much, despite being reinforced on the right by two cavalry divisions under Colonel I. A. Pliev.

Two other attacks occurred off the map. Also attacking on 24 July south-west of Bobruisk (off the map's bottom left margin), a cavalry group of three cavalry and one rifle divisions under General Colonel O. I. Gorodovikov attempted to threaten the rearward communications of both 2. Panzergruppe and 2. Armee. Off the map's top margin, Group Maslennikov, NKVD General Lieutenant I. I. Maslennikov's 29th Army (three rifle divisions) attacked, likewise to no avail.

Army General Major K. K. Rokossovsky attacked directly into the teeth of Hoth's panzer group and contributed markedly to keeping open the route from Smolensk through which Lieutenant General P. A. Kurochkin's trapped men could escape. Rokossovsky began on 28 July with only two rifle divisions, but soon added men and equipment from disorganized Red Army outfits wandering about the battlefield. He simultaneously fought the XXXIX Panzer-Korps to a temporary standstill while keeping open Kurochkin's escape route. Bock dispatched mobile divisions and Luftwaffe CAS to rectify the situation, which they did by the end of the month.

The Timoshenko counteroffensives involved the better part of two dozen divisions fighting along a 300-mile arc for over a week. Most of these formations were either rifle or cavalry divisions, quite often facing German panzer or motorized units, so the overall affect was dissipated. In this way the counteroffensives cannot be considered much more successful than his earlier manoeuvres on the Berezina, but their attacks did coincide loosely with the summer command crisis then afflicting Hitler's headquarters and caused additional casualties and delays. As part of the death-by-a-thousand-cuts strategy, these counterattacks added a good number of wounds to Hitler's hopes for *Barbarossa*.

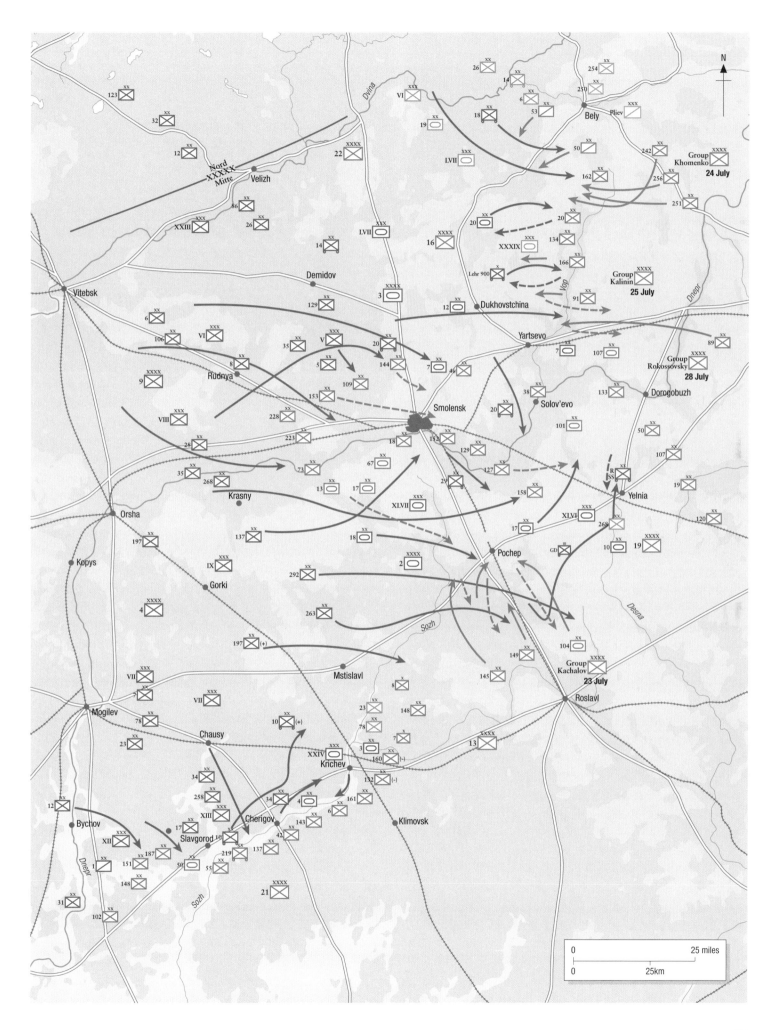

MAP 13: OPERATION *TYPHOON* (I), VIAZMA AND BRYANSK – 30 SEPTEMBER TO 15 OCTOBER, 1941

By early September, Hitler could anticipate Leningrad's isolation and successful battles in the Ukraine. Führer Directive No. 35, issued on 6 September, considered conditions ripe for the destruction of 'Army Group Timoshenko' and for continuing the drive toward Moscow. Ten days later, Bock issued his order to attack the Western, Reserve and Bryansk fronts. Operation *Typhoon* consisted of a triple envelopment conducted by three pairs of infantry armies for breakthroughs and panzer groups for exploitation: 3. Panzergruppe and 9. Armee in the north, 4. Panzergruppe (transferred from Leeb) with 4. Armee as the *Schwerpunkt* in the centre and 2. Panzergruppe plus 2. Armee in the south (reinforced by XLVIII Panzer-Korps from Rundstedt). Controversy attended *Typhoon*'s planning as Hitler, Halder, Bock and various field commanders argued their own opinions and theories of how to conduct the operation. Wehrmacht intelligence performed above average, since the two sides had been involved in toe-to-toe combat for nearly a month. Logistics would be the Germans' Achilles heel again, however, since the hoped-for logistics pause failed to amount to much against constant Soviet counterattacks. Nevertheless, for *Typhoon* Bock mustered a force second only to that of 22 June: 1,929,000 men in 78 divisions, 14,000 mortars and artillery pieces, 1,000 panzers and 1,390 aircraft.

Red Army forces on the other hand were battered, as conducting the death by a thousand cuts defence was very costly. Correctly, however, they would focus their delaying efforts on roads and built-up areas since these would be critical to the Germans, especially as the weather worsened. The normally astute Soviet intelligence expected continued attacks along the Smolensk–Moscow continental divide, so they were surprised by the location of Bock's three thrusts. Likewise, the defenders' logistics were also stretched. More than 1,250,000 soldiers in 95 divisions and 13 tank brigades, 7,600 indirect-fire weapons, 990 tanks and 863 planes manned the line; this translated to 1,000 men, 7.5 guns and one tank per mile. Significantly, there was no single overall commander... yet.

Two days before the rest of the army group, on 30 September, Guderian attacked from north-eastern Ukraine. His tankers quickly overwhelmed the local defenders and bewildered leaders at higher echelons, who did not know what to make of this apparent one-off offensive. Heeresgruppe Mitte's other attack occurred on the morning of 2 October when 2. and 4. Armeen infantry fought through defences

which had been weeks in the making. Later that same day, 3. Panzergruppe penetrated between the Soviet 19th and 30th Armies while 4. Panzergruppe rolled over the 43rd Army; soon both Hoth and Hoepner were in the open field. General Boldin's counterattacks supported by 300 tanks were ineffectual. Otherwise, the preferred defensive technique was to stand fast in prepared positions. By 3 October the panzers had advanced 50 miles and, with most of their reserves already heading south to counter Guderian, Soviet commanders in the northern and central sectors had nothing with which to stop them. Stalin, the Stavka and tactical commanders froze in inaction, reminiscent of June.

Fortunately for them, 48 hours into *Typhoon* anaemic German logistics crippled the offensive. By 5 October, 3. Panzergruppe, refuelled and now commanded by Georg-Hans Reinhardt, renewed its assault as the Stavka finally gave its permission for nearly-encircled forces to retreat. Red Army defenders had barely disengaged when Reinhardt and Hoepner's panzers met at Viazma on the morning of the 7th, trapping elements of 19th, 20th, 24th and 32nd Armies. To the south Guderian wilfully headed for Moscow rather than another *Kessel*, while 2. Armee infantry struggled to advance. Leading elements of these two formations did manage to link up north of Bryansk, also on the 7th, encircling most of 3rd, 13th and 50th Armies. Of the 1,250,000 defenders present on the battlefield ten days earlier, 332,000 had died and 668,000 were POWs, while over 100,000 escaped eastward. German losses totalled 48,000.

Between September and October, at Kiev and Viazma–Bryansk, 1.3 million Soviet troops marched into captivity while half a million died in battle. Almost no other nation or army could sustain two million casualties in four weeks, but in October and November the Soviets were able to send 1.5 million new troops to take their place. Clearing the two *Kesseln* required two weeks' effort by most of Bock's men while advancing panzer spearheads went it alone, by 15 October reaching the line Kalinin (off map to the north)–Mozhaisk–Kaluga–Mtensk. Just as the triple encirclement became an accomplished fact, the autumn rains and attendant *rasputitsa* (muddy season, when roads become difficult to travel) arrived to slow the Wehrmacht further. Then on 10 October Stalin ordered Zhukov back to Moscow from Leningrad to breathe new life into the capital's defences.

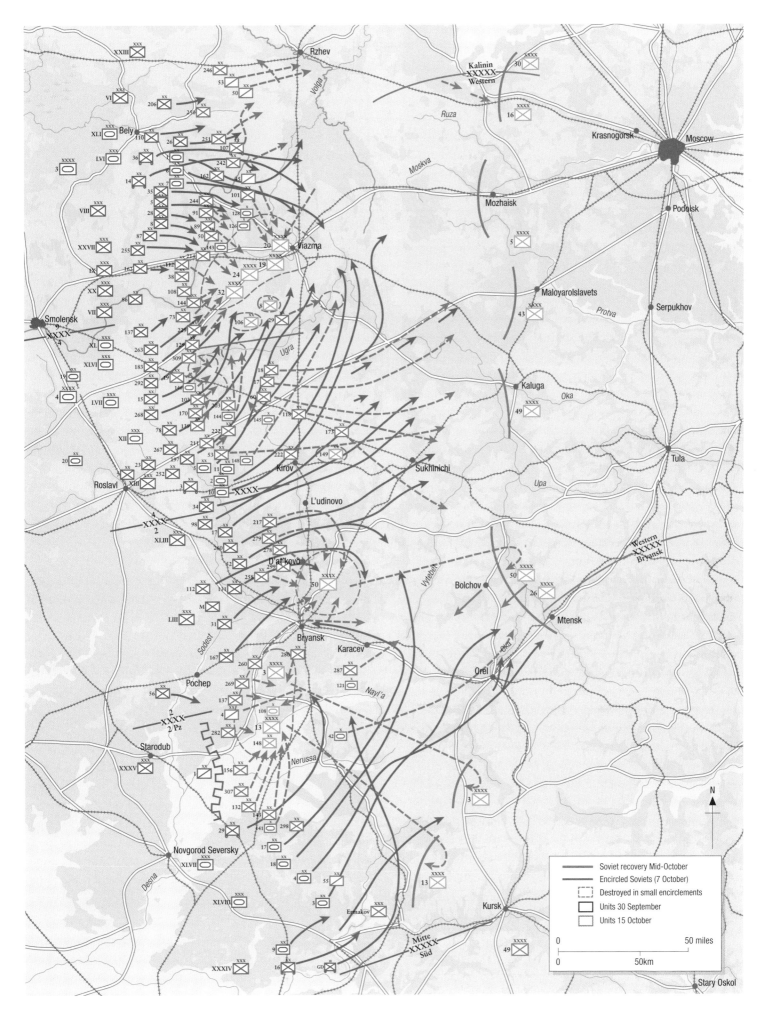

XXIII XXX

246
53
50

VI XXX
206 XX
259 XX

XLI XXX
Bely 110 XX
36 XX
26 XX 251 XX 68 XX
107

LVI
3
14 XX
35 XX
28 XX
8 XX
87 XX

VIII XXX
255 XX

XXVII XXX

IX XXX
162 XX
XX XXX
86 XX

VII XXX

Smolensk
9
XXXXX
4

XI XXX
XLVI XXX
9 XX
4

LVII XXX

242
162
244 XX
91 XX
89 XX
50 XX
214 XX
112 XX
38 XX
108 XX
144 XX
73 XX
229 XX
137 XX
263 XX
183 XX
292 XX
15 XX
268 XX
170 XX
78 XX
139

101
128 XX
126
143
32 XX
106 XX
309 XX
18 XX
60 XX
303 XX
144 XX

Rzhev

Volga

Kalinin
XXXXX
Western
30 XXXX
16 XXXX

Ruza

Krasnogorsk
Moscow

Moskva

Mozhaisk

Podolsk

Viazma
20 XX
XXXX 19
24 XX
XXXX
29 XX
129
117 XX
145

5 XX
5

Maloyaroslavets
43 XXXX

Protva
Serpukhov

Ugra
Kaluga
49 XXXX
Oka

XII XXX
267 XX
20 XX
23 XX 252 XX
XIII XXX
197 XX
53 XX
11 XX
148 XX
2 XX
3
10

Roslavl

222 XX
149 XXXX
118 XX
173 XX
222 XX

Kirov
Sukhinichi

XXXX

Tula
Upa

34 XX
98 XX
17 XX
260 XX
52 XX
258 XX
112 XX
131 XX
LIII M
31 XX

XXXXX
2
XLIII XXX

L'udinovo

217 XX
279 XX
278 XX
299 XX
50 XX

Western
XXXXX
Bryansk
50 XXXX
26 XXXX

Vytebet
Bolchov
Mtensk

D'at'kovo

Bryansk

167 XX
260 XX
28 XX
3 XXXX
269 XX
137 XX

Karacev
287 XX
121
Nayl'a

Orel

Oka

56 XX
Pochep
XXXX
2
2 Pz
282 XX
4
13 XX
148 XX

108
XXXX
42

Starodub

XXXV

Nerussa
1
156 XX
307 XX
132 XX
143
29 XX 298
17
18

3 XXXX

Novgorod Seversky
XLVII
4
55 XX
13 XXXX

Desna
XLVIII XXX
3 XX
Ermakov XXX

Kursk
49 XXXX

9
16 XX
Mitte
XXXXX
Süd
GD

XXXIV XXX

Stary Oskol

N

	Soviet recovery Mid-October
	Encircled Soviets (7 October)
	Destroyed in small encirclements
	Units 30 September
	Units 15 October

0   50 miles
0   50km

39

MAP 14: OPERATION *TYPHOON* (II), DRIVE ON MOSCOW – 15 NOVEMBER TO 5 DECEMBER, 1941

The Soviet state and its army survived the loss of nearly two million combatants in just a matter of weeks. As they had in nearly every encirclement battle during *Barbarossa*, trapped Red Army soldiers either fought tenaciously before escaping, dying, or more commonly, being captured. Many German mechanized formations moved eastward at the conclusion of the encirclement battles, but others had to contribute to reducing huge *Kesseln*, a form of almost defensive static fighting for which they had not been designed.

On the same day the Viazma and Bryansk *Kesseln* shut, 7 October, Bock issued orders for Heeresgruppe Mitte to continue operations toward Moscow, Phase II of *Typhoon*. The earlier pairing of field armies and panzer groups remained from Phase I. Already on 7 October, fearing high casualties, Hitler had forbidden his soldiers from entering Moscow or other major Soviet cities. Therefore the plan called for a deep encirclement of the city, with the twin jaws meeting far to its east, but by the end of October the pace of operations along the Moscow axis slowed. Many explanations have centred on weather as the cause of the Germans' failure before Moscow that autumn, but in fact rainfall was slightly below normal in October and November while temperatures were only 2–4 degrees (F) colder than the average. More science and less wishful thinking would have helped them better anticipate cold weather, which hampered their mobility.

Informed by Stalin's spies that Japan no longer intended to attack the Soviet Far East and instead was turning toward the Pacific, the Red Army began to transfer units west. Some of the first fighting by newly arrived Siberian formations occurred on the Napoleonic battlefield of Borodino, about five miles west of Mozhaisk. Stalin determined to stay in Moscow, bolstering the morale of the capital's defenders. Zhukov, newly arrived to take charge of the situation, immediately saw the danger to Moscow. He concentrated what defensive forces he could near the Mozhaisk River. Fieldworks consisted of 225 miles of parallel anti-tank obstacles augmented by bunkers, dragons' teeth and wire entanglements. Behind these stood the new Moscow Defence Zone. Zhukov threw everything he could into the line: militias, local 'destroyer' security forces and nearly half a million armed factory workers. True to his plan, Zhukov poured more units into this central sector, the anchor of the entire front. He did not simply establish another fragile thin line

that the Germans could easily pierce and overrun, but instead emplaced an integrated system reaching back dozens of miles to Moscow.

Accordingly, once colder weather arrived to restore its mobility, Heeresgruppe Mitte would attempt to neutralize Moscow via the indirect approach against its flanks. Reinhardt's 3. Panzergruppe represented the direst threat to Moscow via Hitler's pet project, Operation *Volga Reservoir*. Beginning on 17 November, it was joined a day later by 4. Panzergruppe, breached the Lama River and continued north-eastward to Klin (22nd), Rogachevo (24th) and Yakhroma (27th) (Map 16). To Zhukov's frustration, Soviet armies, such as the 30th, obliged the enemy by falling back away from Moscow. Hoepner's 2. Panzer-Division reached Krasnaya Polyana on the last day of November, the closest a major German unit would get to the Soviet capital.[15] Guderian's advance from the south looks impressive, but during the second half of October his men had to fight for every yard – against Soviet defenders and their own logisticians. After overcoming enemy resistance at Mtensk his advanced guard made it into Tula, only to be thrown out hours later (Map 15). With the panzer thrusts exhausted north and south of Moscow, between 1 and 3 December the feckless Kluge launched the supposed *Schwerpunkt* up the middle into the teeth of Zhukov's defensive system with predictably unsatisfactory results.

On 1 November, Bock fielded 2.7 million men in 136 divisions (full-strength equivalent of 83), while Zhukov could call on 2.2 million men in 269 divisions and 65 brigades (also very understrength). Over the course of the month Heeresgruppe Mitte would receive no reinforcements worthy of mention, while Moscow's defences added almost another two million men in 81 divisions and 33 brigades. One week into December, *Typhoon* peaked and, along with it, *Barbarossa*. Both operations succumbed to the 'four horsemen' of Nazi strategic overstretch: troop exhaustion, personnel and materiel attrition, anaemic logistics and the continued inability to settle on attainable objectives.[16]

---

15 It is doubtful that any Germans actually saw 'the Kremlin's golden domes'. Earlier the entire fortress had been heavily camouflaged and the gold leaf domes painted over.

16 Robert Kirchubel, *Barbarossa* (Oxford: Osprey, 2014,) p. 374.

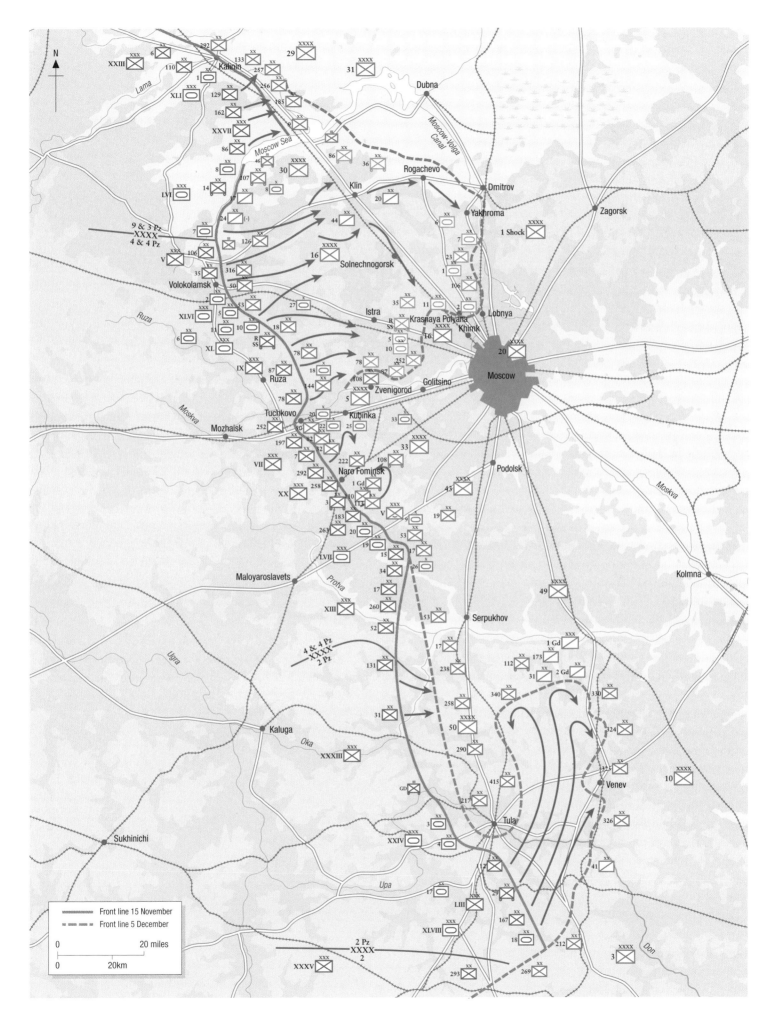

N

Lama

XXIII XXX | 6 XX
110 XX
Kalinin
292 XX
133 XX
29 XXXX
31 XXXX
Dubna

257 XX
XLI XXX | 129 [ ]
246 XX
185 XX

162 XX
XXVII XXX
86 XX
Moscow Sea
Rogachevo
Dmitrov
Zagorsk

46 XX
86 XX
36 XX
Yakhroma

8 [ ]
30 XX
8 X
Klin
20 XX
6 XX
1 Shock XXXX

LVI XXX | 14 [ ]
107 XX

24 XX (-)
44 XX
7 [ ]
23 [ ]
1 [ ]

9 & 3 Pz
XXXX
4 & 4 Pz
7 [ ]
126 XX
16 XXXX
Solnechnogorsk
106 [ ]

V XXX | 106 XX
316 XX
35 XX
11 [ ]
2 XX
Lobnya

Volokolamsk
50 XX
27 [ ]
Istra
Krasnaya Polyana
Khimk
16 XXXX

2 XX
53 XX
5 [ ]
35 XX
R SS
XLVI XXX | 5 [ ]
10 [ ]
18 XX
R SS
5 [ ]
10 [ ]
20 XXXX
Moscow

11 [ ]
6 [ ]
XL XXX
78 XX
78 XX
252 XX

Ruza
IX XXX | 87 XX
18 X
108 XX
67 XX
Zvenigorod
Golitsino

144 XX
78 XX
5 XX

Moskva
78 XX
Tuchkovo
20 X
Kubinka
33 [ ]

Mozhaisk
252 XX
50 XX
22 X
25 XX
33 XX
Podolsk
Moskva

197 XX
82 X
12 X
108 XX

VII XXX | 7 XX
222 XX
Naro Fominsk
43 XXXX

292 XX
1 Gd XXXX
Kolmna

XX XXX | 258 XX
3 XX
10 [ ]
V XX
19 XXXX

183 XX
20 [ ]
9 XX
53 XX
17 X

263 XX
19 XX
15 XX
17 X
26 [ ]
49 XXXX

LVII XXX | [ ]
34 XX

Maloyaroslavets
Protva
17 XX
260 XX
53 XX
Serpukhov

XIII XXX
52 XX
17 XX
1 Gd XXX
Tula

4 & 4 Pz
XXXX
2 Pz
131 XX
238 XX
112 XX
173 XX
31 XX
2 Gd XXX

Ugra
258 XX
340 XX
330 XX

31 XX
50 XXXX
224 XX

Kaluga
Oka
290 XX
415 XX
325 XX
Venev
10 XXXX

XXXIII XXX
GD III
217 XX
326 XX

3 [ ]
Sukhinichi
XXIV XXX | [ ]
4 [ ]

12 XX

Upa
17 [ ]
29 XX
41 XX

Front line 15 November
Front line 5 December
LIII XXX
167 XX
212 XX
Don

0   20 miles
XLVIII XXX | [ ]
18 [ ]
269 XX
3 XXXX

0   20km
2 Pz
XXXX
2
XXXV XXX
293 XX

41

MAP 15: BATTLES FOR TULA AND KASHIRA 18–30 NOVEMBER, 1941

Little the Red Army did slowed Guderian during *Barbarossa*'s first four months as he contributed to victories at Minsk, Smolensk, Kiev, Bryansk and numerous smaller locales. More vociferously than many Wehrmacht generals, he wanted Moscow, and now stood among the handful of his peers actually in position to attack the city. German plans called for his 2. Panzer-Armee to act as the southern pincer with a final goal of Noginsk, about 35 miles east of the Soviet capital. Intermediate objectives were the rail junction town of Tula with its airfield, more than 100 miles from Moscow's centre, and Kashira on the Oka River, nearly 75 miles distant. Kashira represented the southern terminus of Zhukov's Moscow defensive system, held by the 50th Army under General Major A. N. Yermakov and random NKVD troops plus workers' regiments, partisans and other civil militia forces organized by the Communist Party Tula Defence Committee.

Guderian knew of Tula: between 30 October and 9 November, 3. Panzer-Division and the Grossdeutschland Motorized Infantry Regiment temporarily held the town. In the meantime Yermakov had turned the place into a fortress known as 'little Moscow'. During the second week of the month, Guderian tried to win an advantageous position from which to assault Tula. The XXIV Panzer-Korps attacked on 18 November, driving a 30-mile wedge between the Western and Southwestern fronts and reaching Dedilovo. The LIII Armee-Korps and XLVII Panzer-Korps covered the thrust's exposed right flank while simultaneously pushing eastward. Defending Red Army divisions numbered 1,000 to 2,000 men each. Soon the Germans' advance slowed to 3–6 miles per day and after four days Guderian was ready to quit even though he had half-encircled Tula, now under Boldin as per Stalin's directions. On 23 November the panzer general flew to army group headquarters to plead for reinforcements. Bock emphasized destroying Soviet rail lines and suggested bypassing Tula to the east and making instead for Venev, which XXIV Panzer-Korps captured on the next day after destroying 50 tanks of the Venev Operational Group. Additionally, corps commander General der Panzertruppen Leo *Freiherr* Geyr von Schweppenburg dispatched 17. Panzer-Division farther north toward Kashira.

Meanwhile around Tula, Guderian had consolidated approximately 110 panzers from 3., 4. and 17. Panzer-Divisionen under Colonel Heinrich Eberbach. This *Kampfgruppe* would swing counterclockwise north of the town with the intention of meeting the XLIII Armee-Korps coming east. In blizzards colder than -30 degrees Fahrenheit Guderian personally led attacks in order to share the extreme discomfort of his troops. Eberbach earned oakleaves to his Knights Cross while Generalleutnant Gotthard Heinrici pushed his *Landsers* – both in losing efforts. Boldin's men held on and launched countless counterattacks while the Red Army Air Force (RAAF) generally ruled the skies. Zhukov sent the 2nd Cavalry Corps to Kashira, which on 26 November received the honorific 1st Guards Cavalry Corps for its pains. The 17. Panzer-Division under Oberst Rudolf-Eduard Licht just missed taking Kashira by coup before the cavalry arrived, and it eventually fought its way to within two miles of Kashira, but could get little closer. With the help of numerous tanks and Katyusha batteries, on the 27th General Major P. A. Belov's horsemen drove back the panzers. That day is considered 2. Panzer-Armee's high water mark. Guderian must be held to account for wasting scarce resources on secondary tasks such as capturing bridgeheads of the Don River in the LIII Armee- and XLVII Panzer-Korps sectors. On 28 November, Heeresgruppe Mitte downgraded his mission to merely 'take Tula', but ultimately he could not achieve even this task.

North of Tula, on 3 December elements of 3. and 4. Panzer-Divisionen temporarily cut the main road to Serpukhov but could not hold their position. As late as the 4th, Guderian still believed he could capture 'little Moscow'. This was clearly beyond the capabilities of his men, and besides Stalin would launch his own massive counteroffensive only hours into the future. Soon it would be Guderian fighting to avoid encirclement. In the meantime, all he could do was complain about the inactivity of Kluge. After more than two years of phenomenal personal and organizational success, the egotistical panzer general had lost his first battle.

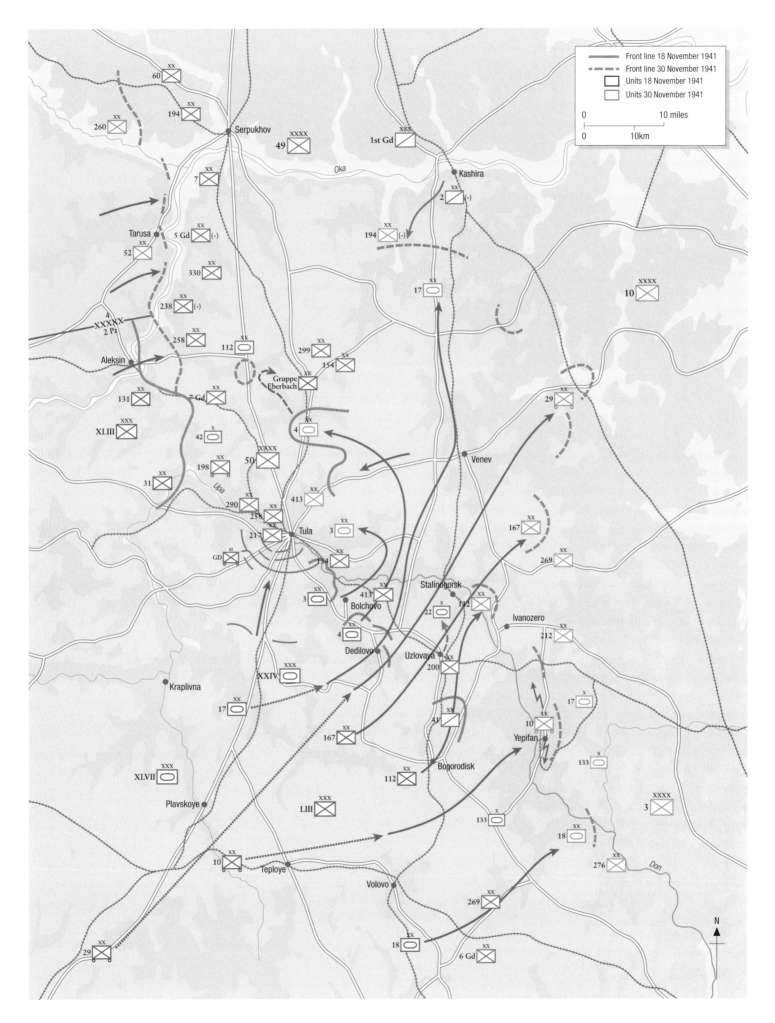

MAP 16: THE YAKHROMA BRIDGEHEAD 28-29 NOVEMBER, 1941

The Germans' main hope for success against Moscow rested with 3. and 4. Panzergruppen attacking the city's north. According to Hitler's plan of 30 October, beginning in the middle of November 3. Panzergruppe would attack over Klin and across the Moscow–Volga Canal (connecting the Moskva and Volga Rivers). Operation *Schneesturm* (Snowstorm, one of numerous German operations by that name) began on 15 November with 233,000 men, 1,880 guns and 1,300 panzers supported at times by upwards of 800 aircraft. Facing them were the 16th and 30th Armies numbering a quarter of a million men, 1,254 guns, 500 tanks and nearly 700 planes.

The two panzer groups attacked on 16 November with LVI and XLVI Panzer-Korps leading the way. They split the two Soviet armies and raced through the resulting gap, taking Klin from Rokossovsky's troops a week later. Contrary to its mission of defending Moscow, the 30th Army slipped north from Klin toward Kalinin and away from the capital. Exploiting this blunder, the panzers rolled eastward fairly unhindered. On the 27th Reinhardt's 7. Panzer-Division reached the canal at Yakhroma – the last sizeable obstacle barring the way to Moscow. Without waiting for orders, assuming such a manoeuvre would contribute to any advance on Moscow, very early on 28 November Oberst Hasso von Manteuffel used an existing bridge to push his 6. Schützen-Regiment[17] and a company of the 25. Panzer-Regiment over the canal at Yakhroma. Like Rokossovsky, Manteuffel would be promoted over the next three and a half years and play increasingly important roles in the war.

To both sides, the bridgehead looked like the start of another dangerous salient on the seam between two Soviet armies. Stalin made sure he had two new armies in place, the 20th and the 1st Shock, to man the gap.[18] That morning Manteuffel's men established a thin defensive perimeter and throughout 28 November held their exposed hasty positions despite the climate and little winter clothing or equipment. During the day the 1st Shock Army repeatedly pounded the bridgehead from all three sides with its 29th and 50th Rifle Brigades and 58th Tank Division, supported by armoured trains, Katyusha rocket launchers and CAS. The Germans fended off each of these with defensive fire and local counterattacks. In face of mounting losses, men inside the bridgehead maintained high morale since they represented the advanced guard in the battle for Moscow. However, higher headquarters decided against a major effort east of the canal and instead ordered a concentrated panzer drive west of the watercourse; by pivoting south perhaps Bock could enfilade defenders directly to the capital's west who had halted Kluge. Therefore barely 24 hours after creating the bridgehead 6. Regiment received orders to evacuate. By sunrise on 29 November Manteuffel's men were back on the near bank, their spirits 'crushed'. The LVI Panzer-Korps would hold these advanced positions for another week, withdrawing on 6 December.

In accordance with Heeresgruppe Mitte's new plan, Reinhardt's XLI Panzer-Korps, commanded by future field marshal (now General der Panzertruppen) Walther Model, drove on Moscow. His attack was meant to support Hoepner's more direct assaults against the city's northern suburbs, which had already culminated days earlier. These assaults, specifically that of 2. Panzer-Division at Khimki on 30 November, reached positions much closer to Moscow than the Yakhroma bridgehead had been. Although they stood nearer to the Kremlin than either Guderian or Kluge, Reinhardt and Hoepner's depleted panzer groups mounted no serious threat to a metropolis of many millions. The Yakhroma bridgehead battle was an interesting tactical episode, but could not compensate for the overall terminal weakness of Hitler's eastern army in December 1941.

17 The infantry in panzer divisions were referred to as Schützen (rifle) units, I will retain the original German to avoid confusion with Red Army 'rifle' designations.

18 The Stavka created shock armies at this time and place to help defend Moscow.

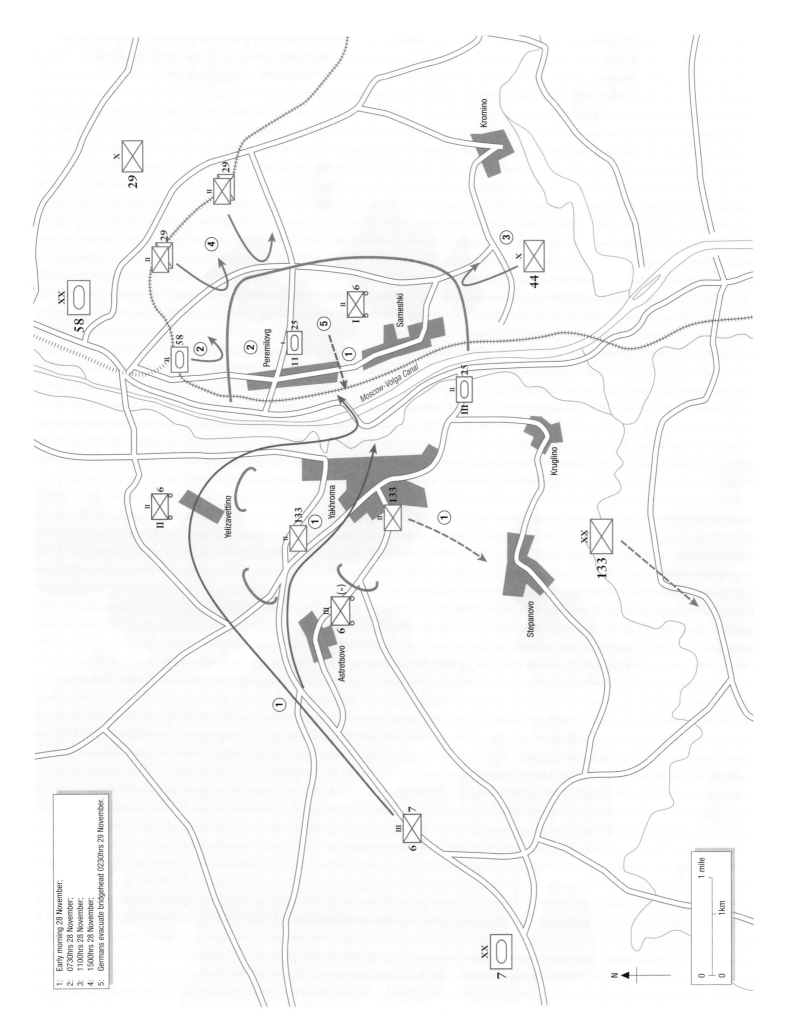

Early morning 28 November;
0730hrs 28 November;
1100hrs 28 November;
1500hrs 28 November.
Germans evacuate bridgehead 0230hrs 29 November.

Kromino

29

29

29

58

58

Peremilovg

11 25

6

Sameshki

44

25

6

Yelizavettino

133

Yakhroma

133

Moscow-Volga Canal

Kruglino

6

133

Astretsovo

Stepanovo

7

6

1km   1 mile

0   0

N

45

MAP 17: FRONTIER BATTLES SOUTH 22–30 JUNE, 1941

Heeresgruppe Süd had perhaps the most daunting planning challenges of the three army groups. It would not reach its strategic objectives in two years of desperate fighting, much less one. Opposite stood the Red Army's defensive main effort and its best commander and troops. Commander Feldmarschall Rundstedt had to manage the Third Reich's version of coalition warfare, with Italian, Romanian, Slovak and, eventually, Hungarian formations in his order of battle. Hitler did not permit any co-ordination with the Hungarians before *Barbarossa*, and lingering historical animosities meant that after the campaign began Hungarian soldiers had to remain separated from the Romanians. Therefore Rundstedt had to deal with a 200-mile gap in his initial front lines between Slovakia and Romania. Romania's primitive infrastructure and the Germans' Balkan invasion that spring also negatively affected operations in the far south. Like Leeb, Rundstedt had only one panzer group and also had the same expanding funnel-shaped sector. With the deepest and ultimately widest theatre of any army group, OKH allocated Rundstedt 6. and 17. Armeen and 1. Panzergruppe on *Barbarossatag*. The 11. Armee and two Romanian armies became part of the battle with Operation *Munich* on 2 July, with other Axis contingents joining the conflict at various times.

The Kiev Special and Odessa Military Districts, under General Lieutenants Kirponos and I. V. Tyulenev respectively,[19] as the Soviets' main effort enjoyed advantages their comrades north of the Rokitno Marches did not. While their 3,700 tanks outnumbered German panzers on all fronts combined, individual divisions within the mechanized corps were often separated by over 100 miles. Any attempted concentrations attracted the attention of the Luftwaffe, which had air superiority that June. Mechanized or motorized units, such as anti-tank brigades, frequently went into battle without all of their trucks, which had been commandeered by higher headquarters. Kirponos commanded the 5th, 6th, 12th and 26th Armies, including eight mechanized corps, while Tyulenev led the 9th Army with two mechanized corps.

Rundstedt's army group erupted across the entire Ukrainian frontier that Sunday morning. Kirponos' troops met them resolutely in some places while giving way elsewhere. He promptly ordered his mechanized corps to assemble from their widely dispersed garrisons. By the second day leading infantry divisions of 6. Armee north of the sector penetrated the forward defences and created conditions for Generaloberst Ewald von Kleist's 1. Panzergruppe to pass through and into the Soviet rear. Here they encountered Red Army anti-tank brigades and had to stop their advance and take stock of the situation. Their main axes of advance were the Lutsk–Rovno–Novgorod Volynsky road on the left (III Panzer-Korps), the Ostrov –Dubno–Shepetivka route in the centre (XLVIII Panzer-Korps) and the Brody–Kremenets route on the right (XIV Panzer-Korps). South of the sector, General Carl-Heinrich von Stülpnagel's 17. Armee, led by the hard-charging alpine troops of the XLIX Gebirgs-Korps, almost kept pace with the panzers to their left as they advanced through L'vov on their way to Ternopil.[20]

By 23 June, Kirponos already had some of his mechanized corps in position to challenge Rundstedt's spearheads. The 22nd Mechanized in the north near Lutsk and the 15th in the south around Ostrov appeared close to cutting off Kleist's lead units. However, German skill, individual and corporate, mastered every crisis and Soviet inexperience hamstrung Kirponos' plans. At the same time, the 4th Mechanized hit the 71. Infanterie-Division north-east of L'vov but did little damage. By the 25th, Kirponos had two more mechanized corps ready; the 9th attacked III Panzer-Korps near Rovno while the 19th hit the XLVIII Panzer-Korps in the area between Ostrov and Dubno. After a long road march, the 8th Mechanized joined the fray around Dubno under Zhukov's critical eye.[21] Desperate fighting often forced German divisions into all-around *Igel* (hedgehog) defensive positions, while Luftwaffe CAS played a critical role in stabilizing the situation. Red Army thrusts stood only six miles apart, but neither Kirponos in Kiev nor the Stavka in Moscow had any idea they were so close.

The South-western Front had certainly acquitted itself better than its peers from a Soviet perspective during *Barbarossa*'s first week, but by the end of June Kirponos had to withdraw if he hoped to keep his command intact. Kleist's panzers had split the 5th and 6th Armies and Stalin had little between Novgorod Volynsky and Kiev to throw in his way. Until 11. Armee and Romanian units opened the Bessarabian front, Rundstedt fretted over his exposed right flank, but no Red Army threat in that quarter ever materialized. Heeresgruppe Süd had broken into the open.

---

19 When Barbarossa began Stalin removed Tyulenev from his post at the Moscow District and sent him to Odessa. He assumed command there on 24 June (the Odessa MD became the Southern Front).

20 Stülpnagel was a member of the anti-Hitler opposition of long standing.

21 Great distances between garrison towns and attack positions, Luftwaffe interdiction and mechanical breakdowns meant most of the mechanized units arrived at the fighting in drastically reduced condition.

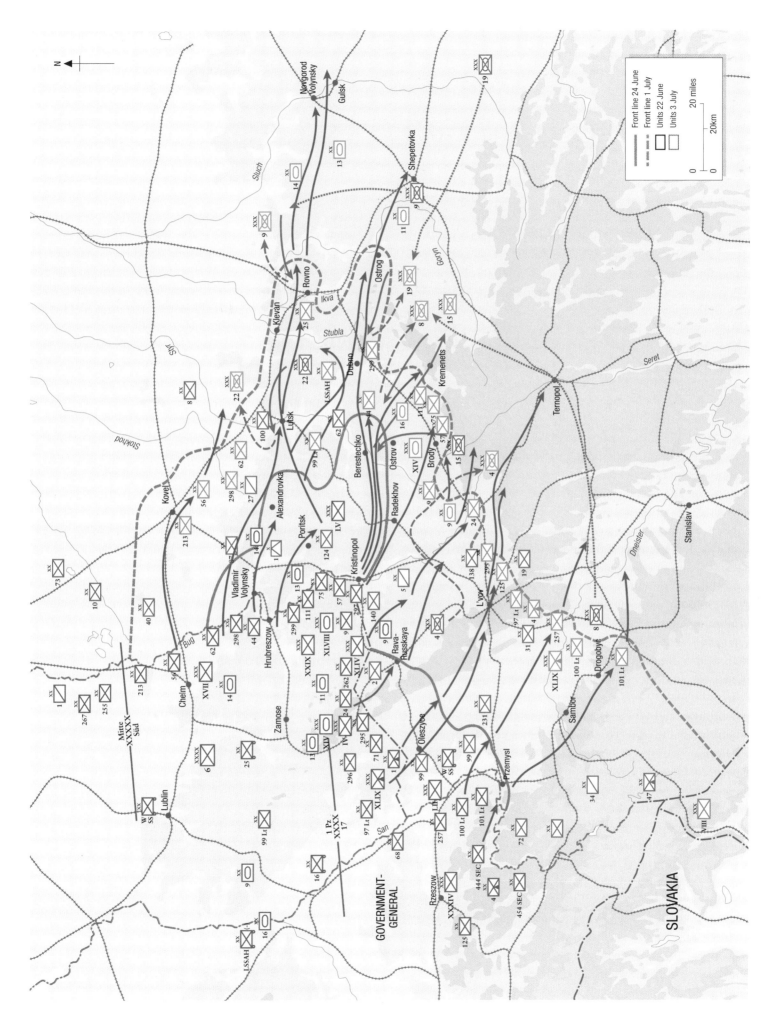

N

Front line 24 June
Front line 1 July
Units 22 June
Units 3 July

20 miles
20km

Novgorod Volynsky
Gulsk
Shepetovka
Sluch
XXX 19
XX 13
XX 14
XXX 9 9
XXX 9
O 11
Goryn
Ostrog
XXX 19
Rovno
Ikva
Klevan
XXX 25
Stubla
XXX 22
XX 8
XXX 22
XX 22
Dubno
XXX 22
LSSAH
Seret
XXX 8
XXX 15
XX 299
O 16
XXX 11
XX 75
Kremenets
XXX 57
Lutsk
XX 62
XX 99 Lt
XX 41
Berestechko
Ostrov
XIV
O
Brody
XXX 57
XXX 15
Stochod
Kovel
XX 8
XXX 22
XX 62
XX 298
XX 27
XX 56
Alexandrovka
Poritsk
XXX LV
XXX 124
Radekhov
Ternopol
O
XXX 4
XX 213
XX 73
XX 10
XX 40
Vladimir Volynsky
XX 14
X 1
O
XX 13
XXX 75
XXX 57
XX 299
O
XX 140
Kristinopol
XX 5
XX 4
XXX 24
L'vov
XXX 125
Stanislav
Dniester
Bug
XX 62
XX 298
XX 44
Hrubreszow
XXIX
XLVIII
XLIV
O 9
O 9
Rava-Russkaya
XX 4
XX 138
XX 29
XX 19
XX 97 Lt
XX 4
XX 31
XXX 257
XXII 8
XX 59
XVII
O 14
Zamose
XIV
O 111
IV
XX 262
XX 2
O
XX 4
XLIX
Drogobyc
Sambor
XX 100 Lt
XX 101 Lt
XX 1
XX 267
XX 255
Chelm
XXXX 6
XX 25
XX 296
XX 71
XX 295
Oleszyce
XX 1
XX 99
W SS
XX 231
Przemysl
XX 34
XX 47
XXX VIII
Mitte
XXXXX
Süd
99 Lt
1 Pz
XXXX
17
San
XX 97 Lt
XX 68
XXXIX
XX 257
XX 1 Lt
XX 100 Lt
XX 101 Lt
XX 72
W SS
Lublin
O 16
XX 16
O 9
Rzeszow
XXXIV
XX 444 SEC
XX 454 SEC
XX 125
GOVERNMENT-
GENERAL
LSSAH
O 16 (-)

SLOVAKIA

47

MAP 18: THE UMAN *KESSEL* 20 JUNE TO 9 AUGUST, 1941

On 30 June, Kirponos conceded the border region and began to withdraw to the Stalin Line in accordance with the Stavka's instructions. Two days later the German 11. and Romanian 3rd and 4th Armies crossed the Prut River into Moldavia, initiating Operation *Munich*. Combat was uneven as defenders stood and fought in some locales and fled in others. Back on the main front, within a week Kleist's men reached Zithomir. On the important Kiev axis, Zhukov wanted to make a stand at Berdichev but the Germans moved too fast for him to stabilize the front anywhere. Three days later, on 10 July, 13. Panzer-Division reached the Irpen River, the Ukrainian capital's first line of defence, between 10 and 20 miles from its Kremlin. The remainder of III Panzer-Korps was strung out along a tenuous 70-mile corridor. Kirponos kept up a series of counterattacks that sorely tested the panzer group. Making parallels with Verdun, German commanders from Hitler down eschewed a direct assault on the big city. Meanwhile, to Kleist's north, 6. Armee's support left much to be desired, but to the south 17. Armee did its best to keep pace with the slashing mechanized troops. Hitler had hoped to execute a *Kessel* in the region of Vinnitsa, but by mid-July around 50,000 Red Army soldiers successfully withdrew and evaded capture. This set the stage for a later encirclement west of Uman.

The Wehrmacht had two options for trapping the bulk of Kirponos' troops in central Ukraine. Both involved swinging Kleist in a clockwise arc in order to smash Soviet armies against the anvil represented by Stulpnagel's 17. Armee. Halder favoured a wide manoeuvre that hugged the right bank of the Dnepr River while Hitler wanted a less ambitious inner pincer; the Führer's plan prevailed. As always in military operations the enemy has a vote, and the Stavka did not remain passive but ordered attacks against both of the panzer group's flanks. The new 26th Army attacked both the panzers' left and Group Schwedler's infantry detailed to protect this exposed flank segment; Kleist eventually dispatched the

III Panzer-Korps to neutralize this threat. At about the same time, Kirponos' 6th Army and 4th Mechanized Corps (minus most of its tanks) inside the developing trap sensed the impending doom and tried to break out. The XLVIII Panzer-Korps, spearheading Kleist's effort, had the dual tasks of reaching the 17. Armee plus preventing a Soviet escape. For its part, by 27 July Stulpnagel's army had fought its way through the Stalin Line past Vinnitsa and headed for a rendezvous with the panzers. The 1. Gebirgs-Division led the way with the Hungarian Fast Corps in support, covering the alpine troops' exposed right. This manoeuvre threatened the boundary of the South-western and Southern fronts, so Tyulenev sent his 18th Army north with the mission of preventing a dangerous split in their common front.

Similar to Timoshenko in the theatre's centre, Stalin delegated to Marshal Budenny the job of co-ordinating the operations of Kirponos and Tyulenev. Even if the old Civil War hero had been qualified for the high-level command, he had no chance to show it as Rundstedt's infantry, panzers and Luftwaffe CAS gave the Soviet troops no respite. The trap slammed shut on 2 August when 9. Panzer-Division and 1. Gebirgs-Division elements met near Troyanka, while a day later 16. Panzer-Division captured Pervomaisk, completing the outside encirclement. Kirponos' 6th and 12th Armies had escaped destruction at Vinnitsa only to suffer the same fate at Uman a fortnight later, while a large portion of Tyulenev's 18th marched north to disaster. Reducing the *Kessel* of 25 Red Army divisions took an additional week. Rundstedt's first cauldron battle netted 103,000 POWs plus 317 tanks, 858 artillery pieces and 242 other guns captured or destroyed. On 28 August, Hitler and Mussolini arrived at Heeresgruppe Süd's Uman headquarters for a briefing on the course of the battle. By then its soldiers had cleared the enemy from most of the west bank of the Dnepr River. They also redirected their attention across the river and toward the upcoming Kiev battle.

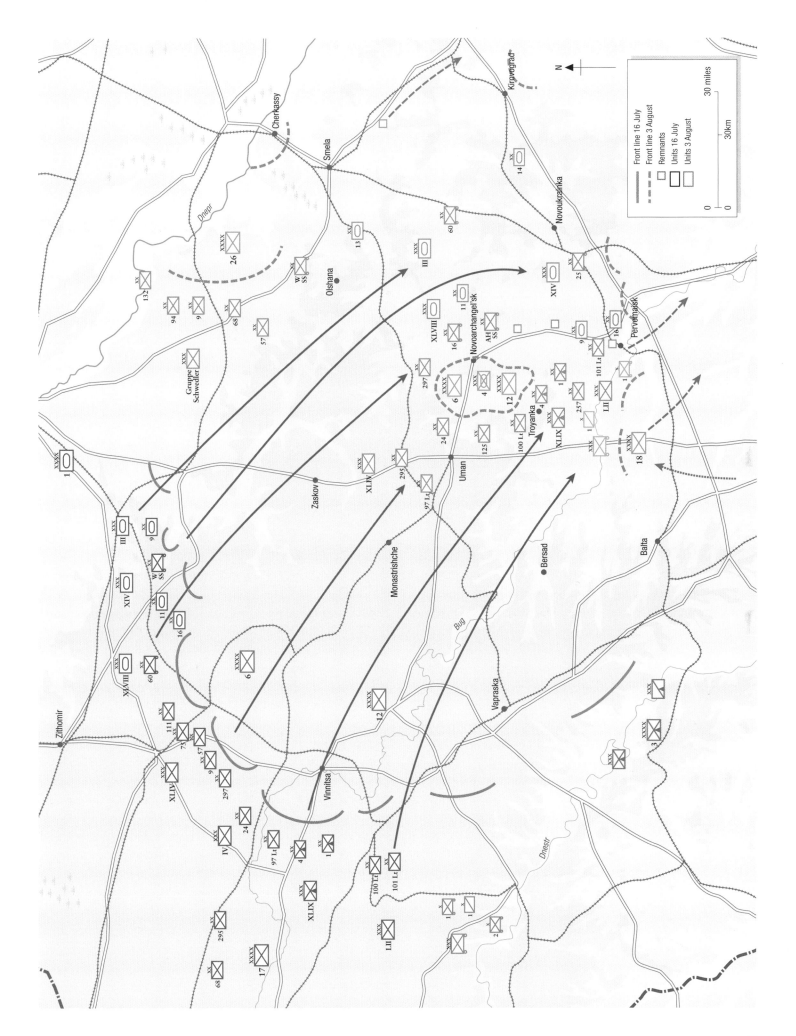

Front line 16 July
Front line 3 August
Remnants
Units 16 July
Units 3 August

N

30 miles
30km

Cherkassy
Smela
Kirovograd
Novoukrainka
Olshana
Novoarchangel'sk
Pervomajsk
Zaskov
Uman
Troyanka
Monastrishche
Bersad
Balta
Zlthomir
Vinnitsa
Vapraska

Dnepr
Bug
Dnestr

49

MAP 19: KIEV POCKET
24 AUGUST TO 24 SEPTEMBER, 1941

The stout defence of the Ukrainian capital plus the stubborn resistance of the neighbouring 5th Army hugging the Rokitno Marshes combined against the lamentable leadership of Feldmarschall Walter von Reichenau to create a salient jutting well over 100 miles west into the German lines. Kirponos' increasingly dangerous position (under the dubious overall control of Budenny's South-western Direction – an echelon of command above fronts introduced in World War I) represented the late-summer equivalent to Pavlov's Bialystok salient earlier that season. The situation screamed for a solution, as generals on both sides could easily see. Strangely, some of the Soviets' most determined fighting threatened to become yet another serious Red Army defeat.

Wehrmacht planners had realized a year earlier that Heeresgruppe Süd could not close the expected Kessel by itself, so would require Bock's assistance. This came in the form of Panzergruppe Guderian supported by 2. Armee, coming south from the Starodub region during the last third of August. The Stavka gave General Lieutenant A. I. Yeremenko's patched-together Bryansk Front the unenviable task of stopping the panzers. But the Soviet counterblows brought only temporary relief. On 24 August 3. Panzer-Division at the vanguard of Geyr von Schweppenburg's XXIV Panzer-Korps captured the critical Desna River bridge at Novgorod-Seversky. Troops from 2. Armee captured Chernigov on 7 September, further hemming in forces that Stalin ordered to remain around Kiev. To the city's north-east, over 20 miles now separated the South-west Front from outside relief.

The Stavka ordered army-size counterattacks against Guderian from the west and east (i.e., from both in- and outside the quickly forming pocket) but these were too small, poorly led and unsupported to have any decisive effect. Within days the gap in Red Army lines had grown to 40 miles while Kirponos' doomed command had to guard a front greater than 500 miles long. Reinforcements poured into Kiev along with a new commander for the South-western Direction, Marshal Timoshenko.

Meanwhile to the south, Rundstedt's men closed on the Dnepr River following their victory at Uman. By 25 August Kleist had won bridgeheads at Dnepropetrovsk and Zaporozhe, while 17. Armee captured another at Kremenchug. Kirponos threw everything he could against these incursions, but with Luftwaffe CAS the Landsers held out despite severe losses. Rundstedt would use Kremenchug to launch his half of the Kiev battle. The German plan went through a number of permutations in early September before deciding to pull XLVIII Panzer-Korps out of its downstream bridgeheads and then pass it through 17. Armee. This formation, its panzer strength hovering around 50 per cent, commanded by General der Panzertruppen Werner Kempf, would move out on 11 September under V Flieger-Korps CAS. Blocking the tankers stood the new 38th Army, an ad hoc collection of 40,000 Soviet soldiers holding a 120-mile perimeter.

Rain pushed back the attack until the 12th when the southern pincer finally moved out, achieving total surprise. With the additional support of II Flak-Korps and Nebelwerfer rocket launchers, Kempf blasted 38th Army defenders and scattered its commanding general and his field headquarters. The 16. Panzer-Division led the effort with 9. Panzer-Division close behind; together that day they covered more than half of the 75 miles to the planned rendezvous with Guderian. The 17. Armee protected the panzers' exposed right by driving on the ancient city of Poltava. The last defensive stands by Kirponos' men took place on 13 September against 3. Panzer-Division at Romny in the north and 16. Panzer-Division at Lubny in the south. The next day both divisions covered the remaining distance across the rolling terrain and cultivated fields, meeting at Lokhvitsa at 1820 hours.

Debate within the Soviet high command over how to respond raged at the same time. Red Army generals urged withdrawal from the obvious death trap, but Stalin stood his ground. More than 72 hours following Lokhvitsa the dictator relented, but by then it was clearly too late. On the morning of 18 September Kirponos gave the order to break out; two days later German troops killed him trying to escape the pocket. Next came the difficult twin tasks of capturing Kiev itself and of reducing the massive Kessel. Fighting in the city lasted until the 24th, and processing two-thirds of a million POWs and mountains of captured equipment took until 4 October.

Hitler finally prevailed over wilful generals like Halder and got the battle of annihilation in the south that he wanted. On the other hand, Stalin ignored warnings from Zhukov and others and blundered into another massive defeat. In the end, Kiev represented Stalin's defeat as much as Hitler's victory.

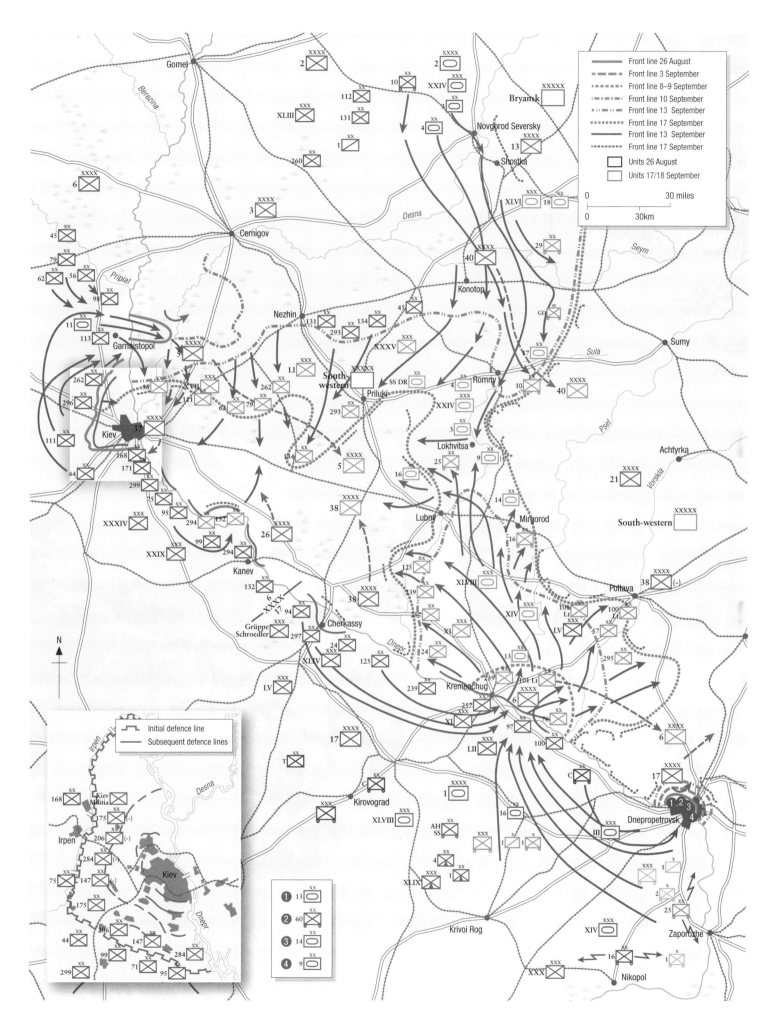

Gomel

Berezina

Pripiat

2 XXXX

112 XLIII XXX

131 XX

1 XX

260 XX

6 XXXX

45 XX

79 XX

62 56 XX

98 XX

11 XX

113

Garnaistopol

5 XXXX

262 XX

296 XX

56 XXVII XXX

111 XX

Kiev 37 XXXX

111 XX

168 XX

44 XXXX

171

299 XX

75 XX

95 XXXX

XXXIV XXX

294 XXXX

99 XX

294 XXXX

XXIX XXX

Kanev

132 XX

6 XXXX
17

94 XX

Grüppe
Schroedler

297

XLIV XXX

LV XXX

24 XXXX

125 XX

38 XXXX

Cherkassy

Dnepr

17 XXXX

T XX

C XXXX

Kirovograd

1 XXXX

XLVIII

AH
SS

4 XX

XLIX XXX

1 XX

Krivoi Rog

XIV XXX

Cernigov

3 XXXX

Desna

Nezhin

131 XXX

293 XX

134 XX

45 XXX

LI XXX

262 XX

79 XX

62 XX

South-
western

XVII XXX

134 XX

5 XXXX

38 XXXX

Lubny

SS DR XXX

Priluki

293 XX

XXXV XXX

XXIV XXX

3 XX

Lokhvitsa

25 XX

9 XX

16 XX

8

14 XX

16 XX

125 XX

239 XXXX

257 XXX

XLVIII XXX

XIV XXX

LV XXX

13 XX

24 XX

239 XXXX

Kremenchug

257 XXX
XXX

XI XXX

97

LII XXX

100

16 XX

1 XX

2 XX

25 XX

10 XX

XXIV XXX

Bryansk XXXXX

13 XXXX

Novgorod Seversky

Shostka

XLVI XXX

18 XX

29 XX

40 XXXX

Konotop

GD III

17 XX

10 XX

40 XXXX

Romny

4 XX

3 XX

9 XX

Mirgorod

16 XX

XLVIII XXX

101
Lt

239 XXX

101 Lt XXX

6 XX

76 XXX

100 XXX

C XXX

III XX

Sumy

Psel

Seym

Sula

Achtyrka

21 XXXX

Vorskla

South-western XXXXX

Poltava

38 XXXX (-)

100
Lt

57

295 XX

6 XXXX

17 XXXX

1 2 3 4

Dnepropetrovsk

1 XX

XIV XXX

16 XX
1 XX

Zaporozhe

16 XX
1 XX

XXX

Nikopol

Front line 26 August
Front line 3 September
Front line 8–9 September
Front line 10 September
Front line 13 September
Front line 17 September
Front line 13 September
Front line 17 September
Units 26 August
Units 17/18 September

0   30 miles
0   30km

N

Initial defence line
Subsequent defence lines

Irpen

Desna

168 XX

Kiev
Militia

175 XX (-)

206 XX (-)

Irpen

284 XX (-)

75 XX   147 XX (-)

Kiev

175 XX

206 XX

44 XX   147 XX

99 XX   284 XX

299 XX   71 XX   95 XX

Dnepr

1 13 XX
2 60 XXXX
3 14 XX
4 9 XX

51

MAP 20: BATTLE ON THE SEA OF AZOV 17 SEPTEMBER TO 7 OCTOBER, 1941

Following its victory at Kiev, the Wehrmacht's eastern army temporarily outnumbered its Soviet counterpart. The South-western Front ceased to exist, but along the Black Sea coast the Southern Front maintained itself in the field. A month earlier, after Uman, with the German 11. Armee and Romanian 3rd and 4th Armies applying pressure along the Dniestr River, Tyulenev had skilfully evacuated Bessarabia and the western Ukraine. While Marshal Ion Antonescu's 4th Army detoured south to besiege Odessa,[22] Generaloberst Eugen *Ritter* von Schobert's men closed on the lower Dnepr. For nearly two months the Romanians committed organizational suicide against well-prepared and well-led defenders before finally walking into the unoccupied port on 16 October; over a period of days the Black Sea Fleet had secretly evacuated over half the encircled garrison to the Crimea. During the third week of August, the Germans first threw bridgeheads across the Dnepr River at Kherson and Berislav and then spent the next couple of weeks expanding them. Simultaneously with the Kiev battle they pushed across the steppe, isolating the Crimea on 17 September and reaching the Sea of Azov coast. Axis exhaustion and Red Army determination then brought most movement to an end as the front stabilized along a line running south of Zaporozhe, west of Melitopol and to the sea coast. Tyulenev had his troops dig prepared positions behind anti-tank ditches and minefields.

Meanwhile, both senior commanders had been replaced within a month of each other; Tyulenev received battlefield wounds in mid-August, so General Lieutenant D. I. Ryabyshev, who formerly led the 38th Army, took over the South Front. Meanwhile on 12 September Schobert died when his liaison aircraft landed in a minefield, and Manstein replaced him in command of 11. Armee. In an attempt to regain the initiative, on 26 September Ryabyshev launched an assault by a dozen divisions under the 18th and 9th Armies (main effort and supporting attack respectively) against the northern sector of the German front. Units of the Romanian 3rd Army had just taken responsibility for defending this 'quiet' front in relief of the XLIX Gebirgs-Korps, which had been sent south to complete the capture of the Crimea (Map 22). Despite sending in two tank brigades in the

exploitation role, both Soviet armies had been in continuous combat for longer than two months, so lacked the strength to defeat the Romanians. To be on the safe side, Manstein had his mountain troops turn back north. The 1. Gebirgs-Division, definitely out of its preferred Alpine element, continued to excel in these manoeuvres, as did SS Division Leibstandarte Adolf Hitler (SSLAH). By 28–29 September the Soviet offensive was spent.

Feldmarschall Rundstedt had already sensed a perfect chance to follow up success at Kiev, and on the day before Ryabyshev's attack had planned a stroke of his own. The III and XIV Panzer-Korps[23] had not participated in the Kiev operation and so he wanted them to attack out of their Dnepr bridgeheads, get behind the South Front and head for Berdyansk on the coast. Accordingly Kleist's men struck out of the region of the great bend of the Dnepr River on 1 October and soon had the Southern Front pinned; the panzers would be the hammer while Manstein's infantry acted as the anvil. With the XIV Panzer-Korps on the right and III Panzer-Korps on the left, they took Melitopol after just 48 hours and Berdyansk four days later. The 11. Armee's SSLAH, attacking from the west, contributed significantly by splitting the two Soviet armies. The Italian cavalry/motorized *Celere* division Duca d'Aosta took part as well, guarding Kleist's exposed eastern flank as he drove on Berdyansk.[24]

When the *Kessel* closed on 7 October, 106,000 POWs, 212 tanks and 766 guns fell into the Germans' hands. General Major A. K. Smirnov, 18th Army commander, fell in battle, while Ryabyshev received wounds and was in turn replaced by 9th Army commander General Lieutenant Y. T. Cherevichenko. Heeresgruppe Süd had great hopes of continuing east toward Kharkov, the Donbas region and Rostov, plus finishing off the Crimea to the south. Halder had delusions of Rundstedt reaching Stalingrad or even the Caucasus oil region before *Barbarossa* was over.

---

22 General N. Cuiperca commanded the Romanian 4th Army.

23 All that now remained of Kleist's panzer group, after Kiev he transferred XLVIII Panzer-Korps to Guderian for Operation *Typhoon*, Map 13.

24 Not to be confused with the various cavalry-mechanized organizations fielded by the Red Army later in the war.

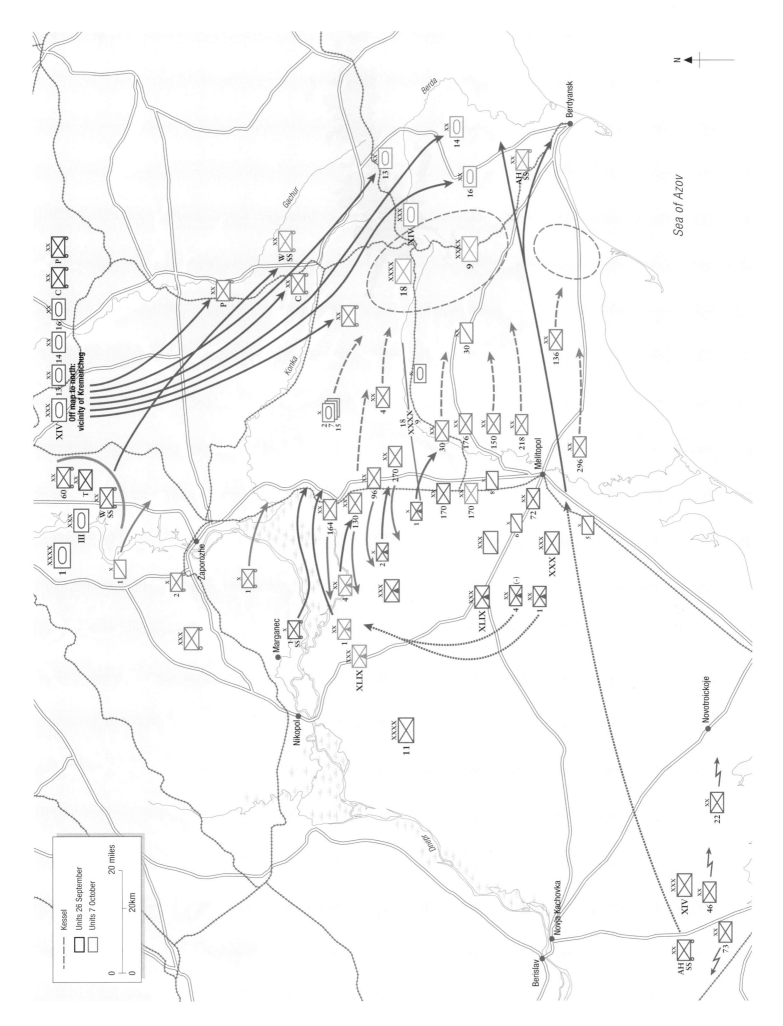

N

Sea of Azov

Berda

Berdyansk

Gachur

Konka

Zaporozhe

Marganec

Nikopol

Dnepr

Melitopol

Novotroickoje

Novja-Kachovka

Berislav

Off map to north:
vicinity of Kremenchug

Kessel

Units 26 September

Units 7 October

0   20km

0   20 miles

53

MAP 21: DONBAS TO ROSTOV
4 OCTOBER TO 15 NOVEMBER, 1941

Key reasons for launching *Barbarossa* in the first place, and among Hitler's major objectives in the south of the USSR, were the natural resources and industrial infrastructure in eastern Ukraine. These areas included the iron mines of Krivoi Rog and the shipyards of Nikopol, but even more the massive factories of Kharkov and the coalmines and steel factories of the Donbas. Farther south-east lay the hoped-for El Dorado of the Third Reich, the Caucasus oil region and energy independence. After obliterating the South-western Front in and east of Kiev, German leaders expected continued success represented by more large *Kesseln* as they advanced east against a cobbled-together defence. For his part, Stalin knew the USSR needed the Caucasus as much as Hitler did and, with the world's attention again focused on fighting around Moscow, he planned to gain some advantage in the secondary southern theatre.

After requiring weeks to process Kiev's 660,000 POWs and consolidating their gains in the central Ukraine, in early October Rundstedt's two infantry armies, 6. and 17. Armeen, moved out toward Sumy and Poltava.[25] Fighting alongside 17. Armee was the Italian Expeditionary Corps in Russia (CSIR, 62,000 men in two infantry and one *Celere* divisions). Understandably, the Stavka had difficulty reestablishing credible resistance following the devastation of Kiev. As already weak Wehrmacht logistics became more tenuous, the eastern army's advances slowed. Reichenau continued toward Kharkov while Hoth divided his effort between Izyum on the Donets River and

Stalino, industrial heart of the Donbas. Both generals had the additional challenge of maintaining communications with a neighbour: 6. Armee keeping close to Heeresgruppe Mitte heading for Moscow on its left, and 17. Armee remaining in contact with 1. Panzer-Armee (as Kleist's command had been re-designated) veering toward Rostov on its right.

While the Soviets might have wanted to hold on to Kharkov, they were not going to do so at the price of another massive encirclement; German intelligence indicated defending units were fleeing to the east. During the third week of October, 6. Armee came at the city from the north, and in a large clockwise arc manoeuvred behind nine Red army divisions holding it. The USSR's fourth city fell on the 24th in the first of many battles in and around the city. The Wehrmacht struggled into Belgorod, but did not get much farther that autumn. To the south, 17. Armee inched eastward hampered by the lack of mobile forces under command except for the Hungarian Fast Corps (24,000 men in two motorized and one cavalry brigades – it would be combat ineffective by November). In a foretaste of future urban combat between the two regimes, workers and peasant militias numbering 150,000 men joined regular Red Army troops defending Stalino's blast furnaces and mine heads. A sizeable Soviet bridgehead on the west bank of the Donets River remained at Izyum, but by November Hoth's men had closed in on the middle of the river near Slavyansk and Lisichansk. On its southern edge, 17. Armee got sucked into the battle for Rostov, with 1. and 4. Gebirgs-Divisionen involved in both heavy offensive and defensive fighting around Krasny Luch during the second half of November. However, for most of 17. Armee the Donets River marked the end of *Barbarossa*.

---

25 17. Armee had a new commander. In early October Rundstedt relieved Stülpnagel over differences in leadership. Herman Hoth took over command of 17. Armee on 5 October.

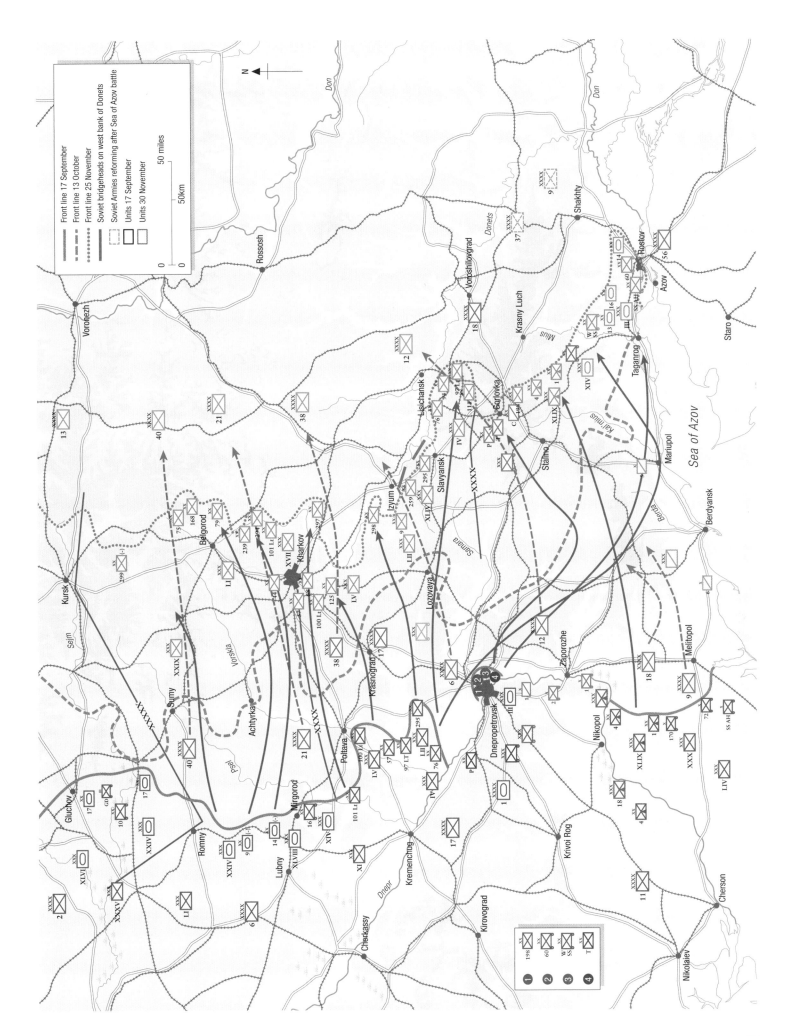

MAP 22: STRUGGLE FOR THE CRIMEA 13 SEPTEMBER TO 15 NOVEMBER, 1941

Hitler wanted the 10,000-square-mile Crimean Peninsula for a number of reasons: in order to avoid a Soviet presence in his rear areas, to eliminate any possible threat to the Romanian oilfields, and to dominate the Black Sea. A by-product of owning the peninsula might be bringing Turkey into the war against the USSR. Meanwhile Tyulenev tried to create some semblance of a legitimate defence following Uman. In mid-August he received orders from the Stavka to defend the lower Dnepr, notably to keep the Germans penned in their Dnepropetrovsk, Berislav and Kherson bridgeheads.

Neither Tyulenev nor his successor Ryabyshev could do much more than slow 11. Armee, under Manstein since 13 September. He withdrew the Southern Front from the Dnepr River to a line running south of Zaporozhe to the Sea of Azov, and so had to detach a separate garrison to the Crimea – the 51st Independent Army. The Crimea joined mainland Ukraine via a narrow isthmus; the first line of defence was the 5-mile-wide narrows at Perekop and the second was a 7-mile-wide line a bit farther south near Ishun. The Soviets tied modern bunkers and obstacles to the centuries-old Tartar Ditch. Four rifle and two cavalry divisions manned the first line, backed up by two rifle and one cavalry divisions. The entire line was supported by extensive indirect fire weapons and 100 tanks. The Black Sea Fleet kept the Crimea relatively well supplied from its bases at Novorossisk and elsewhere. Meanwhile, Manstein could devote only the LIV Armee-Korps to the Crimea breakthrough battles since he had to contend with overall numerical inferiority, active Red Army forces north of Melitopol and a logistics tail many hundreds of miles long.

In one of the classic tactical operations of *Barbarossa*, 46. and 73. Infanterie-Divisionen attacked the Perekop defences on 24 September. Supported by *Nebelwerfer* and Stukas, they took 24 hours to reach the Tartar Ditch and another 24 to cross it. By the 28th they had defeated the first defensive belt and readied to assault the second. However, Ryabyshev's own attack north of Melitopol (Map 20) interrupted the German plans. When the situation was mastered and further operations in the Ukraine became now exclusively Kleist's responsibility, after two weeks (which the Soviets had used to work on their defences and to add nearly 100,000 reinforcements evacuated from Odessa) Manstein prepared to renew his assault. He added 22. Infanterie-Division to the mix, and with heavily reinforced Luftwaffe CAS, LIV Armee-Korps attacked anew on 18 October. Manstein switched his *Schwerpunkt* from east to west and back, but it took his men a week to negotiate the nine defensive belts 6 miles deep. He pushed the LIV Armee-Korps despite debilitating losses until Red Army defenders, having had enough, broke and ran. After the 26th, there was no place north of Sevastopol or the Yalta Mountains for them to turn and fight. Both retreating Soviets and pursuing Germans, moving at the pace of marching men, divided into two main groups, the Coastal Army made up mainly of Odessa evacuees followed by the XXX and LIV Armee-Korps heading west for the fortified port, while the 51st Army which made for the 10-mile-wide Parpach isthmus was chased by the XLII Armee-Korps. In the mountainous far south, the Romanian Mountain Corps fought large partisan forces. The 51st Army, failing to mount a credible defence at either Feodosia or Parpach, was quickly bypassed on 3 November by the XLII Armee-Korps, which won the race to the port of Kerch, capturing it on the 15th.

Sevastopol was another matter altogether. Originally only defended from the sea, new fortifications were now oriented inland as well. Three concentric lines, thousands of bunkers linked by trenches, anti-tank ditches and mines, combined with Red Army Air Force planes and Black Sea Fleet guns and supply ships, equalled a very formidable fortress. The rough terrain favoured the defenders, and logistics continued to hamstring 11. Armee. These factors did not dissuade Manstein from planning an attack for later in November. Reality intruded, however, and would eventually push back his attack another seven months. Nevertheless, in two months his army captured over 100,000 POWs and nearly 800 field pieces, while he had cleared the Crimea except for Sevastopol and some mountainous areas.

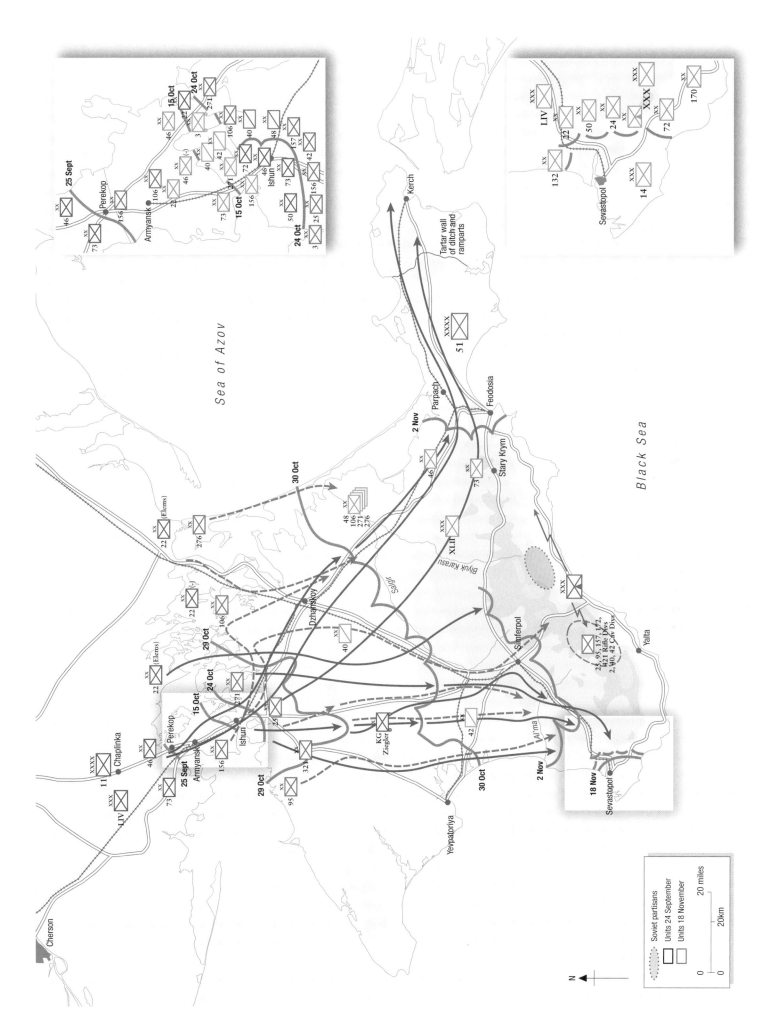

Sea of Azov

Black Sea

Cherson

Kerch

Tartar wall
of ditch and
ramparts

Parpach

Feodosia

2 Nov

Stary Krym

51

73
XX

XLII
XXX

Blyuk Karasu

Salgit

Simferopol

Yalta

25, 95, 157, 172,
421 Rifle Divs
2, 40, 42 Cav Divs
XXX

30 Oct

48
106
271
276

22 (Elems)

276

22 (-)

106

40

Dzhankoy

29 Oct

22 (Elems)

24 Oct

271

KG
Ziegler

42

Al'ma

2 Nov

30 Oct

18 Nov

Sevastopol

Yevpatoriya

95

321

25

156

73

Ishun

25 Sept

Amyansk

15 Oct

Perekop

Chaplinka

46

11
XXXX

LIV
XXX

73

29 Oct

Inset (upper left)

25 Sept

Perekop

156

73

Amyansk

106

46

15 Oct

22

40

271

46

42

1
(-)

40

42

72

156

73

24 Oct

15 Oct

Ishun

46

3
22

106

40

48

57

42

156

25

3

24 Oct

Inset (upper right)

LIV
XXX

22

132

50

24

XXXX

72

170

14

Sevastopol

Legend

Soviet partisans

Units 24 September

Units 18 November

N

0   20 miles
0   20km

MAP 23: THE BATTLE FOR ROSTOV 22 OCTOBER TO 30 NOVEMBER, 1941

Following the successful conclusion of the Sea of Azov battles, Rundstedt arranged his army group with 6. Armee at Belgorod and Kharkov, 17. Armee along the middle Donets, 1. Panzer-Armee in the Donbas and 11. Armee on the Crimean cul-de-sac. By early November, only Kleist had any significant manoeuvring abilities left. Reorganized by losing XLVIII Panzer-Korps to Guderian but gaining XLIX Gebirgs-Korps from Manstein, he also had III and XIV Panzer-Korps plus SSLAH and CSIR. Rundstedt's Directive No. 10 of 22 October instructed 1. Panzer-Armee to launch its final offensive against Rostov. During the last days of October and first days of November, it pushed small mobile groups across the Mius River with whatever little fuel they could scrape together. Expecting a successful conclusion to the in-progress *Typhoon* battles on the main Moscow axis, Heeresgruppe Süd soldiers assumed Rostov would be their last major fight before the USSR collapsed under the combined effects of *Barbarossa*'s blows.

The XIV Panzer-Korps passed over the Mius at Golodayevka, but by 7 November Red Army defenders holding the Tuslov River brought it to a halt. Kleist then made III Panzer, hugging the coastline under IV and V Flieger-Korps CAS, his main effort. The 1. Panzer-Armee took advantage of freezing weather starting on 13 November to continue its advance. Unfortunately, it began to outrun the flank cover; XLIX Gebirgs-Korps experienced difficulty keeping pace through the heavily industrialized Donbas while 17. Armee even farther north had reached its limit of advance. By the 17th, Kleist's extended left presented Timoshenko with an opportunity for a well-placed counterattack, as he had briefed Stalin a week earlier. With the panzers arcing north-east of Rostov nearly 150 miles out in front of the rest of the army group, the newly arrived 37th Army under General A. I. Lopatin came out of Sverdlovsk to hit the XIV Panzer-Korps' northern flank the next day. At the same time from positions west of Rostov, General Lieutenant F. N. Remezov's 56th Independent Army attacked III Panzer's southern flank. The Soviet force totalled seven armies consisting of more than 50 divisions plus seven tank brigades. Together with 17. Armee units, the XIV Panzer-Korps and XLIX Gebirgs-Korps handled the threat on the left while III Panzer-Korps kept advancing on the right, reaching both outer Rostov and the Don River by 19 November. Timoshenko had learned from his earlier Smolensk battles that only a large, well co-ordinated assault would slow the Germans, and he would soon renew his efforts. The III Panzer-Korps under Generalleutnant Eberhard von Mackensen entered the city the next day, even pushing SSLAH over the river, representing *Barbarossa*'s deepest penetration of the USSR.

Marshal Timoshenko assembled another counterattack force of new and rebuilt armies. Their objective was 1. Panzer-Armee; if they could defeat Kleist, then Rostov would be theirs. Despite Halder urging the army group on to the Baku oil region, Rundstedt and even more Kleist knew to prepare for a Red Army counterattack by creating alarm units and writing withdrawal plans. First to move on 25 November came 56th Army against the SSLAH south of Rostov. Ferocious fighting along the Don River and in the city took place for two days. On the 27th, Timoshenko turned loose the entire Southern Front against Kleist's exposed salient. It took the panzer general a mere 48 hours to realize that only giving up Rostov would save his command. After an additional 48 hours, on the last day of November, Rundstedt authorized retreating all the way to the Mius River, the only viable defensive terrain west of Rostov. Timoshenko spurred his men to keep up a vigorous pursuit over the frozen steppe.

Hitler had been away from his headquarters during these moves and when he discovered them he was livid, immediately accepting Rundstedt's resignation. On 1 December, he placed 6. Armee commander Reichenau atop Heeresgruppe Süd as well, with orders to halt the retreat and renew eastward movement. The field marshal had been a Hitler supporter since the late Weimar Republic, so dutifully passed down the unrealistic directions only to give in and cancel them later the same day. Hitler flew to Mariupol over 2–3 December to look into the absolutely novel development of an entire German army retreating in the face of Soviet attacks. Little did he know that within a very few days that would be the case for much of his eastern army.

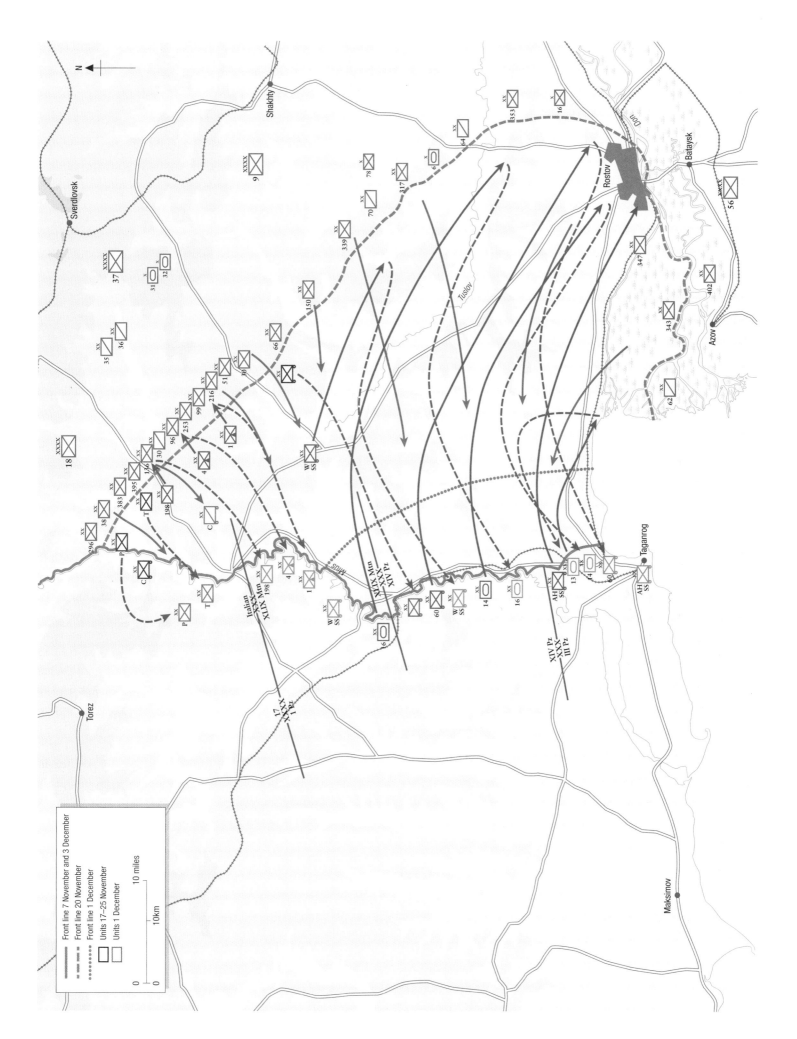

MAPS 24 & 25: OPERATIONS *PLATINFUCHS* AND *POLARFUCHS*

The Arctic theatre is one where the paucity of strategic thinking and the disregard for logistics characteristic of the Third Reich stands out. World War I had demonstrated the importance of convoys to Archangel and Murmansk in keeping Russia in contact with its allies and the outside world. Hitler never devoted the land or air resources necessary to ensure Arctic success much beyond occasional bombing of both ports and less frequent cutting of the rail line to Murmansk.

MAP 24: OPERATION *PLATINFUCHS* – 29 JUNE TO 21 SEPTEMBER, 1941

The Wehrmacht's AOK Norwegen under Nikolaus von Falkenhorst was one of its largest, but due to Hitler's paranoia concerning possible Royal Navy amphibious operations along the Norwegian coast, he devoted only two of its corps to Barbarossa. Ardent Nazi Party member and 'Hero of Narvik' General der Gebirgstruppen Eduard Dietl commanded Gebirgs-Korps Norwegen, made up of the 2. and 3. Gebirgs-Divisionen plus a selection of support troops. Facing him were elements of General Lieutenant V. A. Frolov's 14th Army, specifically the 14th and 52nd Rifle Divisions and eventually the very understrength Polyarnyy ('Polar') Militia Division.

Dietl attacked on 29 June with his Schwerpunkt, 2. Gebirgs-Division augmented by a company of tanks (1/ Panzer-Battalion 40) hugging the coast, while 3. Gebirgs-Division moved out further inland. Within one day 3. Gebirgs-Division came to the end of roads in its sector, so Dietl placed it behind 2. Gebirgs-Division. Henceforth he would attack along a one-division front and generally follow the one road east from Petsamo. During the first week of July his alpine troops pushed across the Litsa River only to be beaten back by Frolov's counterattacks. To compound Dietl's problems, on numerous occasions Soviet Northern Fleet ships landed troops at various places behind his lines.

Falkenhorst and Dietl joined forces to convince Hitler they would need reinforcement and a few days later he agreed to send 6. Gebirgs-Division from Greece – by which time the short Arctic fighting season would almost be over. Dietl attacked without the reinforcements on 8 September. The 2. and 3. Gebirgs-Divisionen slogged forward, but by 21 September Dietl had to admit failure. His men had covered less than half of the 50-odd miles to Murmansk and would never get appreciably closer.

MAP 25: OPERATION *POLARFUCHS* – 1 JULY TO 10 OCTOBER, 1941

Perhaps Falkenhorst would have better chances attacking toward Kandalaksha on the White Sea, cutting the rail line and achieving basically the same results: rendering Murmansk ineffective. General der Infanterie Hans Feige commanded the XXXVI Armee-Korps consisting of 169. Infanterie-Division and 6. SS-Division Nord, the latter a partially motorized occupation force. The Finns initially contributed their 6th Division. Defending was the 42nd Rifle Corps (104th and 122nd Rifle Divisions) under General Major R. I. Panin, augmented by Frolov with the 1st Tank Division.

Feige attacked on 1 July with the 169. Infanterie-Division and 6. SS-Division Nord against the 122nd Rifle Division, which manned the front lines and acquitted itself well, especially against the untried SS. The Axis forces attacked again three days later with army and Finnish troops making progress, while the SS troops came up short again, some even fleeing the fighting in a panic. Feige's men attacked yet again on 6 July, this time supported by Panzer-Abteilung 40 (minus its 1. Company in Petsamo) and Panzer-Abteilung 211, both restricted to the main roads. This manoeuvre levered the 122nd Rifle out of Salla. The 104th Rifle Division and remnants of the 122nd manned Panin's next defensive position halfway to the old 1939 border.

Feige planned to defeat this line with a large encirclement, with his 169. Infanterie-Division reinforced by an additional infantry regiment swinging around from the north and the Finnish III Corps coming from the south. By 24 August the Red Army divisions had been trapped, although poor weather and the difficult tundra landscape meant the small Kessel was full of gaps through which many of Panin's men escaped (but not the 1st Tank Division). Axis forces captured Allakurtti on 1 September but did not advance much beyond five miles before Soviet defences in the terrain of lakes and marshes interlaced with rivers. To the south, Finnish troops made decent advances beyond Kasten'ga (off map to the south-east), but with so much of the AOK Norwegen tied down in unnecessary garrison duty, its efforts against the 14th Army suffered.

That autumn two Führer directives, 36 (22 September) and 37 (10 October) alternately restarted and then halted Feige's operations. Soviet forces frequently seemed to be on the brink of collapse, but manoeuvring in the environment of the far north was always harder than it looked. By mid-November the climate made any more large-scale manoeuvres impractical, and, still 40 miles from the rail line, any disruption of lend-lease shipments fell to infrequent minuscule Luftwaffe raids.

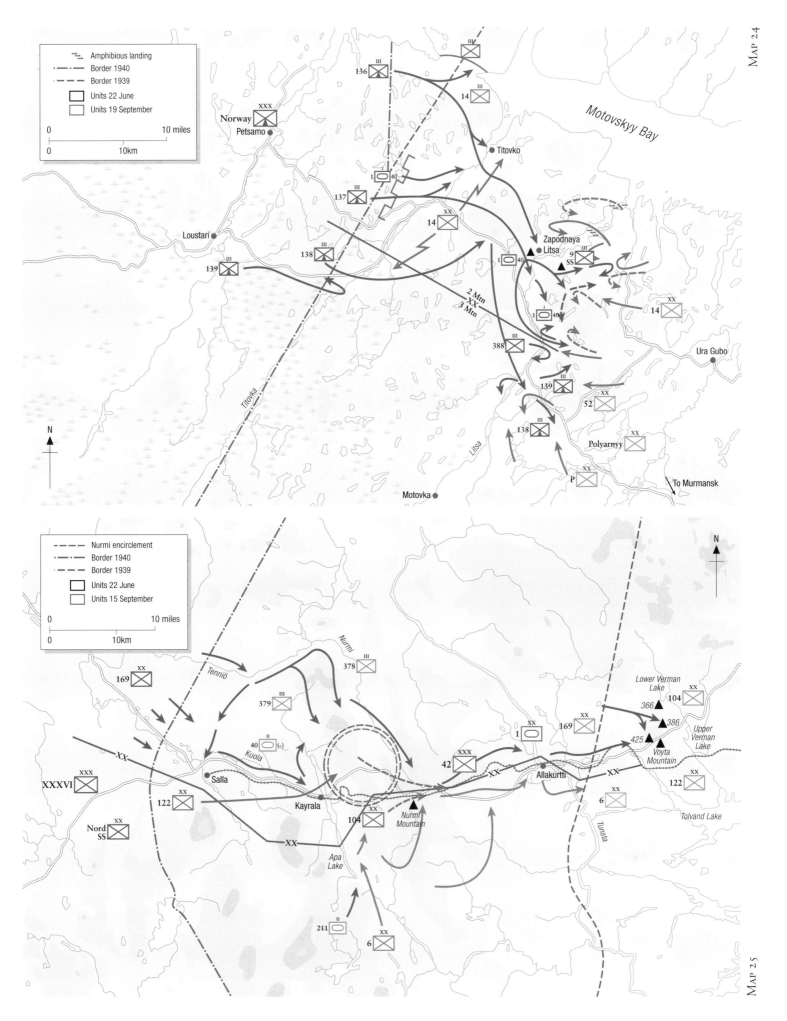

Map 24

Amphibious landing
Border 1940
Border 1939
Units 22 June
Units 19 September

0 ————— 10 miles
0 ————— 10km

Norway
Petsamo

Motovskyy Bay

136

14

Titovko

1 40

137

14

138

Zapodnaya
Litsa

9 SS

1 40

139

Loustari

2 Mtn
3 Mtn

1 40

14

388

Ura Gubo

139

52

138

Litsa

Polyarnyy

N

Motovka

P

To Murmansk

Nurmi encirclement
Border 1940
Border 1939
Units 22 June
Units 15 September

0 ————— 10 miles
0 ————— 10km

N

169

Nurmi

378

Tenniö

379

Lower Verman
Lake

104

366

386

40 (-)

Upper
Verman
Lake

1

169

Kuola

425

Voyta
Mountain

XXXVI

Salla

42

Allakurtti

122

122

Nord
SS

Kayrala

104

6

Nurmi
Mountain

Tunsta

Tolvand Lake

Apa
Lake

211

6

Map 25

MAP 26: KARELIAN FRONT 10 JULY TO 15 OCTOBER, 1941

Finland's greatest contribution to Hitler's war against the USSR came in Karelia, on either side of Lake Ladoga. Unfortunately for Hitler, its main objectives were to regain territory lost at the Moscow Peace Treaty (1940) and to secure a more defensible frontier, not to provoke its massive southern neighbour. The country did not join the Third Reich by treaty until 1944, so was merely a co-belligerent fighting against a common enemy. It managed to turn both its small size and geographical separation from Germany into significant advantages, and, even in defeat, managed to avoid total domination by the Soviet Union as happened to Stalin's other former enemies. During the Winter War Finland grudgingly gave ground in Karelia, but by March 1940 Finnish troops were almost 75 miles farther away from Leningrad than when they started. This arguably saved the city from capture in 1941.

Twelve of Finland's 18 divisions and all of its independent brigades were in General Axel Heinrichs' Army of Karelia. During most of the inter-war period, the Finnish military had been equipped by nearly every army on the continent, but in the year preceding *Barbarossa* Germany had become its primary supplier. Across the front General Major P. S. Pshennikov's 23rd Army (five rifle divisions and one mechanized corps) defended the approaches to Leningrad, while the 7th Independent Army under General Lieutenant F. D. Gorelenko (four rifle divisions) guarded the area between lakes Ladoga and Onega. Quite unnecessarily, on 2 July Stalin provoked Finland into active warfare by bombing Finnish cities and even invading the country.

Heinrichs attacked on 10 July along the southernmost 200 miles separating Finland from the USSR. Moving in the north half of the front, Group 'O', reinforced by the German 163. Infanterie-Division, broke through the Soviet lines at Kopisel'kaya and swung around in a clockwise arc toward Lake Ladoga. When they reached Koirinoye on the 16th, they isolated much of the 7th Army against VI and VII Corps troops coming at them from the front. Red Army commanders regained their composure after two weeks of combat and initiated counterattacks that gave the Finns and Germans reason to pause. Encircled Soviet forces held on tenaciously and by the end of the month a major battle developed around Sortavala. A month later the Ladoga Flotilla succeeded in evacuating most of the 142nd, 168th and 198th rifle Divisions to temporary safety around Leningrad. Operations on the front's southern half continued with a II Corps attack toward Lake Ladoga on 31 July, followed by IV Corps attacking toward Vyborg on 22 August. Within weeks the Finns had worked their way around isolated pockets of Red Army troops and the Vyborg fortress. Three rifle divisions were initially trapped within the fortress, but all eventually managed to escape. By the last day of August, the 23rd Army had given up most of the gains won during the Winter War. Finnish troops did not push their luck but halted just miles inside the 1939 borders. This left Leningrad with a large surrounding region that would dissipate the Germans' later efforts to reduce the city.

East of Lake Ladoga, the Finnish VI Corps blasted out of the general area of the 1939 border in the direction of the Svir River. On its right flank, VII Corps joined in the assault. Men of VI Corps reached the Svir in just three days and cut the Murmansk railway a day later. On their left II Corps and Group 'O' advanced through the first half of October into the region of Lake Lizhm and the Stalin Canal. Although Finland had admittedly limited objectives for its Continuation War, one would have to conclude that by reaching the right bank of the Svir River the Finns kept up their end of the bargain. It remained to be seen if Leeb's Heeresgruppe Nord could reach the left bank; it never did.

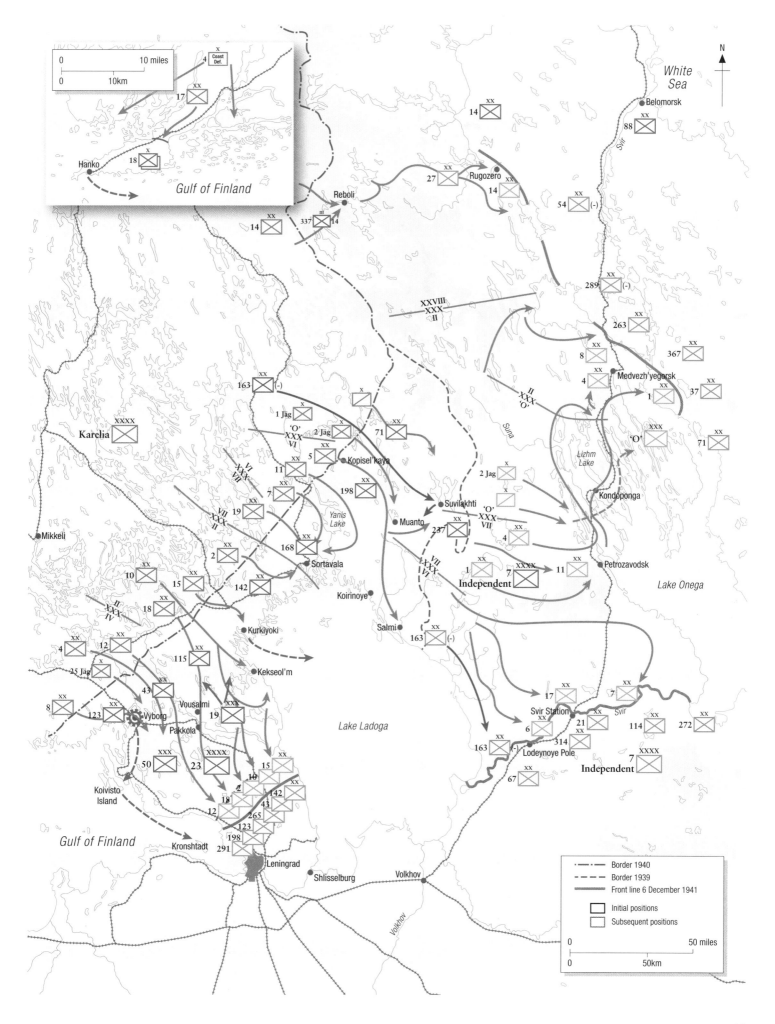

Inset (top left)

0 ____ 10 miles
0 ____ 10km

4 | Coast Def. (X)

17 (XX)

18 (X)

Hanko

Gulf of Finland

Main map labels

White Sea

Belomorsk

88 (XX)

14 (XX)

27 (XX) Rugozero 14 (XX)

54 (XX) (-)

14 (XX) 337 (III) 14

Reboli

289 (XX) (-)

263 (XX)

XXVIII
XXX
II

8 (XX) 367 (XX)

4 (XX) Medvezh'yegorsk

163 (XX) (-)

II
XXX
'O'

1 (XX) 37 (XX)

Karelia (XXXX)

1 Jäg (X)
'O'
XXX
VI
2 Jäg (X)

71 (XX)

Suna

'O' (XXX) 71 (XX)

Lizhm Lake

Kondoponga

2 Jag (X)

11 (XX)
5 (XX) Kopisel'kaya

VI
XXX
VII

7 (XX)

198 (XX)

19 (XX)

Yanis Lake

Muanto 237 (XX)

Suvilakhti

'O'
XXX
VII

4 (XX)

VII
XXX
II

2 (XX) 168 (XX)

Sortavala

1 (XX) 7 (XXXX) 11 (XX) Petrozavodsk

Lake Onega

Mikkeli

10 (XX) 15 (XX) 142 (XX)

Koirinoye

VII
XXX
VI

Independent

18 (XX)

II
XXX
IV

Kurkiyoki

Salmi

163 (XX) (-)

4 (XX) 12 (XX)

25 Jäg (X)

115 (XX)

Kekseol'm

17 (XX) 7 (XX)

8 (XX) 123 (XX) Vyborg

43 (XX)

Vousalmi 19 (XXXX)

6 (XX) Svir Station

21 (XX) *Svir*

114 (XX) 272 (XX)

Pakkola

314 (XX)

Lodeynoye Pole

50 (XXX) 23 (XXXX) 15 (XX)

10 (XX)

2
18 (XX) 142 (XX)
12 43
265
123
198
291

Koivisto Island

163 (XX) (-)

67 (XX)

7 (XXXX) **Independent**

Gulf of Finland

Kronshtadt

Leningrad

Shlisselburg Volkhov

Lake Ladoga

Volkhov

Legend

- - · - Border 1940
- - - - Border 1939
——— Front line 6 December 1941

☐ Initial positions
☐ Subsequent positions

0 ____ 50 miles
0 ____ 50km

63

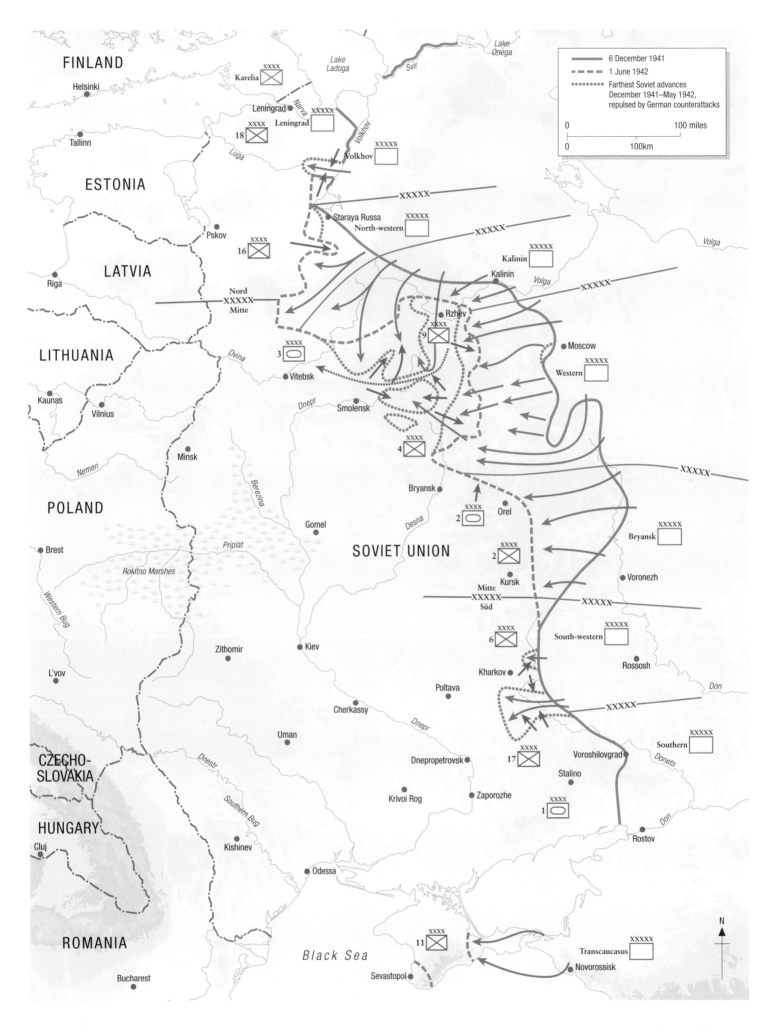

FINLAND

Helsinki

Lake Ladoga

Karelia XXXX

Leningrad
Leningrad XXXXX
18 XXXX

Svir

Lake Onega

6 December 1941
1 June 1942
Farthest Soviet advances
December 1941–May 1942,
repulsed by German counterattacks

0 ——————————— 100 miles
0 ——————————— 100km

Tallinn

ESTONIA

Pskov

LATVIA

Riga

Narva

Volkhov

Volkhov XXXXX

Luga

Staraya Russa
North-western XXXXX

16 XXXX

Volga

Kalinin XXXXX

Kalinin

Volga

Nord
XXXXX
Mitte

Dvina

Rzhev

9 XXXX

Moscow

Western XXXXX

3 XXXX

LITHUANIA

Kaunas

Vilnius

Vitebsk

Smolensk

Dnepr

4 XXXX

Minsk

Nemen

Berezina

POLAND

Brest

Rokitno Marshes

Pripiat

Gomel

Bryansk

2 XXXX

Orel

SOVIET UNION

2 XXXX

Bryansk XXXXX

Voronezh

Western Bug

Desna

Mitte
XXXXX
Süd

Kursk

Zithomir

Kiev

6 XXXX

South-western XXXXX

Rossosh

L'vov

Poltava

Kharkov

Don

CZECHO-
SLOVAKIA

Dnestr

Cherkassy

Dnepr

Uman

Southern Bug

Southern XXXXX

Donets

HUNGARY

Cluj

Kishinev

Dnepropetrovsk

17 XXXX

Voroshilovgrad

Stalino

Krivoi Rog

Zaporozhe

1 XXXX

Don

Rostov

Odessa

ROMANIA

Bucharest

Black Sea

11 XXXX

Sevastopol

Transcaucasus XXXXX

Novorossisk

N

CHAPTER 2
SOVIET WINTER COUNTEROFFENSIVES, 1941–42

During Operation *Typhoon* the Germans' eastern army threw every last man and bullet against Moscow. Across the front lines, although clearly sorely tested by *Barbarossa*, the Soviets had been setting aside fresh reserves for the right occasion. On 5 December, Hitler bowed to the realities of the situation and halted the Germans' attacks; by general consensus this date is considered the end of Operation *Barbarossa*.

Fronts and armies fighting to defend Moscow just hours earlier switched to the offensive starting the following day. Surprise was complete, since the Wehrmacht intelligence branch had assumed its adversary had no reserves to speak of. At the same time partisan groups launched co-ordinated actions against bridges, railways, supply depots and telephone/telegraph lines. Reflecting the most serious threat to their capital, the first counterattacks concentrated against the German positions north of the city. Stalin eventually threw 17 armies against Heeresgruppe Mitte. Despite a slight German superiority in numbers, fresh Soviet units enjoyed success during the first days. Operating close to their logistics bases and able to choose the time and location of their assaults, numerous attacks built local dominance. The cold adversely affected everything the Wehrmacht had: men and horses froze to death, wheels of artillery pieces became stuck to the frozen ground and would not budge. Vehicle and aircraft engines froze and, if they did not fail outright, would not turn over.

The German Army had not been challenged like this since October–November 1918. Determined Red Army attacks sorely tested the Wehrmacht's flexibility and mobility, its key strengths. These assaults were aided by a new combined-arms formation, cavalry-mechanized groups, which drew on the strengths of both branches. Bock requested permission to withdraw, but to Hitler cancelling attacks was one thing, retreating entirely another. Having used all its resources in *Barbarossa*'s closing weeks, the Wehrmacht had no reserves to give the hard-pressed fighting troops. Their defence faltered as the retrograde movement threatened to become a rout. Urged from above, Heeresgruppe Mitte's leader relinquished command on 18 December, followed the next day by the commander of the entire German Army, Generalfeldmarschall Walther von Brauchitsch. Like their soldiers, both generals were beaten down.[26] Hitler then added Army Commander in Chief to his many

26 'Retiring for reasons of ill-health', in the Third Reich a euphemism for being relieved from duty, was true

titles, essentially completing his takeover of the military begun in earnest in 1938.

Slowly but surely, Stalin's men pushed back the invaders away all along the Moscow sector. New formations arrived from Siberia and the Urals helping local counterattacks grow in size, so that after a dozen days the Soviets had many reasons to be satisfied. The tactic of employing mainly infantry, supported by armour limited to brigade size, restricted their success, however, so hoped-for decisive results evaded them. The situation was a reversal of the previous autumn; as the Red Army advanced away from its logistics, the Germans fell back on theirs, getting closer to food and shelter. Winter clothing, having sat in rail cars in Germany for months, began to arrive at the front. With better conditions, German discipline and morale improved. Snowdrifts many feet deep also slowed the Red Army, while the panzers' mobility often allowed them to escape entrapment and destruction. Despite these factors, Soviet forces inexorably levered the Wehrmacht from one temporary position to another, although moving slower than planners would have liked. Doomsday predictions for Heeresgruppe Mitte by Bock's successor Kluge failed to materialize, which seemed to justify the Führer's calls for 'fanatical defence'. Unrealistic war-winning breakthroughs likewise evaded the Red Army, despite numerous penetrations by large and free-ranging cavalry formations. New to larger offensive manoeuvres, the Soviets had not yet mastered the technique. Additionally, their own intelligence service had likewise overestimated Wehrmacht fragility.

Toward the end of December, the Germans managed new threats in an increasingly organized fashion while sustaining losses that were large but not crippling. In an effort to encircle Heeresgruppe Mitte, Zhukov shifted his main effort from one point to another, temporarily gaining ground at various places until opposing defenders forced him to try elsewhere. Throughout December his emphasis migrated from Moscow's north to the west then to the south. In early January 1942 he moved it back north and then once more to the city's west. On some days that month severe weather brought even the attackers to a standstill. Three weeks into 1942, the Wehrmacht's retreat generally came to an end along the Königsberg Line running Rzhev–Gzhatsk–Kaluga; by *Barbarossa*'s standards Moscow remained within easy striking distance (60–70 miles away). Neither side knew it at the time, but the war would get no closer to the city. The Germans, or more specifically Hitler, drew false lessons from the winter fighting. He believed anecdotal yet apocryphal evidence that his own version of 'not one step back' orders represented the difference between success and failure that winter. At the same time he learned to trust his own intuition and wisdom over the advice of his generals. These twin notions would haunt Germany for the remainder of World War II.

Based on Stalin's insistence and against the recommendations of many generals, in early 1942 the Soviets expanded their attacks from the Gulf of Finland to the Black Sea. By resorting to this 'attack everywhere' mentality, Stalin sacrificed mass in one sector as he dissipated Red Army strength over the entire front. Before the end of 1941, the Stavka ordered amphibious landings on the Crimea, but these succeeded only in temporarily liberating the Kerch Peninsula from mainly Romanian forces. Stout German positions at the Feodosia Isthmus held against renewed breakout attempts in February, March and April, incompetently led by one of Stalin's political hacks. The key port of Sevastopol provided one bright spot for the defenders, withstanding a lengthy siege. In the far north, Red Army forces attacked both Finns and Germans, on either side of Lake Ladoga, throughout the depths of winter and early spring. Their success at Tikhvin re-opened rail traffic to the south-eastern shore of Lake Ladoga, from where supplies were transferred over water to Leningrad. They registered gains north and south of Lake Il'men, creating encirclements at Demyansk and Kholm that cost Leeb his job. Again, however, larger Soviet objectives in this sector – to lift the siege of the city and if possible to destroy Heeresgruppe Nord – were at variance with their capabilities. Superior German operational leadership proved to be a decisive factor against poorly prepared, resourced and supervised attacks in this especially brutal climate.

Between these two geographical extremities, the second phase of Soviet countermoves in the centre did not enjoy the success of the first phase. The Stavka's planners had little idea of Red Army capabilities and gave some commanders objectives as far away as Smolensk (to which their units came, and remained, dangerously close). Granted, in early February encirclement of Heeresgruppe Mitte looked tantalizingly achievable. Unfortunately for Zhukov, the jaws of his trap consisted of small, isolated, widely separated, poorly supplied and often tenuously commanded units. Whatever success they did have in the early stages succumbed to Wehrmacht powers of recovery and skill, not to mention climate and overstretch. Just as Zhukov had warned, firstly Soviet losses during *Barbarossa* had been tremendous but had not been made good, secondly they had forsaken the element of surprise as winter progressed, thirdly proper breakthrough forces had not been provided for and, finally and most critically, their leadership skill at this early point simply was not equal to the task of co-ordinating complex widespread combined-arms operations.

With each side punch-drunk, weakened from earlier losses and suffering from horrible weather – first blizzards then the *rasputitsa* – both offence and defence were sporadic. The infrequent Soviet penetration bypassed the rare German strongpoints, so much of the central sector became a series of alternating tactical salients jutting into the other's territory, giving the front a castellated appearance. Isolated pockets from each side dotted the countryside, exaggerating the jagged lines. Another dangerous precedent that developed and would come back to haunt the Wehrmacht was its solution for fully or partially encircled German units, which was the unrealistic assumption that the Luftwaffe could provide indefinite aerial resupply. In the same vein, as spring arrived the Soviets proved incapable of maintaining many of their most exposed gains: distant penetrations, isolated airborne and cavalry raiding groups plus wary forces trying to reduce various enemy

in the case of both field marshals and many other senior (i.e. older) generals that terrible winter. In December alone Hitler cashiered 35 generals of the rank of Generalleutnant or above. Of course individual German soldiers could not just go home regardless of illness or weather.

defences. Meanwhile, the Germans had somewhat regained their equilibrium and largely succeeded in managing these same penetrations, raiding groups and attacking forces. However, in some cases it would be July before many of these Soviet outliers were close to being fully defeated.

There remained one last major Red Army offensive of the winter/spring 1942 season near Kharkov. Timoshenko's South-western Direction had the mission of executing a double envelopment using some of the best troops and equipment still in the field. Their large Izyum bridgehead jutting into the Wehrmacht lines (won in January and target of a planned German attack pre-empted by the Soviets) served as the main assault position. The Stavka's planners expected a weak defence manned by shattered units, but instead found the most powerful German concentration of ground and air forces since *Typhoon*. In addition to the usual Red Army leadership and logistical woes common at that stage of the war, German intelligence caught wind of the attack's build-up. The Soviet leadership, specifically Stalin, offers a curious model of lessons from the preceding few months, both learned and not learned. Evidently wary of overambitious attacks covering large areas, here it wisely chose a limited frontage. Conversely, however, it downplayed indications from its own forces in contact that the Germans had been improving and recovering as the weather warmed. Two further factors conspired to doom the Kharkov attack: continued command and control problems when it came to orchestrating complex and large-scale operations, and Wehrmacht preparations for its own summer 1942 offensive taking place right in the same neighbourhood.

After a momentous start, in less than one week that May (12–19) Red Army units moved out, fell behind schedule attacking into the teeth of the Germans' two biggest formations, came to a virtual standstill and, finally, received permission to withdraw. The Soviets failed to provide adequate exploitation forces to move through their initial breakthroughs, to anticipate and prepare for the inevitable German countermoves and to execute a proper retrograde. An orderly retreat in the face of Wehrmacht air and ground attacks proved impossible. The offensive's small frontage represented a double-edged sword; it meant the operation was conducted with an eye toward Red Army limitations, but also that Hitler had to be concerned with only a local emergency. On 23 May, the Germans launched a revised version of their assault planned in March. Their pincer in the southern sector snapped shut near Balakleya, while the on the 26th they eliminated the penetration to the north around Belgorod. By the end of the month the fighting had concluded, with Soviet losses approaching a quarter of a million men, much equipment and many top leaders. In common with other battles that winter and spring, the Wehrmacht had given up a few breaches but no major penetrations. As bad as the winter retreat had been for the Germans, casualties of all types in the first four months of 1942 (277,000, or about 2,900 per day) compare favourably to those of the five months of *Barbarossa* (830,000, or 4,300 per day). Stalin had actually done Hitler a favour by offering this twin sacrifice of men and equipment plus surrendering improved jumping-off positions for the Führer's summer offensive, scheduled to begin the following month. In a year and a half of disaster for the USSR, May 1942 rates as one of the communist leader's worst failures.

Both dictators assumed they could win the war in its first year; neither seems to have realized they were in a marathon. The numerous Soviet offensives conducted in the six months after *Barbarossa*'s culmination are frequently offered up as examples of Stalin's dilettantism plus the USSR's continued inexperience and unpreparedness, strategic overstretch mirroring that of Hitler in 1941. Indeed, they were all those things, but also the latest instalments in the nation's death-by-a-thousand-cuts approach that would drive Germany, and its eastern army, to ruin. Five factors would affect German operations during the coming campaign season: firstly, losses in men, horses and equipment during the winter offensives had to be replaced;[27] secondly, in the centre, if Hitler chose to make Moscow his 1942 *Schwerpunkt*, his men would have to recapture most of the land taken during Operation *Typhoon*; thirdly, in the north Leningrad was no closer to falling; fourthly, in the south Red Army forces still occupied Sevastopol while Wehrmacht forces preparing for Operation *Blau* needed to recover from unexpected action; and finally, Luftwaffe elements across the entire front been weakened by combat and operational wear and tear. As the Nazi-Soviet War entered its second year, Stalin now knew he still had much work to do to achieve success; Hitler on the other hand thought victory was just around the corner. In any event, both knew that they were in for a long fight and would have to completely rethink their future conduct of the war.

---

27 Axis armies began *Barbarossa* with 500,000 horses, of which half died in the first 11 months.

MAP 28: LYUBAN OPERATION 5 DECEMBER, 1941 TO 29 JUNE, 1942

Operation *Barbarossa* failed to knock the USSR out of the war in one deadly, quick campaign. Heeresgruppe Nord's zenith occurred during its month-long Tikhvin and Volkhov attacks, but by early December Soviet counterattacks had pushed the front line trace back to the Volkhov River, between Novgorod and Kirishi where it cut north-west toward Shlisselburg (Map 8). The 18. Armee under Generaloberst Georg von Küchler had the unenviable double mission of reducing the Leningrad pocket and holding the northern portion of the Volkhov River line, the latter with the XXVIII and I Armee-Korps. Busch's 16. Armee, generally on either side of Lake Il'men, defended the southern Volkhov with the XXXVIII and X Armee-Korps forward and XXXIX Panzer-Korps back. Opposite stood the Leningrad Front (8th and 54th Armies) under General Lieutenant M. S. Khozin and Volkhov Front (4th, 59th, 2nd Shock and 52nd Armies) commanded by General K. A. Meretskov. Their missions were to attack toward Volosovo nearly 100 miles to the west and, if possible, break the siege of Leningrad. The 11th Army coming around from the south of Lake Il'men provided flank support.

As part of the Soviets' larger general offensive, during the first week of January 1942 their units attacked all along the front between lakes Ladoga and Il'men. Most advances were very shallow. Meretskov's main effort came on 13 January in the southern part of the sector where the 2nd Shock Army achieved a breakthrough along the seam dividing the 126. and 215. Infanterie-Divisionen. With elements of the 4th and 59th Armies providing support, the 2nd Shock established a bridgehead over the Volkhov on the following day, creating a deep bulge in the Wehrmacht line. The Soviet's exploitation force, 13th Cavalry Corps, cut the Novgorod–Chudovo road and rail line. Farther north, near Pogostye, the 54th Army overwhelmed the 269. Infanterie-Division and temporarily split the boundary separating 18. and 16. Armeen, but German counterattacks quickly restored the original front. By 21 January only 2nd Shock could make any progress, but was still more than 70 miles from Leningrad. On the 24th the Red Army penetration measured 25 miles deep but only 1 ½ miles wide at its base. Despite

numerous attempts, they could not subdue the Germans' *Igel* at Spaskaya Polist. Both sides poured reinforcements into the area.

During the last days of February, the Stavka urged 2nd Shock and 59th Armies to keep pressing toward Lyuban and Chudovo respectively. The paucity of men, ammunition and CAS conspired to forestall these plans, however. Meanwhile by early March 18. Armee, now under General der Kavallerie Georg Lindemann, began assembling counterattack forces north and south of the 2nd Shock Army bulge. On 15 March, I Armee-Korps from the north and XXXVIII Armee-Korps from the south attacked to cut off the bottleneck. Four days later, troops of SS Polizei-Division and 58. Infanterie-Division met, encircling the bulk of the 2nd Shock and 52nd Armies, nearly 130,000 men, in the frozen forests and marshes. Within a week 54th Army near Pogostye launched a rescue operation over the same ground as before, coming within five miles of Lyuban. The Wehrmacht cordon was porous and approximately 1,000 Soviet soldiers escaped the *Kessel* every day. By early April the Red Army could add the spring thaw to its list of woes as it turned the entire area into a quagmire. Toward the end of the month, Stalin disbanded the Volkhov Front as superfluous and transferred its functions to the enlarged Leningrad Front.

Despite heavy losses, during the last days of May I and XXXVIII Armee-Korps continued to squeeze the pocket from all sides. Conditions inside were terrible under combined-force commander General Lieutenant A. A. Vlasov, soon to play a role as the Red Army's most famous defector and traitor. In early June, Zhukov ordered renewed rescue attempts by the 52nd and 59th Armies while 2nd Shock kept up attempts to break out. Numerous narrow lanes allowed for some escapes, while on 10 June the 29th Tank Brigade momentarily opened a passage at Miasnoi Bor. Though nearly 100,000 Soviets eventually escaped, by the third week of June the pocket had been fully reduced and 33,000 POWs marched off to German captivity. The six-month battles east of Lyuban make for an interesting tactical study of both sides in early 1942.

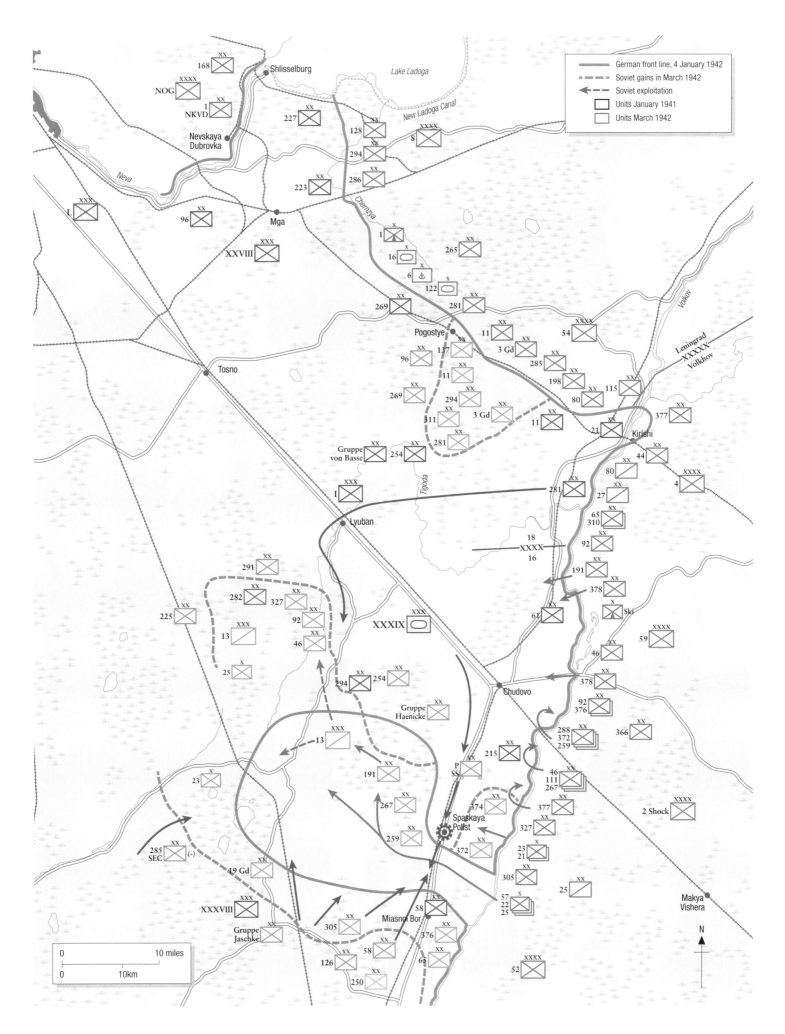

Shlisselburg

Lake Ladoga

New Ladoga Canal

168 NOG

1 NKVD

227

Nevskaya Dubrovka

128

294

8

286

223

Neva

L

96

Mga

XXVIII

1

16

6

122

265

269

281

Chernaya

Pogostye

11

3 Gd

54

Tosno

96

137

285

Volkhov

11

269

198

115

Leningrad
Volkhov

294

80

377

311

3 Gd

11

21

Kirishi

281

80

44

Gruppe
von Basse

254

Tigoda

4

281

27

I

65
310

Lyuban

92

18
16

191

291

378

Ski

282

327

13

46

59

225

92

46

61

XXXIX

294

254

378

25

Chudovo

92
376

Gruppe
Haenicke

288
372
259

366

13

46
111
267

23

191

215

377

2 Shock

267

P
SS

374

285
SEC

259

Spaskaya
Polist

327

19 Gd

372

23
21

XXXVIII

305

25

Gruppe
Jaschke

58

57
22
25

Miasnoi Bor

376

305

58

65

52

126

250

N

German front line, 4 January 1942
Soviet gains in March 1942
Soviet exploitation
Units January 1941
Units March 1942

0   10 miles
0   10km

69

MAP 29: DEMYANSK OPERATION (I) 4–16 JANUARY, 1942

As part of the January 1942 Soviet general offensive and simultaneous with the Lyuban Operation, the North-western, and later Kalinin, Fronts attacked south of Lake Il'men in the direction of Toropets. The North-western Front under General Lieutenant Kurochkin initially consisted of the 11th, 1st, and 34th Armies plus 3rd and 4th Shock Armies, but would be reinforced later. Its assigned missions were to push back Heeresgruppe Nord and ideally assist the Leningrad and Volkhov fronts to relieve the siege of Lenin's city and reach Smolensk. Blocking their way stood the 16. and 9. Armeen. The two southern corps of Busch's 16. Armee, X and II, held the western slope of the Valdai Hills between Staraya Russa and Lake Seliger. The XXIII and VI Armee-Korps held the sector from the reservoir to Rzhev as part of 9. Armee, commanded by Generaloberst Adolf Strauss until 15 January (when deteriorating health forced him to surrender his post – again) and afterwards by Model.

North-western Front began its offensive on 6 January against the supposedly passive sector, its mobility assisted by frozen lakes and rivers. On the far north 11th Army, using ski battalions for enhanced mobility, soon had the 18. Infanterie-Division (Mot.) streaming back toward Staraya Russa (where it was supposed to be 'resting' after Tikhvin), the 290. Infanterie-Division nearly encircled near Pola and other German units isolated in Vzvad on the southern shore of Lake Il'men. Kurochkin brought forward the 1st and 2nd Guards Rifle Corps and prepared to pass them through the assaulting infantry; they would represent the northern jaws of his intended encirclement. At the same time the 34th Army hit the II Armee-Korps front but could not make significant headway against the 30., 12. and 32. Infanterie-Divisionen or SS Division Totenkopf. It was a different story to the south, however. Units from the 34th Army crossed frozen Lake Seliger and near Molvotitsy began to work their way behind the 123. Infanterie-Division.

During the early going, some Red Army formations advanced up to 30 miles per day and bypassed numerous Wehrmacht strongpoints consisting of ad hoc *Kampfgruppen* that frequently held out for many weeks. Within 48 hours, the two guards rifle corps were close to breaking into the open country behind the shattered front of the X Armee-Korps, which had been cut in two. With the road from Staraya Russa cut, the better part of six Wehrmacht divisions, nearly 100,000 men, were isolated. According to Kurochkin's plan, the 1st Guards would now angle south-eastwards to close the inner trap, while the 2nd Guards was to head south-westwards to create the outer encirclement. Phase II of the operation began on 9 January when 3rd and 4th Shock Armies burst across Lake Seliger (another 'quiet' sector) in the direction of Kholm. Their objectives were to drive deep into the rear areas of Heeresgruppe Mitte. Their manoeuvre nearly marked the end of the 123. Infanterie-Division and some difficult days for the 253. Infanterie-Division to its right, both of which weakly manned dozens of miles of front. Nearly ten rifle divisions and a like number of rifle brigades began to threaten the boundary between Heeresgruppen Mitte and Nord, a vulnerable point since *Barbarossa*'s earliest days. By 12 January, Leeb told II Armee-Korps to prepare to abandon their exposed and incoherent front, but Hitler countermanded these instructions.

By mid-January, in the north 11th Army elements advanced on Dno, a key transportation hub and 16. Armee headquarters. In the south, the two shock armies fanned out to invest Kholm, cut the Velikie Luki–Toropets road and generally endanger the hinterland of both German army groups (Map 34). This dispersal of effort eventually revealed uncovered flanks and deficient logistics that slowed the Soviet advance but not before causing another shake-up in the German command structure. Personal differences between Hitler and Leeb, by far the weakest of *Barbarossa*'s original army group commanders and an opponent of the Führer's plan to starve Leningrad into submission, came to a head during the Demyansk crisis. After refusing the field marshal's earlier request to relinquish command, Hitler accepted it on 16 January. The 18. Armee commander Küchler took his place the next day, while L Armee-Korps Commander Lindemann now moved from the Leningrad siege lines to lead 18. Armee. During the last week of January, the Stavka did some re-organizing of its own by giving Kurochkin the 1st Shock Army and sole responsibility for the northern thrust, and re-assigning 3rd and 4th Shock Armies to General Lieutenant I. S. Konev's Kalinin Front to the south.

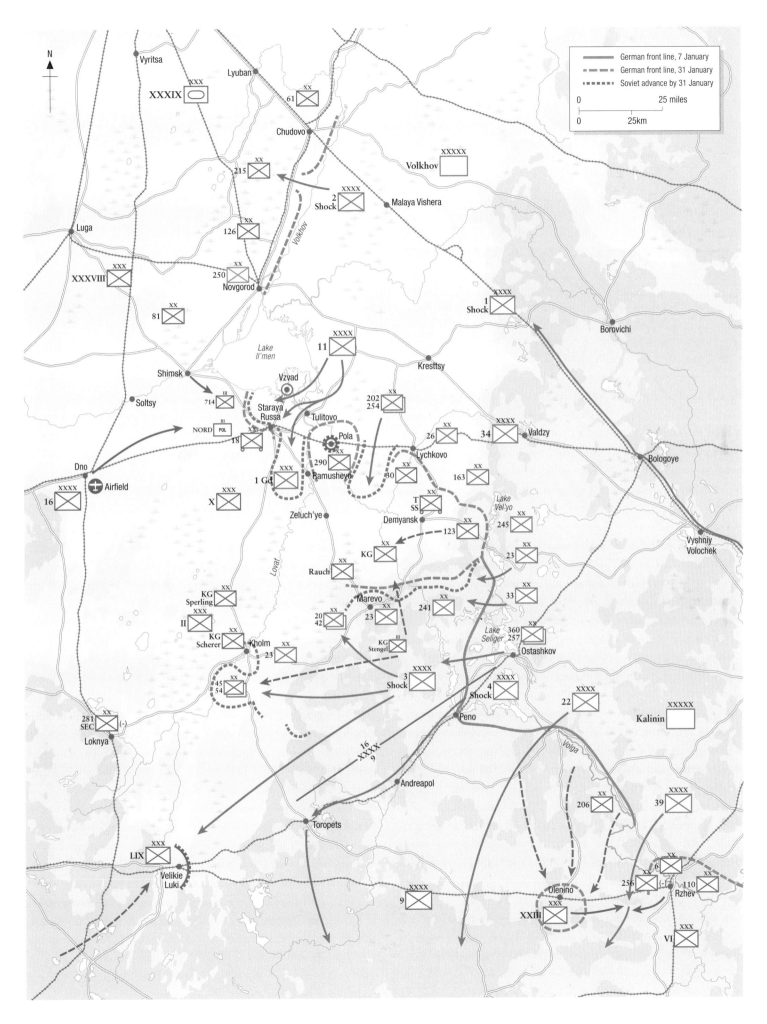

MAPS 30 & 31, DEMYANSK OPERATION (II) 17 JANUARY TO 21 APRIL, 1942

Soviet attacks against Heeresgruppe Nord had been more successful south of Lake Il'men than north and seriously threatened Heeresgruppe Mitte as well. During January 1942 the North-western and Kalinin fronts had rent huge holes in 16. and 9. Armeen lines, surrounded Staraya Russa on three sides, invested Kholm and reached Velikie Luki and Rzhev. The 3rd and 4th Shock Armies, commanded by Generals M. A. Purkaev and A. I. Eremenko respectively, had penetrated Wehrmacht lines to a depth of nearly 100 miles. While all these manoeuvres were taking place around it, II Armee-Korps stubbornly held on to its original positions with elements of half a dozen divisions, now in a dangerously extended salient. By the end of the month Red Army formations began to run out of steam as remnants of German divisions, individual regiments, eponymously named *Kampfgruppen* and thrown-together local defence divisions clung to scattered crossroad towns.

Map 30

By early February, II Armee-Korps under General der Infanterie Walter Graf von Brockdorff-Ahlefeldt was in danger of being completely encircled.[28] The 1st Guards Rifle Corps from 34th Army and Group Ksenofontov of 3rd Shock Army finally accomplished this task on 8 February when they linked hands at Zeluch'ye. The resulting pocket, approximately 20 by 40 miles (the defensive perimeter measured *c*.190 miles), contained between 90,000 and 100,000 soldiers and almost 20,000 horses. Hitler designated the pocket a 'fortress', with the implication that it would not surrender. By 12 February the Luftwaffe had organized an airlift from bases in Pskov and Ostrov, near the borders of Estonia and Latvia. Brockdorff-Ahlefeldt reckoned his men needed 200 tons of supplies per day (100 plane loads). The airlift started slowly, 80–90 tons per day, but soon ramped up and over the first three months the Luftwaffe transport service achieved a daily average of 273 tons. Eventually they evacuated 22,000 wounded and flew in 15,000 reinforcements. On some days aircraft losses equalled 40 per cent of sorties flown, but Hitler demanded the air-bridge remain in operation.

28 Brockdorff-Ahlefeldt had long been active in the anti-Hitler opposition.

On 15 and 25 February, Soviet airborne units up to brigade size parachuted into the pocket to create diversions and confuse the defenders; these fell short of having the desired effect and resulted in significant Soviet airborne losses. Meanwhile X Armee-Korps had solidified its front south of Staraya Russa to the point where it could attempt a relief attack through 25 miles of Red Army-occupied frozen marshes. Two light and two infantry divisions from X Armee-Korps (commanded by General der Artillerie Walther von Seydlitz-Kurzbach) would first launch Operation *Brückenschlag* (to build a bridge or bridgehead) toward Demyansk. When they reached the Lovat River at Ramushevo, approximately 8 miles from the pocket, the encircled forces spearheaded by Kampfgruppe Ilgen (a regiment-sized force under 32. Infanterie-Division deputy commander Oberst Max Ilgen) part of Korps-Gruppe Zorn (led by Generalleutnant Hans Zorn, 20. Infanterie-Division (Mot.) commander) would execute the breakout operation code-named *Fallreep* (Gangway). Perhaps the worst enemy of both the German and Soviet soldiers would be the approaching *rasputitsa* season of rain and mud.

Map 31

Under all the CAS that Luftflotte I could muster, X Armee-Korps moved out on 21 March (not shown on map). Four days later its forces were halfway to the Lovat when the ground turned into a swampy morass. At a cost of 10,000 casualties they slogged forward for nearly three more weeks. They had not yet reached Ramushevo when on 14 April Zorn jumped the gun and began his own assault under worsening *rasputitsa* conditions. Assisted by the anti-tank battalion of SS Division Totenkopf, on 20 April Brockdorff-Ahlefeldt's men reached, but did not cross, the Lovat. The following day they joined hands with Ilgen's *Kampfgruppe* when its forces finally reached Ramushevo. No longer an isolated pocket, Demyansk was nevertheless a very hazardous appendage jutting into the Soviet lines, nearly 50 miles deep and up to 35 miles wide. A deathtrap for his soldiers, Hitler insisted on holding on to it as a possible jumping-off site for future attacks. Needless to say, given the developing realities of the Nazi-Soviet War, Demyansk never served this intended purpose.

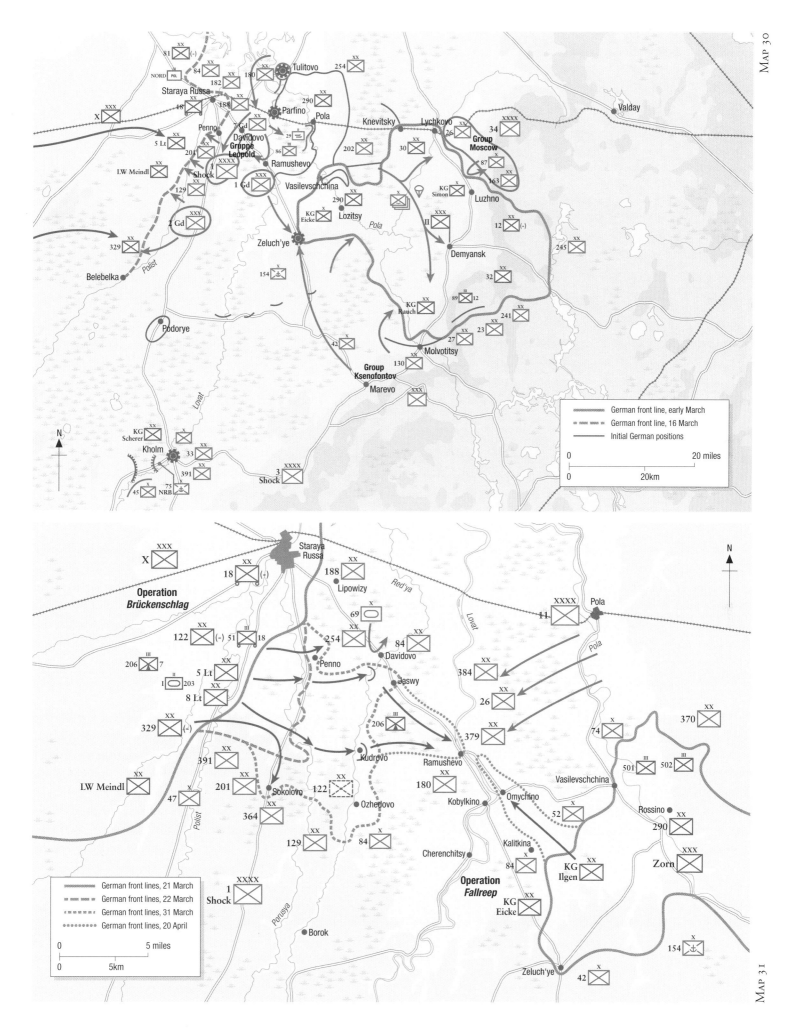

MAP 30

81 (-)
NORD POL
84
182
180
254
Staraya Russa
18 188
X XXX
290
5 Lt
201
Penno
1 Gd
Davidovo
Gruppe
Leopold
Ramushevo
86
29
Pola
Knevitsky
Lychkovo
26
34 XXXX
Group
Moscow
87
Valday
LW Meindl
129
1 Gd
Shock
1 Gd XXX
Vasilevschchina
202
30
KG
Simon
Luzhno
163
329
KG
Eicke
290
Lozitsy
Pola
12 (-)
245
Belebelka
Polist
Zeluch'ye
154
Demyansk
32
Podorye
89 12
241
KG
Rauch
27 23
42
Molvotitsy
Lovat
130
Group
Ksenofontov
Marevo
KG
Scherer
N
Kholm
33
391
3 XXXX
Shock
45 75 NRB

Legend:
— German front line, early March
– · – German front line, 16 March
— Initial German positions
0 — 20 miles
0 — 20km

MAP 31

X XXX
Staraya
Russa
18 (-)
188
Lipowizy
Red'ya
Operation
Brückenschlag
69
Lovat
11 XXXX Pola
122 (-) 51 18
254
84
206 7
Penno
Davidovo
384
5 Lt
203
Jaswy
26
8 Lt
206
379
74
370
329 (-)
501 502
LW Meindl
391
Kudrovo
Ramushevo
Vasilevschchina
47
201
122
180
Omychino
Kobylkino
Rossino
364
Sokolovo
Ozhedovo
52
290
129
84
Cherenchitsy
Kalitkina
84
KG
Ilgen
Zorn
Operation
Fallreep
KG
Eicke
154
1 XXXX
Shock
Porusya
Borok
Zeluch'ye
42

Legend:
— German front lines, 21 March
– · – German front lines, 22 March
······ German front lines, 31 March
········ German front lines, 20 April
0 — 5 miles
0 — 5km

73

MAP 32: MOSCOW, SOVIET DECEMBER COUNTERATTACKS (I) – 5–15 DECEMBER, 1941

During the second half of November 1941, a German victory parade in Moscow that year had a very low order of probability. Within a couple of weeks Hitler, Bock and Halder, as well as Stalin, Zhukov and the Stavka, plus subordinate commanders and staffs of both sides, basically reached that conclusion. As Heeresgruppe Mitte expended its last energies before the Soviet capital, the Stavka created a counterattack force that utterly surprised the Germans. Exact numbers are hard to reconcile, but along the 600-mile-long greater Moscow front, Bock probably had an overall advantage, especially in armour. However, Zhukov concentrated his forces at critical points of assault, one of the common advantages of the attacker. Also, free to strip the eastern ('Siberian') armies of their divisions, numerous of these relatively fresh, winter-equipped formations reported directly to the Moscow sector.[29]

With 3. and 4. Panzergruppen pressing on Moscow from the north-west, Zhukov placed his main effort there. On 5 December a phalanx of Kalinin and Western front Armies, 1st Shock, 20th, 29th, 30th and 31st, smashed into XLI and LVI Panzer-Korps, with Kalinin and Klin as their immediate objectives. A secondary operation by 10th and 50th Armies (also under the Western Front) hit 2. Panzer-Armee south of the capital the same day. Soon the 3rd and 13th Armies of Timoshenko's South-western Front joined the fray from Yepifan to Yelets; at the latter, the three divisions of XXXV Armee-Korps suffered temporary encirclement. The Wehrmacht's usual remedy in this situation, panzer counterattacks, fell short. When South-western Front joined in on 6 December, the whole 600-mile front was aflame as 2., 4. and 9. Armeen also came under attack.

Zhukov considered Klin the anchor of 3. and 4. Panzergruppen positions, toward which Reinhardt was already retreating. By 7 December the 16th Army threatened to unhinge the two panzer groups' defences, attacking in a north-westerly direction toward Solnechnogorsk into Hoepner's right flank. Conditions on either extremity of the

Moscow theatre hung in the balance. To the north, 29th and 31st Armies continued to threaten XXVII Armee-Korps at Kalinin. By the 16th, they had forced 9. Armee to retreat from the city. Around Tula the hunter became the hunted, and on 8 December Guderian had to withdraw Geyr von Schweppenburg to save the panzer corps from encirclement by the 10th and 50th Armies. On the same day, Belov's reinforced 1st Guards Cavalry Corps liberated Kashira; within days it did the same at Venev and Stalinogorsk. Hoping to sustain the momentum, Zhukov threw 49th Army into the fight against Guderian. After a week of additional fighting by two very weakened adversaries, the front lines stabilized generally due south from Tula to Volovo.

Most attention, however, focused on the key sector around Klin, where 1st Shock, 16th, 20th and 30th Armies assaulted Reinhardt and Hoepner's hard-pressed men. Both commanders attempted to rally troops manning the defences and to launch division-size counterattacks where possible. The intended object of a 1st Shock and 30th Army encirclement, on 9 December 3. Panzergruppe seemed to be in the most danger. A day later a thrust from the three armies of Zhukov's Solnechnogorsk cut the last road out of Klin, putting the entire garrison in jeopardy. He dispatched General Major L. M. Dovator's 2nd Guards Cavalry Corps deep into the German rear to hamper any withdrawal attempts; Zhukov scheduled his trap to shut on 13 December, but on that day Hitler authorized rereat by 3. Panzergruppe from the Klin bulge, which it executed 24 hours later. The 1st Shock and 30th Armies liberated the town on the 14th.

In mid-December Phase I of the December counteroffensives came to an end. Essentially using forces on hand around Moscow, in ten days Stalin and Zhukov had removed the dangerous panzer salients north and south of Moscow, pushing them back 30 and 50 miles respectively. As for the Wehrmacht, these reverses certainly came as a shock, but it had allowed no massive, deep penetrations of its lines nor had it suffered permanent, large encirclements of its forces. The Red Army had ripped open some large holes in the wide open southern segment, but around Moscow, affected by many units jammed into a narrow space, the front appeared to be stable. However, on 13 December Zhukov issued orders for Phase II of the offensive, and that would all change.

---

29 'Siberian' seems to have been German shorthand for just about any Red Army organization that came from east of European Russia, i.e., Urals, central Asian Republics, etc. as well as Siberia itself.

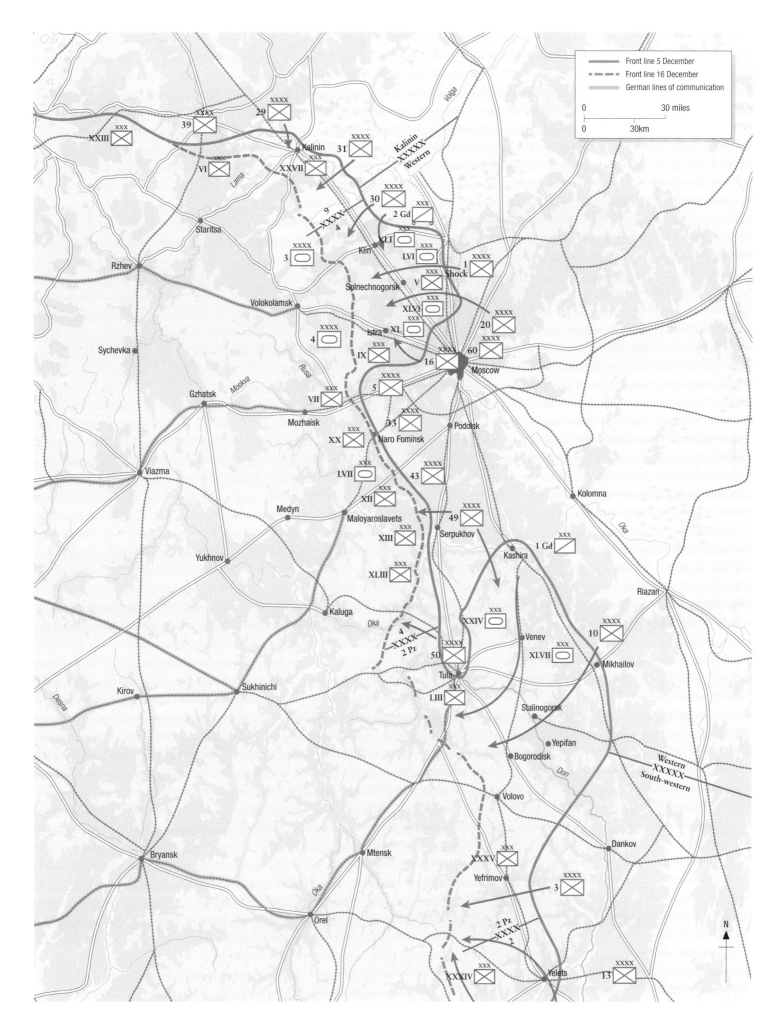

XXXX 39

XXXX 29

XXIII XXX

XXXX 31

Kalinin

Kalinin
XXXXX
Western

XXVII XXX

VI XXX

Lama

XXXX 30

XXX 2 Gd

XXXX 9 4

Staritsa

XXXX 3

Klin

XLI XXX

XXX LVI

XXXX 1 Shock

Rzhev

Solnechnogorsk

XXX V

Volokolamsk

XLVI XXX

Rusa

XXXX 4

Istra

XL XXX

XXXX 20

Sychevka

IX XXX

XXXX 16

XXXX 60

Moscow

Gzhatsk

Moskva

VII XXX

XXXX 5

Mozhaisk

XXX 33

Podolsk

XX XXX

Naro Fominsk

Kolomna

Oka

Viazma

LVII XXX

XXXX 43

Medyn

XII XXX

Maloyaroslavets

XXXX 49

Serpukhov

XIII XXX

Kashira

XXX 1 Gd

Yukhnov

XLIII XXX

Riazan

Kaluga

Oka

XXXX 4 2 Pz

XXIV XXX

XXXX 10

Venev

XLVII XXX

XXXX 50

Tula

Mikhailov

Kirov

Desna

Sukhinichi

LIII XXX

Stalinogorsk

Yepifan

Bogorodisk

Don

Western
XXXXX
South-western

Volovo

Dankov

Bryansk

Mtensk

XXXV XXX

Oka

Yefrimov

XXXX 3

Orel

2 Pz
XXXX
2

N

XXXIV XXX

Yelets

XXXX 13

	Front line 5 December
	Front line 16 December
	German lines of communication

0 — 30 miles
0 — 30km

MAP 33: MOSCOW, SOVIET DECEMBER COUNTERATTACKS (II) – 20–31 DECEMBER, 1941

In mid-December, the various high command organs of the Soviet Union had good reason to be satisfied with events of the previous ten days. *Barbarossa* had suffered a bloody nose, Moscow stood beyond immediate danger and the Red Army had achieved most of the objectives that Zhukov had set out for it. His goals for the next stage of attacks would be to push Heeresgruppe Mitte back to at least its pre-*Typhoon* positions, an average of 100 miles west. To accomplish this, he assigned many of the same armies that had been attacking since the first week of the month, plus additional armies on the far flanks and those guarding the central Moscow axis opposite 4. Armee. The Wehrmacht had only superficial reasons to believe it had the situation under control. Not only did the front appear stabilized, but now Hitler, decorated veteran of front-line combat during World War I, had taken personal command of the eastern front. The affection and blind faith that the German people and soldiery put into the person of the Führer is one of the outstanding, and bewildering, aspects of the Third Reich.

North-west of Moscow, the Volga, Lama and Ruza Rivers looked to Bock's men like the foundations of a coherent defence, but the south seemed ready to disintegrate. In many places along the fighting front the Germans had broken contact and the Soviets were slow to react, contributing to the sense of calm. Delays in renewing Phase II of the offensive frustrated Zhukov, but by 20–22 December his forces began to attack at various places along the Moscow sector.[30] They attacked aggressively in the 2. Panzer-Armee and 3. Panzergruppe areas, where, during the mid-month slowdown, Guderian had not been able to make good large gaps in his defences. Zhukov expanded operations northward from the Tula region with assaults by the 5th, 33rd, 43rd and 49th Armies augmented by the much-reinforced and marauding 1st Guards Cavalry Corps. He was keen to take Kaluga, at the southern edge of the Smolensk-Moscow ridge, in which particularly fierce fighting took place until the end of the year. New 4. Armee commander, General der Gebirgstruppen Ludwig Kübler, proved unable to master the situation presented by 33rd and 43rd Armies (although the attack's progress disappointed Zhukov) and soon fell foul of Hitler. Neither could the

Führer's darling, Guderian, come up with countermeasures to attacks by the resuscitated Bryansk Front, which threatened the critical logistics bases at Orel and Kursk (off map to the south). Emaciated Wehrmacht divisions held frontages many times the distance called for by doctrine in the face of gaps dozens of miles wide.

For the moment, the situation west and north-west of Moscow was much less volatile. The front could burst open at any time but despite losses in men and equipment, for the time being 3. and 4. Panzergruppen and 9. Armee fell back slowly and managed to keep Kalinin and Western Front attackers squarely in front of them. Zhukov sensed that the time was ripe for fresh efforts in this sector. The 16th and 20th Armies were already nearing Volokolamsk and he wanted them to reach Gzhatsk within another week. Meanwhile Konev now had Rzhev in his sights and activated the 22nd and 39th Armies to join the 29th, 30th and 31st Armies in the attack. Although Strauss complained that his 9. Armee could not hold the heavily forested region, by the end of 1941 Konev had not progressed much west of Staritsa. German fortunes in the north managed to hold.

The same cannot be said for the south, where, from the German point of view, the situation between Mozhaisk and Orel continued to deteriorate. Both Guderian and Schmidt reported huge gaps in their lines full of Soviet corps and divisions. The 10th and 50th Armies were especially aggressive, cutting the railway line north from Bryansk in numerous places and exploiting the virtually undefended sector between Sukhinichi and Kaluga, which led directly to Smolensk. One can hardly imagine two more opposite personalities than Kluge and Guderian; the two had clashed since *Barbarossa*'s earliest days, through *Typhoon* and into the present crisis. By Christmas the plodding Kluge had convinced Hitler of the panzer general's disobedience and the dictator relieved Guderian the following day. For the next month the 2. Armee commander also controlled 2. Panzer-Armee as the renamed Armeegruppe Schmidt.[31] On the last day of 1941 Hitler refused to allow any withdrawal, not even to the Königsberg Line position (Map 34), while Zhukov planned to continue ripping Heeresgruppe Mitte apart in the new year.

30   The third week of December generally coincided with the German high-command personnel shake-up begun a bit earlier with Rundstedt, but now hitting the very top with Brauchitsch and Bock.

31   Army Group (Armeegruppe) in this sense is a temporary command arrangement within the larger Army Group (Heeresgruppe) South.

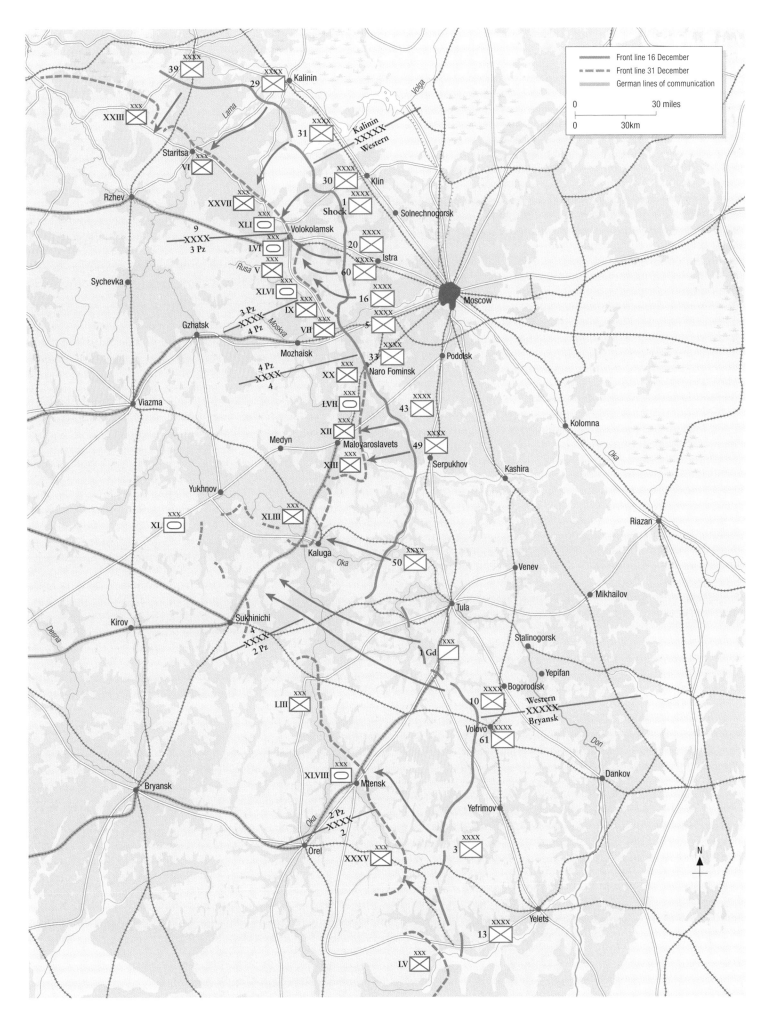

MAP 34: MOSCOW, SOVIET WINTER COUNTEROFFENSIVE (I) – 4 TO 15 JANUARY, 1941

On the Moscow front between Ostashkov and Kursk, New Year's Day came and went with little more than proclamations from Hitler and the prospect of more brutal winter weather. If it had not been obvious to Wehrmacht leaders in 1941 that Zhukov intended to encircle Heeresgruppe Mitte, that vision became clearer in 1942. Earl Ziemke compares the pending German disaster to that which they had created at Kiev just four months earlier.[32] As they had in the previous weeks, Soviet flank Armies struck first.

On 4 January, Konev's Kalinin Front, unable to take Rzhev from the direction of Staritsa, tried to swing around and capture the town from the south and west. Meanwhile his new 3rd and 4th Shock Armies (eight rifle divisions and three rifle brigades, reinforced with tanks and Katyusha rocket launchers) came plunging down from the Ostashkov area heading for yet another major German logistics base, this time at Toropets (off map to northwest). Within days the 29th and 39th Armies had penetrated 9. Armee while the 9th Cavalry Corps approached Sychevka on the road to Viazma. Meanwhile in the south, Bryansk Front had run out of steam 20–25 miles from the essential rail hubs of Orel and Kursk.[33] The southern flank of 2. Panzer-Armee stiffened below Belev, as did the northern flank of 4. Armee above Kaluga. But in between stood a gaping 50-mile hole pointed directly at Smolensk, deep in the army group's rear area. By mid-January less than 100 miles separated the two spearheads of the Kalinin and Bryansk fronts.

Heeresgruppe Mitte's prime concern was closing off the bulge reaching out toward Viazma, Roslavl and Bryansk. Wehrmacht formations positioned to intervene were mere shadows of themselves: for example, the XXIV Panzer-Korps near Sukhinichi was hardly worthy of the name, with only a couple of battalions under command and no panzers. While the Soviets manoeuvred around Kluge's flank armies in an effort to form a trap, they sought to bludgeon to death the German armies holding out in the centre, the 4. Armee, 3. and 4. Panzer-Armeen and, to a certain degree, 9. Armee. Pounded by artillery and assaulted frontally by infantry, this campaign of attrition often centred on villages and hamlets that could offer some shelter from the elements. Under these circumstances the eastern army lost another

senior commander when Hitler not only relieved 4. Panzer-Armee's Hoepner for an unauthorized retreat but also declared him 'dishonoured'.[34] Near the boundary with 4. Panzer-Armee, 4. Armee's line jutted out to Maloyaroslavets, more than 50 miles east of the giant Red Army salient. The 50th Army threatened both to sever Kübler's main supply route (the *Rollbahn*) and overrun his command post at Yukhnov as well. With the memory of Hoepner's example fresh in the mind of every German general, Kluge argued back and forth on the telephone with Hitler's headquarters about pulling back 4. and 4. Panzer-Armee, now squarely in Stalin's crosshairs. On 7–8 January, just as Zhukov issued attack orders to eliminate the German Gzhatsk–Mozhaisk salient by 1st Shock, 20th, 16th, 5th, 33rd, 43rd, 49th and 50th Armies (clockwise), Hitler relented and authorized a token 10-mile retreat from the exposed positions.

At staggered times the new Soviet offensive opened up from 7–10 January. Continuous and brutal winter combat took place around the familiar-sounding locales of Volokolamsk, Mozhaisk, Kaluga and Yukhnov. Against the 9. Armee and 3. Panzer-Armee, Zhukov sought an advantage by shifting his main effort between three attacking armies, a tactic often used by the Germans. In the far south of the offensive, Stalin added 61st Army to Zhukov's order of battle with orders to press on toward Kirov, which it liberated on the 11th, as well as to secure the seam between Western and Bryansk fronts. The 2nd and 1st Guards Cavalry Corps, operating with the northern and southern thrusts respectively, infiltrated through the many gaps in the German lines and sowed confusion in Kluge's rear areas. The 43rd Army fought its way through Maloyaroslavets to the 4. Armee strongpoint of Medyn, which it captured on 14 January. This last event finally convinced Hitler of the need to permit withdrawal to the Königsberg Line. Such a move would considerably shorten Kluge's jagged front, close gaps such as that on the boundary between 4. Armee and 4. Panzer-Armee north of Maloyaroslavets and also free up some divisions with which to launch local counterattacks. Still mistrustful of his generals, however, Hitler would micromanage the retreat to the Königsberg Line from his headquarters.

---

32 Ziemke, Earl, *Moscow to Stalingrad*, p. 125.

33 Schmidt left 2. Armee on 26 December to replace Guderian at 2. Panzer-Armee. The 2. Armee was re-assigned to Heeresgruppe Süd on 15 January, so was no longer part of the greater Moscow battles.

34 As a retired general and civilian in Berlin, Hoepner became involved in the anti-Hitler resistance, which ended with the 20 July 1944 bomb plot. He was tried in a Nazi court on 8 August and hanged the same day.

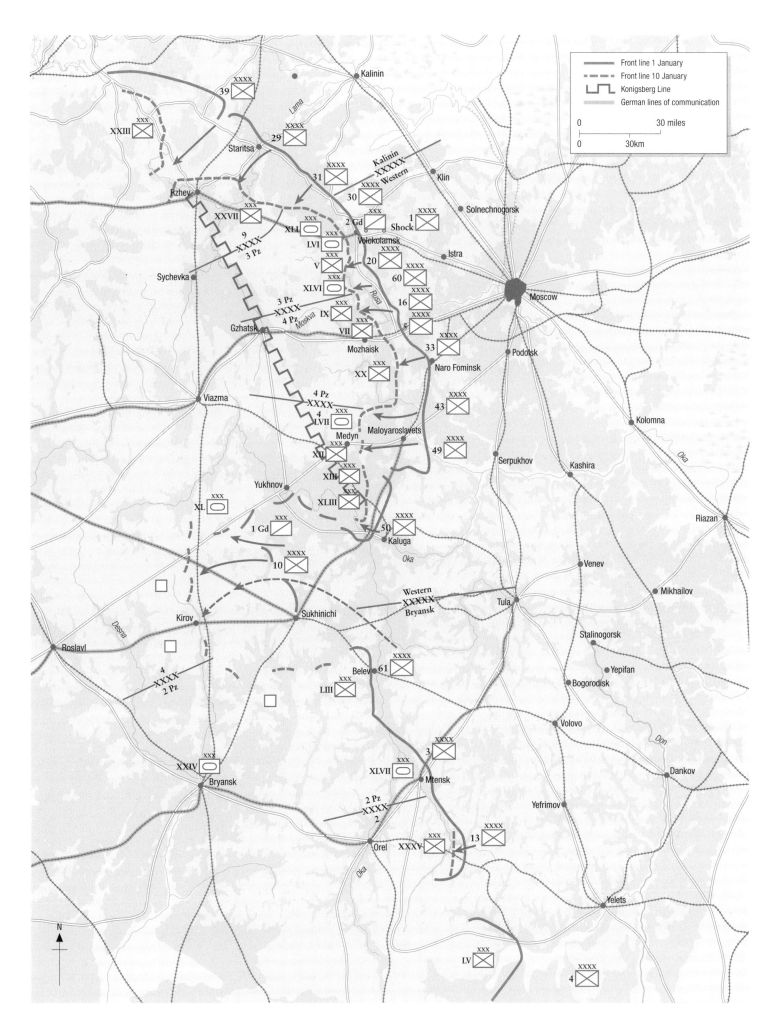

MAP 35: MOSCOW, SOVIET WINTER COUNTEROFFENSIVE (II) 18 JANUARY TO 30 APRIL, 1942

While Kluge dutifully argued to convince his subordinate commanders and men that the move to Königsberg Line was a good one, Stalin planned to expand his winter counteroffensive. As agreed by the Soviet Politburo and Stavka, a 'general' counteroffensive would erupt from Leningrad to Rostov, with the main effort coming from around Moscow. Zhukov argued for concentrating only on the Moscow axis where he had Hitler's eastern army on the ropes, but Stalin would not listen.

In the centre of the main sector, on 18 January Kluge prepared for the deliberate withdrawal to the Königsberg Line, to be conducted in small steps over the next week. Once reached, the northern portion of the line, generally between Rzhev and Gzhatsk, surprisingly held for months. In the south it did not stand up as well, however. The 5th Army made decent progress around Mozhaisk while other units moved through the thick forests east of Viazma; Yukhnov changed hands more than once.[35] In the north Konev's drive immediately began to suffer when Stalin redirected the 1st Shock Army to the Volkhov Front. A similar fate befell the Western Front's right wing when Stalin transferred 16th Army from Volokolamsk to Sukhinichi; he clearly wanted to expand the southern bulge and seek a decisive encounter there. But in the Sukhinichi sector the Germans began to regain their footing and launched counterattacks, which, although limited in scope, halted the Soviets in some places and fully turned them back in others.

Badgered by Stalin to open up the Moscow front and regain the initiative, Zhukov co-ordinated Red Army efforts with a brigade (8th Airborne) of the 4th Airborne Corps dropping near Ozerechnya, plus partisan ambushes behind German lines. In conjunction with these, the 33rd Army, 1st and 11th Cavalry Corps[36] plus other formations, by early February Viazma became the focus of much offensive activity. However, as the Red Army around Moscow entered its third month of constant attacks, it began to suffer from mounting losses and overextended lines. At the same time the Germans showed signs of recovering from their earlier shock; Heinrici, just beginning a career as a defensive expert that he would burnish throughout the war, and new 4. Panzer-Armee commander General der Infanterie Richard Ruoff,

combined forces around the Viazma threat. The leading Soviet units there, expecting only to round up routed Germans, instead found divisions and corps full of fight and panzer divisions that actually had some panzers. Around Rzhev Model managed to launch counterattacks both to shore up his 9. Armee[37] position and to contribute toward Soviet misfortune; he encircled portions of the 29th Army there.

In mid-February, the Stavka upped its pressure on Zhukov to complete the destruction of Heeresgruppe Mitte, which had seemed assured just weeks earlier. Other portions of the front were doing their share; for example, the North-western Front's new assaults from the Ostashkov region toward Kholm and Vitebsk necessitated flying the 3. Panzer-Armee headquarters hundreds of miles west by 1 February in order to take control of that rapidly deteriorating situation. Both dictators dispatched organizations and men (70,000 for Kluge, 60,000 for Zhukov) into the critical central sector. The remainder of 4th Airborne Corps tried another assault west of Yukhnov on 17 February, but this drop suffered from a shortage of transport aircraft, widely dispersed landing zones and an effective response by the German V Armee-Korps. Stalin's hoped-for rendezvous of the Kalinin and Western fronts near Viazma and the encirclement of the 9. Armee, 4. Panzer-Armee and 4. Armee began to look problematic. Soviet failure and German success at that town mean that Kluge maintained open communications along the essential Smolensk–Moscow ridgeline.

Heinrici gave up Yukhnov in early March and settled in behind the Ugra River. This made defensive sense, but Zhukov did not weaken in his desire to crush Kluge's centre. In a race against the pending *rasputitsa*, he ordered his units to redouble their efforts all along the front: at Rzhev, Viazma and Kirov. The mission of the now-isolated Viazma group (33rd Army, 1st Guards Cavalry and 4th Airborne Corps) changed from defeating Germans to saving themselves. During the first half of April breakout attempts in just about every direction were considered, but few succeeded. Many Red Army troops simply melted into the forests to join partisan bands, so their combat value was not completely lost. By the end of the month the front stabilized: although it was only about 350 miles as the crow flies, the many undulations nearly tripled the actual frontage.

---

35   All of this proved too much for Kübler, in whom Hitler lost confidence, and he turned over command of 4. Armee to General der Infanterie Gotthard Heinrici.

36   These two cavalry corps belonged to Western and Kalinin fronts respectively, the 11th having come south all the way from the neighbourhood of Rzhev.

37   General der Panzertruppen Walther Model replaced Strauss as commander of 9. Armee on 15 January.

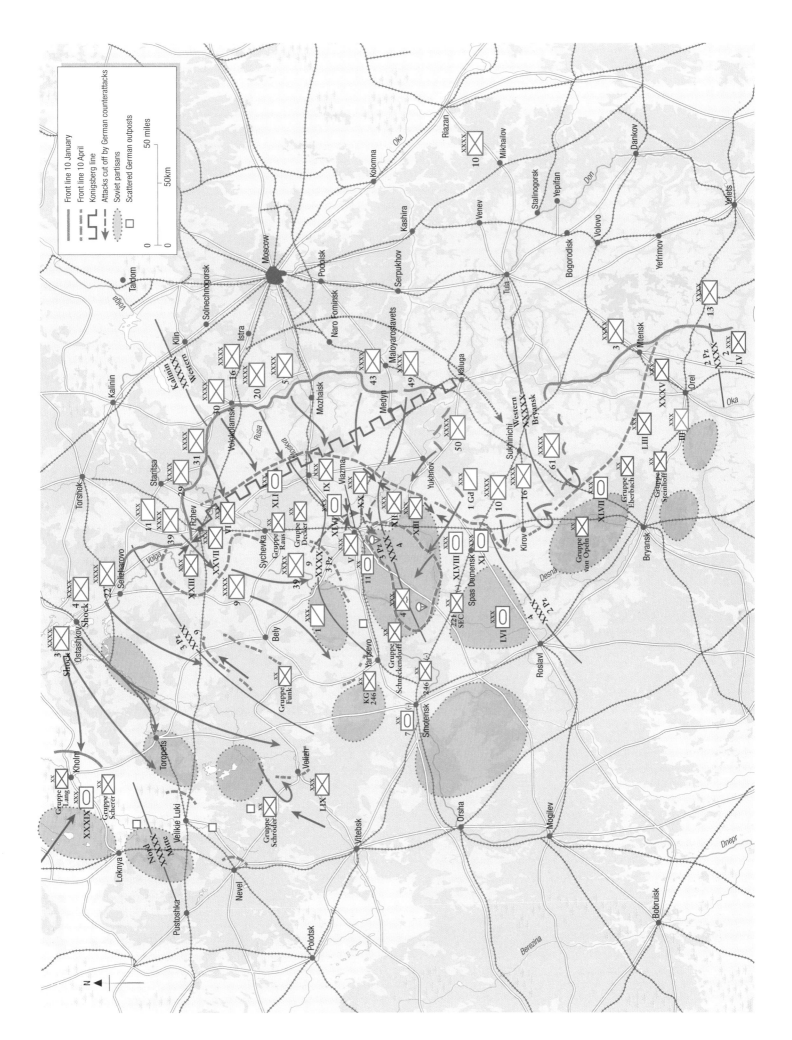

MAP 36: KERCH PENINSULA 26 DECEMBER, 1941 TO 9 APRIL, 1942

By mid-November, Manstein's 11. Armee had overrun all of the Crimea except for the fortified port of Sevastopol. Just weeks later Stalin decided he wanted to take back the peninsula and, flush with success, on 7 December the Stavka directed the Trans-Caucasus Front to prepare amphibious assaults across the 2–6 mile-wide Kerch Strait. Front commander General Lieutenant D. T Kozlov would lead the ground forces, 44th and 51st Armies, while commander of the Black Sea Fleet Vice Admiral F. S. Oktyabrsky led the landing operations. These commanders and their staffs had two weeks to come up with a plan to threaten 11. Armee besieging Sevastopol as well as trap and then destroy Axis forces occupying the Crimea.

On 26 December, one and a half months after it had been chased off the Kerch Peninsula (Map 22), the 51st Army came roaring back. Commanded by General Lieutenant V. H. Lvov in place of the disgraced Kuznetsov, in heavy seas the Azov Naval Flotilla put 13,000 of his troops ashore along the peninsula's eastern (302nd Rifle Division) and north-eastern (224th Rifle Division) shores. By nightfall Red Army forces had secured all beachheads except for Eltigen. Although the odds against it were not overwhelming, the defending 46. Infanterie-Division immediately began to waver. After two days, the division's higher headquarters, XLII Armee-Korps, ordered the Romanian 8th Cavalry Brigade to attack and dispatched the Romanian 4th Cavalry Brigade to the area. On 29 December, the Soviet 44th Army under General Lieutenant A. N. Pervushin conducted an additional landing at Feodosia and at other locales along the peninsula's southern shore, which eventually numbered 26,000 men. These manoeuvres threatened the isthmus separating Kerch from the rest of the Crimea and prompted Manstein to order 170. Infanterie-Division and two more Romanian brigades eastward to the rescue. Based on real and imagined reports, that same day XLII Armee-Korps commander, Generalleutnant Hans *Graf* von Sponeck began to fear for his command and ordered 46. Infanterie-Division back 60 miles to Parpach. Most of the 20,000 51st Army soldiers now ashore on Kerch took up the pursuit. Manstein, starting to doubt Sponeck's nerve, tried but failed to countermand the retreat order in time and so replaced him with General der Infanterie Franz Mattenklott (commanding general of XXX Armee-Korps, then

on the main Sevastopol front).[38] As 46. Infanterie-Division withdrew westward in a series of forced marches during the last days of 1941 (abandoning most of its heavy equipment), nearby Romanian formations took note of the impending débâcle and began to fall back themselves, usually not in good order.

As the number of 44th Army troops in Feodsia also approached 20,000, German defences began to coalesce around Stary Krim. Both sides seemed somewhat content with a stalemate along the line Feodosia–Vladislavovka; weather and logistical woes hampered *Landser* and *frontoviki* alike. Manstein probably stood to benefit more from the situation than Kozlov (his command now re-named the Crimean Front), as the interior of the Crimea was ripe for the picking if the Soviets had been able to capitalize on it. During the first week of January, Manstein shifted 132. Infanterie-Division from the now (relatively) quiet Sevastopol front and waited for auspicious weather to launch a counterattack (not shown). During the second week of the month he added 170. Infanterie-Divison plus some Romanian units to 46. Infanterie-Division, now declared by Heeresgruppe Süd commander Reichenau to be in forfeit of its honour. Mattenklott assaulted the poorly defended Soviet lines on 15 January. Three days of half-hearted resistance later, the two Soviet armies pulled back east of the Parpach isthmus into positions prepared the previous autumn. This was as far as 11. Armee would make it that winter. Kozlov, fresh reinforcements rolling in directly over the frozen Kerch Straits, and Oktyabrsky planned a combined amphibious and overland assault of the Feodosia lines for mid-February. The attack finally went off at the end of the month, but Manstein had received reinforcements too, so that the narrow isthmus was impacted with nearly 20 divisions of both sides. By early March Kozlov had accumulated nearly 300,000 troops between Parpach and Kerch. In the middle of the month he launched attacks by up to eight divisions and two tank brigades that severely tested the infantry divisions manning the line. On 9 April, the Crimean Front tried again with six rifle divisions supported by 150 tanks, but could not overthrow Manstein's defences.

---

38 Manstein had Sponeck court-martialled for unauthorized withdrawal of his corps (Hermann Göring presiding). The SS executed him on 23 July, 1944.

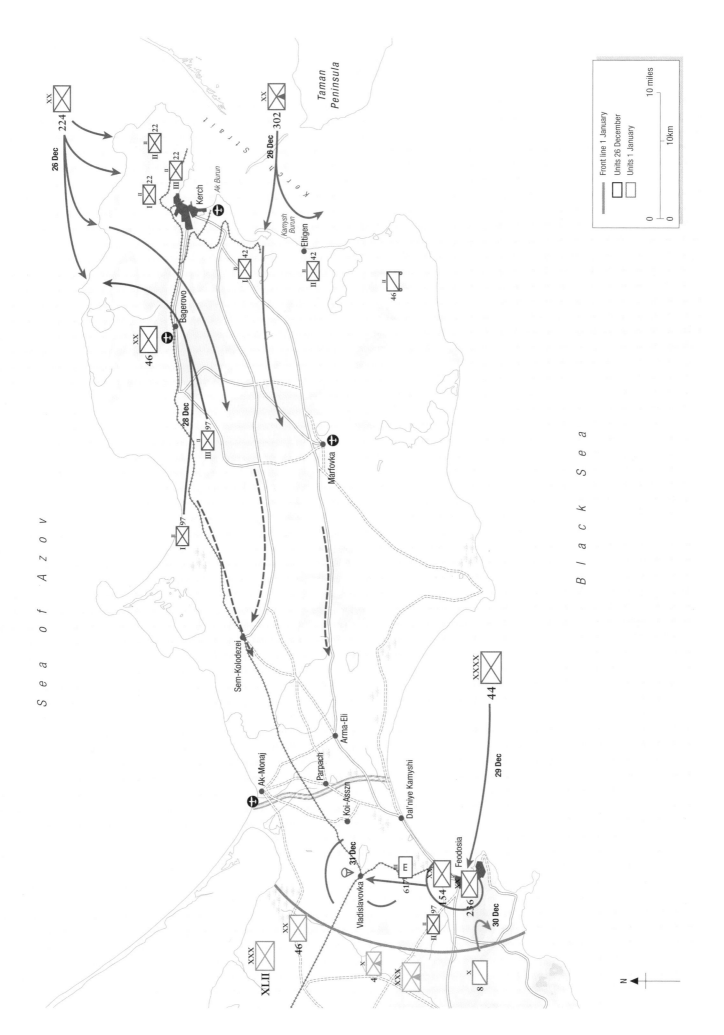

Sea of Azov

Taman
Peninsula

Kerch Strait

Ak Burun

Kerch

Kamysh
Burun

Eltigen

26 Dec 224

26 Dec 302

22

22

22

22

42

42

46

Bagerovo

28 Dec

97

97

46

Marfovka

Sem-Kolodezei

Black Sea

Arma-Eli

44

29 Dec

Ak-Monaj

Parpach

Koi-Asszn

Dal'niye Kamyshi

31 Dec

Feodosia

617

154

236

97

30 Dec

XLII

46

4

8

Vladislavovka

Front line 1 January

Units 26 December

Units 1 January

0   10km
0   10 miles

N

MAP 37: BARVENKOVO OPERATION 18 JANUARY TO 15 FEBRUARY, 1942

Major Soviet offensives to turn back *Barbarossa*'s spearheads began in the south during the second half of November 1941, when Marshal Timoshenko's South-western Direction kicked 1. Panzer-Armee out of Rostov and back to the Mius River (Map 23). These continued in January as he shifted attention north to the Kursk–Belgorod area, where the Bryansk and South-western Fronts attempted to run yet another seam between two German army groups, in this case the boundary separating Heeresgruppen Mitte and Süd. His operational mission was to reach Dnepr crossings at Dnepropetrovsk, Melitopol (120–200 miles distant) and ideally to crush Heeresgruppe Süd against the Sea of Azov. Except in the north of the sector, where they benefited from significant Soviet gains around Moscow, the Red Army could not pull off another such operation, and in fact the 13th, 40th, 21st and 38th Armies failed to make much of a dent in 2. and 6. Armeen lines.

Accordingly, Timoshenko redirected new, loosely connected attacks by two fronts, South-western (General Lieutenant F. Ya. Kostenko, 6th Army and 6th Cavalry Corps directly involved) and Southern (General Lieutenant R. Y. Malinovsky, 57th, 9th, 37th Armies plus 1st and 5th Cavalry Corps), against the boundary of 6. Armee (LI Armee-Korps) and 17. Armee (XI and IV Armee-Korps) north of Izyum.[39] Here the Red Army had held on to a small bridgehead on the west bank of the Donets River. Their 50-mile-wide attack began on 18 January against the front of German strongpoints.[40] The 57th Army assault hit 17. Armee hardest, which began to evacuate its rearward services after barely 24 hours. Hoth recommended that Bock immediately create counterattack forces and attempt to gain the initiative. Within four days Heeresgruppe Süd had sustained an enemy breakthrough nearly 100 miles wide and half as deep. Only stubborn defences on the breakthrough's shoulders, at Balakleya in the north (6. Armee) and

Slavyansk in the south (17. Arme) prevented the rupture from widening, while both organizations threw their last reserves into the fighting. Timoshenko ordered the 9th Army against the Slavyansk strongpoint. At this point, 22 January, he figured the moment was right to commit his exploitation forces, the three cavalry corps being held back. By the 24th it looked like his men could peel off right and left to roll up the two Wehrmacht armies; they were also halfway to Dnepropetrovsk, while Kharkov appeared uncovered. To buck up the weaker southern defences, Bock attached 17. Armee to 1. Panzer-Armee to form the temporary Armeegruppe Kleist.

Unfortunately for Timoshenko, just at this point his fortunes began to fade. The Germans had turned the numerous villages and hamlets that dotted the Ukrainian countryside into small forts. The undersized Soviet cavalry divisions had not been designed for sustained, set-piece battles. Brutal winter weather battered man, beast and machine. Stalin's senior marshal requested reinforcements, but eventually received only four rifle brigades plus 315 tanks. Toward the end of January his offensive looked more like disjointed cavalry raids, but did have some successes, including capturing Hoth's huge supply dump at Lozovaya and threatening the Dnepropetrovsk–Stalino rail line. Meanwhile, Kleist had taken his new combined command seriously and with the northern edge of the bulge seemingly under control he moved to secure the southern. Here, with the help of Stuka CAS, in one week 257. Infanterie-Division holding Slavyansk had beaten back 200 assaults; at a cost of 652 dead and 1,663 wounded they had killed 12,500 *frontoviki*. The panzer general dispatched III Panzer-Korps commander General der Kavallerie Eberhard von Mackensen north with a panzer division, a detachment of 75 panzers and a light division toward the most dangerous looking Red Army threat. On the last day of January, the panzers encountered Soviet horsemen 40 miles south of Barvenkovo at Sergeevka. Seeing his opportunity, Bock ordered every spare formation that could still move to attack the Izyum bridgehead from every direction. Only Mackensen had more than token success, taking ten days to even get close to Barvenkovo. The end result by mid-February was that both sides suffered from exhaustion due to combat and climate. Timoshenko's bulge remained, a jumping-off point for future operations.

---

39 The new 6. Armee commander was Friedrich Paulus, promoted to General of Panzer Troops on the same day he was named to the new post, 1 January. He had had minimal troop leading experience during the first months of World War I, but had not commanded troops since he led a reconnaissance battalion as a lieutenant colonel in 1934.

40 That same day Bock arrived to take command of Heeresgruppe Süd. On the 17th, army group commander Reichenau died from complications of a stroke suffered two days earlier. Therefore between 15 and 18 January Hoth temporarily commanded both the army group and his 17. Armee.

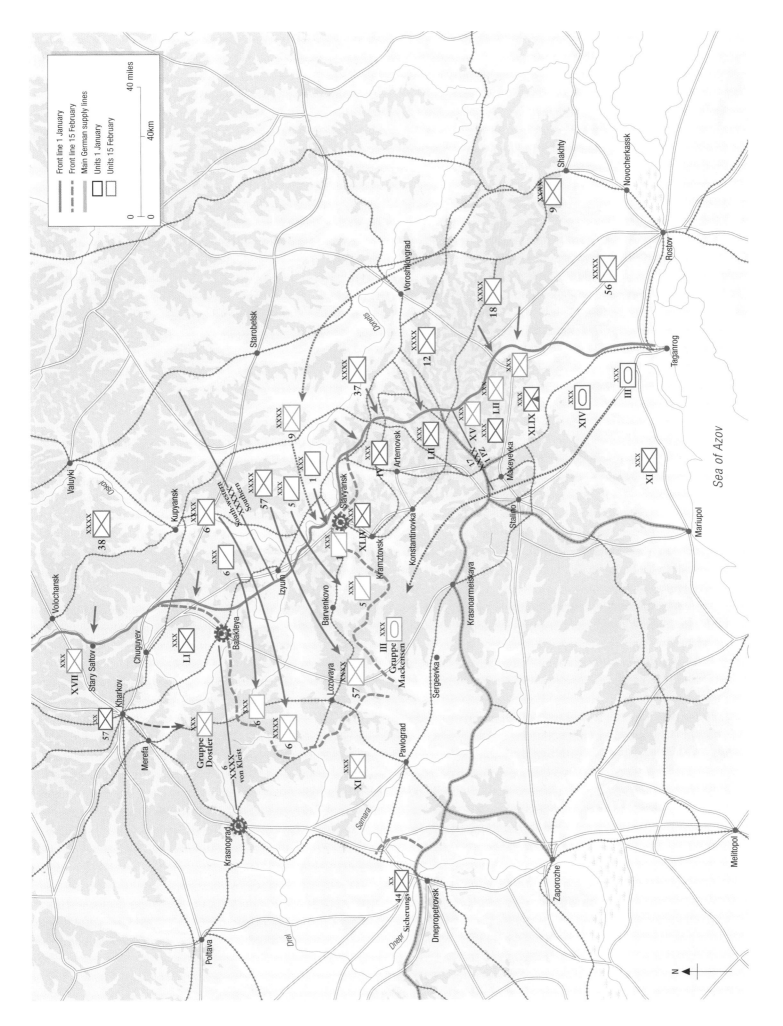

MAP 38: SECOND KHARKOV, EVE OF BATTLE 11 MAY, 1942

The situation on 11 May represented another of the perfect storms of German advantages and Soviet disadvantages that had marked much of the first 11 months of the Nazi-Soviet War. The Wehrmacht's emphasis for the 1942 campaign season lay in the south and accordingly by May it had rebuilt many of its formations there. While the highest echelons of Soviet leadership saw a healthy debate regarding the course of continued operations in 1942, their intelligence missed this development. Assuming Moscow would be Hitler's main objective, the Stavka anticipated that only weak and emaciated German units manned the front around Kharkov, Marshal Timoshenko's next intended target.

As he had since November, Timoshenko commanded the South-west Direction, made up of the South-western (Kostenko) and Southern fronts (Malinovsky). The boundary between the two fronts ran down the middle of the Izyum bulge, 50 miles deep and more than 60 miles wide, created the previous winter. The Red Army knew that the rail-crossroad city of Kharkov housed a huge Heeresgruppe Süd logistics base that seemed vulnerable to renewed attacks following the spring *rasputitsa*. The salient already practically encircled Kharkov from the south; a little effort here, plus a matching thrust from a smaller Donets bridgehead to the north, should certainly doom Paulus's centre. According to the Stavka's plan, General Lieutenant A. M. Gorodniansky's 6th Army and Army Group Bobkin (General Major L. V. Bobkin) had responsibility for the southern attack, while 28th Army under Ryabyshev assaulted from the north supported by the 21st and 38th Armies. For the offensive, Timoshenko assembled 640,000 men, 1,200 tanks, 13,000 indirect fire weapons and 926 aircraft. Presumably once Kharkov had fallen, the critical Dnepr bridges at Dnepropetrovsk and Zaporozhe, barely 50 miles from the farthest west Red Army units, could be easily threatened. The Stavka gave South-west Direction five

to six weeks to perfect its plans, which, uncharacteristically, German intelligence learned of in some detail.

These Soviet forces would run right into Paulus, himself preparing for Operation *Fredericus*, the Wehrmacht manoeuvre to nip off the Izyum bridgehead and due to begin in a week. Opposite 28th Army stood XVII Armee-Korps under General der Infanterie Karl Strecker,[41] while General der Artillerie Walter Heitz's VIII Armee-Korps and Seydlitz-Kurzbach's LI Armee-Korps faced 6th Army and Group Bobkin.[42] Their 16 German and one Hungarian infantry divisions faced half again as many Red Army divisions. The 6. Armee also held two rebuilt panzer divisions and other formations in reserve. General der Infanterie Karl Hollidt's corps had escaped the Barvenkovo–Lozovaya fighting in January, so was well dug in. Adding to Timoshenko's pending troubles was Armeegruppe Kleist to the south of Izyum, also rebuilding and recovering. Further, top Soviet staffs evidently wishfully assumed that a secondary effort by the 9th and 57th Armies south of Barvenkovo would serve to distract Kleist as the two main efforts destroyed Paulus and captured Kharkov. Lastly, the lingering effects of the spring thaw, Luftwaffe interdiction, ammunition shortages and other logistical woes hamstrung the offensive just as it began. Although the Red Army had learned some valuable lessons about modern warfare during the Nazi-Soviet War's first year, the Wehrmacht still had some finer points left to teach it.

41 Officially General der Infanterie Karl Hollidt commanded XVII Armee-Korps, but former police major general Strecker held temporary command from 2 April to 12 June 1942.

42 Heitz had spent some of the interwar years in the German Army's leagal system, including witnessing the shameful 1938 Fritsch trial. He followed Paulus to Stalingrad, joined him in Soviet captivity and died a year later in Moscow.

87

MAP 39: SECOND KHARKOV, NORTHERN SECTOR 13–19 MAY, 1942

Compared to Izyum, South-western Front's January offensive between Belgorod and Kharkov had been disappointing. Kostenko now possessed a long shallow bridgehead across the Donets River centred on Stary Saltov. General Ryabyshev's 28th Army occupied the bulk of the sector, and he crammed five rifle divisions into a 15-mile frontage. Elements of the 21st and 38th Armies covered his flanks. According to the plan, once these organizations achieved penetrations of the German first-echelon defences then the 3rd Guard Cavalry Corps (three cavalry divisions and one motorized infantry brigade) would exploit past the riflemen to the west of Kharkov and rendezvous with two new tank corps coming up from Izyum. Across the front lines Bock's army group, specifically Paulus's 6. Armee, basically held the same positions it had occupied since early February.

Attacking on 13 May, 28th Army enjoyed early success, creating penetrations and encircling 294. Infanterie-Division *Landser*s holding the thin front. Despite roadblocks such as Kampfgruppe Grüner at Ternovaya, Red Army divisions in places advanced up to a dozen miles during that first day, with some advance detachments subsequently reaching the outer defences of Kharkov itself. On the offensive's third day Timoshenko was supposed to dispatch his cavalry, but he delayed in order for it to complete its attack preparations and because he expected more favourable weather conditions in a day or two. Meanwhile Paulus shifted 73., 113. and 305. Infanterie-Division elements to threatened sectors. Also on the 13th, Heeresgruppe Süd began to dispatch fresh divisions, 3. and 23. Panzer-Divisionen plus 71. Infanterie-Division, to launch counterattacks against Ryabyshev's advance units. Committing divisions earmarked for Operation *Blau* was no easy matter, since although a large number of unengaged Wehrmacht formations occupied the Kharkov region, these belonged to OKH and not to Bock. Seeing the danger to Kharkov (if not to the entire upcoming summer offensive as well), Hitler released portions of his hoard. Starting on the southern edge of the penetration, over the next three days the two panzer divisions worked their way northwards, blunting Soviet attacks, plugging holes in the line and relieving encircled

German outposts. Supporting the entire army group, Luftwaffe Generaloberst Alexander Löhr's Luftflotte 4 flew CAS missions overhead, and soon received reinforcements from the elite VIII Flieger-Korps, which Hitler pulled off the Crimea just for the Kharkov battles.

Starting on the 15th, on the southern edge of the fighting the LI Armee-Korps, not seriously engaged, threw its northern units against the 38th Army, tasked with covering Ryabyshev's left. Along with the two panzer divisions, LI Armee-Korps manoeuvres spilled over against the 28th Army, endangering the entire Stary Saltov pincer. At about the same time, three divisions from the Belgorod area began arriving to stabilize the XVII Armee-Korps on the northern shoulder; this manoeuvre had the additional effect of robbing 21st Army of the success it had been enjoying up to that point. On 17 May Kostenko played his last ace, the 3rd Guards Cavalry, not as the intended battle-winning exploitation force but as a stopgap to prevent the frustration of his plan and the destruction of his front's best units. It seems he waited too long, however, since by then the matter was close to being settled in the Germans' favour; on the same day a Kleist counterattack was crushing Timoshenko's southern pincer and the entire Izyum bulge along with it (Map 41).

On 17 and 18 May, the Stavka and Soviet operational headquarters debated back and forth over the wisdom of cancelling or continuing the offensive and to what extent. Many of Stalin's generals counselled a halt to the twin operations, which he refused to sanction.[43] After more than two days of arguments, during which the danger to his command became only more acute, late on the 19th Timoshenko unilaterally called off the attack. His hand forced, Stalin agreed to the fait accompli. The northern pincer avoided the annihilation suffered by its southern cousin. Nevertheless, pushed back by 6. Armee countermoves, a week after attacking, the chewed up remnants of the 21st, 28th and 38th Armies had retreated back to their start lines, very much worse for wear.

43 Post-war histories have not settled the issue, however: see Ziemke, *Moscow to Stalingrad*, pp. 279–80.

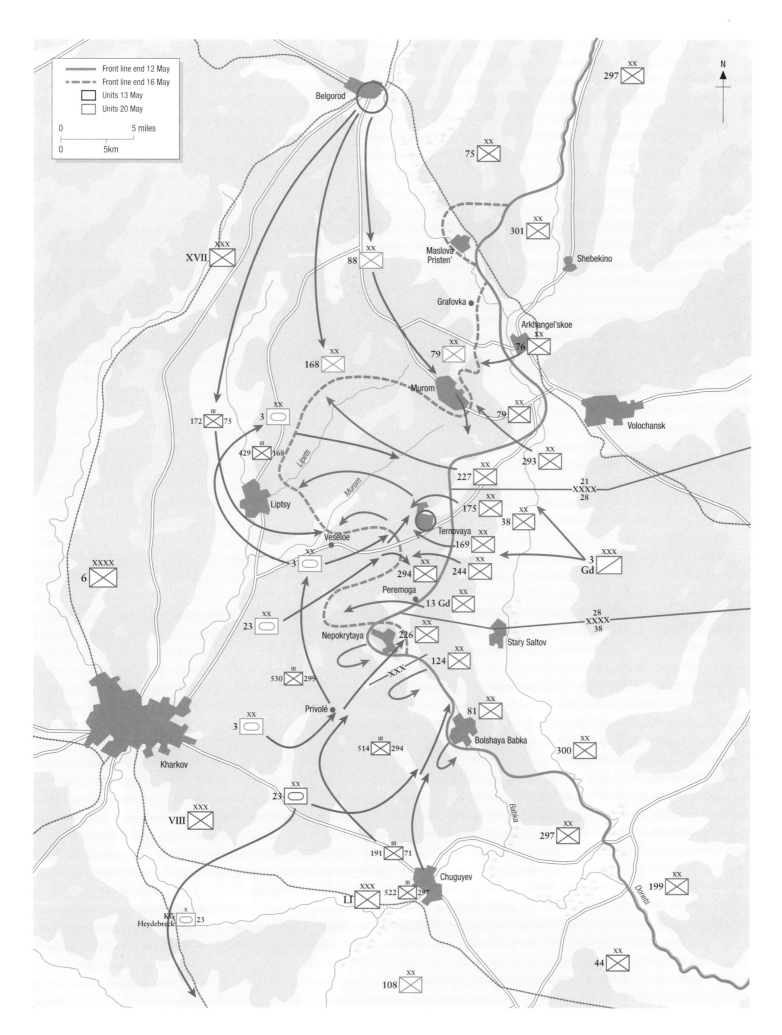

MAP 40: SECOND KHARKOV, SOUTHERN SECTOR 12–19 MAY, 1942

Marshal Timoshenko's assault from the Izyum bulge against Bock's centre represented the main effort of the South-western Direction's offensive that spring. Between them, the orders of battle of 6th Army and small army-sized Group Bobkin included ten rifle divisions and five tank brigades, with two tank and one cavalry corps standing by to exploit the expected ruptures in the 6. Armee front. Cavalry corps had proven their value during the earlier winter counteroffensives, but tank corps were a new Red Army development in an attempt to fine-tune larger operational formations after the disappointments of the *Barbarossa*-era mechanized corps.[44] The immediate objective of 6th Army and Group Bobkin was to surround and capture Kharkov from the south. General Heitz's VIII Armee-Korps, made up of two German and one Hungarian divisions, barred their way.

After a one-hour artillery bombardment on the morning of 12 May, troops under generals Gorodniansky and Bobkin quickly overwhelmed VIII Armee-Korps, splitting its two front-line divisions and advancing 15 miles that day. Paulus reacted by dispatching his reserve 113. Infanterie-Division to Efremovka to plug the hole. By the 13th Bobkin had already passed the 6th Cavalry Corps through his infantry and soon its horsemen neared the rail hub of Krasnograd, more than 25 miles from their starting point a day earlier. Taking and holding this town would provide invaluable flank security to the 6th Army's drive on Kharkov.

As Heitz fell back northwards toward Kharkov, the neighbouring XI Armee-Korps of 17. Armee drifted toward the south-west, so that by 14 April a dangerous tear had appeared along the army boundaries. On that same day, cavalry scouts working their way through this growing gap neared Poltava, site of both Bock's headquarters and another massive army group logistics base, an additional 75 miles west of Krasnograd. Little more than 48 hours into Timoshenko's offensive, even Hitler could see the danger to 6. Armee and Heeresgruppe Süd. Another day later near Zmiev, the Hungarian 108th Division began

finally to give way, threatening to expose the flank of the neighbouring LI Armee-Korps, in particular 44. Infanterie-Division, holding its critical Balakleya strongpoint. The VIII Armee-Korps planned to withdraw to the line Taranovka–Krasnograd; Heitz's men might be giving up ground, but they did so in a controlled and organized fashion.

The 16–17 May period represented a critical time for both sides. The Soviets smelled blood and prepared to commit the two armoured corps of more than 250 tanks against the VIII Armee-Korps. Hitler, Bock and their staffs sensed the precarious position, but concluded that the best defence was a good offence. Kleist had been prepared to launch the southern pincer of Operation *Fredericus* against the Izyum salient, scheduled to begin on 18 May. However, the German high command realized Paulus was too engaged fighting back two attacks north and south of Kharkov, so Kleist would have to go it alone, and in view of the dire situation, attack a day earlier than originally planned. The 17th was a big day for all concerned with the Izyum bulge; to the north the 21st and 23rd Tank Corps smashed into the VIII Armee-Korps line on either side of Ryabukhyne, while to the south Kleist took the offensive against the 9th Army in the direction of Barvenkovo (Map 41).

In the face of stiffening German defences, the two tank corps did not have the hoped-for decisive impact and gained less than ten miles. To make matters worse, the 305. Infanterie-Division had only just arrived from France, and Heitz immediately threw it into the battle in front of the tanks and to strengthen his Krasnograd position. Only hours into Kleist's attack, Timoshenko began to worry over his southern flank and told Gorodniansky to pull 23rd Tank, the more successful of the pair of corps, out of the line the next day and send it south to assist the 57th Army. The 21st Tank Corps continued alone toward Merefa (location of VIII Armee-Korps headquarters). On the 18th it ran into Kampfgruppe Heydebreck, detached from 23. Panzer-Division the day before, and halted. On 19 May, Timoshenko realized that with his drive on Kharkov stymied and Kleist rampaging in his rear areas he had to call off the offensive. He ordered 6th Army and Group Bobkin over to the defensive and redirected 21st Tank south-east to add its weight against the panzers. Defeat turned into disaster two days later when Kleist and Paulus linked up near Balakleya.

44 Tank corps were about the size of a panzer division, with two to three tank brigades totalling 100–140 tanks. In these battles the 21st and 23rd Tank Corps included lend-lease British tanks.

Chuguyev

Zmiev

Merefa

Valki

Borki

KG Hedebrock

Ryabukhyne

Berestovenka

Petrovka

Krasnograd

Savintsy

Chepel

Balakleya

Andreevka

Verkhniy Bishkin

Velikaya Bereka

Taranovka

Efremovka

Pavlovka

Grushino

Kegichovka

Mikhailovka

Lozovenka

Krasnopavlovka

Artelnaya

Ligovka

Mar'evka

Petrovskaya

Smirnovka

Lozovaya

Barvenkovo

Northern Donets

Bereka

Berestovaya

199

304

297
523

132
44

194

62
190

253

108

294 179
515

337

47

103
48

37

41

5 Gd

411

23

38

266

208 179

454
375

610

393

6

270

4

2

912

20

21

4

VI

113

Group Georgescu

454 Sicherungs

Gruppe Konrad

454 Sicherungs

6 von Kleist

6 von Kleist

XXXX von Kleist

150

21

23

113

305

113

23

305

378

305

576

E

21
AG BOBKIN

AG BOBKIN
57

28
XXXX
38

LI
XXX
VIII

VIII
XXX

248

AG BOBKIN
XXXX

21
XK

6

6

7

Front line 12 May
Front line 14 May
Front line 16 May
Front line 17 May
Units 12 May
Units 17 May

10 miles
10km

N

91

MAP 41: SECOND KHARKOV, KLEIST'S ATTACK 17–26 MAY, 1942

Timoshenko had been too focused on the battles around Kharkov and had not devoted enough attention to the southern edge of the Izyum salient. He assumed that some spoiling attacks by the 9th and 57th Armies would be enough to hold off any danger from Germans in that quarter. In this the old marshal seriously underestimated Kleist, and it turns out that Soviet intelligence let him down concerning Wehrmacht intentions as well. The 9th Army's six rifle divisions and two depleted tank brigades (barely 40 tanks combined), backed up by the 5th Cavalry Corps, defended front lines largely unchanged since the end of January but nevertheless poorly prepared. Against this the panzer general hurled Mackensen's III Panzer-Korps and the XLIV Armee-Korps, totalling three infantry and two light divisions plus the hard-charging 1. Gebirgs-Division and two panzer and one motorized infantry division. As noted earlier, Bock moved up Operation *Fredericus* one day (to the 17th) to help relieve pressure on Paulus's 6. Armee (Map 41).

Under clear skies, the IV and VIII Flieger-Korps pounded the Red Army positions early on the 17th, and soon German mechanized formations had advanced 15 miles, more than halfway to Izyum and completely through Barvenkovo, creating a dangerous threat to the entire Kharkov offensive. With his southern flank stoved in, Timoshenko lost no time redirecting units south, most notably the 23rd Tank Corps just then making good progress against Paulus, with orders to hit Mackensen on the 18th. However, by the second day of *Fredericus*, Kleist's men had created a 40-mile gap in Red Army lines, burst into Izyum and isolated the 57th Army and 2nd Cavalry Corps in their extended western positions. In its two-day battle the 5th Cavalry Corps proved no match for the panzers. Divisions of the 9th Army east of Kleist's counterattack began to fall back across the Donets. By 19 May, Timoshenko still retained a corridor between Balakleya and Petrovskaya to units to the west, but must have anticipated the pending disaster, as on that day he created Group Kostenko made up of remnants of the 6th, 9th and 57th Armies and Group Bobkin.

Wehrmacht units slowed to a crawl during 19–20 May, but still pushed to the north and west. Unaware of the debates in the Kremlin over whether to continue attacking or not, Bock and Kleist wondered why they had detected no Soviet reaction to their offensive. Their curiosity was answered on the 19th when pressure against VIII Armee-Korps began to slacken as Timoshenko redirected his attacks toward the growing danger in the south. That evening, Hitler and Bock knew they stood on the brink of a major victory and agreed to keep pushing toward Balakleya. The army group commander in turn ordered Paulus to prepare to attack southwards in order to meet Kleist part way. On the 21st the latter re-oriented his mechanized units in the direction of 6. Armee's LI Armee-Korps. The 14. Panzer-Division reached the 44. Infanterie-Division coming out of Balakleya late the next day, officially severing the Izyum bulge, the original mission of *Fredericus*. Early in the morning of 23 May, Mackensen's 16. Panzer-Division and 60. Infanterie-Division (Mot.), which along with three infantry divisions had been pushing the *Kessel* toward the west, made contact with 3. Panzer-Division sent down by Paulus. Ten miles now separated Group Kostenko from the remainder of Timoshenko's command, dooming the bulk of four armies.

On the 23rd elements of 57th Army, which had escaped encirclement, immediately launched ineffective rescue attempts in the direction of Chepel. Two days later, trapped Red Army units tried attacking over Lozovenka to friendly lines. By this time Bock's cordon was solid and well supported by IV Flieger-Korps' CAS. German and even Romanian forces squeezed the *Kessel* from all sides. Occasionally Soviet breakout attacks came close to succeeding, but by the 26th the remnants of Timoshenko's offensive had been pushed into a lozenge-shaped deathtrap in the Bereka valley, measuring two by ten miles. Fighting continued while the better part of four army-sized organizations and their valuable commanders and staffs, including Gorodniansky and Kostenko, languished inside. It took Bock's men until the end of the month to reduce the pocket. Reminiscent of *Barbarossa*, a quarter of a million soldiers marched off to captivity while the Germans inventoried booty numbering more than 1,200 tanks and 2,500–3,000 guns. Wehrmacht losses approached 20,000 men, not to mention time lost launching Operation *Blau*.

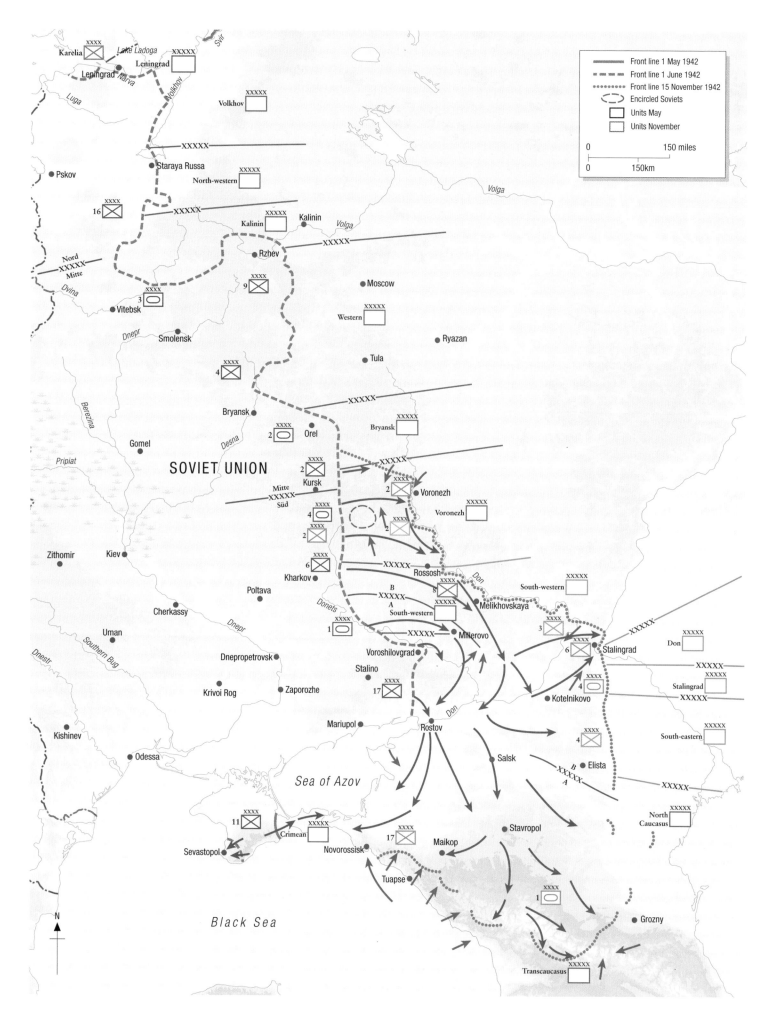

Karelia
Lake Ladoga
Leningrad
Leningrad
Svir
Volkhov
Volkhov
Narva
Luga
Psков
Staraya Russa
North-western
16
Nord
Mitte
Dvina
Kalinin
Kalinin
Volga
Rzhev
Moscow
9
Western
Ryazan
Vitebsk
3
Dnepr
Smolensk
Tula
Berezina
4
Bryansk
Bryansk
Gomel
Desna
Orel
2
SOVIET UNION
Mitte
Süd
Kursk
2
Voronezh
Voronezh
Pripiat
4
2
Zithomir
Kiev
6
Kharkov
Rossosh
Don
South-western
Poltava
8
Cherkassy
Donets
B
South-western
A
Melikhovskaya
Uman
Dnepr
1
Millerovo
3
Stalingrad
Don
Dnepropetrovsk
Voroshilovgrad
6
Stalingrad
Dnestr
Stalino
17
Kotelnikovo
Krivoi Rog
Zaporozhe
Stalingrad
Kishinev
Mariupol
Rostov
Don
4
South-eastern
Odessa
Salsk
Elista
B
A
Sea of Azov
North
Caucasus
11
Crimean
17
Sevastopol
Novorossisk
Maikop
Stavropol
Tuapse
N
1
Grozny
Black Sea
Transcaucasus

Front line 1 May 1942
Front line 1 June 1942
Front line 15 November 1942
Encircled Soviets
Units May
Units November
0   150 miles
0   150km

CHAPTER 3
OPERATION *BLAU*, 1942

While some German generals at the time and afterwards, plus many historians since, believe that the capture of Moscow would have won the war in 1941, Hitler knew better. Already in November 1941, part way between *Typhoon*'s spectacular start and its anticlimactic conclusion, Hitler made plans for the 1942 campaign he knew must come. Again the *Schwerpunkt* would be in the south, once more chosen for economic and political – not military – reasons and again Moscow played the role of decoy. At war with the United States since 8 December, Germany would now need Soviet resources even more. Hitler figured that he had one year, or at the most two, before American men and materiel would negatively affect his war in Europe. When Stalin's own winter and spring offensives came up short, Hitler indeed got his second chance.

Germany would be in no better position to win than the year before, however. With army commander added to his list of executive titles, Hitler could now bless that body with his disorganized managerial style. Only in Hitler himself did the three primary services, plus myriad private armies like the SS and other paramilitary organizations, come together. He dealt with commanders in the field and inserted himself into the operations of increasingly lower-echelon units. The tension between OKH and OKW increased, while Halder was marginalized to the point where his departure near the end of *Blau* would be no great loss. The destruction of Germany's war machine dating from *Barbarossa*, and the defence against Stalin's counteroffensives, not to mention the Battle for the Atlantic, the north African campaign and growing air war, had not been made good over the winter. Trained men, and even horses, could not be instantaneously found and made ready for action. The nation's economy was basically leaderless, while Hitler insisted that its industry, such as it was, continued to produce consumer goods in order to maintain civilian morale and avoid another domestic calamity like 1914–18. All of these factors, along with resources squandered on Hitler's fascination for 'wonder weapons', conspired to make Germany's eastern army and air force much smaller than 12 months earlier. To compound matters, the first year of the Nazi-Soviet War had been disastrous for Hitler's already weak coalition allies.

Before turning to Operation *Blau*, it is important to mention one prelude, the Germans' final conquest of the Crimea. The Wehrmacht did this in a brief, self-contained set of battles that coincided with the Red Army offensive around Kharkov and the opening moves of *Blau*. Soviet attempts to liberate the peninsula through early spring had failed. With the return of decent weather, on 8 May the Germans attacked at Feodosia. They immediately scattered the half-hearted Soviet defenders, captured the port of Kerch within a week and eliminated the Red Army bridgehead altogether on the 21st. Hitler dedicated considerable Luftwaffe CAS assets and massive railway siege guns to the initial bombardment of the fortress of Sevastopol, which began on 2 June. Although heavily fortified like Singapore, which had fallen to the Japanese only a couple of months earlier on the other side of the globe, its defences were primarily oriented against a seaborne attack that did not materialize. After four days of preparation, the ground attack began, and a week later German assault troops entered the city proper (but generally avoided costly urban warfare). At the same time, the Soviets began to evacuate their last toehold on the Crimea. Fighting against rearguards dragged on for another three weeks until 3 July, when the victor, Erich von Manstein, earned his field marshal's baton. After taking the Crimea, 11. Armee did not remain in the south as a much-needed operational reserve for *Blau* but instead was broken up, with a major portion going to Leningrad at the other end of the theatre.[45]

Planning for Operation *Blau* by the OKH began in February, became formal on 5 April and called for the southern part of the eastern army to cover distances greater than during *Barbarossa*. Despite destroying nearly 7,000 Red Army Air Force aircraft during *Barbarossa*, the Luftwaffe was at a disadvantage, providing less air support than during the previous two years.[46] Dennis Showalter calls the campaign 'audacious to the point of recklessness',[47] but risky behaviour was a long-standing Prussian/German military characteristic. The first order of business consisted of destroying Red Army forces in encirclement battles along the Donets and Don Rivers. Next came securing the shoulders of the advance at Voronezh and Stalingrad and creating more *Kesseln* before moving south-east to take Maikop, Grozny and Baku, absolutely critical Soviet oil-producing regions.[48] Stalin, partly due to inclination and partly due to the Germans' Operation *Kremlin* deception plan, believed Moscow to be Hitler's objective. The fact that *Blau* began at Voronezh on the far left of the offensive and closest to Moscow served to confirm Stalin's assumptions.

The German offensive began on 28 June. Red Army forces fought tenaciously for Voronezh against German and Hungarian forces until the first week of July, as if they knew they were defending their capital in the process. Farther south along the Don Front starting on 30 June,

other panzer-heavy armies aiming for Rossosh easily swept aside two Soviet armies already ravaged by the fighting around Kharkov in May. To their right another panzer army made good progress near Lisichansk along the middle Donets. In early July Hitler began to tweak *Blau*'s plans with a series of directives and orders, and it is here that many historians consider the 1942 campaign to have lost its compass. First, on 9 July he divided Heeresgruppe Süd, under Bock since January (when its commander died from a heart attack), into two further army groups, unimaginatively named 'A' and 'B', and commanded by Feldmarschall Wilhelm List and Bock, respectively.[49] Although previously arranged as part of *Blau*'s original plan, this de jure split exacerbated the existing de facto partition of effort and objectives. Around Voronezh the offensive had failed to achieve any massive encirclements and had fallen behind schedule; the Führer needed a scapegoat. Blame fell on Bock, who retired for good on 13 July with Generaloberst Maximilian *Reichsfreiherr* von Weichs taking command of Heeresgruppe B. Ten days later the dictator issued a directive making the roles of the two new army groups clearer; Heeresgruppe B would have responsibility for taking Stalingrad while Heeresgruppe A headed for the Caucasus and oil. In addition to setting objectives at right angles from each other, more critically the document reversed *Blau*'s earlier priorities; from now on Stalingrad, not Soviet oil, would be the operation's *Schwerpunkt*. In between these two decisions Hitler made another change of plans that probably cost him Stalingrad and possibly cost him a chance of success for Operation *Blau* overall.

On 16 July, the dictator diverted a panzer army south to the lower Don River that until then had an open shot straight at the city on the Volga (on the same day he moved his headquarters to the Ukraine). Granted, destroying sizeable Red Army forces in and east of Rostov looked like a worthy target for two panzer armies, but unlike the Kiev decision 11 months earlier, this manoeuvre did not bear the expected fruit ('only' 54,000 POWs), so this diversion of additional assets was not really necessary. The purposeless 90-degree turn south by *Blau*'s best unit only wasted valuable time and fuel. Two weeks later, Hitler recognized his mistake and ordered the same formation to make a 90-degree turn back east. Here we can see how a seemingly minor operational decision could have tremendous strategic reverberations. To make matters worse, unlike *Barbarossa*, *Blau* did not create the anticipated huge *Kesseln*. It turns out that, unlike 1941, the Stavka had finally recognized that it could not fight a mobile defence on anything approaching equal terms against the Wehrmacht, so on 6 July decided instead to trade space for time as its Russian ancestors had. At the end of July and beginning of August, when the Soviets did stand and fight against a single German army, their sacrifice sufficed to delay the attackers just long enough to keep them from rushing Stalingrad.

For centuries Prussian/German doctrine had focused on the enemy in the field, but now Stalin prevented his forces from becoming fixed and trapped. Lacking other terrain features of military significance in Asiatic Russia, Stalingrad acted as a magnet. With the wolves at the gates of 'his' city, the communist dictator reconsidered and issued

---

45 In lacking a significant reserve, *Blau* had much in common with *Barbarossa*.

46 The Luftwaffe began the 1942 campaign with 2,900 planes on the main front; in 1940 it had 3,700 machines and in 1941 it had 3,400.

47 *Armor and Blood*, p. 8.

48 The straight-line distance Heeresgruppe Süd was expected to cover in 1942, from the Mius River to Baku, exceeded that travelled from occupied Poland to Rostov in 1941. Additionally, during *Blau* the USSR was on a total war footing, while the infrastructure between the Black and Caspian Seas was infinitely more primitive than that to the west. Before *Blau*, the Caucasus region extracted and refined upwards of 70 per cent of the USSR's oil. Even if the Germans had captured the wells, their 'plan' to get any oil home was based largely on wishful thinking.

49 List dabbled on the fringes of the anti-Hitler opposition.

another 'not one step back!' order. In addition, Soviet armies counterattacked whenever an opportunity presented itself. Heeresgruppe B closed on the Volga and reached the outskirts of Stalin's city on 23 July.[50] Over the next two days Luftwaffe bombing raids torched large portions of the city. The Wehrmacht spearhead, now two armies strong again, stood at the end of yet another tenuous logistical trail – a looming disaster. Whole armies had to take turns attacking, since the Germans could supply only one of the two at a time. To compound German problems, a weak cordon of non-mechanized Hungarian, Italian and Romanian armies held their nearly 500-mile-long left flank from Voronezh almost to Stalingrad. The Hungarian Second and Italian Eighth armies were not only new to the east, but were brand new organizations. They seemed happy to let the Don River do most of the defensive work for them, but the river line was by no means completely secure; depleted and overly-hasty German withdrawals left many active Red Army bridgeheads intact on the right bank. Not only were Wehrmacht mechanized forces initially too small given its divergent twin missions, but in July threats near Moscow, Leningrad and even France caused Hitler to pull away additional valuable mobile units from *Blau*.

While Heeresgruppe B's situation on the road to Stalingrad looked bad, Heeresgruppe A had it worse as it neared the Caucasus Mountains. Its mission expanded to include occupation of the Black Sea coast and it had to depend more and more on the Luftwaffe for resupply. As usual, the Germans did not have resources adequate for their objectives, while Soviet defences contributed to slowing the invader. The Germans indeed captured Maikop, but found the oil wells smoking ruins.[51] They would never reach the Grozny oil region, much less the more distant Baku. In the midst of one of the globe's greatest oil-producing regions, camels with jerry cans strapped to their backs refuelled stranded panzers and Stukas. On 9 September, as punishment, List followed Bock into forced retirement, with Hitler temporarily taking on the job of army group commander as well. Two weeks later the dictator fired army chief of staff Halder, ending four years of fatal dysfunction in that critical

relationship at the very peak of the Third Reich's military. The atmosphere at Hitler's 'advanced' headquarters at Vinnitsa became more poisoned. Personality conflicts spilled over from OKH to OKW, the latter his own creature and in practice almost a personal staff.[52] It is a tribute to the men of Heeresgruppe A that it managed to keep advancing at all as summer turned to autumn. There is never a good time in the middle of a war to have a meltdown in a nation's high command, but this was becoming an annual occurrence in Hitler's Germany. The tendency began slowly in the days leading up to Dunkirk in 1940, while the 1941 version took a month to work itself out. In mid-1942, the Germans' command crisis took place in the shadow of some of the worst fighting of World War II.

The battle for Stalingrad is one of the best-known episodes of the war. When Heeresgruppe B's *coup de main* failed in July, the Germans condemned themselves to a long, deliberate battle of attrition against a resolute enemy 35 miles beyond the last natural line of defence, the Chir River. The defenders rationed new troops into the city from the relative safety of the left bank of the Volga. As David Glantz has pointed out, once again the USSR's ability to create and properly employ reserves rectified a dangerous situation (and distinguished it from Germany).[53] The principal Red Army commander deliberately ordered his men to stay as close to the enemy as possible in order to negate German indirect fire and CAS. Urban fighting degenerated into countless brutal and deadly, block-by-block, building-by-building and often room-by-room small-unit actions in bombed-out rubble, in what the Germans called *Rattenkrieg* (war of rats). It was a war in which they were increasingly outclassed and it looked doubtful that they would prevail. Nevertheless, by October they succeeded in breaking the Soviet defences into smaller and smaller isolated bridgeheads barely hugging the banks of the Volga. In an interesting contrast, Wehrmacht forces felt more and more anxiety over the perceived need to take the city before the arrival of winter, while the Red Army welcomed cold weather as a harbinger of the counteroffensive they had been preparing for most of the summer.

50 At the same time Hitler took away two panzer divisions from Weichs and sent them to Heeresgruppe Mitte.

51 Any quantity of Caucasus oil taken by the Germans was minuscule. Retreating Soviets demolished the oil-producing infrastructure – wells, refineries, transport – in the entire Armavir, Krasnodar and Maikop area. The German effort, including the 6,500-strong Technical Brigade 'Mineral Oil', would have produced better results in existing Romanian and Hungarian oil regions.

52 Although at first blush the OKW may look like the modern, overarching 'department of defence', being developed by the better-managed Allies, it was little more than a political tool for Hitler to dominate the German military and circumvent the general staff.

53 Glantz, David and House, Jonathan, *When Titans Clashed*, p. 123.

MAP 43: OPERATION *TRAPPENJAGD* 8–19 MAY, 1942

An essential prerequisite to Hitler's plans for the summer of 1942 included removing the Soviet presence from the Crimea. Thanks to Red Army landings on the Kerch Peninsula the previous winter, Manstein now had two separated lodgements to defeat. He held LIV Armee-Korps and some Romanian units on an economy of force mission facing the Sevastopol garrison. On the Parpach he placed two corps headquarters, six German and a couple of Romanian divisions ready to assault 23 Red Army divisions distributed among three armies, almost an exact inverse of the ideal 3:1 (attacker: defender) ratio. The VIII Flieger-Korps, amphibious landings and Soviet mistakes would have to compensate for the numerical inferiority. According to Manstein's plan, XLII Armee-Korps would hold in the north while XXX Armee-Korps led the main effort in the south. Specifically, 50. and 132. Infanterie-Divisionen plus 28. leichte Infanterie-Division would create the breakthrough, through which 170. Infanterie-Division, 22. Panzer-Division and Brigade Groddek (truck-mounted German and Romanian infantry) would exploit. Most of the Crimean Front defenders expected the blow and in fact had prepared their own offensive against the XLII Armee-Korps on the northern side of the Parpach. Arrayed in four successive lines of prepared positions, under an average commander the Kerch defences could have been almost unassailable. Unfortunately for the Soviets, the front's military and political leaders, General Kozlov and his commissar Mekhlis, put on a display of incompetence exceptional even for the first months of the Nazi-Soviet War.

Recognizing the key role Richthofen's aviators would play, Manstein described *Trappenjagd* as a ground operation with a Luftwaffe *Schwerpunkt*. As the operation began on 8 May, VIII Flieger-Korps flew nearly continuous sorties and maintained complete air superiority for the entire battle.[54] After a massive preparatory artillery barrage, 132. Infanterie-Division on the coast and 28. leichte Infanterie-Division to its left advanced through defensive positions 44th Army had occupied for months but made minimal efforts to defend. For added insurance, XXX Armee-Korps commander General der Artillerie Maximilian Fretter-Pico sent a battalion of 132. Infanterie-Division in assault boats on a dangerous mission across the Black Sea to land behind the Soviet defences. Disordered, Kozlov's men fell back in droves as the Germans advanced up to 6 miles by the end of that first day. The 11. Armee had cleared its most difficult hurdle at the cost of barely 100 killed. That night Fretter-Pico brought 22. Panzer-Division forward in order to begin exploitation operations the next day. Following Brigade Groddek through the shattered 44th Army defences, 22. Panzer-Division swung left toward Arma-Eli and into the rear of the neighbouring 51st Army. With Stuka support overhead, the panzer men smashed a counterattack by the 56th and 39th Tank Divisions. Groddek continued due east, penetrating the weak Nasyr Line 10 miles behind the Parpach defences and continued an additional dozen miles to the stout Sultanovka Line by evening. The 47th Army offered minimal resistance; the weather did much more to delay Manstein's men.

Heavy rain and Soviet defences slowed 22. Panzer-Division on 10 May, but the division reached the Sea of Azov coast on the 11th, completing the encirclement of the 51st Army. While 132. Infanterie-Division followed Brigade Groddek east, 50. Infanterie-Division and 28. leichte Infanterie-Division helped 22. Panzer-Division seal off and reduce the 51st Army *Kessel*. The three divisions then turned over mopping up operations to XLII Armee-Korps troops and continued east to give Kozlov no chance to catch his breath. By the 12th the Red Army retreat had turned into a rout pursued by XXX and XLII Armee-Korps, with the Romanian 7th Corps joining the chase in the north. Manstein's second objective, now that *Trappenjagd*'s frontal assault had been a complete success, was to reach the port of Kerch and the Kerch Straits in order to prevent a Soviet withdrawal. The Axis formations moved faster than their Crimean Front counterparts, overcame the Sultanovka Line on the 13th and 170. and 132. Infanterie-Divisionen reached Kerch two days later.

Fighting against bypassed groups of Kozlov's men continued until 18 May, and the Red Army managed to evacuate approximately 40,000 troops to the Taman Peninsula. Manstein declared the battle over on the 19th, with approximately 150,000 POWs captured. One enemy threat on the Crimea eliminated, the general had the freedom to turn on Sevastopol.

---

54 Hitler kept VIII Air Corps on a very short leash under his personal control.

Taman
Peninsula

Kerch Strait

Ak Burun

Kamysh Burun

S e a   o f   A z o v

B l a c k   S e a

Kerch

Bagerovo

Marfovka

Groddeck

Sem-Kolodezei

Arma-Eli

Ak-Monaj

Parpach

Koi-Asszn

Dal'niye Kamyshi

Feodosia

Front line 7 May 1942	
Soviet anti-tank ditch	
Soviet reserve positions	
Units 7 May	
Units 16 May	

0   10km

0   10 miles

22
46
170
132
156
XLIII
19
XXX
XXX
VII
XLII
XXX
50
XXX
72
11 NKVD
44 XXXX
156 XXX
47
51 XXXX
404
39
56
55
396
57
40
138 390
224 77 236 302
271 320 400 398
8 170 19
46
50
28 Lt
132
276
63
436
22
XLII XXX

99

MAP 44: PREPARING TO CONQUER SEVASTOPOL APRIL 1942

During Operation *Barbarossa*, 11. Armee finally halted after surrounding Sevastopol (Map 22). By early November the fortress's defences consisted of three concentric lines bristling with thousands of bunkers, 140,000 mines and anti-tank ditches, all over-watched by turreted naval guns. Manstein assembled LVI and XXX Armee-Korps, but a series of hasty and under-supported attacks during the second half of November accomplished little. His men tried again during the third week of December from both the northern and south-eastern quadrants. They progressed to the Belbek Valley, where the front stabilized as Manstein had to tend to renewed fighting on the Kerch Peninsula (Map 36). During the winter and spring, the Black Sea Fleet and Red Army Air Force reinforced and resupplied Sevastopol. Meanwhile throughout the Crimea, 11. Armee was stretched to its limit by local counterattacks, pinprick amphibious landings and increasingly bold partisan ambushes. As the overall situation stabilized in the spring, Manstein prepared to take Sevastopol as the Red Army prepared to keep it.

The adjacent map shows dispositions of both sides on the eve of Manstein's month-long assault, Operation *Störfang* (Sturgeon Catch). General Major I. Y. Petrov's Independent Maritime Army was the cornerstone of Admiral Oktyabrsky's Sevastopol Defence Region. It divided the fortress defences into four sectors, defended by seven rifle divisions, five naval infantry brigades, seven artillery regiments and nearly 40 tanks. He was lavishly outfitted with anti-aircraft regiments, anti-tank battalions and other combat support units. Most worrisome to the Germans were batteries of 305mm, 203mm, 152mm and 120mm guns totalling nearly 600 tubes of artillery (not counting 2,000 mortars), in addition to numerous well-built forts codenamed by the Germans after Soviet luminaries and Russian place names. The biggest of the forts were World War I-era concrete and earth constructions with thick armour-protected turrets that could fire in 360 degrees and against which the Germans devoted much special planning and weaponry.

Overall man- (and woman-) power around Sevastopol stood at nearly 190,000, of which more than 100,000 manned the combat formations. Petrov's first defensive belt measured between 1 and 2 miles deep and contained trenches and wire entanglements. The second belt defended the harbour from the relatively flat northern Sector IV behind the Belbek stream and included most of the famous forts: Maxim

Gorky I, Molotov, GPU, Siberia, Stalin, Volga, and others. The eastern and southern portions of the perimeter included rough terrain that favoured the defenders. The third defensive belt wrapped around Sevastopol itself. Together, the port's defences covered over 200 miles. The garrison suffered shortages of some types of ammunition, for example, but generally was well provisioned.

The 11. Armee anticipated a difficult fight to subdue Sevastopol. Manstein did not have unlimited personnel, so allowed World War II's largest collection of massive siege artillery, Richthofen's VIII Flieger-Korps experts and specialized pioneer units make the task easier. He planned a very deliberate set-piece battle with General der Kavallerie Eric Hansen's LVI Armee-Korps as the *Schwerpunkt* in the north. Fretter-Pico's XXX Armee-Korps contributed supporting attacks along the south.[55] Between the two German corps stood the Romanian Mountain Corps of two divisions. Both Wehrmacht corps received significant combat engineer reinforcements in the form of specialized pioneer battalions. Manstein also gave each corps *Nebelwerfers*, but he retained most heavy artillery assets at the army level. In addition to railway and other super-heavy artillery (800mm, 420mm, 355mm and 305mm), he had six battalions and numerous batteries at his disposal. The VIII Flieger-Korps represented his other ace: 70 Stukas, 100 Bf 109s and 160 He 111s or Ju 88s.

In mid-April Manstein personally briefed Hitler at the latter's headquarters on his concept of the Sevastopol operation, essentially an updated and up-gunned version of earlier assaults. The 11. Armee plan of attack concentrated on the north, not only due to favourable terrain, but because roads were better there, essential for supplying the siege artillery. Almost all of the super-heavy guns were in the north, where their limited deflection could take most of Petrov's fortifications under fire. Four days of intense 'annihilation' barrage by artillery and CAS would open the attack and prepare the way for the *Landsers*. After penetrating the initial defences, Hansen's intermediate objectives were the northern edge of Severnaya Bay and the Gatani Heights to the east. The XXX Armee-Korps' supporting attack aimed for the Sapun Ridge, which overlooked the port city from the south-east.

---

55 The XXX Armee-Korps headquarters plus 50., 132. and 170. Infanterie-Divisionen and 28. leichte Infanterie-Division had completed Operation *Trappenjagd* just weeks beforehand (Map 43) and were slow re-deploying to Sevastopol.

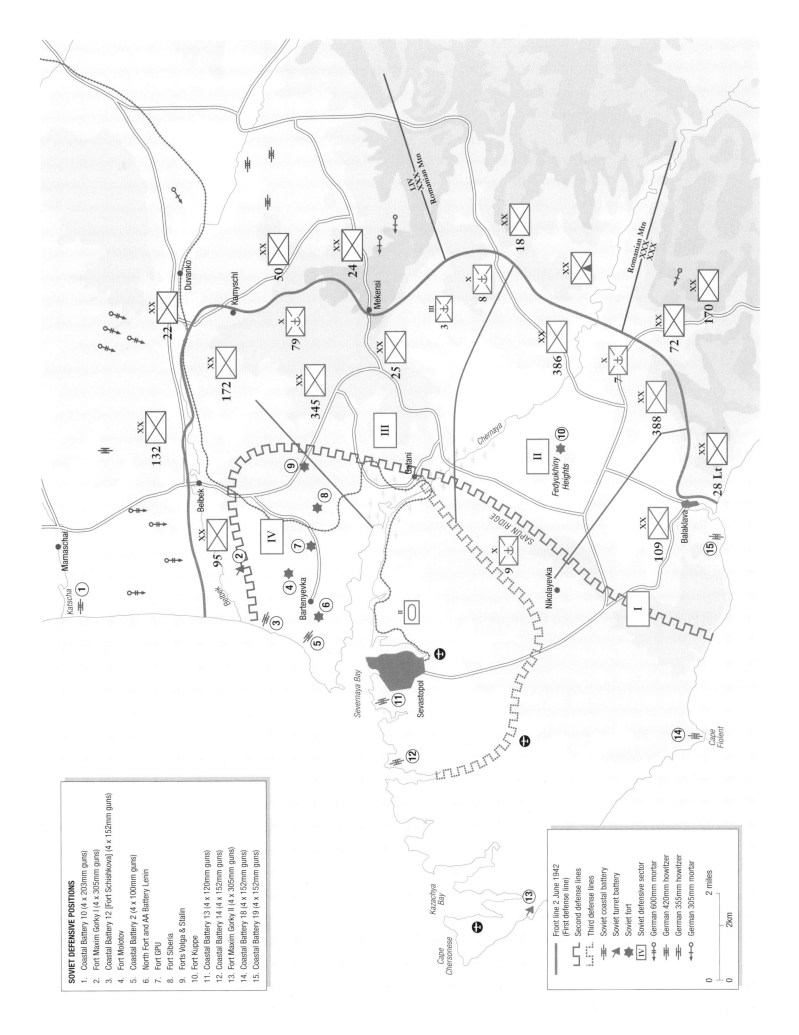

SOVIET DEFENSIVE POSITIONS

1. Coastal Battery 10 (4 x 203mm guns)
2. Fort Maxim Gorky I (4 x 305mm guns)
3. Coastal Battery 12 [Fort Schishkova] (4 x 152mm guns)
4. Fort Molotov
5. Coastal Battery 2 (4 x 100mm guns)
6. North Fort and AA Battery Lenin
7. Fort GPU
8. Fort Siberia
9. Forts Volga & Stalin
10. Fort Kuppe
11. Coastal Battery 13 (4 x 120mm guns)
12. Coastal Battery 14 (4 x 152mm guns)
13. Fort Maxim Gorky II (4 x 305mm guns)
14. Coastal Battery 18 (4 x 152mm guns)
15. Coastal Battery 19 (4 x 152mm guns)

Front line 2 June 1942
(First defense line)
Second defense lines
Third defense lines
Soviet coastal battery
Soviet turret battery
Soviet fort
Soviet defensive sector
German 600mm mortar
German 420mm howitzer
German 355mm howitzer
German 305mm mortar

0   2km
0   2 miles

MAP 45: SEVASTOPOL (I) – 2–27 JUNE, 1942

The Wehrmacht 'annihilation fire' bombardment of prolonged, co-ordinated and closely directed artillery began on 2 June and climaxed five days later. Luftwaffe CAS flew non-stop in the summer-like weather, sending up between 1,000 and 2,000 sorties on some days. Hardest hit were defensive positions and forts in the north between Belbek and Severnaya Bay, basically a 4 by 6 mile killing zone. Concrete bunkers and battleship-type steel turrets were demolished, as were ordinary earthen or timber fieldworks and simple trenches and fighting positions. Aside from explosive power and shell splinters, the overpressure created by projectiles weighing between 2 and 5 tons killed men caught in the open. Much is made of huge German guns like the 800mm 'Dora', but this monster actually shot fewer than 50 times during the entire battle, while 600mm 'Karl' shot only 120 rounds. Richthofen's VIII Flieger-Korps, desperately needed by Heeresgruppe Süd for Operation *Blau*, remained on station over Sevastopol past the planned three days.

Somehow many Red Army units avoided the slaughter and were ready when Hansen's infantry began its assault on 7 June; on that first day the Germans would be hard pressed to find a single opening to capitalize on. Following a one-hour preparatory artillery barrage, LIV Armee-Korps attacked with all four infantry divisions abreast (right). Sappers usually led the way, clearing minefields and other obstacles, while in places *Sturmgeschütze* from attached Sturmgeschütz Abteilungen 190 and 197 contributed their guns. In addition to stout defences, 132. and 22. Infanterie-Divisionen had to negotiate the Belbek Valley while 50. and 24. Infanterie-Divisionen were faced with the Kamyshiy Ravine. Many German units sustained heavy casualties, but, driven by Manstein, they kept advancing nonetheless. By late afternoon they had captured the town of Belbek and numerous Soviet strongpoints. Red Army units launched counterattacks, but these usually failed to dislodge the attackers. By evening both sides were exhausted, but in places the Germans had gained up to 2 miles, most notably in the north-east corner of the front.

Despite all the military technology available to him in 1942, Manstein was still fighting against a numerically superior enemy. Progress by LIV Armee-Korps was slow and casualties mounted. By 11 June, XXX Armee-Korps entered the fight to the south, having recovered somewhat from *Trappenjagd* at Kerch, but found the going very slow against an intact enemy in the tangled terrain. The Romanians generally failed to make themselves felt. A day later at his Poltava headquarters, army group commander Bock began to have doubts about *Störfang's* prospects. Things began to look up on the 13th when forts Maxim Gorky I and Stalin fell to 132. Infanterie-Division and 22. Panzer-Division respectively; most of the forts' big guns had been silenced days earlier.[56] On the same day 72. Infanterie-Division troops took Fort Kuppe in the south. Hansen re-organized to gain further advantage; he pulled 24. Infanterie-Division out of its fight at the far end of the Kamyshiy Ravine and placed it between 132. Infanterie-Division and 22. Panzer-Division. Romanian Mountain Corps commander Major General G. Avramescu brought forward his 4th Mountain Division to take the place of 24. Infanterie-Division in the line.

Manstein issued fresh orders on 17 June and re-positioned his siege mortars. LIV Armee-Korps's success continued and on that same day it captured forts Bastion, Malakov, Cheka, GPU, Siberia and Volga while advancing to within 1 mile of Severnaya Bay. At the other end of the front, XXX Armee-Korps fought its way past the initial defences of defence zones I and II and the following day reached the base of Sapun Heights. Soon Hansen reached the edge of the bay, but it would take Fretter-Pico and the Romanians days to consolidate their positions. On the 27th, Manstein paused to re-organize his army for the final assault on Sevastopol proper.

---

56 The 22. Infanterie-Division had tried but failed to capture Fort Stalin on 9 June.

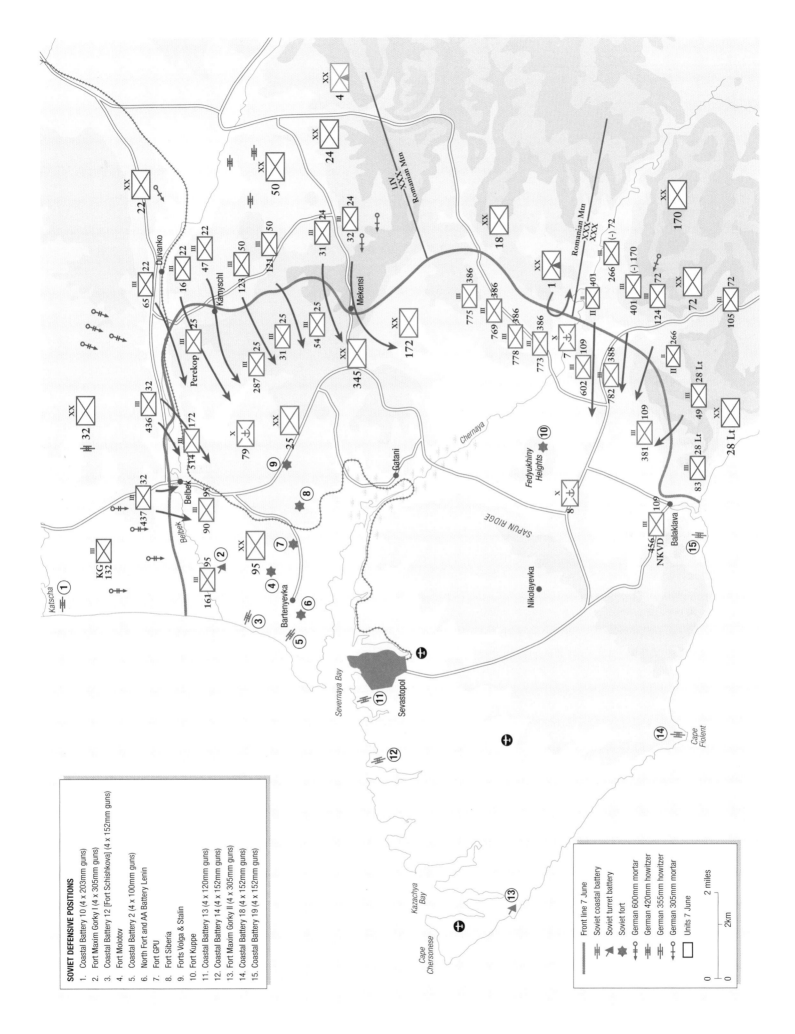

SOVIET DEFENSIVE POSITIONS

1. Coastal Battery 10 (4 x 203mm guns)
2. Fort Maxim Gorky I (4 x 305mm guns)
3. Coastal Battery 12 [Fort Schishkova] (4 x 152mm guns)
4. Fort Molotov
5. Coastal Battery 2 (4 x 100mm guns)
6. North Fort and AA Battery Lenin
7. Fort GPU
8. Fort Siberia
9. Forts Volga & Stalin
10. Fort Kuppe
11. Coastal Battery 13 (4 x 120mm guns)
12. Coastal Battery 14 (4 x 152mm guns)
13. Fort Maxim Gorky II (4 x 305mm guns)
14. Coastal Battery 18 (4 x 152mm guns)
15. Coastal Battery 19 (4 x 152mm guns)

Front line 7 June
Soviet coastal battery
Soviet turret battery
Soviet fort
German 600mm mortar
German 420mm howitzer
German 355mm howitzer
German 305mm mortar
Units 7 June

0   2 miles
0   2km

MAP 46: SEVASTOPOL (II), 28 JUNE TO 1 JULY, 1942

By the third week of June, 11. Armee had the worst of Sevastopol's defences behind it, the large forts and other positions dug into the bedrock around the city. Petrov's defenders meanwhile had lost both the outer defences they had worked so hard to improve and any room to manoeuvre as well.

Manstein had created a tight ring around the port: the LIV Armee-Korps occupied the northern shore of Severnaya Bay while the XXX Armee-Korps and Romanian Mountain Corps both sat atop the Gatani Heights just below the Sapun Ridgeline, face-to-face with the Soviets. Petrov had the bulk of his men generally along the high ground Inkerman–Sapun–Balaklava. The critical point in his defences was the marshy area where these heights, the bay and the Chernaya River all met. The Germans surrounded his troops inside this sharp angle on two sides. On the 26th, Manstein decided on a novel approach to crack the city's last line of defences. While Fretter-Pico and the Romanians made a frontal attack against the ridge, Hansen would execute a surprise amphibious assault across the eastern end of Severnaya Bay and swing around behind Inkerman. He hoped that Soviet planners had put too much faith in the bay's half-mile width. In this way, even if Red Army defenders on the ridges held back XXX Armee-Korps and the Romanians, the *Landsers* coming across the water would unhinge Petrov's positions.

During the night of 28–29 June, Hansen's engineer troops eased 100 assault boats into Severnaya Bay and began to lay a smokescreen along their northern shore. German artillery pounded Soviet positions in the rocky cliffs on the opposite shore. The naval infantry defending that section of front failed to notice the activity until the German boats were on top of them. Just then, XXX Armee-Korps artillery began to fire in order to soften up the positions along Sapun. By 0400 troops of 22. and 24. Infanterie-Divisionen had secured their bridgehead. Simultaneously 170. Infanterie-Division assaulted the centre of the Sapun line and the Romanian 1st Mountain Division moved into Novo Shuli. Both found themselves in tough fights, either in a tangle of hilltop trenches or a toughly defended village. Stukas from VIII Flieger-Korps harassed Red Army artillery and interdicted the movement of Petrov's reserves. Around 0700 both German and Romanian divisions had prevailed, threatening to penetrate the Sapun position. Fretter-Pico already had his reserve 105. Infanterie-Regiment on the move, and soon it crossed the ridgeline and broke into the rear of the Soviet line. Manstein ordered the regiment straight to Cape Chersonese deep in Sevastopol's rear area.

Meanwhile, men of 50. and 132. Infanterie-Divisionen on Hansen's left began working over the vulnerable angle between Inkerman and Gatani. By noon a *Kampfgruppe* of 50. Infanterie-Division linked up with the bridgehead, encircling a good number of Petrov's men. The Soviet defences were compromised in numerous places by the afternoon and XXX Armee-Korps had occupied the entire Sapun a few hours later. On the next day 11. Armee units pressed Red Army remnants from the outskirts of Sevastopol to Balaklava. Assault parties and rearguards fought to the death. Richthofen's aviators pounded the city as the garrison began to run low on ammunition, food and drinkable water.[57] Admiral Oktyabrsky switched Black Sea Fleet ships from a diversionary attack on the Kerch Peninsula to evacuating the city's beleaguered defenders. Stavka approved this move on the 30th, which was certain to be dangerous given Luftwaffe air superiority. As rearguard engagements raged over the next three days, 25,000 Soviets, mainly soldiers and sailors, managed to escape the city.

On 1 July, before the fighting had ended, Manstein had earned his field marshal's baton. Three days later the battle was officially over when the last fort fell – Maxim Gorky II – although small groups held out for days longer. The 11. Armee claimed nearly 20,000 Red Army troops killed and over 90,000 POWs captured at a cost of more than 40,000 Axis casualties.

---

57 By this point Sevastopol's only tangible contact with the outside world was via submarines.

SOVIET DEFENSIVE POSITIONS

1. Fort Maxim Gorky I (4 x 305mm guns)
2. Coastal Battery 12 [Fort Schishkova] (4 x 152mm guns)
3. Fort Molotov
4. Coastal Battery 2 (4 x 100m guns)
5. North Fort and AA Battery Lenin
6. Fort GPU
7. Fort Siberia
8. Forts Volga & Stalin
9. Fort Kuppe
10. Coastal Battery 13 (4 x 120mm guns)
11. Coastal Battery 14 (4 x 152mm guns)
12. Fort Maxim Gorky II (4 x 305mm guns)
13. Coastal Battery 18 (4 x 152mm guns)
14. Coastal Battery 19 (4 x 152mm guns)

Front line 29 June
Soviet coastal battery
Soviet turret battery
Soviet fort
German 600mm mortar
German 420mm howitzer
German 355mm howitzer
German 305mm mortar
Outposts

0 — 2km
0 — 2 miles

MAP 47: OPERATION *BLAU* (I), DRIVE ON VORONEZH, 28 JUNE TO 18 JULY, 1942

Without the benefit of hindsight, blinded by poor strategic intelligence and crippled by massive pathologies and prejudices, Hitler believed both that *Barbarossa* had been more successful than we now know it was and likewise that a 1942 campaign could win World War II for the Third Reich. During Stalin's winter general counteroffensives, the OKH began to develop plans to grab the industrial and resource areas of the lower Volga and the Caucasus in the following summer. The Führer's Directive 41 of 5 April made Operation *Blau* official.[58] By stripping Heeresgruppen Nord and Mitte, Hitler rebuilt much of Heeresgruppe Süd's combat strength. For the campaign Generalfeldmarschall Bock commanded 54 German divisions – 38 infantry, nine panzer and seven motorized infantry – plus 20 Axis divisions – eight Romanian and six each Hungarian and Italian. Stalin expected the assault to aim for Moscow and arranged his defences accordingly. What capability he did have in the south was massed around Izyum and Kharkov, and in any event suffered encirclement and destruction in May (Maps 37–41). The Bryansk and South-western fronts were held by the 13th, 40th, 21st and 28th Armies. For *Blau*, Wehrmacht planners expected Timoshenko to stand fast, become encircled and destroyed just as in 1941. In order to succeed, like *Barbarossa*, the Germans needed every aspect to go their way.

The *Schwerpunkt* in the north belonged to 4. Panzer-Armee under the stalwart Hoth, which during the spring had been transferred from Heeresgruppe Mitte and strengthened and assembled east of Kursk, along with Paulus's 6. Armee, between Kharkov and Belgorod and recovering from its Izyum bridgehead battles.[59] The 2. Armee plus the Hungarians and Romanians had support missions. Delayed by their Izyum counterattacks and the Crimean siege operation, *Blau* kicked off on 28 June with Voronezh the immediate objective in the north. The 40th Army absorbed the brunt of Hoth's blows and collapsed after 48 hours while the 13th Army gave way to the north, allowing 4. Panzer-Armee through. Prodded by the Stavka, the next day Timoshenko launched counterattacks with a pair of new tank corps – 1st and 16th, generally converging on Volovo – with five more tanks corps on the way. Paulus joined the offensive on 30 June, easily levering 21st and

28th Armies out of their positions. By 2 July, Hoth's men had covered half the 100 miles to Voronezh. His southern pincer, XLVIII Panzer-Korps, had reached Stary Oskol, barely 25 miles from Paulus's XL Panzer-Korps at Chernianka; in between these two stood elements of the 40th and 21st Armies. To save the situation, Timoshenko ordered the 4th and 24th Tank Corps against Stary Oskol.

With 4. Panzer-Armee driving ever closer to Voronezh, on 3 July Hitler flew to Bock's headquarters to say he no longer cared about the city but wanted to turn south instead.[60] This latest adjustment lasted barely 24 hours as XLVIII Panzer-Korps reached the Don River just miles from Voronezh on the 4th, but the episode demonstrates Hitler's increasing micromanagement of operations. A compromise plan where 2. Armee would take the city in order to free 4. Panzer-Armee to manoeuvre southwards failed when Infanterie-Division (Mot.) Grossdeutschland captured an intact bridge over the Don at Semiluki. By 5–6 July Hoth was tied down in a costly urban combat when he should have been freewheeling southwards. In Stalin's mind the battle for Voronezh only confirmed his belief that Hitler intended to attack Moscow that summer, albeit indirectly from the far south. The large city proved a tough nut to crack as both sides threw more and more into the fight. Timoshenko had rallied the 40th Army, which made high-value German mechanized units struggle for every block. As if to frustrate *Blau* even more, 4. Panzer-Armee ran low on fuel.

Meanwhile to the south, 6. Armee made steady progress over the steppe but could not achieve a *Kessel*. By 6 July it had reached the Don in a couple of places including a sizeable bridgehead near Korotoyak. More closely aligned with *Blau*'s original purpose, however, Paulus began to veer to the south. His XL Panzer-Korps captured Kamenka and had Rossosh, on the main north-south railway line, on its line of march. Fighting in Voronezh dragged on until 13 July, but the Germans neither captured the whole city nor created a pocket; Timoshenko managed to withdraw his troops north-east over the Voronezh River. The damage had been done to *Blau* at a very early stage when 4. Panzer-Armee became bogged down in a city instead of encircling retreating Red Army forces.

---

58 Führer Directive 45 gave Manstein's 11. Armee the mission of capturing Leningrad once it had conquered the Crimea.

59 On 1 June Hoth and Ruoff swapped command of 4. Panzer-Armee and 17. Armee.

60 Evidently despite the fact that Voronezh played a very large part in Blau's Führer Directive 41.

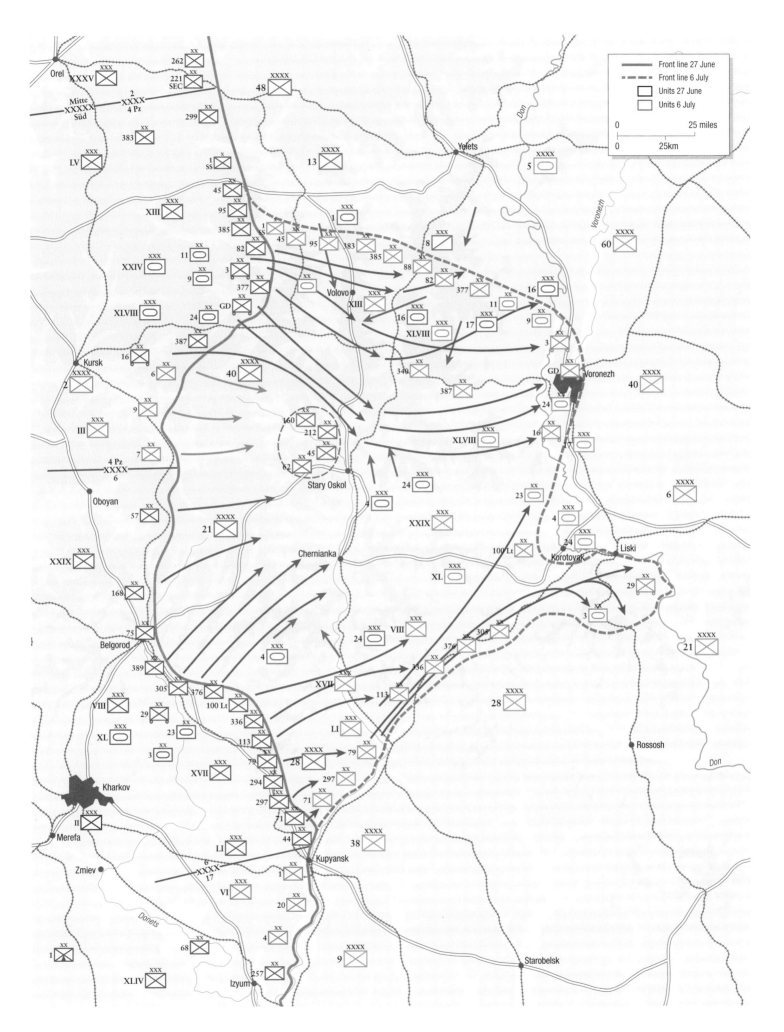

Orel

XXXV
262 XX
221 SEC XX
Mitte
XXXXX 2 XXXX
Süd 4 Pz
383 XX
LV XXX

48 XXXX
299 XX
13 XXXX

1 SS x
45 XX
95 XX
385 XX
1 SS
45 XX
95 XX
383 XX
385 XX
8 XX
XIII XXX
1 XXX
XIII XXX

XIII XXX
11
XXIV XXX
9
82 XX
3 XX
377 XX
GD XX
24 XX
387 XX
Kursk
16 XX
6
40 XXXX
88 XX
82 XX
377 XX
16
11
17
9
3
24
16
17
GD XX
Voronezh
40 XXXX

XLVIII XXX
2 XXXXX
III XXX
9 XX
7 XX
4 Pz XXXX
6
Oboyan
57 XX

160 XX
212 XX
45 XX
62 XX
Stary Oskol
4 XXX
24 XXX
XXIX XXX
349 XX
387 XX
XLVIII XXX
24
16
17
23
4
24
100 Lt
Korotoyak
Liski
29

21 XXXX
XXIX XXX
168 XX
75 XX
Belgorod
389 XX
305 XX
376 XX
100 Lt XX
VIII XXX
29 XX
XL XXX
23 XX
3 XX
XVII XXX
336 XX
113 XX
79 XX
294 XX
297 XX
71 XX
Chernianka
4 XXX
24 XXX
VIII XXX
XVII XXX
113 XX
336 XX
28 XXXX
79 XX
297 XX
71 XX
LI XXX
XL XXX
40 XXX
28 XXXX
3 XX
305 XX
376 XX

Kharkov
II XXX
Merefa
Zmiev
LI XXX
44 XX
VI XXX
1 XX
20 XX
4 XX
6 XXXX
17
Kupyansk
38 XXXX
9 XXXX
Rossosh
Starobelsk

1 XX
68 XX
XLIV XXX
257 XX
Izyum
Donets

Yelets
5 XXXX
60 XXXX
Don
Voronezh

Don

Front line 27 June
Front line 6 July
Units 27 June
Units 6 July
0   25 miles
0   25km

107

MAP 48: OPERATION *BLAU* (II), CLEARING THE DON RIVER BEND – 9–23 JULY, 1942

Two weeks into Operation *Blau*, massive problems could already be seen. Was this the best that Halder and Bock and their staffs could come up with? Their prime striking force, 4. Panzer-Armee, had rushed 100 miles to Voronezh only to have reached a deadly, resource-consuming and momentum-robbing dead end. By the middle of July, Hoth had to pull his army out of the city, restock, turn 90 degrees and move out again. The 6. Armee had a slightly easier task, which was to keep moving forward, albeit at a slightly oblique angle to the right. Now 1. Panzer-Armee and 17. Armee attacked the Southern Front in the Donbas.

With *Blau* I off to such an unsatisfactory start, *Blau* II began on 9 July, earlier than originally planned, with Kleist's panzers still not ready. As planned before, on that same day Heeresgruppe Süd divided into the unimaginatively named Heeresgruppen A and B. Bock retained command of B while Feldmarschall Wilhelm List would lead A. Along the Gulf of Taganrog coast, 17. Armee infantry could do little more than assault stout Red Army Mius River defences, but somehow Kleist's depleted panzers were expected to break through from Lisichansk to Starobelsk on an azimuth to meet Hoth's spearheads coming south. Hitler and Halder had hopes of destroying the bulk of 38th, 9th and 37th Armies in this manner. As happened earlier against Hoth and Paulus, however, the Soviets withdrew before Kleist and Ruoff rather than suffer encirclement. Hitler saw any chance of a *Kessel* slip away. Somebody besides Hitler would take responsibility for this situation, but on 13 July he relieved Bock for bungling *Blau*'s opening gambit and put Weichs in his place at Heeresgruppe B.

A day later, on the 15th, Hoth and Kleist's panzers did indeed meet at Millerovo, where Paulus soon joined them. They had indeed trapped elements of the 9th and 38th Armies, but the catch had been far less than expected. Half the panzers of Hitler's eastern army milled around the steppe in a huge, out-of-fuel and poorly maintained mass.[61] The Führer cast about for a new victim for *Blau* and decided on Rostov,

which Kleist had captured and lost eight months earlier (Map 23). While 2. Armee beat back Soviet counterattacks at Voronezh and 6. Armee and the Hungarian Second Army guarded the middle Don and cautiously pushed east, he concentrated 1. and 4. Panzer-Armeen and 17. Armee against Rostov. In untangling the concentration around Millerovo, the combat trails of the German mechanized divisions looked like a handful of cooked spaghetti noodles tossed on a plate.

The 1. Panzer-Armee took the inside track with Mackensen's III Panzer-Korps leading the way over the steppe, while the heavily reinforced 4. Panzer-Armee covered the outside flank against non-existent Red Army counterattacks. With what fuel and other supplies he could muster, Hoth fanned out to occupy most of the lower Don River and even threw some bridgeheads over to the right bank of the big river. By 19 July, 17. Armee had overcome the Southern Front's Mius line and closed in on Rostov from the west. For a while it looked like List might pull off a sizeable encirclement against portions of the 12th, 37th, 18th, 24th and 56th Armies apparently pinned between Voroshilovgrad and Rostov. The Soviets refused to die in place to no purpose, however, and when the fighting ended on the 26th approximately 85,000 POWs were taken. The 1. and 4. Panzer-Armeen vehicles had moved from Millerovo to the lower Don, an additional 100 miles from their supplies.

Although stripped of XL Panzer-Korps, during the Rostov manoeuvre, Paulus kept moving east and by the third week of July had come close to occupying the great bend of the river. Certainly, if the German high command had kept 4. Panzer-Armee and 6. Armee paired after Millerovo, List could still have taken Rostov and Weichs would have been much closer to Stalingrad in far greater force. Before Rostov fell, but probably two weeks too late, on the 23rd, Hitler issued his Führer Directive 45. It transformed *Blau* into Operation *Braunschweig*, in turn divided into two, non-mutually-supporting halves: Heeresgruppe A's Operation *Edelweiss* would fulfil *Blau*'s original purpose of capturing the Baku and Caucasus oil regions and the Black Sea coast, and Heeresgruppe B's Operation *Fischreiher* henceforth had the task of taking Stalin's city.

---

61 Kleist's panzers especially had not recuperated from May and June battles around Izyum.

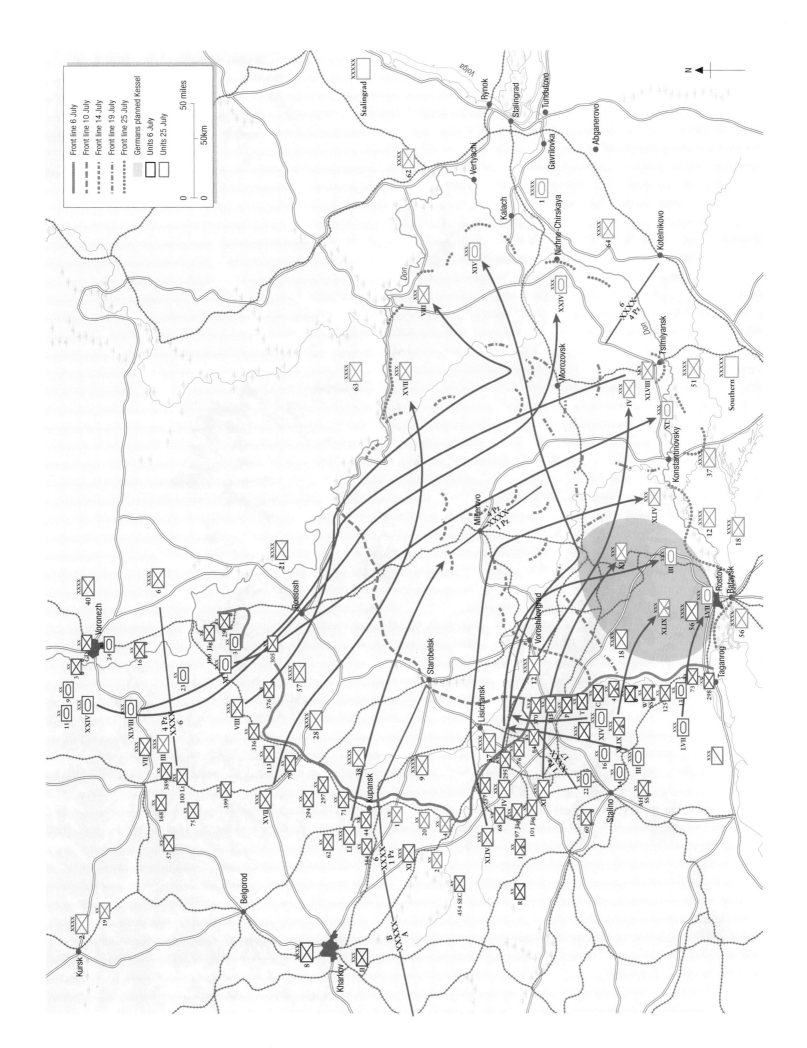

MAP 49: OPERATION *FISCHREIHER*, FINAL DRIVE ON STALINGRAD – 26 JULY TO 30 AUGUST, 1942

Compared to Führer Directive 41, number 45 was a model of clarity, with two army groups given distinct missions. What Hitler wanted was not clear to everyone, however: Hoth seemed to be adrift between List and Weichs, while the Soviets had no idea what the Germans might do next. To deal with any expected Wehrmacht course of action Stalin decided to continue withdrawing, to the Volga and Caucasus if necessary, and evacuating industry to the Urals; the intervening arid steppe would be grudgingly conceded to Hitler. In mid-July the Stavka created the Stalingrad Front out of the 21st, 62nd, 63rd and 64th Armies plus the 1st and 4th Tank Armies under General Lieutenant V. N. Gordov to defend the city.

By the last week of July, 6. Armee had closed up to the Don everywhere except for a Red Army bridgehead at Kalach. Paulus's next step would be to eliminate the enemy there and seize bridges over the Don. His attack began on 26 July and immediately XXIV Panzer-Korps in the south succeeded in splitting the seam between the 62nd and 64th Armies and driving on Nizhne–Chirskaya. In the north the XIV Panzer-Korps likewise broke through the Chir line and came around behind 62nd Army. On the 27th the 1st Tank Army, backing up the 62nd, mounted a counterattack against this northern prong that achieved little. General der Infanterie Gustav von Wietersheim's XIV Panzer-Korps continued to take abuse the next day as 4th Tank Army hit it and neighbouring LI Armee-Korps. At this critical juncture, 6. Armee experienced problems getting ammunition, fuel and other supplies to its spearheads. It looked doubtful whether the army had the strength to take Stalingrad alone.

On the last day of July, Paulus received much-needed support from an unexpected quarter; Hitler changed his mind again and ordered Hoth out of his Konstantinovsky and Tsimlyansk bridgeheads and against Stalingrad's uncovered left flank (a distance of 200 miles for the farthest west units). In a surprise move, 4. Panzer-Armee, now only XI Armee-Korps, XLVIII Panzer-Korps and Romanian VI Corps, dutifully turned 90 degrees north-east, routed the 51st Army in the process and by 2 August began to make contact with Stalingrad's outer defences. Meanwhile Paulus advanced and managed to create a couple of small *Kesseln* within the Kalach

bridgehead. Perhaps combined, the two German armies could capture the city of 600,000.

The Soviets re-organized their defensive scheme and pumped new armies into the region. A defensive line longer than 400 miles was more than one headquarters could reasonably control, so on 4 August the Stavka divided the Stalingrad Front in two, re-naming the southern part the South-western Front under Eremenko. At the same time, along with other new formations, the 66th and 57th Armies began to arrive north and south of the city respectively. During the first week of August on the Aksay River the 64th Army even handed 4. Panzer-Armee and its Romanian allies a sharp reverse.

On 8 August, within the Don bend, XIV and XXIV Panzer-Korps finally joined forces west of Kalach, encircling nine rifle divisions and seven mechanized brigades. Mopping-up operations took until the 16th, but now Paulus stood less than 50 miles from Stalingrad. Covering the last distance to the city would not be easy, however, as 4. Panzer-Armee still struggled against the 64th Army around Abganerovo. To help remedy the disparity in forces, VIII Flieger-Korps transferred north from the Caucasus sector; soon it would be flying out of the Morozovsk airfield. With resistance in the Kalach bridgehead finally broken, Weichs planned his final drive on Stalingrad.

The 4. Panzer-Armee's new attacks near Abganerovo and Tundutovo beginning on 20 August did not fare much better than earlier assaults, however. On the 23rd Paulus's XIV Panzer-Korps on the far north crossed the Don, courtesy of a 195. Infanterie-Division pontoon bridge over the river, raced 60 miles over Vertyachi, and went on to the Volga and the northern Stalingrad suburb of Rynok. Eremenko launched counterattacks here the next day that failed to dislodge the Germans, while Hoth's men finally began to make headway south of the city. To soften up its defenders, the Luftwaffe launched more than 2,000 sorties over 23–24 August. However, Paulus's intended date to capture Stalingrad, the 25th, came and went. On the 30th, Hoth's *Landsers* broke through Red Army defences at Gavrilovka and Weichs ordered Paulus to join in with his infantry. On 2–3 September Eremenko pulled back his defences into Stalingrad proper; the bloody siege was about to begin.

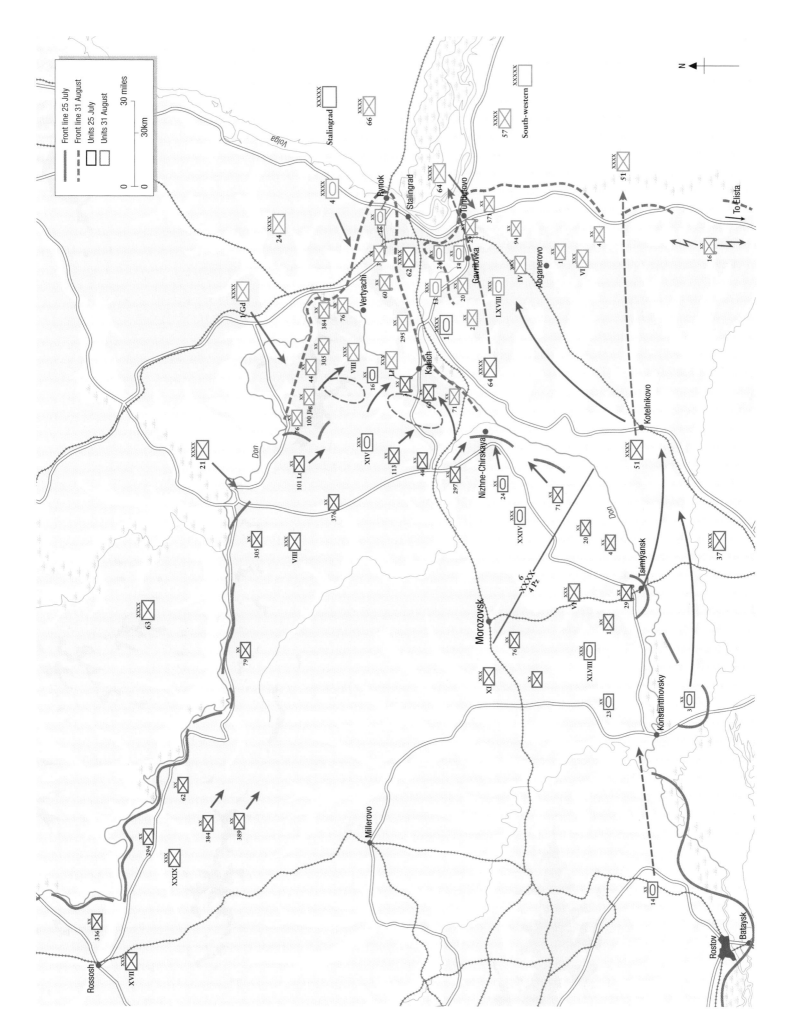

Front line 25 July
Front line 31 August
Units 25 July
Units 31 August

0   30km
0   30 miles

Stalingrad

Volga

Rynok

Stalingrad

Tundutovo

South-western

To Elista

Gavrilovka

Abganerovo

Vertyachi

Kalach

1 Gd

VIII

Lt

Don

Nizhne-Chirskaya

Kotelnikovo

Morozovsk

Tsimlyansk

Konstantinovsky

Millerovo

Rossosh

Rostov

Bataysk

MAP 50: OPERATION *EDELWEISS* (I) 20 JULY TO 10 AUGUST, 1942

Hitler launched the 1942 campaign in order to secure the Baku–Caucasus oil region for Germany (and deprive the USSR of it). According to Führer Directive 41 outlining Operation *Blau*, attacking Stalingrad was only a tactically prudent manoeuvre to shield the left shoulder of the drive to the south-east; simply bringing the city under heavy artillery fire was good enough. That all changed with Directive 45 and Operation *Braunschweig*, where the two objectives became co-equal. With its Operation *Edelweiss*, List's Heeresgruppe A alone had the twin missions of capturing the oil and clearing the Black Sea coast against Budenny's Northern Caucasus Front.

The Wehrmacht plan called for 1. Panzer-Armee to cross the Don, after which 17. Armee would follow and swing south-west toward Krasnodar and the Black Sea in conjunction with a corps crossing from Kerch to Taman. Initially 4. Panzer-Armee had a vague mission between *Braunschweig*'s two army groups, but Hitler soon clarified this and Hoth joined the fight for Stalingrad. Ideally, 1. Panzer-Armee, sweeping clockwise, could crush any defenders between 17. Armee and the mountains and the sea; this would then theoretically leave open the road to Baku.

German units crossed the Don even before the battle for Rostov had concluded.[62] From 20–25 July they established bridgeheads at Nikolsaevskaya (XL Panzer-Korps on 20 July), Melikhovskaya (III Panzer-Korps on 23 July) and Bataysk (LVII Panzer-Korps on 25 July).[63] The 17. Armee crossed over the Don on the 26th. Arrayed against Heeresgruppe A stood the 56th, 18th, 12th, 37th and 51st Armies, but these seemed less steady as one went east. Once south of the Don, the three panzer corps made good time traversing the Kalmyk Steppe, while Red Army countermeasures, such as the attack at Martynovska by two tank brigades against XL Panzer-Korps, could not appreciably slow them. The III Panzer-Korps worked its way upriver in the Manich Valley despite demolished reservoir dams and extensive flooding, while LVII Panzer-Korps approached Salsk, which fell on the 30th. Ruoff's infantry made constant progress due south toward Krasnodar, winning a bridgehead over the Yeye River on the last day of July.

Except for their own logistics problems,[64] little on the open steppe could appreciably slow Kleist's panzer corps. Stavropol fell to the XL Panzer-Korps on 3 August, while three days later III Panzer took Armavir and LVII Panzer took Kropotkin. The III and LVII Panzer-Korps captured Maikop on the evening of the 13th with the help of Luftwaffe CAS. That day German troops recorded temperatures of 125 degrees Fahrenheit in the sun. By 10 August, Geyr von Schweppenburg's men had crossed the Kuma River and captured Piatigorsk. The Germans had now reached the western Caucasus foothills in some force along a broad front.

To the west, 17. Armee and the Romanians moved at a slower pace on foot and horseback. Since the beginning of August, they had been pushing the Soviets south of Krushchevskaya, moving against an enemy without much fight in him. After a week they reached Timoshevskaya, assisted by capturing a number of bridges intact, and kept up the pursuit. Due north of Krasnodar there existed no natural obstacles, but the Germans encountered anti-tank ditches and strong fieldworks about 15 miles from the city. To the east, Red Army troops turned to make a stand on the southern bank of the Kuban River. However, 1. Panzer-Armee units working their way west in the general direction of Maikop, trying to create the hoped-for *Kessel*, threatened to roll up the river line. By 9 August, *Landsers* had penetrated the defences in the north and advanced down the Kuban River toward Krasnodar. By the 10th they had attacked the city from west, north and east as the Soviets retreated into its centre. Serious urban combat ensued, with both road and rail bridges (which the Germans would later need) being demolished. Fighting for the southern parts of the city continued until the next day.

The *Kessel* that the designers of Operation *Edelweiss* hoped to create around Krasnodar and Maikop failed to materialize. The better part of five Soviet armies remained intact between the Sea of Azov and Maikop. In addition, with Luftwaffe assets spread so thin over the huge theatre of war, Black Sea Fleet freedom of movement along the coast went unchallenged. For phase II of *Edelweiss* 17. Armee had the mission of clearing the Black Sea littoral all to itself. Kleist turned east toward the oil wells.

---

62 Some consider the area south and east of the Don River to be Asia, yet call Mount Elbrus, 300 miles south-east of Rostov, 'the tallest mountain in Europe'.

63 Before turning toward Stalingrad, Hoth detached XL Panzer-Korps to Kleist.

64 During these operations the German war diary often uses phrases such as 'with his last drops of fuel General Breith…'

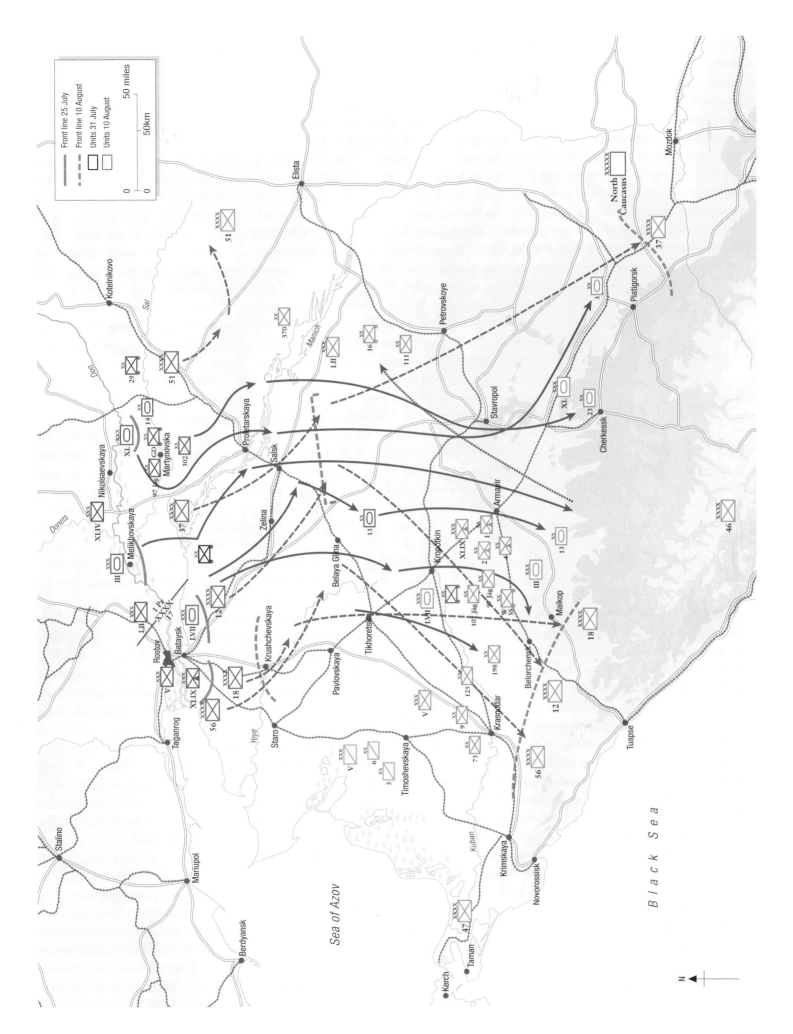

MAP 51: OPERATION *EDELWEISS* (II) 11 AUGUST TO 15 NOVEMBER, 1942

During Phase I of Operation *Edelweiss* Heeresgruppe A claimed over 300,000 POWs captured, plus nearly 2,400 guns and more than 500 tanks destroyed. However, with its failure to create a decisive *Kessel* in the relatively open country around Krasnodar–Tikhoretsk, in Phase II it would face two very difficult, distinct battles in the passes and ridges of the Caucasus and in the immense steppes before Baku. Both would be rather straightforward; movement restrained in the first by severe terrain, in the second by limited supplies. Meanwhile, during the past year Stalin had demonstrated that he had learned to choose more carefully where to retreat and where to make a stand.

BATTLES FOR THE BLACK SEA COAST

Over the Caucasus passes, Ruoff had V and XLIV Armee-Korps attack toward Tuapse and XLIX Gebirgs-Korps attack toward Sukhumi.[65] With V Armee-Korps clearing Krasnodar until 14 August and XLIV Armee-Korps still marching across the steppe, from the 11th to the 16th LVII Panzer-Korps attempted to rush the oilfields centred on Neftyanaya, but could not overcome the Red Army defenders. To the south, by mid-month 1st Gebirgs-Division troops fought their way to Teberda on the Sukhumi Military Road, but would advance little more. While the Romanians endured hard combat on the Kuban Peninsula, the remainder of 17. Armee found it very tough going in the rough terrain of the Neftyanaya oil region.

Three weeks into August, the German high command had serious doubts about the further prospects for the western half of *Edelweiss*, either in the highlands south of Krasnodar or the alpine passes above Sukhumi. Their personnel shortages compounded by casualties (many from non-combat causes) and inadequate logistics, added to determined Soviet resistance enabled by naval mobility, all combined to frustrate the enterprise. Following Jodl's 7 September visit to the Stalino headquarters of Heeresgruppe A, Hitler's lack of faith in Feldmarschall List was complete. He voiced concerns that the Caucasus campaign required new leadership and when, two days later List requested to be relieved, Hitler immediately agreed. The dictator took over personal command of the army group on the 10th.[66]

Despite this new leadership and the capture of Novorossisk on 10 September, on the main front opposite Tuapse every small German advance over the next six weeks was hard won. Finally on 26 September the XLIV Armee-Korps achieved a breakthrough on the main mountain road. Although 18th Army gave up some ground, it soon recovered and re-established a coherent defence. On 25 October, new army chief of staff General der Infanterie Kurt Zeitzler returned from his visit to 17. Armee and gave a very pessimistic report. This basically marks the end of any further German offensive manoeuvres in the Tuapse area.

BATTLES FOR THE GROZNY OILFIELDS

By the second week of August, Kleist reached Piatigorsk and prepared to move on the Terek River, one of the last natural obstacles barring the road to the Caspian Sea and also where the Trans-Caucasus Front intended to make a stand. Around Elista in the vast Kalmyk Steppe, his LII Armee-Korps attempted to mind the massive gap separating 1. and 4. Panzer-Armee while harassing the enemy wherever possible.

On 25 August 1. Panzer-Armee moved out and, discovering a bridge over the Lenin Canal, XL Panzer-Korps captured Mozdok. With strong Red Army Air Force CAS backing them, the defenders showed few signs of weakening. Nevertheless, by the end of the month III Panzer-Korps' advanced guards reached the Terek River at Isherskaya. They created a bridgehead on 2 September, but it would be the 20th before the Germans crossed the river in any strength. Reacting to Hitler's obsession with Caucasus passes and roads, toward the end of the month III Panzer-Korps diverted toward Ordzhonikidze, the logistics hub for the Red Army's Caucasus operations. Such was its disastrous logistics situation that 1. Panzer-Armee required another month to accumulate supplies for further assaults. When these were finally launched during the last week of October, they achieved only modest success before losing momentum. By early November, the 9th and 44th Armies had built up enough strength to seriously challenge the Wehrmacht and initiate their own counterattacks. The Germans were on the move again by mid-month, when winter weather and the impending Soviet counteroffensive at Stalingrad demanded all of their attention. To deflect possible criticism of his own leadership of *Edelweiss* over the previous two months, Hitler handed over command of Heeresgruppe A to Kleist.

---

65 Some sources refer to XLIV Armee-Korps as a 'Jäger' corps as it had 97. and 101. Jäger Divisions assigned.

66 At the same time Hitler floated the idea that new blood in the army chief of staff position might be needed, marking the beginning of the end for Halder, who was replaced on 24 September.

Front line 31 August
Front line 25 October
Units 31 August
Units 25 October

50 miles
50km

North
Caucasus

Transcaucasus

Grozny

Ordzhonikidze

XXXX 44
XX 10 Gd
Gruppe
XL von Bodenhausen
13
3
111 Mozdok Ishcherskaya
XX
370 LII 111 11 Gd 9
0
13
23 370
Gruppe
Steinhauer
0 2
3 37
Piatigorsk

Elista

94 1 4
VI 16
LII

Petrovskoye

Kotelnikovo

Stavropol

Cherkessk
23

Teberda
XLIX

Sukhumi

46

Armavir

13

Proletarskaya
Salsk

Nikolsaevskaya
Martynovska

Zelina

Belaya Glina

Kropotkin

Maikop
XLIX

Sea of Azov

Stalino

Mariupol

Berdyansk

Taganrog
Rostov
Bataysk

Tikhoretsk

Pavlovskaya

Krushchevskaya

Staro

Timoshevskaya

Krasnodar

Krimskaya

Kuban

Novorossisk

Kerch
VII
Taman
47

Black Sea

LVII
Belorchensk
XLIV
Neftyanaya
101 Jäg
97
46
W
SS
97 Jäg
Gruppe
Lanz
198
101 Jäg
18 Tuapse
125
125
198
56
9
V
13
5
6
9
47

N

MAP 52: STALINGRAD (I) – 14–26 SEPTEMBER, 1942

There are very few logical reasons that Stalingrad should have attracted such attention. It was an administrative centre with a couple of good-sized factories but otherwise a third-rate city, even by the standards of the USSR at the time. Unfortunately we may never know what drew Hitler to sacrifice an entire army there, so are left to speculate.

During the first days of September, Weichs' troops neared Stalingrad and reached the Volga River to the north and south. Hoth definitely played the more aggressive role, as the field marshal kept prodding Paulus to attack. On the 3rd Eremenko withdrew into a defensive ring only a few miles from the built-up areas (Map 49). To deny the Wehrmacht troops any rest, the Soviets launched attacks whenever and wherever they could, including against vulnerable Hungarian and Italian positions upriver along the Don. On 7 September, LI Armee-Korps under General der Artillerie Walther von Seydlitz-Kreuzbach, destined to be Paulus's hammer at Stalingrad, reached Gumrak, site of a critical airfield half a dozen miles from the city. Meanwhile, on the 12th Eremenko consolidated his hold on the defensive effort, replacing the unsteady General Lieutenant A. I. Lopatin atop the 62nd Army with General Lieutenant V. I. Chuikov and cramming into the threatened area every formation the Stavka sent.

Hitler had demanded that 6. Armee capture Stalingrad by 15 September and was furious at Paulus's perceived delays. On the 11th the general briefed him at the Führer's Werwolf headquarters at Vinnitsa concerning plans to take the city. Paulus would attack with two 'shock groups', aiming for the spot on the right bank where the Volga ferry-boats landed men and materiel, opposite Krasnaya Slobada, site of Eremenko's headquarters and a key logistics base. Hoth would simultaneously assault the 64th Army to the south. The relatively fresh Germans had an initial numerical advantage of 3:1 in men and 6:1 in AFVs, while the Luftwaffe dominated the skies.

The German attack began at 0630 on 14 September and made good progress in the centre and south. By noon they had progressed through the suburbs and into the city centre, using artillery to kick Chuikov from his command post on the Mamayev *kurgan* (burial mound, also known as hill 102) a couple of hours later. The 4. Panzer-Armee assault

parties reached the Volga in numerous places and approached the large grain elevators. Both the central and southern train stations seemed in danger of falling to the Germans. The 71. and 76. Infanterie-Divisionen made spectacular advances into the city centre and threatened to chase Chuikov out of another command post. Eremenko rushed reinforcements including the 13th Guards Division across the broad river and into the fight. In the south the battle stabilized with the Red Army still in possession of the grain elevator. On the 15th, the central railway station changed hands numerous times, but by nightfall it too remained in Soviet possession.

Stalingrad was in real danger of falling on 14 September when Hoth's 24. Panzer-Division reached the Volga and then wheeled north, threatening to roll up both the 64th and 62nd Armies. A day later, Stalin dispatched two brigades across the river to further secure the ferry-boat staging area and to halt the panzers. The latter, the 92nd Naval Infantry Brigade, arguably saved the day. For his part, Hitler gave Paulus overall control of the Stalingrad battle, detaching the XLVII Panzer-Korps from Hoth. Given the inexperience of Paulus contrasted with Hoth's excellent field leadership throughout the first three years of World War II, this was a curious, if not decisive, decision. By the 18th, 71. Infanterie-Division indeed forced Chuikov out of his Pushkin Street command bunker, while the 13th Guards almost ceased to exist. Eremenko was becoming desperate, and 24 hours later began launching low-odds counterattacks everywhere.

With both sides nearing exhaustion, by the third week of September the battle hung in the balance. As of the 21st, only the 92nd Naval Infantry remained south of the Tsaritsa River. In the centre, the Soviets held only a few slivers of land right on the Volga banks. They had lost many ferry-boat staging areas, absolutely critical to keeping the defence of Stalingrad going. Desperate counterattacks on the 22nd, they failed to lever the Germans off their hard-won positions. On 22 September, troops belonging to XLVIII Panzer-Korps captured the grain elevator and the following day the 92nd Brigade withdrew to the far bank of the Volga. Paulus's men had suffered grievously as well, but appeared on the verge of victory.

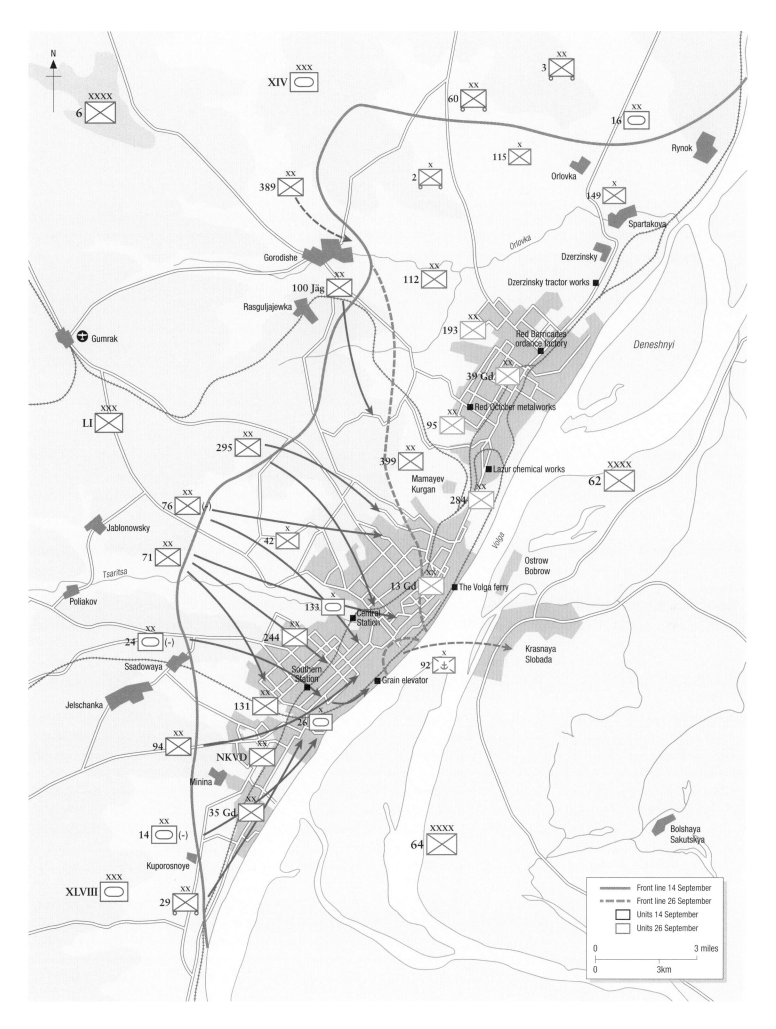

N

6 XXXX

XIV XXX

3 XX

60 XX

16 XX

Rynok

115 x

Orlovka

2 x

389 XX

Orlovka

149 x

Spartakova

Gorodishe

Dzerzinsky

100 Jäg XX

112 XX

Dzerzinsky tractor works

Rasguljajewka

Deneshnyi

193 XX

Red Barricades
ordance factory

Gumrak

39 Gd. XX

LI XXX

Red October metalworks

95 XX

295 XX

399 XX

Lazur chemical works

Mamayev
Kurgan

62 XXXX

76 XX (-)

284 XX

Jablonowsky

42 x

Volga

71 XX

Ostrow
Bobrow

Tsaritsa

13 Gd XX

The Volga ferry

Poliakov

133 x

Central
Station

244 XX

24 XX (-)

Krasnaya
Slobada

Ssadowaya

92 x

Southern
Station

Grain elevator

Jelschanka

131 XX

26 x

94 XX

NKVD XX

Minina

35 Gd XX

14 XX (-)

64 XXXX

Kuporosnoye

Bolshaya
Sakutskya

XLVIII XXX

29 XX

	Front line 14 September
	Front line 26 September
	Units 14 September
	Units 26 September

0   3 miles

0   3km

117

MAP 53: STALINGRAD (II)
27 SEPTEMBER TO 7 OCTOBER, 1942

Up to 26 September, the Germans had made significant progress against the Soviet defenders of Stalingrad but could not land the knockout blow. Their main effort had cleared much of the administrative and residential central and southern sections, causing Paulus to declare the city secured. Chuikov's forces were severely pressed in the process, to the point where he required a change in tactics; he admonished his subordinate leaders against committing full companies or battalions and instead warned them to operate in small groups using mostly close-in weapons. If they hugged Paulus's troops as closely as possible, this would largely negate the Wehrmacht advantage in large-calibre guns and Luftwaffe CAS.

Both sides planned to take the offensive on 27 September, but while the 62nd Army could do little more than launch ineffective small assaults, Paulus had prepared Phase II of his own offensive. The 6. Armee would clear the southern portion of the city, reach the River Volga in the critical central portion where the ferry-boats landed, and he would open operations in the city's north, which had been quiet for the previous weeks. By the end of the first day, LI Armee-Korps (71., 76. and 94. Infanterie-Divisionen) had indeed captured Stalingrad's centre, except for a small toehold where the Tsaritsa River emptied into the Volga. Other German units attacked the Red October workers' housing settlement.[67] On the 28th, Chuikov set the 95th and 284th Rifle Divisions against the Mamayev *kurgan* and although the hill changed hands many times, Red Army troops could not maintain their gains. Paulus changed his approach on 29 September, shifting his *Schwerpunkt* from the frustrating task of city fighting and instead attacked the bulge on either side of the Orlovka River, sticking out approximately five miles west into the German lines. Chuikov reinforced the area but could not halt the XIV Panzer-Korps from nipping off the salient at its base, although he successfully evacuated most units from impending encirclement.

As September came to a close, Paulus had constricted 62nd Army into a small bridgehead anchored on the Dzerzinsky Tractor Works, Red Barricade ordnance factory and Red October steel mill and their surrounding workers' settlements. From the relative safety of the Volga islands and the left bank, Stalin created an artillery reserve to support the defenders. The Stavka continued to rush reinforcements to the embattled bridgehead, but in this new area the ferry-boats had much more trouble getting safely across than previously down river. Nevertheless, by 1 October numerical advantage had begun to tilt in the Soviets' favour as more than ten divisions arrived during the second half of September. Paulus continued to drive his men forward and on that same day it looked as if they might take the Red October factory. Luftwaffe sorties averaged nearly 1,000 per day. As for Chuikov, he narrowly escaped death on 2 October when Stukas destroyed his command bunker with the general still inside and set nearby oil tanks aflame.

The Soviets somehow managed to get more new troops and weaponry across the Volga, while the anaemic German formations somehow managed to advance deeper into Stalingrad's northern industrial heart. The only Wehrmacht units available to reinforce Paulus were those manning the Volga upriver from Stalingrad, and this was still dangerous territory sprinkled with Soviet bridgeheads on the German bank that had been bypassed in Hitler's haste to reach the city. The patently unreliable Romanian Third Army was soon to replace these German units so they could join Paulus. Urged by Weichs, 6. Armee launched yet another series of attacks against the three principal remaining factories on 4 October. Paulus employed five divisions abreast on a 3-mile frontage while the 193rd and 308th Rifle Divisions took the brunt of the punishment. Fighting raged for two days until, with most infantry companies reporting fewer than 100 men, Paulus ordered a pause on the 6th. The Germans renewed their efforts on the following day, but with the loss of almost four battalions of troops in a matter of hours the general again temporarily called off the assaults. It was beginning to look like the 62nd Army just might outlast 6. Armee.

67 Most of the main industrial enterprises had a housing development with a corresponding name, so this settlement housed workers of the Red October steel plant.

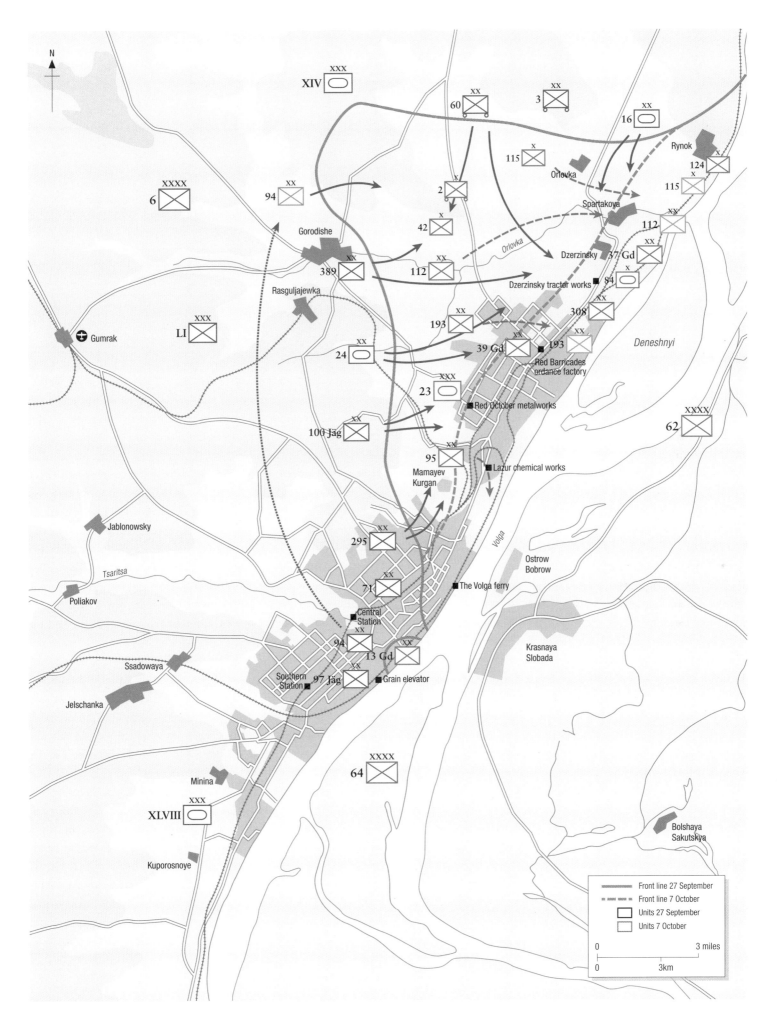

N

XIV ⬚XXX

60 XX
3 XX
16 ⬚XX

Rynok

94 XX
115 X
Orlovka
124 X

6 XXXX

2 X
Spartakova
115 X

Gorodishe

42 X
112 XX
112 XX
37 Gd XX

Rasguljajewka

389 XX
Dzerzinsky
84 X

Gumrak

LI XXX

Dzerzinsky tractor works

193 XX
308 XX

Deneshnyi

24 XX
39 Gd XX
193
193 XX

23 XXX
Red Barricades ordance factory

Red October metalworks

62 XXXX

100 Jäg XX

95 XX
Lazur chemical works

Mamayev Kurgan

295 XX
Volga

Jablonowsky

Ostrow Bobrow

Tsaritsa
71 XX
The Volga ferry

Poliakov
Central Station

Krasnaya Slobada

Ssadowaya
94 XX
13 Gd XX

Jelschanka
Southern Station
97 Jäg XX
Grain elevator

Minina
64 XXXX

XLVIII ⬚XXX

Kuporosnoye

Bolshaya Sakutskiya

———— Front line 27 September
----- Front line 7 October
⬚ Units 27 September
⬚ Units 7 October

0   3 miles
0   3km

MAP 54: STALINGRAD (III) – 14–29 OCTOBER, 1942

Toward mid-October Paulus ordered another pause in German attacks. Yeremenko took the opportunity to have Chuikov's men launch new attacks near the tractor factory where advances were measured in 200–300-yard increments. He could afford to be patient: just a few days earlier the Stavka had informed him of the upcoming counteroffensive that would soon hit the entire Army Group B front, paying special attention to Paulus's exposed salient. On the other hand, Germany's tense strategic situation forced Hitler to issue his Operations Order No. 1, halting all Wehrmacht offensive operations except those in Stalingrad and the eastern Caucasus.

Nevertheless, 6. Armee accumulated enough forces to launch its third major attack against the city on 14 October, this time five divisions aimed in the direction of the tractor factory with four specialized sapper companies in the lead. The 14. Panzer-Division managed to mass nearly 200 AFVs to drive over the 37th Guards Rifle Division and down the Mechetka River. It bypassed the Dzerzinsky facility, reached the banks of the Volga, splitting 62nd Army in two, and then pivoted south toward the Red October factory. The 14th surrounded the tractor factory on three sides, but on that day 3,000 men from both sides died in the fighting. At the same time the Volga ferry-boats set a new one-day record for transferring reinforcements across the river: 3,500 men. Weichs could not hope to compete with these figures. On 15 October Paulus added 305. Infanterie-Division to the 14. Panzer and 94. Infanterie-Divisionen's tractor factory battle, which seemed to be tipping the fight in his favour, and put his *Landser*s within a couple of hundred yards of Chuikov's latest command post. The 14. Panzer and 94. Infanterie Divisionen concentrated against the ordnance factory. But 16 October saw another German pause, and while Chuikov received some reinforcement Paulus got none. On 18 October 14. Panzer and 389. Infanterie-Divisionen moved out again, nearing the brick furnaces, the Lazur chemical works and 'tennis racket' railway yards. With this Chuikov authorized 308th Rifle Division to execute his army's first retreat of the Stalingrad battle.

During the fourth week of the month Paulus concentrated on the Red Barricades and Red October factories, using what strength he had remaining. The troops of 6. Armee made significant progress into the heart of both installations by 23 October, occupying more than half of each. A 64. Armee supporting attack begun that same day south of the city against 4. Panzer-Armee failed to significantly distract the Germans. All around Stalingrad divisions of both armies suffered tremendous casualties, yet somehow maintained cohesion despite reporting personnel numbers of only a few hundred souls. As Wehrmacht units closed in on the Volga in more places, they were able to take ferry-boats under direct fire, making river transit very hazardous. Red Army units that did cross the river were obliterated almost as soon as they reached the right bank, but in numerous places a rifle company here or there served to save the situation. Paulus committed the 79. Infanterie-Division to the fight over the Red October. On the 25th gun boats of the Soviet Volga Flotilla joined the battle, contributing to turning the Germans back in places.

The 25 October also marked 14. Panzer-Division's final assault on Red Barricade factory, which it finally captured two days later. On the 29th, 16. Panzer and 94. Infanterie Divisionen captured the Spartakovka suburb (on the far north of Stalingrad) from two brigades, reaching the Volga yet again and isolating another Soviet grouping at Rynok. The 39th Guards Rifle Division defending the steel mill had been divided into three small parts. Everywhere along the river at the end of the month 62nd Army units had been reduced to maintaining thin toeholds only a couple of hundred yards from being shoved into the Volga. At this point, however, Paulus could ask no more from his battered troops, although they would push on in a limited fashion for another fortnight. Weichs had already scoured the army group for all the German reinforcements he could spare. Already on the 6th Army's deep flanks, the Italian, Hungarian and Romanian units noticed a troubling increase in aggressive Soviet activity.

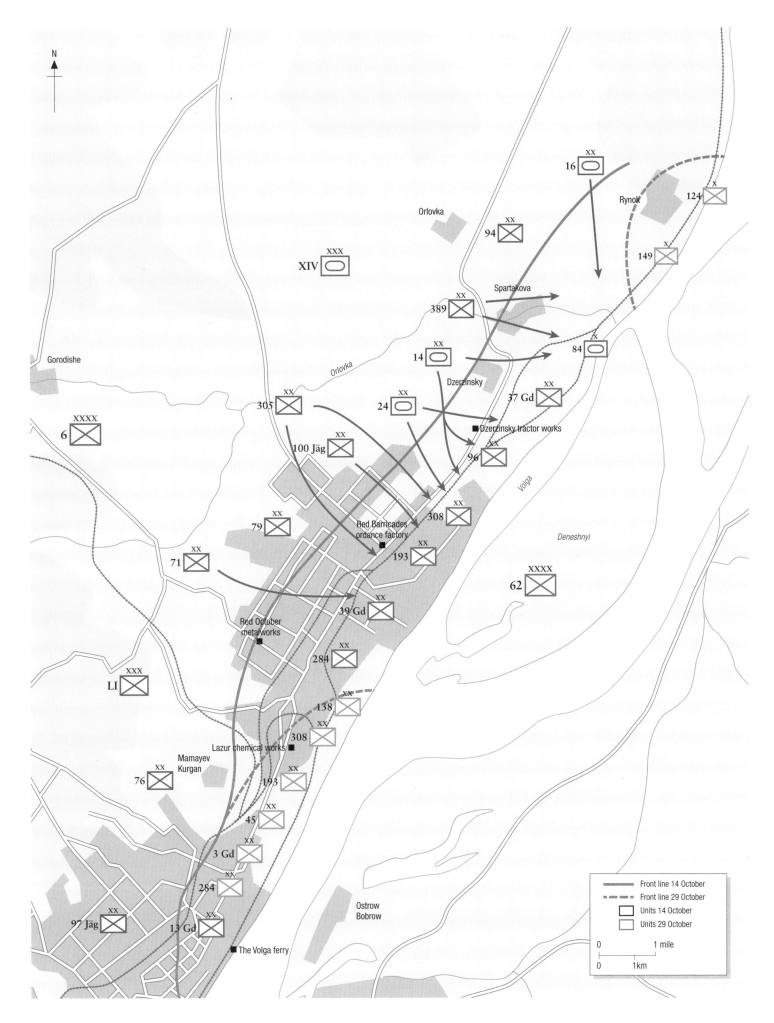

N

6 XXXX

Gorodishe

XIV XXX

Orlovka

94 XX

16 XX

Rynok

124 X

149 X

Orlovka

305 XX

389 XX

Spartakova

14 XX

84 X

Dzerzinsky

24 XX

37 Gd XX

100 Jäg XX

■ Dzerzinsky tractor works

96 XX

Volga

79 XX

308 XX

Red Barricades ordance factory ■

71 XX

193 XX

Deneshnyi

Red October metalworks ■

39 Gd XX

62 XXXX

LI XXX

284 XX

138 XX

308 XX

Lazur chemical works ■

76 XX

Mamayev Kurgan

193 XX

45 XX

3 Gd XX

284 XX

97 Jäg XX

13 Gd XX

■ The Volga ferry

Ostrow Bobrow

	Front line 14 October
	Front line 29 October
□	Units 14 October
□	Units 29 October

0 — 1 mile

0 — 1km

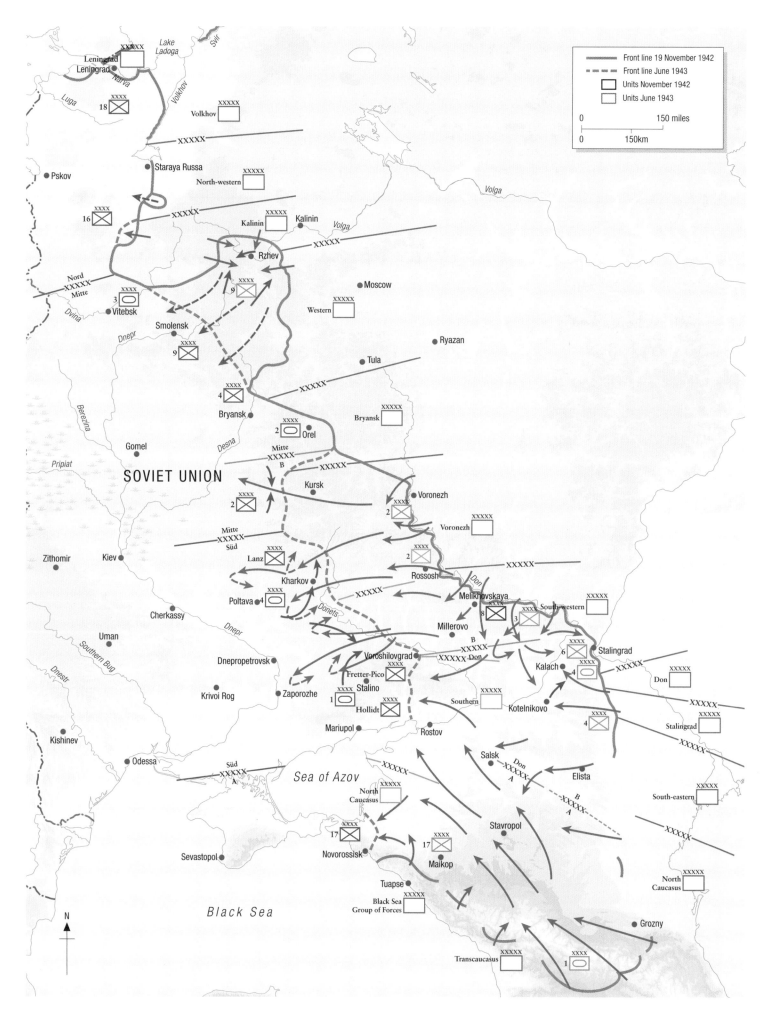

Lake Ladoga

Svir

Leningrad
Leningrad
XXXXX

Narva

Luga

18 XXXX

Volkhov
XXXXX

Volga

Pskov

Staraya Russa

North-western
XXXXX

XXXXX

16 XXXX

Kalinin XXXXX
Kalinin

Volga

Nord
XXXXX
Mitte

3 XXXX
Vitebsk

9 XXXX

Rzhev

Moscow

Dvina

Smolensk

9 XXXX

Western
XXXXX

Dnepr

Ryazan

Tula

4 XXXX

XXXXX

Bryansk XXXXX

Bryansk

Gomel

Desna

Mitte
XXXXX
B

2 XXXX
Orel

Pripiat

SOVIET UNION

Kursk

2 XXXX

XXXXX

Voronezh

2 XXXX

Berezina

Mitte
XXXXX
Süd

Lanz XXXX

Voronezh
XXXXX

Zithomir

Kiev

Kharkov

2 XXXX

XXXXX

Rossosh

Don

XXXXX

Poltava 4 XXXX

Donets

Melikhovskaya

South-western
XXXXX

Cherkassy

Dnepr

Millerovo

8 XXXX

3 XXXX

Uman

B
XXXXX
Don

6 XXXX
Stalingrad

Southern Bug

Dnepropetrovsk

Voroshilovgrad

XXXXX Don

Kalach
4 XXXX

Don
XXXXX

Dnestr

Krivoi Rog

Fretter-Pico XXXX

Zaporozhe

1 XXXX
Stalino

Hollidt XXXX

Southern
XXXXX

Kotelnikovo

4 XXXX

Stalingrad
XXXXX

Kishinev

Mariupol

Rostov

Salsk
Don
XXXXX
A

Elista

South-eastern
XXXXX

Odessa

Süd
XXXXX
A

Sea of Azov

XXXXX

North
Caucasus
XXXXX

B
XXXXX
A

17 XXXX

17 XXXX

Stavropol

North
Caucasus
XXXXX

Sevastopol

Novorossisk

Maikop

Tuapse

Black Sea
Group of Forces
XXXXX

Grozny

Black Sea

N

Transcaucasus
XXXXX

1 XXXX

Front line 19 November 1942
Front line June 1943
Units November 1942
Units June 1943

0   150 miles
0   150km

CHAPTER 4
SOVIET WINTER COUNTEROFFENSIVES, 1942–43

In mid-October 1942 General der Panzertruppen Friedrich Paulus, the German commander at Stalingrad, said he would capture the city within a month. The ten reserve armies that the Soviets had created that summer and had concentrated largely intact around the city and its periphery would dispute that claim. This time the Stavka made reasonable objectives commensurate with Red Army doctrine, leadership and skills; all three of these had evolved markedly over the preceding year and a half. It also concentrated its initial blows against the suspect Romanians on Paulus's flanks. Throughout the summer the Soviet high command had remained focused on an eventual counteroffensive despite Hitler's apparent successes. Operation *Uranus*, which began on 19 November, aimed at encircling Paulus by exploiting his extended and weak flanks. The Red Army enjoyed an overall 2:1 superiority, with overwhelming advantages in critical locales. For its part, the Wehrmacht knew of this vulnerability, but fell victim to both its own wishful thinking and typically abysmal intelligence, helped by skilled enemy disinformation. Of course, Hitler had no alternative; by 1942–43 his understrength coalition had to fight on the cheap in nearly every theatre. Anthony Beevor considers Paulus's worst tactical error to be placing his mechanized divisions, 16. and 24. Panzer-Divisionen and 3. and 60. Infanterie-Divisionen (Mot.), deep in Stalingrad's *Rattenkrieg* rather than holding them back as a mobile reserve.

Romanian armies on either side of Stalingrad took the worst of the blunt force trauma that day begun by a 3,500-gun barrage. Soviet units generally enjoyed success even where they encountered the occasional German unit. Along the Don River front the attackers overcame Axis resistance by evening and passed mechanized exploitation elements through the breakthrough infantry. In the south they required two days to cautiously break into the open country. Approximately 48 hours later, mechanized spearheads from both sides met at Sovetsky in the steppe between the Don and Volga Rivers. They cut off a third of a million Axis soldiers in 22 divisions.[68] So great was the surprise that Hitler was in Bavaria at the annual celebration of the 1923 Nazi Putsch and his military headquarters was afraid to act in his absence. At first he directed the Wehrmacht's reactions from his Alpine retreat. When he did return to his command post on the day before the trap slammed shut, he resorted to the defence that had seemingly served him so well the previous winter at Moscow: stand fast. Initially Paulus had no

68   At first Paulus was not inside the pocket; he actually flew back to Stalingrad and eventual captivity.

organized defence to his rear, so he had to create it on the fly. The Führer re-organized various forces outside the pocket in view of the current dire realities. To the newly created Heeresgruppe Don under Manstein he gave the twin missions of stabilizing the defence and organizing a relief of the encirclement. Fortunately for the Wehrmacht, the Red Army achieved only a few breakthroughs but little in the way of penetrations. The Soviets made accomplishing the first task easier by concentrating on the inner encirclement rather than expanding the outer. But Heeresgruppe Don would have to accomplish its second task without the assistance of Paulus, who was prohibited from leaving Stalingrad and did not have the strength to fight his way out of the trap, even if Hitler had allowed it. Neither did other German forces fight their way into the pocket; from 12–21 December two panzer corps allotted the mission as part of Operation *Wintergewitter* could not get closer than 25 miles. There were two main reasons for the relief effort's failure: proper reactions and stubborn resistance by the Red Army, and Hitler's curious refusal – given the emotional value he attached to Stalin's city – to release available mobile assets to the endeavour. He would repeat this error in Normandy.

The Stavka then ordered the overall co-ordinator of *Uranus*, General Lieutenant A. M. Vasilevski, to build upon his success by keeping up the pressure on the Germans. His solution was Operation *Saturn*, an expansion of the Stalingrad bulge that included the destruction of the Italian army manning the Don, upriver from the now nonexistent Romanians. The renewed offensive's goal was Rostov and its numerous railway connections, plus the extermination of all Germans to the south-east: Heeresgruppe A still hugging the Caucasus foothills, plus the new Heeresgruppe Don. But the size of Paulus's garrison far exceeded Soviet estimates and would prove a tough, time-consuming nut to crack. The poor results of Operation *Mars* near Rzhev (see below) and the Wehrmacht attack to relieve Stalingrad also gave the Soviet leadership cause to hesitate. After two weeks of debates, Stalin's high command downgraded the plan to *Little Saturn*, basically expanding Stalingrad's outer encirclement. Earlier objectives were considered overly ambitious, especially given the forces tied down reducing the stubborn Stalingrad pocket. The fact that this was a hastily planned attack was demonstrated by the relatively slow *Little Saturn*; it took troops from 16–20 December to break through the Italian positions and create a gap 100 miles wide. Penetrating the Italians' second line defences caused high losses, while freewheeling mechanized troops captured airfields critical to the Luftwaffe's hard pressed resupply efforts. During the first half of December, the XLVIII Panzer-Korps had been fighting a tactical battle along the Chir River against the 5th Tank Army, so was unable to address the operational threat posed by *Little Saturn* when that offensive hit. But despite that, dealing with German ground and resurgent air forces throughout the sector was even more expensive and the operation came to a halt by year's end.

During late January the situation inside the Stalingrad pocket went from bad to worse. Exhaustion, starvation and Red Army pounding decimated the isolated outpost, which nevertheless exacted a severe toll on the would-be liberators. Paulus's remaining large airfield fell on 24 January, 1943 while Red Army units split the pocket into two parts on

the 26th. Paulus surrendered a week later. Casualties amounted to a quarter of a million Axis and twice as many Soviets. Outside on the main front, the Stavka ordered new attacks along the Don farther upriver for the second half of January on either side of Voronezh. These assaults smashed one Hungarian army south of the city and a fortnight later one German army to the north. Other Red Army formations pressed on Rostov, the last escape route of Heeresgruppe A, still hugging the Caucasus in dangerously exposed positions. From Voronezh through Rostov to the Caucasus foothills, single panzer or motorized infantry divisions were often all that stood between minor and major disaster. Stalin expected German resistance to experience total failure at any moment.

Decisive success evaded the Soviets, however, as they suffered overstretch in the form of combat losses, breakdowns in logistic support, nonexistent reserves and insufficient planning time. Meanwhile, the Germans regained their footing. In December and January they had managed to reinforce the southern sector with over 25 divisions. Just as Manstein stabilized the front and created his own counterattack reserve, the Stavka planned to keep up the pressure with two more offensives. Axes at right angles would aim south-east for Mariupol – Operation *Gallop* – and north-east for Kharkov – Operation *Star*. If these succeeded, the advance would continue to the great bend of the Dnepr, and in a best-case scenario, they would throw a bridgehead over the massive river. Finishing before the impending spring *rasputitsa*, which usually arrived in March, gave the Soviets a sense of urgency.

After much German dithering while Hitler reconciled his desire to keep attacking toward the Caucasus oil region with the conflicting realities of Stalingrad, on 21 January he finally gave Heeresgruppe A permission to evacuate the steppe beyond the Don. After sloughing off forces to maintain a forlorn beachhead on the Kuban, barely five divisions escaped through Rostov. These joined other Wehrmacht formations, including 100,000 troops (minus their equipment) amazingly airlifted from the Taman garrison, creating a viable defence on the Mius River. In the *Gallop/Star* sectors, the Soviets enjoyed initial success until two panzer divisions at Slavyansk caused a significant change of plans. In response to this German resistance, the Stavka reoriented Operation *Gallop* away from Mariupol on the Sea of Azov and instead toward the Dnepr. To the north Operation *Star* continued unabated, liberating Kursk on 8 February, Kharkov (temporarily) the following week and creating a very deep penetration of German lines. However, four developments soon favoured the Wehrmacht. Firstly, its various headquarters in the area were consolidated into a new Heeresgruppe Süd, again under Manstein; secondly the Germans had conducted a fairly orderly retreat from Rostov, Voroshilovgrad and points north without tremendous losses; thirdly sizeable reinforcements, including panzers and motorized infantry, began to arrive in the region from the west; and fourthly Soviet overstretch was about to raise its ugly head again.

Hitler flew to Manstein's Zaporozhe headquarters on 17 February for a 48-hour visit, probably to relieve the field marshal. Only 36 miles of undefended, frozen grain fields stood between Red Army tanks and the dictator. However, the Führer ended up freeing large panzer and

Luftwaffe elements while backing an audacious plan to strike a counterblow against the dangerously overextended Soviet spearheads. Oblivious to these developments, the Stavka shifted triumphal but battered forces from Stalingrad to the Moscow region to launch a revived *Mars*-type offensive that had as its final objective Smolensk and the upper Dnepr. However, Manstein's attack began with significant Luftwaffe CAS the day after Hitler's arrival, and by the end of the month the Operation *Gallop* grouping had been routed (and the new attacks against Heeresgruppe Mitte likewise halted). Other panzer forces attacked toward Kharkov on the 28th, stubborn SS troops retaking the city on 14 March and Belgorod four days later after a brief engagement. With massive mechanized forces concentrated in the northern Ukraine and with momentum on his side, Manstein advocated continuing northward into the Red Army bulge west of Kursk. This manoeuvre had a good chance of succeeding if only the weather and Heeresgruppe Mitte's timorous commander Kluge, now master of the situation around Orel, would co-operate; neither did.

Within a week of Operation *Uranus* against Stalingrad, the Stavka launched its northern cousin, *Mars*. No less a personage than First Deputy Commissar for Defence Zhukov led this effort to destroy the German salient at Rzhev, still perhaps 125 miles from Moscow. With its prestigious commander and proximity to the capital, *Mars* must be assumed to be as important to Stalin's plans that winter as the battles on the Volga. Phase I consisted of two pincers attacking south of Rzhev, one each driving due east and due west. After success predicted to match that of Stalingrad, phase II would advance on Viazma to lop off the much larger base of Heeresgruppe Mitte's bulge.

As usual, the Soviet attacks caught German intelligence unaware and achieved complete surprise. The eastward assault, on the far western side of the German position, achieved some early but modest success. The same cannot be said about the westward manoeuvre, closest to Moscow. Despite Zhukov's personal intervention in leading the battle, it could not overcome Wehrmacht defences. Soviet losses were massive. By the second week of December, even Zhukov admitted he could do

no more. In March 1943 the Germans voluntarily vacated Rzhev during Operation *Büffelbewegung*, de facto conducting *Mars* on their own terms and reducing the length of these lines by one-third.

Why the unsatisfactory outcome for the offensive around Moscow? Strategically, the Red Army had not arrived at the place where it could launch two massive and simultaneous offensives. The main operational reason must be Heeresgruppe Mitte's mobile reserves around Rzhev (precisely what was lacking around Stalingrad), amounting to initially four, and later an additional three, mechanized divisions. These first halted and then destroyed the Red Army thrusts. Another cause was the northern defensive positions themselves; all the soldiers were battle-tested Germans who had occupied and improved basically the same lines for many months prior to the attack. Some historians minimize the importance of *Mars* to the 1942 Soviet strategy, saying its purpose was merely to keep the Germans from feeding these same reserves into the Stalingrad battle. In that case the operation would be considered a success, but then there is also no reason for the operation to have been edited out of post-war Soviet histories to the extent it was. I consider *Mars* to be a failure of both the Soviet military and Zhukov personally, one of the few black marks on his record.

The month before Manstein captured Kharkov, Paulus and his men surrendered at Stalingrad, vastly overshadowing one month's tactical success in the Ukraine. In the 17 months between *Barbarossatag* and the beginning of Operation *Uranus* the Germans had lost about 50 divisions; in the five months of *Uranus*, *Little Saturn*, *Gallop* and *Star* they lost 45 more, plus 40 of their allies. From November to March the Soviets had liberated all the territory the Germans had captured during Operation *Blau* (June–November). Elsewhere in Europe, the United States Army Air Force (USAAF) fully entered the air battle for Germany alongside the RAF and, only a few weeks after Heeresgruppe Süd ground to a halt short of Kursk, Anglo-American armies ejected the Wehrmacht from north Africa. The year 1943 would prove to be one of retreat and defeat for Nazi Germany.

MAP 56: OPERATION *URANUS* 19–24 NOVEMBER, 1942

While German attacks against Stalingrad petered out during the first half of November, Zhukov had actually begun withholding reinforcements from Chuikov, as he wanted to build up offensive strength on 6. Armee's flanks. On 3 November at 5th Tank Army headquarters he briefed all commanders of the new South-western Front on the winter offensive that would exploit the weak Romanian armies on Stalingrad's flanks and attempt to encircle as much of 6. Armee and 4. Panzer-Armee as possible.

For Operation *Uranus* the Stavka assembled five armies north-west of Stalingrad and another pair to the south, totalling more than one million soldiers, 13,500 artillery pieces, nearly 900 tanks and 1,100 aircraft. Less than a week later, Wehrmacht intelligence apprised Hitler of the growing danger to his Stalingrad project. Better late than never, Hoth gave up the decimated XLVIII Panzer-Korps to buttress the Romanian Third Army, the weaker of two allied armies guarding Paulus's flanks. At slightly more than one million men, 10,300 guns, 675 panzer and 1,200 aircraft, Axis numbers were not significantly inferior, but of course the Red Army would choose the time and place of its offensive.

Vatutin's South-western Front, the offensive's main effort, moved across the Don on the morning of 19 November as General Lieutenant P. L. Romanenko's 5th Tank Army and the 21st Army under General Major I. M. Chistyakov smashed into the Romanians. In some sectors they held, in others they fled in disorder. Rifle divisions quickly created penetrations through which both army commanders poured tank and cavalry exploitation corps. The 4th Tank Corps on Chistyakov's right was especially successful, advancing 20 miles by nightfall. On *Uranus*'s western edge, 1st Tank Corps hit XLVIII Panzer-Korps, which barely amounted to the strength of a division, and the Germans gave way toward the Chir River. Generalleutnant Ferdinand Heim managed to get his panzers and Romanian tankers turned around and counterattacking north-eastwards into 5th Tank Army. At the cost of the Romanian 1st Armoured Division they barely slowed Romanenko, who kept driving toward Kalach. Meanwhile to the east, Rokossovsky's Don Front launched supporting attacks by the 65th and 24th Armies while his 66th Army fought to tie down Paulus.

Twenty-four hours into *Uranus*, Romanian 3rd Army had broken and the Soviets rushed through gaps 20 miles wide. The XI Armee-Korps attempted to protect 6. Armee's rear by covering the gap between the Don and the Volga. To compound Weichs' problems, Eremenko's Stalingrad Front launched its attack against the Romanian Fourth Army with General Major F. I. Tolbukhin's 57th and General Major N. I. Trufanov's 51st Armies; the 4th Mechanized Corps stood by to punch through to Kalach and a rendezvous with Vatutin. Hoth ordered 60. Infanterie-Division (Mot.) to make a futile counterattack into Trufanov's left. By the 20th the danger posed by *Uranus* was clear, and Paulus halted any pretence of further attacks in Stalingrad and withdrew 14., 16. and 24. Panzer-Divisionen from the city and dispatched them toward the rupture on the Don. In the south he had 29. Infanterie-Division (Mot). try to staunch the flow of Eremenko's men.

By 21 November, three corps, 3rd Guards Cavalry, 4th and 26th Tank, were 60 miles beyond the Don and deep into the Axis lines, racing for Kalach. Eremenko's 4th Mechanized Corps took Abganerovo and continued on toward Zety, where the Germans managed finally to halt it. All along the front Axis units vaporized and Red Army formations poured through; in the north in particular they fanned out almost immune to German countermeasures. On the 22nd Vatutin's 26th Tank Corps reached the Don, crossed the bridge at Kalach and captured the town itself. From the south-east, Eremenko's 14th Mechanized closed to within a dozen miles of Kalach. Kampfgruppen of 16. and 24. Panzer-Divisionen attempted to blunt the two spearheads, but this appeared to be a losing proposition. Paulus informed Weichs that an escape route to the south still existed and requested freedom of action, but was ordered to stay put.

Men of the 26th Tanks and 4th Mechanized Corps linked up just east of Kalach on the morning of 23 November and closed any remaining escape route. Vatutin's troops had advanced 100 miles, those of Eremenko more than 60. By the end of the day the cordon was ten miles thick. Inside the trap were 22 divisions, a total of 250,000 soldiers.[69] On the 24th Paulus again requested permission to break out of the trap, only to have Hitler repeat his refusal.

---

69 Encircled were 14 infantry, three motorized infantry and three panzer divisions plus two Romanian divisions, along with Luftwaffe, specialist and auxiliary troops.

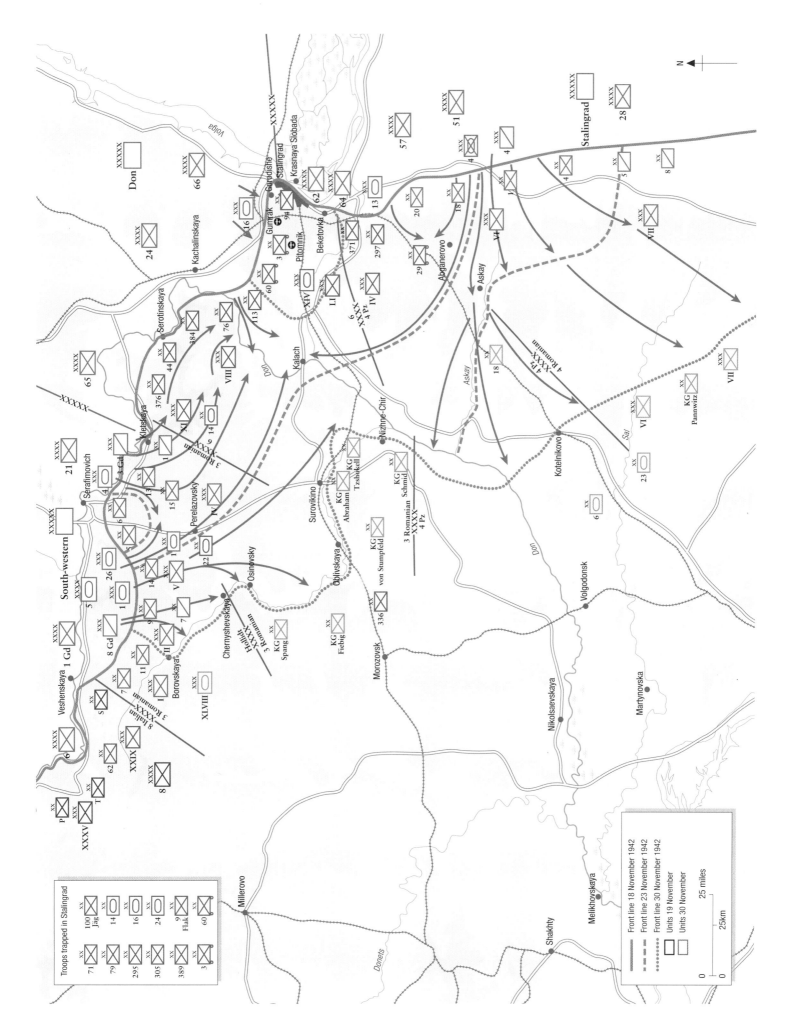

Don

Volga

Stalingrad
Gumrak
Krasnaya Slobada
Pitomnik
Beketovka

Kachalinskaya

Serotinskaya

Kletskaya

Serafimovich

South-western

Veshenskaya

1 Gd

8 Gd

Kalach

Abganerovo

Askay

Askay

Kotelnikovo

Stalingrad

Sal

Perelazovsky

Osinovsky

Chernyshevskaya

Borovskaya

Surovikino

Nizhne-Chir

Obilivskaya

Morozovsk

Nikolsaevskaya

Volgodonsk

Martynovska

Millerovo

Shakhty

Melikhovskaya

Donets

Don

KG
Tzshokell
KG
Abraham
KG
Schmid
KG
von Stumpfeld
KG
Fiebig
KG
Spang
KG
Pannwitz

3 Romanian

4 Pz
4 Romanian

3 Romanian

8 Italian

3 Romanian

N

Troops trapped in Stalingrad

| 100 Jäg | 14 | 16 | 24 | 9 Flak | 60 |
| 71 | 79 | 295 | 305 | 389 | 3 |

Front line 18 November 1942
Front line 23 November 1942
Front line 30 November 1942
Units 19 November
Units 30 November

25 miles
25km

MAP 57: OPERATION *LITTLE SATURN* 16 DECEMBER, 1942 TO 1 JANUARY, 1943

During the last week of November, the Red Army consolidated around the prize of the Stalingrad pocket. On the 24th, Stalin issued orders to prepare to meet the expected German counterattack and for the destruction of 6. Armee. At the same time the Stavka's co-ordinator, Marshal Vasilevski, met with top Soviet commanders to discuss their next move, Operation *Saturn*. It would expand Stalingrad's outer encirclement and trap Heeresgruppe A in the Caucasus. Reinforced by the new 1st Guards Army, Vatutin would re-orientate toward the south-east and overrun the Italian Eighth Army on his way to Rostov, while Rokossovsky again filled the supporting role. They would face an additional opponent, Manstein, brought down from Leningrad (also on 24 November) to take command of Heeresgruppe Don, essentially the ruined remnants of Heeresgruppe B's southern half.[70] Along with Hoth and General der Infanterie Karl Hollidt, he set about attempting to contain *Uranus*.

Seesaw battles raged, principally along the Chir River, but the Stalingrad garrison proved bigger and more difficult to reduce than Soviet plans expected, while conversely getting a rescue force to Paulus proved beyond the capabilities of Hoth's men (Map 58). In view of these last two developments, from 10–14 December the Stavka first delayed and then downgraded Operation *Saturn* to *Little Saturn*, i.e. expanding the outer encirclement and threatening the rear areas of Heeresgruppe Don. South-western Front's 1st and 3rd Guards and 5th Tank Armies smashed into the Italian Eighth Army on 16 December. With the support of the Voronezh Front's 6th Army on the west and after an inauspicious start, within 24 hours Vatutin had demolished numerous Italian divisions. To the east 5th Tank Army threatened to roll up the fragile Chir River line on the left of Army Detachment Hollidt. Also on the 17th, Eremenko launched the 2nd Guards Army against Hollidt's right. Manstein scoured his new army group for formations with which to plug gaps and shore up the faltering Italians.

By 19 December, Vatutin had ripped a hole 30 by 20 miles in General Italo Gariboldi's lines and fanned out to run down the beaten enemy.[71] On the next day OKH placed another ad hoc expedient, Army Detachment Fretter-Pico, in the area of the critical Millerovo airbase and logistics hub.[72] By this point numerous cavalry and tank corps were rampaging deep in the German rear areas, often 100 miles from the main front and dangerously close to the airfields attempting to resupply Stalingrad (one of these, the 24th Tank Corps, had ventured too far toward Tatsinskaya airfield and had itself been encircled). Considering the myriad threats to his army group, plus Hitler's refusal to allow Paulus to attempt a breakout (Operation *Donnerschlag*), Manstein cancelled Hoth's sputtering Operation *Wintergewitter*. By Christmas Day Eremenko had regained the initiative on this front, and soon his units would be back on the Aksay River.

The Soviets had expanded their breach of the Wehrmacht lines to a length of 200 miles, with only the occasional German unit to offer any resistance. Meanwhile they had also compressed the 6. Armee into a lozenge-shaped perimeter 40 miles wide and 20 miles deep. The 24th Tank Corps was still in some danger near the Tatsinskaya airfield, but other than that on 25–26 December everything was going the Red Army's way. Eremenko's Kotelnikovo operation, conducted by General Lieutenant R. Y. Malinovsky's 2nd Guards Army, first reversed Hoth's stalled rescue mission and then overran his hasty defences along the Aksay River. His 7th Tank Corps led the way into the town, where Soviet troops cut all communications in the area and captured its airstrip. The 2nd Guards Mechanized Corps swung north and overran two more airfields near Budarin south of Tormosin, amongst the closest Luftwaffe bases to Stalingrad. The 51st and 28th Armies joined in to push back Hoth to the Sal and Manych rivers. On 27 December, Kleist began the phased withdrawal of Heeresgruppe A from the Caucasus (off map to the south).

Toward the end of the year, Vatutin's main front forces began to run out of steam, though 24th Tank Corps did finally escape Tatsinskaya – closely pursued by the Germans. Otherwise, by New Year's Day Operation *Little Saturn* stabilized for a couple of weeks starting with Heeresgruppe B still in possession of Rossosh, Millerovo and Morozovsk. The Soviets turned their attention to destroying 6. Armee and liberating Stalingrad.

---

70 Manstein technically commanded 6. Armee as well, but he calls this 'a fiction' (Lost *Victories*, p. 300) since Hitler retained total control of the Stalingrad pocket.

71 On that same day the Stavka assigned 6th Army to the South-western Front from the Voronezh Front.

72 Fretter-Pico arrived fresh from his victory at Bely against Operation *Mars* (Map 60).

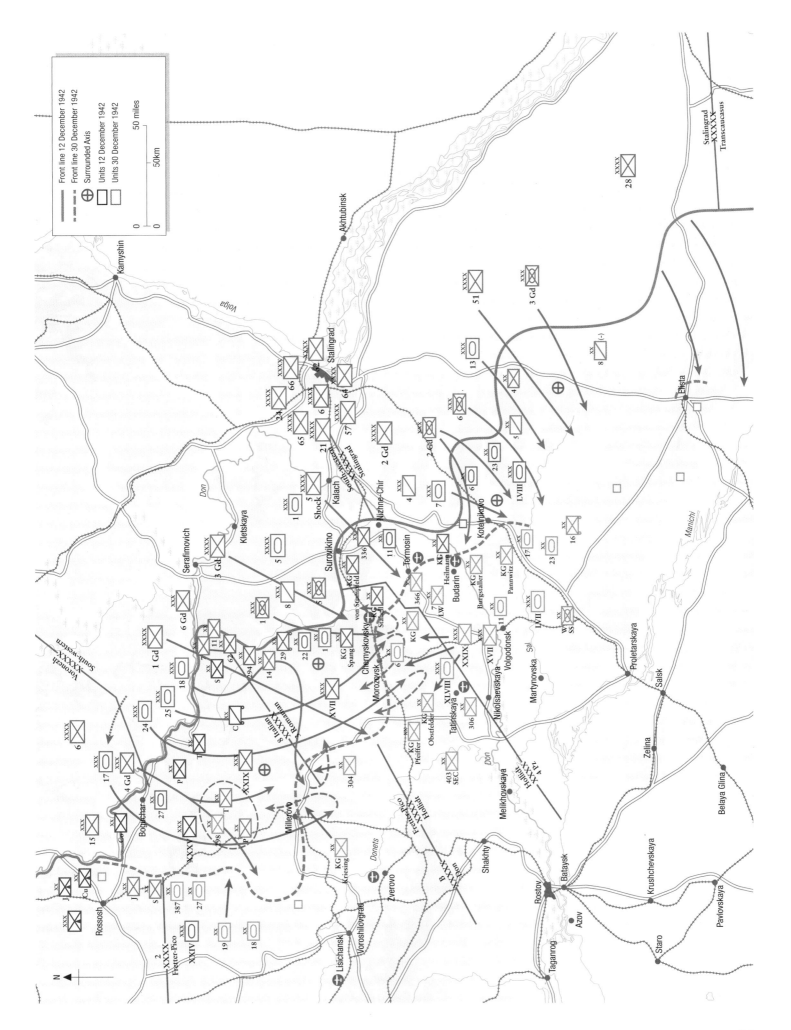

Front line 12 December 1942
Front line 30 December 1942
Surrounded Axis
Units 12 December 1942
Units 30 December 1942

0   50 miles
0   50km

N

Kamyshin

Volga

Akhtubinsk

Stalingrad

XXXXX Stalingrad

66

24

65

21

57

64

62

XXXX Sovietskaya Stalingrad

Don

Kletskaya

Kalach

Nizhne-Chir

5 Shock

2 Gd

Serafimovich

3 Gd

Surovikino

336

11

Tormosin

KG Stumpfeld

von Stumpfeld

KG Spang

Chernyskovsky

KG Stahel

Morozovsk

6 Gd

1 Gd

Voronezh
XXXXX
South-western

24

25

18

294

14

29

22

1

XVII

XXIX

Boguchar

4 Gd

17

27

T

Millerovo

Donets

Rossosh

Cu

387

27

19

18

XXXX
Fretter-Pico
XXIV 2

Lisichansk

Voroshilovgrad

Zverovo

KG Kriesing

KG Pfeiffer

KG Obstfelder

403 SEC

Tatsinskaya

306

XLVIII

XXIX

XVII

Volgodonsk

Nikolsaevskaya

Martynovska

Sal

LVIII

W SS

Budarin

KG Heilmann

Burgstaller

KG Pannwitz

11

LVIII

Holidt
XXXX
4 Pz

Melikhovskaya

Don

Shakhty

Rostov

Batajsk

Azov

Taganrog

Staro

Krushchevskaya

Pavlovskaya

Belaya Glina

Zelina

Salsk

Proletarskaya

Manich

Elista

Stalingrad
XXXXX
Transcaucasus

28

51

3 Gd

13

8

4

6

23

5

2 Gd

7

LVIII

16

17

23

129

MAPS 58 & 59: OPERATIONS *WINTERGEWITTER* AND *KOLTSO*

MAP 58: OPERATION *WINTERGEWITTER* (WINTER STORM), 12–25 DECEMBER, 1942

By 12 December, Manstein had created a force to relieve Stalingrad under Hoth. Starting near Kotelnikovo, it would attack north generally along the railway line toward the city 60 miles away.[73] Kirchner's LVII Panzer-Korps would control 6. and 23. Panzer-Divisionen as the *Schwerpunkt* and the Romanian Fourth Army on its right. All of these formations were heavily attrited. Barring their way stood Trufanov's 51st Army, and later, Malinovsky's 2nd Guards Army.

Hoth attacked on 12 December and neared the Aksay Kurmoyarsky River that night. By the 13th he had two divisions up to and across the river, as the 4th and 13th Mechanized Corps put up a stout defence until 2nd Guards arrived. At Nizhne-Chir the 5th Shock Army halted the supporting attack by Hollidt's XLVIII Panzer-Korps. Despite these defensive successes, Operation *Wintergewitter* caused the Stavka to launch *Little Saturn* initially with South-western Front alone; the Stalingrad Front's main task was to halt the relief effort. It seemed to be succeeding by 15 December, as at numerous places between the Aksay Yesaulovsky and Myshkova rivers, Red Army defenders dealt Kirchner's men a series of reversals. Two days later, both sides received reinforcements in the form of the repatriated 17. Panzer-Division and leading elements of 2nd Guards. Manstein tried to entice Paulus into launching a breakout (*Donnerschlag*), but without Hitler's approval neither would order the forlorn attempt.

By 20 December, 6. Panzer-Division had finally earned a small bridgehead over the Myshkova at Vasilyevka. This marked 2nd Guards Army's main line of resistance and also *Wintergewitter*'s high point. Two days later, threats elsewhere in the Heeresgruppe Don area caused the Germans de facto to halt the operation, still 30 miles away from Stalingrad. On the 23rd, Hoth had to give up 6. Panzer-Division and so began retiring back to the Aksay line. By Christmas Day, the 2nd Guards and 51st Armies were threatening Kotelinkovo.

MAP 59: OPERATION *KOLTSO* (RING), 10 JANUARY TO 2 FEBRUARY, 1943

Seven Soviet armies encircled 6. Armee's 20 German and two Romanian divisions. On 25 November the first Luftwaffe supply planes arrived, but they could never make good on Göring's boast to fly in 600 tons per day. Paulus planned an all-around defence, but by the end of the month had lost half the pocket's territory, finally halting the Soviets in early December. Distracted by *Little Saturn* and *Wintergewitter* (against which Operation *Koltso*'s main effort, 2nd Guards Army, was dispatched), the Red Army settled for pounding the Stalingrad pocket with artillery. Attrition and wastage reduced the 6. Armee's actual combat strength to a small fraction of its quarter of a million reported strength. Rokossovsky's seven armies included only slightly more men, but they enjoyed superior morale and logistics.

On 8 January the Soviets issued a surrender ultimatum to Paulus, which he rejected. Two days later, 21st and 65th Armies launched *Koltso* from the west and within two days had pushed three German divisions out of 'the Nose' and behind the lower Rossoshka River. After a week of fighting, and joined by the 57th, 24th and 66th Armies, they had overrun the western half of the pocket, including the Pitomnik airfield. From the German point of view this looked disastrous, but the Soviets were dismayed by their failure to land the knockout blow. Wehrmacht numbers far exceeded the Stavka's intelligence estimates. Rokossovsky paused to re-organize and then resumed his assault against the northern perimeter on the 20th. In these two weeks, 6. Armee's combat strength had dropped from 80,000 to fewer than 20,000.

Rokossovsky resumed his attack on 22 January with the 57th Army leading the way from the south-west. Paulus wanted to surrender on humanitarian grounds, but this argument had no effect on Hitler. By this time, 6. Armee was mainly a collection of the unattended wounded, sick and starving. The Soviets captured Gumrak airstrip on the 23rd and the Mamai *kurgan* two days later; the 62nd and 21st Armies had split the pocket in two. On 29 January the southern group was further subdivided. Germans in the northern pocket began surrendering the next night, while Paulus waited until the last day of the month to do so. The remnants of six divisions of XI Armee-Korps held out around the tractor factory until 2 February. German losses amounted to nearly 150,000 dead and more than 90,000 taken prisoner. Soviet casualties totalled 1.1 million, including almost 500,000 dead.

---

73 Hollidt, at Nizhne-Chir, was 25 miles closer to Stalingrad than Hoth.

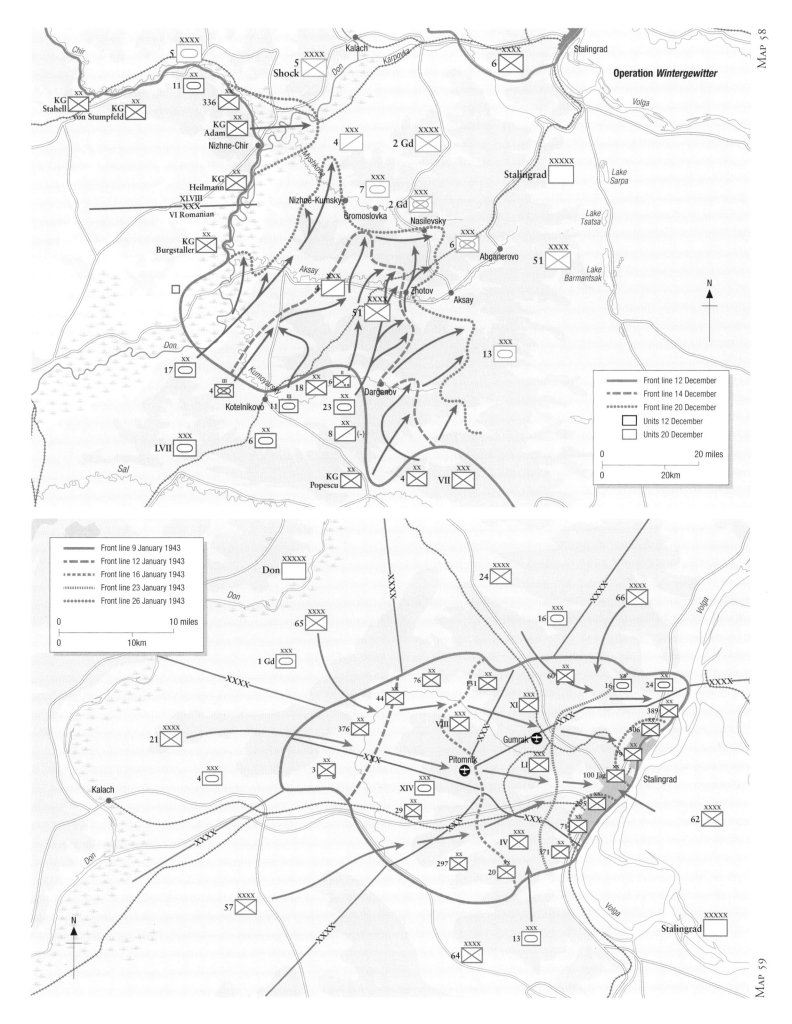

MAP 58

Map 58

Operation _Wintergewitter_

Chir

XXXX
5

KG
Stahell
von Stumpfeld

KG

11

336

KG
Adam
Nizhne-Chir

XLVIII
VI Romanian

KG
Heilmann

KG
Burgstaller

Don

17

4

Kotelnikovo 11

LVII 6

KG
Popescu

Kalach
Don Karpovka

5
Shock

4 XXX

7

Nizhne-Kumsky

Gromoslovka

2 Gd

Nasilevsky

6

Abganerovo

51

Aksay

4 XXX

51 XXXXX

Zhotov

Aksay

13

18 6

23

Darganov

8 (-)

4

VII

Stalingrad

Volga

2 Gd XXXX

Stalingrad XXXXX

Lake
Sarpa

Lake
Tsatsa

Lake
Barmantsak

N

	Front line 12 December
	Front line 14 December
	Front line 20 December
	Units 12 December
	Units 20 December

0   20 miles
0   20km

Sal

MAP 59

Map 59

	Front line 9 January 1943
	Front line 12 January 1943
	Front line 16 January 1943
	Front line 23 January 1943
	Front line 26 January 1943

0   10 miles
0   10km

Don

Don

65

1 Gd

24

66

16

60

16   24

76   31

44

VIII

XI

389

306

306

21

376

3

XIV

4

29

IV

297

20

57

64

13

Kalach

Pitomnik

Gumrak

LI

100 Jäg

295

71

71

Stalingrad

62

Stalingrad

N

MAP 60: OPERATION *MARS*
25 NOVEMBER TO 16 DECEMBER, 1942

Operation *Uranus* was not Stalin's only offensive planned for that autumn. In the Heeresgruppe Mitte sector, the Stavka wanted to destroy 9. Armee, which sat in the 150-mile-tall Rzhev salient, still considered a threat to Moscow. An additional benefit of Operation *Mars* would be to threaten Smolensk. Konev's Western Front would attack from the east while General Purkaev's Kalinin Front came from the west. After *Mars* had eliminated 9. Armee at Rzhev, the follow-on Operation *Jupiter* would destroy 3. Panzer-Armee east of Viazma. Purkaev's 3rd Shock Army would launch a supporting assault against the small German salient at Velikie Luki. Zhukov planned and co-ordinated the offensive, scheduled to coincide with the operations against Stalingrad.

On either side of Rzhev, Konev's 30th and 21st Armies would lead with 45 divisions and two tank corps, while in the area of Bely, Purkaev assembled 25 divisions plus two mechanized corps. Model's 9. Armee counted the XLI Panzer, XXII, XXVIII and XXXIX Panzer-Korps made up of 15 infantry, one SS cavalry, two motorized infantry and three panzer divisions. His intelligence officer accurately anticipated the Red Army offensive. Zhukov struck on both sides of the Rzhev salient and at Velikie Luki on 25 November, two days after the trap around Stalingrad had slammed shut, virtually assuring success in the southern theatre. Penetrations came quickly that first day, and near Bely the 1st and 3rd Mechanized Corps with over 500 tanks began to exploit through the gaps. For all of his experience, Konev did not fare as well, as General Major N. I. Kiriukhin's 20th Army. The XXXIX Panzer-Korps, with the active commitment of 5. and 9. Panzer-Divisionen, accordingly handled the initial shock. The corps' 102. Infanterie-Division halted the 31st Army largely singlehandedly. After two days, 20th Army's 6th Tank Corps had pushed half a dozen miles into Model's lines with the support of 2nd Guards Cavalry Corps. On the 28th, 5. and 9. Panzer-Divisionen struck and cut off the entire cavalry corps of three divisions plus four tank-mechanized brigades. Zhukov ordered an immediate breakout attempt. Over the next two days, these failed in the face of tenacious German defences at a cost of tens of thousands of dead Soviet men and horses and hundreds of smashed tanks.

Attacks by Kalinin Front went more according to plan for at least the first few days. By the end of November tank-mechanized forces had created two penetrations. Toward the north, the 22nd Army had advanced nearly 10 miles up the Luchesa River valley along the boundary dividing XLI Panzer-Korps and XXIII Armee-Korps. South of Bely General Major G. F. Tarasov's 41st Army drove 20 miles deep into Model's lines. Wehrmacht units in desperate combat, including 2. Luftwaffe-Feld-Division to the south, held the shoulders of the narrow breakthrough.[74] This allowed 1. Panzer-Division and elements of Infanterie-Division Grossdeutschland (Mot.) to begin executing counterattacks with the promise of help from the substantial reinforcements that had just arrived in sector: 12., 19. and 20. Panzer-Divisionen from Heeresgruppe Mitte reserves. Fretter-Pico's XXX Armee-Korps headquarters was just arriving as well to take command of this powerful force. During the first week of December, the Germans mainly blunted the attack and pushed back its lead formations, while Fretter-Pico organized his counterattack.

The main striking force, 19. Panzer-Division, finally moved out on 7 December from the southern shoulder and drove straight for Bely. On the next day it reached German defenders south of the town, encircling the bulk of nine brigades of 1st Mechanized and 6th Rifle Corps totalling approximately 40,000 men. For another week Model squeezed the *Kessel* and fought off weak breakout and rescue attempts. On the 14th Zhukov relieved Tarasov and took on the additional post of commander of 41st Army. Fewer than 10,000 troops escaped, making the disaster complete. In the face of Wehrmacht reinforcements, the Luchesa River attack had also petered out by mid-month, costing the 22nd Army commander his job as well. The one bright spot on the central front was 3rd Shock Army's tactical victory at Velikie Luki (off map to north-west). By the 16th, Operation *Mars* had come to an inglorious end, the worst black mark on Zhukov's record.[75] In three weeks, the catastrophe cost the Red Army one-third of a million men, 100,000 of them dead and missing, plus 1,800–1,900 out of 2,000 tanks destroyed. Model's victory had been extremely costly as well, and by the end of winter 9. Armee would evacuate the deadly Rzhev salient.

---

74 Aircraft losses up to the end of *Barbarossa* generally correspond with the Luftwaffe's new role as primarily a ground force (including increased flak for the air defence of the Reich). Hitler therefore wanted Göring to give the army the equivalent of seven divisions worth of underutilized 'volunteers'. In late 1942 the Reichsmarschall countered with an offer to create Luftwaffe field divisions of poorly-prepared de-planed navigators, aircraft mechanics, communications specialists and airfield construction troops, etc.

75 Zhukov finally officially admitted failure on 20 December.

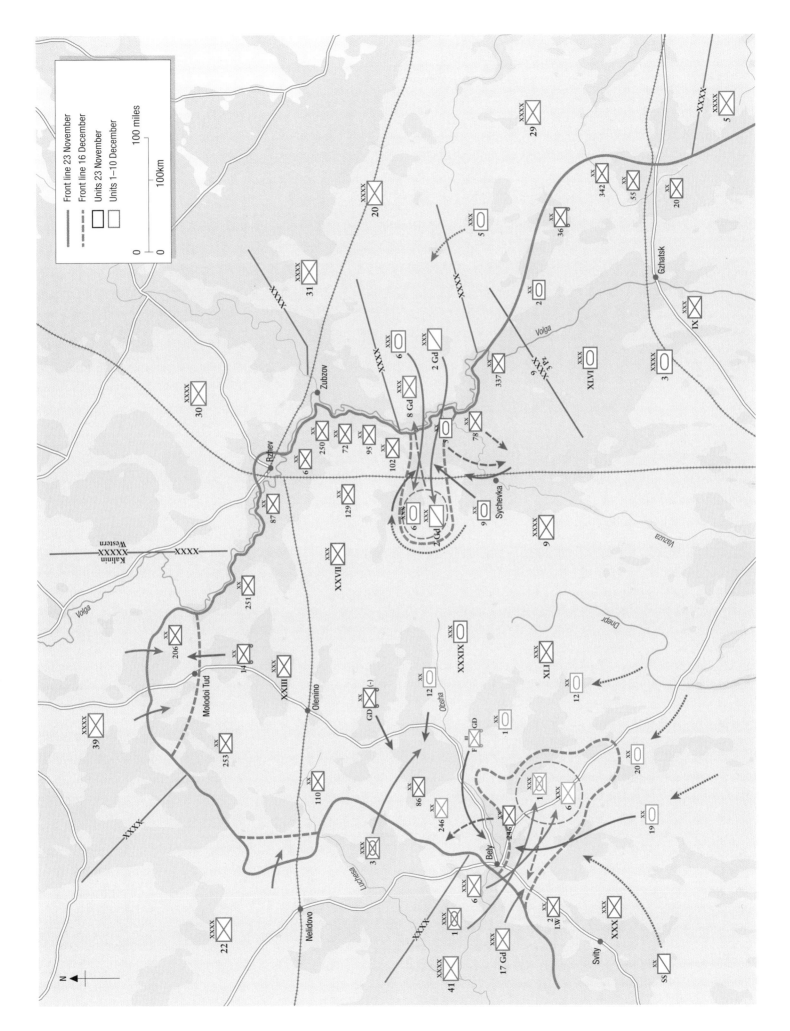

MAP 61: OPERATION *ZIETHEN*, EVACUATION OF DEMYANSK – 3 JANUARY TO 26 FEBRUARY, 1943

Prodded by the disaster at Stalingrad, in early 1943 the German high command realized that they would not be heading back toward Moscow or even encircling the Kalinin Front and so no longer needed their salients at Demyansk and Rzhev. With Heeresgruppe Nord under constant pressure and with the southern theatre threatening to collapse, reserves were sorely needed. The divisions defending these useless appendages (29 in Rzhev and 12 in Demyansk) could be reduced to a fraction of that number, with the balance put in reserve. On 2 January Timoshenko began attacking all around the perimeter of the Demyansk salient, especially its thin neck, but his men could find no weak spots to exploit. By the second week of January casualties on both sides exceeded 10,000 men. On 31 January Hitler relented and agreed to permit the evacuations of both positions.

Heeresgruppe Nord and II Armee-Korps had been planning for just such an order, so were ready. Starting on 1 February II Armee-Korps passed down Hitler's order and began making serious arrangements to evacuate the salient. They had to move judiciously: fast enough in case Hitler reversed himself, but not so quickly as to lose stockpiled equipment. General der Infanterie Paul Laux had II Armee-Korps construction troops build new roads through the neck of the corridor and began to evacuate its equipment and materiel. His troops staged demonstrations to deceive the Soviets to believe that units were only being rotated in and out of the salient. Almost simultaneously, as part of a larger set of offensives in the northern theatre, Timoshenko launched yet another series of assaults by elements of the 11th and 27th Armies (north) and 1st Shock Army (south) against the salient's base. Fourteen rifle divisions, including airborne troops and a tank brigade, smashed into four infantry divisions fighting to keep the 6-mile-wide passage open. Evenly divided north and south, 100,000 Red Army frontoviki hit the 290th, 58th and 54th Infanterie-Divisionen in the north and 126th Infanterie-Division in the south. The Germans sustained numerous penetrations but no breakthroughs.

On the 17th, Laux commenced Operation Ziethen, the actual evacuation of Demyansk. He pulled out 329. and 32. Infanterie-Divisionen to the first of seven intermediate resistance lines. Over the next week – one line per day – 16. Armee withdrew from the salient. On the 19th, the Red Army units opposite the abandoned positions realized they had been duped and took up the pursuit on horseback or skis. Terrible blizzards, especially on the night of 19/20 February hindered their efforts. The heaviest fighting fell on the divisions holding the corners – called 'corner posts' by the Germans – 30. and 122. Infanterie-Divisionen to the north and 12. Infanterie-Division to the south.

On 26 February Laux's men had halted on the Robya stream, with one more line behind them under construction on the Lovat River. The ten-day battle ended the next day: Timoshenko had liberated 1,200 square miles of Russian homeland. Busch's divisions had evacuated 8,000 tons of equipment, 5,000 horse-drawn wagons and 1,500 motor vehicles. Three divisions now guarded the stump of a salient that used to require eleven. Those men could be put to good use as Heeresgruppe Nord reserves or even in the Ukraine. The Soviets stood to benefit from the shorter lines as well and immediately began transferring units to the area around Kursk, where at the moment scene of the Backhand Blow battles (Maps 67 and 68) and future operation Zitadelle offensive (Maps 72–74).

Valdai

161

245

146
171

329
32

241

182

86

III Fortified Region
91

Luzhno

30

225

Molvotitsy

166

200

Lychkovo

XXX
II

Demyansk

12

348

235

Marevo

144

Knevitsky

122

126

163

254

Pola

123

129

370

Lozitsy

XXX
Höhne

282

58

Vasilevshchina

290

126

53 Gd

380
397

167

XX 53
XXXX
1 Shock

68

Group-Khozin

Pola

Tulitovo

20

87

8 Jäg

Zeluch'ye

23

North-western
XXXXX
Kalinin

Parfino

188
202

Davidovo

5 Jäg

Ramushevo

30

254

391 Gd
1 Gd

250

3
Shock

127
161

Staraya
Russa

122

Penno

32

2 Gd
3 Gd
4 Gd

Lovat

8 Gd

225

290

18

329

6 Gd

9 Gd

Poddorye

44

21

33

16

X

254

21 LW

218

Kholm

12

58

254

Belebelka

Lake
Seliger

XXXX
53

Front line, 17 February
Front line, 18 February
Front line, 20 February
Front line, 22 February
Front line, 26 February
Front line, 28 February
Soviet attacks, 15–17 February
Units initial positions
Units subsequent positions

10km
10 miles

N

135

MAP 62: OPERATION *BÜFFEL*, EVACUATION OF RZHEV – 31 JANUARY TO 31 MARCH, 1943

By the end of January, Heeresgruppe Mitte's exposed Rzhev salient represented another tempting target for the Red Army's growing confidence. Operation Mars had been an unmitigated disaster, but had also cost the Germans dear. During the winter of 1943, loosely coordinated with Operations Gallup and Star, Red Army forces had roughed-up 2. Armee on Mitte's southern flank, driving 25 miles west of Kursk. Now 2. Panzer-Armee also occupied an exposed salient, centered on Orel. This made holding on to Rzhev even more risky and the intelligence staff at OKW predicted that the Kalinin and Western Fronts would be back. In late January Kluge briefed Hitler on his plan to withdraw 9. and 4. Armeen while he still had the means to do so on his own terms. On 6 February the dictator grudgingly authorized clearing out the protuberance, even though it meant falling back 100 miles and giving up Rzhev and Viazma, symbols of Barbarossa's past glories. Two weeks later Kluge tried his luck again, recommending that 2. Panzer-Armee also give up its Orel salient, but Hitler would not hear of it.

As with Operation Ziethen, Büffel would be a scorched-earth affair. Destroying or removing anything of value, including as many able-bodied civilians as could be evacuated, was almost as important to Hitler as safely getting 9. and 4. Armeen out of their dangerous positions, with most of their equipment if at all possible. Model employed 29,000 men building a fortified line at the base of the salient, running generally from Dukhovschina to Dorogobuzh to Spas Demensk. Military and Reichsarbeitsdienst construction troops also built new roads and railways radiating from Rzhev southwards.

The withdrawal began on 1 March and two nights later 129. Infanterie-Division rearguards demolished the Volga River bridge at Rzhev; the 30th Army did not notice their departure. Again the Germans fell back on a series of prepared intermediate positions, the first leap retreating 30 miles in three days. Attacking from the east, the 5th Army liberated Gzhatsk on the 5th and 33rd Army freed Viazma on the 12th. Severe weather intervened here as well, hindering both Wehrmacht staff withdrawal timetables and the Soviet pursuit. Fierce combat took place in the numerous villages that the Germans had fortified to facilitate their retrograde movement. Many tank-supported assaults attempted to throw off the 9. Armee from its plan, but after 23 days the retreat was complete by 25 March; the 330-mile front was only one-third as long, while four corps headquarters, 15 infantry, three panzer and two motorized infantry divisions had been freed up for use elsewhere. The manoeuvre had been too late to save Voronezh and Kursk, but Operation Zitadelle would fix that, especially with the units freed-up by Büffel. Of course shortened lines meant that many of the ten Soviet armies formerly surrounding the bulge were likewise now available for other tasks. The 3. Panzer-Armee and 4. Armee took over the new sector, while Model's headquarters moved to Smolensk to plan for the German's summer 1943 offensive. As they moved west and liberated territory, the Soviets saw firsthand the effects of the brutal Nazi occupation of the USSR. Likewise, the Stavka resolved in the future to not be caught unaware, but to anticipate German withdrawals and be ready to take up the pursuit..

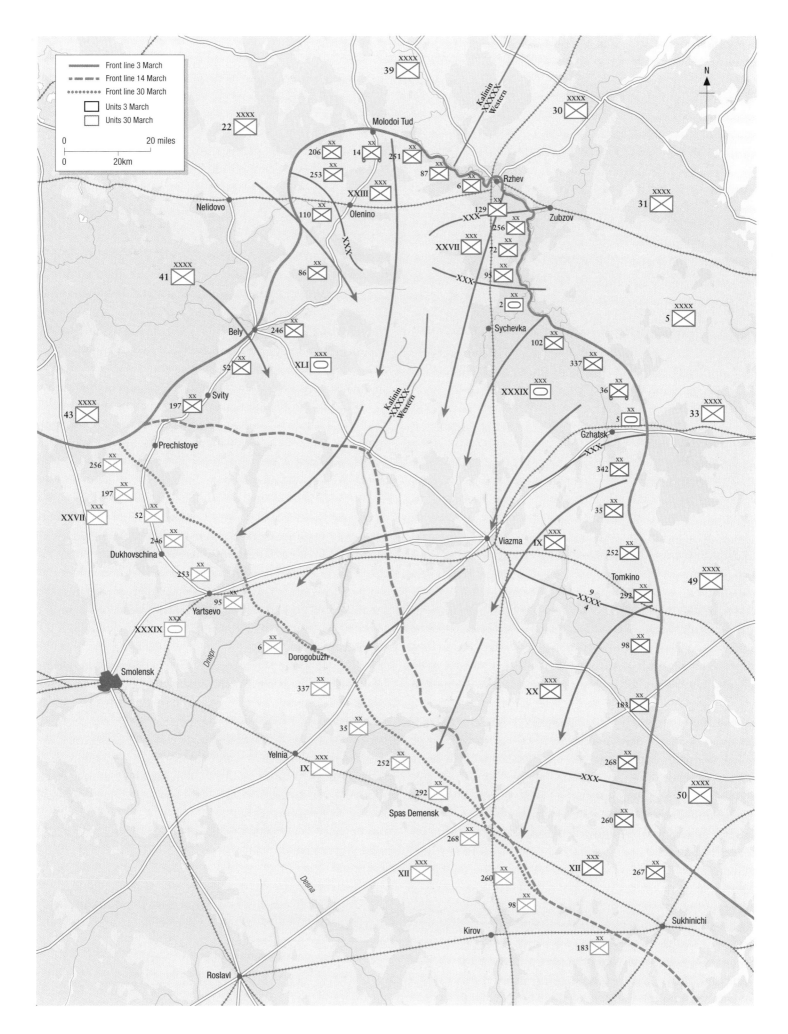

MAP 63: ROSTOV, KUBAN AND MIUS RIVER 29 DECEMBER, 1941 TO 18 FEBRUARY, 1943

Don River bridges at Rostov loomed large in both Soviet and German calculations. As Operation *Little Saturn* wound down, South-western Front units near Millerovo stood about 125 miles from the city; the 4. Panzer-Armee and Romanian formations south of Stalingrad were twice as far away, while 1. Panzer-Armee in the Caucasus foothills was three times as far. Further, between Voronezh and Rostov Heeresgruppe Don had only a collection of ad hoc units like those bearing Hollidt's and Fretter-Pico's names to bar the way of Vatutin and his compatriots. Manstein needed to get Hoth and Kleist out, not only to avoid another Stalingrad but also to use these armies to block the Soviet's advance into the Ukraine.

With the failure of Operation *Wintergewitter*, Hitler finally relented on 29 December and authorized 1. Panzer-Armee to retreat as far as Piatigorsk and the Kuma River. At the Kuma, Kleist could link up with Hoth's forces on the upper Manich River, essentially 16. Infanterie-Division (Mot.). On 4. Panzer-Armee and Armee-Abteilung Hollidt fell the responsibility of keeping open the lifeline through Rostov. As soon as the South-western, Don and Southern fronts regained their breath after *Little Saturn*, these two headquarters could expect a massive attack. Chased by the 44th Army, Kleist had reached the Kuma River on 7 January, where his men paused for four days. At the same time, German mountain troops began to withdraw north out of the Caucasus passes. Further North Caucasus Front assaults on the 10th levered 1. Panzer-Armee off the Kuma and back to the Kalaus River, really an intermittent stream. Kleist was too weak at this point to offer serious resistance.

Meanwhile, much closer to Rostov 2nd Guards and 51st Armies had renewed their drive south-west along the railway line from Kotelnikovo toward Salsk and threatened to overwhelm 16. Infanterie-Division (Mot.). At the Manich River bridge at Proletarskaya, LVII Panzer-Korps plus 5. SS Panzer-Grenadier-Division Wiking dealt a severe reversal to the 2nd Guards during the third week of January. With skilful, well-placed counterattacks by his limited mobile reserves, Hoth kept the Soviets at arm's length from Rostov long enough for Kleist to escape via an ice road across the far-eastern tip of the Sea of Azov. Trains passed through Rostov in both directions; in mid-January Hitler ordered much of Heeresgruppe A, 17. Armee and elements of 4. Panzer-Armee to fall back to the Taman Peninsula (Gotenkopf) where supplies were stockpiled. Eventually nearly 400,000 Germans were

isolated there.[76] All the while the Soviets continued pushing westward from Voronezh to the Caucasus. The Red Army liberated Armavir on 23 January, Maikop six days later and Krasnodar on 12 February. The 17. Armee, ten German divisions of V and XLIV Armee-Korps and XLIX Gebirgs-Korps, plus three Romanian and one Slovakian division, settled down to a seven-month siege before retreating across the Kerch Straits in October.

During the second half of January, the 4. Panzer-Armee had generally stabilized the situation around Rostov. The Southern Front did not make much of an effort here, although on the 20th four Soviet corps had briefly threatened its main airfield. Hitler's order of 22 January creating 17. Armee's Gotenkopf position also instructed 1. Panzer-Armee to fall back to the city.[77] Starting on 1 February, combined with Hoth's LVII Panzer-Korps under Manstein's overall control it would hold the critical Don River crossings as long as possible. Once through, 1. Panzer-Armee continued westward to create the counterattack force Manstein was forming south of Izyum. While the Stavka detailed a guard force to keep watch on the Kuban bridgehead, it began to assemble significant forces around Rostov, including forces freed up by Paulus's final surrender at Stalingrad. In early February, Malinovsky launched new attacks against Fretter-Pico at Voroshilovgrad,[78] endangering Rostov from a new direction: the north.

On 6 February, Manstein reported to Hitler's East Prussian headquarters and successfully lobbied for permission to withdraw again, this time from the Donets to the Mius. Two days later, Fretter-Pico, Hollidt and Hoth began their retrograde movement. South-western Front kept up the pressure and the Germans employed scorched-earth tactics once again. On 15 February the 4th Guards Mechanized Corps briefly penetrated the Mius line, only to beaten back by a 16. Infanterie-Division (Mot.) and 23. Panzer-Division counterattack. The withdrawal lasted until the 18th, when Hollidt's men occupied the Mius River positions from which Operation *Blau* had begun eight months earlier.

---

76 Although in one of the Luftwaffe's transport services' real successes in February–March 100,000 troops largely of LII Armee-Korps were flown out of the bridgehead to the southern Ukraine.

77 In a series of temporary command moves Kleist took over Heeresgruppe A (from Hitler!), General der Kavallerie Eberhard von Mackensen moved up from III Panzer-Korps to 1. Panzer-Armee while Generalleutnant Hermann Breith left 3. Panzer-Division to replace Mackensen.

78 Malinovsky had taken over from Eremenko on 2 February.

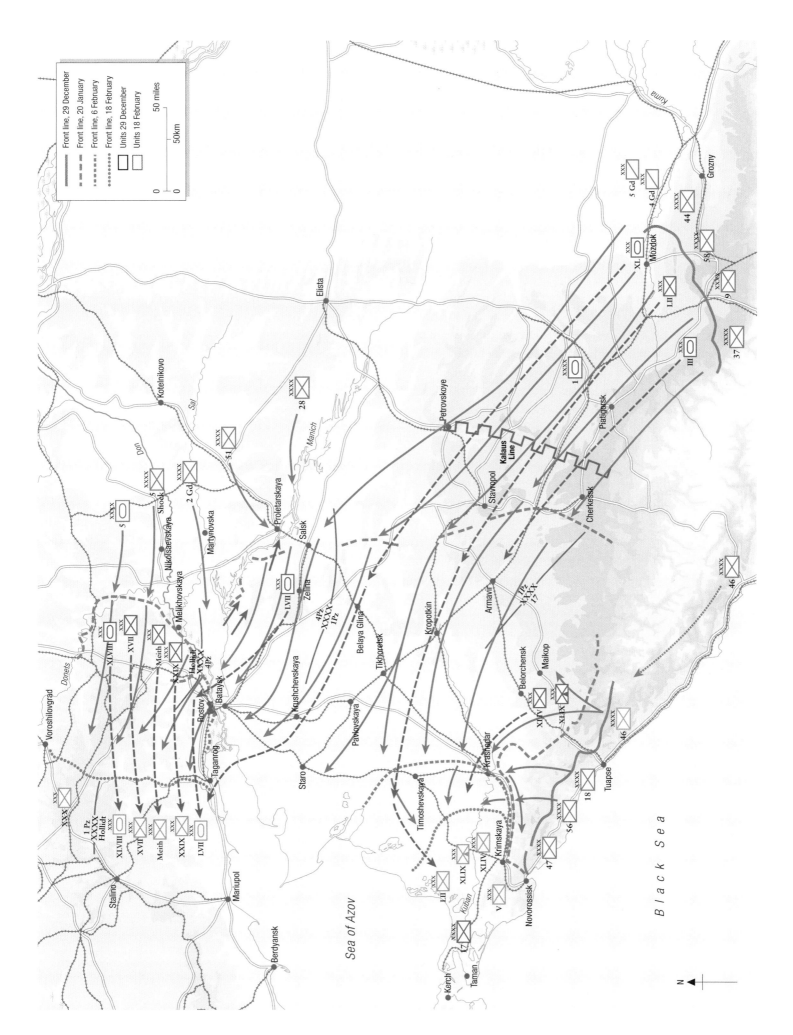

Black Sea

Sea of Azov

MAP 64: VORONEZH TO KURSK 12 JANUARY TO 12 MARCH, 1943

As early as 22 December, the Stavka issued orders to the Voronezh Front to prepare for operations to build upon the success of *Uranus* and *Saturn*. General Lieutenant F. I. Golikov's men were to continue hounding the routed Italian Eighth Army while initiating new assaults on the Hungarian Second Army. The offensive would later expand to include the German 2. Armee as part of the planned campaign to shatter Hitler's southern theatre. However, as elsewhere, Soviet underestimation of Wehrmacht defences, especially within the Stalingrad pocket, would come back to haunt Red Army plans.

Attacking from 12 to 14 January, Golikov's 40th and 3rd tank Armies brushed aside the Hungarians, killing and capturing 150,000, and scattered the XXIV Panzer-Korps command post.[79] Within a week they had also finished off what had remained of the Italians, causing over 100,000 casualties in total and creating a 150-mile gash in the Axis lines reaching from Liski to Voroshilovgrad. It was then the Wehrmacht's turn, and on 24–25 January the 48th, 13th and 38th Armies of the Bryansk Front joined Golikov's 60th army against 2. Armee's flanks on either side of Voronezh, which Generaloberst Hans von Salmuth had just abandoned days earlier. The two jaws linked up four days later at the rail hub of Kasternoye, encircling VII Armee-Korps and seven infantry divisions.[80] It took only a couple of days for the Stavka co-ordinator Vasilevski to suggest and for Stalin to approve follow-on operations against the threadbare defence; this would be the larger Operation *Star* (Map 65). *Star*'s greater operational objective was the long-held but oft-frustrated Soviet goal of liberating Smolensk.

The Voronezh Front renewed offensive operations toward Kursk on 2 February as the 60th Army pursued the severely attrited 2. Armee. Ten days later the Bryansk Front opened its attack with 48th and 13th Armies against the southern flank of 2. Panzer-Armee holding the region around Orel, but made disappointing progress. By mid-month Rokossovsky, with two armies from the Stalingrad battle, 2nd Tank and 65th, had re-deployed to the neighbourhood of Voronezh and, with the untried and newly assembled 70th Army made up of NKVD border troops, was ready for the next mission: the town of Bryansk and another massive encirclement battle in conjunction with the Western Front coming south. On the offensive's first days, 25–26 February, in the face of fresh winter snow General Lieutenant A. G. Rodin's reinforced 2nd Tank Army penetrated 20 miles into 2. Panzer-Armee's defences. Despite prodigious Red Army Air Force CAS as they continued to advance, they could not maintain such a pace, so by early March the Germans regained their balance. With only one panzer corps, the relatively new XLVI, 2. Panzer-Armee was a panzer army in name only, but Schmidt's men knew their sector. On the 7th, Rokossovsky changed Rodin's objective from Pochep to Karachev. Two days later, 2nd Tank came up against two infantry divisions, 45. and 72. Infanterie-Divisionen, and ground to a halt.[81] The reinforced 2nd Guards Cavalry Corps slipped around Rodin's stalled tankers and made for the Desna River bridge at Novgorod-Seversky, widely separating 2. Panzer-Armee and 2. Armee in the process. Seizing bridgeheads over the Desna for future operations represented key Stavka tasks.

By 10 March, Rokossovsky's horsemen stood 175 miles west of Kursk astride an army boundary; certainly this threat would cause a German reaction that Vasilevski could exploit. Instead, Kluge dispatched more Heeresgruppe Mitte reserves to the threatened area. The 2. Panzer-Armee counterattacked southwards with an estimated half-dozen divisions while 4. Panzer-Division took the lead as 2. Armee manoeuvred northwards. Around 12 March the Stavka attempted to re-organize on the fly, basically concentrating the entire Orel operation under Rokossovsky's command. Simultaneously German pressure forced his spearheads back nearly 80 miles to the east. As supplies dried up and the spring thaw set in, the front lines in this sector stabilized from Sevsk to Rylsk. The Soviet offensive had pushed back the Wehrmacht, but failed to register the hoped-for decisive victory. The stage was set for the northern half of the upcoming summer's Operation *Zitadelle*.

79 The panzer corps lost two commanders killed (Wandel and Eibl) within four days.

80 This was all Hitler needed: he relieved Salmuth on 3 February, replacing him with General der Infanterie Walter Weiss. Some German units escaped the pocket to avoid total destruction.

81 As if to confirm the wisdom of *Büffel* (Map 62), 72. Infanterie-Division had just left the Rzhev bulge.

MAP 65: OPERATION *GALLOP* 12 JANUARY TO 19 FEBRUARY, 1943

The Soviets had deliberately planned Operations *Uranus* and *Little Saturn* with an eye toward their growing, but still somewhat limited, operational abilities. Their successes in the war's southern theatre, below Orel, had continued with the Rostov and Voronezh offensives that ended with significant tactical victories, bringing Red Army formations well west of Kursk, to the Mius River and Taman Peninsula. By the second half of January, however, Stalin and the Stavka again overestimated their skills plus German weaknesses, and tempted fate by planning ever bolder manoeuvres. Operation *Gallop*, set to begin at the end of the month, meant to build on momentum that had brought them to the Donets River and propel them to the Dnepr and possibly beyond. Manstein still had a difficult situation to master, but with significant portions of 1. and 4. Panzer-Armee safely west of Rostov and with strategic reserves that Hitler had released earlier beginning to arrive in theatre, he had cause to be guardedly optimistic.

On 29 January, Vatutin's South-western Front attacked on a broad front from Zmiev to where the Donets met the Don, with 6th, 1st Guards, 3rd Guards and 5th Tank Armies plus Mobile Group Popov, all of which had been greatly weakened by the previous three months' fighting. The Heeresgruppe Don lines, always in danger of breaking, finally did so on 1 February when Group Popov, inserted between 6th and 1st Guards Armies, forced its way over the Donets near Lisichansk. To the south-west the 3rd Guards Army crossed the Donets behind Voroshilovgrad the next day. Izyum fell four days later as the 3rd and 4th Tank Corps were poised to burst into Manstein's insecure rear areas. Seeing his Donets position disintegrate and fearing the loss of his far-southern anchor, on the 8th the field marshal began withdrawing Army Detachment Hollidt to the Mius (Map 64). A week later the rupture ran from Zmiev to Krasny Liman, with no Wehrmacht units to be seen besides scattered regiments and remnants dotting the Ukrainian countryside.

Finally Hitler seemed to have heard his general's warnings and took additional positive steps to stabilize the situation. Acknowledging the fact that German soldiers would never man the Don River again, he re-named Manstein's command Heeresgruppe Süd. He also re-organized the army group boundaries by transferring Armee-Abteilung Lanz at Kharkov (Map 66) from Heeresgruppe Mitte to Süd, thereby subordinating the entire crisis in the Ukraine under one man. On the Soviet side, Vatutin determined to maintain the momentum and, to reinforce his own success, committed the fresh 1st Guards and 25th Tank Corps to the breakthrough, and in mid-February the latter stood at the gates of Pavlograd, 30 miles from the Dnepr. In the north 6th Army units neared Krasnograd, south-west of Kharkov and with a straight shot to Poltava. At the same time, to the south Popov reached Krasnoarmeiskaya cutting the rail line from Dnepropetrovsk into the Donbas; only 5. SS Panzer-Grenadier-Division Wiking blocked its way to Stalino and the rear of Army Detachment Hollidt's Mius river line.

Again Hitler responded to the deteriorating situation. On 17 February he flew to Heeresgruppe Süd headquarters at Zaporozhe with Jodl and Zeitzler, probably to relieve Manstein of his command. As he had been doing for the past three weeks, the field marshal painted a bleak picture, even though at far away Rastenburg Hitler surely had had the same maps showing the 80-mile gap between Army Detachment Kempf and 1. Panzer-Armee. However, with the 111th Tank Brigade at Chervonoarmeiskaya, less than 20 miles away from the person of the 'greatest field commander of all time', the Führer had a new appreciation of the danger to his entire eastern army.[82] He finally agreed with Manstein's concept of allowing the Soviets to continue overextending themselves before launching large counterattacks (Maps 67–68). Red Army intelligence duly reported these developments, while Popov and other field commanders tried to convince their superior of friendly weaknesses and growing enemy strength. The 5th Tank and 3rd Shock Armies in the far south began new assaults on Hollidt's Mius positions and made numerous penetrations. Stalin was still convinced that Soviet forces stood on the brink of a tremendous operational victory. But when Hitler departed Zaporozhe on 19 February he left intact Manstein's bold plan. The Wehrmacht's last victory of the Nazi-Soviet War began the next day.

---

82 In July 1940, after the fall of France, Keitel referred to Hitler by that term, also known by its German acronym 'Gröfaz'; it became a secret joke during the Third Reich, especially after Stalingrad.

MAP 66: OPERATION *STAR* – 2–28 FEBRUARY, 1943

The Soviet high command was intent on riding down the shattered Wehrmacht units all the way to the Dnepr. With Golikov's Voronezh Front already committing one army to the battles around Kursk (Map 64), the Stavka ordered it to commence new attacks in the direction of Kharkov with its 69th and 3rd Tank Armies.[83] Defending the region of Belgorod and Kharkov stood Armee-Abteilung Lanz,[84] another ad hoc headquarters, but one with an ace up its sleeve, the new SS Panzer-Korps. The USSR's fourth city acted as another symbolic lightning rod for both Hitler and Stalin.

The Voronezh Front opened its new offensive on 2 February, with the boundary separating its two armies splitting Kharkov in two. General Lieutenant S. Rybalko's 3rd Tank Army (two tank and one cavalry corps plus four rifle divisions) covered the 50 miles between the Oskol and Donets rivers in two days, elements of 2. SS-Panzer-Grenadier-Division Das Reich not defending any better than 298. Infanterie-Division. South of Belgorod Korps Cramer (Grossdeutschland and 168. Infanterie-Division)[85] also fell back to the Donets. Less than a week into the attack it looked like Lanz might stabilize his front along the river, but Vasilevski, co-ordinating operations *Gallop* and *Star* for the Stavka, brought new pressure from north and south, the 40th Army veering away from Kursk and into Lanz's rear and the 6th Army bypassing Kharkov on his right. Eventually these manoeuvres bore fruit as Belgorod fell on 9 February, while in costly frontal attacks 69th and 3rd tank Armies fought their way across the frozen Donets on the following day. In short order they stood inside Kharkov's outer defences and by mid-February had the city surrounded on three sides. Under attack from north, west and south, the SS could not launch the corps-sized counterattack Hitler had promised they would. A limited assault on 11–12 February by a detachment from Das Reich against the 6th Guards Cavalry Corps south of Merefa was no substitute.

By 13 February, pressure, in particular against Kharkov's north, caused Hitler to issue another 'defend to the last man' order. Echoing the Führer's demands, Lanz in turn ordered Obergruppenführer Paul Hausser to hold Kharkov. Hausser requested permission to retreat and Lanz said no, but after much disingenuous prevarication by the SS general he abandoned the city to Golikov on the 16th anyway. With the single escape route to the south-west down to one mile wide, this move may have saved a high-value outfit but it infuriated the Nazi dictator. Semi-professional Waffen SS leaders like Hausser usually had good relations with their army superiors, but in this case blatant SS disobedience cost Lanz his job;[86] XLVIII Panzer-Korps commander Kempf took over the re-named army detachment on the next day. At the same time, on 17 February, Golikov ordered Rybalko's tank army to continue its attacks toward Poltava and, if possible, to Kremenchug on the Dnepr. Barely 24 hours later Voronezh Front had overrun the Udy River line and closed up to the Mzha River, and it took Merefa on the 19th and Akhtyrka on the 22nd. These last dates coincide directly with Hitler's visit to Manstein's Zaporozhe headquarters and the German decision to counterattack against the weakened and overstretched Red Army spearheads (Map 65). But while Vatutin's cavalry and tank outliers came under immediate attack, the Voronezh Front still had a few days of progress ahead of it.

On 21 February, Golikov even believed he could launch a relieving counterattack against the panzers threatening South-western Front. Within two days this manoeuvre by Red Army foot infantry augmented by freshly liberated militia levies came to grief against Grossdeutschland's *Landser*s. By the last day of February, the Stavka had transferred 3rd Tank from Golikov to Vatutin in another vain attempt to halt Hoth (Map 68). On the same day, advance guards of 5th Guards Tank Corps took Veprik, dangerously splitting the 2. Armee (Heeresgruppe Mitte) and Armee-Abteilung Kempf (Heeresgruppe Süd) seam. However good driving practically to Poltava looked on the Stavka's maps, its far-flung and unsupplied units were ripe targets for Manstein's developing countermove.

---

83 The 69th Army was a new formation under General Lieutenant M. I. Kazakov, centred on the 18th Independent Rifle Corps and consisting of four rifle divisions. The 3rd Tank Army began Operation *Star* with 165 tanks.

84 Commander of 1. Gebirgs-Division Hubert Lanz took command of the detachment and was promoted to General der Gebirgstruppen on 28 January. He would barely last two weeks in this position.

85 Commanded by XLVIII Panzer-Korps deputy commander General der Panzertruppen Hans Cramer until 1 March, when he departed to command the Afrika Korps; the British captured him ten weeks later.

86 The 62-year-old Hausser served in staff positions during World War I, rose to major general during the Weimar Republic and retired in January 1932 with brevet (Charakter) rank of lieutenant general. In 1934 he joined the SA as a Standartenführer (colonel) but quickly transferred to the SS with the same rank.

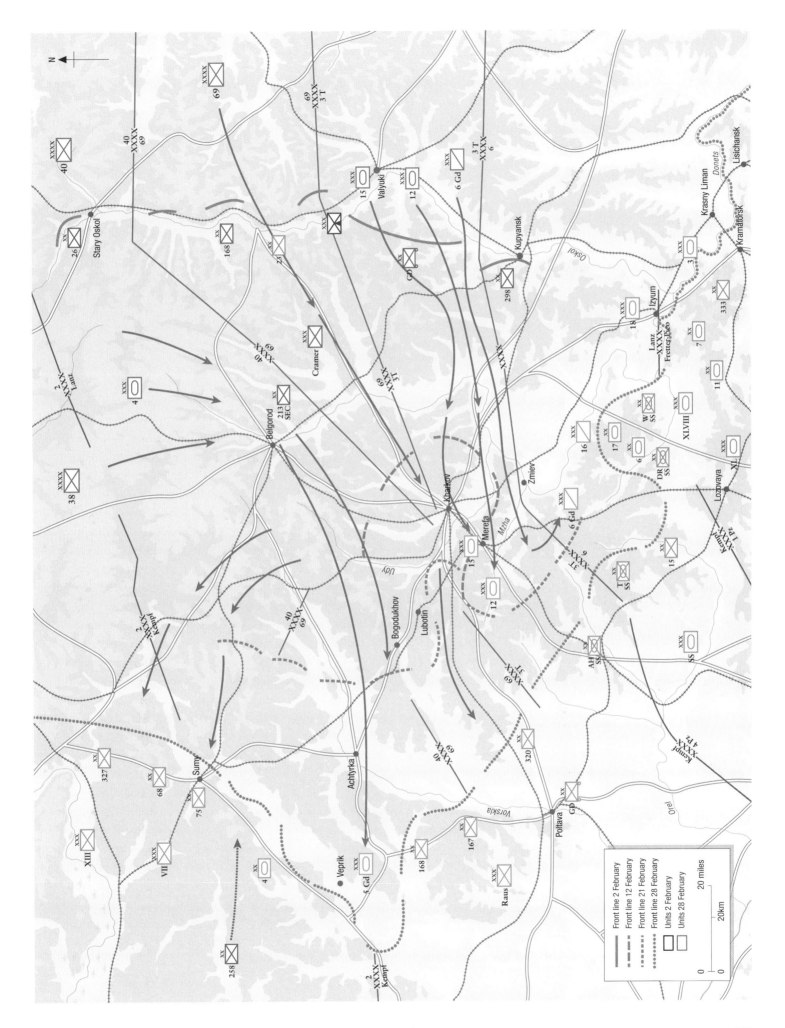

N

40 XXXX 69

69 XXXX 69

69 3 T

XXX 6 Gd

3 T XXXX 6

Lisichansk

Donets

Krasny Liman

Kramatörsk

40 XXXX 40

Stary Oskol

26 XX

168 XX

23 XX

15 XXX

Valyuki

12 XXX

Kupyansk

3 XXX

333 XX

XXX GD

298 XX

Oskol

Izyum

18 XXX

Lanz XXXX Fretter-Pico

Oskol

7 XX

XXX 69 Lanz

2 XXXX Lanz

4 XXX

Cramer XXX

213 SEC XX

Belgorod

69 XXXX 40

3 T XXX 69

11 XXX

W SS XX

XLVIII XXX

38 XXXX

Kharkov

16 XXX

17 XXX

6 XXX

DR SS XX

XL XXX

Lozovaya

4 Pz XXXX Kempf

2 Kempf XXXX

Merefa

Mzha

6 Gd XXX

15 XXX

15 XXX

6 XXXX 3 T

T SS XX

Udy

Bogodukhov

Lubotin

12 XXX

2 Kempf XXX

40 XXXX 69

AH SS XX

SS XXX

320 XX

3 T XXXX 69

327 XXX

68 XX

Sumy

75 XX

Achtyrka

69 XXXX 40

4 Pz XXXX Kempf

GD XX

Poltava

Vorskla

Orel

XIII XXX

VII XXX

258 XX

4 XX

Veprik

5 Gd XXX

168 XX

167 XX

Raus XXX

2 Kempf XXXX

Front line 2 February
Front line 12 February
Front line 21 February
Front line 28 February
Units 2 February
Units 28 February

20 miles
0
20km
0

145

MAP 67: BACKHAND BLOW (I), DONBAS 15–24 FEBRUARY, 1943

For the Germans, the three months between mid-November 1942 and mid-February 1943 had been a series of disasters. For the Soviets, the same period had been one of strategic, operational and tactical success. Over the next month, Hitler would manage one more victory while Stalin would sustain one final loss. For the Third Reich defeat was no longer a question of if, only when.

Since the beginning of Operation *Uranus* the Wehrmacht had been trying to regain its balance and along with it the initiative, but nothing had succeeded. On 11 February Hitler ordered Lanz[87] to attack southwards to link up with Manstein and cut off Vatutin's thrusts. However, with only three mechanized divisions, SSLAH, SS Das Reich and Grossdeutschland, Lanz lacked the resources. A day later, Hitler issued his Operations Order 4, again demanding closing the gap between the two army groups and establishing a defensive line along the Donets and Mius rivers. Besides simply issuing more orders, he also transferred seven divisions from the Reich to the Ukraine with an expected arrival date of early March. As the Red Army celebrated continued success and liberated territory, the Germans began husbanding counterattacking forces; in addition to the three divisions mentioned above, headquarters 1. and 4. Panzer-Armeen and mobile units brought with them across the Don River became the focus of Manstein's efforts to rebuild a viable defensive front.

Still under Mackensen since 11 February, 1. Panzer-Armee (XXX Armeekorps plus III and XL Panzer-Korps) had been defending the middle Donets on either side of Lisichansk. Its order of battle included six severely weakened panzer and five infantry divisions, with SS Wiking just arriving. Ten days later, contact with Lanz was non-existent, while Vatutin's 6th, 1st Guards and 3rd Armies had compressed 1. Panzer-Armee's front into an arc resembling an umbrella over Stalino. By mid-month the 8th Cavalry Corps had worked its way into XXX Armeekorps' rear at Debal'tseve while SS Wiking brought 4th Guards Tank Corps, belonging to Mobile Group Popov, to a standstill at Krasnoarmeiskaya;

87 Still part of Heeresgruppe B until 14 February.

60 miles separated these units. As much as a week later, Popov believed that he had Mackensen on the ropes and prepared to deliver the knockout blow.

However, what few in the leadership of the South-western Front knew was that days earlier 1. Panzer-Armee had already initiated the southern portion of Manstein's Backhand Blow against Popov's spearheads. While Wiking held fast around Krasnoarmeiskaya, Mackensen cut off the mobile group's rear communications. The XL Panzer-Korps, 7. and 11. Panzer-Divisionen, partially accomplished this task by attacking east to west toward Stepanovka. A few days later XLVIII Panzer-Korps was ready, and it closed the pocket's western edge. Inside were 18th, 3rd and 10th Tank Corps plus the 4th Guards Tank Corps. Again, believing he had the upper hand, Popov made no attempt to break out. On the 23rd, down to 50 functioning tanks, out of supply and facing a breakdown of discipline, he finally saw the danger, but it was too late; Vatutin then refused his request to withdraw. His trapped units resorted to *sauve qui peut* and broke in every direction. The Germans lacked the strength to create airtight encirclements, so as the mobile group broke into smaller parts these fragments succeeded in avoiding capture. By 24 February, individual Red Army units were fleeing north back toward the Donets with XLVIII (now part of 4. Panzer-Armee), XL and III Panzer-Korps in hot pursuit.

With Vatutin finally admitting failure, around Barvenkovo and Slavyansk 1st Guards Army formations ran out of fuel, halted and made a hasty defence. A couple of days later these battered regiments and divisions were pulling back again, and by the end of the month had given up most gains south of the Donets River below Izyum almost to Voroshilovgrad. They walked or drove across the frozen river to relative safety; Mackensen's equally exhausted men were in no condition to pursue them farther. Meanwhile, to the south-east Hollidt had consolidated its positions on the Mius. Aided immensely by the Soviets' failure to appreciate their own weak position, Manstein's manoeuvre had brought to a halt the rampage begun nearly half a year earlier on the Volga.

MAP 68: BACKHAND BLOW (II), KHARKOV 20 FEBRUARY TO 14 MARCH, 1943

The last part of Manstein's counterattack puzzle fell into place on the night of 18 February when 'Papa' Hoth's command train pulled into Zaporozhe. Hitler was still in town and Manstein immediately briefed the general on his plan to recreate 4. Panzer-Armee around new panzer corps headquarters and mechanized divisions. He had two missions: firstly with Mackensen's help (Map 66) to eliminate 1st Guards and 6th Armies driving on the Dnepr bend, and secondly once on the Donets to change direction and join Kempf to reconquer Kharkov and, if possible, continue northwards past Belgorod. Overhead would be Richthofen's rejuvenated and re-organized Luftflotte 4, ready after the terrible winter.

Hoth's first moves on 19 February were directed against the advanced units and right flank of the 6th Army heading for the big river. The SS Panzer-Korps, now SS divisions Das Reich and Totenkopf, drove south from Krasnograd on to Novo-Moskovsk just miles from the Dnepr, where it linked up with other German units – thereby removing the immediate danger to Dnepropetrovsk. From there it turned 90 degrees east following the Samara River and the next day took Pavlograd, effectively cutting off the 25th Tank Corps on its lone mission to Zaporozhe. It made another right-angle turn to the north, and, now parallel to XLVIII Panzer-Korps to its right, headed toward the Donets. In concert with 1. Panzer-Armee (Map 66) the XLVIII Panzer-Korps, 6. and 17. Panzer-Divisionen, hounded much of Mobile Group Popov, pushing the tank corps' remnants before them. In the first five days of Manstein's offensive, 1. and 4. Panzer-Armeen neutralized six Soviet corps in a box 60 miles to a side and removed the immediate threat to Heeresgruppe Süd's rear areas and the Dnepr River crossings. During the final days of February, Hoth and Mackensen chased crumbs of the South-western Front's 6th and 1st Guards Armies to and across the Donets. Manstein operated under pressure from the calendar; the spring thaw and *rasputitsa* could arrive any day.

To the north, however, the Voronezh Front was having its way with Armee-Abteilung Kempf, by the end of February pushing Korps Raus[88]

[88] Korps Cramer became Korps Raus on 13 February when Generalleutnant Erhard Raus left 6. Panzer-Division and took over for the departing Cramer.

to Chutovo, barely 25 miles from Poltava, a key army group command, control and logistics node. This turned out to be a temporary situation, though. A couple of days later Golikov's troops were also streaming back, reeling from Hoth's onslaught after his latest 90 degree turn, this time at the Donets. The XLVIII Panzer-Korps hugged the river's right bank, and with the SS Panzer-Korps to its left they drove on Zmiev and Merefa, southern gateways to Kharkov. Supported by Richthofen's Stukas and reunited with SSLAH, Hausser's panzer corps caught Rybalko's exposed spearhead around Staroverovka, mauling a number of divisions and pocketing some others. With the thaw creating mud all around them, both sides struggled to manoeuvre, but cold weather returned on 7 March and from positions near Merefa Hoth moved out again.

With Kempf applying pressure to the north-west, by 9 March 4. Panzer-Armee had split the seam between Golikov's 69th and 3rd tank Armies. The XLVIII Panzer-Korps attacked Kharkov from the south-west, SS Panzer-Korps from the north-west. Hausser encircled the city with Totenkopf, keeping any eye open for a chance to recapture it by *coup de main* in accordance with Hoth's instructions. Again Hausser and his army superiors disagreed over the method, and the SS began its assault on the 11th. Hausser's battle to recapture the city in March was as controversial as his decision to give it away in February. In what many historians consider to be wasteful frontal urban combat, SSLAH and Das Reich required three days of house-to-house fighting to re-take the city on 14 March.

Manstein still had one more mission remaining, to get Belgorod back. In the first half of March, as Hoth had been pushing toward Kharkov, Kempf had been aiming north-eastwards at Belgorod. Grossdeutschland led the way against a disorganized 69th Army, and by the time Kharkov surrendered had fought to within 25 miles. The cold weather remained and following Kharkov the SS Panzer-Korps re-oriented northward and in three days fought its way into the town. Manstein now considered his offensive concluded. By one count, his operations had destroyed 52 Red Army divisions and brigades, including 25 tank brigades. Heeresgruppe Süd occupied basically the same Donets–Mius line it had prior to Operation *Blau* nine months earlier – only much worse for wear and facing a new, confident Soviet military.

MAPS 69 & 70, THIRD AND FOURTH BATTLES OF KHARKOV

Arguably few Soviet cities saw as much combat as Kharkov. The Wehrmacht and Red Army had already fought over it in October 1941 and May 1942 (Maps 21 and 37–41) and would do so again in August 1943 (Map 76). Toward the end of winter of 1943 the city changed hand twice in one month (Maps 69–70). The adjoining map shows the third and fourth battles, parts of Operation *Star* and the Backhand Blow.

Map 69: Temporary Liberation – 2–16 February, 1943

The Stavka not only wanted Voronezh Front to smash German defences along the Donets River, capture Kharkov and scatter Wehrmacht reserves, it also told Golikov to surround the city and exterminate all enemy forces it trapped there. Supported by the 69th Army, Rybalko's 3rd Tank Army would sweep south of the city through Chuguyev to Lyubotin, where it would rendezvous with the 40th Army coming southwards. German defences were spread thin, centred on village strongpoints with two SS panzer grenadier divisions in Kharkov proper.

The 3rd Tank Army moved out on 2 February, but did not make anticipated progress; during the attack's first days SSLAH and Das Reich formations kept showing up at its front. The 40th Army began its assault on the 3rd and advanced as planned. Rybalko adjusted plans, ordered deliberate crossings of the Donets and by 6 February was once again on the march. Wehrmacht resistance slackened by the 9th and Lanz ordered the SS divisions back toward Kharkov. Meanwhile, 69th Army had its share of problems fighting Grossdeutschland, so Golikov ordered the 40th Army to pick up its pace; Belgorod fell on the 8th. This unhinged Lanz's left and signalled a general Wehrmacht withdrawal.

A frustrated Rybalko dropped ideas of fancy encirclements and on 10 February ordered a direct assault. Major portions of 3rd Tank and 69th Armies, to include 12th and 15th Tank Corps, finally got under way on the 12th against the two SS divisions, now joined by the retreating Grossdeutschland. For the next two days both sides engaged in deadly city fighting. By 14 February divisions of the 40th Army threatened Kharkov's northern suburbs and Lanz's rearward communications. Hausser could not decide whether or not his black SS uniform entitled him to disobey Hitler. By noon on the 16th German defences were hopelessly disorganized and the city lost.

Map 70: Temporary Reconquest – 5–14 March, 1943

By early March, Manstein's offensive was a dozen days old and the Soviets were reeling. Vatutin's 6th and 1st Guards Armies were streaming back, while Golikov had just seen his 3rd Tank Army chewed up south of Staroverovka and could expect similar treatment for his 40th and 69th Armies next. Voronezh Front shifted from offence to defence and even withdrew in places. By 5 March the XLVIII and SS Panzer-Korps engaged his positions south of Merefa as Manstein's *Schwerpunkt*, while Kempf also showed signs of taking up the attack in support of Hoth. Between 6 and 9 March 4. Panzer-Armee began rolling up the spread-out and depleted Red Armies. Confusion at the top level of Soviet field commanders made the job easier. Soon German units stood along Kharkov's last natural obstacles, the Mzha and Udy rivers, while the massive SS Panzer-Korps plus Grossdeutschland drove along the seam dividing the 69th and 3rd Tank Armies. On the 9th a small 40th Army counterattack from Bogodukhov failed to make much of a dent in the panzer juggernaut.

A day later, four of the Wehrmacht's biggest divisions stood abreast roughly north of Kharkov, creating a gap between Golikov's two southern-most armies 30 miles wide. With Grossdeutschland angling toward Belgorod (threatening to encircle the 69th Army) and SS Totenkopf executing the far encirclement of Kharkov, SSLAH entered the city from the north and Das Reich from the west. The 11. Panzer-Division of XLVIII Panzer-Korps came in from the south while also holding broken remnants of the 3rd Tank Army in the vicinity of Merefa and Zmiev. In Kharkov, commandant General Major E. E. Belov tried to organize a viable defence with his 19th Rifle Division, 17th NKVD Brigade and 86th Tank Brigade. A steady stream of Richthofen's CAS aircraft added to his problems. On 13–14 March SS Totenkopf continued its encircling manoeuvres east of Kharkov, while 11. Panzer-Division kept up its counterclockwise movement to the south. By the evening of the 14th the city had been cut off from outside succour. That same day, SSLAH and Das Reich worked their way through the nearly ruined Kharkov, breaking out of its eastern outskirts and into the Ukrainian countryside.

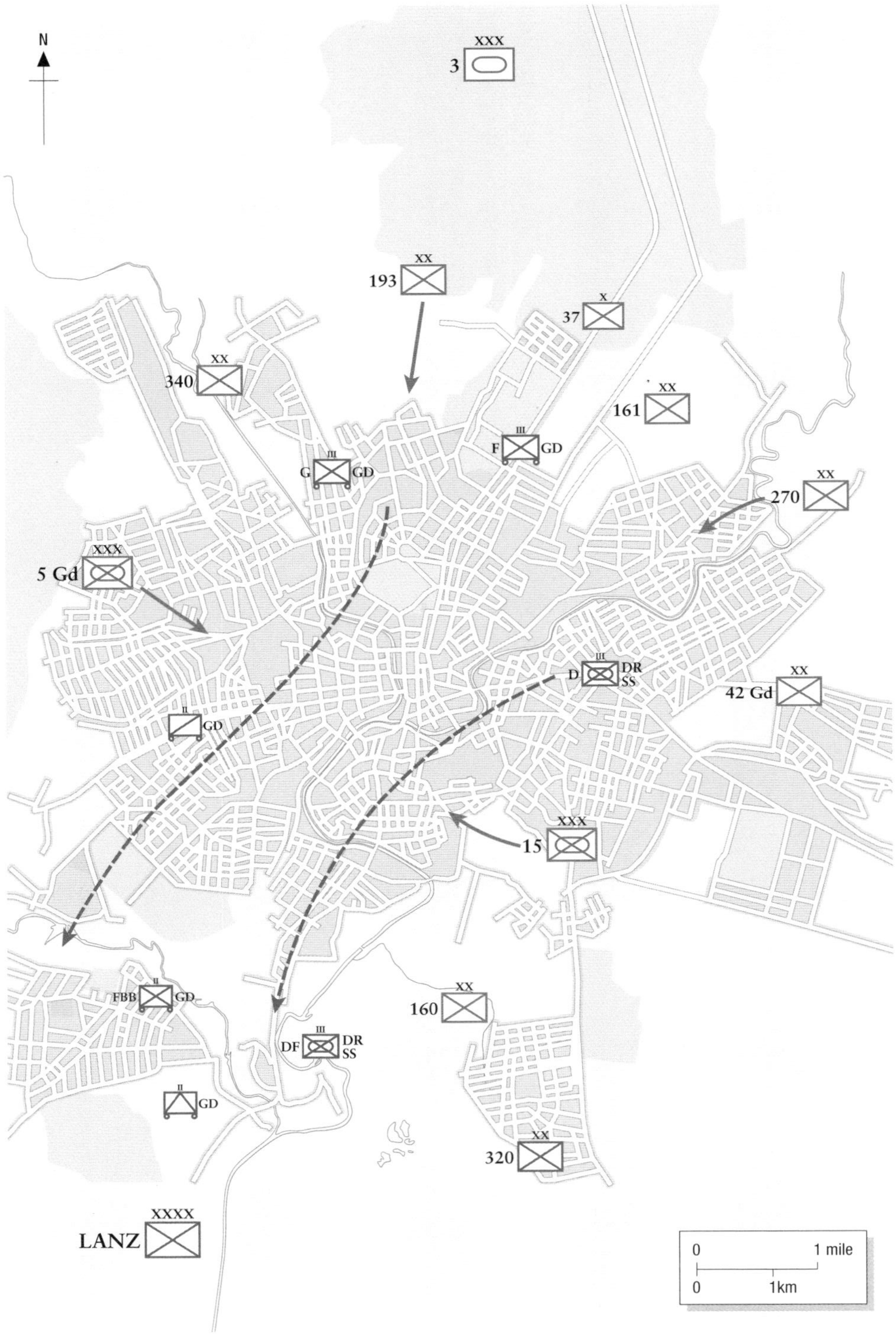

XXXX
69

III AH SS
1

AH SS XX
183 XX
AH SS XX

T SS XX

II AH SS

III AH SS
2

XX
19

III DR SS
DF

SS XXX

III DR SS
D

XX
DR SS

XX
303

O XX
11

XXX
XLVIII O

Front line 15 February

0   1km
0   1 mile

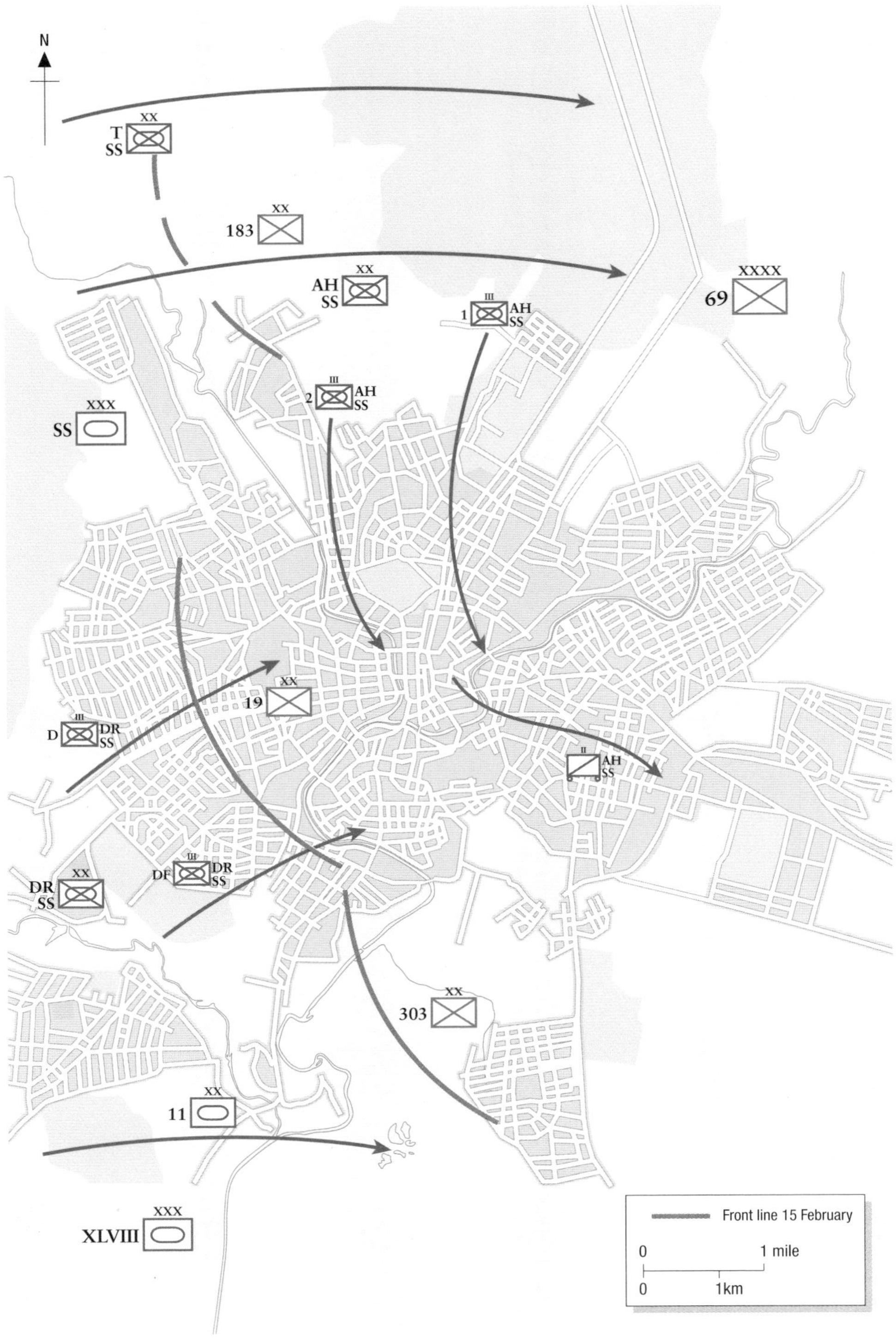

MAP 70

XXX
3 O

X
37 XX

XX
161

III GD
F

XX
193

III GD
G

XX
340

XXX
5 Gd

XX
270

XX
42 Gd

III DR SS
D

XXX
15 XX

XX
160

XX
320

III DR SS
DF

II GD

III GD
FBB

GD

LANZ XXXX

0   1km
0   1 mile

MAP 69

151

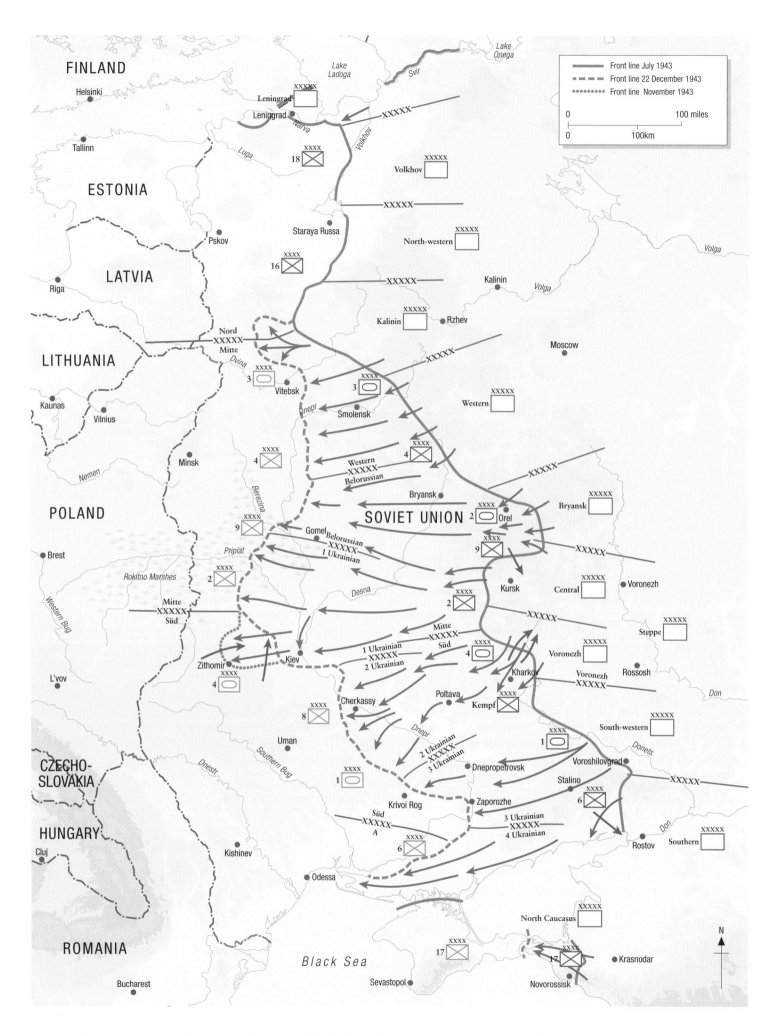

FINLAND

Helsinki

Lake
Ladoga

Svir

Lake
Onega

XXXXX · Front line July 1943
XXXXX - - Front line 22 December 1943
XXXXX · · Front line November 1943

0   100 miles
0   100km

Leningrad
Leningrad

Tallinn

Narva

18   XXXX

Volkhov

XXXXX

ESTONIA

Luga

Volkhov

Pskov

Staraya Russa

North-western   XXXXX

Volga

LATVIA

Riga

Dvina

16   XXXX

XXXXX

Kalinin

Volga

Kalinin   XXXXX   Rzhev

Moscow

LITHUANIA

Kaunas

Vilnius

Nord
XXXXX
Mitte
Dvina

3   XXXX
Vitebsk

Dnepr

3   XXXX

Smolensk

XXXXX

Western   XXXXX

Nemen

Minsk

4   XXXX

Western
XXXXX
Belorussian

4   XXXX

XXXXX

POLAND

Berezina

9   XXXX

Bryansk

SOVIET UNION

2   XXXX
Orel

Bryansk   XXXXX

Brest

Gomel
Belorussian
XXXXX
1 Ukrainian

Pripiat

Rokitno Marshes

2   XXXX

9   XXXX

XXXXX

Western Bug

Mitte
XXXXX
Süd

Desna

Kursk

2   XXXX

Central   XXXXX

Voronezh

XXXXX

Steppe   XXXXX

L'vov

Zithomir

4   XXXX

Kiev

1 Ukrainian
XXXXX
2 Ukrainian

Mitte
XXXXX
Süd

4   XXXX

Voronezh   XXXXX

Voronezh
XXXXX

Rossosh

Don

8   XXXX

Cherkassy

Poltava

Kharkov

Kempf   XXXX

South-western   XXXXX

Donets

CZECHO-
SLOVAKIA

Dnestr

Uman

Southern Bug

1   XXXX

2 Ukrainian
XXXXX
3 Ukrainian

Dnepropetrovsk

1   XXXX

Voroshilovgrad

Stalino

6   XXXX

Don

HUNGARY

Cluj

Kishinev

Krivoi Rog

Süd
XXXXX
A

6   XXXX

Zaporozhe

3 Ukrainian
XXXXX
4 Ukrainian

Rostov   Southern   XXXXX

ROMANIA

Bucharest

Odessa

Black Sea

17   XXXX

Sevastopol

North Caucasus   XXXXX

17   XXXX

Novorossisk

Krasnodar

N

CHAPTER 5
SUMMER AND AUTUMN 1943

Conventional wisdom holds that Germany and Japan had to win the war in 1942, or at least create successful conditions to do so in the first half of 1943. But between limited ability or inclination to co-operate, poor strategic thinking, limited resources, economic and industrial inferiority, occupation policies sure to create hostile populations, a USSR that could not be knocked out and the arrival of the USA, the two main Axis powers could do neither. Instead of a victorious period, at Stalingrad and its aftermath and in the Pacific, the tide of war had turned against both. In Europe the Soviets took the strategic initiative at Stalingrad, never to give it back; operationally the Germans briefly got the upper hand at Kharkov, never to have it again. Neither side knew it at the time, but by that March the Red Army had suffered its last major defeat while the Wehrmacht had won its last victory of any size.

Owing to exhaustion and *rasputitsa* around Kursk, where both sides came to rest in the spring of 1943, a large salient projected into German lines. Stung by Manstein's Backhand Blow, the Stavka decided to stand back during the approaching campaign season, improve Soviet defences, create reserves and welcome Hitler's next summer offensive, which it knew was on the way. The Soviets took this decision not from a position of weakness, as in 1941 and 1942, but from one of strength. It held the high ground in the battle over intelligence as Ultra intercepts, strategic reconnaissance and partisans provided a wealth of information about German deployments and intentions. Despite enormous losses caused by the various operations associated with Stalingrad, German numbers had recovered by mid-1943. The difference this time, however, would be improvements in the Red Army's situation. Manstein had taught it an expensive lesson in the advantages of a flexible defence followed by stinging counterattacks.[89] Command and control arrangements, organizational makeup of divisions, corps and armies, interaction of infantry, artillery, armour, CAS and support branches, plus other doctrinal, manpower and equipment issues, were either solved or close to being worked out and would carry the Red Army to Berlin with minor adjustments. The Stavka placed its best leaders, soldiers and weapons in the region of the Kursk salient in at least eight defensive echelons, and, as importantly, in ready reserve behind it.

89 The growing power of the defence that would continue through the end of the war, including such individual anti-tank weapons as the shaped-charge Panzerfaust, helps explain the huge numbers of Soviet forces employed in their subsequent attacks and defensives.

As for the Germans, the main significance of the Kursk battle is not its failure but the fact that they squandered panzer and air assets on such a low pay-off enterprise. Even shortening their lines and dealing the enemy a setback on a limited frontage would not have been much of an achievement on so huge a front. Wehrmacht losses even in victory would have left them poorly positioned to defend against an expected Soviet counterblow. As I have argued elsewhere,[90] faulty doctrine and leadership, not shrinking numbers of armoured fighting vehicles, cause us to mark Manstein's Backhand Blow as the end of German operational-level manoeuvre. Likewise, declining Axis fortunes in the Mediterranean, specifically the need to fight a two-front war in Sicily and Mussolini's ignominious dismissal two weeks later, stretched German resources. Halfway through 1943, political realities had not yet caught up with their geostrategic counterparts. Hitler's Third Reich required forward movement, which meant going on the offensive that summer when perhaps that was not really the best course of action. Lingering hubris, still somehow in the Wehrmacht's subconscious after Stalingrad, further demanded that it attack and presumably destroy the best Red Army elements on the battlefield. Operation Zitadelle at Kursk, the largest of a number of operational-sized attacks planned all along the front for that summer, would do the most work in accomplishing this goal.

For the offensive, the Germans assembled 430,000 men and more than 3,100 AFVs against 1,500,000 men and approximately 4,800 AFVs. Famously, Hitler kept delaying the attack's start date until new Panther and Tiger tanks and Ferdinand tank destroyers rolled off the assembly lines and joined operational units. Along with increased industrial output under Albert Speer, these new panzers were meant to erase the quality deficit in armoured forces that Germany had suffered from since Barbarossa's first day. Soviet defenders put the extra time to good use, improving their defences. As late as the second half of June, many of Hitler's advisers strongly recommended Zitadelle's cancellation. Starting on 5 July, Heeresgruppe Mitte would attack from the north of the bulge and Heeresgruppe Süd from the south.[91] By this time the situation on the ground since the original order in April had changed markedly. The Soviets deployed two fronts up and one back, all three well prepared and resourced and led by a trio of skilled and experienced generals of the post-Barbarossa generation: N.F. Vatutin, Rokossovsky and Konev.

Such was the state of decline and neglect of mechanized operational manoeuvre thinking in the Wehrmacht that an infantry army led Mitte's operation, while a panzer army, the largest and best resourced during Barbarossa 24 months earlier, watched from the sidelines in defensive positions. Despite being commanded by one of Hitler's darlings, Generaloberst Walter Model – also a skilled leader – this northern effort ground to a stop in a matter of days after gaining barely 10 miles. The southern pincer's commander, one of the panzer branch's most solid performers, Generaloberst Hermann Hoth (himself an

infantry general), had a much better weapon at his disposal and made more progress against the Soviets. Throughout the theatre, German success often depended on Luftwaffe CAS and fighter cover. However, the new marks of panzers suffered from debilitating maintenance problems. After a week Hoth's men, aided by an infantry army covering their right outer flank, had pierced approximately five defensive lines. This set the scene for the war's largest tank battle at Prokhorovka between 10 and 13 July. Though Soviet tank losses were almost double those of the Germans, they had many more to give. On the following day Hitler had Manstein (and his counterpart from Heeresgruppe Mitte) report to his command post at nearby Vinnitsa, where he cancelled the offensive; the field marshal resisted, believing that his troops stood on the verge of victory. But Zitadelle had peaked, and, sated with the human and materiel sacrifice, petered out ten days later.

Partial proof that Zitadelle did not cause system overload within the Red Army as Barbarossa and Blau had in earlier years is that partway through the offensive it was able to launch its own attacks against elements of both German army groups directly involved around Kursk. In the Heeresgruppe Mitte sector, Operation Kutuzov achieved no significant breakthroughs against prepared Wehrmacht defences, but in a matter of hours helped hasten the end of Model's Zitadelle attack and in another five weeks eliminated the Orel salient altogether. Against Heeresgruppe Süd, Soviet forces attacked defences along the Mius River that had stood for six months. The Wehrmacht overreacted to this tactical threat by dispatching the equivalent of a panzer army to the Donbas.[92] This move could have hardly played into the Stavka's hands better. While the panzers temporarily restored the Mius Front, it meant that Germany's premier operational weapon was out of place when it was really needed.

Not long after Zitadelle culminated, assuming that the offensive had been harder on the enemy than his own troops, Manstein predicted the Soviets could not quickly or easily transition to the attack. He turns out not to have been quite as prescient as he liked to think. The day after the field marshal's forecast, a dozen Soviet armies, which had sat out the Zitadelle battle and totalled almost 100 divisions, blasted Heeresgruppe Süd's defenders in a sophisticated series of co-ordinated assaults. First hit were infantrymen in their re-occupied pre-Zitadelle positions (which had likewise been strengthened during the spring and early summer). From that point, Operation Rumiantsev spread north and south in attacks cleverly sequenced by the Stavka in such a way as to keep the Wehrmacht either off balance or guessing what would come next. German mobile reserves were in short supply; besides the burnt hulks in Zitadelle's wake, many of Manstein's best formations manned the fragile front line or else stood hundreds of miles from the main action, such as the three panzer corps ill-advisedly sent to the tangential sector in the Donbas. Such counterattacks as he could manage did not appreciably slow the enemy. Rumiantsev seemed like a larger and more destructive version of Uranus, only with perfect summer weather, even more skilled Soviet leadership, no hapless Romanians for Hitler to blame, and dangerously was much closer to Germany. Operations like

---

90 *Hitler's Panzer Armies on the Eastern Front.*

91 A less intuitive indicator of German weakness is that their 1942 and 1943 summer offensives each began later in the valuable campaign season: *Blau* started a week later than *Barbarossa*, *Zitadelle* a week later than *Blau*.

92 Two army and one SS panzer corps.

Rumiantsev were not just Cyrillic copies of the blitzkrieg, but represented unique expressions of Soviet military art tailored to their new skillset. The Red Army would keep up its drab but remorseless pressure along a broad front until nearly 1944; it gave Heeresgruppe Süd no respite.

The Soviet offensives transitioned from summer to autumn, punctuated only by brief logistics halts and barely interfered with by Manstein. Natural barriers did not cause significant delays, as the assaults continued despite *rasputitsa* or rivers like the Dnepr. They were not things of beauty, but carried forward largely thanks to firepower. The Red Army Air Force ruled the skies, while German soldiers on the ground lamented the disappearance of the Luftwaffe, increasingly chased from the sky from Brittany to Berlin to Belorussia. However, Soviet attacks lacked the finesse of deep penetrations and, despite periodically losing contact with Heeresgruppe Mitte, Manstein managed to keep Soviet forces squarely in front of him, avoiding large encirclements. German success consisted primarily in maintaining itself on the battlefield in the face of blistering attacks and executing the occasional panzer corps-sized counterblow.

Kharkov, which Hitler still wanted held, changed hands for the fourth and last time during World War II on 22 August.[93] Around the same time Red Army troops levered the defenders off the Mius River to the south. Without these two anchors at the army group's extremities, the broad Ukraine did not possess much in the way of terrain features around which to focus a defence. To exacerbate the situation, without sufficient mechanized forces it proved difficult if not impossible to fight an elastic or mobile defence. All Hitler's eastern army could do was fall back as the Stavka concentrated on the southern theatre. This included the far south as well: Hitler conceded on the senseless Kuban beachhead and in late September allowed the beleaguered garrison to cross the Kerch Straits. Relief was short-lived, however, since barely a month later the same men were trapped on the Crimea as advancing Soviets closed off the Perekop isthmus on their way to the mouth of the Dnepr. The Führer likewise relented concerning holding the river's largely featureless left bank and gave permission to withdraw toward the west and the imagined security of an eastern bulwark.

Throughout late summer the Red Army pushed the Wehrmacht back to, and then across, the Dnepr River. The Germans placed inordinate credit on shortened fronts, their scorched-earth retreat, enemy attrition and lengthening supply lines, plus other illusory and transitory factors. Despite the river's broad width, it gave them just as little defensive benefit in 1943 as it did to the Soviets during *Barbarossa*. By the second half of September 1943, Red Army groups large and small had crossed at numerous points, often barely disputed by the Wehrmacht. Satisfied, they did not put much effort into anything more than simply advancing on a broad front. A month later, near Krivoi Rog, Manstein managed to launch a multi-corps-sized counterattack, large for that stage of the war, and earn some breathing space, but little more. His men could not prevent the Red Army from liberating Kiev on 6 November or from pushing into the western Ukraine in December. The Wehrmacht did manage to assemble a two-panzer-corps counterattack force near Zithomir and Fastov, dealing the Soviets a sharp reverse during the third week of November. Elsewhere late that autumn, the Germans gave up ground around Gomel in the Heeresgruppe Mitte area and near Nevel on Heeresgruppe Nord's right.

Two months into *Barbarossa*, Hitler told Goebbels that if he had known earlier of the true capabilities and size of the Soviet military, he might have made another decision about going to war in the east. There are plenty of reasons not to believe his retroactive good sense and prudence. Respected historians have likewise speculated that if two years later he had known of the stout defences around Kursk he would not have launched *Zitadelle* either.[94] There is good cause not to believe this as well, mainly since Hitler was not the sort of man to allow logic and statistics to influence his decisions. Red Army advances during the second half of 1943 were relentless. If Hitler thought that year was bad, he needed only to wait for 1944.

---

93 This was the fifth battle of Kharkov. The Soviets got close but did not capture the city in May 1942.

94 Willmott, H.P. The Great Crusade, p., 304. Glantz and House, When Titans Clashed, p. 165.

MAP 72: OPERATION *ZITADELLE* (I), SOUTH 5–10 JULY, 1943

Over the previous four years, spring or summer had brought victorious campaigns to Hitler. Unfortunately for him, the winter and spring of 1943 had been so disastrous, with Stalingrad and north Africa lost, that Germany would be in the unenviable and unusual position of resorting to the strategic defensive. The Third Reich no longer had the resources for a prolonged offensive and clearly the growing strength of the USSR and USA would give Hitler no rest. Therefore in March and April the German high command came up with a viable option of using Manstein's newly won positions and reserves, freed up by such common sense tactics as the *Büffelbewegung*, to fight a mobile defence throughout the entire eastern theatre. According to their plan, when mobility returned in the spring they would eliminate irregularities in the southern front, including the Kursk bulge, subdue Leningrad in the summer, and then wait for Stalin.

Lingering doubts caused by sceptical generals, new weapon production, weather and intelligence on the Red Army led to numerous delays. Hitler came close to cancelling *Zitadelle*, but he was a politician and the political need to demonstrate the Third Reich's vitality trumped military logic: the attack would go forward. The Wehrmacht plan was straightforward: to cut off the Kursk bulge with Hoth's 4. Panzer-Armee (Manstein's *Schwerpunkt*, six mechanized divisions) and Armee-Abteilung Kempf (three panzer divisions) from the south and Model's 9. Armee from the north (Map 74). Hoth and Kempf commanded 168,000 men, 3,600 guns and 1,700 AFVs. Supporting all of Heeresgruppe Süd, but concentrated for *Zitadelle*, Fourth Air Fleet had over 2,300 aircraft, including 1,071 Stukas. Arrayed against Manstein stood Vatutin's Voronezh Front (six armies), in deep, well-prepared strongpoint defences, totalling 1,087,000 men, 13,013 guns and 3,275 AFVs. In a cruel reversal of fortunes, they were backed up by five field and three tank armies in reserve. From the beginning, the Stavka's plan was to wait for the Germans to exhaust themselves and then unleash these reserve forces; Zhukov and Vasilevski would co-ordinate operations.

The Soviets learned of *Zitadelle* in April and spoiled the 5 July start with a pre-emptive artillery barrage. Over 1,000 Luftwaffe aircraft then heralded the beginning of the offensive, and by the end of the day panzer spearheads had pierced the first defensive belts. The Red Army's minefields and inter-connected fields of fire created a nasty welcome.

The Germans made advances in 2–3 mile increments but the XLVIII Panzer-Korps kept its eyes on the Psel River bridge at Oboyan. That day Vatutin dispatched his front reserve corps to the threatened area: 3rd Mechanized plus 6th Tank and 5th and 2nd Guards Tank Corps. By the evening of 6 July, Hausser's SS Panzer-Grenadier-Regiment 4 Der Führer had reached the village of Luchki, 20 miles deep in the Soviet positions, but were met by 5th and 2nd Guards Tank Corps. To the west, near Alexieva on the Pena River, Grossdeutschland likewise encountered the 6th Tank Corps. To the right, Kempf's forces struggled to keep pace.

By 7 July the II SS Panzer-Korps had smashed 6th Guards Army, and, now past Luchki, SSLAH and Totenkopf fanned out. Vatutin began to despair of Oboyan and its bridge just half a dozen miles from his own headquarters at Bobryshevo. A day later, 2nd Guards Tank Corps continued to harass Totenkopf on Hausser's right until the timely arrival of Luftwaffe CAS. Tank attacks pinned down Totenkopf on the 9th as well. However, all eyes were on 4. Panzer-Armee's *Schwerpunkt*, 3. and 11. Panzer-Divisionen, Grossdeutschland, SSLAH and Das Reich, with four infantry divisions on flank security duty, pushing up the motorway from Belgorod to Oboyan. Fresh units of 1st Tank Army at Kalinovka joined remnants of 6th Guards Army near Kochetovka to halt them.

At this juncture, the Germans made a critical decision to divide their main striking force: XLVIII Panzer-Korps would continue to Oboyan while SS Panzer-Korps would angle to the north-east and Prokhorovka (Map 73). General der Panzertruppen Otto von Knobelsdorff urged his men on and on 10 July Grossdeutschland crossed the tiny Pena at Verkhopenye. Along with 11. Panzer-Division it attacked the high ground separating that stream from the Psel, but halted 7 miles from Oboyan and was re-directed toward the developing battle at Prokhorovka. At the opposite end of the battlefield, III Panzer-Korps had finally begun moving generally parallel to the SS, but found itself on the wrong side of the Donets River, more than a dozen miles from Prokhorovka. Generalleutnant Hermann Breith crossed the river at Rzhavets, but the 2nd Guards Tank Corps kept him from joining in the battle. On that same day the Western Allies landed on the coast of Sicily.

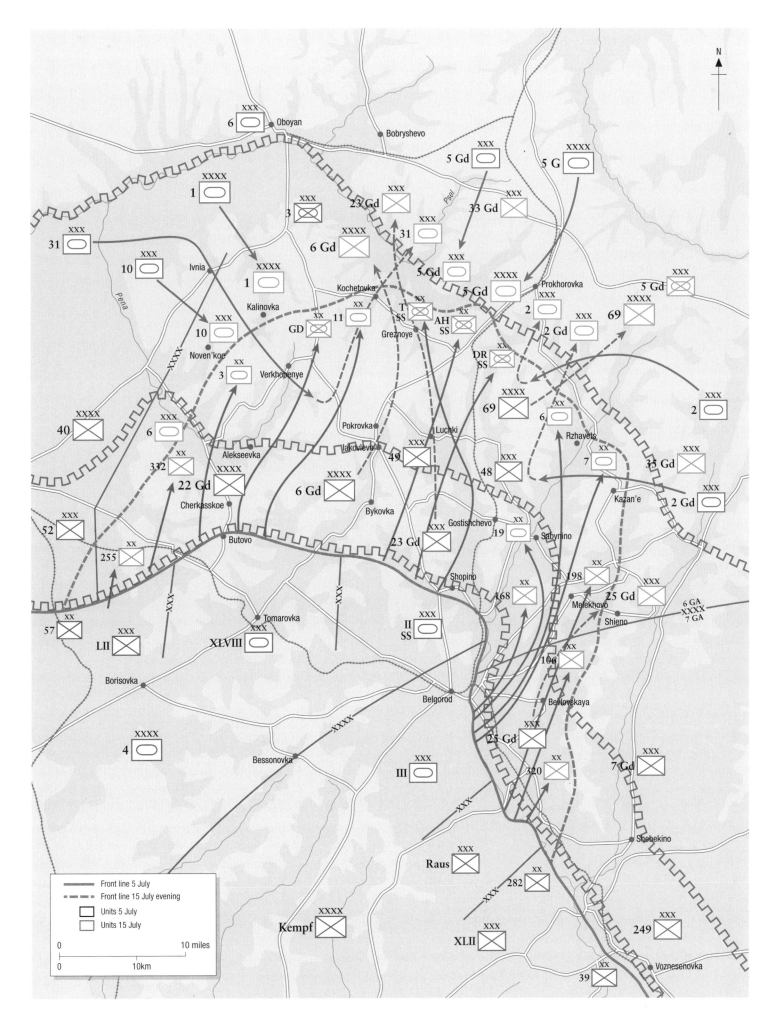

6 Oboyan
Bobryshevo
5 Gd
5 G

1
3
23 Gd
31
33 Gd

31
6 Gd
5 Gd
5 Gd

10
Ivnia
1
Kochetovka
5 Gd

Kalinovka
T SS
2
2 Gd
69

10
GD
11
Greznoye
AH SS

Noven'koe
DR SS

3
Verkhopenye

40
Pokrovka
Luchki
69
6
2

6
Rzhavets

332
Alekseevka
Jakovlevo
49
7
35 Gd

22 Gd
Cherkasskoe
48
Kazan'e
2 Gd

52
Bykovka
Gostishchevo
19
Sabynino

255
6 Gd
23 Gd
198
25 Gd
6 GA
7 GA

57
Butovo
Shopino
25 Gd

LII
XLVIII
Tomarovka
468
Melekhovo
Shieno

II SS
106

Borisovka

Belgorod
Bervlovskaya

4
Bessonovka
III
25 Gd
320
7 Gd

Shebekino

Raus
282

Front line 5 July
Front line 15 July evening
Units 5 July
Units 15 July
0   10 miles
0   10km

Kempf
XLII
249

39
Voznesenovka

157

MAP 73: OPERATION *ZITADELLE* (II), PROKHOROVKA – 10–13 JULY, 1943

Marshal Vatutin noticed the move by Hausser's panzer corps toward Prokhorovka, and on the evening of 10 July reported his plans to Stalin. He had two fresh guards armies moving south into the area to blunt the SS drive: General Lieutenant P. A. Rotmistrov's 5th Guards Tank Army (approximately 850 AFVs) and General Lieutenant A. S. Zhadov's 5th Guards Army. The help arrived at a critical time, since 6th Guards Army had been locked in mortal combat for nearly a week while 1st Guards Tank Army was also heavily engaged. In places the Germans had penetrated three army defensive belts, but two layers of front defences still guarded Kursk.

Meanwhile, Hoth thought *Zitadelle* had finally reached a point where his panzers were about to break into the open; he expected a decisive battle on the 12th. Totenkopf had a bridgehead north of the Psel River and Manstein ordered the XXIV Panzer-Korps (23. Panzer-Division and SS Wiking, about 100 AFVs) north from the 1. Panzer-Armee area to exploit the expected success (off map to the south). To the south-east, Kempf's men had redoubled their efforts and were one day away from crossing the Donets, with 6. Panzer-Division in the lead and 7. and 19. Panzer-Divisionen close behind (approximately 300 AFVs, also off map to the south). With any luck, in a couple of days Manstein's panzers would decisively outnumber Vatutin's tanks. Unknown to him, however, there was no 'open field' in the Kursk battlefield; Red Army defensive belts ran throughout the entire bulge.

On 11 July, Hoth tried to pound the battered 1st Guard Tank Army into submission before Rotmistrov and Zhadov could contribute in a meaningful way. With XLVIII Panzer-Korps holding the salient's western shoulder, the main task of creating the critical penetration fell on Hausser's three SS divisions (600 AFVs). The 12th was *Zitadelle*'s critical day for two reasons: a new Soviet offensive against Heeresgruppe Mitte's Orel positions caused the 9. Armee's northern pincer to be cancelled (Maps 74–75), and Vatutin's two new guards armies smashed directly into the SS Panzer-Korps. On the 12th barely a dozen miles separated Manstein's two subordinates, and Vatutin intentionally

inserted Rotmistrov between 4. Panzer-Armee and Kempf to keep the two armies from joining. Massed around Prokhorovka, late on the night of the 11th the 5th Guards Tank Army drove south-west along the road to Luchki with three tanks corps abreast, followed by the 5th Mechanized Corps. Its 18th and 29th Tank Corps ran straight into SSLAH attacking north-eastwards while its 2nd Tank Corps hit Das Reich around Kalinin. On the right flank of Das Reich, 2nd Guards Tank Corps added its weight to make sure Hausser and Breith, now less than 10 miles distant, remained separated.

The heaviest fighting that day, and the largest tank battle in history, took place in a box 4 by 6 miles in size centred on the plain between the Psel and the railway line coming out of Prokhorovka. The three regiments of SSLAH and the 18th and 29th Tank Corps were locked in a life and death struggle, while the lead elements of the 5th Guards Army attacked from the march against Totenkopf attempting to expand its bridgehead over the Psel. Over 500 panzers, including more than 100 Tigers, fought it out against better than 800 Soviet tanks, mostly T-34s. Amidst the mechanized slaughter, the 9th Guards Airborne Division defended the road into Prokhorovka against the SSLAH spearhead, 1 ½ miles from the town. Aircraft from both sides on CAS missions filled the skies. With Breith's III Panzer-Korps across the Donets that afternoon, Manstein pushed Kempf to encircle the 69th Army, now dangerously exposed between the two panzer thrusts.

This was not 1941 or 1942, and Hoth and Kempf could not pull the trigger on the *Kessel*. On 13 July, Manstein and Kluge reported to Hitler at Rastenburg to hear that *Zitadelle* had to be cancelled, mainly due to the situations in Italy and the Heeresgruppe Mitte sector. Manstein, overestimating his strength and progress and underestimating remaining Soviet defensive belts and lurking reserves, argued to continue the attack. That day, Wehrmacht and Soviet forces continued to sway back and forth over the battlefield around Prokhorovka and the Psel bridgehead. But III Panzer-Korps was nowhere to be seen and Hitler had made up his mind.

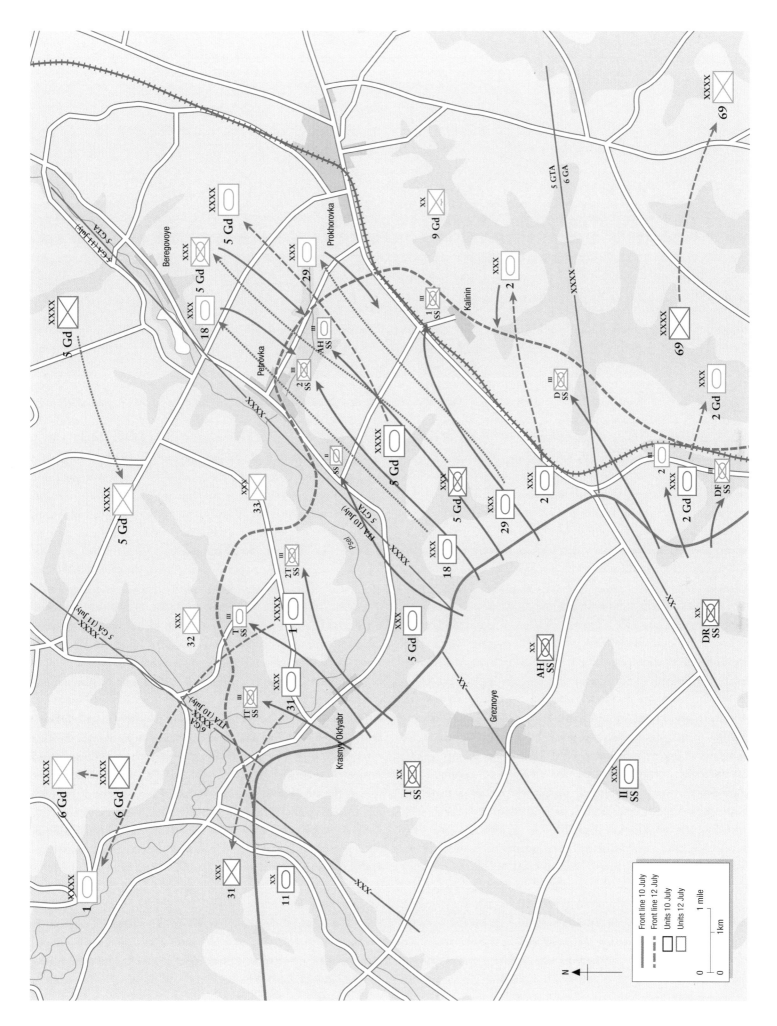

5 Gd

Beregovoye

5 Gd

XXX
18 5 Gd

Petrovka

33

XXX
32

6 GA
XXXX
1TA (10 July)

TT
SS
31

6 Gd

6 Gd

1

31

11

29

Prokhorovka

AH
SS

2
SS

5 Gd

5 Gd

18

5 GTA
1TA (10 July)
Psël

2T
SS

1

T
SS

Krasny Okfyabr

T
SS

9 Gd

Kalinin

2

1
SS

2

D
SS

2

5 GTA
6 GA

69

69

2 Gd

2

2 Gd

DF
SS

Greznoye

AH
SS

DR
SS

II
SS

N

Front line 10 July
Front line 12 July
Units 10 July
Units 12 July

0   1km
0   1 mile

159

MAP 74: OPERATION *ZITADELLE* (III), NORTH 5–12 JULY, 1943

Generaloberst Model's 9. Armee's thrust from the north was clearly *Zitadelle*'s secondary effort. Of the offensive's senior commanders, Model was perhaps the most pessimistic, trying in April, May and June to talk Hitler and the two army group commanders out of attacking such a well-defended position. The 9. Armee looked like a Panzer-heavy army considering its three panzer corps (XLVI, XLVII and XLI) and two army corps (XXIII and XX) and Model had near-parity in AFVs, 1,455:1,745. However, XLI Panzer-Korps had only one panzer division on its order of battle (18. Panzer-Division), while XLVI Panzer had none. The XLVII Panzer-Korps, with 6. Infanterie-Division and 2., 9. and 20. Panzer-Divisionen under General der Panzertruppen Joachim Lemelsen, was Model's *Schwerpunkt*, with 4. and 12. Panzer-Divisionen and 10. Panzer-Grenadier-Division in reserve. Model had 266,000 men and almost 6,336 indirect fire weapons under his command. Approximately 730 aircraft from Luftflotte 6 would provide CAS from airfields around Orel.[95]

Like the Voronezh Front to the south, Rokossovsky's Central Front was well-resourced and dug into stout defences. He had five field armies (13th, 48th, 70th, 65th and 60th) and the 2nd Tank Army with Konev's Steppe Front in reserve east of Kursk, at the base of the salient backing the entire effort. As mentioned previously (Map 72), the Kursk defences included extensive fieldworks constructed by pioneer troops with recently liberated and newly impressed civilian teams; defensive densities were orders of magnitude greater than those found at Moscow or Stalingrad. Facing Model stood 667,000 Red Army soldiers, 14,163 guns and mortars all supported by three Red Army Air Force aviation corps. Partisan bands conducted co-ordinated actions against the Germans throughout the *Zitadelle* area. In common with many Soviet operations at that point of the war, they held the bulk of their artillery at higher headquarters behind the front, while Rokossovsky had many reserve formations backing up his front line.

As in the south, alerted by excellent intelligence, Red artillery conducted a pre-emptive counter-preparation barrage two hours before the Germans moved out. On the morning of 5 July, 9. Armee attacked the left of General Lieutenant I. V. Galanin's 70th and the right of

General Lieutenant N. P. Pukhov's 13th Armies, with the *Schwerpunkt* mainly hitting the latter. Model moved out along a 35-mile frontage with three corps side by side, with XXIII Armee-Korps in reserve and XLVII Panzer-Korps ready to exploit through any penetrations. A key distinction between Model's and Hoth's techniques was that the former led with his infantry; nine of his first echelon divisions were infantry. Tigers and the new Ferdinand heavy tank destroyers of the lone panzer division accompanied the infantry forward to deal with Soviet AFVs and strongpoints. Having broken into the first defensive belt by a depth of 3–4 miles by afternoon, the Germans pushed on as Red Army units occupied rearward positions and continued their defence, which had bowed but not broken.

Later during that first day, Model, having achieved an initial breakthrough, was ready to develop his *Schwerpunkt*, so ordered Lemelsen's XLVII Panzer-Korps out of its assembly areas and into the fighting. Most combat took place in the 20-mile space between the road and railway line leading from Orel to Kursk. Model had crammed four panzer and two infantry divisions into this area, and had advanced only about 8 miles at a cost of 25,000 casualties and 200 AFVs out of action that first day alone. On 6 July, his men had to start again through trench after trench against defenders seemingly as prepared and strong as the day before. Rokossovsky clearly identified the enemy's main thrust and spread out three tank corps to hold the arc from Molotychi (19th Tank) to Olkhovatska (16th) to Ponyri Station (3rd). Wehrmacht troops gained an additional 2–3 miles that day, but no more. By the 7th, with ten infantry and four panzer divisions inside a crescent 30 miles wide and perhaps 10 miles deep, there was no room to manoeuvre. Rokossovsky had his T-34s dug into hull-down positions, which, operating with large anti-tank brigades, the panzers could not defeat. On 8 July, Model brought forward Gruppe von Esebeck, his reserve, which mainly added to the congestion. He tried to build new *Schwerpunkt*s shifting between Olkhovatska and Ponyri Station without success.

Ponyri Station became the focus of the heaviest fighting as both sides attacked and counterattacked, advanced and gave ground. By 10–11 July *Landser*s and *frontoviki* shared the village between them, like a miniature Stalingrad according to Geoffrey Jukes. On the 12th, Central, Bryansk and Western fronts launched an attack to pinch off the Orel salient (Map 75), and Kluge called off *Zitadelle*'s northern portion.

95 As of early July Luftflotte 6 counted more than 2,000 aircraft, not all of them operational, in support of the entire Heeresgruppe Mitte, including 647 Stukas.

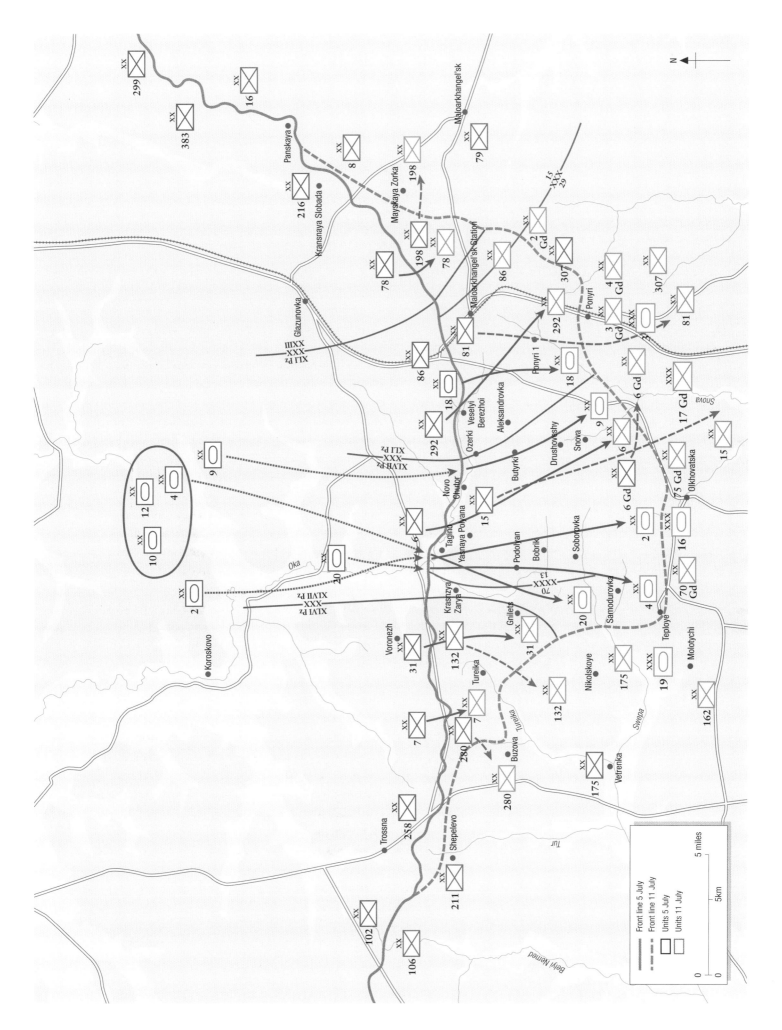

N

Korostovo

Trossna

Panskaya

Krasnaya Slobada

Glazunovka

XXX
XLI Pz
XXIII

XXX
XLVIII Pz
XLVII Pz

XXX
XLVII Pz
XLVI Pz

Oka

Novo
Chutor

Tagino

Yasnaya Polyana

Krasnaya
Zarya

Voronezh

Gnilets

Tureika

Shepelevo

Buzova

Ozerki
Veselyi
Berezhoi

Aleksandrovka

Butyrki

Drushoveshy

Snova

Podolyan

Bobrik

Soborovka

Samodurovka

Nikolskoye

Vetrenka

Molotychi

Teploye

Olkhovatska

Maloarkhangel'sk

Mayskaya Zorka

Maloarkhangel'sk Station

Ponyri

Ponyri 1

XXX
15
29

Snova

Swepa

Tur

Belyi Nemed

Tureika

XXXX
70

XXXX
13

299

16

383

8

216

198

78

78

198

86

79

198

2 Gd

307

307

4 Gd

81

3 Gd

3

6 Gd

17 Gd

81

86

18

292

292

18

15

6

9

16

75 Gd

6 Gd

2

16

4

70 Gd

15

20

19

162

175

175

132

31

7

7

280

280

31

132

6

258

211

102

106

12

4

10

9

6

20

2

5 miles

5km

0

0

Front line 5 July
Front line 11 July
Units 5 July
Units 11 July

161

MAP 75: OPERATION *KUTUZOV* 14 JULY TO 14 AUGUST, 1943

During the spring of 1943, both Hitler and his high command and Stalin and his staff knew that operations over the summer and autumn would go to the side with the strongest and most well rested reserves. In the first two years of the Nazi-Soviet War Hitler and Stalin would attack, become intoxicated with victory, push the troops too far and then have no reserves remaining when the inevitable counteroffensive struck. With *Zitadelle* Hitler consumed Germany's mobile reserves in less than two weeks of fruitless, almost World War I-style attacks against an established defence, and opened the door to Stalin's countermoves.

Unlike 1941 and 1942, in 1943 Stalin did not wait and launched Operation *Kutuzov* at the height of *Zitadelle*. True, the smaller northern effort had culminated, but the southern portion had yet to reach its anticlimactic ending. According to the Stavka plan, West and Bryansk fronts would attack against Heeresgruppe Mitte's Orel bulge on 12 July, and Rokossovsky would join battle as soon as he was able, which would not be too long since the damage caused by Model had been moderate compared to that which Manstein had dealt to Vatutin. General Colonel V. D. Sokolovsky's Western Front (50th and 11th Guards Armies) would attack through the ancient Bryn Forest toward Khotynets, while General Colonel M. M. Popov's Bryansk Front (61st, 3rd and 63rd Armies) was to cave in the north face around Mtsensk. Each front had an air army in support. Total combined Red Army forces were 1,287,000 soldiers, over 21,000 guns and mortars, 2,400 AFVs and more than 2,000 aircraft. Marshal of Artillery N. N. Voronov acted as the Stavka co-ordinator.

Operation *Kutuzov* went up against the weak centre of Kluge's army group: Schmidt's 2. Panzer-Armee (not a single panzer division assigned!) and Model's 9. Armee, still decisively engaged with *Zitadelle's* northern attack. In addition to a thin outer crust of infantry divisions, German defences included fortified cities and the towns of Bolchov, Mtsensk, Karachev, Orel and Zmievka. Soviet intelligence reckoned that the Wehrmacht had five divisions in reserve in the entire theatre, and Kluge had only one panzer division not involved in *Zitadelle*, 5. Panzer-Division. Almost 600,000 German troops occupied the salient, supported by 7,000 artillery pieces, 1,000 panzers and 1,100 aircraft. On 14 July Hitler put Model in overall control of the battle.

Operation *Kutuzov* began with pre-emptive airstrikes and a 2½-hour artillery barrage. The 11th Guards, 61st, 3rd and 63rd Armies assaulted on individually narrow fronts and by the end of the day had advanced between 10 and 15 miles. The 11th Guards created a breakthrough near Ktsyn through which it passed the 5th Tank Corps, while the 61st Army penetrated initial German defences at Telchye. German defences maintained cohesion, but as discussed above (Map 74), Kluge halted Model's *Zitadelle* attack and stripped him of 12., 18., and 20. Panzer-Divisionen, which he sent to the Bolchov region. Model began giving up his modest gains on 14 July with the 2nd Tank Army in pursuit. On the same day Rokossovsky let his 13th Army loose to the tank army's right over relatively open country. By the 19th, the 9. Armee had passed its pre-*Zitadelle* positions on its way north-west.

Also on 19 July, the Soviets added 4th Tank and 3rd Guards Tank Armies to the Western and Bryansk fronts, but heavy rains delayed their arrival on the battlefield. A day later Sokolovsky tried to insert the new 11th Army between his 50th and 11th Guards Armies, but in this case, a 100-mile approach by marching infantry likewise held up its employment. Only after another week, on the 26th, did the 4th Tank Army enter the battle around Bolchov, but German defenders managed to hold on to the strongpoint city for another three days. Pre-occupied by fighting in Italy and elsewhere, Hitler did not interfere. In addition, on 26 July OKH ordered Model to begin to withdraw to the Hagen position, which he began on the 31st with minimal micro-management. Due to heavy rains it took Rybalko's 3rd Guards Tank Army an additional week to capture the smouldering wreck of Orel, liberated on 5 August, but at this point Red Army forces began to prevail over their enemy. In an attempt to overwhelm Kluge, the Stavka expanded the offensive against 4. Armee. Assisted by partisan raids, the Soviets picked up the pace while the retreating Germans scorched the earth. Fierce resistance met each Soviet attack: a breakthrough now would be disastrous. On 14 August Model's troops began reaching the prepared Hagen defensive positions, just east of Bryansk. Three days later, the rearguard also arrived; they fully occupied the new defensive line. The Red Army had liberated a sizeable chunk of territory, but the Germans had avoided a major disaster.

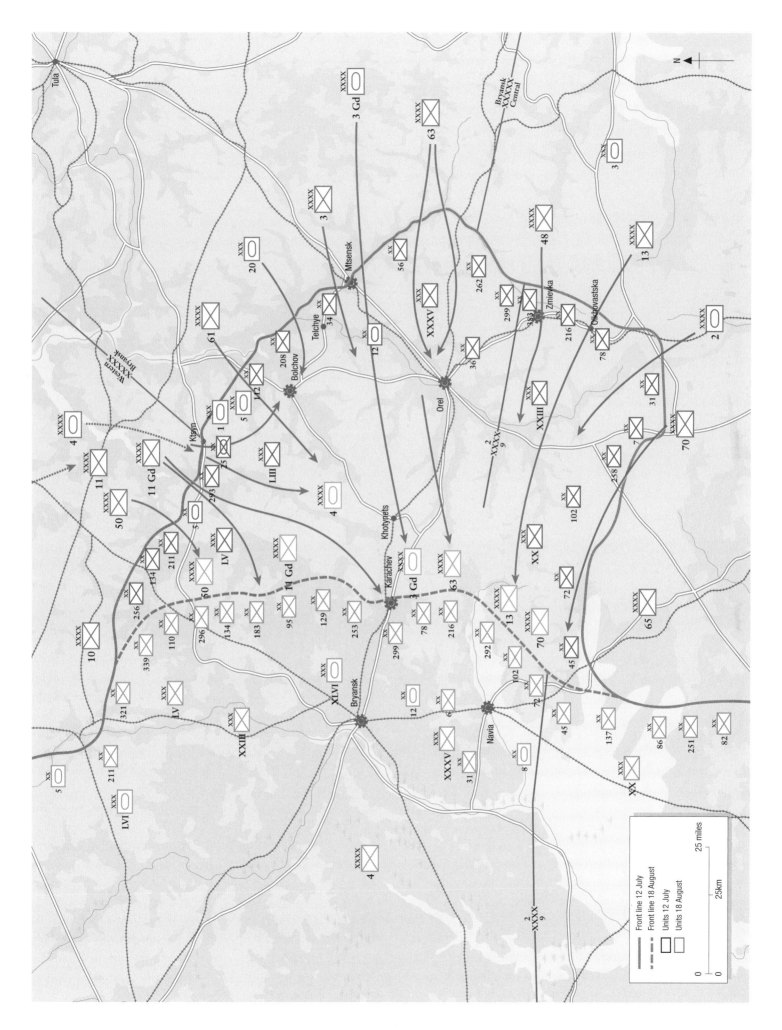

MAP 76: OPERATION *RUMIANTSEV* 3–24 AUGUST, 1943

The Soviet plan all along had been to transition to the counterattack once the Germans had attrited, exhausted and overextended themselves with their offensive. However, 4. Panzer-Armee and 5th Guards and 5th Guards Tank Armies continued to fight over Prokhorovka through the middle of July. Bowing to the inevitable, on the 17th Hitler ordered *Zitadelle* cancelled, its hard-won gains surrendered and the II SS Panzer-Korps entrained for Italy.[96] In early August Manstein's retreating soldiers were imprudently ordered to halt before reaching their pre-*Zitadelle* positions (which they had been improving since March). They would defend the region of Kharkov with 300,000 men, 3,000 guns and 600 panzers. Mobile reserves, already devastated by *Zitadelle*, were further weakened by the departure of the three SS divisions, Grossdeutschland and other mobile formations.

On 18 July the Stavka activated Konev's Steppe Front (previously in reserve) and moved it opposite Belgorod between the Voronezh and South-western fronts (Malinovsky). By the end of the month Vatutin had been reinforced somewhat and, despite Manstein's assurances to the contrary, was clearly prepared to take the offensive with the other two fronts. With Zhukov as the Stavka co-ordinator, Vatutin and Konev would surround Kharkov from north and east while Malinovsky would drive down the seam between Hoth and Kempf. Zhukov had almost as many armies (11) as Hoth and Kempf had emaciated divisions (15).

Enjoying a 6:1 superiority and an armour density of more than 100 AFVs per mile, the Red Army hit on the morning of 3 August. To Manstein's discredit, the attack surprised the Germans and initial fighting was especially brutal where their lines made a right angle north-east of Belgorod. Within hours 5th Guards, 6th Guards and 53rd Armies had penetrated many miles into the hasty new defences and pushed a 7-mile wedge between the two Wehrmacht armies. Hitler, applying his normal level of micro-management, unintentionally made the job of the breakthrough armies easier when he pulled the XI Armee-Korps out of the line and dispatched it to hold Kharkov.[97] Konev's troops liberated Belgorod on the second day of *Rumiantsev* and on 5 August Zhukov expanded the offensive to the west by ordering 40th and 27th Armies to join in. That day Hitler recalled his four heavy

mechanized divisions, plus 3rd Panzer and SS Wiking, from their dispersed outposts to the Kharkov sector, but the rupture between Hoth and Kempf now measured 30 miles. Decimated infantry units, suffering particularly from Red artillery, got some relief as they fell back into Kharkov's well-prepared fortified belts. As the Germans' heavy divisions began arriving (despite partisan interdiction of the railways) they were immediately thrown into counterattacks, which in the case of XLVIII Panzer-Korps near Achtyrka, for example, uncharacteristically almost ended in disaster. In an echo of the previous winter, only one division in Poltava stood between Zhukov and the Dnepr.

By 8 August, Vatutin and Konev had Kharkov surrounded on three sides, while to the south Kempf struggled to avoid encirclement. The heavy divisions, often rolling off railway cars directly into battle, temporarily stabilized the situation: 3. Panzer-Division against the gap between the two German armies, and SS Das Reich, Totenkopf and now also Wiking against the 1st Tank Army's spearheads near Bogodukhov. As the fifth and final battle for Kharkov raged in the city, 5th Guards Tank Army came to Kautukov's aid, and during 13–17 August the mechanized struggle raged between two tank armies and three SS panzer grenadier divisions, ultimately ending in a draw. General Kempf's indiscreet opinions concerning the hopelessness of the situation inside Kharkov caused Manstein to relieve him on the 14th and the next day General der Infanterie Otto Wöhler took his place in the re-named 8. Armee.[98] Throughout mid-August armoured combat continued to rage south and west of Kharkov: around Achtyrka 7. Panzer-Division and Grossdeutschland joined Totenkopf to turn back the 4th Guards Tank Corps, and near Bogodukhov, where III Panzer-Korps and Das Reich, Totenkopf (elements) and Wiking struggled against 6th Guards, 1st Tank and 5th Guards Tank Armies.

Such occasional tactical victories could not hold 4. Panzer-Armee's fragile front, however, and while Vatutin was thereby frustrated on the direct road to Poltava, his 38th, 40th and 47th Armies now represented a dagger pointed at Kiev. Wöhler had been requesting permission to abandon Kharkov from the time he arrived at 8. Armee, always to be refused by Manstein and/or Hitler. Manstein finally gave permission on 22 August and XI Armee-Korps abandoned the city two nights later, ending the Belgorod–Kharkov operation.

---

96 Only SSLAH ever got to Italy. Das Reich and Totenkopf remained with Heeresgruppe Süd, albeit on the Mius River.

97 The original XI Armee-Korps had been destroyed at Stalingrad. On 20 July Korps Raus was designated XI Armee-Korps.

98 Wöhler had just distinguished himself near Lake Ladoga (Map 81). Kempf would spend the next nine months in the Führer Reserve.

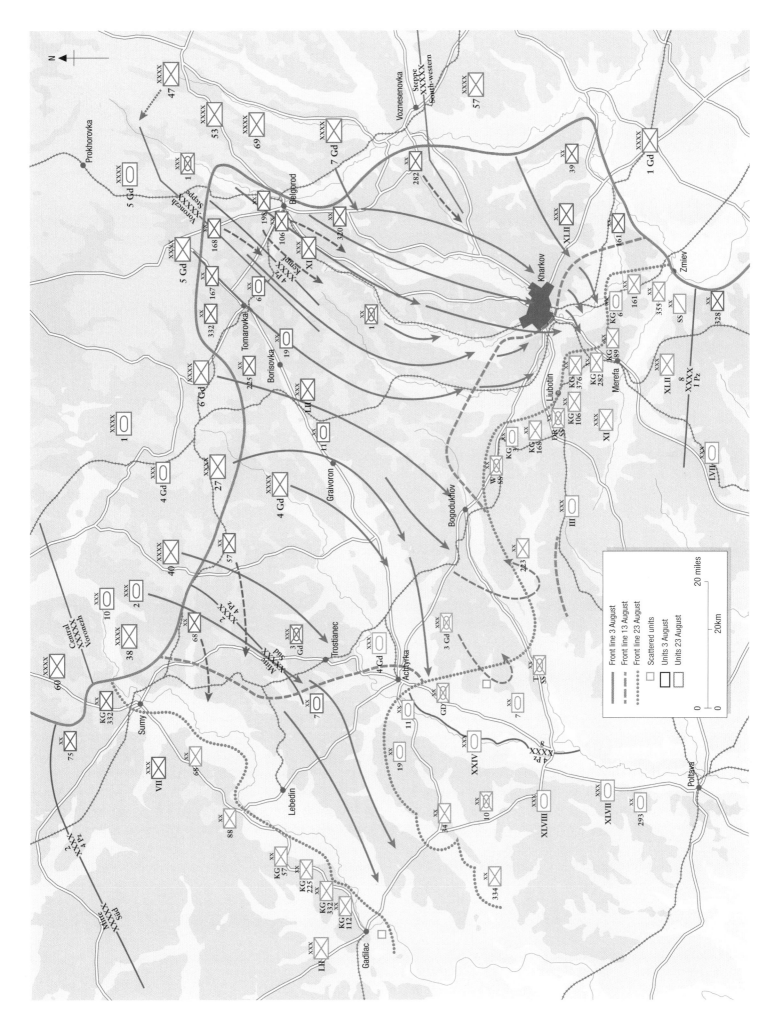

MAP 77: LIBERATING EASTERN UKRAINE, NORTH – 25 AUGUST TO 30 SEPTEMBER, 1943

If he did not already do so, in the coming weeks Hitler would wish he still had the soldiers and panzers squandered to such little purpose during *Zitadelle*. Kharkov had been a worthy prize, but Stalin had bigger things in mind. During the summer of 1943 the Red Army would realize the objective goal denied them in their two previous winter campaigns: the Dnepr River. Meanwhile, lacking adequate mobile reserves, Hitler had decided to put his faith instead in fixed fortifications; his 'Eastern Wall' would run overland from Melitopol on the Sea of Azov to Zaporozhe, then follow the Dnepr and Desna rivers, somehow work its way north-west through the northern Russian forests until it met Lake Pskov on the Latvian border.[99]

Achtyrka changed hands for the sixth and last time on 25 August as Vatutin applied gentle pressure along Manstein's left. Hoth struggled to maintain a viable defence on the Merefa, launching one- or two-division counterattacks when possible. In general, both sides were suffering from exhaustion at the end of six weeks of intense fighting. Rokossovsky, Vatutin and Konev re-built their commands, prepared for the next lunge and shared some of the limelight with Malinovsky and Tolbukhin (Map 78). Manstein and his principal subordinates laboured to create their own hasty defensive lines between their current positions and the Dnepr. One supposedly ran generally from Konotop–Romny–Mirgorod–Poltava–Krasnograd, while the other guarded the approaches to Kiev along the line Chenigov–Nezhin–Lubny. Featureless rolling terrain, a paucity of built-up areas to anchor a defence and rivers generally running perpendicular to any lines of resistance complicated their work. However, two other factors, much more mundane, dominated the thinking of Wehrmacht leaders. These were the railway lines running west and south-west to the imagined safety of the big river's right bank and its major crossing points (Chernigov, Kiev, Cherkassy, Kremenchug, Dnepropetrovsk, Zaporozhe, Nikopol, and Kherson – the last two off the map to the south). Manstein's men largely lined up on the first and aimed for the second. He complained to Hitler about the 55 divisions facing him.

Rokossovsky struck first, on 26 August, down against Kluge's right. A small counterattack at Sevsk toward the end of the month brought only momentary relief. Soon, with the 65th Army running the boundary between Heersgruppe Mitte and Süd, Hitler allowed them to withdraw to Krolevets. On 4 September the Soviets' main effort, Vatutin, hit Manstein's northern flank. The severely weakened 4. Panzer-Armee, a mere shadow of its former self, buckled under the weight of six tank and two mechanized corps. Within days Rokossovsky took up the chase again, driving past Konotop (liberated on the 8th) to Bakhmach, further dividing the two army groups as 2. Armee swung north-west and 4. Panzer-Armee south-west. Once again, Hitler flew to army group headquarters at Zaporozhe and promised reinforcements to be surrendered by Kluge. But the Führer would not agree to Manstein's request to fall back to the Dnepr; this move would completely isolate Heeresgruppe A, currently occupying the Crimea (Kleist also attended the conference). While Hitler dawdled, Vatutin approached Romny and Poltava, cleared the last of the Germans' Kharkov positions and neared Krasnograd. Partisan bands stepped up their activities dramatically. By mid-month Central Front troops stood barely 50 miles from Kiev, while the Voronezh Front had reached a point only 75 miles from Cherkassy.

On 15 September, Hitler reluctantly authorized retreating to the Dnepr. Hoth fell back in 'two great leaps' in order to separate himself from pursuing Soviets and gain a modicum of freedom of manoeuvre. A full-blown rout began as Wehrmacht units streamed west; at each of the five Dnepr crossing points between Kiev and Dnepropetrovsk, they looked like an hourglass on its side with the actual bridge representing the thin neck.[100] The Stavka reinforced its obvious success by detailing 52nd and 61st Armies and 3rd Tank Army to Rokossovsky and Vatutin and 5th Guards, 37th and 46th Armies to Konev. During the second half of September, both sides turned the move to the Dnepr into a race, in which the Red Army would not be limited to crossing only at the major bridge sites. By the fourth week of the month, the Soviets had won nearly 40 bridgeheads across a 300-mile frontage, some of them large and promising.

---

99 Hitler's sincerity is open to question since he believed such works only encouraged his troops to retreat faster. Besides, true to form, he would not devote the resources necessary to build such a wall.

100 In addition to German troops, as part of their scorched-earth policy the army and Nazi Party functionaries drove hundreds of thousands of Ukrainian citizens and several million head of cattle to the same crossing sites.

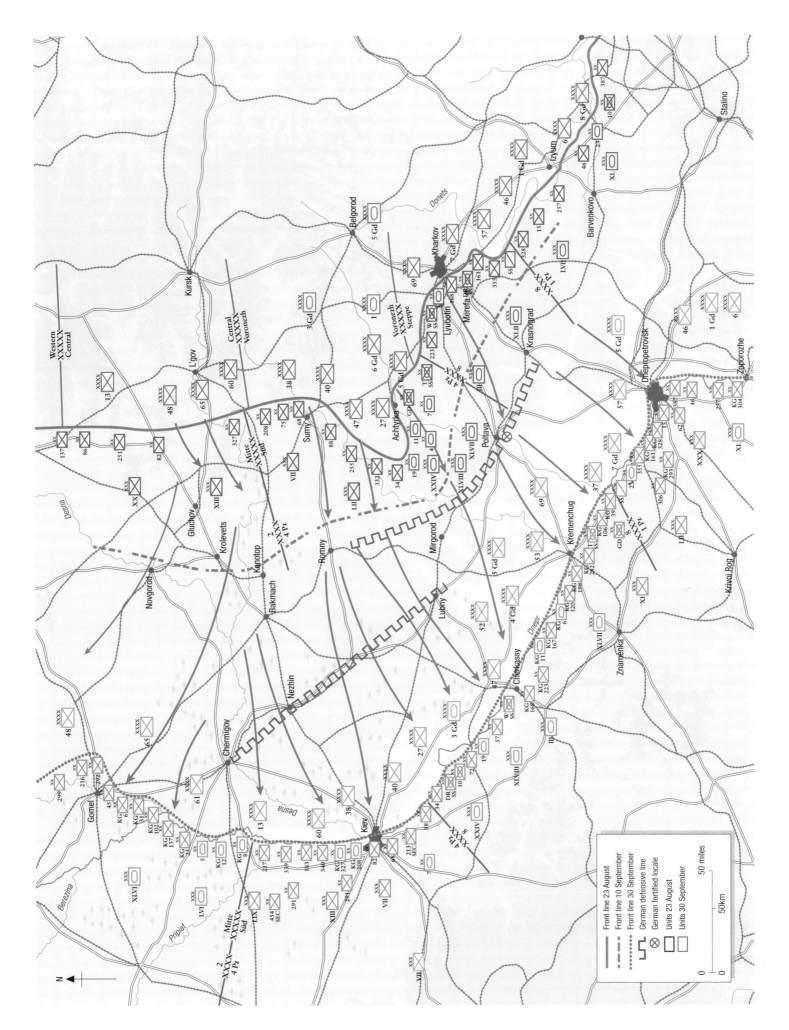

N

Belgorod

Kursk

Kharkov

Izyum

Barvenkovo

Stalino

Dhepropetrovsk

Zaporozhe

Krivoi Rog

Znamenka

Kremenchug

Cherkassy

Lubny

Mirgorod

Poltava

Krasnograd

Merefa

Lyubotin

Achtyrka

Sumy

L'gov

Gluchov

Krolevets

Konotop

Bakmach

Romny

Nezhin

Chernigov

Novgorod

Gomel

Kiev

Western XXXXX Central

Central XXXXX Voronezh

Voronezh XXXXX Steppe

Mitte XXXXX Süd

Mitte XXXXX Süd

Donets

Dnepr

Desna

Desna

Berezina

Pripiat

2 XXXX 4 Pz

2 XXXX 4 Pz

4 Pz XXXX 8

4 Pz XXXX 8

8 XXXX 1

8 XXXX 1

1 XXXX 8

167

MAP 78: LIBERATING DONBAS AND EASTERN UKRAINE, SOUTH – 17 JULY TO 23 OCTOBER, 1943

A key feature of this new period of the war was the Soviets' ability to conduct simultaneous large operations across broad fronts. Just as Hitler called off *Zitadelle* and Stalin launched *Kutuzov* against Heeresgruppe Mitte, on 17 July the Southern and South-western fronts began offensives against Manstein's right. Malinovsky's troops attacked from the familiar battlefield of the Izyum bridgehead against 1. Panzer-Armee's centre. In a ten-day battle the XXIV Panzer-Korps succeeded in limiting the damage. The Germans had a much stronger reaction to Tolbukhin's assault on the 6. Armee's Mius River positions.[101] Assuming it would take Voronezh and Steppe fronts many weeks, if not months, to recover from *Zitadelle*, Manstein promptly sent III Panzer-Korps and the SS Panzer-Korps to the Mius sector. From 30 July to 2 August these two formations counterattacked and restored the German positions along the river, capturing 18,000 POWs and destroying 700 AFVs in the process. However, this was a pyrrhic tactical victory in the sense that these two corps were completely out of position when Vatutin and Konev attacked Kharkov a day later, on the 3rd.

Capitalizing on German attention being fixed on the Kharkov area, days later Malinovsky (13 August) and Tolbukhin (16 August) attacked again in the exact same places. The 2nd Guards and 5th Shock Armies pushed 6. Armee back through prepared defences, within a few days creating a 20-mile-deep bulge halfway between Stalino and Taganrog. By the end of August the 2nd Guards Mechanized Corps had liberated the coastal town while encircling most of the XIX Armee-Korps in the process. With Manstein's far right thus compromised, Hitler established the Tortoise Positions (a fallback defensive line) guarding Stalino. Attempting to keep pace with 8. Armee to his left and 6. Armee on his right, Mackensen withdrew in an orderly fashion through the first week of September. On the 6th Malinovsky opened a new attack on the boundary between Mackensen and Hollidt; soon his 3rd Guards Army reached Konstantinovka, a manoeuvre which threatened 6. Armee's rear. South-western Front unhinged the new Tortoise Line and a day later liberated Stalino. Two days later, Tolbukhin did the same at Mariupol. In between these two events Hitler met with Manstein and

Kleist (Map 77), the significance of which for the far southern theatre was permission to withdraw to the Wotan Line, generally Zaporozhe to Melitopol.

On 11 September, a 9. Panzer-Division attack re-established contact between Mackensen and Hollidt simultaneously, but briefly isolating 1st Guards Mechanized and 23rd Tank Corps heading for the Dnepr. By mid-month 1. Panzer-Armee had reached the river's bend and began to cross to the western bank. At the same time 6. Armee occupied the overrated Panther Line, its retreat aided by the well-developed Donbas rail system. The last remaining Wehrmacht outpost east of the Dnepr was all that stood in the way of Heeresgruppe A's isolation. Fortunately for them, as of 17 September Tolbukhin was still 40 miles east.[102] Over the next ten days the Southern Front closed in on 6. Armee, 11 German and two Romanian divisions. Southern Front opened the two-week battle to overthrow the defensive position on 9 October. Its 45 divisions, two tank corps, two guards mechanized corps and two cavalry corps with 800 tanks faced 13 Axis divisions with 181 AFVs. The 51st Army and 12th Tank Corps' attack against Melitopol saw some of the worst fighting, lasting two weeks. A German relief counterattack out of the Zaporozhe bridgehead was beaten back after three days. On 13 October Malinovsky opened operations against Zaporozhe, the Wotan Line's northern anchor. Within four days 1. Panzer-Armee had lost the city, and soon Red Army units were across the middle Dnepr in force (Map 80).

With the river line breached in strength in so many places, Manstein could no longer afford to send reinforcements or reserves to Hollidt. By the fourth week of October the Soviets had come close to liberating Melitopol, which, with the loss of Zaporozhe, would undo the Wotan Line. Tolbukhin's re-named 4th Ukrainian Front unleashed its final assault on the 22nd, and his men liberated Melitopol the next day.[103] The 28th and 51st Armies cut 6. Armee in two, pushing one part north to the Dnepr and the other south toward the Perekop Isthmus. The 2nd Guards Army burst through the gap and made for Kherson. Disaster had befallen Hitler's far southern flank.

---

101 The original 6. Armee had been obliterated at Stalingrad. Army Detachment Hollidt was re-named 6. Armee on 6 March, retaining its same commander.

102 On 17 September 6. Armee was subordinated to Kleist's Heeresgruppe A.

103 On 20 October Voronezh, Steppe, South-western and Southern fronts were re-named 1st, 2nd, 3rd and 4th Ukrainian Fronts.

Rostov

Taganrog

Mius

Voroshilovgrad

Sea of Azov

Mariupol

Berdyansk

Stalino

Konstantinovka

Izyum

Barvenkovo

Donets

Krasnograd

Dnepropetrovsk

Zaporozhe

Melitopol

Nikopol

Dnepr

Dnepr

XXXX 46

South-western XXXXX Southern

XXXX 51

XXXX 5 Shock

XXXX 2 Gd

XXXX 28

XXXX 44

XXXX 3 Gd

XX 3

XX 3

XXXX 304

XX 302

XX 3 SS

XX T SS

XX DR SS

XX 23

XX 16

XX 336

XX 17

XX 15 LW

XX 111

XXXX 12

XX 62

XX 335

XX IV

XXX XXIX

XXXX 6

XXXX 8 Gd

XX 387

XXX XXX

XXXX 6 XXXX 11

XXXX 1 Gd

XX 333

XX 46

XX XL

XX 17

XX W SS

XX 75

XX 257

XXX XXIV

XXX LVIII

XXXX 8 Gd

3 Ukrainian XXXXX 4 Ukrainian

XXXX 51

XXXX 44

XXXX 2 Gd

XXXX 12

XXXX 6

2 Ukrainian XXXXX 3 Ukrainian

XXXX Gd

XX 17

XX 123

XX 333

XX 9

XX 335

XX 3 Gd

XX 302

XX 101 Lt

XX 3

XX 5 LW

XX 13

XX 111

XX 15 LW

XX KG 336

III 5

XXXX 5 Shock

XXXX 5 Gd

XX 38

XX 46

XX 257

XX KG 404

XVII

1 Pz XXXX 6

IV

XXX XXIX

XX 24

XX 17

XXXX 46

XX 15

XXXX XXX

XXXX 57

XX KG 328

XX 355

XXXX 7 Gd

XX KG 306

N

MAP 79: LIBERATING KIEV AND THE MIDDLE DNEPR – 30 SEPTEMBER TO 26 NOVEMBER, 1943

With the exception of the Zaporozhe–Melitopol–Kherson wedge, by the end of September the Red Army had liberated the eastern Ukraine and had captured numerous bridgeheads west of the Dnepr River. From their newly won positions the Stavka had two objectives for the autumn's operations: to liberate Kiev and to create conditions for continuing westward, building on the momentum begun at Kursk and Kharkov. Since Heeresgruppe Süd already held the 'usual suspects' of the permanent bridge sites, Soviet leaders would create their own expedient crossing sites.

Such was the mystique of the Dnepr that Soviet leaders promised all sorts of rewards to soldiers and organizations achieving bridgeheads. Alerted by partisans to the absence of any Germans, during the third week of September elements of the 3rd Guards Tank Army crossed at Bukrin (upriver from the Kanev bridge). From here Rybalko could turn either north against Hoth in Kiev (most likely) or south against Wöhler at Cherkassy or drive due west between the two. Wöhler reacted to the danger of the 40th and 27th Armies at Bukrin, with three airborne brigades on the way, by sending XXIV Panzer-Korps to the area. He soon added XLVIII Panzer-Korps to the list of forces hemming in the bridgehead. Eventually ten German divisions surrounded the Red Army forces, which suffered from lack of ammunition, rough terrain, poor communications with the east bank but, worst of all, resolute *Landsers*. After a number of failed attempts to break out of Bukrin between 12–15 and 23–25 October, Vatutin developed a new plan: to extract Rybalko out of Bukrin in secret and to reinsert the 3rd Guards Tank Army at another bridgehead.

During the last days of September, the 38th Army had wrested a Dnepr crossing from XIII Armee-Korps at Lyutezh north of Kiev. Farther north a week later, 61st and 65th army units of the Belorussian Front created another at Loev, where the Sozh joins the Dneper (off map to the north). Lyutezh was the more important of the two and by late October had expanded to the point where it had Kiev within artillery range. At this point, following unsuccessful attempts at Bukrin, Vatutin shifted Rybalko, his supporting artillery and other units to Lyutezh. An elaborate deception plan tricked German intelligence about the tank army's whereabouts. With Stalin demanding Kiev be liberated in time to mark the anniversary of the October Revolution, Vatutin created a massive assault force.[104] On 3 November, 4. Panzer-

Armee's XIII (208. Infanterie-Division) and VII Armee-Korps (68. and 88. Infanterie-Divisionen) first sustained an artillery barrage of nearly 3,000 tubes of artillery and then a frontal infantry assault. Hoth rushed in 7. and 8. Panzer-Divisionen and 20. Panzer-Grenadier-Division but could not plug the 6-by-6-mile breach. The 60th Army launched a supporting attack against Garnaistopol, and within two days the combined offensive overwhelmed the 14 understrength divisions of the Wehrmacht defenders. On the 4th Vatutin ordered Rybalko to pass through the infantry; Hoth concluded that Vatutin's objective was to continue west into his operational depth. Instead, on the next day 3rd Guards Tank Army turned south behind Kiev, surrounding the city on three sides. Hoth saw no option but to retreat to the south, his troops' only escape route. The Red Army liberated the Ukrainian capital the next day, killing 15,000 Germans and capturing 6,000, an event Stalin marked with a massive artillery salute.

Vatutin did not dawdle but immediately ordered 60th, 3rd Guards Tank, 1st Tank and 38th Armies to fan out west and south. By 7 November Rybalko had taken the important Heeresgruppe Süd logistical base of Fastov, while soon the 1st Tank Army neared the city of Zithomir and the 60th Army approached the gates of Korosten. The 4. Panzer-Armee was now broken into three separated parts. Manstein had to beg his Führer to release mechanized divisions in order to stop the Soviets expanding along a 130-mile arc and secure his rear communications. With the fall of Zithomir the dictator relented, and Hoth began to assemble a sizeable counterattack force centred on XLVIII Panzer-Korps, which eventually numbered six mechanized and six infantry divisions.[105] General der Panzertruppen Hermann Balck, latest commander of the XLVIII Panzer-Korps, attacked on 14 November and recaptured Zithomir five days later, but, by the 20th, Red Army resistance had stiffened and his advance slowed. For the next few days the Germans pushed forward, although the attack had no chance of reaching Kiev, much less re-taking the city. Unexpectedly warm weather on the 26th turned the frozen ground to mud, halting Hoth's forward movement. At Korosten the 60th Army and LIX Armee-Korps reached a stalemate. The duel between Hoth and Vatutin subsided for the moment.

---

104 Accounting for differences in Gregorian and Julian Calendars, the anniversary fell on 7 November that year.

105 That October–November, XLVIII Panzer-Korps went through four commanders in as many weeks.

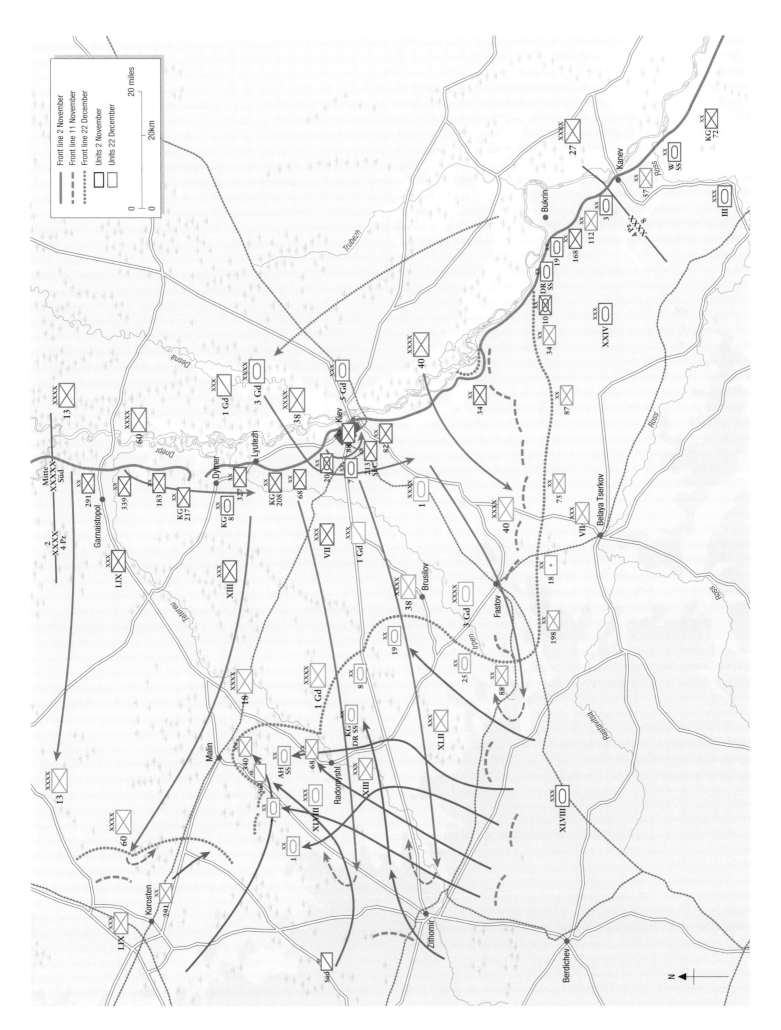

MAP 80: LIBERATING THE DNEPR BEND 1–31 OCTOBER, 1943

Along with operations against the Wotan Line and Kiev, the Soviets did not neglect Manstein's 8. Armee and 1. Panzer-Armee between Cherkassy and Zaporozhe on the great bend of the Dnepr. Wöhler and Mackensen's troops reached their designated bridge sites during the last week of September and, along with their civilian captives, undertook the time-consuming task of crossing the river. Meanwhile mechanized units fought desperate rearguard actions to keep the bridges and ferries open for as long as necessary, despite the disruptive efforts of the Red Army, partisans and aviation assets.

Once west of the Dnepr, things did not automatically improve for the Germans. Weakly held stretches of riverbank occurred in the gaps between their few bridge sites,[106] where the limited numbers of mechanized formations did not suffice to eliminate Soviet incursions into them. By the beginning of October, Konev and Malinovsky faced off against Wöhler and Mackensen and paused to contemplate the riverine assault. The 1. Panzer-Armee's one remaining bastion east of the Dnepr, XL Panzer and XVII Armee-Korps at Zaporozhe (and northern foundation of the Wotan Line), immediately drew the attention of the 3rd Ukrainian Front. After a brief battle from 10 to 13 October, Malinovsky's 12th, 8th Guards and 3rd Guards Armies settled the matter in the attacker's favour. The 1. Panzer-Armee gave up the Dnepr's right bank and henceforth Hollidt's men were on their own holding the Wotan Line.

Hundreds of miles north, Wöhler attempted to hold his stretch of the Dnepr against a determined 2nd Ukrainian Front. By 10 October, Konev had assembled 37th and 57th Armies and 5th and 7th Guards Armies to assault, plus his exploitation force, 5th Guards Tank Army, opposite Mishurin Rog, downriver from Kremenchug. He made his move on the 14th, hitting the four infantry divisions of Fretter-Pico's XXX Armee-Korps hardest, aiming right down the seam dividing Manstein's two centre armies. With partisans disrupting the Germans' reactions, within 24 hours Soviet troops had three small bridgeheads, and a day later Konev let loose Rotmistrov's 5th Guards Tank Army in the direction of the iron ore mines at Krivoi Rog. By 16 October, 2nd Ukrainian Front, which had ripped a hole nearly 30 miles wide in the German lines, had three armies west of the Dnepr. At the same time,

3rd Ukrainian Front renewed its attacks against 1. Panzer-Armee at Dnepropetrovsk and Zaporozhe. That day Manstein told Mackensen, down to 18 infantry, two panzer and one panzer grenadier divisions, to prepare to abandon the Dnepr bend as his position had clearly become untenable. An unexpected Soviet manoeuvre north from Nikopol could cut off three of the panzer army's five corps. Hitler would not, and did not, concur. By 19 October, Konev's advanced units were 35 miles south of the river. As was his inclination, Mackensen wanted to launch an immediate counterattack, but Kirchner's LVII Panzer-Korps was already decisively engaged in the urgent defensive fighting. He would have to wait for the arrival of two panzer divisions promised by the army group, plus 14. and 24. Panzer-Divisionen coming from Italy by rail.

By the last week of October, Malinovsky's 8th Guards had just begun to cross the Dnepr midway between Dnepropetrovsk and Zaporozhe in conjunction with the 46th Army. However, the Soviets were running out of steam. This caused Konev, barely a dozen miles from Krivoi Rog, practically to go it alone within the river's bend. With the Germans finally beginning to recover, Wöhler and Mackensen had managed to assemble 20 divisions along the line Znamenka–Dolinskaya–Krivoi Rog–Apostolovo Station–Nikopol. Wehrmacht mobile reserves also began arriving in the area and 8. Armee readied III Panzer-Korps for its own counterattack. Rotmistrov's lead elements nosed into Krivoi Rog on the 25th, only to have XL Panzer-Korps (14. and 24. Panzer-Divisionen plus SS Totenkopf) eject them with the help of Luftwaffe CAS. Repeatedly humbled over the next five days, the roughly handled 5th Guards Tank Army did not stop retreating until it reached the Ingulets River, 20 miles back. By the end of October Manstein's troops still hung on to the Dnepr near Cherkassy, immediately east of Zaporozhe and at the manganese mining city of Nikopol. Though the Soviets had carved out a huge balcony nearly 200 miles wide and up to 50 miles deep between these two dots of German resistance, Wöhler and Mackensen (later Hube) had stabilized their defences for the time being.[107]

---

106 For example, nearly 100 miles separated German bridges at Kremenchug and Dnepropetrovsk.

107 On 29 October Mackensen departed 1. Panzer-Armee to take command of 14. Armee in Italy; General der Panzertruppen Hans-Valentin Hube took his place on 5 November.

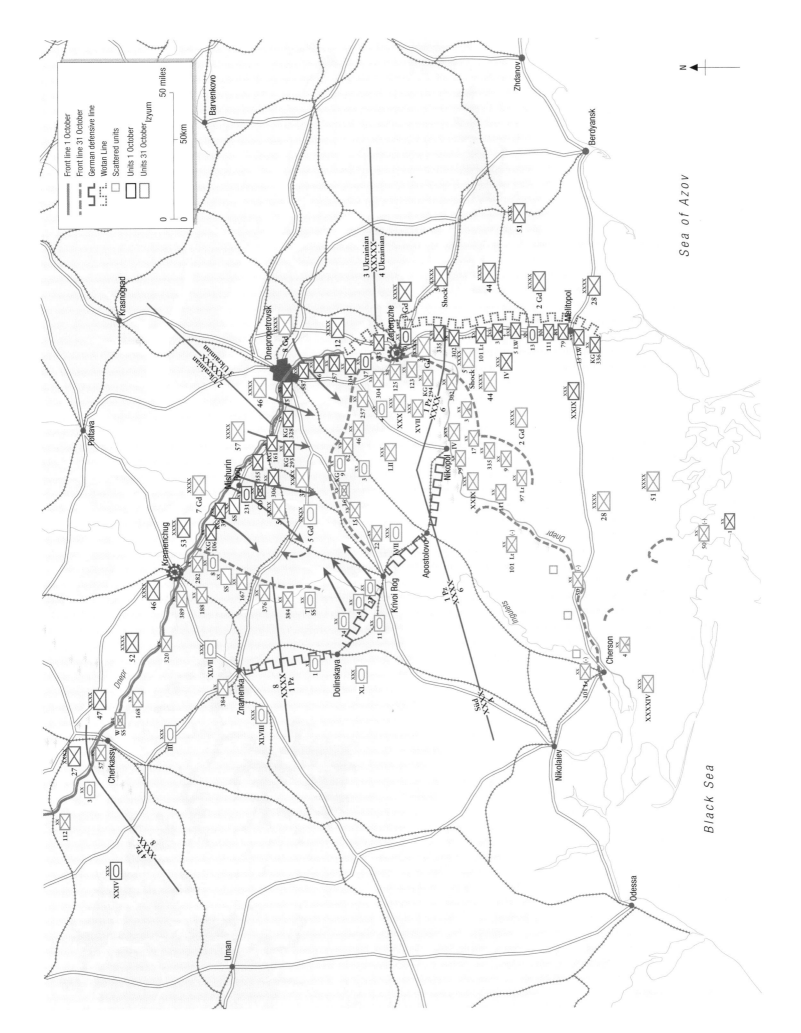

MAP 81: LENINGRAD FRONT, LATE 1943
6 OCTOBER TO 23 DECEMBER, 1943

In 1942 and 1943, the northern theatre of the Nazi-Soviet War resembled World War I more than World War II. With minor exceptions (Maps 29, 61 and 62) front lines had remained fairly static. The Finns, satisfied with their 1941 gains, sat idle, while the Germans could not create the preconditions to do more than occasionally antagonize the Soviets. The Gulf of Finland plus Lakes Ladoga and Il'men gave the combatants formidable natural terrain features on which to anchor their lines, so for nearly two years the positions of the two sides looked like World War I trenches, complete with a shell-cratered no man's land and advances measured in a few hundred yards. Heeresgruppe Nord served as a manpower reservoir to be tapped whenever another army group needed to re-build prior to an attack or be reinforced following a defeat. A lively air war developed; the Germans even conducted a leaflet-dropping propaganda campaign, though it was of doubtful utility. The Baltic Fleet mostly remained holed up in Kronstadt, short of fuel and contributing brigades of naval infantry to other theatres.

Generalfeldmarschall Georg von Küchler remained atop Heeresgruppe Nord with 16. (General der Artillerie Christian Hansen) and 18. (Lindemann) Armee under command.[108] Throughout 1943 strength remained around 750,000 men in 40 divisions, including many new Luftwaffe field divisions and Volksdeutsche SS divisions and brigades, with 10,000 artillery pieces and 300–400 panzers. It also provided a training ground for inexperienced Luftwaffe and SS corps staffs.[109] Throughout its existence, the army group fought extensive and violent actions against partisans throughout the region. General Colonel L. A. Govorov's Leningrad Front, the Vokhov Front and the Oranienbaum bastion had 1.2 million men between them, 10,000 guns and mortars, more than 1,000 tanks and were under pressure to take action. In January 1943 the 67th and 2nd Shock Armies attacked XXVI Armee-Korps at Shlisselburg and opened a very narrow path (6 miles wide) to the besieged city. After 500 days Leningrad's isolation technically came to an end and the rail connection re-opened a month later, albeit under the threat of German artillery interdiction; both sides claimed victory. Attacking to re-establish the full blockade in the late summer supposedly would follow a successful conclusion to *Zitadelle*.

As the war dragged on, Küchler and Govorov developed competing plans for the coming year. Heeresgruppe Nord, locked into the siege of Leningrad that wasn't, considered giving it up altogether and withdrawing to the Panther Line. These positions, running from the Narva River to Lakes Peipus and Pskov to Heeresgruppe Mitte, would reduce its frontage by 25 per cent and free up resources for other purposes. The Soviets, on the other hand, sought to join Oranienbaum to Leningrad while also expanding the overland link to the Volkhov Front. The comparative personalities of Hitler and Stalin make it seem likely that Hitler would veto Küchler's proposal, while Stalin would applaud Govorov's plan. The Leningrad Front would be the centrepiece of an operation that included an offensive along the new boundary between Heeresgruppen Nord and Mitte, at Nevel, between Velikie Luki and Vitebsk and dangerously close to Latvia. The first stage of that plan commenced on 6 October when Eremenko's Kalinin Front attacked and made unexpectedly good progress, taking Nevel on the first day. Within a couple of days the gap along the army group seam had expanded to 15 miles wide and about as deep. Küchler, not the most decisive leader, responded to Hitler's demands for action by merely plugging holes. Unexpectedly, Eremenko came to the German's aid by drastically slowing his assault starting on 10 October. His command, re-named 1st Baltic Front on the 16th, sat idle until 2 November, when the 3rd and 4th Shock Armies renewed their drives along the army group boundary. After advancing an additional 35 miles west, the two armies split north and south, eventually creating a mushroom-shaped breakthrough that threatened the rear areas of both 3. Panzer-Armee and 16. Armee. Hitler demanded (again) counterattacks from all directions, but his commanders had no forces with which do so. Ever indecisive, Küchler put off counterattacking from one week to the next and Hitler had to summon him to Rastenburg three times in one month. By the end of November, Busch and 3. Panzer-Armee's Reinhardt could not agree on how to halt the Red Army. Unseasonable warm weather generated a sea of mud, however, which accomplished that task. Cold weather returned in mid-December and on the 23rd the 4th Shock, 11th Guards, 39th and 43rd Armies attacked Reinhardt's LIII and VI Armee-Korps defending Vitebsk. Red Army troops made significant advances, but by Christmas Day the Germans had enough reserve divisions in the general area that they were able to reinforce the town and prevent any major breakthroughs. The northern front quietened down… for the time being.

---

108 When Kluge was injured in a car wreck in October, Busch moved from 16. Armee to Heeresgruppe Mitte, Hansen advanced from commanding X Corps to replace Busch on 4 November.

109 The development of Luftwaffe field divisions has been summarized above (fn. 72); its corps headquarters were equally underwhelming. As manpower shortages beset the Third Reich, the SS gave up its pretensions of racial purity and accepted large numbers of Volksdeutsche (Germans living throughout Europe for many generations) and non-Germans, mainly in its higher-numbered units of questionable quality.

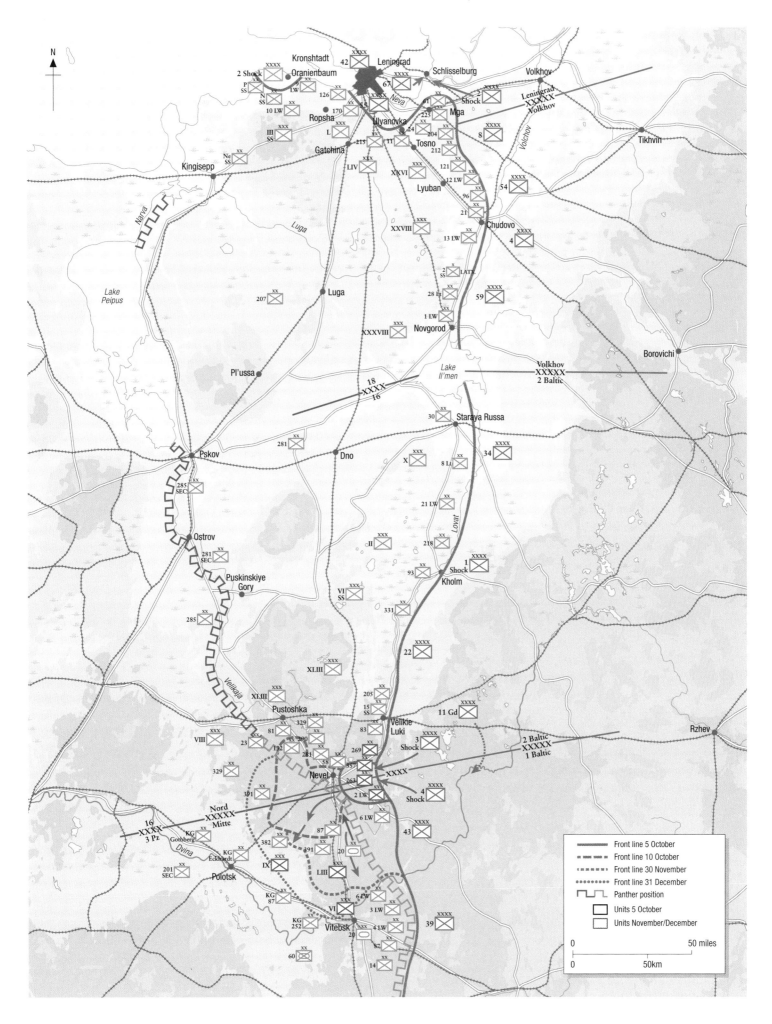

N

Kronshtadt
42
XXXX
Leningrad
Schlisselburg
Volkhov

2 Shock
XXXX
Oranienbaum
P SS
N SS
10 LW
67
XXXX
Neva
2 Shock
XXXX
Leningrad
Volkhov
Tikhvin

126
55
55
170
Ropsha
91
225
Mga
8
XXXX

III SS
L
Ulyanovka
24
204
212
Tosno

Ne SS
Gatchina
215
11
121
12 LW
54
XXXX

Kingisepp
LIV
XXVI
Lyuban
96
21

Luga
XXVIII
XXXX
13 LW
Chudovo
4
XXXX

Lake Peipus
207
2 SS
LATV.
28 I
59
XXXX

Luga
1 LW
XXXVIII
XXXX
Novgorod

Pl'ussa
Lake Il'men
Volkhov
XXXXX
2 Baltic
Borovichi

18
XXXX
16
30
Staraya Russa

281
XXXX
Dno
34
XXXX

Pskov
X
XXX
8 L
281 SEC
XXX

285 SEC
XXX
21 LW
XX

Ostrov
281 SEC
XXX
218
XX

Puskinskiye Gory
II
XXX
1 Shock
XXXX

Lovat
93
Kholm

285
XX
331

VI SS
XX
22
XXXX

XLIII
XXX

Velikaia
XI.III
XXX
205
XX
11 Gd
XXXX

Pustoshka
15 SS
XX
Velikie Luki
Rzhev

VIII
XXX
81
329
83
3 Shock
XXXX
2 Baltic
XXXXX
1 Baltic

23
290
269
XXXX

329
XX
132
281
58
55
263
4 Shock
XXXX

351
2 LW
XXXX

16
XXXXX
Nord
Mitte
6 LW
XXXX

KG Gothberg
3 Pz
87
43
XXXX

Dvina
KG Eckhardt
382
391
20

201 SEC
XX
IX
XXX
LIII
XXXX

Polotsk
6 LW
XXXX

KG 87
3 LW
VI
4 LW
39
XXXX

KG 252
Vitebsk
20

60
XX

14
XX

	Front line 5 October
	Front line 10 October
	Front line 30 November
	Front line 31 December
	Panther position
	Units 5 October
	Units November/December

0   50 miles

0   50 km

MAP 82: LIBERATION OF SMOLENSK 7 AUGUST TO 25 SEPTEMBER, 1943

Smolensk had cultural significance as one of western Russia's ancient cities, along with a tactically valuable location atop the continental divide on the portage between the Dvina and Dnepr rivers. It was also the first major city of the USSR lost in the Nazi-Soviet War – symbolic of one of Stalin's earliest defeats. Stalin hoped to take the city during the winter counteroffensives of 1942 and 1943, but failed. These earlier attempts had been made on the cheap, i.e., as the by-product of some other operation or in a finesse move hoping to catch the Germans napping. To correct these previous shortcomings, the Stavka now planned to re-capture the city with an old-fashioned head-on mass assault.

Operations over the past few months, the elimination of the Rzhev and Orel salients to name the most important, had created pre-conditions for a successful offensive. With Voronov again acting as Stavka co-ordinator, General Colonel V. D. Sokolovsky's Western Front represented the main effort, assisted by the Kalinin and Bryansk Fronts on his flanks. They would enjoy a 10:1 advantage over the defenders. The first stage of their plan was to destroy the small bulge east of Spas Demensk using the 5th, 10th Guards and 33rd Armies with the 68th Army in reserve. The second stage would expand north and south with the addition of the 31st, 49th, 10th and 50th Armies attacking on a 150-mile-wide front centred on Yelnia, the site of Hitler's first reverse of World War II; the Bryansk Front would join in here. The third stage added the Kalinin Front and would take Yartsevo and Roslavl on the extremes while aiming for the operation's real prize: Smolensk.

Over the previous two years Heeresgruppe Mitte had given up much ground and taken many beatings, but so far had avoided catastrophic losses. Like Heeresgruppe Nord, over the past half year it had been forced to contribute many men and numerous formations to shore up the disastrous situation in the south. By mid-summer it consisted of 55 divisions divided among 3. Panzer-Armee (Reinhardt), 4. Armee (Heinrici), 2. Panzer-Armee (Model), 9. Armee (Model)[110] and 2. Armee (Weiss).

Following an increase in air and partisan raids, the offensive began on 7 August, ripping a hole in Kluge's front from Gorodok to Kirov. The 4. Armee managed to keep its defences intact, claiming 214 tanks

destroyed on the 9th. Both air forces flew great numbers of CAS sorties. Slowly and steadily, the Red Army pushed forward with heavy artillery support while the Germans launched local counterattacks whenever possible. Spas-Demensk fell on the 13th and Sokolovsky's men inched forward against the stubborn Wehrmacht defenders for one more week. On 20 August operations slowed while the Stavka re-evaluated its options as the Germans reinforced the new positions and lashed them to 2. Panzer-Armee's Hagen Line (Map 75). After the two-week pounding, Heinrici's order of battle had dropped to 11 divisions and seven *Kampfgruppen* as he awaited the Soviets' next move.[111]

The Western Front took up the attack again on 28 August; the Germans estimated that the Red Army Air Force flew 2,700 sorties that day and more than 1,000 the next. The Soviets created a penetration 12 miles wide and 5 miles deep; on the 30th, 10th Guards Army troops took Yelnia. Dorogobuzh fell the following day, but Kluge's defences generally remained solid as he slowly retreated. After only five days Sokolovsky halted once again to re-organize. When he resumed, it was clear that Smolensk would be his main objective, with Roslavl and Yartsevo relegated to a very distant second. The Western Front moved out again on 14 September, almost overwhelming Heeresgruppe Mitte's ability to resist. With his forces very much weakened and little in the way of defensible terrain, Heinrici's men fell back, now joined by 3. Panzer-Armee and 9. Armee, which were being hounded by the Kalinin and Bryansk Fronts.[112] Yartsevo fell on 16 September and Bryansk on the 17th (off map to the south). To hinder the German retreat, partisans detonated over 100 bridges in one day. By the 19th the 39th Army had seriously compromised the seam between 3. Panzer-Armee and 4. Armee almost to Demidov, and on the 20th Heinrici began pulling back everywhere. On 24 September his rearguards put Smolensk to the torch, and a combined 5th Army and 10th Guards Army force liberated the city a day later. By the end of the month, fighting had stabilized along a line around 25 miles east of Vitebsk, Orsha and Mogilev.

---

110 During Operation *Kutuzov* (Map 75) Model had been given temporary command of both 2. Panzer-Armee and 9. Armee; Austrian General der Infanterie Dr Lothar Rendulic took over on 15 August.

111 At this stage of the war 'Kampfgruppe' had taken on a new meaning. Instead of a purpose-built task force, the term now referred to the shattered remains of a division, often +/-1,000 men, named after its commander. Occasionally they were pulled out of the line and rebuilt.

112 Upon reaching the Hagen Line, 2. Panzer-Armee headquarters transferred to Yugoslavia, so will no longer figure in this story. The 4. and 9. Armeen absorbed its units.

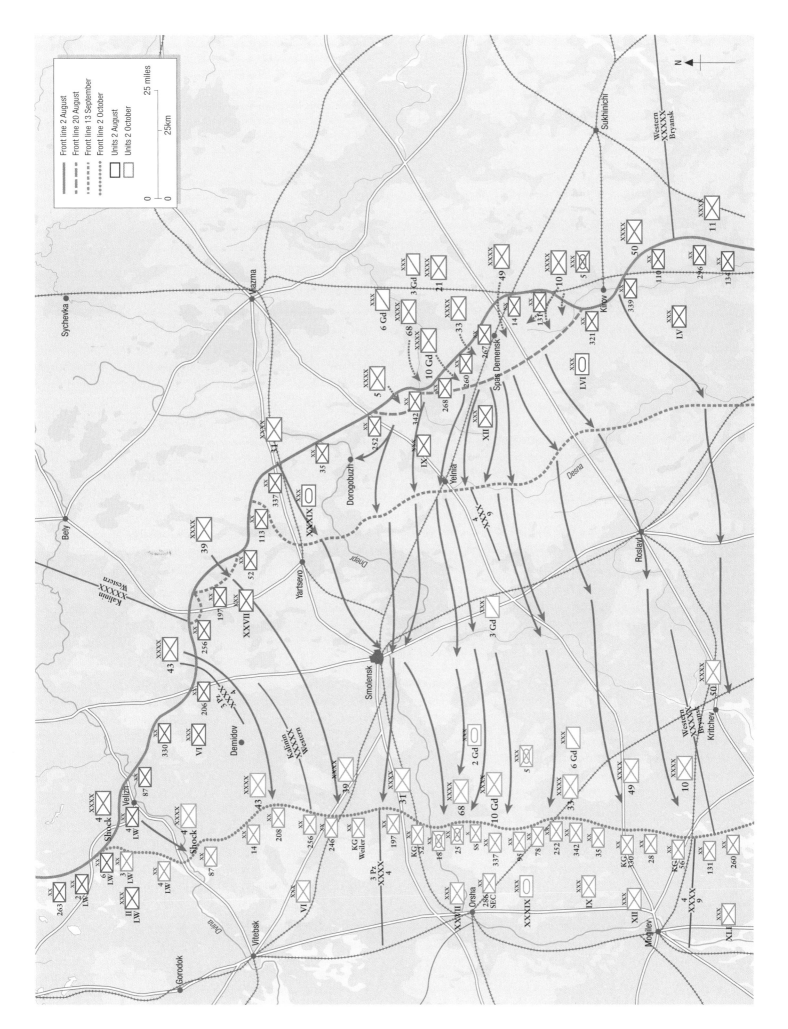

MAP 83: KUBAN PENINSULA 4 FEBRUARY TO 9 OCTOBER, 1943

With delusions of returning to the Caucasus oil region, Hitler insisted on maintaining the Gotenkopf position on the Kuban Peninsula after the Soviets had chased the Germans over the Don River (Map 63). For the first eight months of 1943, when the rest of his eastern army was pressed for manpower, weapons and equipment, one quarter of a million men and more than 75,000 horses, 20,000 vehicles and 2,000 guns and panzers languished at the far south-eastern corner of the Third Reich.

During late January and early February, German and Romanian units retreated up to 250 miles in four weeks into the flat peninsula named after the Kuban River and established the Gotenkopf Line. Kleist's Heeresgruppe A had responsibility for the Kuban and the Crimea.[113] Ruoff's 17. Armee consisted of XLIX Gebirgs-Korps, XLIV and V Armee-Korps, eight German divisions plus five divisions of the Romanian Mountain Corps and the Slovak Mobile Division as its reserve. Surrounding them stood a ring of, at times, seven Soviet armies of General Colonel I. E. Petrov's Northern Caucasus Front: the 58th, 9th, 37th, 46th, 56th, 47th and 18th.

It only took a few days for the Red Army to begin to harass the Axis beachhead. On 4 February, using the mobility provided by the Black Sea Fleet, it landed troops at Cape Myskhako, the tip of land south of the port city of Novorossisk. After a bloody battle, the Germans were unable to drive out the defenders. In mid-March the 56th Army, helped by the 37th Army's supporting attacks, tried to break into the south-eastern angle of Ruoff's lines. The Germans would not be dislodged, even though the Red Army kept trying through April. Again, thanks to the Black Sea Fleet, the Soviets made several small landing attempts along the peninsula's north and south shores. In these areas, mostly guarded by Romanian divisions, Axis troops had to remain constantly vigilant. In mid-April Ruoff tried but failed again to eliminate the Red Army presence at Myskhako, his final attempt.

At the end of April and in early May both sides attacked and counterattacked at the town of Krymskaya, with 56th Army units prevailing. Within a few days the 56th had made a 10-mile-deep and 30-mile-wide dent in the Large Gotenkopf position, and the Germans fell back to their 70-mile-long Gotenkopf/Blue Line. The centre of the

German position bent but did not break.[114] With Kleist unable to provide the isolated outpost with the logistics required for sustained assaults, all meaningful attempts at attacking the Soviet perimeter failed. This led to a stalemate developing in early summer. On 1 June General der Pioniere Erwin Jaenecke replaced Ruoff as commander of the 17. Armee.

With the failure of *Zitadelle* and the corresponding successes of *Kutuzov* and *Rumiantsev*, by mid-summer the German situation in the southern theatre became acute. Between 17. Armee and forces on the Crimea, Kleist had nearly 400,000 men in 20 divisions supported by almost 3,000 artillery pieces and 100 AFVs; these assets could be of great use in the Ukraine. Therefore on 14 August Hitler agreed to evacuate Gotenkopf, but quickly reversed his decision days later, only to reverse it yet again on 3 September. Petrov did his best to hurry the Axis troops off the peninsula, and on 10 September launched a general offensive all along the Blue Line, complete with amphibious landings at various places on the coast to Jaenecke's rear. Generally the Germans held fast for the attack's first week, but on the 16th, troops of the 18th Army liberated Novorossisk.

Losing the port and biggest city in the region marked the beginning of the end for the Gotenkopf beachhead. As the North Caucasus Front applied pressure everywhere, during the second half of September Kleist began extensive scorched-earth operations and orchestrated an evacuation conducted by the Kriegsmarine's Kerch Strait Flottilla and Luftwaffe transports. German troops fought a rearguard action westward through the Kuban Peninsula, briefly halting to fight in the prepared defensive positions Siegfried, Volker, Hagen and Rüdiger. Over the course of a week, Petrov's armies kept constricting Jaenecke's defences from all sides until 17. Armee held only the port town of Taman and the hook of land to its north. The final Axis defensive positions were named after the German cities Vienna, Bucharest (in honour of their allies), Berlin, Munich, Breslau and Ulm. By the end of September, the Gotenkopf had been evacuated except for Taman itself, which hung on until 9 October. Unlike many previous German evacuations, Kleist managed to remove an entire field army with most of its equipment.

---

113 Not to be confused with the 1944 Gothic Line in Italy.

114 This action was made famous by Willi Heinrich in *Cross of Iron* and the Sam Peckinpah movie of the same name.

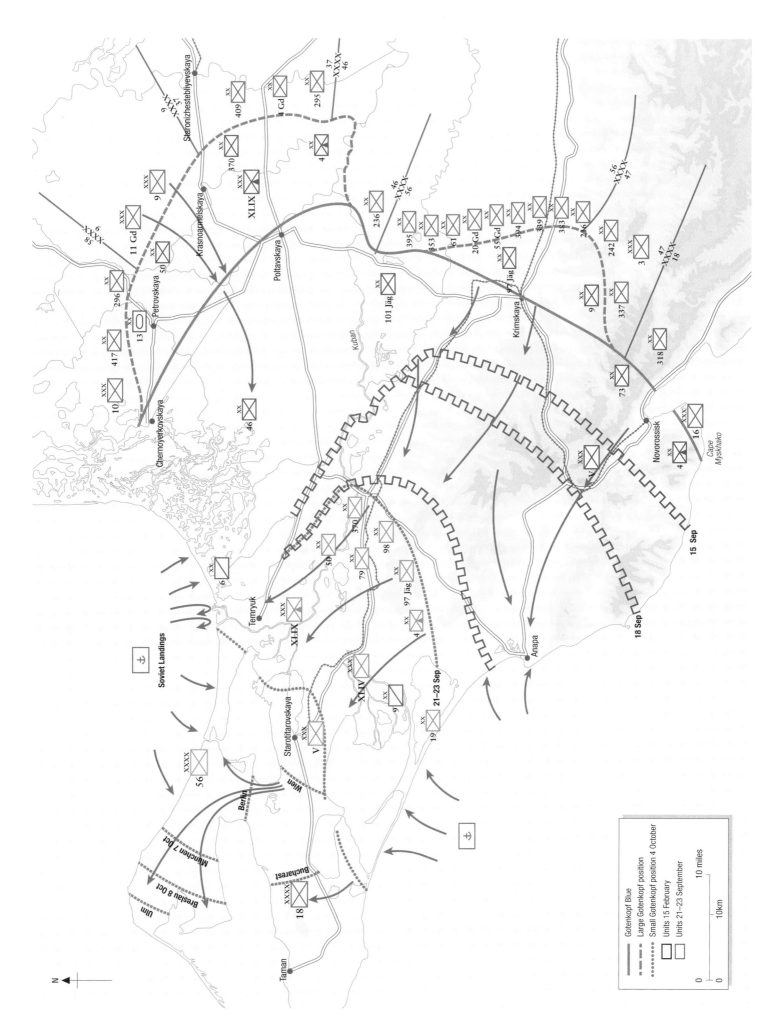

Units 15 February
Units 21–23 September

Gotenkopf Blue
Large Gotenkopf position
Small Gotenkopf position 4 October

0   10km
0   10 miles

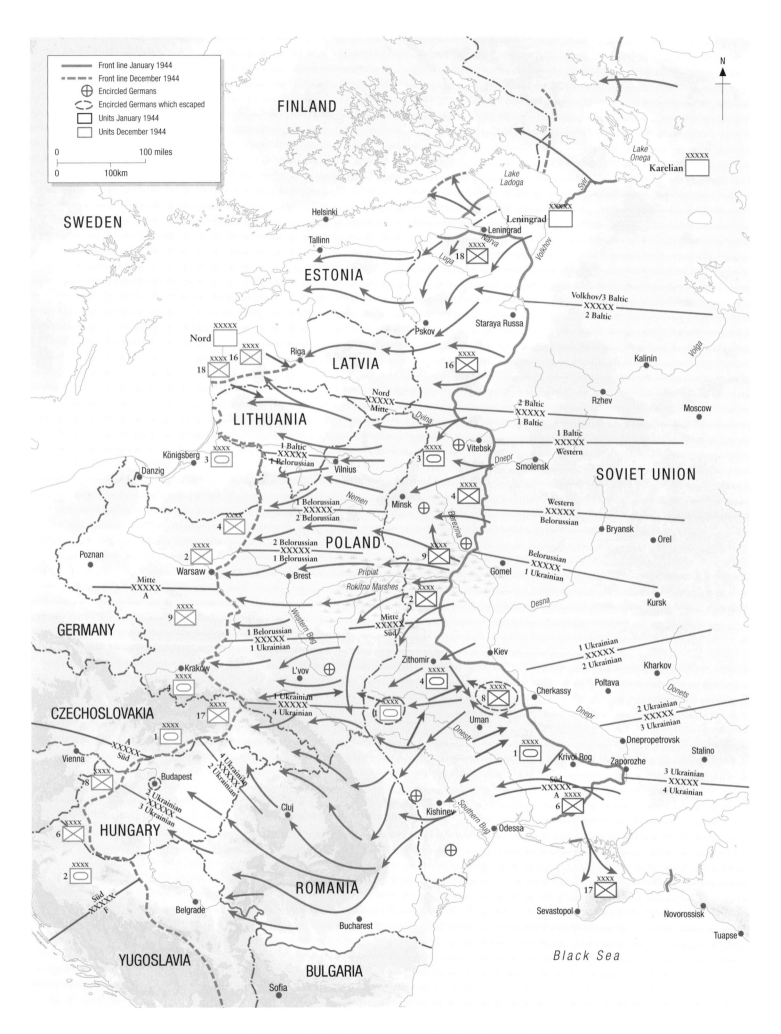

FINLAND

SWEDEN

Helsinki

Tallinn

ESTONIA

Leningrad

Narva

Luga

18

Lake
Ladoga

Lake
Onega

XXXXX
Karelian

Volkhov

Volkhov/3 Baltic
XXXXX
2 Baltic

Pskov

Staraya Russa

Kalinin

Volga

Moscow

Rzhev

Riga

LATVIA

Nord
XXXXX
Mitte

2 Baltic
XXXXX
1 Baltic

16

Nord

18   16

LITHUANIA

Dvina

Königsberg

Danzig

3

Vilnius

1 Baltic
XXXXX
1 Belorussian

Nemen

Vitebsk

3

Dnepr

Smolensk

1 Baltic
XXXXX
Western

SOVIET UNION

Minsk

4

Berezina

Western
XXXXX
Belorussian

Bryansk

Orel

4

1 Belorussian
XXXXX
2 Belorussian

Poznan

2

POLAND

9

Belorussian
XXXXX
1 Ukrainian

Kursk

Warsaw

Brest

2 Belorussian
XXXXX
1 Belorussian

Pripiat

Rokitno Marshes

2

Gomel

Desna

Mitte
XXXXX
A

9

Western Bug

Mitte
XXXXX
Süd

Zithomir

Kiev

1 Ukrainian
XXXXX
2 Ukrainian

Kharkov

GERMANY

1 Belorussian
XXXXX
1 Ukrainian

Krakow

L'vov

4

8

Cherkassy

Poltava

Donets

2 Ukrainian
XXXXX
3 Ukrainian

CZECHOSLOVAKIA

4

17

1 Ukrainian
XXXXX
4 Ukrainian

Uman

Dnepr

Dnepropetrovsk

Stalino

1

A
XXXXX
Süd

Vienna

1

4 Ukrainian
XXXXX
2 Ukrainian

Budapest

18

Krivoi Rog

Zaporozhe

3 Ukrainian
XXXXX
4 Ukrainian

2 Ukrainian
XXXXX
3 Ukrainian

Cluj

Kishinev

Süd
XXXXX
A

6

6

HUNGARY

Southern Bug

Odessa

2

ROMANIA

Süd
XXXXX
F

Belgrade

Bucharest

17

Sevastopol

Novorossisk

YUGOSLAVIA

BULGARIA

Black Sea

Tuapse

Sofia

Front line January 1944
Front line December 1944
Encircled Germans
Encircled Germans which escaped
Units January 1944
Units December 1944

0   100 miles
0   100km

CHAPTER 6
SOVIET OFFENSIVES, 1944

I consider 1944 the reverse of *Barbarossa*; what Hitler did to the USSR in 1941 Stalin did to the Third Reich that year. The main distinction was that after three years of war small Germany was in no position to recover. During the course of 1944, the retreat of Hitler's eastern army would turn into a rout. That January it still stood near Leningrad, plus held Minsk and toeholds on the Dnepr. By December, Soviet troops had liberated their country from any trace of the Wehrmacht, stood on German territory in East Prussia and had the Reich's eastern allies and tribute states in various stages of occupation. Squeezed in a vice-like grip from east, west and south and pounded from above, the country somehow maintained a defence capable of withstanding the overwhelming Allied onslaught. Bearing the brunt of the fighting, the Red Army sustained massive losses but carried forward with superior leadership at all three levels of war (strategic, operational and tactical), plus superior firepower and technique.

Less well-known due to lingering cultural and Cold War prejudices, the Soviets' 1944 campaign was every bit as impressive and arguably more destructive than *Barbarossa*. In places they advanced nearly 500 miles that year and demolished German divisions by the dozen. Two main offensive axes – one due west along the traditional Moscow–Smolensk–Warsaw–Berlin route and the other a clockwise sweep from the Ukraine, through Romania and Bulgaria into Hungary and Yugoslavia – were augmented by smaller operations along the Baltic, into the Carpathians and elsewhere in the unfortunate conflict zone separating the Third Reich from the Soviet Union. Continuing the trend begun at Stalingrad, the Wehrmacht could do little more than take the abuse heaped on it as effective countermeasures became increasingly few and far between. Overwhelming Red Army numbers, one of two post-war fig leaves German generals hide behind to excuse their poor performance,[115] strategically amounted to approximately 1.6:1 overall as the USSR dealt with its own acute manpower shortage. This proportion should have been well within a competent defence's ability to manage, although operationally and tactically, in time and place and in other key indicators, combat ratios significantly favoured the liberators. The Western Allies' Second Front siphoned off the Wehrmacht, especially panzer forces, to the Normandy front. The Soviets came to rely on increasingly complicated operations, using massed artillery, armour and CAS as a compensation for diminishing human material. Meanwhile Hitler compounded his generals' and soldiers'

---

115 The prime fig leaf of course being Hitler, long dead and unable to present his side of the story.

woes by insisting on maintaining unnecessarily lengthy front lines and allowing withdrawals only at the last minute (if even then), not when they were prudent. But it is not dumb luck that allows one side to create circumstances where it can overwhelm the other. Combined arms armies, reinforcing artillery and engineers, specialized reconnaissance and especially mechanized forces overwhelmed the Germans. Stalin's generals used deception, shifting axes and objectives, expert placement and use of reserves, co-ordinated and sequential offensives from the Arctic Circle to Thrace that their opposite numbers in *feldgrau* simply could not match; any qualitative advantage, the Wehrmacht's earlier cornerstone, had all but vanished. Historian H. P. Willmott lists ten Soviet offensives that season:[116]

24 December, 1943 to 17 April, 1944	Western Ukraine
14 January to 1 March, 1944	Leningrad–Novgorod
8 April to 12 May, 1944	Crimea
9 June to 9 August, 1944	Vyborg–Petrozavodsk
22 June to 29 August, 1944	Belorussian (*Bagration*)
13 July to 29 August, 1944	L'vov–Sandomierz
19 August to October, 1944	Romania–Bulgaria–Hungary–Yugoslavia
14 September to 20 November, 1944	Estonia–Latvia
7–29 October, 1944	Petsamo–Kirkenes
20 October, 1944 to 13 February, 1945	Budapest

Since the northern theatre had been relatively quiet for over a year, the best German formations there had been slowly removed to reinforce other areas, so quality suffered. When final operations to lift the siege of Leningrad began on 14 January, German defenders proved unable to prevent the union of the Leningrad garrison with the even more isolated Oranienbaum beachhead. A day later, a Red Army front outside the encirclement attacked in a halting fashion from the direction of Novgorod and eventually opened communications with the beleaguered city on the 27th. The famous 900-day siege (actually 876 days) claimed over one million dead Soviet citizens. Heeresgruppe Nord managed to stabilize its front first along the Narva–Vitebsk line and later along the Narva–Lake Peipus line, but only with a healthy infusion of reinforcements from Heeresgruppe Mitte. Operationally, stripping Mitte of essential divisions would soon have disastrous effects. Strategically, Finland noticed these developments and Hitler would soon lose this 'co-belligerent'.[117]

In the south, where relatively moderate weather made almost year-round manoeuvre possible, Soviet operations begun in December continued into 1944. Multiple fronts co-ordinated by Zhukov attacked all along the Heeresgruppe Süd sector. Their earlier limit of advance plus Hitler's stand-fast orders combined to create a ready-made disaster inside the great bend of the Dnepr. Manstein gave up the river by mid-February and many of his troops considered themselves fortunate to escape destruction in pockets at Cherkassy and elsewhere. Resource

116 Wilmott, The Great Crusade, p. 369.

117 Finland never fully signed on as an Axis ally; it remained only a co-belligerent, in its own war against the USSR.

areas at Krivoi Rog and Nikopol, probably the most rewarding aspects of the Nazi occupation of the USSR, were liberated. Corps of cavalry worked their way through the Rokitno Marches along the seam between two German army groups. By the end of February, Red Army units operating in the Ukraine were approaching Poland and the Carpathians. In March, three fronts consisting of 19 field armies and backed up by six fresh tank armies smashed German defences. By constantly shifting attack axes, before the month was out they had laid waste to whole German corps at more than one locale and had driven into pre-war Poland and Romania. Hitler rushed in reinforcements from France, reversing nine months of precedent. A panzer army consisting of the remnants of 21 divisions first suffered encirclement but then managed to escape total destruction by extricating many of its men and some of its weaponry. By early April, Odessa had been liberated while the Stavka directed the establishment of numerous Dniester and Vistula River bridgeheads from which to launch later offensives. A month later, Hitler's nonsensical Crimean outpost fell to another front-sized assault. Now a theatre of war with Bessarabia under Soviet occupation, Romania, Hitler's largest remaining ally and the source of most of Germany's natural petroleum (and which had just lost seven divisions in the Crimea), stood at a crossroads. In any event, the fighting in early 1944 on the flanks further demonstrated the continued twin trajectories begun at Stalingrad: Soviet improvement and German decline.

As operations in the north and south culminated that spring, Stalin, Zhukov and Vasilevski planned to shift their attention to the sizeable eastward bulge created by Heeresgruppe Mitte. This 'balcony' ran in an arc from Polotsk to Brest and was held by 50 Wehrmacht divisions, each one defending an average of over 20 miles of front. Wehrmacht reserves, especially mechanized, were almost non-existent. Organized in four fronts and loosely associated with operations in the Ukraine and even the Normandy landings, Operation *Bagration* enjoyed almost a 2:1 superiority in men and an even greater preponderance in guns, armour and aircraft. German intelligence staffs again came up short, believing (with the help of enemy deception measures) that the earlier two massive Ukrainian offensives falsely indicated firstly that these had been the Soviets' main efforts in 1944 and consequently their inability to attack elsewhere in any appreciable strength. Launched in stages from 20–23 June, it was days into *Bagration* before Wehrmacht higher staffs came close to appreciating the operation's extent and violence. By that time numerous German corps-sized pockets had ceased to exist at Vitebsk, Bobruisk, Minsk, and Mogilev, often victims of Hitler's orders to defend to the last man. In all fairness, the Red Army successes surprised even its own leaders. Minsk fell on 3 July and along with it more corps of defenders. The Germans assumed *Bagration* would soon run out of steam after the initial thrust crushed 25 of their divisions, but the offensive had just begun. Generals commanding westward-racing mechanized and tank spearheads barely looked back.

Phase II of *Bagration* started on 4 July, greatly expanded from Latvia to Slovakia by four additional fronts. Assisted largely by American-made lend-lease trucks, Red Army logistics could now keep pace with the attacking armies much better. From the initial gains of Phase I, Soviet armies fanned out through the Baltic States and drove deeper into central and southern Poland, the last-named representing the L'vov–Sandomierz and Lubin–Brest operations. Although the Red Army's main effort aimed down the Warsaw axis, it nevertheless created additional pockets of German troops near Vilnius, Brest and L'vov. Desperate rescue attempts by panzer and panzer grenadier (as motorized infantry had been renamed) divisions operating singly or in pairs continued to represent the only exceptions to the otherwise hopeless situation. Hitler fired commanders of Heeresgruppen Mitte and Nord (twice); he had already relieved Manstein, Kleist and Hoth. Could Generalfeldmarschall Model work more of his magic amid these disasters? It did not seem so as Red Army elements invaded Reich territory on 17 July and crossed the upper Vistula River in numerous places toward the end of the month. A double envelopment of Warsaw seemed to be developing until the Wehrmacht began to regain its footing, with Model launching tactical counterattacks near Siedlce south of the city and at Wołomin to the north. However, other offensives pushed Heeresgruppe Nord past Riga in mid-October and toward near-isolation in Kurland. By early August, Soviet losses, extended logistics and stabilizing German efforts had brought further advances to a halt. Decades of controversy sprang up when the Red Army failed to come to the aid of the two-month long Warsaw Uprising late that summer or to liberate extermination camps like Auschwitz, which to some seemed well within its capabilities. Even Roosevelt and Churchill got caught up in the debate as Stalin's abetters.

Exhaustion in the centre of the theatre did not equate to inactivity everywhere. On the extreme flanks Hitler's allies prepared to jump ship, the farther away from the centre of mass of the Reich the better. On the main front in Finland, Red Army offensives in June to August, ranging from Leningrad to Karelia, forced the government first to disingenuously request assistance from Hitler and then to ask for an armistice from Stalin. Fighting between Finland and the USSR ended with an indecisive Soviet 'victory' on 15 September. In the far north German troops around Petsamo technically overstayed their welcome past that date but continued to resist in northern Norway until the end of World War II. Meanwhile the attacking Soviets discovered the same difficulties in manoeuvring in the Arctic that the Germans had experienced three years earlier.

Soviet offensives in the far south during the second half of 1944 carried them to the Adriatic and Alps as the Red Army brought the 'Eastern Front' into the enigma known as the Balkan Peninsula. What the military history of the USSR calls the Jiassy–Kishinev operation began on 20 August with an offensive by two fronts numbering more than a million men and armed with prodigious amounts of weaponry.

In a matter of days double envelopment crushed one German and two Romanian armies belonging to Heeresgruppe Südukraine, which had recently lost 11 divisions (including three-quarters of its panzer divisions) to other hard-pressed fronts. The two Axis allies eyed each other wearily, both ready to bail out on the other as selfish national interests required. On the 23rd the Romanian king dismissed the dictator Ian Antonescu and had him arrested, then two days later the country switched sides and declared war on Germany. This severely tested Wehrmacht soldiers who had to fight their way out of hostile country where they had been 'welcomed' four years earlier. After another week of fighting, they lost the critical Ploesti oil region, a significant blow to the Reich. Soviet troops crossed the Danube into Bulgaria on 8 September, a new popular front government declaring war on Germany the next day. Hungarian prevarication and a healthy dose of prudence caused Hitler to dispatch forces to his last remaining ally in mid-March, both to ensure its continued reliability and secure his south-eastern flank. By late summer, Soviet forces managed to advance through the Carpathian and Transylvanian Alps mountain passes and into eastern Hungary and Slovakia, but only slowly and after suffering stiff losses. When the Red Army entered Belgrade in mid-October, it looked like it might entrap large German forces still on occupation and anti-partisan duty farther south in Greece, Albania and southern Yugoslavia. However, the Soviet priority was not in this south-western direction but to the north and Hungary. Here Wehrmacht defences recovered, stiffened on their Margarethe Line and even dealt the enemy a tactical reverse at Nyiregyhaza. The delay was temporary, and in a final sequel to the Jiassy–Kishinev offensive the two fronts encircled Budapest in late December.

The end of 1944 saw Hitler's armies in possession of little more than his 1939 borders. Certainly American–British armies in France and Italy contributed to this situation, but pride of place goes to the Red Army. Gone were Germany's resource areas and with them the reason to keep its factories working. More importantly, the loss of two million soldiers (plus a quarter of a million draught animals) and destruction of mountains of equipment rendered the Wehrmacht increasingly helpless. The Soviets caused most of this misfortune. Heeresgruppe Mitte absorbed most of the carnage that summer, half of its 890,000 strength vanishing in a couple of months. Red Army losses in the same fighting amounted to nearly 250,000 dead and 810,000 wounded. All the while its generals consistently outperformed their German counterparts. These factors combined to demolish the argument that it was only Hitler's meddling and the Soviet Union's superior numbers that defeated the eastern army of the Reich.

MAP 85: LIBERATION OF LENINGRAD (I) 14–28 JANUARY, 1944

Considering Leningrad's importance as a cultural, economic, military and political symbol to both Stalin and Hitler, neither had put much effort into the northern theatre. Taking note of the unfavourable German situation in Heeresgruppe Mitte and Süd through the autumn of 1943, Küchler and his staffs concluded that the siege of Leningrad had become a military liability to the entire eastern army (although it remained a strategic necessity in order to keep Finland in the war), and so prepared to withdraw to the Panther Line, which was generally along the Soviet borders with Estonia and Latvia. Hitler naturally baulked at making such a decision, but constantly dangled a carrot in front of Küchler that he would authorize a withdrawal any day. Heeresgruppe Nord's 40 understrength divisions manned a 500-mile front of mainly forests and marshes teeming with an estimated 35,000 partisans; it had perhaps 200 AFVs, but no reserves worthy of mention. Across the front lines the Leningrad (33 divisions) and Volkhov fronts (23 divisions), plus three divisions in the Oranienbaum pocket, counted over a million soldiers with 1,200 AFVs in a dozen tank brigades covered by over 1,500 aircraft. The first phase of their plan was to join Oranienbaum to Leningrad while pushing 18. Armee away from Leningrad to the Luga River, thereby completely breaking the siege. Phase II would add the 2nd Baltic Front (45 divisions) coming east from its positions south of Lake Il'men. Lake Peipus and the Velikaya River represented the Soviets' operational objective and coincidentally Küchler's portion of the Panther position; theoretically both sides would be satisfied reaching that line.

Barely 10 miles separated Oranienbaum from Govorov's closest positions in western Leningrad. Following a preparatory artillery barrage that included Baltic Fleet guns, the attack began on 14 January with a goal of the two forces linking up at Ropsha. Five divisions of General Lieutenant I. I. Fedyuninsky's 2nd Shock Army quickly overran 9. Luftwaffe-Feld-Division, but 30th Guards Rifle Corps had more difficulty versus the L Armee-Korps *Landser*s. On the same day, the Volkhov Front's 54th and 59th Armies hit 18. Armee's right flank near Novgorod, some Red Army troops crossing the frozen Lake Il'men. On

the 15th, Govorov's 42nd Army in Leningrad proper joined the offensive while his 67th Army launched a diversionary attack against Mga. Now under attack from Oranienbaum to Lake Il'men, Lindemann struggled to master the situation. By 16 January Fedyuninsky and Maslennikov's men had almost joined forces, and a day later the OKH advised Küchler to make preparations to pull away from Leningrad. Closest to Lake Ladoga his troops were falling back to the south. His XXVI Armee-Korps was about to lose Lyuban, while XXXVIII Armee-Korps was in danger of encirclement if it did not retreat soon. Five days into the offensive, on 19 January, 2nd Shock and 42nd Army forces did indeed meet at Ropsha, cutting off two German divisions stranded on the coast. Almost simultaneously, on the 20th, 54th Army liberated Volkhov and 59th Army liberated Novgorod. In a short time, Govorov and Meretskov had accomplished many key tasks: ended Oranienbaum's isolation, pushed Heeresgruppe Nord away from Leningrad and generally had the Germans in full retreat along the entire front. Govorov ordered his armies to expand their attacks south-west toward Kingisepp (2nd Shock), Gatchina (42nd) and Ulyanov–Tonso (67th). Overall he wanted to reach the Luga River and threaten the 18.–16. Armee boundary.

The last German artillery shells fired against Leningrad fell on 20 January, and then the guns moved out of range. Two days later Lindemann ordered his troops out of the exposed Mga salient and back to the Rollbahn Position (the pre-war Leningrad–Moscow railway), but the enemy had already compromised this defensive line. The Soviets did not allow Heeresgruppe Nord any respite, but maintained constant pressure everywhere. By 25 January, not only did the 67th and 54th Armies threaten the intended Luga River position from the north, but 59th Army did so from the south as well. The past ten days had cost Küchler 40,000 casualties, and on 28 January he ordered his army group back to the Luga on his own authority. Two days later Hitler summoned the field marshal to Rastenburg and relieved him over 'differences of opinion'. By the end of January, Red Army troops had already crossed the Luga.

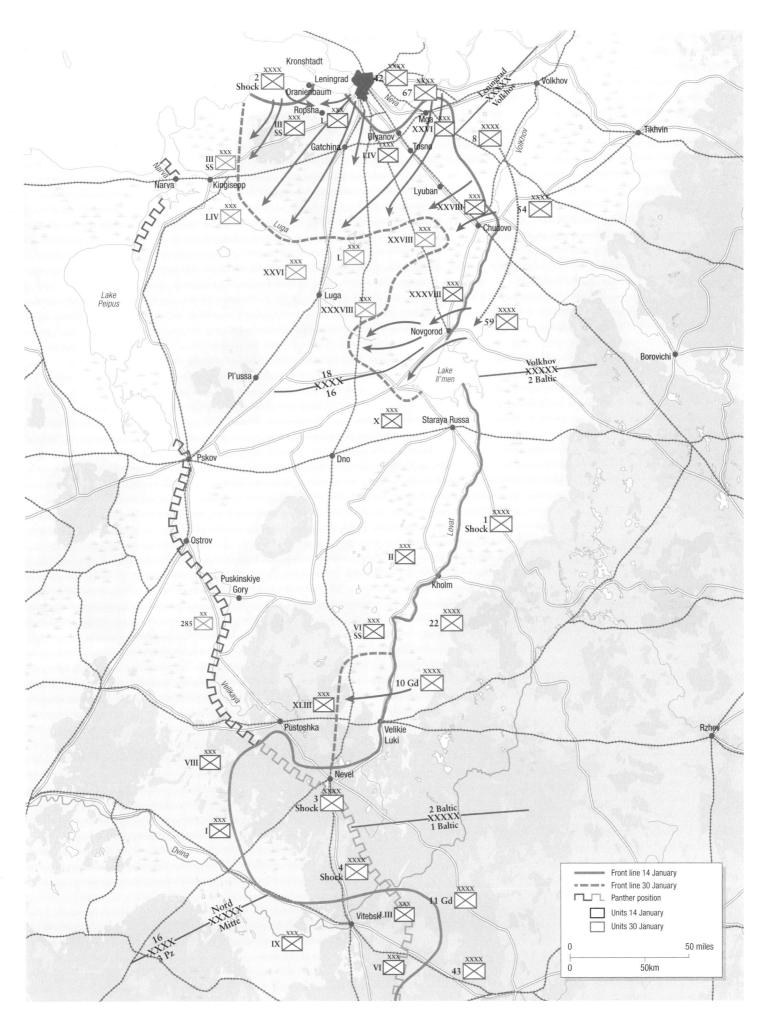

Kronshtadt

Leningrad

Oranienbaum

2
Shock XXXX

Ropsha

III
SS XXX

L XXX

Gatchina

Ulyanov

XXXX 42

XXXX
67

Mga
XXVI XXX

Leningrad
XXXXX
Volkhov

Volkhov

Tikhvin

LIV XXX

Tosno

8 XXXX

Volkhov

Narva

Narva

Kingisepp

III
SS XXX

LIV XXX

Lyuban

XXVIII XXX

XXVIII XXX

Chudovo

54 XXXX

L XXX

XXVI XXX

Luga

XXXVIII XXX

XXXVIII XXX

Novgorod

59 XXXX

Borovichi

Lake
Peipus

Pl'ussa

Luga

18
XXXX
16

X XXX

Staraya Russa

Volkhov
XXXXX
2 Baltic

Lake
Il'men

Pskov

Dno

Lovat

1
Shock XXXX

Ostrov

II XXX

Kholm

Puskinskiye
Gory

285 XX

VI
SS XXX

22 XXX

Velikaya

10 Gd XXXX

XLIII XXX

Pustoshka

Velikie
Luki

Rzhev

VIII XXX

Nevel

I XXX

3
Shock XXXX

2 Baltic
XXXXX
1 Baltic

Dvina

4
Shock XXXX

11 Gd XXXX

Nord
XXXXX
Mitte

Vitebsk

III XXX

16
XXXX
3 Pz

IX XXX

VI XXX

43 XXXX

	Front line 14 January
	Front line 30 January
	Panther position
	Units 14 January
	Units 30 January

0   50 miles
0   50km

185

MAP 86: LIBERATION OF LENINGRAD (II) 4 FEBRUARY TO 3 MARCH, 1944

In place of Küchler, Hitler brought in Model from 9. Armee, who was sure to shake up Heeresgruppe Nord. For their part, the Soviets were going to keep driving westwards from the Leningrad region toward the Baltic States. Model arrived at army group headquarters in Pskov and had the first couple of days of February to re-motivate his new command and to introduce Hitler's new war-winning tactic, *Schild und Schwert* (shield and sword, a new name for thrust and parry), to his troops. He ordered Lindemann back to the Luga River without even asking Hitler's permission. By the 4th the Leningrad, Volkhov and 2nd Baltic fronts had re-organized and were ready to attack again.

The three fronts moved out, concentrating on 18. Armee, although 2nd Baltic continued its efforts, begun a month earlier, to nibble away at the south-eastern corner of 16. Armee. Red Army commanders had little of the offensive flair of their peers in the Ukraine, but their progress felt unstoppable. Model's immediate task was to secure the Panther Line, especially on his left where 2nd Shock Army units easily crossed the lower Luga River and approached the Narva. His second task was to assemble a counterattack force with which to execute the 'sword' portion of his new mission. His only suitable mobile division, 12. Panzer-Division, attempted to accomplish a long list of operations, including closing the gap between 18. and 16. Armeen, which it did on 6 February. Infantry, artillery and pioneers of Govorov's 42nd and 67th Armies worked to overthrow the middle Luga line, while Meretskov's 59th and 8th Armies expanded their bulge west of Lake Il'men. The two fronts combined to liberate the town of Luga on 12 February.[118] This proved a disastrous loss for Model, as it made doubtful Busch's continued defence of Staraya Russa, although the general told his Führer that he did not intend to surrender the Lake Il'men mainstay. As of mid-February, Lindemann's front line ran almost due east from the narrows connecting lakes Peipus and Pskov on his centre to Lake Il'men on his right, but he managed to secure his front line with the bare minimum of troops.

118 The Stavka disbanded the Volkhov Front on 13 February, giving most of its units to the Leningrad Front, but sent the 1st Shock Army to the 2nd Baltic Front.

Events began to unravel quickly, however, and threw Model's good intentions into doubt. On 14 February, the Soviets made an amphibious landing behind the city of Narva while ski troops negotiated the narrows between lakes Peipus and Pskov, both moves threatening the Panther Line. To the east, the Germans began to abandon Staraya Russa, and avoided real disaster for a couple of days when the 1st Shock Army failed to notice or take up the chase. Soon Popov's 2nd Baltic Front shifted its forces from the unrewarding attacks around Velikie Luki and the boundary with 3. Panzer-Armee to the north near Lake Il'men. This move complete, the 22nd Army joined the 1st Shock Army pushing back 16. Armee, taking Kholm on 21 February. Along with these threats to his flanks, Model had to worry about a Red Army manoeuvre against Pskov anchoring his centre and the tens of thousands of vengeful partisans killing Germans, destroying their vehicles and sabotaging their infrastructure (bridges, roads, communications wire, etc). Despite this, he conducted an orderly withdrawal. Surprisingly, at the end of February Hitler actually asked him to expedite the withdrawal, an almost unheard-of request. A few days later, in early March, the army group front had come to rest approximately on the Panther Line. In the far north the Soviets had crossed the Narva against the III SS Panzer-Korps, but were eventually halted by its four weakened divisions, while in the south movement stopped on the Velikaya River from Pskov to Ostrov and then generally south-eastwards to Vitebsk. Toward mid-month the Soviets conducted probing raids against the Germans, but little more.

Model was happy to have made it back to the Panther Line without suffering a disaster, although he had used much more *Schild* than *Schwert*. A favourite German tactic had been to break contact with the Red Army, jump back to a new position and catch their breath as the enemy caught up to them again. The Soviet pursuit had been clumsy and full of missed opportunities; their commanders were content to wait out the spring thaw and *rasputitsa*. The summer would bring another round of massive changes.

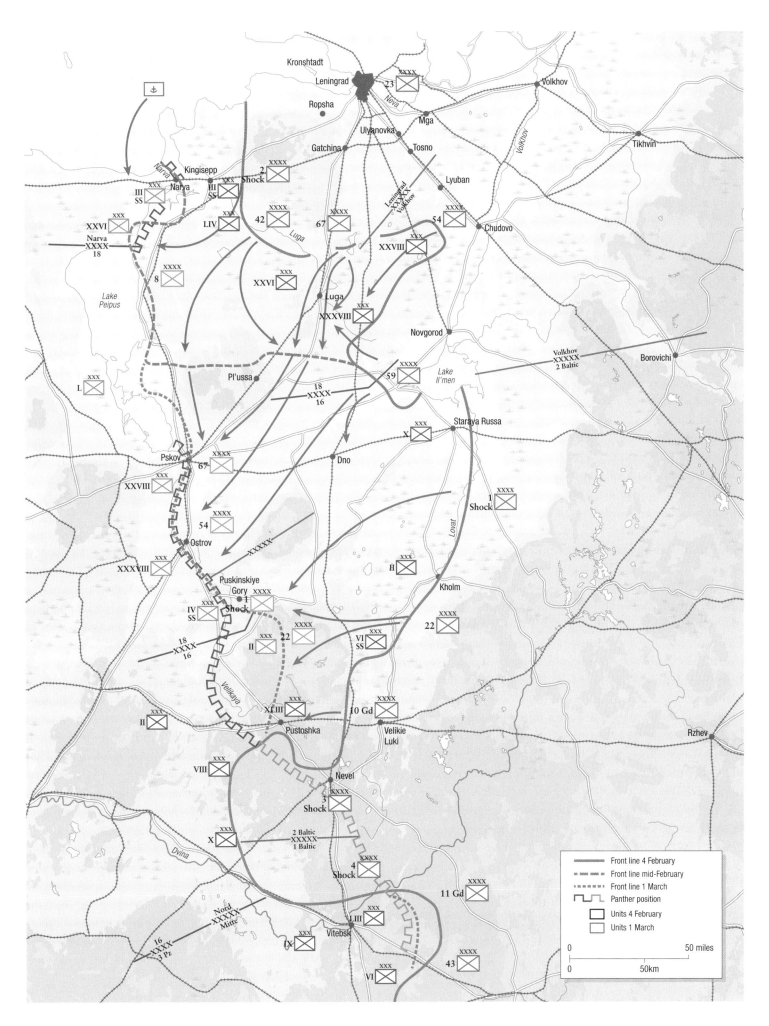

Kronshtadt

Leningrad

Volkhov

Ropsha

Neva

Mga

Tikhvin

Ulyanovka

Tosno

Gatchina

XXXX 23

Kingisepp

XXX Narva

2 Shock XXXX

Lyuban

XXXX 54

Chudovo

III SS

XXX

III SS XXX

LIV XXX

42 XXXX

Luga

67 XXXX

XXX XXVIII

Narva
XXXX
18

Leningrad
XXXXX
Volkhov

Lake Peipus

XXVI XXX

8 XXXX

XXVI XXX

Luga

XXXVIII XXX

Novgorod

Volkhov
XXXXX
2 Baltic

Borovichi

Pl'ussa

18
XXXX
16

59 XXXX

Lake Il'men

L XXX

Staraya Russa

X XXX

Pskov

67 XXXX

Dno

1 Shock XXXX

XXVIII XXX

54 XXXX

Ostrov

XXXXX

Kholm

II XXX

22 XXXX

XXXVIII XXX

Puskinskiye Gory

IV SS XXX

1 Shock XXXX

II XXX

22

Lovat

18
XXXX
16

VI SS XXX

22 XXXX

Velikaya

II XXX

XL III XXX

10 Gd XXXX

Pustoshka

Velikie Luki

Rzhev

VIII XXX

Nevel

3 Shock XXXX

X XXX

2 Baltic
XXXXX
1 Baltic

Dvina

4 Shock XXXX

11 Gd XXXX

Nord
XXXXX
Mitte

Vitebsk

LIII XXX

16
XXXX
3 Pz

IX XXX

VI XXX

43 XXXX

	Front line 4 February
	Front line mid-February
	Front line 1 March
	Panther position
	Units 4 February
	Units 1 March

0   50 miles

0   50km

MAP 87: BALTIC STATES
5 JULY TO 13 OCTOBER, 1944

Major operations in the north came to a halt with the spring thaw. At the end of March Model left for the Ukraine, which had a domino effect on the top leadership of Heeresgruppe Nord.[119] The smallest army group of Hitler's eastern army, it now had responsibility for little more than defending Estonia and Latvia and half of Lithuania. Opposite it stood four front commanders: Govorov, newly promoted Maslennikov (his Volkhov Front re-named 3rd Baltic), Eremenko and General I. K. Bagramian. With the summer's main effort clearly around Minsk, the Red Army in the Baltic region concentrated on the Heeresgruppe Nord (16. Armee) and Centre (3. Panzer-Armee) seam. General Vasilevski acted as the Stavka representative co-ordinating the 1st Baltic and 3rd Belorussian fronts, with the 2nd Baltic Front coming in later and 3rd Baltic and Leningrad fronts even later.

After much wrangling over objectives, Bagramian had his mission: attack Vitebsk with the neighbouring 3rd Belorussian, then veer north-west along the Dvina River toward Dvinsk (Dünaburg), helping cover Operation *Bagration*'s right flank. His 6th Guards and 43rd Armies attacked according to plan on 5 July and within a week had liberated Polotsk, 60 miles beyond Vitebsk. New 16. Armee commander, General der Infanterie Paul Laux, rushed reinforcements to Dvinsk as the 6th Guards Army drew near. Meanwhile the 2nd Baltic Front had moved out on 10 July, aiming ultimately for Riga, with two pairs of two armies: 10th Guards and 3rd Shock in the north and 22nd and 4th Shock below. Together they ripped a 100-mile hole in 16. Armee's defences and soon reached the Velikaya River, taking Opochka on the 15th. That town represented a key bastion on the Panther Line and its loss opened the road into central Latvia, although the forests and marshes in the area favoured the defenders. On the next day, the 3rd Baltic Front attacked 18. Armee, also using two pairs of two armies: 42nd and 67th against Pskov, and 1st Shock and 54th Armies aiming for Ostrov. The Germans in both towns held out for a week and then retreated, bypassing the defenceless terrain west of the Estonian towns.

The situation on Heeresgruppe Nord's two flanks began to deteriorate in late July.[120] On 25 July the Leningrad Front stirred itself and set 2nd Shock and 8th Armies against German defences at Narva. With numerous crises elsewhere requiring reinforcement, Armee-Abteilung Narva, a collection of mostly SS units, had dwindled from 12 divisions in May to four divisions and three SS brigades in July. Fedyuninsky's men took the town on the 26th and crossed the Narva River, but could not immediately break out into the open country of the Estonian interior. The Stavka re-organized its forces in south-west Lithuania, adding the 2nd Guards and 51st Armies to Bagramian's order of battle and ordering him to Siauliai, which he reached on 27 July.[121] The same day, after being assaulted and almost surrounded by a host of Red Army units, the Germans pulled out of the smouldering Dvinsk. Near the end of July (the 27th) Bagramian's tankers had reached Tukums on the Gulf of Riga, splitting the two German armies, and Siauliai, 90 miles from Memel, threatening to cut off the entire army group.

It was the loss of Siauliai that the Germans took most seriously. In early and mid-August Generaloberst Ferdinand Schörner managed to launch some ineffective counterattacks in the direction of Siauliai, the latter even including Grossdeutschland. But he also urgently wanted to eliminate the armour salient between Jelgava and Tukums to avoid having 18. and 16. Armeen isolated and defeated in detail. His counterattack by Panzergruppe Strachwitz here initially came up short as the 1st and 2nd Baltic fronts began to squeeze the heavily fortified Riga. The 3rd Baltic Front returned to action, linking up with Bagramian's men west of Lake Peipus. Despite Soviet reinforcement efforts, the line around Siauliai stabilized and Schörner kept pressing west of Riga with panzer counterattacks. During the third week of September, he opened a difficult route to his men still fighting in a narrow, 500-mile-long front running from Riga to Valga to the Gulf of Finland. The Soviets, now re-organized, renewed attacks on 5 October west to Memel and north to Riga. When it was inevitable that these two cities would be lost (they fell on 10 and 13 October respectively), the troops fighting in the area escaped via a narrow path. When 1st Baltic Front fanned out toward the Baltic coast, it sealed the fate of Heeresgruppe Nord. Until the end of World War II, Heeresgruppe Nord and 26 divisions languished on the Kurland peninsula.

---

119 Lindemann moved up from 18. Armee to replace Model, General der Artillerie Herbert Loch moved up from XXVIII Armee-Korps to replace him. Lindemann lasted only until 3 July when Hitler replaced him with Generaloberst Johannes Friessner, commander of Army Detachment Narva.

120 On 20 July, the date of the Hitler assassination attempt, Generaloberst Ferdinand Schörner, a Bavarian, World War I *Pour le mérite* recipient and ardent Nazi, took command of Heeresgruppe Nord.

121 The 51st Army, under General Lieutenant Ia. G. Kreizer, had just liberated the Crimea in May before being re-assigned to the north two months later.

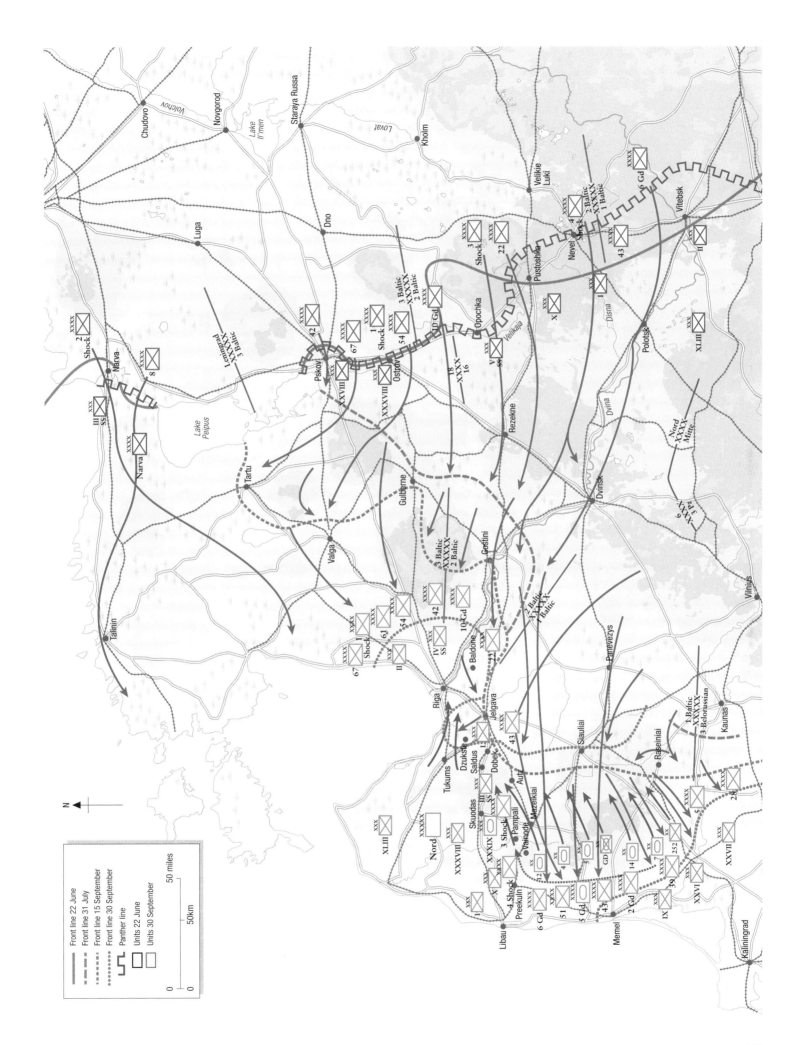

Chudovo

Volchov

Novgorod

Lake Il'men

Staraya Russa

Lovat

Kholm

Luga

Dno

Velikie
Luki

Nevel

XXXX
6 Gd

Pustoshka

4
Shock

2 Baltic
XXXXX
1 Baltic

Vitebsk

XXXX
II

XXXX
3 XXXX
Shock 22

43

XXXX
II

XXX
X

2 Shock
XXXX

Narva

XXXX
8

Leningrad
XXXXX
3 Baltic

Pskov
XXXX
42

XXXX
67

XXXX
1
Shock

3 Baltic
XXXXX
2 Baltic

XXXX
54

XXXX
10 Gd

Opochka

Velikaja

XXX
V

XXX
59

Nord
XXXX
Mitte

III
SS

Narva

Lake
Peipus

XXVIII

XXXVIII

Ostrov

18
XXXXX
16

Rezekne

Dvina

Polotsk

XLIII

Tartu

Valga

Gulberne

3 Baltic
XXXXX
2 Baltic

Gostini

Dvina

Dvinsk

XXXX
9

Vilnius

Tallinn

XXXX
1
Shock

XXXX
61

67
XXX

XXXX
54

XXXX
42

IV
XXX
SS

10 Gd

Baldone

22

2 Baltic
XXXXX
1 Baltic

Panevezys

1 Baltic
XXXXX
3-Belorussian

Kaunas

II

Riga

Jelgava

1

XXXX
43

Siauliai

Raseiniai

XXXX
28

XLIII

Nord

XXXVIII

Dzukste

Saldus

Dobek

Autz

5

XXXX

Tukums

III
SS

Mezeitkiai

GD

XX
14

XX
7

252

XXVII

3 Shock

Pampali

XX

XVI

Skuodas

Vainoda

XX
4

GD
XX

XX
39

IX

XXVII

X

Preekuln

4 Shock

51

43

2 Gd

Libau

6 Gd

5 Gd

Memel

Kaliningrad

N

Front line 22 June
Front line 31 July
Front line 15 September
Front line 30 September
Panther line
Units 22 June
Units 30 September

50 miles

50km

189

MAP 88: FINLAND AND KARELIA 9 JUNE TO 15 JULY, 1944

Finland had no grandiose designs on the USSR, but in 1941 it had both regained territories lost in the Winter War and also kept up its end of the bargain with Germany by reaching the north bank of the Svir River. It noted with interest that throughout 1942–43 Hitler could get no closer to Leningrad, and in fact had even been pushed away at various places and times. Finnish enthusiasm for the Führer and his Third Reich had waned by early 1944 when the Leningrad and Volkhov fronts broke the siege. During the lull between this event and Operation *Bagration*, Stalin planned to push back Axis forces from Leningrad's northern approaches and, if possible, encourage his smaller neighbour to drop out of World War II altogether. The Stavka's plan envisioned Govorov attacking against Vyborg on 10 June with the 21st and 23rd Armies while Meretskov (now commanding the Karelian Front) would clear the far side of Lake Ladoga with the 32nd and 7th Separate Armies, starting on the 21st. With the Red Army's 1.5:1, 5:1, 7:1 and 5.5:1 superiority over the Finns in men, artillery, armour and aircraft, there could be but one outcome to these battles.

To avoid an unlikely repetition of 1939–40, the Stavka planned carefully and built up a massive materiel advantage. Artillery and bombs began falling on Finnish positions on 9 June, surprising the defenders; evidently they never expected to be attacked. Govorov's tactics – firepower preferred over manpower – came as news to the Finns, who it seems had not been paying much attention to the war the Germans had been fighting for the past year. Ten rifle and three tank divisions assaulted three and a half Finnish divisions. The Finns, sitting statically in neglected front-line fieldworks, had not modernized their military. Their three subsequent defensive lines extended back behind the primary positions, which likewise had not been maintained or modernized during the previous three years. Along the coast the 21st Army struck IV Corps hardest, forcing it back to the second defensive line within 48 hours. Marshal Carl Mannerheim assembled such reserves as he could and pulled back its northern neighbour III Corps

in order to maintain the integrity of his defences. The Finns confided in the senior German commander on the scene, Generaloberst Eduard Dietl, that if the Soviets overcame their second line of positions (the best of the lot), they would be forced to withdraw from the Svir as well. Indeed, Govorov attacked the Finns' second line 24 hours after the conversation with Dietl, using the same deadly combination of artillery, tanks and CAS. A day later III and IV Corps were falling back after suffering an 8-mile breach in their lines near Kutersel'ka. The Soviets moved faster in their tanks and trucks than the Finns could on foot, and Mannerheim worried that the enemy might reach the third line of defences before his own troops could. Sure enough, on 20 June both sides made it to the positions almost simultaneously. Around this time, the Finnish government opened secret negotiations with Stalin, while also begging Hitler to airlift weapons to them. The already abandoned Vyborg fell to Govorov on 21 June, into which he shipped the 59th Army.

True to his word, Mannerheim issued orders on 16 June for the evacuation of the Svir River positions and those north of Lake Onega. In this eastern portion of Karelia his forces were outnumbered by 4:11 in divisions and 2:6 in brigades. The Finns pulled out on the 18th and Meretskov began his assault on the 19th. Red artillery therefore fell on empty space, but 7th Separate Army especially made up for it with a lively pursuit. Two weeks later, it liberated Salmi from the retreating VI Corps. A further week later fighting came to a rest along the U-line, practically back to the old international boundary. The Finns lobbied Hitler hard for additional German units, especially assault gun brigades; the Führer gave them the absolute minimum support he thought he could get away with. The Soviets kept up subtle pressure all along Mannerheim's lines until mid-July, when their aggressiveness began to slacken. Both sides were exhausted: the Finns had no more replacements to put into their front-line units, while the Soviets wanted to transfer their troops south to the main fighting.

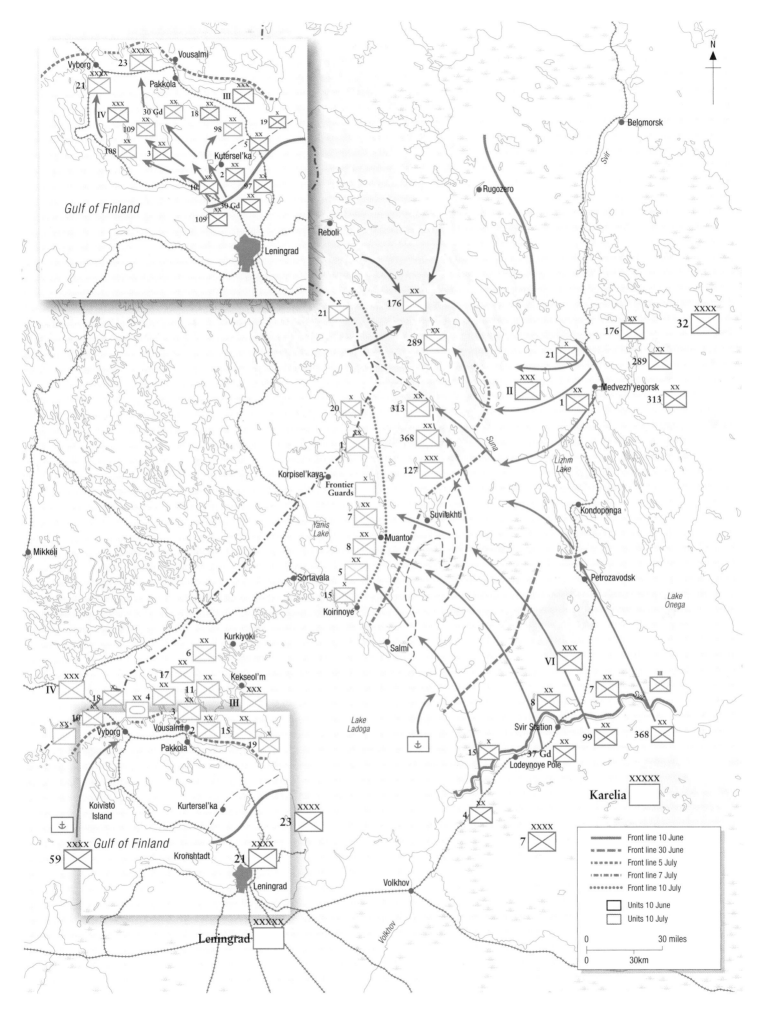

Inset (top left)

Vyborg
23 XXXX Vousalmi
21 XXXX Pakkola
IV XXX
30 Gd XX 18 XX III XXX
109 XXX 98 XX 19 XX
108 3 XX 5 XX
Kutersel'ka
2 XX
10 XX 97 XX
30 Gd XX
109 XX

Gulf of Finland

Reboli

Leningrad

Main map

N

Belomorsk

Svir

Rugozero

176 XX
289 XX

21 X

32 XXXX
176 XX
289 XX
21 X
II XXX
1 XX
Medvezh'yegorsk
313 XX

Suna

Lizhm Lake

313 XX
368 XX
127 XXX

Kondoponga

Korpisel'kaya
Frontier Guards X
7 XX
8 XX
Muanto
5 XX
15 X
Koirinoye

Suvilakhti

Petrozavodsk

Lake Onega

Mikkeli

Sortavala

Yanis Lake

Salmi

Kurkiyoki
6 XX
17 XX
Kekseol'm
11 XX III XXX
IV XXX
18 XX 4 XX 3 XX 15 XX 19 X
Vyborg
Vousalmi
Pakkola
10 X

VI XXX
8 XX
7 XX III
99 XXX
368 XX

Svir Station
37 Gd XX
15 X
Lodeynoye Pole

Lake Ladoga

⚓

Kurtersel'ka
23 XXXX
59 XXXX
Koivisto Island
Kronshtadt
21 XXXX
Leningrad

⚓

Volkhov

Volkhov

4 XX

7 XXXX

Karelia XXXXX

Leningrad XXXXX

——	Front line 10 June
—·—	Front line 30 June
····	Front line 5 July
—··—	Front line 7 July
·····	Front line 10 July
☐	Units 10 June
☐	Units 10 July

0 ———— 30 miles
0 ———— 30km

MAP 89: FINLAND EVACUATED AND PETSAMO–KIRKENES OPERATION 1 OCTOBER TO 3 NOVEMBER, 1944

Throughout 1944 the Finns watched the Soviets raise the siege of Leningrad, push the Germans back to their pre-war frontier and finally in late summer observed the Red Army dismantle Heeresgruppe Nord in the three Baltic States. The writing was on the wall and in mid-July the Finns began the self-serving process of secret negotiations with their once and future masters: Hitler for support and Stalin for peace. On 4 August, the Finnish parliament gave Mannerheim the additional office of president and soon thereafter he nullified the previous president's 26 June, 1942 agreement not to seek a separate peace with the USSR. A month later, after negotiations hosted by neutral Sweden, Stalin informed Mannerheim that peace between their two nations depended on Finland breaking off relations with Hitler and expelling, by force if necessary, German troops from its territory by 15 September. The Germans had three mountain corps headquarters, two infantry, three mountain, one SS mountain, and one fortress division and two ad hoc 'division groups' in Finland.

The deadline for German removal came and went, with the Germans keeping up appearances that they were leaving, the Finns seeming to hurry them on their way and the Soviets pretending not to notice what was going on between the two former co-belligerents. A gentlemens' agreement allowed the Germans to continue their way north toward Lapland and eventually Norway through late September. The Germans executed a mini scorched-earth policy that ensured the Finnish army could not follow too closely, but did not create too much of a hardship for local civilians. Actual fighting between the two occurred around the port of Tornio on the Swedish frontier between 1 and 8 October. The better part of four Finnish divisions attacked Divisionsgruppe Kräutler and sent it packing north. Henceforth the Germans practised a thorough scorched-earth policy across Lapland. On 3 October Hitler made the decision to remove the German forces on the Arctic Circle from Soviet soil to northern Norway as well. Not only would XIX Gebirgs-Korps have to contend with brutal polar weather during its withdrawal, but also General Lieutenant V. I. Shcherbakov's 14th Army was sure to give pursuit.

Outnumbering the Germans 113,000 to 45,000 and supported by more than 2,000 indirect fire weapons, 110 AFVs and 750 aircraft, the Red Army troops under Meretskov's Karelian Front attacked on 7 October, mainly against 2. Gebirgs-Division on the right. The 131st and 99th Rifle Corps created the breakthrough and ski troops of the 126th and 127th Light Rifle Corps began the exploitation. A month later, the Soviets had split the two German divisions apart, while the Arctic Fleet units landed naval infantry in brigade strength on the coast in the mountain corps rear areas. The 20. Gebirgs-Armee diverted the XXXVI Gebirgs-Korps (headquarters and 163. Infanterie-Division), supposedly evacuating the Salla front north-west through Finland but instead moving north-east to the endangered Petsamo area. A week into the attack, the Soviets had demolished the entire German arctic position. Though Divisionsgruppe van der Hoop tried to hold the town against the 126th Light Rifle Corps's determined attacks, it fell on 15 October. By the last week of October, the Germans had their backs to Kirkenes, Norway and they gave up the town on 25 October. The Soviets essentially gave up their pursuit at Tana.

By the end of October, the Germans had still not fully evacuated Finland. The XVIII Gebirgs-Korps had fallen back to the Sturmbock position just inside Finland where that country, Sweden and Norway come together. It would remain there until 12 January 1945. The XXXVI Gebirgs-Korps remained in the Schutzwall Position throughout the month. In early November it reached Lakselv, Norway, where it joined up with XIX Gebirgs-Korps. From there the two moved to Lyngen; here 20. Gebirgs-Armee settled down to wait for the war to end. Thanks to mild weather, an unenthusiastic Red Army chase and a healthy dose of luck, the Germans had skilfully managed a withdrawal of many hundreds of miles at the top of the world. For all concerned, World War II in Finland was over.

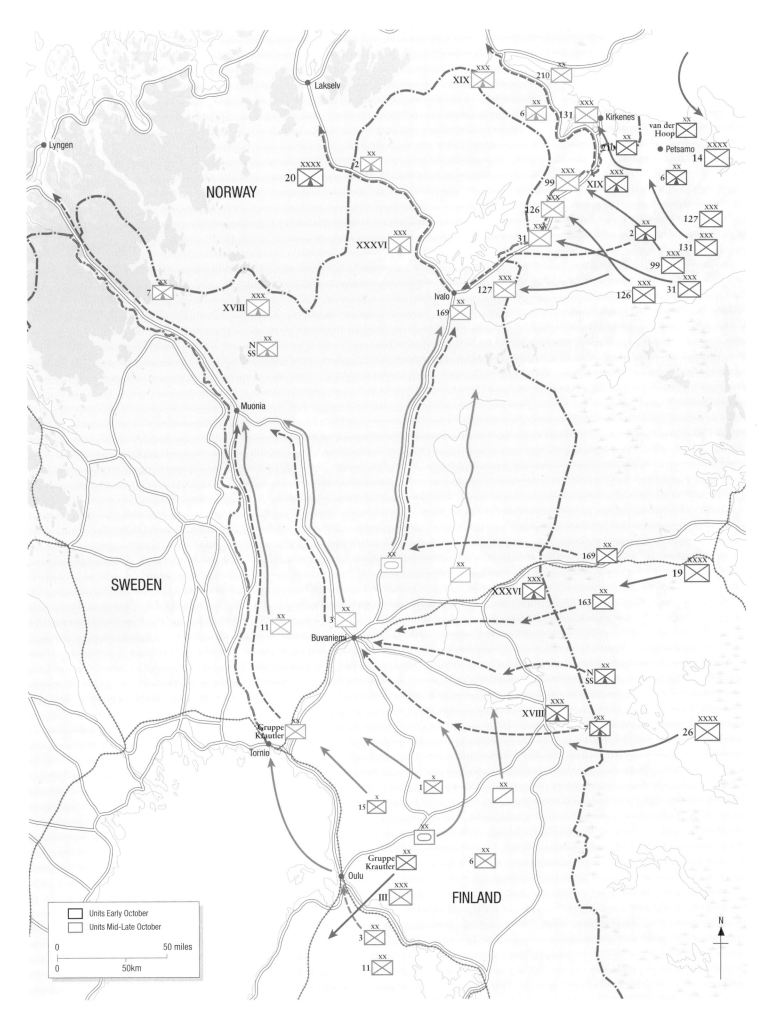

NORWAY

Lakselv

Lyngen

XIX XXXX 210
6 XX 131 XXX Kirkenes
van der Hoop XX
210 XXXX 14
XXX 99 XIX XXX 6 XX
20 XXXX 2 XX 126 XXX 2 127 XXX
31 XXXX 131 XXX
XXXVI XXX 127 XXX 99 XXX
Ivalo XXX 126 31 XXX
7 XX 169
XVIII XXX
N SS XX

Muonia

SWEDEN

169 XX
19 XXXX
XXXVI XXX 163 XX
11 XX
3 XX
Buvaniemi
N SS XX
XVIII XXX
Gruppe Krautler XX
Tornio 7 XX 26 XXXX
1 X
15 X
XX
Gruppe Krautler XX
Oulu 6 XX
III XXX FINLAND
3 XX
11 XX

Units Early October
Units Mid-Late October

0   50 miles
0   50km

N

MAP 90: OPPOSING FORCES AND PLANS SPRING 1944

The winter and spring of 1944 had proved the Red Army's ability to maintain operations in just about any weather and terrain. The northern flank had been cleared east of Lake Peipus down to Vitebsk, while in the south the Germans had been expelled from the Ukraine except for Galicia. The Rokitno Marshes played its usual decisive role, dividing the theatre in two. Above it Heeresgruppe Mitte jutted eastward in the 'Belorussian balcony'. The Stavka came up with numerous possible courses of action, but in the end Stalin chose that best suited to Red Army capabilities: a sequence of massive frontal assaults along most of the entire front. Heeresgruppe Mitte would be hit the hardest, reflecting both its bulge and the fact that it guarded the direct route to Berlin, but no sector of the front would be safe that year.

The Soviets' southern theatre had just cleared the huge area between the Dnepr and Dniester rivers a few weeks earlier, so would need a pause to recover and bring forward logistics for any new drive. Therefore Stalin's first move would be against Karelia, and with any luck, this manoeuvre would also distract Hitler from the central theatre (Map 88). The Red Army's main effort that season would be 1812 and 1941 in reverse, aiming down the high ground from Minsk to Bialystok to Warsaw: Operation *Bagration*. Attacking between Vitebsk and the Pripiat River, the three Belorussian fronts would vaporize the initial German defenders. Their first thrust was expected to carry them considerably past Minsk, while subsequent assaults had East Prussia as their likely objective. Besides capturing ground, commanders had the additional mission of the destruction of a 'significant' portion of the German defensive strength. Planners at the Kremlin anticipated that after this initial blast, adjacent attacks through the southern Baltic States and along the north slope of the Carpathian Mountains by the Baltic and Ukrainian front later in the summer would carry them to Warsaw. The Red Army's best operational-level thinkers, Zhukov and Vasilevski, co-ordinated the main blows for the Stavka. Rounding out a season of devastating Soviet offensives, the end of summer brought new assaults in the far south against Hitler's Hungarian and Romanian allies.

Bagration's opening tactical targets would be Vitebsk, Mogilev and Bobruisk, after which tank armies would encircle Minsk. After much deliberation, final orders went out on the last day of May, with the offensive to begin in two or three weeks. Some of the Red Army's best field generals, Bagramian, I. D. Cherniakhovsky, Rokossovsky and Konev led the attacking fronts. Together they counted 118 rifle divisions, 13 artillery divisions, eight mechanized or tank corps, and two cavalry corps in 15 armies numbering 1.25 million men, nearly 25,000 artillery pieces (plus 2,300 Katyushas), more than 2,000 tanks and 5,300 aircraft. Logistical arrangements were extensive, based on years of bitter experience of running short at the most inopportune moments. As with all Soviet operations at this stage of the war, partisans contributed fully to *Bagration*.

Combat during the second half of 1943 and early 1944 had not been kind to Heeresgruppe Süd, while recent attacks had taken their toll on Heeresgruppe Nord; Mitte had escaped major operations since the liberation of Smolensk (Map 82). Busch had commanded the army group since the previous October when Kluge had received injuries in a car wreck; 2 ½ years of commanding an army in the static northern theatre poorly prepared him for the storm about to hit. Available forces consisted of 42 divisions (34 of them infantry divisions) in four armies, with approximately 700,000 soldiers, fewer than 10,000 guns, and 550 AFVs, supported by 830 aircraft. As usual German intelligence had both misjudged Soviet strategic intentions and failed to notice *Bagration*'s build-up, so operationally it came as a complete surprise, although German units in contact noticed the unmistakable signs. The army group's front lines were thin and brittle with no fallback positions, while Busch had no mobile reserves (in fact no operational-level reserves, mobile or otherwise, existed in the eastern army). Finally, Hitler's requirement to hold the Berezina and Dnepr rivers tied Busch's hands.

The month of June, 1944 possibly represented the zenith of Allied prowess worldwide, as *Bagration*, D-Day and the Battle of the Philippine Sea demonstrate.

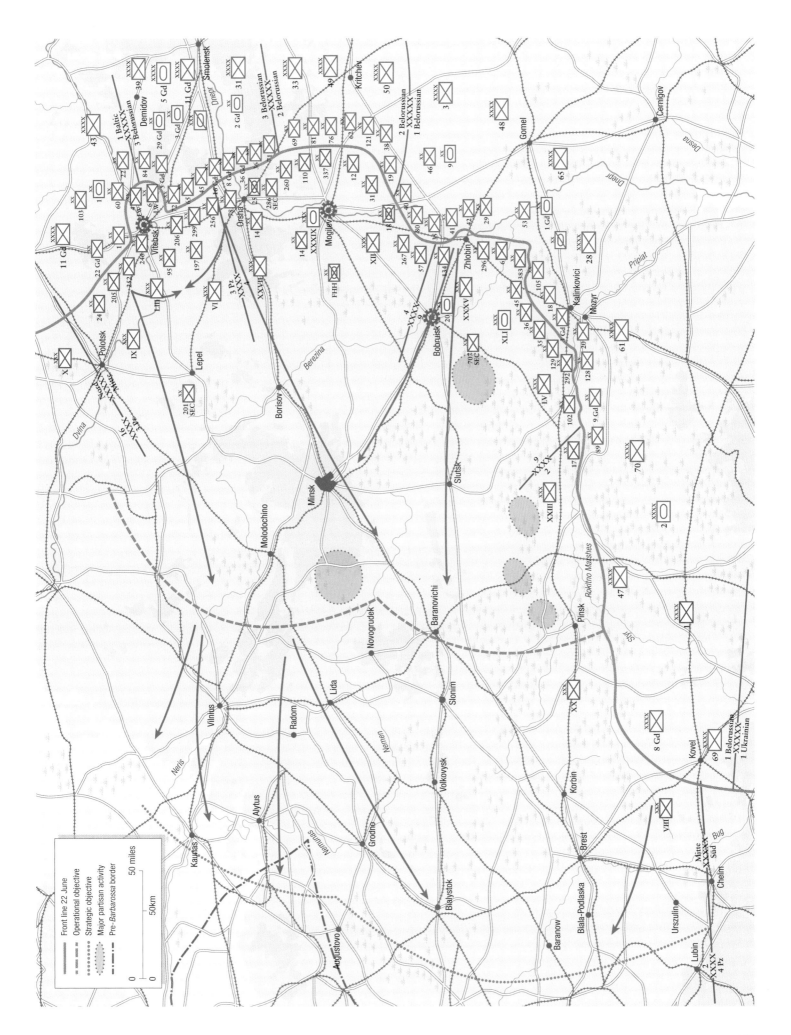

Smolensk
Demidov
Vitebsk
Polotsk
Lepel
Borisov
Minsk
Molodochino
Novogrudek
Vilnius
Alytus
Kaunas
Augustovo
Grodno
Lida
Radom
Slonim
Volkovysk
Białystok
Baranow
Biała-Podlaska
Brest
Korbin
Kovel
Pinsk
Mozyr
Kalinkovici
Gomel
Cernigov
Zhlobin
Bobruisk
Slutsk
Baranovichi
Orsha
Mogljev
Kritchev
Urszulin
Chelm
Lublin

1 Baltic
1 Belorussian
3 Belorussian
2 Belorussian
2 Belorussian
1 Belorussian
1 Ukrainian
3 Belorussian
8 Gd

Dnepr
Dniepr
Desna
Berezina
Dvina
Neris
Nemen
Priplat
Rokitno Matshes
Bug
Neumann

Front line 22 June
Operational objective
Strategic objective
Major partisan activity
Pre-*Barbarossa* border

50km
50 miles
0

195

MAP 91: OPERATION *BAGRATION* (I)
22 JUNE TO 3 JULY, 1944

Demonstrating Stalin's historical flair, Operation *Bagration* began on the third anniversary of *Barbarossa*, 22 June, 1944. In some places the attack obliterated the Germans, while in others they barely noticed its beginning. However, by the offensive's second day, its existence was clear. The 3rd Belorussian Front's 39th and 5th Armies began encircling Vitebsk with the help of the neighbouring 43rd Army, while its 11th Guards and 31st Armies attacked on either side of Orsha; the 2nd Belorussian Front's 49th and 50th Armies worked their way around Mogilev; and the 1st Belorussian Front's 3rd and 65th Armies were in the process of isolating Bobruisk. The 3. Panzer-Armee, 4. and 9. Armeen fought to close gaps and launch local counterattacks; assault gun units and the Panzer-Grenadier-Division Feldherrnhalle (a mere 28 panzers) tried in vain to stabilize the situation. A day later, Vitebsk had been cut off, defences around Orsha were penetrated to a depth of 10 miles and the seam between 4. and 9. Armeen was split open. In the north, by 25 June the LIII Armee-Korps had been trapped in Vitebsk (German engineers demolished escape routes to make sure) while in the south XXXV Armee-Korps looked to suffer the same fate in Bobruisk. As usual, Hitler demanded these 'corner posts' were held. Busch at army group headquarters did little more than pass the Führer's orders down the chain of command.

The time had long passed since Hitler's empty pronouncements, such as naming locales a *fester Platz* (fortress), had any practical effect on a battle; the surrounded towns of Vitebsk, Orsha and Mogilev all fell on 27 June, each with thousands of Germans marching off to captivity. Soviet units, especially cavalry and tank-mechanized corps, left the Dnepr behind and approached the Berezina River. While some mobile units began to arrive in the army group sector, for example 5. and 12. Panzer-Divisionen (the former went straight from the railway platforms into combat), these represented tactical sticking plasters, not operational-level solutions to a massive problem. To compound Wehrmacht woes, when mechanized reserves did get into battle, it was often only in the forlorn hope – and wasted effort – of saving an already lost *fester Platz*. In a trend begun in 1943 in the Ukraine, the cruel realities of the new Red Army war-making used in *Bagration*, combined with Hitler's anaemic response, meant that the tables were now turned and it was now the Germans whose command and control proved inadequate and overwhelmed. On 28 June, Hitler relieved Busch and

9. Armee's leader, General der Infanterie Hans Jordan. Generalfeldmarschall Model took command of Heeresgruppe Mitte (in addition to already leading Heeresgruppe Nord Ukraine) with the expectation of working defensive magic yet again.[122] A day later, the 3rd and 1st Belorussian fronts had advanced up to 100 miles in less than a week and two pincers could clearly be seen developing on either side of Minsk; against the XXXIX Panzer-Korps the 5th Guards Tank Army had reached Borisov on the old post road route.

The Soviets barely paused on the Berezina as, despite another Führer order, the Germans could not offer any serious resistance. Minimal contact existed between Heeresgruppen Nord and Mitte, an event exploited by Cherniakhovsky's spearheads. At the end of June, he ordered Rotmistrov to take his tankers in the direction of Vilnius and eventually Kaunas. The Stavka would leave Minsk to advancing infantry armies. In the meantime 4. Armee's situation looked dangerous; the pincers aiming for Minsk encircled significant portions of one Panzer, five panzer grenadier and 17 infantry divisions in two major pockets, with more than 100,000 men becoming POWs. By the first days of July, 3. Panzer-Armee, 4. and 9. Armeen stood on the brink of real disaster, each headquarters now controlling only remnants of a small handful of shattered divisions. Under relentless Red Army assaults, they fought desperate rearguard actions and tried to escape further pockets. The 5. and 12. Panzer-Divisionen, in the north and south respectively, made little difference with their makeshift counterattacks. The damage had been done: the Red Army had vaporized the better part of six German corps.

The pending battle of Minsk, another *fester Platz*, was sure to be ugly for the Wehrmacht. Even if they had occupied defensible terrain, combat strength fell short as thousands of rear-echelon troops clogged the city, as did thousands of wounded in its many hospitals. On 2 July, Hitler relented and authorized the inevitable abandonment of Minsk just as the Soviets worked their way around to the west. Lead elements of 2nd Guards Tank Corps entered the city the next day with 1st Guards Tank Corps close behind. Late on the 3rd, the Red Army's jaws closed to the west.

---

122 General der Panzertruppen Nikolaus von Vormann moved up from XLVII Panzer-Korps to 9. Armee, but he barely lasted two months in that position.

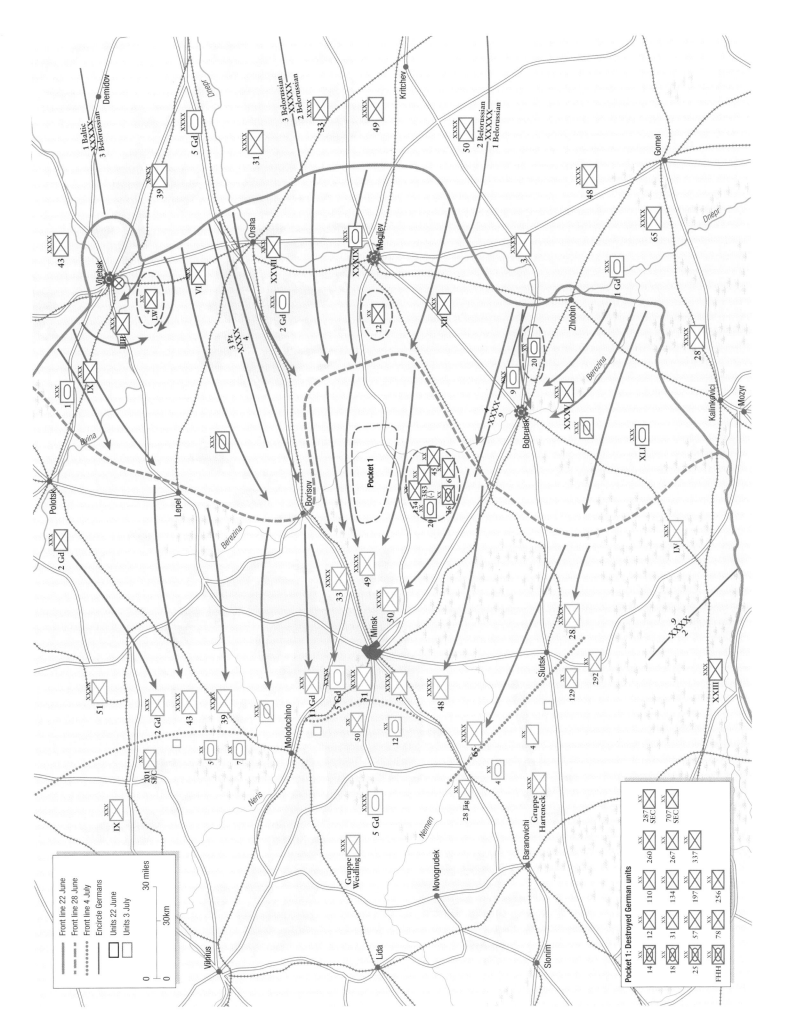

Front line 22 June
Front line 28 June
Front line 4 July
Encircle Germans

Units 22 June
Units 3 July

0   30km
0   30 miles

Demidov

1 Baltic
XXXXX
3 Belorussian

Dnepr

Vitebsk

5 Gd

31

Orsha

Kritchev

33

49

3 Belorussian
XXXXX
2 Belorussian

50

2 Belorussian
XXXXX
1 Belorussian

Gomel

48

65

Dnepr

39

43

XXXVII

Mogilev

3

4 LW

IHH

VI

XX
4

2 Gd

XX
12

XIII

1 Gd

Zhlobin

28

3 Pz
XXX
4

XXX
1

IX

Berezina

Bobruisk

Kalinkavici

Mozyr

Dvina

XXX
9

9

XXX
20

9

Polotsk

Lepel

Berezina

Borisov

Pocket 1

XX
383
(-)

45

6

134

20

36

XLI

2 Gd

XXXX
33

49

50

51

XXX
2 Gd

43

39

Molodochino

11 Gd

5 Gd

31

3

48

XX
292

Slutsk

129

IV

28

2 Gd

5

7

50

12

XXX
IX

5 Gd

Gruppe
Weidling

Neris

Neman

28 Jäg

4

4

65

Baranovichi

Gruppe
Harteneck

Vilnius

Lida

Novogrudek

Slonim

Pocket 1: Destroyed German units

287 SEC	707 SEC	
260	267	337
110	134	197
12	31	57	78
14	18	25	FHH

197

MAP 92: OPERATION *BAGRATION* (II)
3 JULY TO 29 AUGUST, 1944

The 3rd and 1st Belorussian fronts retraced the 1941 routes of Hoth and Guderian, only in reverse. Minsk had been taken on the march by the 11th Guards, 33rd, 49th and 50th Armies with little in the way of organized German opposition, while very few *Kampfgruppen* and broken divisions managed to escape destruction. Mopping up the pocket took 2nd Belorussian Front and partisans more than a week, with approximately 60,000 POWs being taken (in addition to nearly 40,000 killed). Over the short time span of *Bagration*, this brought German casualties to greater than 300,000 (including 30 generals) and AFV losses to over 900; more than 25 divisions had disappeared. At the end of the first week of July, Red Army forces attacking Heeresgruppe Mitte reached a line generally running from Dvinsk to 30 miles west of Minsk to a similar distance west of Slutsk. Model had been in the job for nearly 10 days, but it is hard to see where he made a difference.

For Stalin the liberation of Minsk represented a major political event, but Zhukov and Vasilevski barely paused to notice; the infantry armies progressed at a pace of 10–15 miles per day. Such defences as Model could create had significant holes in them and it was here, near Molodochino and Stolbtsy, where the Soviets continued westward. On their right, the 5th Guards Tank and 5th Armies approached the Vilnius *fester Platz* on 7 July. The 5. Panzer-Division, seemingly everywhere and doing everything in these days, tried to prevent the inevitable. This it could not do and within 24 hours the guardsmen had surrounded the city. Commanded by a Luftwaffe Flak officer, Generalleutnant Rainer Stahel, the division-size garrison held out for three days, but then either surrendered or escaped. The 5th Guards Tank Army headed for its next objective, Kaunas, running parallel to the 1st Baltic Front on Rotmistrov's right.[123] In the centre, finished at Minsk, 2nd Belorussian Front drove due west, reaching Grodno by mid-July and Bialystok on the 27th. To the south, Rokossovsky's 1st Belorussian Front followed the left bank of the Neman River in the general direction of Warsaw, quickly taking Heeresgruppe Mitte's logistics base at Baranovichi.[124] On 16 July, the Soviets had reached a line Alytus–Grodno–Pinsk, having advanced 200 miles in little more than three weeks.[125] In terms of divisions the Soviets now had a 10:1 advantage, but had begun to outrun their rear services, which struggled to keep the pace.

Just days into *Bagration*, the Stavka considered the situation ready to renew the offensive south of the marshes, and the resulting L'vov–Sandomierz operation began two weeks later (Map 93). In the north, a dangerous Baltic Gap (*baltisches Loch*) had developed between Heeresgruppen Nord and Mitte between Dvinsk and Kaunas, exacerbated by 16. Armee's withdrawal to Riga (Map 90). Bagramian's 1st Baltic Front's 2nd Guards Army had worked its way through the gap and was posed to turn south behind Reinhardt's 3. Panzer-Armee (four infantry and one panzer divisions plus *Kampfgruppen* and *Sperrgruppen* [blocking groups], i.e., a large corps), which was concentrating on holding the Neman River east of Kaunas in accordance with Hitler and Model's orders. Cherniakhovsky opened a new offensive with his right on 28 July, and 48 hours later had overthrown the Neman defences. The 2nd Guards Tank Corps passed through the breach on the 29th and 5th Army followed its lead into Kaunas the next day. The Red Army now stood only about 40 miles from the Reich frontier. The Soviet general now pushed his left past Grodno. During the second half of August both thrusts neared East Prussia, and by the last day of the month had actually crossed it in the north, east of Gumbinnen. Operation *Bagration*, considered completed on 29 August, and the collapse of Heeresgruppe Mitte, had been a massive Soviet victory and an unmitigated German catastrophe, worse in terms of casualties than Stalingrad.

---

123 Stalin removed Rotmistrov from command on 8 August, and, after a brief interval, General Lieutenant V. T. Vol'sky replaced him.

124 With the capture of Minsk, Rokossovsky had been promoted to marshal.

125 Far south, below the Rokitno Marshes, at this time 1st Belorussian Front also captured Kovel in northern Ukraine.

SOVIET UNION

POLAND

Rokitno Marshes

Minsk

Slutsk

Stolbsty

Baranovichi

Pinsk

Novogrudek

Slonim

Lida

Molodochino

Neris

Neman

Volkovysk

Vilnius

Radom

Pripiat

LITHUANIA

Korbin

Alytus

Kaunas

Grodno

Brest

Bialystok

Augustovo

Baranow

Biala-Podlaska

EAST
PRUSSIA

Gruppe
von Rothkirch

2 Gd

1 Baltic
3 Belorussian

43

5

5 Gd

11 Gd

33

39

39

50

49

48

65

28

61

203

251

292

102

129

XXIII

50

14

12

367

28 Jäg

W SS

LV

W SS

65

61

70

211 SEC

5 Jäg

VIII

199

MAP 93: THE LUBLIN–BREST OPERATION 18 JULY TO 2 AUGUST, 1944

With *Bagration* less than a week old, the Stavka could already tell that the operation would be successful. Building on that triumph, plus the earlier advances through the northern Ukraine in the winter and spring (Map 99), it planned for the 1st Belorussian Front to launch an assault in conjunction with the final stages of *Bagration* plus Konev's in-progress L'vov–Sandomierz operation (Map 94).

While the left flank armies of 1st Belorussian Front had been manhandling the 9. Armee in the neighbourhood of Bobruisk (Map 91), Rokossovsky's other troops had not been idle. By the second week of July his 61st Army had attacked from Pinsk along the Dnepr–Bug Canal toward Kobrin and Brest. His centre 70th and 47th Armies, now on the 1939 frontier and with the Rokitno Marshes behind them, pushed west. His left flank units had just liberated Kovel and now the 8th Guards, 1st Polish, 69th and General Lieutenant S. I. Bogdanov's 2nd Tank Armies made ready to attack toward Lublin, keeping even with the 1st Ukrainian Front. Facing them stood the 2. Armee commanded by Weiss, weakened like the rest of Hitler's eastern army, but so far generally unscathed by Rokossovsky or Konev. Everywhere along the German side of the front line partisan activity was intense.

Rokossovsky's second offensive began on 18 July out of the Kovel area, against the boundary between 2. Armee and 4. Panzer-Armee. Tasked with creating the initial breakthroughs were 47th, 8th Guards and 69th Armies. Within 24 hours, Chuikov's 8th Guards had forced its way across the Western Bug and two days later had reached Chelm. In fact, by 22 July Rokossovsky's men had penetrated 2. Armee's lines to a depth of 35 miles in numerous places, both north and south of Brest, and more than 40 miles near Urszulin. The front had fallen back even at Brest, where XXIII and XX Armee-Korps stubbornly held out. The 2nd Tank Army broke out of its Urszulin bulge and began to race south-west to Lublin, while a cavalry-mechanized group made up of the 2nd Guards Cavalry Corps and 11th Tank Corps headed north-west toward Warsaw. Lublin fell to the 2nd Tank and 8th Guards Armies on the 24th, while Bogdanov's tankers reached the Vistula River at Demblin with the 1st Polish Army close behind.

Two main developments occurred during the last week of July. The first, which was Hitler's decision for Model to reinforce and hold on to

Brest as long as possible, made the second easier, which was Rokossovsky's decision not to cross the Vistula in force but instead to keep driving to the north-west and Warsaw. Ultimately portions of eight Wehrmacht divisions defended the region around Brest, and by 26 July these were three-quarters encircled by elements of the 65th, 28th, 61st and 70th Armies. Two days later the garrison surrendered, although three divisions attempted to escape east toward Siedlce. The 70th Army tracked down and trapped them, killing 15,000 Germans in a 10-day battle near Biala Podliaska.

Nearly 100 miles west, the 2nd Tank Army and cavalry-mechanized group neared the approaches to Warsaw.[126] Chuikov's men established two Vistula bridgeheads at Magnuszew and Pulawy, with their ultimate goal being the Polish capital. At the end of July Model had taken the wrecked 9. Armee out of the line and given its combat units to 2. Armee. He then re-constituted it by putting 9. Armee in charge of the defence of Warsaw; it had XXXIX Panzer-Korps in the city, VIII Armee-Korps to the south and IV SS Panzer-Korps to the east. Rokossovsky's men neared the city's approaches and by the 29th had closed to within 10–12 miles of the city. Radzievsky split his army into its three tank corps as it entered the Praga suburbs. By the last day of the month, only a railway bridge separated the Soviets from Polish Home Army fighters in the city, ready to rise up against their Nazi tormentors (Maps 95–98).

Unfortunately for them, 19. Panzer-Division, SS Panzer-Grenadier-Division Wiking and the 1. Fallschirm-Panzer-Division Hermann Göring counterattacked just at this moment. Model had been probing for an enemy weak point, and these powerful German formations smashed into Rokossovsky's spearhead after the latter had been manoeuvring continuously for six weeks across hundreds of miles. Capturing Warsaw could not be done from the march, but would require a deliberate and full-scale assault. The Soviets consider the Lublin–Brest operation to have concluded on 2 August. A day, later Model reported to Hitler that he had created a fragile but stable defensive front between Siauliai in Lithuania to Pulawy.

126 Bogdanov had been wounded at the end of July and was replaced by General Major A. I. Radzievsky.

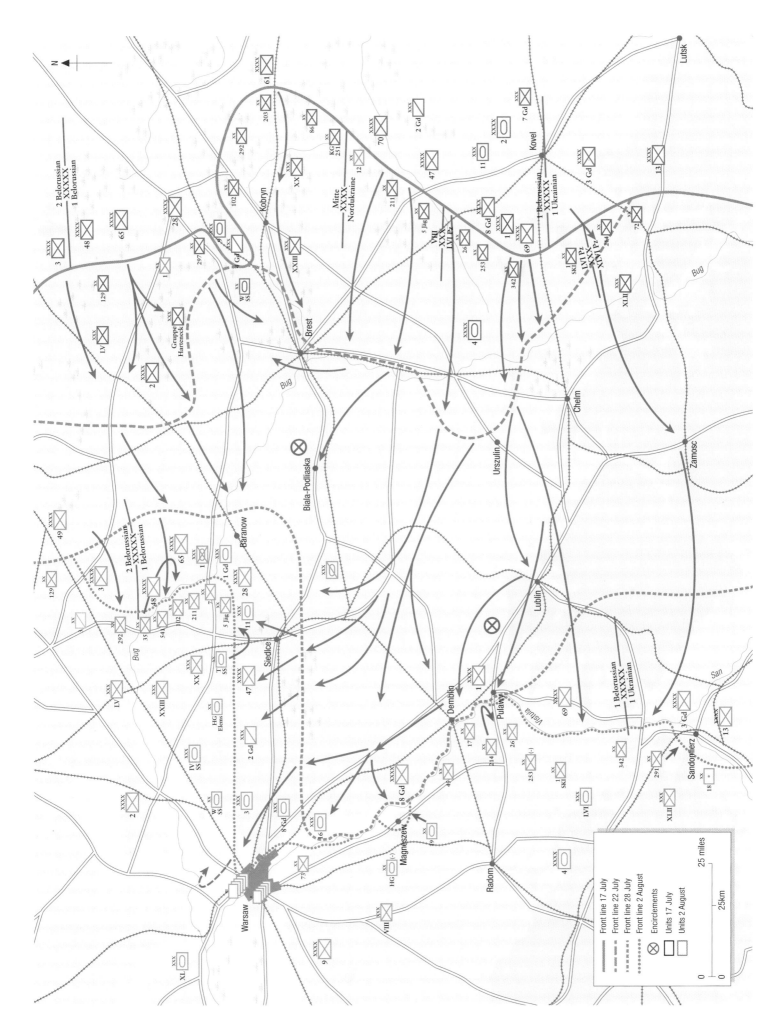

N

2 Belorussian
XXXXX
1 Belorussian

XXXX
3

XXXX
48

XX
65

XXXX
28

XXXX
1

XX
129

XX
297

XXX
LV

XXXX
2

Gruppe
Harteneck

W SS

4 Gd

Kobryn

XX
102

XX
292

XX
201

XX
86

XXXX
61

XX
KG 251

XX
12

XXXX
70

XXX
XXIII

XXXX
2 Gd

Mitte
XXXX
Nordukraine

XX
5 Jäg

XX
211

XXXX
47

XXXX
11

XX
2

7 Gd

XXXX
2 Gd

XXXX
8 Gd

XXXX
1

XX
69

VIII
XXX
LVI Pz

XX
26

XX
253

XX
342

1 Belorussian
XXXXX
1 Ukrainian

XX
SKl

LVI Pz
XIV Pz

XX
2nd

XX
72

XXXX
3 Gd

XXXX
13

Bug

XX
XLII

Brest

Bug

Chelm

Urszulin

Zamosc

Biala-Podliaska

XXXX
49

XX
129

XXXX
3

XX
292

XX
35

XX
54

XX
102

XX
211

XXXX
48

XXX
65

XXX
1

1 Gd

XX
28

XX
11

XX
5 Jäg

XX
7

Baranow

2 Belorussian
XXXXX
1 Belorussian

XXX
LV

XXX
XXIII

XXX
T SS

XXXX
47

HG
Elems

XXXX
2 Gd

IV SS

XXXX
2

W SS

XXXX
3

8 Gd

Siedlice

Lublin

1 Belorussian
XXXXX
1 Ukrainian

Vistula

San

XXXX
1

Dembln

XX
17

XX
214

XX
26

XXXX
69

XX
253

XX
SKl

XX
342

Pulawy

Sandopñerz

3 Gd

XXXX
13

XXX
LVI

XX
XLII

XX
291

XX
18

Magnuszew

XX
46

XX
9

HG (-)

XX
73

XX
8

Warsaw

Radom

XXXX
4

XXXX
9

XXX
XL

0   25 miles
0   25km

Front line 17 July
Front line 22 July
Front line 28 July
Front line 2 August
Encirclements
Units 17 July
Units 2 August

Lutsk

Kovel

201

MAP 94: THE L'VOV-SANDOMIERZ OPERATION 13 JULY TO 31 AUGUST, 1944

Heeresgruppe Nord Ukraine escaped Operation *Bagration*'s opening blows (Map 91), and for three months Model had been able to fine-tune his defences, 25–30 miles deep in places. His 4. Armee and 1. Panzer-Armee each had about a dozen infantry divisions backed up by three to four panzer or panzer grenadier divisions in reserve behind the front.[127] As the Germans' situation deteriorated in White Russia – and Normandy – Hitler even allowed General Harpe to slightly straighten his defensive lines.[128] Facing them, and ready to pounce across the 225-mile front, stood the 1st Ukrainian Front, now commanded by Konev. John Erickson states matter-of-factly that it was the most powerful single front in the Red Army, with four field, three guards and three tank armies plus two cavalry-mechanized groups, all supported by two air armies. Arranged quite thinly on the two flanks, Konev concentrated most of his hitting power between Lutsk and Ternopol, opposite Brody. In terms of manpower the two sides had rough parity (approximately one million men each), but the Soviets enjoyed a massive materiel superiority: AFVs 1,600:900, artillery tubes 14,000:6,000 and aircraft 2,800:700.

Konev began the offensive on 13 July with his northern grouping, which had Rava-Russkaya as its objective, and, a day later with his southern grouping, aiming at L'vov. Many thousands of Soviet and Polish partisans disrupted the Germans' defences and hampered their command and control and logistics. On the Soviet right, the 3rd Guards and 13th Armies advanced until struck by the XLVI Panzer-Korps and halted for three days, causing Konev to commit his second echelon. In the centre, the 60th and 38th Armies likewise gained about 5 miles before being halted by III Panzer-Korps counterattacking from the south. The Red Army infantry overcame this setback and soon opened a breach, through which Konev passed 3rd Guards Tank and 4th Tank Armies. A XLVIII Panzer-Korps counterattack failed to slow Rybalko and General Colonel D. D. Lelyushenko, who bore down on L'vov while the 60th Army and Lieutenant General S. V. Sokolov's cavalry-mechanized group curled around to the north behind Brody. By 17 July Konev's northern group had punched through as well, and Baranov

slipped through the resulting gap with 1st Guards Tank Army close behind. These developments doomed the fortified town of Brody, which held about 50,000 soldiers from portions of at least half a dozen divisions under XIII Armee-Korps. Elements of four Soviet armies closed the trap on the 18th, shortly after which a XLVIII Panzer-Korps relief attack failed to make it through. Resistance in the pocket ended on 22 July with 100 per cent casualties.

Fifty miles west, the two tank armies menaced L'vov. On 18 July Baranov's force had compromised the 4. Panzer-Armee's Bug River positions. Accordingly the 1. Panzer-Armee pulled back from the river and, prudently, German-Hungarian forces in the south began to withdraw as well. Lelyushenko's men entered the suburbs of L'vov on the 21st but could not take the city in a hasty attack, and so four armies settled in for a deliberate battle. It was surrounded on 25 July and liberated two days later. While Konev's left crawled forward toward the Carpathian foothills and his centre focused on L'vov, his right raced across the open country of south-eastern Poland, generally keeping pace with Rokossovsky to their north (Map 93). By 27 July Konev's forces had crossed the San River in a couple of places, including Sokolow and Przemysl.

During the last days of July, 1st Ukrainian Front re-oriented to the north-west and the Vistula River near Sandomierz and Baranow. At Yaroslav the 3rd and 4th Guards Tank Armies turned 90 degrees in that direction with the 5th Guards Army in tow; they would soon join the 3rd Guards and 1st Guards Tank Armies and Sokolov's cavalry-mechanized group already nearby. The 4. Panzer-Armee, recently reinforced with nearly 20 divisions and many AFVs, laboured to create a viable counter to this armoured mass, as well as the 1st Belorussian Front, which had just cleared Lublin. Both sides re-organized for the upcoming battle by bringing up transfers from the Crimea (Map 103). Headquarters 4th Ukrainian Front took over Konev's south opposite the Slovak-Hungarian frontier, while the Wehrmacht placed the resuscitated 17. Armee headquarters between 4. and 1. Panzer-Armeen in front of Krakow.[129] In early August, the Soviet bridgehead west of the Vistula measured 20 by 15 miles and by the end of the month it had doubled in size. At this point, Red Army exhaustion and German recuperation stabilized the front.

---

127 1. Panzer-Armee, now including the Hungarian First Army, was technically named Armeegruppe Raus.

128 When Model took on Heeresgruppe Mitte in addition to North Ukraine on 28 June, 4. Panzer-Armee commander Generaloberst Josef Harpe took on the additional post as Model's deputy. At the height of the present battles, on 5 August, Hermann Balck moved up from XLVIII Panzer-Korps to replace Harpe at 4. Panzer-Armee.

129 The victorious 4th Ukrainian arrived on 5 August; the defeated 17. Armee, evacuated on 12 May, took over in Galicia on 26 July.

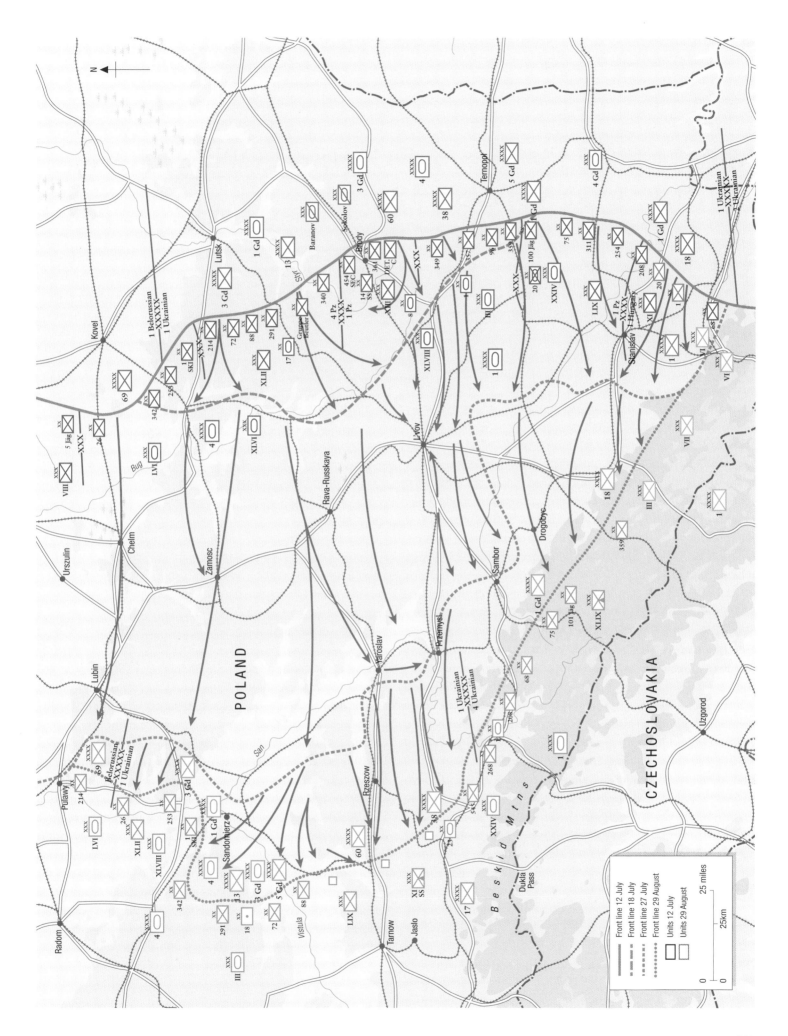

MAPS 95 & 96: WARSAW UPRISING (I) 2–6 AUGUST, 1944

For centuries, the Polish, Russian, Lithuanian and Ukrainian peoples have had their own fascinating history. Frequently the Germans are added, such as with the 1939 Molotov-Ribbentrop Pact, further complicating matters. Adding another layer of complexity, during World War II at least two national liberation movements developed in most Nazi-occupied countries: one pro-western, sponsored by London and Washington, and the other communist, backed by Moscow. In April 1943 the Germans discovered a mass grave of 4,500 Polish officers in Katyn, west of Smolensk. During their occupation of eastern Poland, the Soviets had executed these potential pro-western sympathizers to strengthen the hand of their pro-communist collaborators. After this grisly discovery, the British-supplied Polish Home Army (Armia Krajowa, AK), created in February 1942 to lead the Polish resistance, decided to have no further dealings with Stalin. In January 1944, therefore, the AK had two enemies: the Third Reich and the Soviet Union. The Soviets countered with the pro-communist Polish People's Army (Armia Ludowa, AL).[130]

By early 1944, the AK had grown to 250,000–300,000 fighters (although only 32,000 actually had weapons) in 6,000–9,000 small units or 'platoons' located throughout Poland. The AK planned partisan-like activities across the country against the Germans as the Red Army started advancing into Poland. During the summer, when the Soviets captured Polish cities such as Vilnius and L'vov, they frequently murdered or interned AK fighters while favouring the AL. In late July the 1st Belorussian Front neared Warsaw, but the Stavka's plans did not call for an immediate assault across the Vistula River. This allowed Heeresgruppe Mitte to solidify its defences. With Rokossovsky's troops only a few miles away, on 1 August the AK called for a general uprising in Warsaw. Little did they know that the nearby Red Army could not, or would not, lend any assistance.

The AK had to strike a delicate balance in the city, which still contained one million people, between attacking the Germans and avoiding provoking overly aggressive reprisals. The number of AK members was roughly estimated at 25,000 to 35,000, including thousands of women, perhaps 10 per cent of whom were armed. Additionally, German intelligence had received signs of a pending uprising since about 29 July and knew of the main command post (1, map left). Using assault guns, hand grenades and small mortars, the AK uprising started at 1700 hours on 1 August, when they attacked German strongpoints, administrative buildings, barracks, depots and hospitals throughout the inner city and some suburbs (2). In a number of critical engagements, the AK failed in its attempts to capture Vistula bridges (3) (both to link up with comrades in the eastern suburbs and supposedly enable the Red Army to join the battle). Already on that first day the Germans under Luftwaffe General Stahel divided AK forces into small, non mutually-supporting pockets (4). The main AK success that day consisted of capturing the SS depot on Stawki Street (5) and the Prudential office building (6). Otherwise, their losses amounted to 2,000 fighters, four times the number of German casualties. That night, many platoons retreated out of the city and into the surrounding woods. Outnumbered, outgunned and lacking surprise, the uprising got off to an inauspicious beginning.

Despite these handicaps, 2 August saw many AK successes, such as the capture of much of the old town (7), Czerniakow (8) and the main post office (9). On the next day they took the Nordwache police station (10) and part of the Polytechnic Institute (11) in addition to expanding their holding in the old town and erecting barricades on the main street of Nowy Swiat (12). On the 4th they spread out in the northern suburb of Zoliborz (13), but by this point the Germans began to react forcefully. By 3 August German army units had begun to arrive to augment the garrison and police forces, although not always with complete success, and Stukas had started to bomb AK positions at the main post office. The next day Himmler took over, with Obergruppenführer Erich von dem Bach-Zelewski in charge of a who's who of SS thugs: anti-partisan forces, penal units, concentration camp guards and Soviet POWs. The Germans began counterattacking throughout the 5th, moving up the main thoroughfares toward the old town (A, map right), supported by Luftwaffe CAS and terror bombing. A day later they reached Stahel's besieged command post at the Bruhl Palace (B). Isolated groups of the AK bravely fought, though heavily outnumbered, against Bach-Zelewski's motley force. Afterwards, both sides began building barricades and settled in for a long conflict.

---

130 A minority of Polish resisters even considered creating the Polish Anti-Communist Legion and fighting alongside the Germans. Stalin created a competing pro-Soviet government in exile, the Polish Committee of Liberation (ultimately in Lubin) supported by the AL, which was only one-tenth the size of the AK.

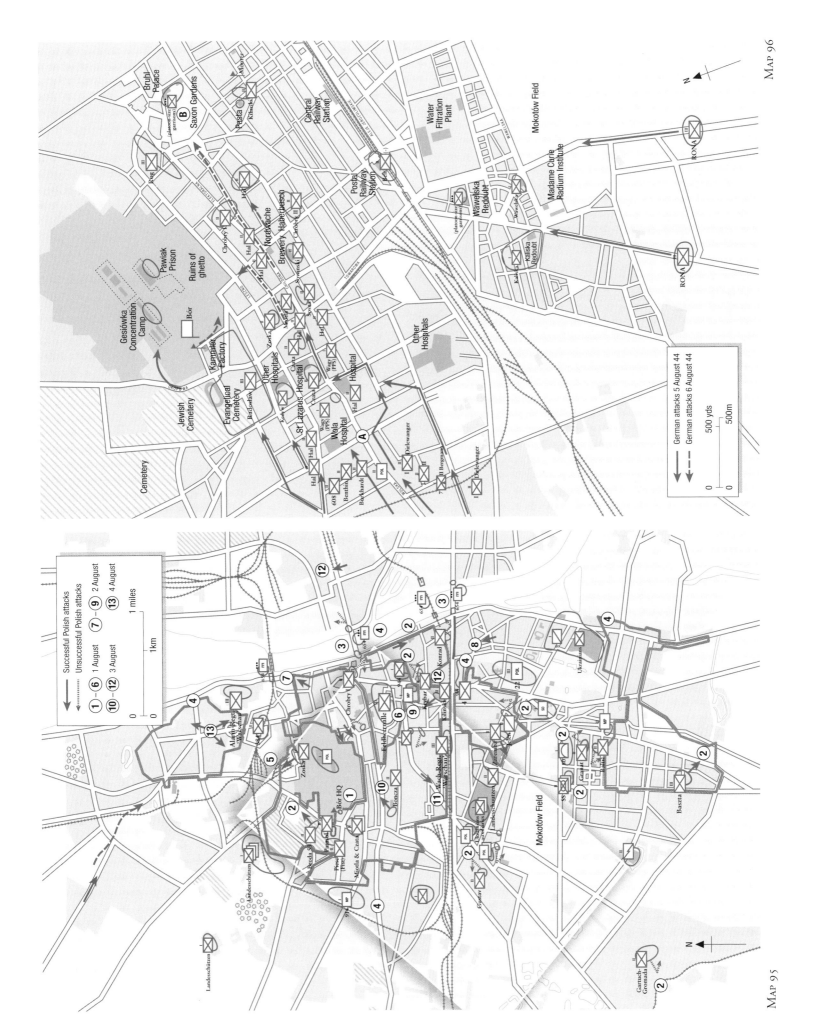

MAP 96

Water Filtration Plant

Mokotów Field

Madame Curie Radium Institute

RONA

Brühl Palace

Saxon Gardens

Pasta

Central Railway Station

Postal Railway Station

Wawelska Redoubt

Kaliska Redoubt

RONA

Gesiówka Concentration Camp

Pawiak Prison

Ruins of ghetto

Jewish Cemetery

Evangelical Cemetery

Cemetery

Kammler Factory

Other Hospitals

St Lazarus Hospital

Wola Hospital

Other Hospitals

Brewery (Haberbusch)

Nordwache

German attacks 5 August 44
German attacks 6 August 44

500 yds
500m

MAP 95

Successful Polish attacks
Unsuccessful Polish attacks

1 – 6   1 August   7 – 9   2 August
10 – 12 3 August   13   4 August

Mokotów Field

Bór HQ

1km   1 miles

MAPS 97 & 98: WARSAW UPRISING (II)
4 AUGUST TO 30 SEPTEMBER, 1944

After a week of initial Polish Home Army (AK) attacks and German countermoves, a stalemate developed while the disinterested Red Army observed from a safe distance. This last point is critical; due to Soviet passivity, the Polish-German fight can be described only as a struggle between David and Goliath. At the beginning, the AK witnessed an approximately equal number of successes and failures. The Germans' reactions were disjointed and inept. Other than a few Wehrmacht battalions and regiments belonging to the 9. Armee, most Germans in Warsaw were constabulary, occupation troops, Luftwaffe airfield staff of doubtful military quality or Nazi administrators and railway workers, among others. During the first days of the uprising, they proved capable of defending individual buildings and bridges (and committing outrageous atrocities), but little else. Only on 4 August did a serious Nazi countermeasure develop with the arrival of Obergruppenführer Bach-Zelewski (supposedly in overall command) and Kampfgruppe Reinefarth and SS Sturmbrigade Dirlewanger, plus numerous auxiliaries and paramilitaries.[131] The latter included two 700-man Azerbaijan battalions of assorted Cossacks, Hungarians and Muslims, a penal brigade of 4,000 convicts and a brigade of 6,000 Soviet POWs. Naturally, this being Nazi Germany, confused and overlapping chains of command abounded.

The AK may have had high morale to begin with and a detailed knowledge of subterranean Warsaw, but it lacked tactical skill. The Germans brought in specialized weapons such as Goliath remote-control tracked explosives, flame-throwers for use in sewers, and others. Two weeks into the uprising, fighting had devolved to two main areas: the old town (7,000 AK men and women under General Tadeusz Bor-Komorowski) and the suburbs and woods on the periphery. The Germans attacked the city centre from all directions with their regular and irregular troops, and brought out siege artillery barely used since Sevastopol. Hitler stressed the use of heavy explosives and ordnance to increase the destruction of Warsaw. At this stage, the German plan concentrated on clearing ('cleansing') the suburbs. Bach-Zelewski consolidated his position as commander of nearly 21,000 men, while Bor-Komorowski called upon all of Poland to send AK fighters to Warsaw as reinforcements. Adding to the misery, 100,000 civilians

crammed into the city centre during the fighting. Nevertheless, the AK actually expanded its perimeter and frequently attacked German outfits around the city, causing over 3,800 casualties.

Toward the end of August the city centre had become untenable for the AK, and its commanders made plans to evacuate through the sewers or any other way possible. Soon the Germans noted that the AK had ceased to fight as an organization, but as individual rebels. On 4 September, Bor-Komorowski informed London that the uprising was almost beaten. A week later, Rokossovsky's 47th Army attacked the German Praga bridgehead east of the city, forcing 9. Armee across the Vistula on the 12th. Retreating Wehrmacht soldiers detonated all the Vistula bridges, so the AK remained isolated from the approaching Soviets. Perhaps sensing that they would soon be ejected from Warsaw, the Germans renewed attacks against the Czerniakow quarter on 12 September, in the north cutting it off from the old town (1, map left). With the sector cut off, the Germans began squeezing from the south and west (2). The AK commander withdrew to the industrial buildings close to the Vistula, where Red Army forces could reach him (3). From 15–16 September, 1,200 soldiers from the 1st Polish Army crossed the river into the embattled AK enclave (4). By the 21st, the AK held only two buildings (5) and the Germans wiped out the remaining Poles four days later.

With the abandonment of the city centre, fighting moved to the Mokotow and Zoliborz neighbourhoods. From 24–27 September at Mokotow in the south of Warsaw, the Germans, mainly battalions of 19. Panzer-Division, eliminated the AK presence. On 29–30 September, north of the city, 19. Panzer-Division attacked Zoliborz from all directions. German pioneer battalions were especially successful attacking from the south-eastern side (A, map right). A surprise attack on the morning of the 30th won ground on the AK's western front (B) and compressed the Poles into a small area (C). The Poles waited for promised Red Army assistance that never arrived. That evening Bor-Komorowski ordered his men and women to surrender, and for the first and only time during the uprising Wehrmacht soldiers treated the AK as POWs, not bandits. In two months the AK had suffered 16,000 dead and missing, 6,000 wounded and 9,000 prisoners, while almost 200,000 Warsaw civilian inhabitants perished. German casualties were 2,000 dead and 9,000 wounded.

---

131 In the sordid history of the Third Reich, SS Oberführer Oskar Dirlewanger stands out among the worst of the worst.

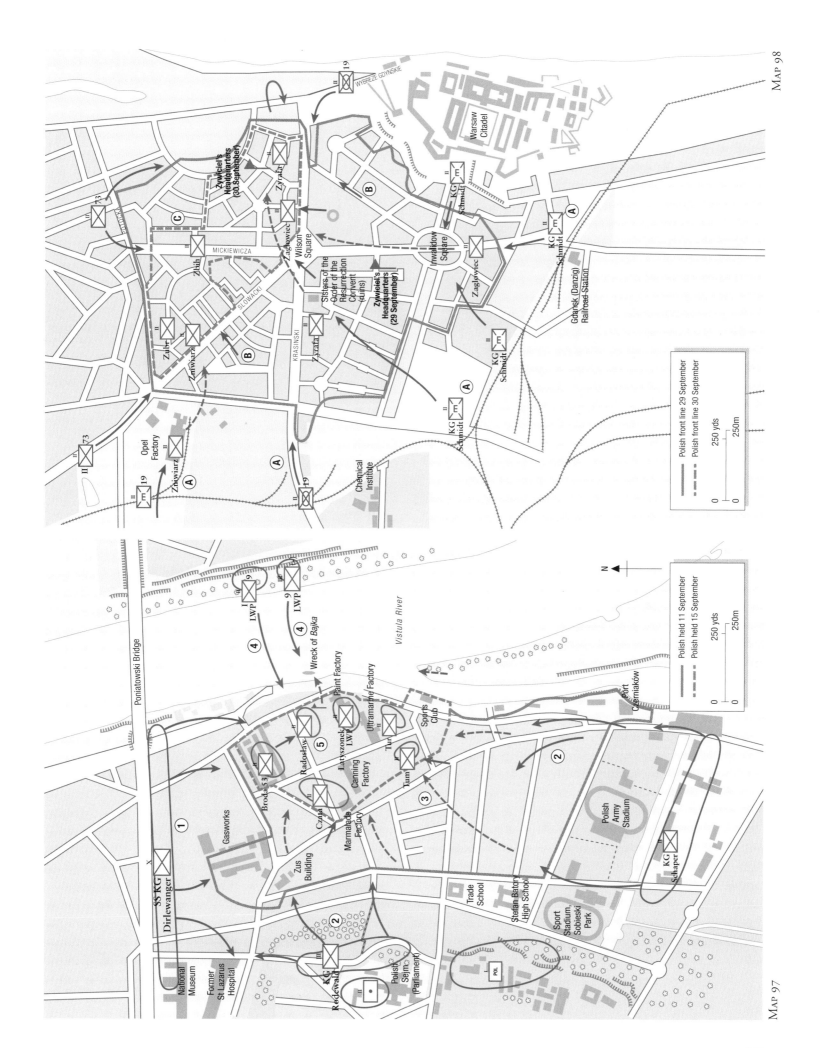

National Museum

Former St Lazarus Hospital

Poniatowski Bridge

SS KG Dirlewanger

① ①

KG Radowald

Polish Sejm (Parliament)

Zus Building

② ②

Gasworks

Broda 53

Radosław ⑤

Czata

Marmalade Factory

Canning Factory

Paint Factory

Latyszonek LWP

Ultramarine Factory

Turz

Tum

Sports Club

④ ④ LWP ⑨ ⑨ LWP

Wreck of *Bajka*

Vistula River

③ ③

②

Trade School

Stefan Batory High School

Sport Stadium, Sobieski Park

POL

Polish Army Stadium

KG Schaper

Port Czerniaków

N

Polish held 11 September
Polish held 15 September

0 ——— 250 yds
0 ——— 250m

MAP 97

19

WYBRZEŻE GDYŃSKIE

73

LITTOCKA

Żubr

Zmiwiarz

C

MICKIEWICZA

Żubr

Zmiwiarz

B

SŁOWACKI

KRASINSKI

Żyrafa

Żyrafa

Zagłowiec

Wilson Square

Sisters of the Order of the Resurrection Convent (ruins)

Żywiciel's Headquarters (29 September)

Żywiciel's Headquarters (30 September)

Żyrafa

Zagłowiec

Inwalidow Square

Warsaw Citadel

KG Schmidt E

KG Schmidt A

Gdańsk (Danzig) Railroad Station

KG Schmidt E

KG Schmidt E A

73

Opel Factory

Zmiwiarz A

19

19

A

B

A

Chemical Institute

Polish front line 29 September
Polish front line 30 September

0 ——— 250 yds
0 ——— 250m

MAP 98

MAP 99: LIBERATING WESTERN UKRAINE (I) 24 JANUARY TO 21 MARCH, 1944

After the successful summer and autumn of 1943, the Stavka began planning for the next offensive in the Ukraine. The huge assemblage of forces, marching and mechanized, that made up the 1st–4th Ukrainian fronts was about to be put to good use. The numerous and complicated attacks detailed in the next four maps (100–103) required extensive co-ordination, were spread over huge distances and showcased the Red Army's increasingly sophisticated planning, execution and logistical support. Manstein's Heeresgruppe Süd would barely survive another year like 1943 (Maps 79–80). Hitler's counter plan was simple and predictable: hold everywhere until forced to retreat, then improvise.

Although technically not the first attack of the series, the Korsun operation by the 1st and 2nd Ukraininan Fronts stands out for demolishing the centre of the Wehrmacht's positions in the Ukraine. Hitler had insisted on retaining the toehold on the Dnepr at Kanev, and throughout December and early January 1944 it had become a dangerous salient bulging north-eastwards from the remainder of his front lines. Fatefully it also marked the inter-army boundary, a favourite Soviet target, between 1. Panzer-Armee and 8. Armee, and it was here that Vatutin and Konev converged.[132] The Stavka had fretted over the two fronts' exposed flanks growing along the salient, but it need not have worried, since manoeuvres like the Backhand Blow were a thing of the past. The two fronts would attack across the 75-mile base of the salient, Vatutin's 6th and 2nd Tank Armies and Konev's 4th Guards and 5th Guards Tank Armies accomplishing the outer encirclement as their 27th and 52nd Armies worked to crush the trapped Wehrmacht defenders.

On 24 January, elements of the 27th Army on the west and 4th Guards and 53rd Armies on the east attacked to breach the 8. Armee and 1. Panzer-Armee positions. They quickly overwhelmed the feeble front-line defences and soon the tank armies passed through the assaulting rifle divisions. On the 28th, the pocket shut when Rotmistrov and Lieutenant General A. G. Kravchenko (6th Tank Army) met at Zveningorodka; 2nd Tank and 4th Guards Armies sealed the trap even tighter when they linked up at Ol'shana. Surrounded near Korsun were

132 On 1 January Manstein pulled 1. Panzer-Armee out of the Dnepr bend and inserted it between 4. Panzer-Armee and 8. Armee.

more than 56,000 soldiers in six divisions of XI and XLII Armee-Korps, which the Soviet armies began to squeeze into a small perimeter. Hitler tied Manstein's hands by refusing to countenance any sort of withdrawal. All the field marshal could do was create a relief force to try and push its way into the encirclement.

While Luftwaffe transport aircraft flew supplies to yet another isolated pocket, Wöhler's XLVII Panzer-Korps (Vormann, with 11., 13. and 14. Panzer-Divisionen) and Hube's III Panzer-Korps (Breith, with 1., 16. and 17. Panzer-Divisionen plus SSLAH) assembled along the southern flanks of 5th Guards Tank and 6th Tank Armies. The III Panzer-Korps moved out first on 4 February, gaining 6 miles that day through mud and Red Army positions. Vormann experienced no similar advances, having attacked into the spearheads of two tank armies. On 7 February inside the Korsun pocket, the Germans began moving the pocket south-westwards toward Breith's oncoming tankers. Under the overall command of XLII Armee-Korps' General der Artillerie Wilhelm Stemmermann, they managed to crawl to Shevchenkovsky and Steblev, but a week later Breith was little farther north than Lysyanka; 10 miles still separated the two. On the 17th, with III Panzer-Korps still over 5 miles away, the pocket had been reduced to 45,000 men. Stemmermann ordered a general breakout, and small groups of Germans streamed south through the mud and snow and a gauntlet of Soviet artillery and small-arms fire. What became of the doomed German garrison is open to debate, but tens of thousands died, including Stemmermann (killed in action on the 18th), or were wounded and captured – few escaped.

Hitler had again squandered valuable mobile reserves attempting to undo another of his 'stand fast' mistakes. After re-grouping for two weeks, Konev renewed the offensive on 4 March, his 6th Tank, 4th Guards and 5th Guards Tank Armies smashing into Wöhler and heading for Uman. The 8. Armee disintegrated. Uman fell on 9 March as small clusters of Germans wandered south-westwards, apparently not part of any coherent larger plan. Two days later, the Red Army had pushed them to the Bug River; Hitler ordered them to halt there, but his instructions had already been overcome by events. With Kravchenko leading the way, Konev's armies closed on the Dniester at Mogiliev-Podolosky and Yampol by the third week of March, and soon won a large bridgehead on its right bank.

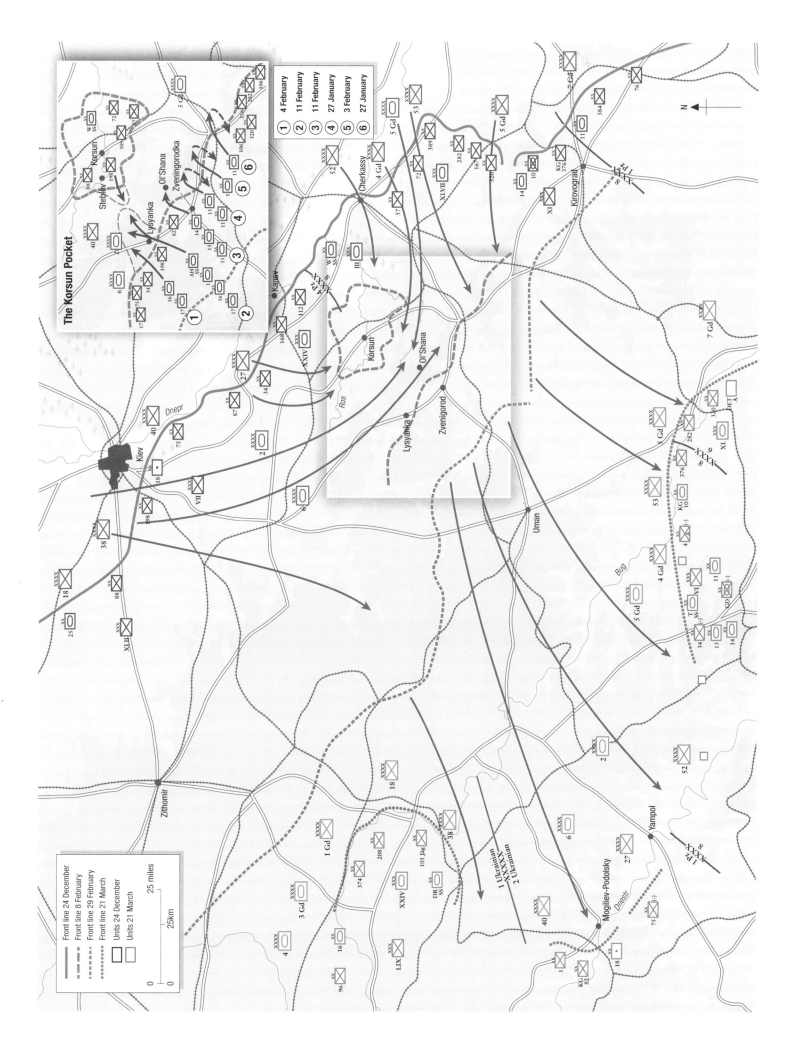

The Korsun Pocket

Korsun
Steblev
Lysyanka
Ol'Shana
Zveningorodka

1 4 February
2 11 February
3 11 February
4 27 January
5 3 February
6 27 January

Cherkassy
4 Gd
5 Gd
5 Gd
Kirovograd
Kaniev
Ros
Korsun
Ol'Shana
Lysyanka
Zvenigorod
Uman
Bug
7 Gd
5 Gd
Dnepr
Kiev
Zithomir
1 Gd
3 Gd
101 Jäg
Yampol
Mogiliev-Podolsky
Dnestr

1 Ukrainian
2 Ukrainian

Front line 24 December
Front line 8 February
Front line 29 February
Front line 21 March
Units 24 December
Units 21 March

25 miles
25km

MAP 100: LIBERATING WESTERN UKRAINE (II) 4 JANUARY TO 21 MARCH, 1944

Even before turning on Korsun, Vatutin had been building on his momentum after liberating Kiev (Map 79). Manstein's panzer riposte at Fastov had caused only a minor delay in the 1st Ukrainian Front's progress. As the year came to an end, Vatutin's men moved out again, and from the beginning Raus had little with which to stop them. On his left and centre, the front erupted from Korosten to Bruislov to Belaya Tserkov. All three towns fell in short order to the 13th, 18th and 27th Armies as 4. Panzer-Armee also struggled on its right to maintain contact with the 8. Armee across a 45-mile gap in Hitler's illogical and resource-consuming Kanev bridgehead.

Just days into 1944, 13th Army units reached the 1939 border at Gorodnitsa on the Slutsk River and took the town from XIII Armee-Korps, reportedly the strength of a regiment. Remnants of XLVI Panzer-Korps attempted but failed to defend the rail node at Berdichev. Raus had only scattered mechanized units to plug the numerous gaps. Manstein tried to locate and send in potential mobile reserves, but, suffering from systems overload across the entire army group front, he could find little. Vatutin sensed this weakness and rushed his 1st Tank and 40th Armies south past Belaya Tserkov and into the void. Manstein had to take drastic action and brought up 1. Panzer-Armee's III Panzer-Korps and began assembling another force of divisions scraped together from all corners of the eastern army under headquarters XLVI Panzer-Korps. Both corps, commanded by Hube, attacked between Vinnitsa and Uman in mid-January, III Panzer-Korps on the 15th and XLVI Panzer-Korps on the 24th. Too late, too small and suffering from the vagaries of the Russian winter, these manoeuvres bought only short-term relief. Meanwhile, on 4. Panzer-Armee's left XIII Armee-Korps briefly stabilized the situation around the army group's logistics centre at Rovno.

Although in late January and early February all eyes might be on the Korsun pocket, Vatutin remained active elsewhere; in the XIII Armee-Korps sector Rovno fell on 2 February, while a week later the 6th Guards Cavalry Corps threatened Dubno. By mid-month, other Red cavalry had spread out unhindered throughout Galicia from Lutsk to Kovel. To face this crisis, Manstein beefed up XIII Armee-Korps and built another counterattack force consisting of the rump of 7. and 8. Panzer-Divisionen under XLVIII Panzer-Korps headquarters. On 22 February Balck's men attacked to the north-west through heavy snow from the vicinity of Dubno, up the Styr River valley through Rovno and on to Kovel. In this way 4. Panzer-Armee's left, now at least scattered strongpoint outposts, temporarily ceased to be a problem, but Manstein knew the Soviets would be back. He took advantage of what appeared to be a Soviet pause following the conclusion of the Korsun battles to tidy up his battered front lines. However, the 1st Ukrainian Front, under Zhukov at that moment, had the 3rd Guards Tank and 4th Tank Armies assembling south of Rovno and ready to strike.[133]

That blow came on 4 March in an almost unmanned sector of the German lines between Yampol and Shepetovka. The 60th Army easily opened a hole and the two tank armies poured through and spread out in three directions. In danger were railway lines south-east from L'vov to Manstein's right flank and Kleist's Heeresgruppe A, plus the borders with Hungary, Romania and Slovakia. In a matter of days, the Soviet tankers approached Ternopol, Volochansk and Proskurov. Heeresgruppe Süd orchestrated hasty counterattacks against the first two by XVIII Panzer and against the third by III Panzer-Korps, but these acted as little more than temporary speed bumps. On the attack's north flank, 13th Army took Dubno and neared Brody. In the south the 30th Army, attempting to keep pace with the 2nd Ukrainian Front to its left, liberated Vinnitsa. In previous years, the Wehrmacht could count on operational and logistical overstretch plus the spring thaw for succour. In 1944, however, the new cohort of skilled Red Army leaders took care of the first two and American-made lend-lease trucks often negated the third. By 20 March, the Red Army was readying for its drive to the Dniester.

133 Ukrainian nationalists ambushed Vatutin on 29 February. He died from his wounds six weeks later.

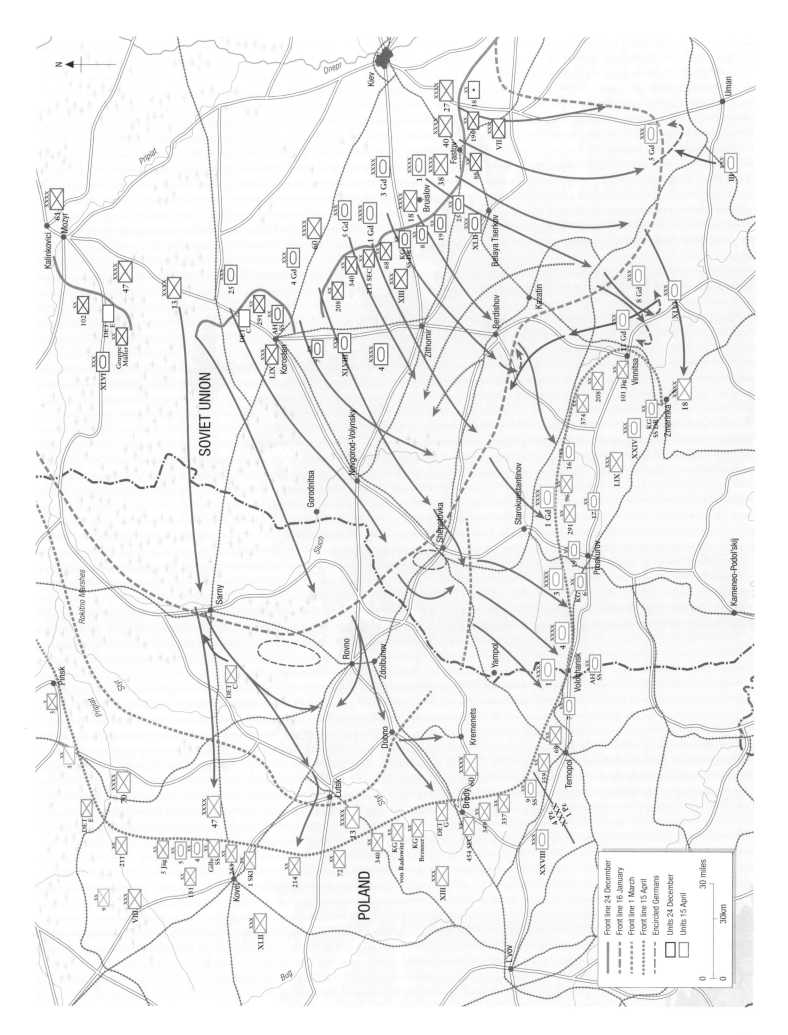

N

Dnepr

Kiev

SOVIET UNION

POLAND

Kalinkovici
Mozyr
61
XXXX
47
XXXX
102
XX
DET
E
Gruppe Müller
XX
XLVII
XXX
13
XXXX
25
XXX
Pripjat
Rokitno Marshes
Pinsk
3
XX
3
XX
70
XXXX
DET
E
211
XX
9
XX
VIII
XXX
131
XX
5 Jäg
XX
5
XX
4
XX
Gille
SS
XX
1 SKJ
Kovel
214
XX
42
XXXX
72
XXXX
XIII
XXX
XLII
XXX
Bug
Sarny
Gorodnitsa
Sluch
Novgorod-Volynsky
Korosten
LIX
XXX
DET
C
XX
291
XX
AH
SS
XX
7
XXX
XLVIII
XXX
4
XXXX
60
XXX
5 Gd
XXX
4 Gd
XXX
1 Gd
XXXX
3 Gd
XXXX
Bruslov
18
XXX
340
XXX
208
XXX
213 SEC
XXX
XIII
XXX
68
XXX
KG
SS DR
8
XX
19
XX
25
XX
1
XXX
38
XXX
40
XXX
Fastov
88
XXX
198
XX
VII
XXX
27
XXX
18
XX
5 Gd
XXX
IV
XX
Zithomir
Berdishov
Kazatin
Belaya Tserkov
Starokonstantinov
8 Gd
XXX
11 Gd
XXX
101 Jäg
XXX
Vinnitsa
208
XX
374
XX
KG
SS DR
XX
Zmerinka
18
XXXX
XXIV
XXX
LIX
XXX
16
XXX
96
XXX
12
XX
1 Gd
XXXX
291
XXX
19
XX
Proskurov
KG
6
XX
3
XXXX
4
XXXX
1
XXX
Volochansk
AH
SS
XX
7
XX
68
XX
Kameneo-Podol'skij
Shepetovka
Rovno
Zdolbunov
Dubno
Kremenets
Yampol
Lutsk
47
XXXX
13
XXXX
340
XXX
KG
von Radowitz
KG
Bremner
DET
G
XX
349
XX
357
XX
454 SEC
XX
Brody
60
XXXX
9
XX
SS
359
XX
Ternopol
1 Pz
XXXX
4 Pz
XXXX
XXVIII
XXX
Lvov

Front line 24 December	
Front line 16 January	
Front line 1 March	
Front line 15 April	
Encircled Germans	
Units 24 December	
Units 15 April	

0   30 miles
0   30km

MAP 101: LIBERATING WESTERN UKRAINE (III) 4 JANUARY TO 28 MARCH, 1944

By the end of 1944, in the far south of the theatre Stalin had the 3rd and 4th Ukrainian fronts inside the Dnepr bend and downstream to the river's mouth. Their mission was to drive west, destroying Axis armies as they went. Hitler had a more difficult job, thanks largely to his own insistence on never letting go of a square mile of territory occupied by his troops. He had one quarter of a million men condemned in the Crimea and a dangerously long line just so he could hold on to the Nikopol manganese mines. Operations over the first months of 1944 would not solve the matter of the Crimea, but would impose some logic on the Wehrmacht's approach to the lower Dnepr.

Wöhler's right flank and the newly expanded 6. Armee held a long, jagged line almost devoid of natural terrain features. Six Soviet armies (three from each front) surrounded the exposed easternmost tip centred on Nikopol on three sides. It was to the southern side of this bulge, the only remaining German presence south of the Dnepr, that Hitler sent one of his favourite troubleshooters, Schörner. Using headquarters XL Panzer-Korps as his basis for command, Schörner took control of the six divisions of XVII, IV and XXIX Armee-Korps in one of the ad hoc relationships preferred by the Führer. Co-ordinated by Vasilevski, in early January the 3rd and 4th Ukrainian fronts opened their newest offensive in a very disjointed fashion. On the 10th, Malinovsky's 8th Guards attacked down the Buzuluk River toward Loskarovka, but XXX Armee-Korps halted it cold with heavy AFV losses. Additional Soviet infantry and artillery could only buy a 5-mile advance, and they called off further slaughter. Days later on the southern front, Tolbukhin's 5th Shock Army assaulted the IV Armee-Korps portion of Schörner's bridgehead. Again, seeing no sense in proceeding after negligible gains, they halted on the 16th. So far, Hollidt had weathered two small storms.

6. Armee, 20 partial-strength divisions with one very weak panzer division in reserve, would not be so fortunate next time. During the second half of January Vasilevski juggled his forces (51 divisions, two each mechanized and tank corps) somewhat and attacked again on the 30th. Fretter-Pico's XX Armee-Korps took the first hits over two brutal days, and for the second time withstood the best Malinovsky's men

could give. At the same time, the 4th Ukrainian Front took on Schörner, this time his far west formation, XXIX Armee-Korps, around Bolshaya Lepatikha. Within 48 hours, however, 8th Guards Army had overrun XXX Armee-Korps and opened a 6-mile hole. Wehrmacht forces were severely affected by the *rasputitsa*, while Chuikov's troops were seemingly only minimally so. Hollidt tried to establish a four-division counterattack force, something large enough to make a difference, but Soviet pressure denied him that luxury. On 4 February, with his left collapsing, Hollidt told Schörner on his right to withdraw north of the Dnepr; Tolbukhin harried his every step. The 46th Army finished the job the next day by taking the Apostolovo station, cutting off Group Schörner. From this railway junction, a central point in the middle of Hollidt's rear areas, Malinovsky's divisions fanned out north, east and south. The 6. Armee managed to extract most of its forces and restore a solid defence, but on 12 February Kleist requested permission from Hitler to begin retreating to the Bug River; he repeated that request numerous times until finally on 26 March he retreated on his own accord. Having failed in the attempt to encircle 6. Armee, on the 21st Malinovsky turned his attention on Krivoi Rog, which fell to the 37th, 46th and 6th Armies a day later.

Losing that city broke Hollidt's army, which had taken 40,000 casualties in the previous six weeks. It paused along the narrow Ingulets River, but this would not do for a long-term defence. Vasilevski prepared for the next stage of the offensive, which now included a huge cavalry-mechanized group under General Lieutenant I. A. Pliev. The Stavka marshal's two fronts attacked on 6 March and soon had the Ingulets behind them. Within two days Pliev's cavalry, perfectly suited for the terrain, had crossed the Ingul River, halfway to the Dniester. Hugging the Dnepr's right bank, the 28th Army liberated Kherson and appeared about to beat 6. Armee in the race to Nikolaev. As it was, seven divisions under Hollidt became trapped near Bereznegovatoe, 50 miles from the large port city. Tolbukhin's men broke the group into smaller parts, but the bulk of 6. Armee escaped through Nikolaev, which remained in German hands until 28 March.

213

MAP 102: LIBERATING WESTERN UKRAINE (IV) 21 MARCH TO APRIL 6, 1944

The catastrophic winter 1944 Ukrainian campaigns proved the undoing of two of the Wehrmacht's best-known field marshals, Kleist and Manstein.[134] Days later, Armeegruppen A and South were dissolved, their armies re-organized into Heeresgruppen Nordukraine and Südukraine under a new generation of hard-charging, Nazi Party member generals, Model and Schörner. Meanwhile, a world away, the Stavka knew its forces had done tremendous damage to Hitler's southern armies and intended to press on until it had driven them into the ground. For about one month, from 20 March to 20 April, the southern theatre was aflame from Ternopol to the Black Sea.

1st Ukrainian Front

Zhukov began on 21 March with three field, three tank and one guards armies. Hube's 1. Panzer-Armee occupied an extended salient around Proskurov, while 4. Panzer-Armee held the line north of Volochansk. The Red Army tankers effortlessly swept aside XLVIII Panzer-Korps divisions to their front and headed due south toward Chortkov, which was taken on 23 March, on their way to the regional city of Chernovtsy and a rendezvous with Konev. Once his spearheads had passed Chortkov, Zhukov mushroomed his forces west toward Stanislaviv and east to Kamenets-Podolsky. The 38th and 40th Armies likewise broke out near Zhmerinka against the XXIV Panzer-Korps.[135] On 26 March the 4th Tank and 38th Armies joined hands at Kamenets-Podolsky, partially trapping 1. Panzer-Armee's 21 weak divisions south of Proskurov. In one of his last acts as Heeresgruppe Süd commander, Manstein convinced Hitler to allow Hube to escape. The question remained as to which direction. Hube wanted to go south toward the Dniester, but Manstein pulled rank and ordered him out to the west instead; the II SS Panzer-Korps would help him out. The manoeuvre caught Zhukov by surprise, since he had prepared for the southern attempt. By the end of March, 1. Panzer-Armee had drifted south near Kamenets-Podolsky and from here Hube moved out westwards, a critical event being the seizure of crossing sites over the Zbruch River on the 29th. Zhukov reacted belatedly by reversing the 4th Tank Army back toward Chortkov, as terrible storms hampered both sides. The

weather cleared a little on 3 April, and Zhukov threw all he had against Hube's ragged masses, but the Germans resisted. Two days later the SS Panzer-Korps had assembled and assaulted through the 4. Panzer-Armee toward the moving pocket, and the two linked up on the 6th. The Germans had turned disaster into defeat, not victory, but they did halt Zhukov; his armies now stood at the gates of Slovakia, Hungary and northern Romania.

2nd and 3rd Ukrainian Fronts[136]

The 2nd Ukrainian Front also drove south on a very wide front from Mogilev-Podolsky to Pervomaisk. Konev also had a very robust force under command of four field, two guards and three tank armies. The front had contributed in the battle against 1. Panzer-Armee, somewhat lessening the pressure on Wöhler. In general he was more interested in pushing on toward Romania than in encircling 8. Armee (or 6. Armee). As Wöhler and Hollidt had found out, he too knew that the underdeveloped Romania was something of a dead end. He had jammed one guards and two tank armies into the salient on the Dniester on either side of Soroki, pointing directly at the Bessarabian city of Beltsy. Mechanized forces crossed the Dniester on 21 March, again pushing down a German inter-army boundary, in this case cutting off 1. Panzer-Armee from 8. Armee, increasing its isolation. Beltsy fell on the 26th and within the first few days of April Konev had reached the Prut River in numerous places. Romania was proper just a few miles from the city of Jiassy.

Malinovsky's 3rd Ukrainian moved out last, crossing the lower Bug close on the heels of Wöhler and Hollidt's retreating rearguards. On 2 April, the 6. Armee joined the Romanian Third Army in Odessa, which Hitler demanded be held at all costs. Taking advantage of a savage winter-like storm, Pliev's cavalry penetrated the thin German-Romanian screen and were soon behind Odessa. By mid-month, the Wehrmacht no longer had any men east of the Dniester, while with an eye toward the future the Soviets had snatched plenty of bridgeheads to the river's west. As Malinovsky's men reached the limits of their endurance, the two biggest problems facing Heeresgruppe Süd Ukraine were how to keep Romania in the war and how to manage their logistics.

---

134 Hitler relieved both on 31 March and never recalled either.

135 The 40th Army belonged to the 2nd Ukrainian Front.

136 The 4th Ukrainian Front had been detailed for liberation of the Crimea.

Cherkassy

Kiev

Zithomir

Dnepr

Rovno

Lvov

Stryl

Stanislav

Ternopol

Proskurov

Starokon

Volochansk

Chortkov

Kamenets-Podolsky

Mogilev-Podolsky

Zbruch

Zhmerinka

Vaph'arka

Pervomaisk

Slobodka

Sorok

Beltsy

Kishinev

Tiraspol

Nikolaev

Odessa

Dniester

Southern Bug

Prut

Prut

Mures

Sluch

Stryl

1 Ukrainian
XXXXX
2 Ukrainian

2 Ukrainian
XXXXX
3 Ukrainian

Front line 20 March 1943
Front line 14 April 1943
Units 20 March 1943
Units 14 April 1943

50 miles

50km

215

MAP 103: LIBERATION OF THE CRIMEA 8 APRIL TO 9 MAY, 1944

With the German situation deteriorating by late 1943 and early 1944, we can assume Hitler's resolve to maintain his Black Sea possessions was, at best, half-hearted. Soon after Tokbukhin's 4th Ukrainian Front overcame 6. Armee at Melitopol, Zhakarov's 2nd Guards Army arrived at the Perekop Isthmus during the last days of October and the 17. Armee could run no farther. Within a few weeks, Red Army units had created beachheads inside the Sivash and north of Kerch.

With fighting in the Ukraine successfully concluded in the winter of 1944, Tolbukhin prepared to take the peninsula. The 4th Ukrainian Front had the 2nd Guards (Perekop) and 51st Armies (Sivash Lake) working in tandem with the Independent Coastal Army under General A. I. Yeremenko (Kerch). In total 470,000 Red Army soldiers plus marines in 30 divisions, covered by 6,000 guns and supported by 560 AFVs and 1,200 aircraft were aligned against the 17. Armee's deep defences.[137] Jaenecke planned to resist initially where his men stood, but without mobile reserves, he then anticipated rushing back to another system of fortifications on either side of Simferpol, the Gneisenau Line. He would then pull back to Sevastopol, where after a noble defensive effort, he fully expected that Hitler would allow him to evacuate the hopeless situation. He had 200,000 soldiers in six German and seven Romanian divisions, plus more than 3,000 artillery pieces, 200 assault guns and perhaps 600 aircraft. The Kriegsmarine and Luftwaffe kept the isolated garrison relatively well provisioned.

Tolbukhin attacked on 8 April following a 2 ½ hour artillery and CAS preparation, and Kreizer's 51st Army immediately made headway against the Romanian division holding half the Sivash line. This manoeuvre surprised Jaenecke, expecting an attack down the Perekop. Tolbukhin did not disappoint, and, backed up by 500 tanks of the 19th Tank Corps, the 2nd Guards Army hit the same Tartar Ditch defences Manstein had attacked years earlier. The XLIX Gebirgs-Korps under General der Gebirgstruppen Rudolf Konrad held on grimly for about two days. But with the Sivash line collapsing quickly, Kreizer's troops threatened the Perekop position from the rear. On the 9th Yeremenko attacked V Armee-Korps from his beachhead, and soon his men had worked their way around the town of Kerch. The next day the Axis Sivash front had essentially vanished, and by evening Red Army tanks had taken the communications hub at Dzhanskoy along with 2,000 POWs. At the same time the Perekop defences became untenable. Assaulted from the front and in danger of encirclement from the rear, Konrad's men fell back in disorder to Ishun.

Barely three days into the offensive, the Soviets had demolished Jaenecke's first line of defences and now stood on the brink of breaking into the centre of the Crimea, and possibly all the way to Sevastopol. In particular danger were the two German and two Romanian divisions of V Armee-Korps, almost 100 miles to the east. On 10 April, therefore, Jaenecke ordered them to make for Sevastopol; Yeremenko took up the pursuit.[138] The following day, Axis units arrived at the Gneisenau Line with Red Army right behind them. In particular Tolbukhin's two armies mercilessly hounded the XLIX Gebirgs-Korps' retreat. In general the Soviets were more mechanized than the Axis troops, so Jaenecke's men could never catch their breath. The 19th Tank Corps penetrated the Gneisenau Line in numerous places on 12 April and liberated Simferpol 24 hours later. Hitler had already made it clear there would be no mass evacuation of the Crimea, but the Kriegsmarine and Luftwaffe worked feverishly doing just that. On the 14th the first Axis units began arriving in force in Sevastopol's outer defences; casualties so far numbered nearly 70,000. Tolbukhin drew up on the 15th and Yeremenko arrived on the 17th. The Romanians no longer fielded combat-worthy units, while six German divisional *Kampfgruppen* faced 29 rifle divisions plus a tank corps. During the second half of April Hitler refused permission for 17. Armee to leave the Crimea. By early May, he had relieved Jaenecke and the two corps commanders. The final Soviet assault began on 5 May behind a massive artillery and CAS barrage. Three days later, the Führer agreed to an evacuation. Sevastopol fell the next day as the Germans retreated to Cape Khersones and continued to withdraw men by sea, bringing the total removed to approximately 50,000 (many died at sea under air attacks).

---

137 Generaloberst Erwin Jaenecke, former LXXXII Armee-Korps commander in the Kuban, took over 17. Armee from Ruoff on 25 June, 1943.

138 The Coastal Army liberated Feodosia for the last time on 12 April.

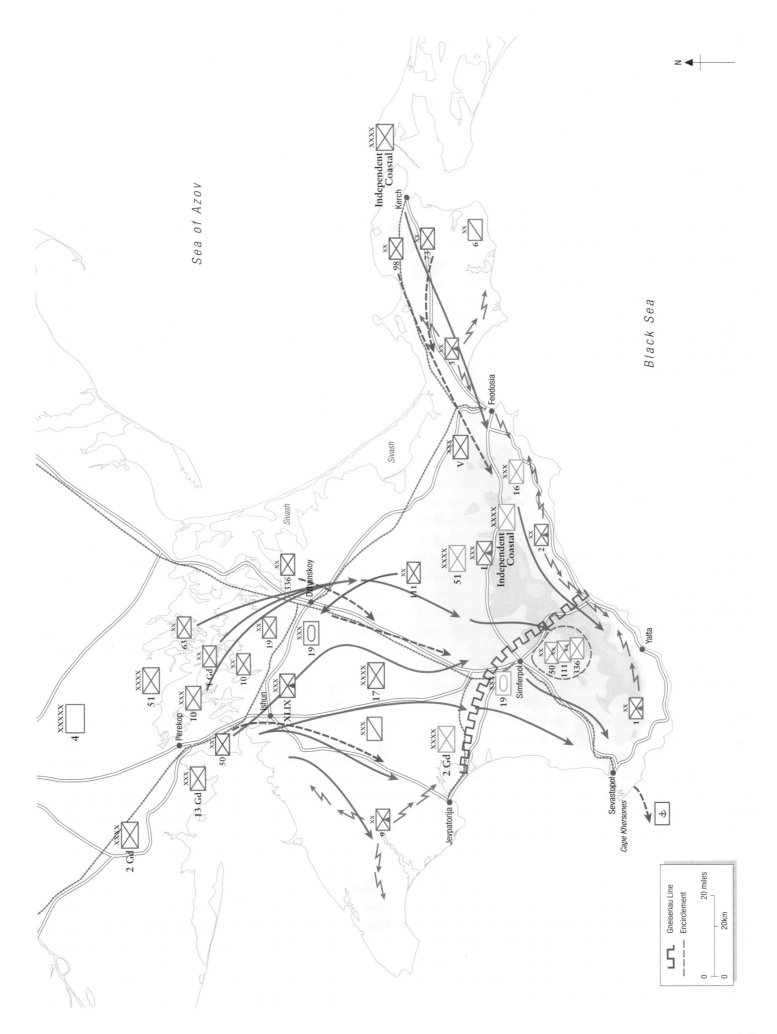

Sea of Azov

Black Sea

Independent
Coastal

Kerch

98

73

6

3

Feodosia

Sivash

V

16

Sivash

Independent
Coastal

51

2

Dzhankoy

336

111

51

Yalta

63

19

19

50

111

336

Hrd

10

Simferopol

51

10

Perekop

Ishun

19

17

XLIX

1

50

2 Gd

13 Gd

9

2 Gd

Jevpatorija

Sevastopol

Cape Khersones

4

XXXXX

Gneisenau Line
Encirclement

0   20km
0   20 miles

N

217

MAP 104: CONQUEST OF ROMANIA 20 AUGUST TO 21 SEPTEMBER, 1944

*B*arbarossa, Stalingrad, the retreat across the Ukraine and the loss of the Crimea had all been costly for Romania. Events throughout mid-1944 justified Hitler's concern over the stability and longevity of Antonescu's legionary state. A 5 August meeting at Rastenburg convinced Hitler that his fellow fascist would remain in the Axis until the end; the Führer should have been more concerned with the contrary opinions of everyone else in the country instead.[139] Militarily, the Third Reich's Balkan flank teetered on the brink. Since Stalingrad the Romanian military had become a shadow of its pre-*Barbarossa* predecessor. The Germans doubted the quality and resolve of its two front-line armies (Third and Fourth, 23 divisions totalling 400,000 men and perhaps 150 AFVs), even in defending their homeland. Friessner's Heeresgruppe Süd Ukraine could also be considered an unknown quantity.[140] His 8. Armee and 6. Armee (also 23 divisions, 500,000 soldiers) were backed up by only two mechanized divisions (170 AFVs) and fewer than 300 aircraft. The German plan was basically to start falling back as soon as the enemy attacked (without Hitler's knowledge).

On the Red Army side were the 2nd and 3rd Ukrainian fronts under Malinovsky and Tolbukhin. The 2nd consisted of six field armies plus Kravchenko's 6th Tank Army, while the 3rd had four field armies and two mechanized corps, totalling 1.3 million men, 1,400 AFVs and 1,700 aircraft. The Black Sea Fleet provided added mobility along the coast. After overrunning Jiassy, Malinovsky planned to crush the Axis front lines and then break in two directions behind the much-abused 6. Armee and toward Bucharest and Ploesti. Tolbukhin would attack out of his Tiraspol bridgehead and then also split in two directions: right to help Malinovsky entrap Fretter-Pico and left to pin the Romanian Third Army against the Black Sea. With these two tasks complete, he would cross the Danube River delta on his way to Bulgaria.

As Friessner's staff had predicted, the Soviet offensive began on 20 August with the usual massive artillery barrage. German units often held their ground, although this was not universal, while Romanian units melted away. The Wehrmacht often interspersed its units among the Romanians (or Italians or Hungarians) in order to fortify the latter, but when the Romanians disappeared, the Germans were left without flank protection. As was common at this point in the war, attacking mechanized and truck-borne Red Army units advanced faster than the Germans could march backwards. With Romanian armies giving way on either side of it, the static 6. Armee appeared doomed. Little remained of the defence on the second day and, with most Romanians nowhere to be seen, many German units thought only of saving themselves. Malinovsky and Tolbukhin committed fresh mobile formations that were soon deep in the German rear, with the latter often unaware. Wöhler and Fretter-Pico strove to bring some order to the crumbling defence.

Just 48 hours into the offensive, King Michael had Marshal Antonescu and other top fascist leaders arrested. The king declared an end of the war and gave the Germans two weeks to evacuate his country. On 24 August the two Soviet fronts joined forces near Husi, conclusively trapping the bulk of 18 divisions (mainly 6. Armee) around Kishinev and eventually claiming more than 100,000 Germans killed and a like number of POWs. To compound Friessner's problems, on the 25th the Luftwaffe bombed Bucharest and the new Romanian government declared war on Germany; he now had responsibility for many German civilians in the country, most of whom depended on the goodwill of the Romanian people for their safety. Militarily, the situation on the Danube plain turned into a rout, with 8. Armee falling back north-west into the Carpathians as the Red Army swung around clockwise like a door, pushing scraps of Wehrmacht out of its way. In this case, Hitler's de rigueur demands for defensive stands and no more retreats rang especially hollow. With no organized resistance in front of them, Soviet armies in essence occupied central and western Romania unopposed.

Most German units, large and small (including the headquarters of 6. Armee), which could maintain cohesion streamed back toward the Transylvanian Alps passes. In the absence of a proper front line, in early September individual columns fought over each pass. Once through the Alps and into Transylvania, large-scale combat flared up again, as from Cluj to the west Hungarians and Romanians fought against each other. By the third week of the month, Hitler had sent reinforcements to the region while the Red Army was overextended, so movement stabilized generally along the Muresul River.

---

139 Some Romanians had been in back-channel communications with the USSR since July.

140 Friessner and Schörner swapped positions on 23 July. Fretter-Pico commanded 6. Armee since 17 July.

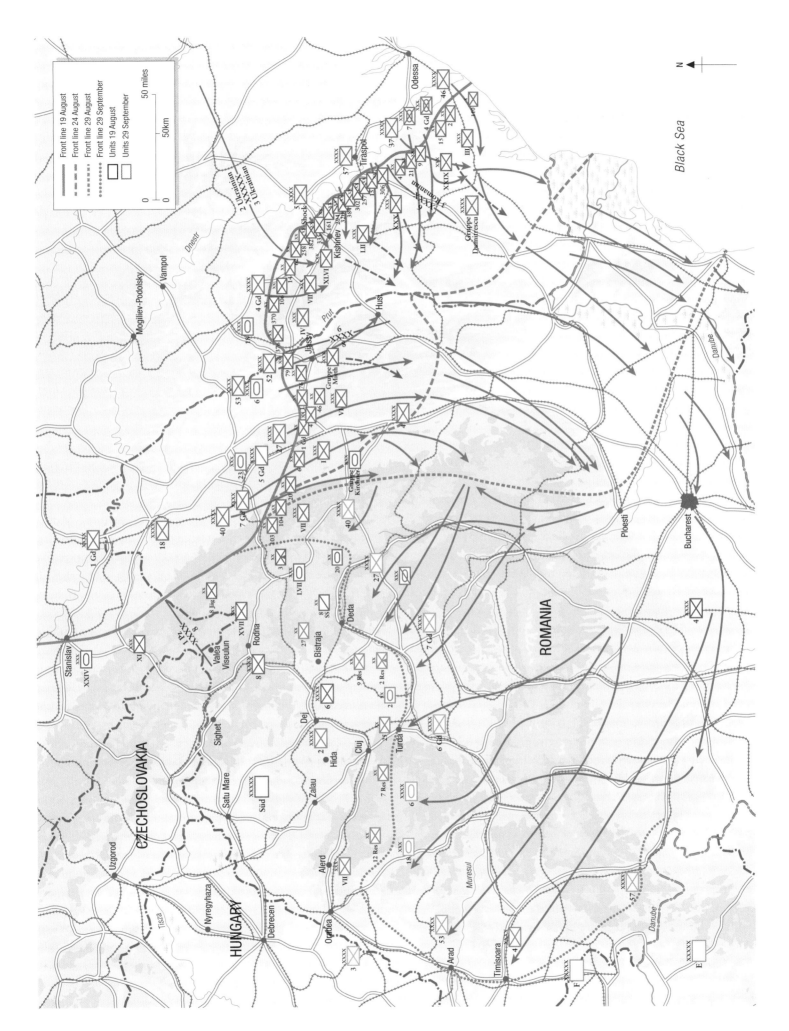

Black Sea

Odessa

Tiraspol

Kishinev

Husi

Mogiliev-Podolsky

Vampol

Iassy

Dnestr

Pruf

Stanislav

Uzgorod

Sighet

Satu Mare

Zalau

Aierd

Debrecen

Nyregyhaza

CZECHOSLOVAKIA

HUNGARY

Viseulun

Rodna

Bistraja

Dej

Hida

Cluj

Turda

Deda

ROMANIA

Ploesti

Bucharest

Arad

Timisoara

Tisza

Muresul

Danube

Danube

Valea

Oradea

2 Ukrainian
3 Ukrainian

Gruppe
Dumitrescu

Gruppe
Mieth

Gruppe
Kirchner

Süd

N

Front line 19 August
Front line 24 August
Front line 29 August
Front line 29 September
Units 19 August
Units 29 September

50 miles

50km

MAP 105: CONQUEST OF HUNGARY (I)
16 SEPTEMBER TO 31 OCTOBER, 1944

For over three years Antonescu had been Hitler's most loyal supporter, and Romania had contributed more troops to the Nazi-Soviet War than any other Axis allied nation. Therefore it is probably not too much of a stretch to say that its precipitous collapse completely ruined the Führer's Balkan strategy. By the first week of September, Bulgaria had switched sides too. This meant Generaloberst Alexander Löhr's Heeresgruppe E in Greece hung by a logistical thread that wound its way through the partisan-infested country of Yugoslavia; it finally left Greece during the second half of October.

With the fall of Antonescu, Hungary became the Third Reich's Balkan shaky bulwark. Hitler's Operation *Margarethe* in March and the arrival of a couple of SS divisions in August put a temporary end to that country's periodic waverings. Now its First and Second Armies (and later, the brand new Third) grudgingly fought alongside Friessner's battered 6. Armee and bruised 8. Armee on the Transylvanian plateau. To the west of the Iron Gate stood Weichs' Heeresgruppe F, equal parts regular army and anti-partisan fighters. The 2nd Ukrainian Front remained a massive force with four field armies (one of them guards, plus two more on the way from Tolbukhin), 6th Guards Tank Army and Gorshkov's 1st Guards Cavalry-Mechanized Group. Later the 3rd Ukrainian Front would join the fight from western Bulgaria. With the 4th Ukrainian Front recently relocated to Galicia, the Soviets' strategic objective was to take Hungary out of the war while their operational goal was to encircle the two German armies. Malinovsky tired of combat in the south-eastern Carpathians and figured his chances were better assaulting Hungary from western Romania. Therefore, in accordance with the Stavka's instructions, he transferred his main striking force to the area between Timisoara and Cluj. Initially the 2nd Ukrainian Front would strike north toward Debrecen in order to meet the 4th Ukrainian Front coming down from the Dukla Pass. With Friessner defeated, it would turn against Budapest.

On 16 September around Cluj, Malinovsky launched a prelude to a new general offensive that came to grief against what was very likely the only viable sector on the entire German-Hungarian front. He then shifted even farther west and on the 21st he took Arad from the untried Hungarian Third Army. On the 25th he attacked in force near Oradea, this time facing Fretter-Pico, whose army consisted of a ragtag collection of 20 battalions, plus random detachments and *Kampfgruppen*.[141] The Germans managed to retake Oradea on 28 September, but Friessner desperately needed the services of the numerous German mechanized divisions 're-fitting' in the area around Budapest (more correctly, ensuring Hungarian loyalty). The Stavka co-ordinator, the venerable Marshal Timoshenko, reworked the earlier plan, including the General I. E. Petrov's 4th Ukrainian Front, to encircle 1. Panzer-Armee, 8. and 6. Armeen in eastern Hungary. The relatively backward Balkan infrastructure created hardships for Malinovsky's logisticians trying to build up supplies for the offensive, while Heinrici's 1. Panzer-Armee[142] held the Dukla Pass over the Carpathian Mountains despite the 4th Ukraine's efforts. Meanwhile Hungary again stepped up its peace negotiations with the Soviet Union.

On 6 October Petrov's men finally prevailed on the Dukla Pass, while on the same day Malinovsky's main effort opened up both near Szeged and Oradea. The eastern attack again came to naught, this time halted by 23. Panzer-Division, but the western attack moved forward as the hastily created Hungarian Third Army essentially quit the field. Within a couple of days, Friessner was worried over the growing danger to Wöhler's rear. Malinovsky shifted Pliev's Cavalry-Mechanized Group from west to east where it came behind 23. Panzer-Division, forcing that division to withdraw and opening the way for 6th Guards Tank Army and Gorshkov's Cavalry-Mechanized Group. Even farther east, Red Army forces finally broke loose the stubborn German positions around Cluj. On his own authority Friessner ordered 8. Armee back, a move made easier by panzer division counterattacks against the 6th Guards Tank Army in the neighbourhood of Debrecen. This blunted Malinovsky's central drive, causing him once more to shift his main effort to his western group attacking toward Szolnok. On the two extreme flanks the 4th Ukrainian made slow headway coming out of the western slope of the Carpathians, so a major pocket of Germans looked doubtful. The 3rd Ukrainian Front began pushing out of Bulgaria against Heeresgruppe F, conducting a low-odds rearguard defence of eastern Yugoslavia. In any event, toward the end of October fighting once again stabilized, this time in central Hungary and Yugoslavia.

---

141 On 23 September, for obvious reasons, Friessner's Heeresgruppe Nord Ukraine was re-named Heeresgruppe Süd.

142 Heinrici replaced Raus on 19 August. The 1. Panzer-Armee combined with Hungarian First Army to become Armeegruppe Heinrici.

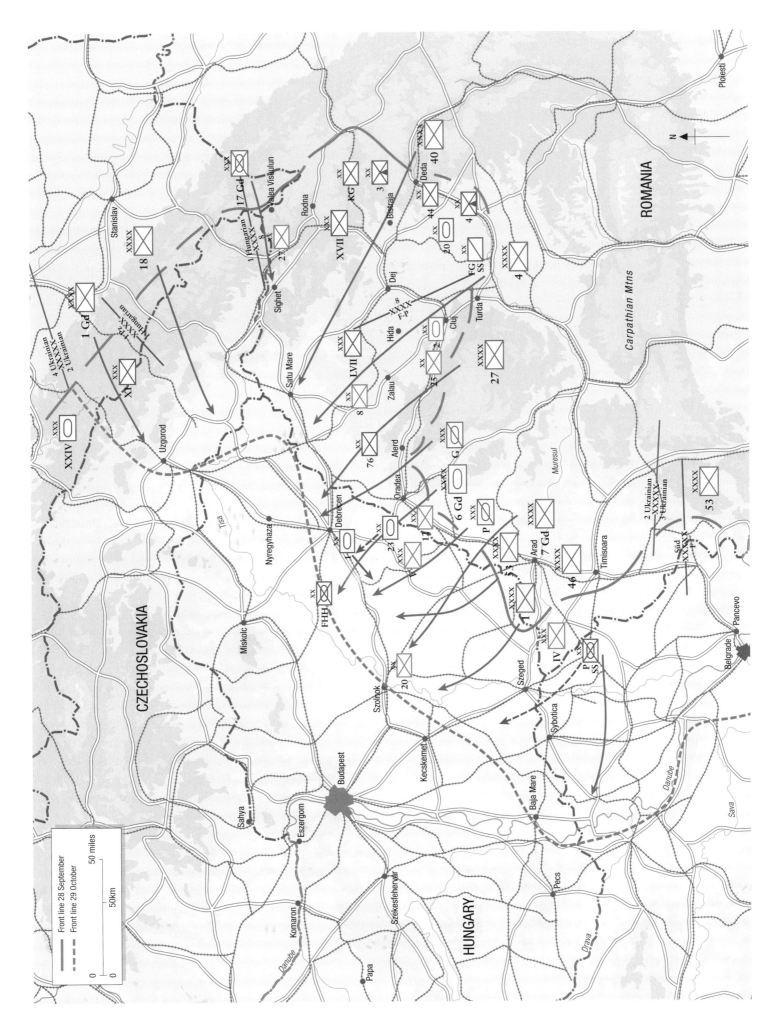

ROMANIA

Carpathian Mtns

HUNGARY

CZECHOSLOVAKIA

Ploiesti

Stanislav

Valea Viseulun

Rodna

Bistrija

Deda

40

44

4

Sighet

Satu Mare

Dej

Cluj

Turda

Hida

Zalau

Alerd

Oradea

Debrecen

Nyregyhaza

Miskolc

Uzgorod

Sahya

Eszergom

Komaron

Papa

Budapest

Kecskemet

Szolnok

Szeged

Arad

Timisoara

Baja Mare

Sybotica

Pancevo

Belgrade

Pecs

Szekesfehervar

Tisa

Muresul

Danube

Sava

Drava

17 Gd

1/Hungarian

KG

3

27

XVII

18

1 Gd

XII

XXIV

8 F-P

LVII

35

8

76

G

6 Gd

P

11

23

FHH

20

53

7 Gd

T

IV

46

P SS

FG SS

20

4

27

4

53

Sud

2 Ukrainian

3 Ukrainian

4 Ukrainian

2 Ukrainian

N

Front line 28 September
Front line 29 October

50 miles

50km

0

0

221

MAP 106: CONQUEST OF HUNGARY (II)
17 OCTOBER TO 26 DECEMBER, 1944

Regent Admiral Miklos Horthy, never as firm an ally as Antonescu, went on the radio in mid-October to tell his countrymen that their war was over. Of course for Hitler political considerations came first, and, with the fighting front little more than 100 miles east, on the following day he ordered German units to restore authority in Budapest despite Friessner's complaints.

On 17 October, Malinovsky renewed the long-delayed plan to trap Wehrmacht formations east of Nyiregyhaza. The 1. Panzer-Armee might avoid capture, but he still hoped to catch 8. Armee. Friessner, hoping to avoid a catastrophe, intended to hold open an escape route. Red Army troops took Debrecen on the 20th, after which Malinovsky passed Pliev's Cavalry-Mechanized Group north in an attempt to block Wöhler, and they captured Nyiregyhaza two days later. Hitler had been sending mobile units to Hungary, and soon Friessner had counterattack forces consisting of 1., 13., 23. and 24. Panzer-Divisionen plus SS police divisions and Panzer-Grenadier-Division Feldherrnhalle.[143] With 8. Armee helping its own cause from the east, Breith's newly arrived III Panzer-Korps attacked from the west. Caught in between were Gorshkov and Pliev, with three mobile corps that had left their infantry support behind. From 23 to 29 October Heeresgruppe Süd re-captured Nyiregyhaza, kept open Wöhler's lifeline and claimed 25,000 enemy casualties inflicted and 600 tanks destroyed. When the 2nd and 4th Ukrainian fronts did finally link up at Uzgorod on 26 October, 8. Armee was long gone. Malinovsky had attacked without proper preparations and paid the price. Friessner withdrew behind the Tisa River and had a solid defensive line for the first time since the Soviets' general offensive over the lower Dniester began nearly two months earlier.

None of this meant that the Germans' Balkan flank was out of danger, however. While they managed to somewhat stabilize the situation to the east, Malinovsky turned up the pressure to the west. Between the Danube and Szolnok, his 46th Army attacked Armeegruppe Fretter-Pico's right on 29 October.[144] Soon the Hungarians routed to the rear. The 2nd and 4th Guards Mechanized Corps had achieved a breakthrough over the Tisa and raced for Budapest. On the last day of the month they reached Kecskemet, 50 miles from the capital. Malinovsky had the 7th Guards Army following close behind, ready to make the final push. In early November his men tried to rush Budapest, but an SS garrison inside and a ring of panzer divisions around the outside first halted them and then sent them back several miles. The Stavka directed Malinovsky to prepare a deliberate assault. In the meantime, Tolbukhin's 3rd Ukrainian Front was on the move again after capturing Belgrade on 20 October, attacking up the Danube and reaching the Hungarian town of Baja in the first week of November. The task of defending from this unexpected direction fell on 2. Panzer-Armee (a mere shadow of its former self) and the Hungarian Second Army.

Malinovsky then shifted his main effort against Budapest from the south to the east, the 7th Guards, 53rd, 27th and 40th Armies attacking Wöhler near Miskolc on 11 November. After five days they took that town and Hatvan, but here 8. Armee stiffened and would not break. Once again Malinovsky changed his emphasis to the west of the big city, which Hitler had demanded be fought over house by house. In early December his 4th Guards Army attempted to drive between Lake Balaton and Budapest in an effort to come around from the north-west. However, Fretter-Pico's army group of 15 divisions, a considerable number of which were mechanized, defended its Margarete Line until losing its grip on the lake in mid-month. Malinovsky attacked from the east again on 8 December, and this time his 6th Guards Tank Army and cavalry-mechanized group reached Vac at the Danube's bend north of the city. Both sides rushed in reinforcements, but through mid-month the Soviets seemed to gain the upper hand and closed in from all directions.

Outnumbering the Axis by a large margin, the 2nd and 3rd Ukrainian fronts opened another series of attacks against Budapest on 14 December. As at Stalingrad and on the Dniester, it was 6. Armee that was encircled and cut off. With difficulty Hitler had dispatched a number of mobile divisions to the area, and Friessner argued with his high command over when to launch a counterattack.[145] On the 26th Red Army units reached Esztergom, completing the deep encirclement of Budapest; two days later Malinovsky unexpectedly stopped.

---

143 This force was not as fearsome as it sounded, having only 67 panzers and 58 assault guns.

144 The name of the combined 6. Armee and Hungarian Third Army command.

145 At the same time Hitler was launching his Ardennes offensive, the Battle of the Bulge.

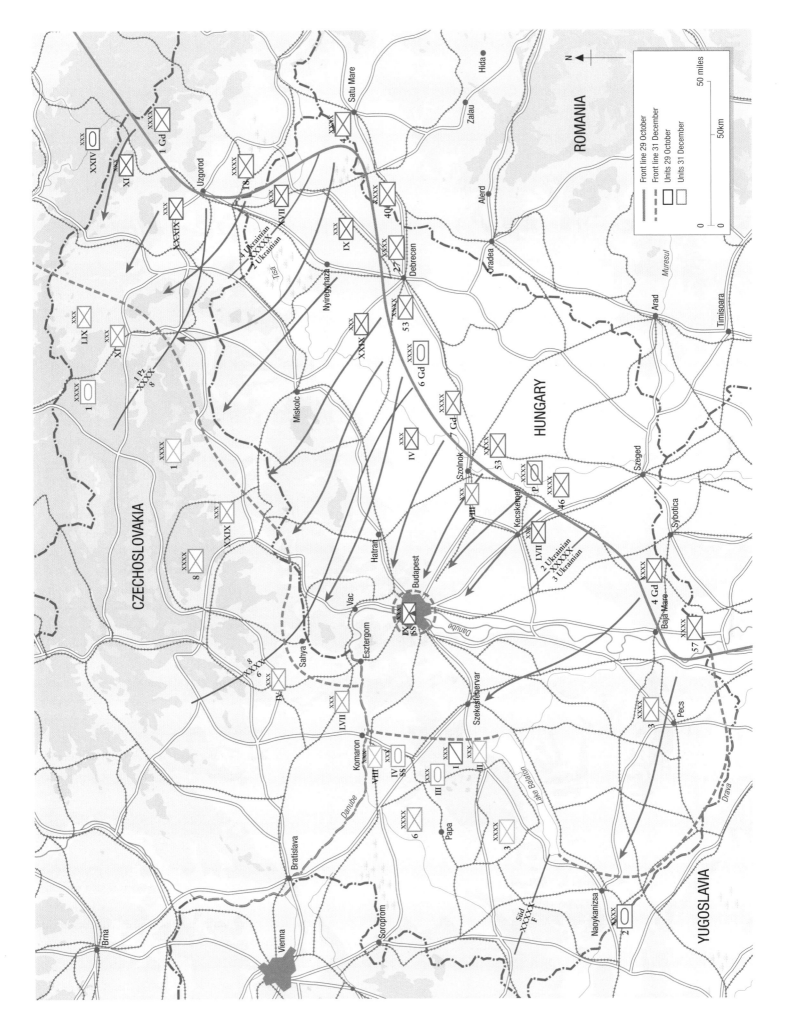

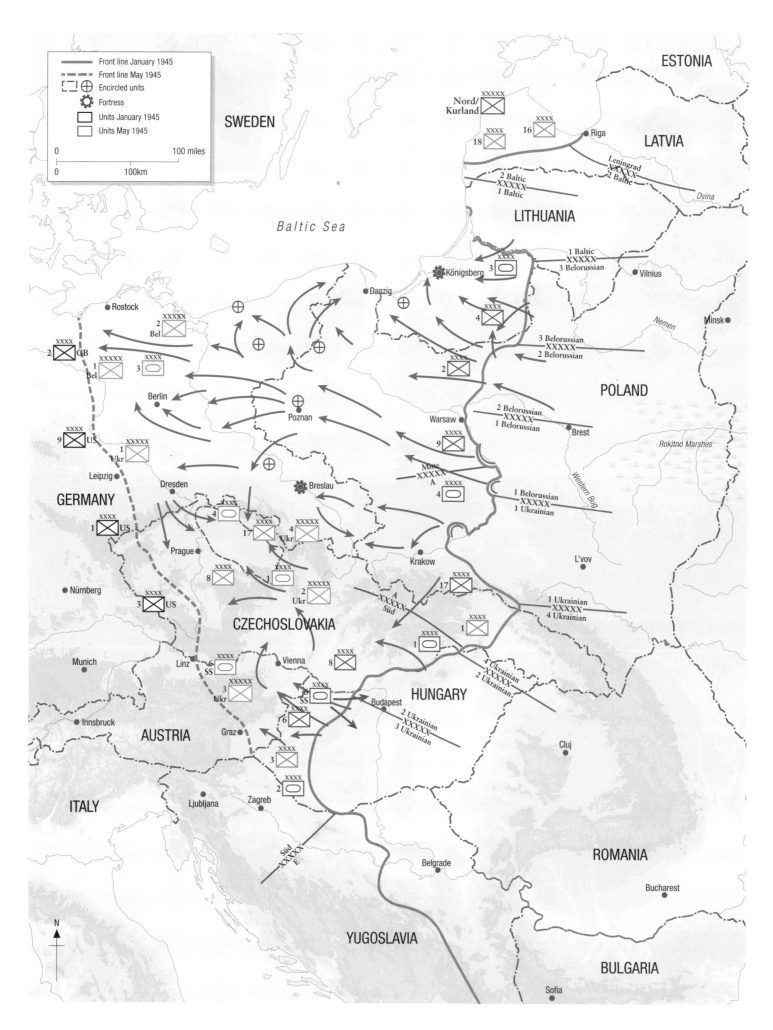

Front line January 1945
Front line May 1945
Encircled units
Fortress
Units January 1945
Units May 1945

0   100 miles
0   100km

SWEDEN

Rostock

Baltic Sea

ESTONIA

LATVIA

Nord/Kurland XXXXX

16 XXXX

Riga

18 XXXX

Leningrad XXXXX 2 Baltic

2 Baltic XXXXX 1 Baltic

Dvina

LITHUANIA

Vilnius

Minsk

Nemen

Danzig

Königsberg 3 XXXX

1 Baltic XXXXX 3 Belorussian

4 XXXX

3 Belorussian XXXXX 2 Belorussian

2 Bel 2 XXXXX

3 XXXX

2 XXXX

POLAND

2 GB XXXX

1 Bel XXXXX

3 XXXX

Berlin

Poznan

2 Belorussian XXXXX 1 Belorussian

Warsaw

9 XXXX

Brest

Rokitno Marshes

9 US XXXX

1 Ukr XXXXX

Leipzig

Dresden

Mitte XXXXX A

4 XXXX

1 Belorussian XXXXX 1 Ukrainian

Western Bug

GERMANY

1 US XXXX

Breslau

4 XXXX

17 XXXX

4 Ukr XXXXX

Krakow

L'vov

Nürnberg

3 US XXXX

8 XXXX

1 XXXX

2 Ukr XXXXX

17 XXXX

1 Ukrainian XXXXX 4 Ukrainian

A XXXXX Süd

1 XXXX

CZECHOSLOVAKIA

Prague

Linz

6 SS XXXX

Vienna

8 XXXX

6 SS XXXX

4 Ukrainian XXXXX 2 Ukrainian

Munich

3 Ukr XXXXX

6 XXXX

Budapest

HUNGARY

Cluj

Innsbruck

AUSTRIA

Graz

3 XXXX

2 Ukrainian XXXXX 3 Ukrainian

2 XXXX

Ljubljana

Zagreb

ITALY

Süd XXXXX E

Belgrade

ROMANIA

Bucharest

N

YUGOSLAVIA

Sofia

BULGARIA

CHAPTER 7
CENTRAL EUROPE AND GERMANY, 1945

Historians like to argue about when the outcome of World War II became assured. Few could dispute that by 1945 it was anything more than a foregone conclusion. Any occupied parts of Europe or Asia beyond the German and Japanese homelands were either inaccessible or useless to them. Enemy armies hemmed in the Third Reich from all sides while Allied air forces ranged its skies with near-impunity. The RAF and USAAF bombed cities like Dresden after they had destroyed almost every other possible target in Germany. Yet whereas their parents in the Kaiser's Germany fought for four years and a few months, a generation later those in Hitler's Germany managed to continue fighting for a few months short of six years. Just as the Soviet state survived the shock of the five-month 'sprint' of *Barbarossa*, the Nazi state survived the shock of a 30-month 'marathon' of a steady barrage of defeats and reverses. Unable to defeat the Third Reich's nation-state enemies on the battlefield with conventional weapons, Hitler's Nazi Germany redoubled the war against its racial enemies with genocidal mass murder.

One can possibly say that Soviet operational art peaked during Operation *Bagration* and the Jiassy–Kishinev offensives. At least the Germans could still field armies worthy of the name in 1944. By 1945, German manpower was scraping the bottom of the barrel: weakly re-constituted divisions, corps and armies plus barely trained *Volksgrenadier* troops and untrained *Volkssturm* masses could do little to halt avenging armies.[146] Petroleum production was so low that it is amazing any of their vehicles, aircraft or ships could move at all. The Red Army of 1945 might even be considered a letdown of sorts, since with Berlin and final victory in sight, only feeble cobbled-together defences were desperately thrown in its way and bloodlust vengeance frequently replaced military discipline. Historians take it to task for coming to a halt for four months at the end of 1944 on the Vistula and for six weeks around March 1945 on the Oder. These arguments aside, the Soviets' early 1945 main Vistula–Oder campaign and its three flank consorts essentially picked up where the autumn 1944 offensives left off.

Wary of overextended penetrations with poor flank security since the winter of 1942–43, the Stavka took care to protect the main thrust on Berlin; it would take no

146 The best example of re-constituted or re-created formations was none other than 6. Armee, originally eliminated at Stalingrad. It would reappear numerous times in later fighting in the Ukraine and Romania, only to be destroyed again.

chances on this cataclysmic finale. Three fronts consisting of 1,600,000 men attacked the region around East Prussia on 13–14 January 1945 and befitting a secondary offensive, fighting against German troops defending their home territory progress was difficult. Stout and deep defensive belts, the marshy countryside and cities of near-mythic importance for the defenders such as Königsberg and Danzig added to the attackers' problems. In addition, the Wehrmacht could count on seaborne logistical support as well as naval gunfire along the Baltic littoral, as Kriegsmarine surface units made their last stand of World War II. Although small pockets of German beachheads held out on the coast until the end of the war, the East Prussian offensive plus a front-sized branch in Pomerania had secured the Red Army's right by late March and early April.

To the south, Soviet operations to clear the Carpathians and overrun Czech, Slovak and Hungarian areas began on the 12th. These were loosely related to the fighting around Budapest. The Red Army encircled the city on the Danube in late December, but in the first weeks of the new year Hitler committed large and, for 1945, well-equipped SS forces to break the siege. Although it took weeks, Soviet commanders managed to master the situation and completed the capture of the twin cities on 12 February after typically brutal urban combat. However, the Nazi dictator continued to lavish attention on the Hungarian theatre that was completely disproportionate to its value. Major combat operations took place on the southern margin of the Reich throughout March and into April, and Vienna fell on 13 April. In a related manoeuvre, from 8 February through to 31 March, two fronts conducted two offensives through Silesia. Hitler designated Breslau and other cities here as fortresses, never to be surrendered. The Silesian capital represented a serious obstruction to the Red Army, and like Prague did not surrender until May.

The Vistula–Oder offensive clearly represented the Soviets' main event that winter, as well as their penultimate campaign of World War II. Over 2,000,000 men, 6,400 tanks and 46,000 guns in two fronts outnumbered the Wehrmacht by ratios of 5.5:1, 5.5:1 and 11:1 respectively. Leading the assault were Stalin's two thoroughbreds, Zhukov and Konev, whose troops would break out of Vistula bridgeheads dating back to October. To compensate for dwindling manpower, these operations would be material-intensive rather than personnel-intensive. In charge of the defence after the first dozen days was, of all people, military neophyte SS Reichsführer Heinrich Himmler.[147] Besides being completely outclassed, Hitler deployed his men too far forward in the featureless north European plain, and they could count on none of the advantages of defensive terrain found in East Prussia or the Carpathians. As had been the case since the very first planning for *Barbarossa* in 1940, the Germans were fatally ill-served by their terrible military intelligence and its flawed estimates of anticipated Red Army intentions, objectives and timing. In addition, Soviet attacks in East Prussia and the Carpathians conformed to Hitler's pre-conceived notions of how events in 1945 would proceed. On top of these

problems, the Führer, never an organized thinker and now as unfocused as ever, on the eve of the assault obsessed over the Ardennes offensive (as did Western Allied leaders) and Budapest and its largely SS garrison and relief effort, so did not have his eyes on the mortal danger rushing straight at his capital.

The offensive began with staggered timing between 12 and 14 January and completely overwhelmed the hapless defenders at every point. At critical points of attack, the Germans were able to maintain themselves on the battlefield for a few hours or a couple of days before tank armies passed through the assault infantry and began to rampage throughout the defenders' operational depth. After two to three days, Heeresgruppe A vanished. On the 17th a Polish army liberated its capital, Warsaw. With few cities upon which to coalesce a stable defence (the Soviets purposefully avoided the built-up areas that did exist) the situation degenerated into a race between the Red Army's advancing mechanized spearheads and the Wehrmacht's retreating de-mechanized mobs. There could be but one outcome to this, although the usual German panzer division and corps-sized counterattacks infrequently brought momentary relief. Soon both Konev and Zhukov were days ahead of schedule. Not even a massive blizzard during the last days of January could alter events much. Few engagements or battles worthy of mention occurred, mainly because the Wehrmacht simply did not have the means to resist on any but the lowest tactical levels. In early February the Red Army's offensive came to rest along the Oder River, including a few bridgeheads on the left bank. Next stop was Berlin.

It took the Stavka nine weeks to prepare for the final three-week offensive of the war. As mentioned above, operations to tidy up the flanks along the Baltic, Carpathians and Danube consumed more time than the dash across central Poland. Securing extended flanks, re-organizing spread-out and attrited formations plus bringing logistics services forward through the devastation of central Europe were legitimate reasons to delay the final push into Brandenburg. However, Zhukov, Konev and other Soviet commanders had a disciplinary nightmare on their hands that had to be brought under control before any serious military operation could proceed; it was payback time for Red Army soldiers. As soon as they reached German territory, they unleashed a de facto terror campaign of murder, rape and destruction on a massive scale. In 1945 they murdered approximately 2,500,000 German civilians in an attempt to even the score for years of Nazi atrocities in the USSR.

As decided by the highest Allied national-strategic leaders at Yalta and elsewhere, the Soviet Union had earned the dubious honour of capturing the bombed-out fortified pile of rubble that was Berlin in the spring of 1945. The same two commanders with similar numbers of Red Army men and weapons as had launched the Vistula–Oder offensive would finish off Hitler's Third Reich. They completed preparations by mid-April, and after some largely self-imposed problems negotiating defences immediately west of the Oder, they covered the last 25 miles to greater Berlin. No matter how unrealistically, the Germans had pinned great hopes on their three-tier Oder position. Although once levered from the river the intervening rolling countryside had little to offer the soon ejected defenders, Berlin's proximity likewise

147 In fact Himmler did listen to his army advisers, and, all things considered, gets above-average marks in a hopeless situation.

limited the Red Army's ability to use operational movement as a substitute for tactical combat. This final campaign of the war would be up close and personal the rest of the way, with all the negative implications that brought. Unlike the fathers' army in the last weeks of World War I, the sons' army in 1945 largely did not implode until the very last days, but made the Soviets pay a steep price for every mile advanced. As for the attackers, on 17 April Stalin bluntly told his two top commanders that Berlin was up for grabs and whichever of them got there first would get the glory. Less than ten days after beginning the assault along the Oder River, tanks belonging to Zhukov and Konev met at Potsdam on 25 April, thereby encircling the capital of the 'Thousand Year Reich', the Führer having finally decided days earlier that the war was indeed lost and that he would remain to the death. The final battle for the city began the next day. Even though a credible German national command structure no longer existed, and losses plus centrifugal force had shattered the once-proud Wehrmacht into countless independent regiment-division-corps-sized entities totalling 800,000 men scattered throughout the 30 square miles of metropolitan Berlin (itself well-prepared for defence), capturing the city required 15 armies. Hitler committed suicide by poison on April 30,[148] and the Berlin garrison commanders began negotiating for terms the next day and capitulated on 2 May. Fighting dragged on another week, most notably in Bohemia, until VE Day on the 9th.

After the Great War there had been no parade through the centre of Berlin by the victorious Allies. This broke millennia of worldwide tradition and was a tragic oversight. Among other things, it contributed to the various inter-war myths in Germany that it, or more particularly its military, had not really been defeated after World War I. After World War II countless parades, victors' memorials, monuments and cemeteries in Berlin, not to mention decades-long armies of occupation and other consequences, made sure there would be no such misconception this time.

148 In a loosely analogous situation, like Wilhelm II in November 1918, Hitler eschewed a soldier's death.

MAP 108: KURLAND – 15 OCTOBER 1944 TO 18 MARCH, 1945

Beginning with Stalingrad, a preferred technique of Hitler's consisted of leaving isolated groups of Wehrmacht soldiers strewn around Europe followed by costly relief attacks by scarce mobile reserves. In most cases, each episode was almost suicidal for both rescuer and rescued. In the ensuing two years, numbers of Germans killed, wounded and captured in this way totalled hundreds of thousands. This strategy was economical in the short term but very costly in the long term, but to his mind the moral victory represented by a desperate evacuation somehow made the disastrous encirclement worthwhile. Quite irrationally, the Führer wanted to hold on to every square yard of territory ever occupied by one of his men, while somewhat rationally he concluded that these sacrificial pockets tied down much of the Red Army, preventing it from being employed against him elsewhere. On the negative side, these groups cost him extensive forces that were then not available on the main fronts, not to mention large Luftwaffe or Kriegsmarine assets required to keep them resisting.

In the autumn of 1944, the Soviets created another huge pocket when they reached Lithuania's Baltic coast and cut off one and a half million Germans in Latvia. The 3. Panzer-Armee counterattacks could not keep open overland communications, but at least now the remaining Kriegsmarine surface fleet had a worthwhile mission to keep it employed during the war's last six months. Ultimately, the remnants of approximately 26 divisions under Schörner became isolated by 52 divisions of the 1st and 2nd Baltic fronts. On his own initiative, and at the prompting of subordinates, Hitler eventually removed many divisions from Kurland, while opposite him Stalin set aside only the minimum required to keep the garrison penned in and make occasional attacks to reduce or destroy it; the Germans number these battles one to six.

The First Battle of Kurland occurred in the first half of October as the Red Army kept up the momentum of its massive summer offensives, captured Riga and generally hoped to either crush Heeresgruppe Nord against the sea or at least force its capitulation (Map 88). This latter option failed to take Hitler's personality into account, so Bagramian and Eremenko's men settled in for a campaign of siege warfare. The second battle began on 22 October with a 2,000-gun artillery preparation. General Rotmistrov's 5th Guards Tank Army attacked with over 400 AFVs against III SS Panzer-Korps and X Armee-Korps between Skuodas and Vainode on the road to Libau (Liepaja) while the

10th Guards Army assaulted an assortment of Wehrmacht units around Autz. Supported by more than 1,800 aircraft and new massive Josef Stalin tanks, a week later the Preekuln sector saw the harshest combat. The German defences managed to hold, and after losing hundreds of AFVs, the Soviets took a break in early November. Schörner re-organized his defences and the Red Army attacked again on the 19th along the seam between 16. Armee and 18. Armee. Over the next week they made very limited gains versus enormous losses for both sides.

Under total Soviet air supremacy, the two fronts attacked again from 21–31 December, the third or 'Christmas' battle. The 3rd and 4th Shock Armies, 10th Guards and 42nd Armies attacked along the pocket's southern face, again aiming for Libau and Saldus. They blasted the front lines of I and XXXVIII Armee-Korps in the Pampali region, making some progress for two days until Schörner mastered the situation with his limited mechanized reserves. Likewise, the 6th Guards Army failed against the II Armee-Korps defending Libau. Again the Red Army suffered massive losses in capturing only a few square miles, although the Germans had suffered 100,000 casualties in the past ten weeks. About the time of the new year Hitler finally saw the folly of keeping so many resources in Kurland and authorized a sizeable evacuation.

The Fourth Battle of Kurland began on 24 January, once more concentrating on the 18. Armee west of Saldus and along the coast. A supporting attack hit 16. Armee positions around Tukums, but in both battles the Germans prevailed as the Soviets sustained heavy losses in men and weapons.[149] The Soviets started the fifth battle on the morning of 20 February in Preekuln (18. Armee) and Dzukste (16. Armee). Two days later they finally fought their way into Preekuln, forcing the Germans back behind the Vartaya stream half a dozen miles west. On the other side of the pocket, Red Army troops captured Dzukste in mid-March before an early *rasputitsa* halted their attacks. Despite the climate, the 10th Guards Army initiated the sixth battle on 18 March, against Saldus but never succeeded. World War II in the Baltic was over.

---

149 Armeegruppe Kurland changed command twice that January: Rendulic (20. Gebirgs-Armee) replaced Schörner on the 18th, and Generaloberst Heinrich von Vietinghoff replaced him on the 29th, but lasted only until 10 March. Kurland's final commander was General der Infanterie Carl Hilpert.

Front line 15 October 1944
Front line 18 March 1945
Soviet attacks (Battles of Kurland)
Units 15 October 1944
Units 18 March 1945

25 miles
25km

Riga

Dvina

Baldone

Lielupa

Siauliai

Venta

Memel

Ventspils

Libau

Mazeikiai

Pampalii

Vainode

Preekuln

Autz

Dobek

Saldus

Dzukste

Tukums

Skodas

Venta

61
1 Shock
67
22
3 Shock
205
42
90
263
281
93
10 Gd
205
Nordland SS
Nordland SS
Leningrad
Nederland
121
12
10 Gd
42
122
218
290
10 Gd
3 Shock
563
87
250
126
132
30
11
11
51
6 Gd
6 Gd
5 Gd
5 Gd
61
14
4 Shock
201
4 Shock
5 Gd
61
I
II
X
16
XXXXX
18
VI SS
XVI
XXXVIII
300
2 LW
24
12

563
227
83
31
24
132
389
87

2 Baltic
XXXXX

229

MAP 109: VISTULA–ODER OPERATION (I) 12–18 JANUARY, 1945

With the massive convulsions of the central theatre brought about by Operation *Bagration* and its smaller sequels, the Red Army had a toehold in East Prussia and a few bridgeheads over the Vistula River but still stood quite a distance from Berlin. Although Königsberg, Danzig and Breslau might be in immediate danger, the western half of Poland – nearly 200 miles wide – separated the Soviets from the German heartland. Hitler had two army groups defending central Poland, consisting of four armies – although two of these, 4. Panzer-Armee and 17. Armee, were in for the worst – numbering 400,000 men with 4,100 tubes of artillery and 1,150 AFVs supported by 1,300 aircraft.[150] Stalin on the other hand had the better part of four fronts, with two – 1st Belorussian and 1st Ukrainian – conducting the main offensive, with over 2.5 million men, 50,000 indirect fire weapons and 7,000 AFVs plus more than 10,000 planes in total.[151] Overall on the Polish front, the Red Army enjoyed a 9:1 or 10:1 superiority in every category, and would create local superiorities at much greater odds. Zhukov's 1st Belorussian Front, formed of seven field (plus one Polish) and one tank army, would smash 9. Armee on a wide frontage and create numerous small encirclements, while Konev, with eight field and two tank armies, would debouch from the large Sandomierz bridgehead against the 4. Panzer-Armee. Sadly for the defenders in *feldgrau*, this coming offensive could have but one outcome.

On 12 January Konev began, with six breakthrough artillery divisions firing 420 guns per mile, pouring shells on General der Panzertruppen Fritz-Hubert Gräser's 4. Panzer-Armee. The barrage obliterated his front-line divisions of XLVIII Panzer-Korps and XLII Armee-Korps, averaging one man per 15 yards of front, in a matter of hours. Later that first day, Rybalko's 3rd Guards Tank Army passed through the numerous large penetrations created by the artillery and infantry. Lelyushenko's 4th Guards Tank Army scattered Graeser's counterattack force, XXIV Panzer-Korps, in its assembly areas before it could get out of the way. Across a 25-mile front infantry advanced up to a dozen miles while tank outfits managed double that distance. The

next day Konev's spearheads reached Kielce and he ordered 59th Army to Krakow.

Zhukov struck on 14 January, his main effort coming out of Magnuszew and a supporting attack launching out of the Pulawy bridgehead. They created breakthroughs 10 and 15 miles wide respectively, with infantry advancing up to 10 miles and the tanks an additional 20 miles. The 9. Armee, now under General der Panzertruppen Smilo Freiherr von Lüttwitz, bore the brunt of the attack: its front-line divisions belonging to LVI Panzer-Korps and VIII Armee-Korps lost half their strength in 24 hours. On the 15th, Zhukov's two bridgeheads had blended into one 75 miles wide. North of Warsaw his 47th Army breached the German line at the same time as Zhukov sent Bogdanov's 2nd Guards Tank and 61st Armies around the city from the south. The XLVI Panzer-Korps did not stick around to witness the capital's encirclement. On Zhukov's right, Rokossovsky began overrunning north-central Poland and East Prussia. The 1st Ukrainian Front approached the Germans' third line of defences behind the Pilica River. With the 4th Ukrainian Front to Konev's left covering the city's south, the Red Army had almost surrounded Krakow on three sides. Four days into the offensive, dozens of German divisions, brigades or their *Kampfgruppen* residue had been completely destroyed or captured.

On 16 January, four Soviet fronts continued to drive west across the breadth of Poland without any sort of effective Wehrmacht counter. Hitler had had enough of watching his most critical front disintegrate and so that day relieved Harpe; two days later he would bring in Schörner to work some of his defensive magic. Meanwhile the Germans had lost the entire Vistula front south of Modlin, and Soviet armies rounded up a number of enemy divisions in small pockets throughout Zhukov and Konev's area. Zhukov had trapped the Wehrmacht garrison inside Warsaw, but would leave the difficult job of liberating their capital to the Polish 1st Army. As usual, Hitler suspected cowardice and perfidy in the city's loss, so therefore relieved Lüttwitz and further clamped down on commanders at every level.[152] The primary fronts fanned out to the west in two lobes separated by an indentation along their common boundary. By the 18th, Zhukov had surrounded Lodz on his way to Poznan; Konev finally encircled Krakow and was aiming for Breslau. A day earlier, the Stavka had told both Zhukov and Konev to speed up their attacks toward the Oder River.

---

150 By 1942, the names of German army groups had lost the simple logic of Nord, Mitte and Süd while lacking the geographic orderliness of the Soviet fronts. After *Bagration*, Heeresgruppe Mitte had slipped north of Warsaw, while to its south Heeresgruppe Nordukraine became Heeresgruppe A. On 26 January 1945, in a cruel joke for historians, Mitte became Heeresgruppe Weichsel and A became Heeresgruppe Mitte.

151 On the flanks, the 2nd and 3rd Belorussian fronts would attack East Prussia while the 4th Ukrainian Front hugged the north slope of the Carpathian Mountains and was fighting in north-west Hungary.

152 The new 9. Armee commander was General der Infanterie Theodore Busse, Manstein's old chief of staff. Lüttwitz later commanded a corps in the post-war Bundeswehr.

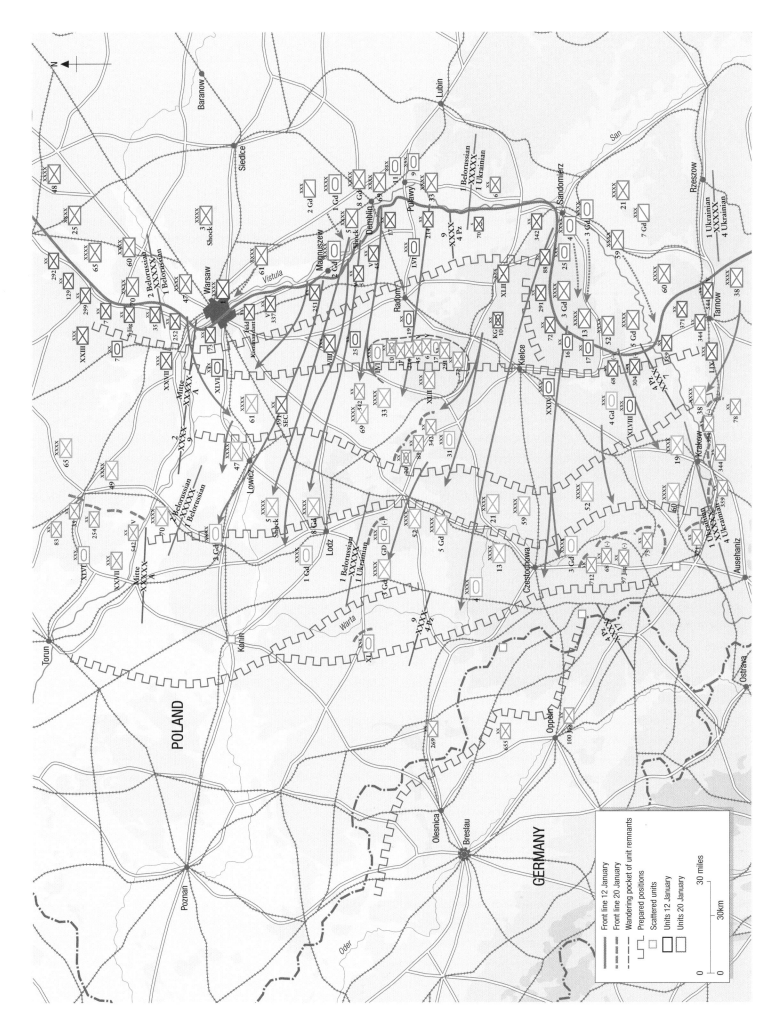

231

MAP 110: VISTULA–ODER OPERATION (II) 21–28 JANUARY, 1945

The Stavka was a harsh taskmaster; on 19 January it again urged on Zhukov and Konev, yet that day the latter was five days ahead of schedule! The Germans had problems of a much more tangible nature. Dozens of divisions, the better part of two armies guarding the direct route to the Fatherland, had vanished, along with most of their elaborate-looking defence in depth. Hitler rushed further dozens of divisions and hundreds of miscellaneous other units toward the rapidly moving front, the Poznan Line. It would remain to be seen if Schörner's Heeresgruppe A could knit this hasty collection into a viable defensive system. The task for the two leading Red Army front commanders would be to break through this line and the next one, the so-called Pomeranian Rampart perhaps 50 miles to the west, before the Wehrmacht occupied it in force. The Germans could offer only sporadic resistance and, with tank armies advancing 25–30 miles per day and field armies approaching 20 miles per day, these missions were not unreasonable.

The 1st Belorussian Front reached portions of the Poznan Line starting the fourth week of January. Busse tried to make a stand along the Bzura River, site of Poland's decisive defeat in 1939, but Bogdanov's 2nd Guards Tank Army brushed the Germans aside. By the 23rd, Bogdanov had cleared Bromberg. A day later, Katukov's 1st Guards Tank Army neared Poznan. At the same time upstream of Breslau, the 1st Ukrainian Front began crossing the Oder River in numerous places. While Konev kept Lelyushenko's 4th Tank Army on a collision course with 4. Panzer-Armee in the Silesian capital, he turned Rybalko 120 degrees to the south-east along with the 1st Guards Cavalry Corps in order to come behind 17. Armee retreating from Krakow. On 22 January, one of Lelyushenko's mechanized brigades created a bridgehead at Steinau north-west of Breslau, meaning that city was already half surrounded. Over the next couple of days, Konev's men reached the Oder everywhere above Glogau. In an act of futility Schörner ordered counterattacks, but his armies lacked the opportunities or resources to execute them.

On 26 January, Hitler re-organized his forces guarding Berlin and paired 2. and 9. Armee to the east and north under the new Armeegruppe Vistula, commanded by Heinrich Himmler of all people, and paired 4. Panzer-Armee and 17. Armee under the latest manifestation of Heeresgruppe Mitte to the south (Map 109, footnote 1). None of these C2 smoke and mirrors tricks slowed down the 1st Belorussian Front. Chuikov's 8th Guards Army, the heroes of Stalingrad, invested Poznan and got ready to besiege its 60,000-man garrison. Zhukov's troops prepared to do the same at other German 'fortresses' of Thorn and Schneidemühl. Toward the end of January a severe blizzard hit central Europe, but this hardly delayed Zhukov. Keen on reaching the Oder River himself, his men entered the Reich in eastern Brandenburg. His dash west created a long and potentially vulnerable right flank, but by 1945 this did not overly concern him. Soon his two tank armies, involved in a race to the west themselves, overran the feeble defences Busse's hard-pressed troops had tried to establish along the Netze and Warthe rivers. On the last day of January Bogdanov reached the Oder below Küstrin, which Hitler demanded be held as a German bridgehead on the river's right bank. Bogdanov's 1st Mechanized Corps crossed the river two days later. South of Frankfurt, Katukov reached the Oder a day behind Bogdanov, but also had a small bridgehead 24 hours later.

Konev continued his assaults on Schörner's 4. Panzer-Armee and 17. Armee manning the central and upper Oder. Arriving from the south to help came Petrov's 4th Ukrainian Front. By 27–28 January, the two fronts had ejected the Wehrmacht from the Silesian industrial basin (no big loss since German industry was not producing much at this stage of the war). Geography and logic meant it no longer made sense to keep 17. Armee fighting the same battle; in late January it began to drift south through the Carpathian passes into Czechoslovakia. At the same time, Kurochkin's 60th Army reached the extermination camp at Auschwitz, confirming the Nazis' bestial 'final solution' for the entire world. In three weeks the Red Army had advanced approximately 350 miles, caused half a million German casualties, destroyed almost 35 enemy divisions and rendered another 25 nearly combat ineffective. Its spearheads stood 40 miles from Berlin.

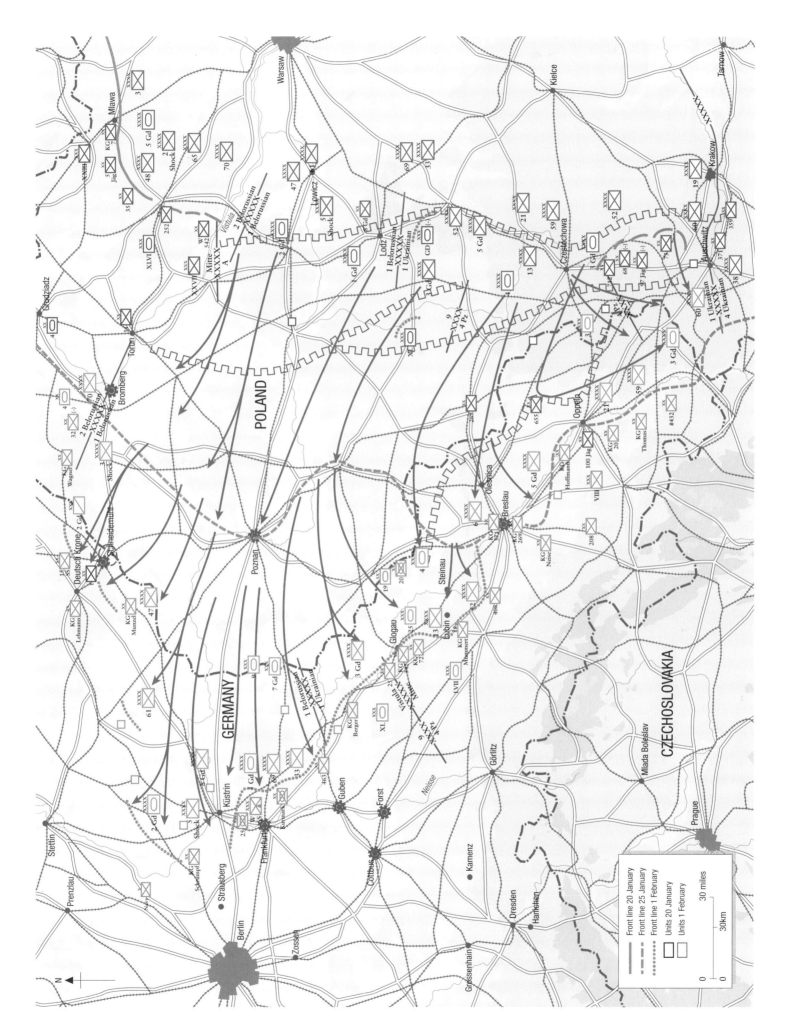

Mlawa

Warsaw

Kielce

Tarnow

Krakow

KG
Jäg

5 Gd

2
Shock

65

70

Grudziadz

252

XLVI

Torun

Bromberg

2 Belorussian
XXXXX
1 Belorussian

32

Schneidemühl

Deutsch Krone

Shock

KG
Wagner

KG
Lehmann

POLAND

Poznan

Mitte
XXXXX
A

Vistula

1 Belorussian
XXXXX
2 Belorussian

Łowicz

5 Shock

Lodz

5 Gd

1 Belorussian
XXXXX
1 Ukrainian

1 Gd

5 Shock

GD

3 Gd

9
XXXX
4 Pz

Czestochowa

Auschwitz

371

60

1 Ukrainian
XXXXX
4 Ukrainian

38

359

21

59

52

3 Gd

68

Jäg

72

76

KG
Thomas

59

21

KG
Hoffmann

100 Jäg

VIII

208

Oppeln

5 Gd

269

Oleśnica

Breslau

KG
51

KG
269

KG
Neisse

GERMANY

7 Gd

3 Gd

KG
Munzel

47

61

Küstrin

Frankfurt

Neumark

Stettin

Prenzlau

Berlin

Zossen

KG
Schümpf

2 Gd

5 Shock

8 Gd

5 Gd

1 Belorussian
XXXXX
1 Ukrainian

KG
Berger

XL

Guben

Forst

Cottbus

Neisse

Görlitz

Kamenz

Dresden

Hamchen

Grössenhain

Glogau

Lubin

KG
72

Mbogmert

XVII

Vistula
XXXXX
NNN

9
XXXX

Steinau

4

20

19

CZECHOSLOVAKIA

Mlada Boleslav

Prague

N

Front line 20 January
Front line 25 January
Front line 1 February
Units 20 January
Units 1 February

0   30 miles

0   30km

233

MAP 111: CONQUEST OF EAST PRUSSIA AND POMERANIA 15 OCTOBER, 1944 TO 22 JANUARY, 1945

EAST PRUSSIA

During the second half of October 1944, the 3rd Belorussian Front tried to rush Königsberg by attacking toward Gumbinnen and Insterburg. The combination of well-prepared positions, fierce defenders and judicious use of panzer counterattacks forced Cherniakhovsky's men to halt after gaining little more than 50 miles, while sustaining heavy losses. Future operations against the German homeland would have to be much more deliberate. As part of the larger Vistula–Oder operation, Cherniakhovsky and Rokossovsky's new attack had two main tasks: firstly to conquer the heavily symbolic East Prussia and its two main cities, Königsberg and Danzig, and secondly to prevent Wehrmacht formations in the region from interfering with Zhukov to the immediate south.[153] Heeresgruppe Mitte, under Reinhardt again, had perhaps 200,000 soldiers in 30 infantry and seven mobile divisions, guarding 360 miles of well-organized and prepared front, quite an achievement for the eastern army in 1945.

The 2nd Belorussian Front would largely avoid the Masurian Lake region and attack with its left to the north-east. While its intermediate objective was Mlawa, its ultimate goal was the mouth of the Vistula. Cherniakhovsky planned to attack straight ahead, above the 4. Armee bulge, slightly north of the Gumbinnen–Insterburg axis toward Königsberg, that he had used the previous autumn. The East Prussian offensive began on 13 January, the day after Konev but a day before Zhukov. The staggered start dates definitely confused the Germans about the Soviets' intentions. The 3rd Belorussian Front moved first. Despite being heavily outnumbered, Raus at 3. Panzer-Armee knew how to fight a defensive battle and a number of towns changed hands more than once that day. The 2nd Belorussian Front attacked a day later, on the 14th, and had the bad fortune of running into Panzer-Korps Grossdeutschland, one of the remaining quality units in the Wehrmacht. As the crisis in central Poland worsened, Hitler sent the panzer corps in that direction, suddenly making Rokossovsky's job much easier. However, any unobstructed movement came to a halt when his troops hit the Mlawa Fortified Region, designated by Hitler as a fortress. On the northern edge of the offensive, Cherniakhovsky shifted his main effort in an attempt to gain freedom of manoeuvre, eventually opening a route over the frozen marshes in the area. By 18 January he had advanced almost 30 miles while Rokossovsky had gained over 50, small progress compared to Zhukov and Konev.

The offensive had stretched German defences to their limits –

Reinhardt had few mobile reserves left. Soldiers fought alongside Kriegsmarine and Luftwaffe men and untrained Home Guard and *Volkssturm* levies. On 19 January the 2nd Belorussian Front broke out across most of its front, in some places covering 40 miles that day; the 3rd Guards Cavalry Corps crossed the Prussian border on the road from Mlawa to Allenstein. Against 3. Panzer-Armee, Cherniakhovsky's 39th Army captured Insterberg. Everywhere the Germans fell back, retreating past prepared 'fortified regions' without halting – and without telling Hitler. Raus began withdrawing to Königsberg on the 20th, and the next day Weiss lost the Tannenberg battlefield, with its shrine to Hindenburg, to Rokossovsky. Simultaneously the 2nd Ukrainian Front advance guard reached Deutsch Eylau, 60 miles from the Gulf of Danzig. On the 22nd, to avoid destruction of his 4. Armee, General der Infanterie Friedrich Hossbach – on his own initiative – began withdrawing from the salient between 3. Panzer-Armee and 2. Armee. After constantly constricting the East Prussian perimeter, 5th Guards Tank Army soldiers reached the coast on 26 January, cutting off the remains of two and a half German armies.[154]

POMERANIA

When 5th Guards Tank took Tolkemit headquarters near the mouth of the Vistula, 2. Armee and three corps were to the west, and Himmler's Armeegruppe Vistula absorbed them.[155] The Germans had been sniping at Zhukov's right flank, but the isolation of Königsberg freed the 2nd Belorussian Front to help address this threat, as had been foreseen by the Stavka's original plans. On 10 February Rokossovsky launched a new attack centred on Grudziadz, but in two weeks gained only 25 miles. Rokossovsky (reinforced from Finland!) and Zhukov opened a new offensive along their entire common 240-mile front on the 24th. The two juggernauts encircled hapless German defenders unlucky enough to be caught between them at Deutsch Krone, Dramburg and Belgard before entrapping a larger garrison at Kolberg. On 4 March, Rokossovsky took control of the entire Pomeranian operation so Zhukov could concentrate on Berlin. His forces fanned out and resistance in the area collapsed by the end of the month. Kolberg capitulated on the 18th and Danzig fell on the 28th.

154 This meant the end of Heeresgruppe Mitte, re-named Nord, and Reinhardt (who also suffered a severe head wound on the 25th while inspecting the front), who was replaced by Rendulic, and Hossbach, who was replaced by General der Infanterie Friedrich-Wilhelm Müller.

155 Armeegruppe Vistula included the re-born 11. Armee, often referred to by its unofficial name, 11. SS Panzer-Armee.

153 Bagramian's 2nd Baltic Front, still heavily engaged against Armeegruppe Kurland, contributed one army against Memel and another against Tilsit.

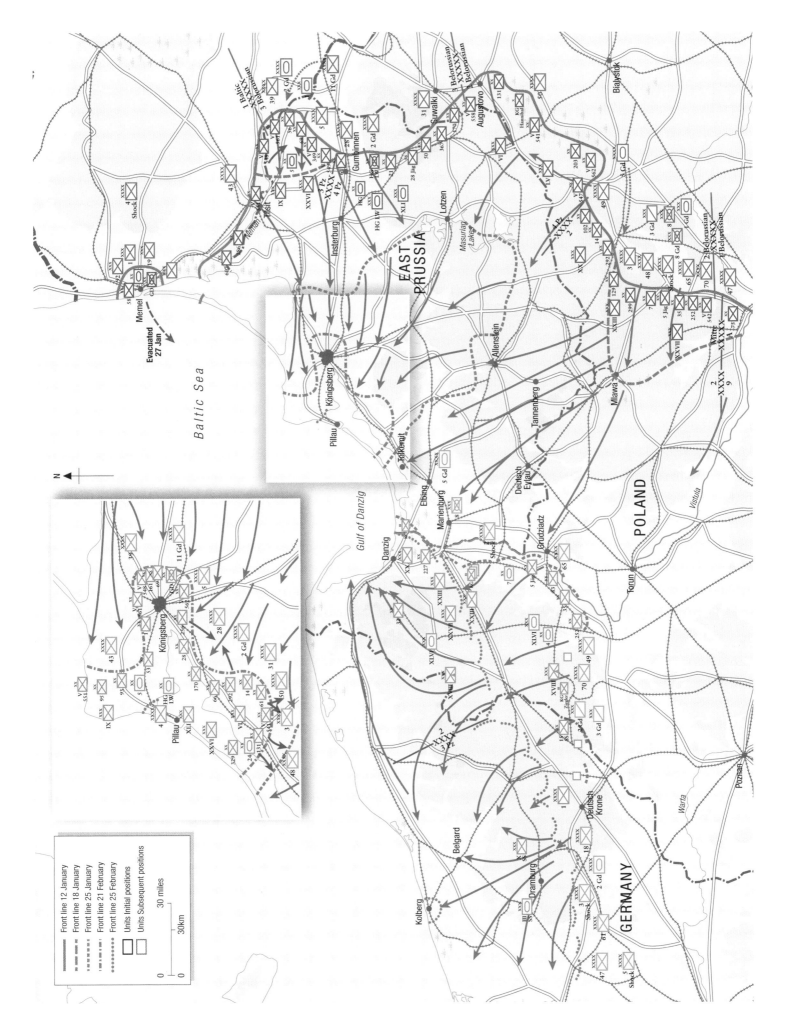

Baltic Sea

EAST PRUSSIA

POLAND

GERMANY

Gulf of Danzig

Königsberg

Pillau

Tolkemit

Danzig

Elbing

Marienburg

Grudziadz

Torun

Poznan

Allenstein

Tannenberg

Deutsch Eylau

Mlawa

Bialystok

Suwalki

Augustovo

Gumbinnen

Insterburg

Tilsit

Memel

Lotzen

Masurian Lakes

Deutsch Krone

Belgard

Kolberg

Dramburg

Vistula

Warta

Evacuated 27 Jan

N

Front line 12 January
Front line 18 January
Front line 25 January
Front line 21 February
Front line 25 February
Units Initial positions
Units Subsequent positions

30 miles
30km

235

MAPS 112 & 113: KÖNIGSBERG AND BRESLAU

Not all of Hitler's decisions to leave behind forlorn 'fortresses' were nonsensical. For example, it is common wisdom that the resistance of the large garrison abandoned at Stalingrad made possible the subsequent escape of much of Heeresgruppen A and B. Likewise, his decision to defend Königsberg and Breslau, on the northern and southern flanks of the Vistula–Oder operation, significantly delayed the final assault on Berlin and possibly extended World War II by at least one month.

MAP 112, KÖNIGSBERG – 13 MARCH TO 8 APRIL, 1945

The Baltic port city, Teutonic Knight outpost, capital of Prussia, site of coronations and burials of Hohenzollern kings, home of Immanuel Kant and symbol of resistance to Napoleon, represented a cultural cornerstone for Germany. Therefore it was important to both dictators: Hitler wanted to hold on to it, Stalin wanted to capture it. Three Red Army fronts first attacked, then isolated, and then commenced squeezing Königsberg and its hinterland, hoping finally to destroy it. Because of its inland position, the Wehrmacht had to protect more than just the city, but also the nearby port of Pillau. A big difference in the story of these two fortress cities is the role of the Kriegsmarine in the Battle for Königsberg. At about the same time in late January as the Soviets cut off East Prussia, Hitler relented and allowed the XXVIII Armee-Korps to evacuate Memel and reinforce Pillau as Group Samland. General Rendulic commanded Heeresgruppe Nord, two armies and initially 23 divisions in a 40-mile perimeter.[156] Approximately 100,000 troops, 4,000 guns, 100 AFVs and 170 aircraft defended the fortress.

Cherniakhovsky's 3rd Belorussian Front, with the 1st Baltic Front subordinated to him, had the mission of capturing Königsberg with about 130,000 men, 5,200 pieces of artillery, over 500 AFVs and 2,100 aircraft.[157] The Soviets did not put February to good use. After initially cutting direct communications between Königsberg and Pillau, they permitted the Germans to restore the overland connection and to build up supplies in the fortress while Vasilevski planned his assault.[158] On 13 March the Soviets attacked against Heiligenbeil to the city's south (off map), but in five days made minimal progress in the face of stout defences. The East Prussian evacuations continued, including the remaining panzer division (7. Panzer-Division), weakening 4. Armee. Vasilevski attacked again on 6 April. Following a large air bombardment, 30 divisions of the 39th, 43rd, 50th and 11th Guards Armies assaulted heavily fortified German positions. For the next two days fighting was fierce and Red Army pioneers were at a premium. On 8 April, 43rd and 11th Guards Army soldiers met, having cut off the Samland. Germans in Königsberg surrendered near midnight on the 9th. Approximately 22,000 made it to Pillau and organized a hasty defence, which held out until VE Day.

MAP 113, BRESLAU – 14 FEBRUARY TO 8 MAY, 1945

The capital of Silesia evoked Frederick the Great, who took the province from Maria Theresa in 1740–41, setting Prussia on the road to becoming a European power. In late January, 4. Panzer-Armee maintained a bridgehead there, but Konev's 6th and 5th Guards Armies surrounded Breslau on 14 February. The front commander sent Rybalko's 3rd Guards Tank Army counterclockwise from Steinau to create a deep encirclement and ensure that the city would not impede his progress toward Berlin. On the next day the Luftwaffe began flying in supplies to the 40,000-soldier garrison, often using the city's wide boulevards as airstrips and losing 165 Ju52s in three months. Nazi Party organs had evacuated many civilians, but well over 100,000 remained and would pay a terrible price. Two genuine infantry divisions, 269. and 371. Infanterie-Divisionen, received orders to break out of the pocket, but only portions of them ever made it out and the remaining *Kampfgruppen* took their places manning the line. The ad hoc 609. Infanterie-Division added to the defence; it consisted of soldiers, sailors, airmen, SS, police, Hitler Youth, *Volkssturm* and other paramilitary groups using ordnance from every corner of Europe.

Outside stood General Lieutenant V. A. Gluzdovsky's 6th Army, tasked with conducting the siege. However, Konev never allowed the 6th Army to lead the all-out assault on the city that its commander wanted; instead, artillery and air power pounded the city. Nazi Gauleiter Karl Hanke did not hesitate to sacrifice the civilian population. He had the fortress's first military commandant replaced in early March because the general showed more concern for reducing hardships for the trapped garrison and its inhabitants than in fanatic resistance. Hanke abandoned Breslau in early May to replace Himmler as Reichsführer-SS. The fortress also surrendered on VE Day.

---

156 General Raus and headquarters 3. Panzer-Armee transferred to Pomerania in mid-February.

157 Bagramian had fallen from favour, so Stalin downgraded his 1st Baltic Front to the Samland Group of 3rd Belorussian Front. Cherniakhovsky, Stalin's only Jewish marshal, died in action leading from the front on 18 February; Marshal Vasilevski replaced him.

158 On 10 March, Rendulic returned to command Armeegruppe Kurland, replaced two days later by Weiss whose 2. Armee had been destroyed in Pomerania.

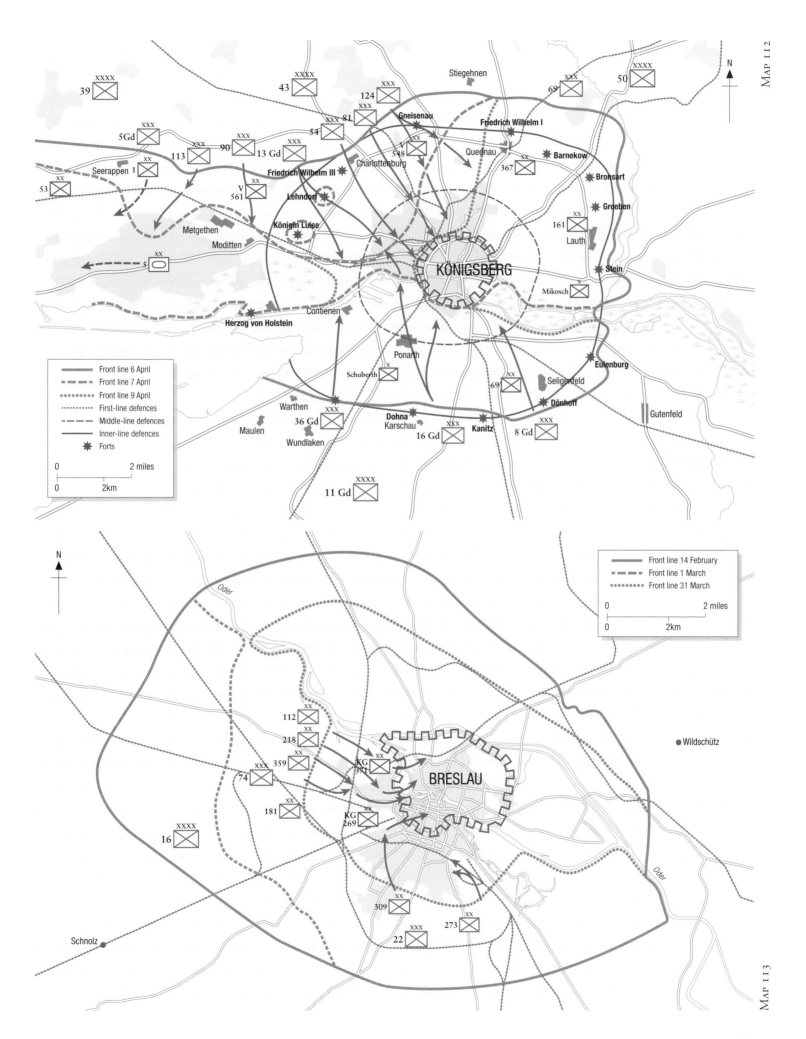

MAP 112

Map 112 (Königsberg)

XXXX 39

XXXX 43

XXX 124

XXX 69

XXXX 50

Stiegehnen

XXX 81

Gneisenau

Friedrich Wilhelm I

XXX 54

V 548

XXX 5Gd

XXX 90

XXX 13 Gd

Quednau

Barnekow

XX 367

XXX 113

Charlottenburg

Bronsart

XX Seerappen 1

Friedrich Wilhelm III

Groeben

XX 53

V 561

Lehndorf

XX 161

Lauth

Metgethen

Königin Luise

Moditten

Stein

XX 5

Mikosch x

KÖNIGSBERG

Contienen

Eulenburg

Herzog von Holstein

Ponarth

XX 69

Seligenfeld

Schuberth x

Dönhoff

Warthen

Gutenfeld

Maulen

XXX 36 Gd

Dohna
Karschau

XXX 16 Gd

Kanitz

XXX 8 Gd

Wundlaken

XXXX 11 Gd

Front line 6 April
Front line 7 April
Front line 9 April
First-line defences
Middle-line defences
Inner-line defences
✳ Forts

0 ___ 2 miles
0 ___ 2km

Map 113 (Breslau)

N

Oder

Front line 14 February
Front line 1 March
Front line 31 March

0 ___ 2 miles
0 ___ 2km

XX 112

XX 218

XX KG 551

XX 359

XXX 74

● Wildschütz

XX 181

XX KG 269

BRESLAU

XXXX 16

Oder

XX 309

XX 273

XXX 22

Schnolz ●

MAP 113

237

MAP 114: SIEGE OF BUDAPEST 28 DECEMBER, 1944 TO 11 FEBRUARY, 1945

Hitler did not like to give ground in any case, but as a son of the old Austro-Hungarian Empire, he may have been even more hesitant to turn away from Budapest, a key part of his eastern defence. On 12 October, a Hungarian delegation tried to make peace with the Soviet Union, but a German coup four days later put an end to such talk; on the 24th the Stavka told its soldiers to treat Germans and Hungarians the same. Throughout November and early December, Malinovsky and Tolbukhin's men made two attempts to capture Budapest on the cheap, but Axis defences were too strong. The 2nd and 3rd Ukrainian fronts began their third and more deliberate assault in earnest on 20 December, encircling the city on the 26th (Map 106). Hitler held Friessner and Fretter-Pico responsible for the debacle, relieving both on the 22nd. In late December, just days after taking command of the reeling Heeresgruppe Mitte, Wöhler asked his Führer only to hold Buda, the smaller, hilly western part of the capital, but Hitler wanted to hold the entire place.[159]

Axis forces in Budapest consisted of the relatively new IX SS Gebirgs-Korps headquarters with 13. Panzer-Division and Panzer-Grenadier-Division Feldherrnhalle, 8. SS Kavallerie-Division Florian Geyer and 22. SS-Freiwilligen-Kavallerie-Division Maria Theresa, elements of 271. Volks-Grenadier-Division and numerous police units, plus the Hungarian I Corps headquarters with their 10th, 12th and 20th Infantry and 1st Armoured divisions, along with many regiments, battalions and gendarmerie units and Arrow-Cross Party militias.[160] Together they totalled approximately 130,000 men under SS Obergruppenführer Paul Pfeffer-Wildenbruch. Around 800,000 Hungarian civilians were also trapped in the capital. Outside initially conducting the siege were 16 Soviet and two Romanian rifle divisions, two tank divisions and other smaller units. Despite German relief attacks meant to raise the siege from the west, Malinovsky's men pushed forward.

The 7th Guards Army's main attack would come from the direction of Pest. During the last couple of days of December and the first week of January, the 30th and 18th Rifle Corps with the 7th Romanian Corps made slow but steady progress through the city's eastern outskirts. West of the Danube in Buda, however, well-organized Axis defences made Soviet assaults prohibitively costly. Red Army casualties mounted in Pest as well, but by 7 January attacks through the Rakospalota and Kispest neighbourhoods had advanced miles, shrinking the Axis holdings by half. During a lull in the action, Malinovsky suggested a new unified command take charge of the Budapest siege. The Stavka took his recommendation, placing the battle under 18th Corps' General Major I. M. Afonin on 11 January. He received orders to drive due west down the main thoroughfare, Kerepesi Street, into the heart of the government quarter on the Danube, and moved out on the 12th. A day later his men had fought to a point halfway to the river, finally reaching the banks of the Danube on 14 January. The defences had been split into three parts, northern and southern Pest plus Buda. Seeing this, the disheartened Hungarians began to surrender in large numbers. By 18 January Malinovsky declared Pest cleared of Axis troops, with over 33,000 killed and nearly twice that number captured.

During the third week of January, the Stavka gave the mission of taking Buda to Tolbukhin's 75th and 37th Corps, but a new German relief effort from west of the capital, Operation *Konrad III*, made the attack quite problematic. Therefore Malinovsky's men received the additional task of capturing Buda as well.[161] The new assault began in late January and made substantial gains in the north through the end of the month. In early February, Managarov shifted his main effort to the south and quickly surrounded the Germans on Sashegy Hill. His men eliminated these positions within 48 hours and squeezed the remaining Axis-held areas toward Castle Hill. These final assaults caused an additional 20,000 Axis casualties and broke the back of the resistance, which ended on 11 February. Another 70,000 troops marched off as POWs. Some Germans attempted to escape to the north-west along the Lipotmezo River, but were intercepted and eliminated. Worst off were the citizens of Budapest, especially women, who the Red Army made to regret ever going to war against the USSR.

---

159 Raus replaced Fretter-Pico at 6. Armee and the re-named Armeegruppe Raus.

160 During these battles Feldherrnhalle is also referred to as a Panzer-Grenadier division, although technically on 27 November it converted to a Panzer outfit.

161 During the second half of January Afonin had been wounded; 53rd Army's General Lieutenant I. M. Managarov took his place.

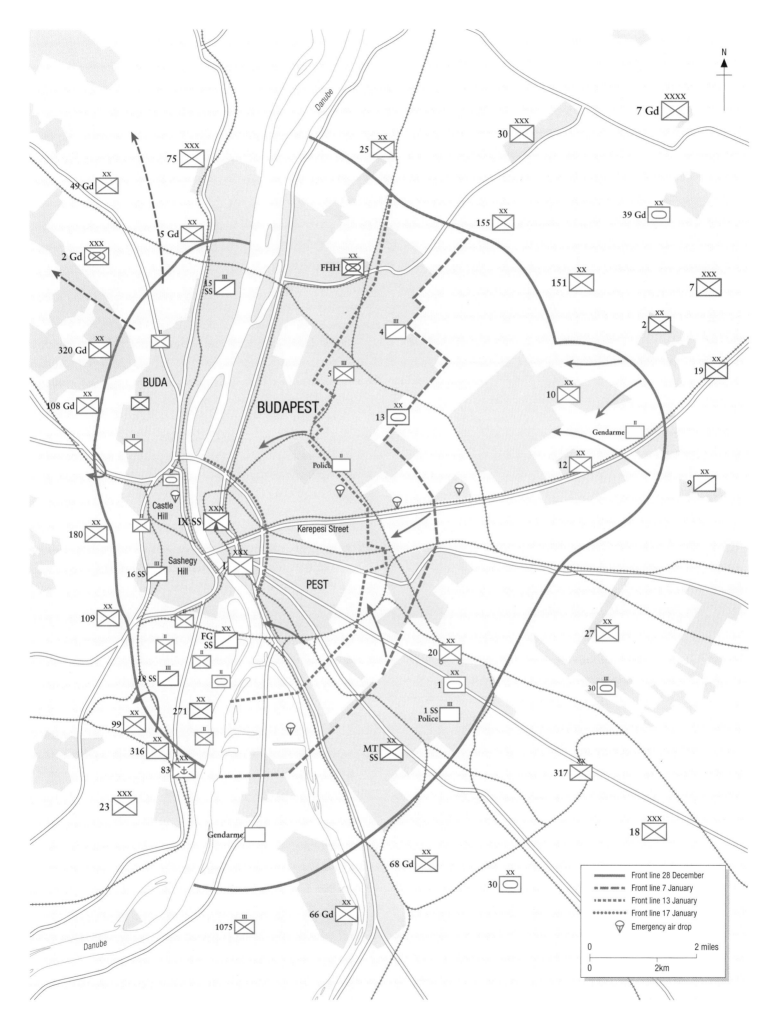

Danube

N

7 Gd
XXXX

30
XXX

25
XX

75
XXX

39 Gd
XX

49 Gd
XX

155
XX

5 Gd
XX

151
XX

7
XXX

2 Gd
XXX

FHH
XX

15
SS
III

4
III

2
XX

320 Gd
XX

II

5
III

19
XX

BUDA

BUDAPEST

10
XX

II

108 Gd
XX

13
XX

Gendarme
II

II

12
XX

9
XX

Police
II

Castle
Hill

XXN

IX SS

Kerepesi Street

180
XX

II

XXX

27
XX

16 SS
III

Sashegy
Hill

I

PEST

109
XX

II

20
XX

FG
SS
XX

1
XX

30
III

II

II

18 SS
III

1 SS
Police
III

271
XX

99
XX

II

MT
SS
XX

316
XX

317
XX

83
XX

23
XXX

18
XXX

Gendarme

68 Gd
XX

30
XX

66 Gd
XX

1075
III

Danube

Front line 28 December
Front line 7 January
Front line 13 January
Front line 17 January
Emergency air drop

0   2 miles
0   2km

239

MAPS 115 & 116: BUDAPEST PANZER COUNTERATTACKS – 1–27 JANUARY, 1945

As mentioned previously, Hitler's encircled pockets were a multi-stage process. Firstly, he would order a force to stay put in an isolated position and relieve some commanders, secondly the Luftwaffe would fly in inadequate supplies at a terrible cost, then a relief force would be assembled and a counterattack with low chances of success launched, and finally the process would end in death and captivity for the garrison. So it was with Budapest. Almost as soon as the 2nd and 3rd Ukrainian fronts cut off the capital, Hitler launched his first rescue counterattack. On 22 December, the same day he dismissed Friessner and Fretter-Pico, he ordered SS Obergruppenführer Herbert Gille's IV SS Panzer-Korps (3. SS Panzer-Division (Mot.) Totenkopf and 5. SS Panzer-Grenadier-Division Wiking) by rail from Bratislava to Komarom.

MAP 115: OPERATION *KONRAD*

Gille attacked on New Year's Day from Tata south-east; the capital's centre was 35 miles away. Totenkopf and Wiking were the obvious *Schwerpunkt*, with 96. Infanterie-Division on their left and Group Pape (elements of 6. and 8. Panzer-Divisionen) covering their right. They immediately caused problems for 4th Guards Army's 31st Rifle Corps, but could not capitalize on these. In four days they had advanced a dozen miles, but the Soviets always managed to throw just enough in their way. After 48 hours more they managed to gain another 4–5 miles, but had to cover as much ground again before they could reach Pfeffer-Wildenbruch, commanding the IX SS Gebirgs-Korps. North of the Danube, the 6th Guards Tank and 7th Guards Armies counterattacked toward Gille's rear at Komarom on 6 January; the remainder of 8. Panzer-Division there managed to turn them back. The Soviets in front of Totenkopf and Wiking not only halted them but also launched local countermoves. The IV SS Panzer-Korps was finished, except for 96. Infanterie-Division's one-regiment push in the north along the Danube's southern bank. This manoeuvre picked up some ground by the 8th, but cannot be considered a serious threat.

To the right of the SS, on 7 January I Kavallerie-Korps attacked north of Szekesfehervar with 3., 23. and 1. Panzer-Divisionen. The Germans had hoped to catch the Soviets napping, but instead hit three guards rifle corps and a mechanized corps with no plans on leaving. The 23. Panzer-Division's 5 miles gained represented the high point of the attack. The

first relief efforts were a flop. Hitler then pulled Gille out of his salient and sent him south on a 70-mile road march in miserable winter weather.

South of Szekesfehervar, IV SS Panzer-Korps attacked again, this time with 1. Panzer-Division on the left and 3. Panzer-Division on the right. Starting on 18 January, it had reached the Sarviz Canal by nightfall. By the afternoon of the 19th, 3. Panzer-Division had reached the Danube at Dunapentele. The next day, with Lake Valencze covering its left, 1. Panzer-Division reached a point 20 miles from its comrades in Budapest. Once again Soviet defences stiffened, and in another week of fighting against the 2nd Guards Rifle Corps, Totenkopf got perhaps 5 miles closer. Only a dozen miles separated the SS from their penetration of earlier that month. This later attempt came up short as well.

MAP 116: OPERATION *FRÜHLINGSERWACHEN* (*SPRING AWAKENING*)

In late January and February, Tolbukhin's troops pushed the SS bulge south of Szekesfehervar 15 miles back and away from the Danube. Meanwhile Budapest fell, and, following the failure of his Ardennes offensive, Hitler found himself with an operational reserve and no place to squander it. This was SS Oberst-Obergruppenführer Sepp Dietrich's 6. SS Panzer-Armee – the I SS Panzer-Korps under Obergruppenführer Hermann Priess and II SS Panzer-Korps under Obergruppenführer Wilhelm Bittrich up the centre and I Kavallerie-Korps to the right. The 6. Armee under Raus sent Breith's III Panzer-Korps to the left just below Szekesfehervar.

Operation *Frühlingserwachen* began on 6 March with I SS Panzer-Korps and on the next day with II SS Panzer-Korps. For 48 hours the SSLAH made remarkable progress west of the Sarviz Canal despite the obstacles presented by thick mud. East of the canal II SS and III Panzer-Korps took much less ground, perhaps 5 miles in as many days. Tolbukhin launched counterattacks by three corps against Bittrich, particularly the spearheads of Das Reich. The Germans advanced for the next couple of days, most of the way up the shore of Lake Valencze (III Panzer-Korps) and closing up to the Sio Canal most of the way to Lake Balaton (II SS Panzer-Korps and I Kavallerie-Korps). With the Wehrmacht in these dangerous positions, the Red Army attacked toward Vienna on 16 March.

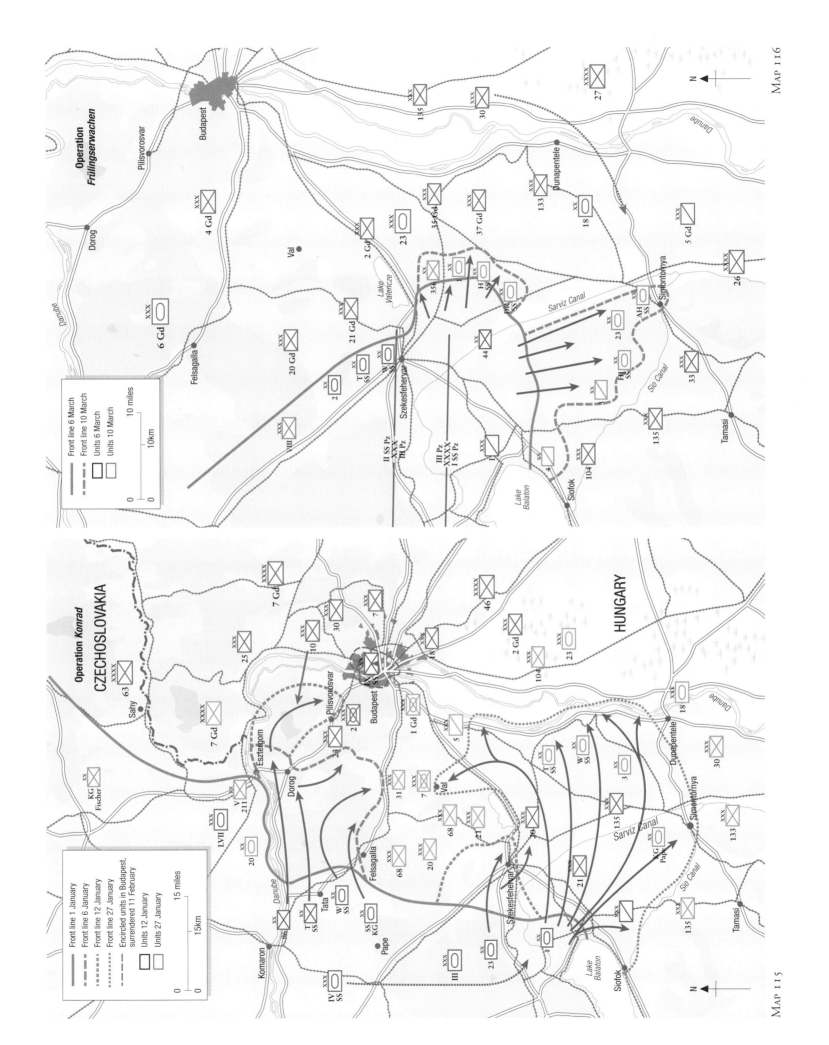

Operation Frülingserwachen

Front line 6 March
Front line 10 March

Units 6 March
Units 10 March

10km
10 miles

Lake Velencze

Sarviz Canal

Sio Canal

Lake Balaton

Danube

Danube

Dorog
Pilisvorosvar
Budapest
Val
Felsagalla
Szekesfehervar
Simontornya
Siofok
Tamasi
Dunapentele

II SS Pz
III Pz
III Pz
I SS Pz

Operation Konrad

CZECHOSLOVAKIA

HUNGARY

Front line 1 January
Front line 6 January
Front line 12 January
Front line 27 January
Encircled units in Budapest,
surrendered 11 February

Units 12 January
Units 27 January

15km
15 miles

Sahy
Komaron
Tata
Pape
Esztergom
Dorog
Pilisvorosvar
Budapest
Felsagalla
Val
Szekesfehervar
Dunapentele
Simontornya
Siofok
Tamasi

Danube

Sarviz Canal

Sio Canal

Lake Balaton

KG Fischer
KG Pape
KG

Map 116

Map 115

241

MAP 117: CONQUEST OF VIENNA 16 MARCH TO 13 APRIL, 1945

The Stavka saw the big picture, not only on the Danube plain but also in front of Berlin. Therefore it did not share the front commanders' concern over Dietrich's desperate gamble, nor did they allow it to slow them down by more than 24 hours. Not only were the Red Army defences very capable of halting the attack, but Malinovsky and Tolbukhin had four relatively fresh armies standing by to renew the offensive into Austria: 46th, 9th Guards, 4th Guards and 6th Guards Tank Armies. Six field armies (one of them a guards army) and numerous Romanian, Bulgarian and Yugoslavian armies plus the 1st Guards Cavalry-Mechanized Groups manned the second echelon. They did not even wait for the German manoeuvre to culminate, but attacked into the panzer spearheads on 16 March.

The 3rd Ukrainian Front, the main effort, moved out first on 16 March against 6. SS Panzer-Armee at Szekesfehervar with the objective of crushing the SS east of Lake Balaton. The 2nd Ukrainian Front followed two days later; the commanders of the two fronts would have loved to encircle Dietrich's army between them. The Germans offered feeble resistance and the Hungarians even less. Just days into the offensive, the Stavka gave 6th Guards Tank Army to Tolbukhin with orders to break into the open as soon as possible. By 22 March, weather and terrain conspired to slow the Soviets as it had the Germans just days earlier. With the gap between the two pincers only a mile apart, Dietrich managed to extricate the bulk of his SS men. Kravchenko's tankers were either not ready in time or just a bit too slow to close off the trap. Nevertheless, Szekesfehervar fell on the 20th. To the north, Malinovsky expanded the right shoulder of the attack past Komarom and Esztergom against the Hungarian Third Army; the former held out until 30 March, the latter could not. Nevertheless, by the 23rd Wehrmacht forces stood on the brink of disintegration. They prepared to give up their current untenable positions and fall back to the Raba River. On 25 March, north of the Danube, Malinovsky launched a broad attack where his 40th and 7th Guards Armies overcame the 8. Armee's Hron River line. With substantial CAS, he passed Pliev's 1st Guards Cavalry-Mechanized

Group through the breach and on its way to Bratislava.

The Soviets' real success came in the south, however, as Tolbukhin overwhelmed the Germans. South of Lake Balaton the 57th Army levered 2. Panzer-Armee off the Nagykanizsa oilfields, the last source of natural petroleum for Third Reich. West of Budapest at Papa, the 4th and 9th Guards Armies and 6th Guards Tank Army smashed the boundary between 6. Armee and 6. SS Panzer-Armee on 27 March. German attempts by Balck and Dietrich to make a stand along the Raba succumbed to the massive Red Army assault. On the first day of April, the sledgehammer represented by Tolbukhin's three guards armies blasted through Soropom and entered Austria. On the 2nd, these armies made for Wiener Neustadt while Malinovsky's men went north of Lake Neusiedler, where Austria, Czechoslovakia and Hungary come together. Wehrmacht rearguards could do little more than snipe at Tolbukhin's troops as they drove by. In early April, the Stavka made plans to encircle and capture Vienna and to continue west into the heart of the Reich. Hitler took the predictable step of naming Vienna a fortress. With the help of the Danube Flotilla, Malinovsky moved the 46th Army north of the river, with the mission of surrounding Vienna from the north. Tolbukhin's 4th Guards would make a direct assault on the city from the south as the 6th Guards Tank Army swung around clockwise for the deep encirclement.

Soldiers of the 4th Guards Army fought vicious battles in the southern outskirts against determined defenders. By 8 April the Ringstrasse had become a battlefield and many of the city's famous landmarks went up in smoke, but Vienna would not become a charred hulk like so many of Hitler's other fortresses. On the 13th, the Soviets declared the capital free of Germans and began to prepare for operations to the west. As Wöhler had told Hitler a few days earlier, after Stalingrad and Budapest the *Landser*s' hearts were just not ready for a third titanic city fight. In mid-April the front generally fell silent from St Polten to the west of Graz to Maribor, and would not move much before the war's end.

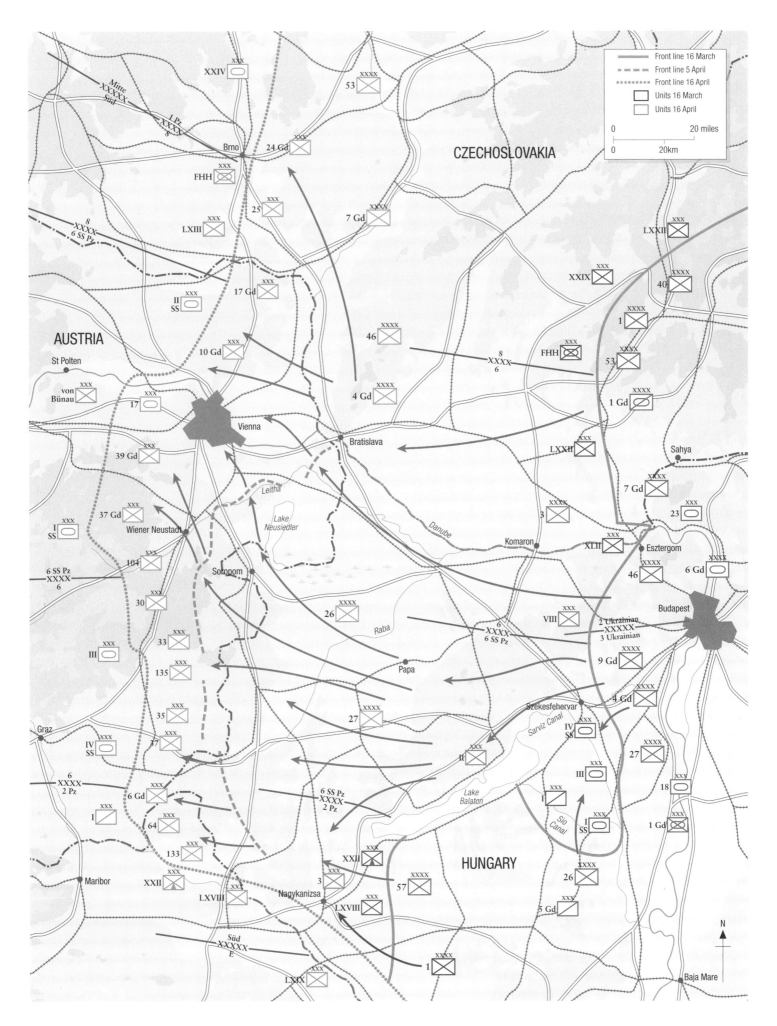

CZECHOSLOVAKIA

AUSTRIA

HUNGARY

St Polten

Brno

Vienna

Bratislava

Komaron

Esztergom

Budapest

Sahya

Wiener Neustadt

Sopron

Papa

Szekesfehervar

Graz

Maribor

Nagykanizsa

Baja Mare

Lake
Neusiedler

Leitha

Danube

Raba

Lake
Balaton

Sio
Canal

Sarviz Canal

Mitte
XXXXX
Süd

1 Pz
XXXX
8

8
XXXX
6 SS Pz

6 SS Pz
XXXX
6

6
XXXX
2 Pz

Süd
XXXXX
E

8
XXXX
6

2 Ukrainian
XXXXX
3 Ukrainian

6
XXXX
6 SS Pz

6 SS Pz
XXXX
2 Pz

XXIV

24 Gd

FHH

25

LXIII

II
SS

17 Gd

10 Gd

von
Bünau

39 Gd

37 Gd

I
SS

104

III

30

33

135

35

57

IV
SS

6 Gd

I

64

133

XXII

LXVIII

17

53

7 Gd

46

4 Gd

26

27

22

3

57

LXIX

LXXII

XXIX

40

1

FHH

53

1 Gd

LXXII

7 Gd

23

XLII

46

6 Gd

VIII

9 Gd

4 Gd

IV
SS

III

I

I
SS

27

18

1 Gd

26

5 Gd

1

Front line 16 March
Front line 5 April
Front line 16 April
Units 16 March
Units 16 April

0   20 miles
0   20km

N

243

MAP 118: CONQUEST OF BOHEMIA AND MORAVIA – 10 MARCH TO 9 MAY, 1945

Czechoslovakia, where the first shots of World War II probably should have been fired in 1938, saw some of its last fighting in 1945. During the summer of 1944, while Stalin first drove toward Warsaw and then through Romania and Hungary, Hitler's small ally Slovakia remained a backwater. Pursued by Petrov's 4th Ukrainian Front, that autumn Heinrici's 1. Panzer-Armee fought its way west, aided by terrain that favoured the defenders. That winter, as the fighting fronts on his north moved west to the Oder River and on south past Budapest, 1. Panzer-Armee jutted out dangerously to the east, but pulled back slowly through January and February. Petrov attacked on 10 March, but made plodding advances thanks to poor artillery co-ordination and the German defences. After gaining about one mile per day for a week, the Stavka replaced him in favour of Eremenko. On the 24th, he renewed the attack with the 38th Army, which did not do much better. Wehrmacht positions around the Moravska–Ostrava industrial area, considerably built up, simply represented a riddle the Red Army could not easily solve. The Stavka reinforced Eremenko with the 60th and 18th Armies and forcefully ordered him to take Moravska–Ostrava immediately. Once that was done, together with Malinovsky he would encircle 1. Panzer-Armee by joining forces at Olomouc.

On 15 April, the 4th Ukrainian Front assaulted the German positions with a 2:1 superiority in divisions and 6,000 guns in support. The 60th and 38th Armies came around from the north-east while the 18th Army attacked from the south-east. The Stavka gave Eremenko three days to overcome the redoubt, but by the 22nd he had captured only Opava. The 1. Panzer-Armee, now under General der Panzertruppen Walther Nehring, defended these positions until the 24th, but then his men could take no more. By now Malinovsky was coming north via Brno with the 53rd Army, 6th Guards Tank Army and Pliev's 1st Guards Cavalry-Mechanized Group. Nehring temporarily blunted Kravchenko's armoured advance with two panzer divisions on the Napoleonic battlefield of Austerlitz (a dozen miles east of Brno), but could not halt the inevitable. On 25 April the two Ukrainian fronts

indeed met at Olomouc, but not before the bulk of 1. Panzer-Armee had escaped. A stay-behind force defended Moravska–Ostrava, just inside Moravia, until the end of April. So far, the Czechoslovakian campaign had cost the Soviets 180,000 casualties.

Stalin now gave Konev, deeply involved in the battle for Berlin, the additional task of turning large portions of his 1st Ukrainian Front south from Saxony to attack over the Sudeten Mountains into Bohemia. The dictator had an eye toward the post-war world, so had Konev turn over parts of his forces fighting in the German capital to Zhukov. The 1st Ukrainian Front committed the 3rd Guards, 5th Guards and 13th Armies, the 3rd Guards Tank and 4th Guards Tank Armies reinforced by five artillery divisions. The 4th Ukrainian Front contributed four field armies coming from the direction of Moravska–Ostrava, while 2nd Ukrainian Front attacked from the Brno region with three field and one guards tank armies. Even the 3rd Ukrainian Front, in south-east Austria, sent its 9th Guards Army. The three-sided offensive included more than 150 divisions backed up by 24,500 guns, 2,100 AFVs and 4,000 aircraft, plus Czech, Polish and Romanian formations. The American Third Army pressed from the south-west. Inside, Schörner's 8. and 9. Armeen and 1. and 4. Panzer-Armeen would conduct the near-hopeless defence.

Not knowing that World War II in Europe was only days from ending, the onslaught began on 5 May. Speed was of the essence, so Konev and Malinovsky's three guards tank armies came barrelling down on Prague from the north-west and south-east. Eremenko created the 60th and 38th Army Mobile Groups, truck-mounted riflemen based on the two armies, to increase his mobility. Red Army soldiers discovered almost no Germans willing to fight back. Along with the Americans, they pushed on toward the Czech capital, where a national liberation committee rose up against the occupiers. While top Wehrmacht officers elsewhere negotiated an armistice, the fanatic Schörner continued to fight. The SS inside Prague offered the only real German resistance. Crushed from all sides, Prague surrendered on 9 May, the day after the rest of Europe.

MAP 119: BATTLE OF SEELOW HEIGHTS 16–19 APRIL, 1945

The 1st Belorussian and 1st Ukrainian Fronts reached the Oder River on 31 January and established small bridgeheads on the left bank, starting the next day. The Red Army spent the next ten weeks securing its operational flanks in East Prussia, Pomerania, Silesia and beyond the Carpathian Mountains. The Soviets brought their logistics trains forward and planned for the final battle against the capital of Hitler's 12-year Reich. By the end of March, the 2nd Belorussian Front had pulled up to the mouth of the Oder, parallel with the other two fronts.

For the assault on Berlin, marshals Rokossovsky, Zhukov and Konev together had 2.5 million soldiers, more than 41,000 artillery pieces, 6,250 AFVs and 7,500 aircraft. The 1st Belorussian Front would lead the way from its 25-mile wide Küstrin bridgehead. Zhukov crammed the 47th, 3rd and 5th Shock, 8th Guards and 69th Armies into the crowded space, with the 1st and 2nd Guards Tank Armies ready to exploit through any breaches and encircle Berlin. For the breakthrough sectors, he arranged for barrages by more than 400 tubes of artillery per mile, and the Red Army Air Force added nearly 4,000 planes. To complete the destruction of the Wehrmacht's Oder River position, Konev would attack a day later in the south, while Rokossovsky's attack in the north would follow four days later (his front had just overrun Pomerania). Holding the bridgehead stood Busse's 9. Armee with a dozen divisions of the CI, LVI Panzer-Korps and XI SS Panzer-Korps under command: seven divisons on the front line, three as tactical reserves and two farther back. Many of them had been thrown together from scraps of army training school cadres, shells of demolished Volks-Grenadier divisions and other formations fighting together for the first time. The 9. Armee possessed 512 AFVs, 344 guns and a like number of flak pieces, equal to the number of weapons Zhukov employed in a single mile of the front. To their benefit, they had flooded the Oder lowlands and built extensive fieldwork buttresses with flak taken from Berlin.

After wide-ranging air and ground reconnaissance, Zhukov attacked early in the morning of 16 April. He illuminated the battlefield with 143 searchlights no longer needed for Moscow's air defences, confusing both defenders and attackers. The Germans had withdrawn from their forward-most positions, so the Red artillery barrage largely fell on empty ground. The 8th Guards Army made minimal progress over the Haupt Canal while the 5th Shock and 69th Armies barely moved. Zhukov made an uncharacteristic beginner's mistake by committing the armour of the two tank armies, only adding to the Soviets' uncertainty in the jumbled bridgehead. Wehrmacht defences held fast against the two shock armies around Letschin and against Chuikov's men below Seelow, and the Kurland Panzer-Division counterattack threw back the 69th Army. Red Army troops fought through one or two German lines only to be stopped at the third. Zhukov ordered the attacks to continue into the night. He urged his men forward the next morning, but the numerous fortified strongpoints continued to resist, augmented by marshy terrain and watercourses that very much favoured the defenders. By evening of 17 April, the 8th Guards had fought part way into Seelow and were working their way around either side of the town, but Zhukov had the sad duty of reporting his slow progress to Stalin. The marshal smelled a rat: he believed that the dictator favoured Konev, who was having a relatively easier time to the south.

Seelow finally fell to Chuikov's frontal assault on the morning of 18 April. To his immediate right the 5th Shock Army achieved a breakthrough south of Letschin. Again, the Germans' strongpoints held for a brief time and a few Luftwaffe bombers made an extremely rare appearance over the battlefield. Feeble counterattacks by the much weakened Panzer-Grenadier-Division Kurmark and Panzer-Division Müncheberg, understrength ad hoc outfits to begin with, battered the attackers, who were dangerously massed in the limited space, but could not reverse the overall flow of the battle. The 9. Armee could not take much more punishment, and soon the Germans were falling back to their fourth line of defence guarding Berlin. On the operational level, developments were becoming much worse than the tactical: Konev's advances to the south endangered Busse's entire position. The 1st Belorussian Front finally shattered the Wehrmacht lines on the 19th. Busse and the XI SS Panzer-Korps plus other formations slid south toward Frankfurt and CI Armee-Korps drifted to the north-west. The LVI Panzer-Korps, left without any flank support, fell back on Berlin. The road was now open for Zhukov.

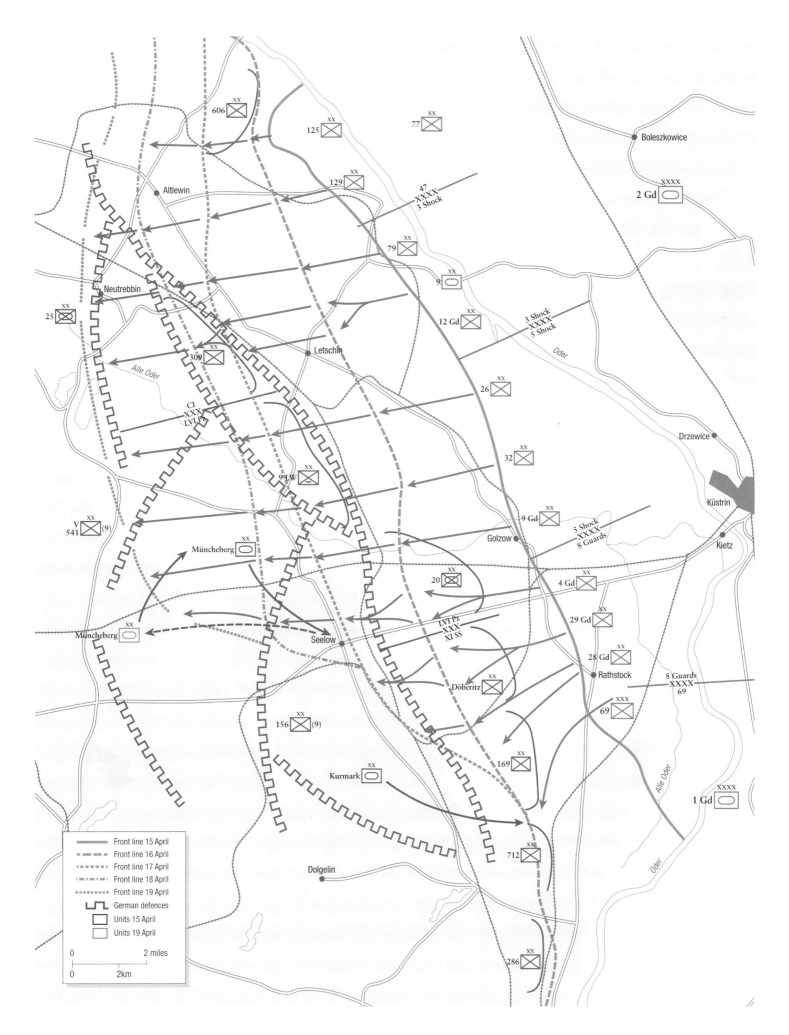

606
125
77
Boleszkowice
Altlewin
129
47
XXXX
3 Shock
2 Gd
79
9
Neutrebbin
25
12 Gd
3 Shock
XXXX
5 Shock
309
Letschin
Oder
Alle Oder
CI
XXX
LVI Pz
26
Drzewice
32
9 IW
Küstrin
V
541 (9)
9 Gd
5 Shock
XXXX
8 Guards
Müncheberg
Golzow
Kietz
20
4 Gd
Müncheberg
LVI Pz
XXX
XI SS
29 Gd
Seelow
28 Gd
Döberitz
Rathstock
8 Guards
XXXX
69
69
156 (9)
169
Kurmark
1 Gd
Dolgelin
712

Front line 15 April
Front line 16 April
Front line 17 April
Front line 18 April
Front line 19 April
German defences
Units 15 April
Units 19 April

0   2 miles
0   2km

286

247

MAP 120: THE DEEP ENCIRCLEMENT OF BERLIN 18–25 APRIL, 1945

No responsible historian would accuse Zhukov of taking the German defences of Berlin lightly, although German resistance on the Seelow Heights did surprise him. The 1st Belorussian Front's pre-assault plans estimated one day to get past it, but in reality it took almost four. While he struggled mightily inside the Küstrin bridgehead, to the south Konev launched another assault from his small lodgement over the Neisse River between Forst and Muskau. The 1st Ukrainian Front consisted of the 13th and 52nd Armies, 3rd and 5th Guards Armies and 3rd and 4th Guards Tank Armies plus other formations, all supported by 2,100 aircraft. Zhukov's straightforward mission, to drive on Berlin, was comparatively simpler than Konev's, which was to drive on the middle Elbe, link up with the Americans, prevent Wehrmacht forces from escaping into Bohemia and, if necessary, assist 1st Belorussian Front conquer Berlin. Konev's main effort would angle to the north-west, while a secondary shot headed south-west for Dresden. Against him stood the 4. Panzer-Armee, now under General der Panzertruppen Fritz-Hubert Gräser and consisting of ten divisions of random provenance common in the German army of 1945. In addition to commanding his front, Zhukov served as the Stavka co-ordinator of the entire Berlin operation.

On 16 April, Konev's artillery preparation hit the Germans with more devastating effect than Zhukov's, with the additional benefit of not ploughing up the earth and limiting mobility World War I-style. Despite their toehold over the Neisse, in practical terms the 3rd and 5th Guards and 13th Armies had to conduct an opposed cross-river assault. They faced the expected fanatical Wehrmacht defence, but soon owned a bridgehead 6 miles deep. By evening, they had expanded it another 3 miles in depth and it had reached 17 miles in width. Konev moved his two tank armies to the left bank over combat bridges, ready to exploit through the penetration early the next day. He also gave 28th Army a warning: be prepared to head north against the south of Berlin. So far German counterattacks (21. Panzer-Division represented Gräser's sole mobile reserve) had little slowing effect on Konev. On the 17th, defensive strongpoints at Cottbus and Spremberg presented Konev's men with tough obstacles, ones that the fast-moving Soviets bypassed. Gräser then fell back on the Spree, getting there ahead of the Red Army, but the small river did not present much of a hindrance. The Stavka was keen to encircle Berlin, and, partially based on Zhukov's delays at Seelow, it instructed Konev to alert the 3rd and 4th Guards Tank Armies to be ready to turn sharply north toward Potsdam in order to cut off Hitler's capital for good. The tankers were to avoid time-consuming combat in towns or against organized defences. On 18 April, so the Red Army slogged forward in the face of the Wehrmacht's final hope of covering Berlin, Zhukov went as far as to tell Rokossovsky that if the Seelow battle continued to vex his troops, the 2nd Belorussian Front might have to take over and encircle the metropolis from the north.

On 19 April Zhukov finally overcame the 9. Armee, while Konev's men crossed the Spree; both marshals now had open shots to Berlin, devoid of any more natural barriers. Along the Baltic coast, Rokossovsky's troops entered the fray on the 20th, five field and one guards tank armies versus the 3. Panzer-Armee. This thrown-together collection of higher-numbered SS and Volks-Grenadier divisions, sailors without ships and other detritus of the once-proud Wehrmacht was commanded by General der Panzertruppen Hasso von Manteuffel. That day Hitler celebrated his birthday, a universe away from the party on the streets above his bunker that all Germany had thrown him just a dozen years earlier, only weeks after President von Hindenburg named him chancellor. Now two of three Red Army fronts were bearing down on him and his capital and his defences had been scattered: 3. Panzer-Armee was about to be pinned against the Baltic, most of 9. Armee and part of 4. Panzer-Armee were in the process of being encircled around Beeskau and Lübben, and the remainder of 4. Panzer-Armee was marginalized in central Saxony. On that day, the 3rd Shock Army was close enough to Berlin to begin lobbing artillery into it, and on the 21st troops of four other armies entered the city's outskirts. Hitler ordered counterattacks against the two fronts by 9. and 12. Armeen and the tragi-comic Armee-Abteilung Steiner (shown on the map as III Panzer-Korps). On 25 April Zhukov and Konev's spearheads met at Potsdam, isolating Berlin; Soviet and US troops met the same day at Torgau.

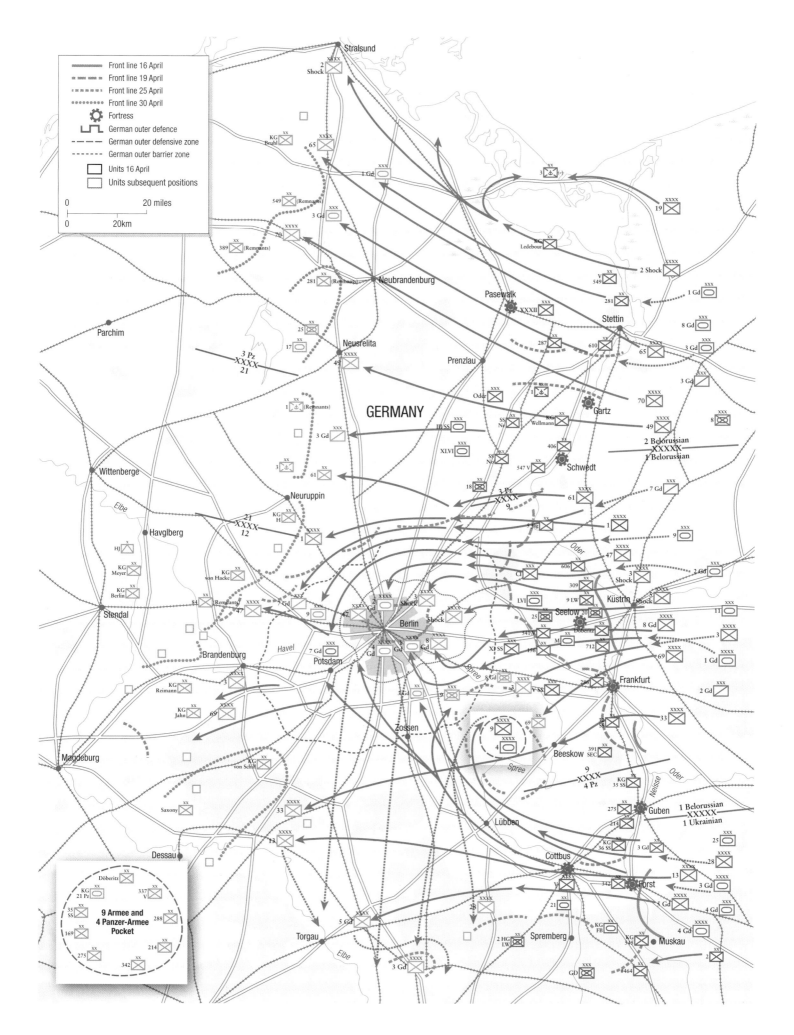

Legend

- Front line 16 April
- Front line 19 April
- Front line 25 April
- Front line 30 April
- ⚙ Fortress
- German outer defence
- German outer defensive zone
- German outer barrier zone
- ☐ Units 16 April
- ☐ Units subsequent positions

0 ——— 20 miles
0 ——— 20km

Stralsund

2
Shock

KG
Beuhl

65

1 Gd

549 (Remnants)

3 Gd

70

389 (Remnants)

Parchim

281 (Remnants)

Neubrandenburg

25

17

Neusrelita

49

3 Pz
XXXX
21

3 (-)

19

KG
Ledebour

V 2 Shock
549

281

1 Gd

8 Gd

3 Gd

Pasewalk

XXXII

Prenzlau

287

610

65

70

3 Gd

8

Stettin

Oder

1

III SS

XLVI

SS
Nd

SS
Nd

547 V

18

406

Gartz

Schwedt

49

2 Belorussian
XXXXX
1 Belorussian

GERMANY

Wittenberge

Elbe

Neuruppin

1 (Remnants)

3

61

3 Pz
XXXX
9

61

1

7 Gd

8

Havglberg

HJ

KG
Meyer

KG
Berlin

21
XXXX
12

KG
H

1

KG
von Hacke

84 (Remnants)

47

Oder

Ch

9

606

309

47

3
Shock

2 Gd

9

1

Küstrin

3
Shock

11

Stendal

9

47

2
Gd

Shock

3

Shock

Berlin

8
Gd

LVI

25

54 V

9 LW

Seelow

Döberitz

8 Gd

3

Brandenburg

Havel

7 Gd

Potsdam

4
Gd

XI SS

156

M

712

69

1 Gd

3

KG
Reimann

3 Gd

9

8 Gd

3

V SS

Frankfurt

2 Gd

Magdeburg

KG
Jahn

69

Zossen

9
4

69

Beeskow

391
SEC

33

2 Gd

KG
von Schill

Spree

9
XXXX
4 Pz

KG
35 SS

33

Saxony

Lübben

275

214

Guben

1 Belorussian
XXXXX
1 Ukrainian

25

Dessau

13

Cottbus

KG
36 SS

3 Gd

28

4464

Torgau

Elbe

5 Gd

3 Gd

23

21

13

3 Gd

5 Gd

4 Gd

Spremberg

2 HG
LW

KG
FB

KG
345

4 Gd

Muskau

2

GD

4464

9 Armee and 4 Panzer-Armee Pocket (inset)

Döberitz

KG
21 Pz

337
V

35
SS

288

169

214

275

342

**9 Armee and
4 Panzer-Armee
Pocket**

MAP 121: THE BATTLE FOR GREATER BERLIN 21–26 APRIL, 1945

The Germans had divided Berlin into three defence zones. Farthest out was the Ring, a belt through the suburbs perhaps 65 miles in circumference. Inside of that was a 50-mile-long middle line that generally traced the city limits. The inner line followed the S-Bahn elevated train lines (not shown on map). Planners had intended for ten divisions to man the Ring and another eight to defend the middle set of defences. But the rapid collapse of the German army and the equally rapid Red Army advance (aided and abetted by Hitler's poor decisions, as discussed below) meant that only a small fraction of these forces were available when Zhukov began his siege. Further, German units actually on hand did not come from trained and cohesive army formations but from frequently irregular paramilitary Nazi Party organs. Security forces, especially the SS, zealously made sure that soldiers retreating into the city centre, individually or in small groups, turned around and returned to the fighting. They frequently summarily executed soldiers who would not obey or whom they deemed cowards.

Berlin was in mortal danger long before it was encircled. On 21 April, elements of Zhukov's 47th, 2nd Guards Tank, 3rd Shock, 5th Shock, 8th Guards and 1st Guards Tank Armies reached its northern and eastern outskirts as close as Weissensee and Marzhahn, less than 5 and 9 miles from the Brandenburg Gate respectively. In the north, Tegel fell as Red Army soldiers approached the Hohenzollern Canal and prepared to assault the heavily industrialized Siemensstadt. On the same day, to the south Konev's 4th Guards Tank Army captured Babelsberg, Germany's Hollywood, and his 3rd Guards Tank Army reached Teltow and began closing in on the Teltow Canal. To the west, 20 miles separated the 4th Guards Tank and 47th Army units driving on Potsdam. Deadly street-to-street fighting began immediately whenever Germans and Soviets encountered one another. Stalin, wanting to keep the competition between his two marshals alive, divided Berlin into sectors for each front to capture, with all the critical government buildings going to Zhukov.

On the 23rd, two events occurred that contributed immensely to shortening the upcoming battle. Firstly, Hitler ordered General der Artillerie Helmuth Weidling's LVI Panzer-Korps to fall back north-west, i.e. toward south-east Berlin, creating a gap between the city and the largest concentration of Wehrmacht troops close by, 9. and 4. Panzer-Armee to the south-east. Secondly, Zhukov sent his 3rd Army into exactly this void. That evening Zhukov's 8th Guards and 1st Guards Tank Armies linked up with Konev's 3rd Guards Tank at Bohnsdorf on the Spree, their numbers adding an additional guarantee of victory. Rifle corps pushed deeper into the city as the front commanders organized the final assault. For this cataclysm, the Red Army assembled 464,000 soldiers and 12,700 tubes of artillery plus 21,000 Katyushas and 15,000 AFVs. Two Red Army Air Force air armies dominated the skies over the city. That evening Hitler made Weidling overall commander of Berlin's defence; only 24 hours earlier, he had wanted the general executed for disobedience.

Red Army troops reached and crossed the S-Bahn line in numerous places. On 26 April, Hitler issued orders in vain to 9. and 12. Armeen (nearly 200,000 men, 2,000 guns and 300 AFVs) currently pocketed 40 miles from central Berlin near Beeskow to come and save him, but this was not 1941 or 1942 and Busse could accomplish little with these shadow formations. Other than tying down three of Zhukov's armies and two of Konev's, they would do little to influence the battle against the dozen Soviet armies surrounding the capital. Hitler ordered a final, futile rescue attack to the west, which gained 10–15 miles against the surprised Red Army troops – this time to rescue himself! The Führer's terminally loyal creatures, Keitel and Jodl, rushed officiously from one end of Berlin to the other, ensuring hapless subordinates carried out his instructions. Besides LVI Panzer-Korps, primarily in the city's south-east, all Hitler had for his personal defence was a disorganized, every-man-for-himself assortment of SS, *Volkssturm*, Hitler Youth, policemen and other misguided diehards. Generals like Manteuffel, who had seen both, said that 1945 was nothing like 1918. Outside the two pockets, Germans facing the Soviets broke and fled west in order to surrender to the Americans and British. World War II in Europe had only one more week of slaughter before the guns would fall silent; 26 April also marked the beginning of the Red Army's final assault on Berlin.

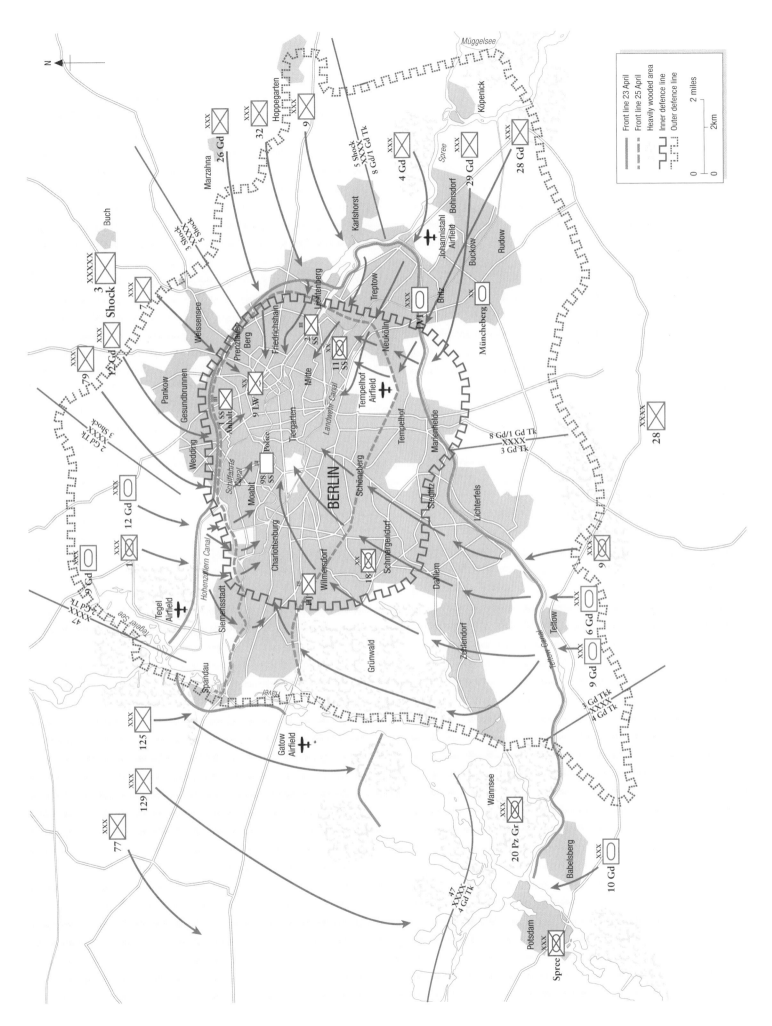

N

Müggelsee

Köpenick

Hoppegarten

Marzahna
26 Gd
XXX

XXX

32
XXX

9
XXX

Karlshorst

5 Shock
XXXX
8 Gd/1 Gd Tk

4 Gd
XXX

Spree

29 Gd
XXX

Bohnsdorf
Johannistahl
Airfield

28 Gd
XXX

Buckow

Rudow

Buch

3
XXXXX
3 Shock
XXX

Weissensee

3 Shock
3 Shock

Treptow

Blitz
O

Müncheberg

XX
O

79
XXX

12 Gd
XXX

Lichtenberg

Prenzlauer Berg

Friedrichshain

2
SS
III

XX
11 SS

Neukölln

Pankow

Gesundbrunnen

III
1 SS
Anhalt

XX
9 LW

Mitte

Tiergarten

Landwehr Canal

Tempelhof
Airfield

Tempelhof

Marienfelde

Steglitz

28
XXXX

Wedding

Schifffahrts Canal

Police

98
SS
III

BERLIN

Schöneberg

8 Gd/1 Gd Tk
XXXX
3 Gd Tk

Lichterfels

2 Gd Tk
XXXX
3 Shock

12 Gd
XXX
O

1 Gd
XXX

Moabit

Charlottenburg

Wilmersdorf

XX
18
III

Schmargendorf

Dahlem

9
XXX
O

6 Gd
XXX
O

Zehlendorf

Teltow Canal
Teltow

9 Gd
XXX
O

Hohenzollern Canal

Siemensstadt

Tegel
Airfield

Tegel See

47
XXXX
2 Gd Tk

Grünwald

3 Gd Tkk
XXXX
4 Gd Tk

125
XXX

Spandau

Havel

Gatow Airfield

129
XXX

Wannsee

20 Pz Gr
XXX

77
XXX

47
XXXX
4 Gd Tk

Babelsberg

10 Gd
XXX
O

Potsdam

Spree
XXX

Front line 23 April
Front line 25 April
Heavily wooded area
Inner defence line
Outer defence line

0   2 miles
0   2km

251

MAP 122: THE BATTLE FOR CENTRAL BERLIN 28 APRIL TO 8 MAY, 1945

In late April 1945, only one man on the planet could keep World War II in Europe raging: Adolf Hitler. Abandoned by Göring and Himmler but not Goebbels, 30 feet underground he went through the motions of running the country and leading the war. The most amazing fact, however, is that millions of ordinary German citizens and servicemen kept obeying orders and fighting and dying. Nearly 1.75 million Berliners still lived in the city throughout the battles described here.

The iron vice of Zhukov from the north and east and Konev from the south and west during the last week of the war had squeezed the Berlin garrison into an east–west strip of the inner city approximately 10 miles long and 2–3 miles wide. Panzer-Division Müncheberg and its 50 AFVs held the southern edge of the city against the amalgamated 8th Guards and 1st Guards Tank Armies until retreating to the Anhalter train station on 28 April.[162] 11. SS-Freiwilligen-Panzer-Grenadier-Division Nordland had already fortified the station and the surrounding neighbourhood, so the Münchebergers continued to the Potsdam station, closer to the chancellery and government quarter. Nearby General Weidling made his last report to the Führer, saying he had only enough ammunition for two more days' fighting. At that point his defences hinged on the Spree River in the north and the Landwehr Canal in the south.

The assault across the Landwehr Canal set for the morning of 28 April was delayed as Chuikov and Katukov untangled their troops. Not only was Zhukov concerned about possible fratricide if the two armies were not careful, but he wanted to reserve the symbolic centre of Berlin (Mitte) for the equally symbolic 'heroes of Stalingrad' of the 8th Guards Army. Across the Spree that afternoon, 3rd Shock Army men captured the old prison (and Goebbels' 'headquarters') in Moabitt, freeing 7,000 inmates including many Allied POWs. From its perch atop the Customs Building, Kuznetzov's 79th Rifle Corps could see the Reichstag. In Berlin's eastern quarters, Lieutenant General N. E. Berzarin's 5th Shock Army fought through building by building. Everywhere in Berlin, Soviet companies and battalions had to clear more than 300 city blocks of desperate Germans, also operating in small groups with tank-hunter teams. Meanwhile, Stalin re-drew the boundary between Zhukov and Konev, shifting it so that Konev's sector now stood west of the Tiergarten. His men were still involved in heavy fighting in Charlottenburg, Grünewald, Spandau and Potsdam, far from the glory.

General Major S. N. Perevertkin's 79th Rifle Corps received the coveted but dangerous mission of capturing the Königsplatz area dominated by the Reichstag building. This charred hulk, torched under suspicious circumstances during Hitler's very first days as chancellor, somehow represented the core of the Third Reich to the Soviets. Perevertkin's men would have to assault over the Spree at the bend of the river using the Moltke Bridge, which was barricaded, covered by pillboxes and wired for demolition. The Reichstag shell, Interior Ministry, Kroll Opera House and embassy quarter, defended by machine-gun nests, trenches and obstacles, represented their main targets. Perevertkin attempted to rush the bridge shortly after midnight, but was thrown back; by dawn it was cluttered with the destroyed wrecks of Soviet AFVs. Shortly after sunrise, the 150th and 171st rifle divisions managed to cross to the southern bank, but a Wehrmacht counterattack brought them to a standstill. This resistance limited Soviet gains during 29 April to the Interior Ministry ('Himmler's house') and immediate vicinity. Reinforced that night by the 207th Rifle Division, fighting on the 30th spread to the diplomatic quarter, opera house and Reichstag building. A couple of hundred yards away on the opposite side of the Brandenburg Gate, SS Brigadeführer Wilhelm Mohnke led hundreds of SS defending the Reich Chancellery and a now-dead Hitler. An hour before midnight, 150th Rifle Division troops placed the Red victory banner on the Reichstag.

Word of Hitler's 30 April suicide spread among the defenders. Soviet attacks had divided them into four groups, often numbering a few thousand men. On 1 and 2 May, fighting continued as surrender negotiations began between the two sides. Soviet armies pounded buildings at point blank range as surviving civilians huddled in cellars and fanatical defenders tried to fight back. The Germans denied Stalin the pleasure of surrendering on May Day, but Weidling met Chuikov early on the 2nd and Zhukov accepted the Berlin garrison's surrender at 0645 that morning.[163] Sporadic fighting against 1.5 million Germans still under arms died away over the next few days, officially halting on 8 May.

---

162 Tremendous losses sustained by both during Seelow Heights battles caused Zhukov expediently to combine the two armies.

163 Fittingly, the house near Tempelhof airfield where Weidling capitulated to Chuikov had been owned by Jews and confiscated by the Nazis after coming to power.

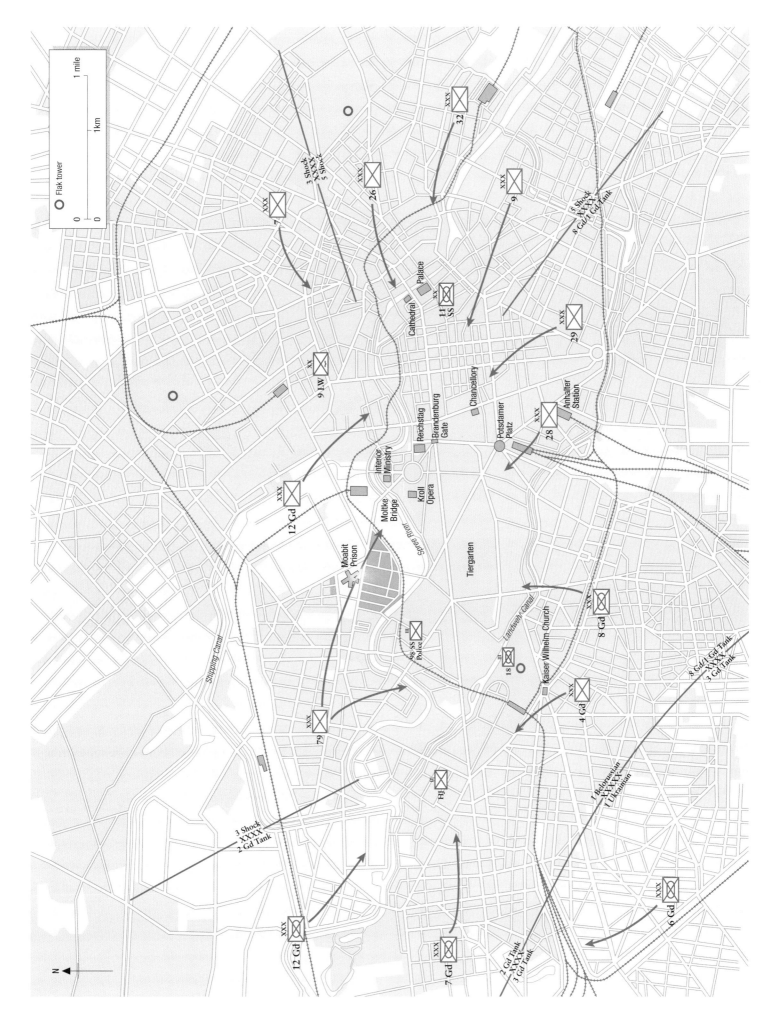

253

APPENDICES

APPENDIX 1: MAP 123, AIR OPERATIONS (I), *BARBAROSSA* TO *ZITADELLE*

Air operations during the Nazi-Soviet War got off to a spectacular start on *Barbarossatag*, 22 June, 1941. Luftwaffe planners targeted Soviet airfields, assembly areas, command and control centres, defensive positions, rail lines and other installations for attack by half of its functioning aircraft from *Barbarossa*'s first minutes. As is well known, they achieved complete surprise and caused destruction on a wide scale. Their aircrews, experienced after combat in Spain, Poland, France, Britain, the Balkans and elsewhere, enjoyed great success. They destroyed more than 2,000 Red Army Air Force (RAAF) machines that day, most of them on the ground. The carnage continued for a few days, but went downhill after 22 June. In an apocryphal statistic, despite the Luftwaffe's surprise and human and technological advantages, it lost more aircraft that day than in the worst day of the Battle of Britain (78 vs 61). Along with the United States, the Soviet Union had the world's largest aviation industry, and would quickly overwhelm the Germans.

Aerial operations fell into four main categories, generally based on airframe type: fighters (air defence, combat air patrol, pursuit), fighter-bomber (close air support or CAS, close interdiction,[164] strafing), bomber (usually level-flight, deep interdiction, 'strategic' bombing) and transport (men and supplies, but also delivering airborne forces by parachute); the last three are shown on maps 123 and 124. The Luftwaffe usually had an air fleet (Luftflotte) assigned to each army group, with subordinate air corps (*Fliegerkorps*) usually detailed to support specific missions, in attack or defence. It had one especially large and well-known air corps, VIII, which was an operational asset, usually controlled by Hitler himself and assigned to only the most critical tasks. The RAAF normally had one air army supporting a single 'front', with subordinate air divisions and air regiments underneath.

Barbarossa's ever-expanding, funnel-shaped area of operations dissipated the Luftwaffe's effectiveness as the campaign went on. The war of production also went the Soviets' way from the beginning; the Luftwaffe never had as many operational aircraft as it did in June 1941, while the Red Army Air Force grew constantly, aided by British and later American machines. Within weeks of the war's beginning, the Luftwaffe was a very infrequent participant or visitor over huge portions of the battlefield. German ground troops often shot at their own planes, since they so seldom saw one of their own and they assumed anything that flew must be the enemy. This situation became more pronounced and much worse as the war went on.

Strictly speaking, the Germans did not conduct many 'strategic' bombing campaigns, for a number of reasons. Most Soviet heavy industry had been moved far to the east; the Luftwaffe was over-committed to other missions; the range of German bombers, designed for central and western European distances, was inadequate; and Soviet air defences were formidable, exceeding anything seen over Britain. Likewise, transport missions during the war's early stages mainly consisted of ferrying supplies to far-flung spearheads. Later, the Luftwaffe had the mission of trying to resupply isolated pockets of Wehrmacht soldiers, the largest of these of course being Stalingrad. Therefore the Luftwaffe's primary task quickly became CAS – either by fighters, dive-bombers (Stukas) or bombers flying low-level attacks. In this sense, the air force became flying artillery for the army, and lost much of its independent reason for existence. Reflecting that, most of the Luftwaffe's missions on the adjacent map are CAS, as commanders attempted to apply greater violence to critical battles, or battles where panzer forces outpaced their army artillery.

The Red Army Air Force had much to learn during *Barbarossa* from fighter tactics to ground-air co-ordination of CAS. But even during its darkest, early days it went on the counterattack, flying thousands of sorties per day even by the end of June 1941. It made bombing raids against German cities in East Prussia, the capitals of Hitler's Axis allies and Romania's Ploesti oilfields. It attacked Luftwaffe airfields throughout the theatre. As part of the 1942 winter counteroffensives they made numerous airborne drops into the Heeresgruppe Mitte area. Like the Luftwaffe, the RAAF's main task consisted of supporting ground operations. The RAAF flew thousands of missions during the major battles around Smolensk, Kiev and Viazma–Bryansk, plus countless smaller battles and engagements. It contributed markedly to operations *Uranus* and *Little Saturn* around Stalingrad and to pre-emptive attacks against *Zitadelle*.

---

164 CAS attacks the enemy in contact with friendly troops, while interdiction attacks the enemy before it reaches the battlefield, often in convoys or on rail, farther to the rear.

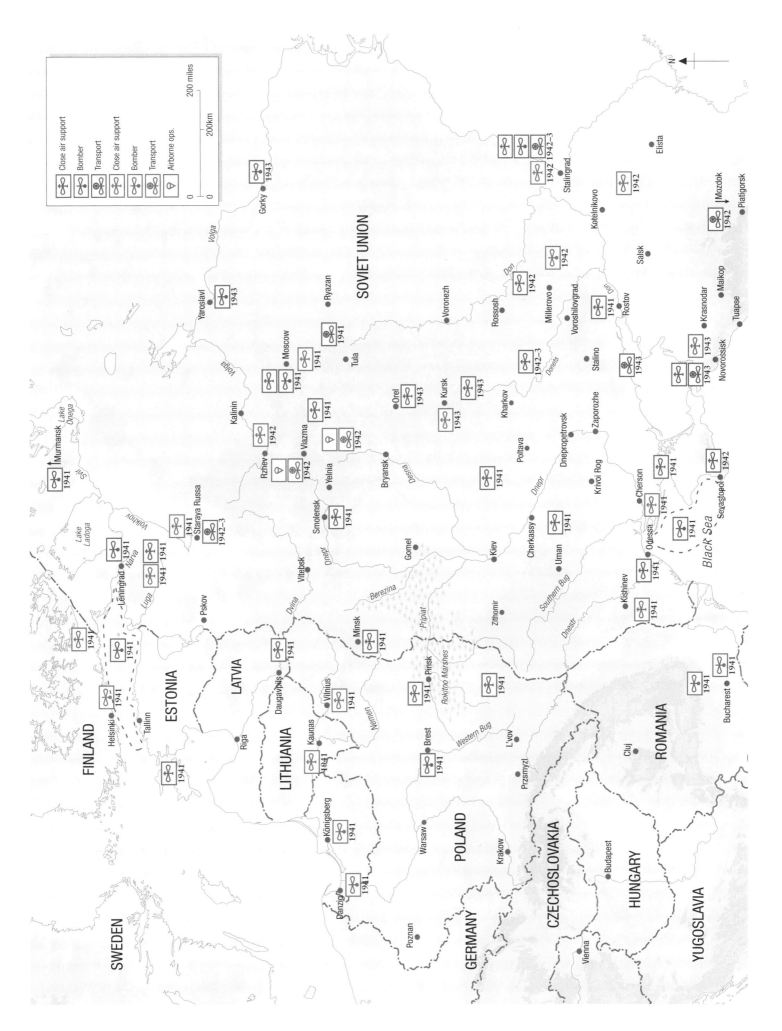

Close air support
Bomber
Transport
Close air support
Bomber
Transport
Airborne ops.

200 miles
200km

N

SWEDEN

FINLAND

Murmansk 1941

Lake Onega
Lake Ladoga

Svir
Volkhov
Narva
Luga

Leningrad 1941 1941
1941

Helsinki 1941
Tallinn

ESTONIA

Pskov

1941
1941

1941

LATVIA

Riga

Staraya Russa 1941
1942-3

Dvina

Kalinin

Yaroslavl 1943

Volga

Gorky 1943

Volga

Moscow 1941 1941 1941

Ryazan

Tula

SOVIET UNION

LITHUANIA

Daugavpils 1941

Vilnius 1941

Kaunas 1941

Königsberg 1941

Danzig 1941

Poznan

GERMANY

Warsaw

POLAND

Krakow

Przsmyzl

L'vov

CZECHOSLOVAKIA

Vienna

Budapest

HUNGARY

Cluj

ROMANIA

Bucharest 1941 1941

YUGOSLAVIA

Minsk 1941

Nemen

Brest 1941

Western Bug

Pinsk 1941

Rokitno Marshes

Pripiat

Berezina

1941

Gomel

Zithomir

Dnepr

Smolensk 1941

Yelnia 1941

Bryansk

Desna

Rzhev 1942 1942

Vyazma 1941 1942

Orel 1943

Kursk 1943
1943

Kharkov

Poltava

Kiev 1941

Cherkassy

Uman 1941

Southern Bug

Dnepropetrovsk

Zaporozhe

Krivoi Rog

Dnestr

Kishinev 1941

1941

Odessa 1941
1941

Kherson 1941

Dnepr

Voronezh

Rossosh 1942-3

Donets

Millerovo 1942-3

Stalino

Voroshilovgrad

1941 1943

Rostov

Don

Kotelnikovo

Stalingrad 1942 1942 1942-3
1942

Elista

Salsk

Mozdok
Piatigorsk 1942

Maikop

Krasnodar 1943

Tuapse

Novorossisk 1943 1943

Sevastopol 1942

Black Sea

APPENDIX 2: MAP 124, AIR OPERATIONS (II), *ZITADELLE* TO BERLIN

By mid-1943 the Luftwaffe had taken a severe beating, and this trend would continue for another year, by which time it almost ceased to be a major factor in the war. Continental commitments, such as Hitler's rush to save north Africa and the Western Allies' growing strategic bombing campaign over the Reich, further sapped strength from the east. Attempting to keep Stalingrad supplied during the winter of 1942–43 decimated its transport services. Quick Red Army advances had overrun airfields from the Caucasus foothills practically to the Dnepr River. Under Albert Speer German aircraft production had grown, but pressure to get as many units to the field as possible, for example, meant that the aviation industry could not afford the luxury of halting old model manufacture and re-tooling to newer jets. In addition, shrinking German oil reserves meant that new pilots arrived in front-line units with greatly diminished training hours, forfeiting the Luftwaffe's earlier qualitative advantage.[165] Meanwhile, the Soviet aviation industry had recovered from the disruptions of 1941–42 and was setting new production records, while pilot, ground crew and commander skills improved all the time.

Operation *Zitadelle* devastated the Luftwaffe's CAS reserves just as it had done to the panzer reserves. Whether flying over the tightly constricted battlefield or sitting on airstrips, the battle had been very costly. Reflecting the fighting on the ground, for the next nine months both sides concentrated their air forces in the region of the Ukraine. Again, fast advances across the open country frequently gobbled up airfields that did not displace westward in time. Wehrmacht ground troops would go days and weeks without seeing one of their own machines overhead. On the infrequent occasions when friendly aviators would arrive over the battlefield and chase off RAAF planes, up rose the cheer 'Sieg heil der Luftwaffe!' The war's momentum had clearly changed, and the Soviets grew in ability and boldness. The Dnepr proved to be only a temporary barrier, and during the winter of 1943–44 the Red Army pushed through the western Ukraine. The Luftwaffe's main contribution again was to fly supplies, at a terrible cost to itself, into forlorn pockets around Korsun and Kamenets–Podolsky. That following spring, preceding D-Day, the American and British air forces absolutely obliterated Luftwaffe forces defending the Reich and western Europe, requiring it to be reinforced from the east.

Operation *Bagration* in June caught the Luftwaffe flat-footed, just as it did the army; most of its forces were manning the Ukrainian front. Across the entire eastern theatre the RAAF outnumbered the Luftwaffe 13,400 to 2,700, and nearly half of these Soviet planes supported the massive offensive in the centre. In just a few days, the RAAF supporting *Bagration* flew around 28,000 sorties: the Germans had no way to counter this onslaught. Railway lines, key to moving Wehrmacht reserves, were paralysed and retreats turned into routs. German front-line units were either obliterated or neatly pocketed and bypassed. Soviet CAS kept pace with the ground forces by occupying abandoned German airfields, many of which had been occupied and improved upon for three years. *Bagration* was just the centrepiece of a season of huge Soviet offensives from Leningrad to the Crimea, and the RAAF supported them all. During the peak months, the Soviets claim to have flown over 150,000 sorties, while the Germans admit 11,000 losses. That autumn the Soviets took up operations through the Balkans, an area with almost no Luftwaffe presence. German air activity returned only when the fighting reached Transylvania and Hungary late in the year.

When 1945 arrived, the RAAF practically had the skies above the battlefields to itself. German industry and infrastructure had been bombed to rubble, Germany had lost its foreign resource supplies (principally oil) and idle factory workers now manned the Volkssturm. Wehrmacht ground forces could occasionally throw up antiaircraft fire from their dwindling ammunition supplies but very few Luftwaffe planes took to the air. As Soviet, American and British armies began to squeeze the last of Hitler's Reich, Allied aviators looked unopposed for targets of opportunity, almost out of sheer boredom.

---

165 This trend affected the entire German manpower pool, diminishing the quality of infantry, Panzer troops, U-boat crews, etc. as well.

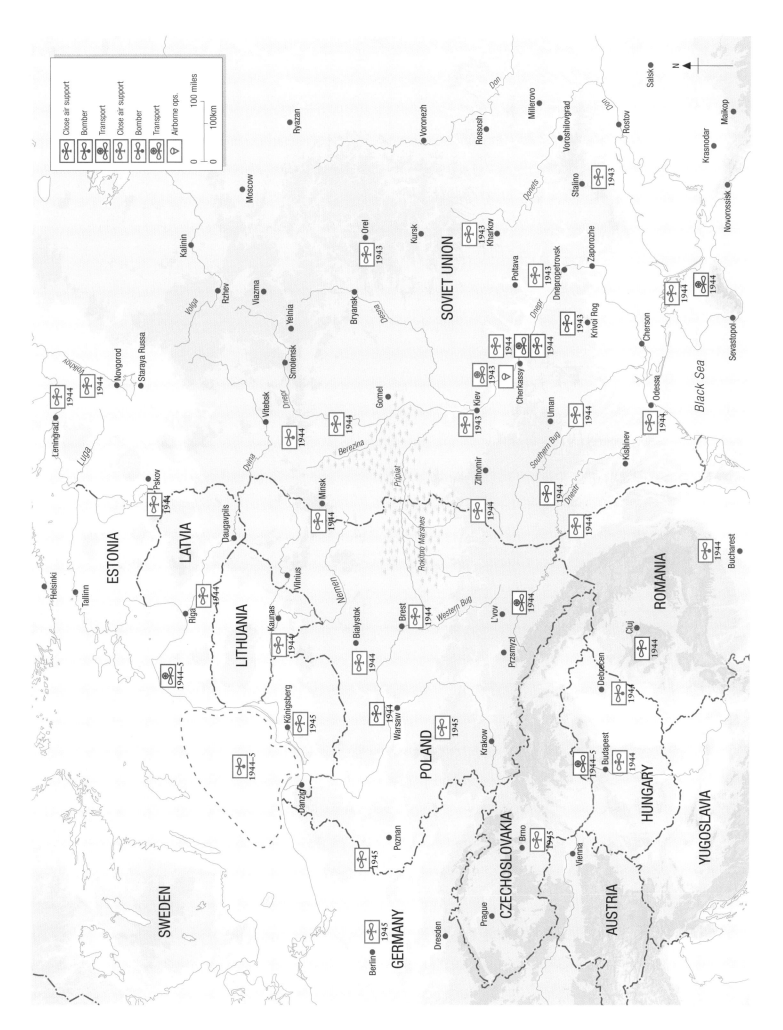

Salsk

N

Maikop

Krasnodar

Novorossisk

Sevastopol

Black Sea

Odessa

Kishinev

Bucharest

ROMANIA

Cluj

Debrecen

HUNGARY

Budapest

YUGOSLAVIA

Vienna

AUSTRIA

Brno

Prague

CZECHOSLOVAKIA

Krakow

Poznan

Danzig

Warsaw

POLAND

Dresden

Berlin

GERMANY

SWEDEN

Königsberg

Kaunas

LITHUANIA

Vilnius

Riga

LATVIA

ESTONIA

Tallinn

Helsinki

Daugavpils

Pskov

Leningrad

Novgorod

Staraya Russa

Volkhov

Luga

Dvina

Minsk

Brest

Bialystok

L'vov

Przsmyzl

Nemen

Western Bug

Rokitno Marshes

Pripiat

Berezina

Dnepr

Gomel

Vitebsk

Smolensk

Yelnia

Viazma

Rzhev

Kalinin

Moscow

Ryazan

Volga

Bryansk

Desna

Orel

Kursk

Voronezh

Don

Rossosh

Millerovo

Voroshilovgrad

Donets

Rostov

Don

SOVIET UNION

Kiev

Zhitomir

Cherkassy

Uman

Poltava

Kharkov

Dnepr

Dnepropetrovsk

Zaporozhe

Krivoi Rog

Stalino

Kherson

Southern Bug

Dnestr

Close air support
Bomber
Transport
Close air support
Bomber
Transport
Airborne ops.

100 miles
100km
0
0

257

APPENDIX 3: MAP 125, GERMAN OCCUPATION POLICIES (I) – POLITICAL AND RACIAL

Like every other war, Hitler's conflict with the USSR had a political basis, arguably a more important factor than its purely military aspects. The genesis of *Barbarossa* had many features for his domestic German audience: domination of Slavic and Jewish 'races', space to live and colonize and toppling the hated Bolshevism. *Barbarossa* (and later, the entire Nazi-Soviet War) represented the convergence of Nazi racism and expansionism; here domination, colonization and toppling focused increasingly on mass murder, ruthless exploitation and absolute destruction.

Hitler did not personally create every Nazi plan or procedure; he had legions of empowered subordinates 'working toward the Führer' in order to bring his notions of a German racial paradise to reality. These men were unrestrained by humane concepts, organizational checks and balances or detailed guidance from the Führer. Depending on their position in the Nazi hierarchy and therefore their access to resources (including slave labour and plunder), various leaders created individual plans, private empires and specialized infrastructures. Mirroring Hitler's own troubled mind, these configurations were competing, unco-ordinated and frequently duplicated or negated another plan or private empire.

Nazi leaders began developing occupation plans as soon as Hitler decided on *Barbarossa*. Himmler's *Generalplan Ost* (p. 9) provided an early foundation. One month into the campaign, Hitler created the Reich Ministries for the Occupied Eastern Territories under Alfred Rosenberg. Nazi Party participation in the occupation is the main distinction between World War II and World War I, when the army practically ran occupied areas as its own private bailiwick. The Germans divided occupied areas of the USSR into two Nazi- (i.e. 'civilian') controlled Reich commissariats, Ostland (Baltic States and Belarus) and Ukraine. The three Baltic states were uncommonly well managed. They planned two more, Moscow and Caucasus. Areas to the east of the commissariats remained under military control. Civilian or Nazi Party agencies included the German railways, post, interior ministry, Reich labour service and Organization *Todt*. The military maintained major forces in the commissariats, primarily to guard and maintain infrastructure (railway and telephone/telegraph lines, supply depots) and to combat partisans. While exploitation remained the primary purpose of the civilian occupation, the military wanted security. Every command echelon from army group to army to corps had its own rear area of responsibility. As the war went on, fighting partisans ('insurgents' in modern parlance) consumed ever-larger military elements, especially as it became obvious that the Germans would lose.

Nazi racial thinking was the key aspect of the Germans' occupation. Jews, communists – especially the hated commissars attached to military units – were usually summarily executed. As in the case of the massacre of Jews in the Babi Yar ravine outside Kiev in 1941, this could include tens of thousands of people murdered within a few days. In the immediate post-war period, the main perpetrators were assumed to be SS, while the army merely fought a clean war. At least since the 1980s, regular German servicemen have been revealed to have been full participants in the brutality and slaughter. Purpose-built execution organizations, *Einsatzgruppen*, were organized into four groups, A–D. While the Nazis' industrialized genocide at concentration camps like Auschwitz is well known, by far the majority of their victims died at the hands of a 'first person shooter', face to face.

Treatment of each other's POWs in captivity by both sides can charitably be described as passive neglect, in the worst case as savage, with large grey areas in between. Military hospitals full of wounded, abandoned by their own retreating troops and overrun by the enemy, commonly became slaughterhouses. *Barbarossa's* logistical arrangements for the Germans' own men were terrible, so it is no surprise that arrangements for Soviet POWs were much worse. Pre-war German plans had somewhat correctly estimated the number of Soviets they believed they would capture, but preparations were completely inadequate. With German logistics strained, in 1941 most Red Army POWs were confined in temporary camps near *Barbarossa* battlefields. Of approximately 3.7 million POWs captured during that campaign, only 1.1 million survived until February 1942; 2.5 million perished that winter, mainly to starvation, disease and climate. After *Barbarossa's* failure, and with the prospect of a long war of attrition, the Nazis viewed Soviet POWs as potential labour, so they sent hundreds of thousands to work in Germany. Of a total 5.7 million Soviet POWs taken throughout the entire war, perhaps 500,000 fled or were liberated and 1 million survived until 1945, so around 3.3 million died. The Soviets captured nearly 3.3 million Germans, of whom approximately 10 per cent died in captivity.

APPENDIX 4: MAP 126, GERMAN OCCUPATION – ECONOMIC

With its relatively small population and territory, plus limited mineral deposits – particularly strategic metals and petroleum – modern Germany has had to depend on foreign sources for vital materials, acquired via commerce or force. The economic resources of the USSR would give Hitler the self-sufficient state with which to compete against the USA and UK. No people or nation willingly works for a dominating conqueror, and Nazi ideas of their own superiority made conditions in occupied Europe even worse. For these and other reasons, occupied regions of the USSR never became the agricultural, mineral and industrial El Dorado that Nazi theorists anticipated and that Hitler's war machine needed to compete on the world stage.

Hitler knew that in 1918 the Ukraine had failed to fulfil its hoped-for role as the Central Powers' bread basket. However, Nazi agricultural experts assumed that with their expertise and the existing Soviet collective farm system, 7 million tons of grain could be shipped annually from the east to Germany. Nazi brutality, a surly workforce, poor administration, partisans, and other factors made this notion obsolete within six months; it did not work in peacetime for the communists and it would not work in wartime for the Nazis. In February 1942, the Germans dismantled the collectives and attempted to reinstate pre-Soviet village communes. Later they privatized eastern agriculture under new corporate trustees, which supervised over 3,000 large farms that were more in line with Nazi concepts of colonial plantations. The already stressed manpower problem in occupied areas was exacerbated in late 1942 when Hitler demanded transfer of able-bodied people (mostly men) to the Reich to work in industry, mining and agriculture there. A year later, German workforce worries became such that Nazi authorities considered making concessions to the peasants and appeasing the general population; this plan was vetoed at the highest levels. From 1941 to 1944 grain production amounted to 100–110 million hectares and other crops 15 million hectares, with priority going to the Wehrmacht and shipments to Germany. Livestock production was 15–20 million head of pigs and horses, 45 million head of cattle and 70 million head of goats and sheep. By 1943, after two years of failed policies, the Germans were retreating along most of the front. As they did so, they practised their own scorched-earth tactics and tried to take captured booty with them. Unfortunately for them, Soviet tank armies moved much faster than peasant carts, and the herds of cattle only jammed up the limited Dnepr bridgeheads needed to get the German military across.

Likewise, the Nazis' brutal and exploitative policies meant they accrued little benefit from the USSR's fabulous mineral wealth. The scorched-earth tactics of retreating Soviets ruined most mines, processing plants and oil wells, and the advancing Germans usually inherited a non-existent or unco-operative workforce. Partisan attacks and worker sabotage were common. Nevertheless, large German corporations followed close on the heels of the army in order to get their hands on what resources they could. Many hundreds of thousands of tons of iron ore, scrap iron and manganese were sent west to the Reich, plus thousands of tons of chromium ore. When the Germans occupied the coal-producing Donets Basin (Donbas, the area around Stalino) only 25 of 178 coal mines were usable due to few miners, wrecked machinery and no electricity. Within a year they extracted 2,500 tons daily. Following a massive effort, including using 60,000 Soviet POWs as miners, after another year the rate had increased to 10,000 tons mined per day. However by this time, late 1943, the advancing Red Army liberated the region. Frequently resource considerations drove military operations, notably in late 1943 when Hitler insisted on defending the dangerously exposed salient around Zaporozhe because of the Nikopol (manganese) and Krivoi Rog (iron ore) mines.

Soviet industrial capacity captured by the Germans never amounted to much. In the first place, the evacuation of almost 1,400 industrial enterprises from the western USSR to the Urals and beyond must rank as one of the Communist Party's great bright spots in 1941.[166] As Alexander Dallin wrote, the Germans found little more than rubble.[167] Major private German corporations – Continental Oil, I. G. Farben, Flick, Krupp, Mannesmann – exploited the situation for their gain. Numbers of small and medium-sized plants eventually operated in occupied areas, mainly producing items for immediate and local military use such as boots, uniforms and horse carts. Electricity was always in short supply; a year into the war, the Germans had managed to restore only 20 per cent of Soviet production, while energy transmission was unreliable.

166 Alexei Kosygin, who managed the evacuation effort, rose to become premier of the Soviet Union during the Brezhnev years.
167 Dallin, Alexander, *German Rule in Russia*, 1941–1945, p. 376.

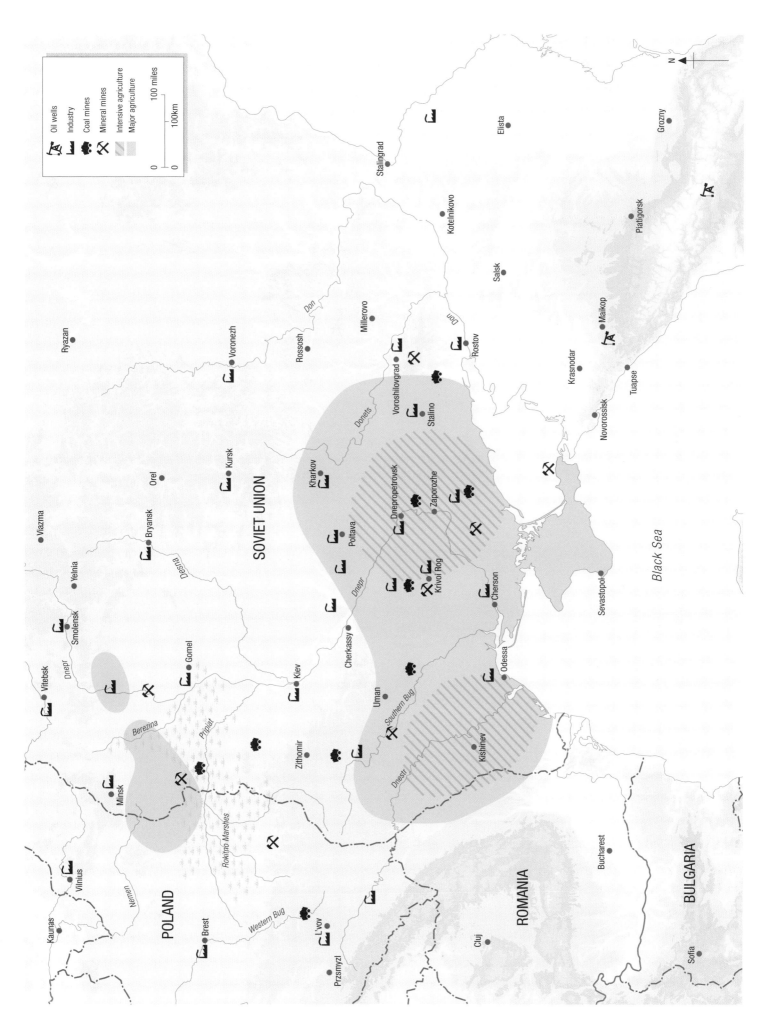

N

Oil wells
Industry
Coal mines
Mineral mines
Intensive agriculture
Major agriculture

0   100 miles
0   100km

POLAND

SOVIET UNION

ROMANIA

BULGARIA

Black Sea

Kaunas
Vilnius
Brest
Przsmyzl
L'vov
Minsk
Vitebsk
Nemen
Dnepr
Berezina
Pripiat
Rokitno Marshes
Western Bug
Zithomir
Kiev
Gomel
Smolensk
Yelnia
Viazma
Ryazan
Bryansk
Desna
Orel
Kursk
Voronezh
Rossosh
Don
Millerovo
Uman
Southern Bug
Dnestr
Kishinev
Cherkassy
Poltava
Kharkov
Dnepr
Donets
Dnepropetrovsk
Zaporozhe
Krivoi Rog
Cherson
Odessa
Stalino
Voroshilovgrad
Rostov
Don
Stalingrad
Kotelnikovo
Elista
Salsk
Millerovo
Maikop
Krasnodar
Novorossisk
Tuapse
Piatigorsk
Grozny
Sevastopol
Cluj
Bucharest
Sofia

261

APPENDIX 5: MAP 127, PARTISAN WARFARE (I), 1941–42

The Gestapo's pre-*Barbarossa* assessment that the Soviet people might support the invaders against the USSR's communist masters had some validity. During the campaign's first few weeks there was virtually no popular mass partisan movement, as most Soviet citizens took a wait-and-see attitude regarding the conquerors. They were not eager to fight for the hated communist regime, which, in any event, seemed doomed. Besides, *Barbarossa*'s speed precluded the organization of a state-led insurgency. Early on, ordinary citizens even helped the Wehrmacht by providing directions or intelligence on the Soviet military. Soon, however, the Germans' brutal policies turned the populace against them and a significant partisan war grew up in the areas behind the front lines.

Red Army soldiers who had evaded capture made up the first partisans, and their main concern was mere survival – food and weapons. Just a week into the war, the Communist Party Central Committee ordered party and government organs in occupied areas to initiate partisan operations. A week later, in his radio broadcast of 3 July, Stalin called for guerrillas to make conditions 'unbearable for the enemy and his accomplices. They must be hounded and annihilated at every step and their measures frustrated'. By-passed soldiers were soon joined by NKVD border guards and party and civilian volunteers. They lacked training, weapons and supplies, but not determination. A split occurred in partisan command and control, mainly between the NKVD, former military and party cadres that would bedevil the partisans for much of the first years. Local, ethno-national and religious differences caused further divisions and tensions. Only that December did Stalin begin to take effective steps to co-ordinate the efforts in the Germans' rear areas. For the war's first 18 months, partisans provided most of the USSR's success stories in face of near-continuous front-line disasters.

One month into *Barbarossa*, the Germans realized they would have no peace in their occupied territory, not even by 1914–17 standards. By late 1941, second-rate security divisions and mobilized police battalions numbering 110,000 men tried to secure 850,000 square miles of hostile landscape. In addition to their terror campaign, they began increasingly harsh countermeasures against partisans, now very broadly defined as almost anyone who resisted them. Harbouring, supporting and even 'tolerating' partisans became subject to individual and corporate punishment. Reprisals for dead Germans were meted out at a rate of 50:1 or even 100:1. By September there were an estimated 87,000 partisans, but four months later German rear security operations had decreased this number by 30,000.

The huge encirclement battles of *Barbarossa*'s later stages, especially around the forested areas between Minsk and Moscow, provided legions of cut-off units, escaped POWs and stragglers. These brought military discipline and experience. During the Soviet counteroffensives of the winter of 1941–42, attacking ground forces (notably cavalry) and even airborne brigades reinforced the partisans. With the Germans on their heels that winter, partisans became bolder and conducted large-scale operations. Partisans preferred the forested and marshy north to the more open Ukraine, while popular support for them fluctuated by region (but was minimal in the Baltic States).

On 30 May, 1942 Stalin created the Central Staff of the Partisan Movement under P. K. Ponomarenko. The arrangement looked organized, but in reality it perpetuated existing chaotic rivalries. Freedom and independent action were hallmarks of the partisan ethos. Continued German brutality combined with increased food requisitions and demands for forced labour requisitions aided the partisan cause. Their numbers rebounded to 70,000 in June and 93,000 in August. By this time the partisan movement was becoming a valuable military adjunct to the Red Army. Detachments ranging in size from tens to many hundreds was the basic building block. Four to seven detachments made up a brigade of 500–2,000 fighters. A complex, created in late 1942 and early 1943, consisted of several brigades. They had a military command structure, with commander, chief of staff, staff and commissar.

Small arms, sub-machine guns, hand grenades, etc. were the partisans' preferred weapons, so they could remain light and conduct ambushes and hit-and-run attacks. At this point in the war, approximately 5 per cent of partisans were women. They concentrated on assaulting isolated outposts, interdicting German infrastructure (especially railways) and destroying crops and livestock. By the end of 1942, they began to experiment with Saburov raids by which thousands of partisans covered hundreds of miles in the enemy rear. These raids elicited a large German response, including the employment of half a million Soviet POWs in anti-partisan duties, a technique that also exploited ethno-national differences.

N

FINLAND

Helsinki

Lake
Ladoga

Svir

Leningrad

Narva

Tallinn

Luga

Volkhov

ESTONIA

Volga

Yaroslavl

Pskov

Staraya Russa

LATVIA

Kalinin

Riga

Rzhev

Volga

Moscow

Daugavpils

LITHUANIA

Dvina

Viazma

Ryazan

Kaunas

Vitebsk

Königsberg

Vilnius

Dnepr

Smolensk

Yelnia

EAST
PRUSSIA

Minsk

Nemen

Berezina

Bryansk

Orel

Warsaw

Brest

Pripiat

Gomel

Desna

Kursk

Voronezh

POLAND

Lublin

Rokitno Marshes

SOVIET UNION

Western Bug

Krakow

Przsmyzl

L'vov

Zithomir

Kiev

Cherkassy

Poltava

Kharkov

Don

Rossosh

Millerovo

CZECHOSLOVAKIA

Southern Bug

Uman

Dnestr

Dnepr

Dnepropetrovsk

Donets

Voroshilovgrad

Budapest

Krivoi Rog

Zaporozhe

Stalino

HUNGARY

Cluj

Kishinev

Don

Rostov

Cherson

ROMANIA

Odessa

Bucharest

Krasnodar

YUGOSLAVIA

Sevastopol

Novorossisk

Maikop

BULGARIA

Black Sea

Tuapse

Sofia

Partisan region
Polish resistance
Partisan base
Partisan unit
Partisan raid

0   100 miles
0   100km

APPENDIX 6: MAP 128, PARTISAN WARFARE (II), 1943–44

In 1943, partisan fortunes rose as the Germans' fell, and counter-insurgency measures had little effect. By February their numbers had increased to 120,000, then to nearly 140,000 in August and more than 180,000 in early 1944, with the largest group in Belorussia. The movement increasingly became 'all peoples' and included previously under-represented groups such as Jews and Crimean Tatars. Augmented by indigenous police forces of questionable quality and released POWs, German anti-partisan forces neared one-third of a million. Despite this sizeable force, they largely resorted to a passive defence of garrison towns, strongpoints and key communications routes.

Command and control problems between independently minded and unco-operative partisan bands limited their effectiveness. A prime example of this came in February 1943 in the Vitebsk region. Under a massive assault from Wehrmacht forces, commanders of two outfits could not agree on command relationships and failed to co-ordinate their actions. As the war turned against the Germans, heretofore sympathetic or ambiguous groups began to switch allegiance from the occupiers back to the Soviets. Soviet authorities became openly suspicious of their motives, and questioned their allegiance. With an eye toward the post-war world, many groups increasingly turned on each other, as in the case of Ukrainians and Soviets or Ukrainians and Polish elements.

German infrastructure continued to be a main partisan target, with fixed railways the most vulnerable. Rail lines, bridges, depots, junctions, and water cisterns plus signalling and switching equipment all came under attack. Along some forest routes the Germans cleared a 150-mile-wide swathe on either side of the rails in order to deny the partisans cover and concealment. Their most effective tactic was the massive sweep through partisan areas with thousands of soldiers with heavy weapons, many taken from front-line units. In the Orel sector, the Germans did just such a sweep in the weeks leading up to their *Zitadelle* offensive there. The partisans established large well-defended fortified regions, complete with barbed wire, minefields and guarded perimeters, just like regular military units.

That summer, with the mediocre results of the German attack, partisan units co-ordinated their operations with the advancing Red Army. Through September, more than 540 detachments made up of 96,000 fighters launched Operation *Rail War* (*rel'soraia voina*). That was followed by Operation *Concert* (*Konsert*), which lasted until December, involved 678 detachments and 120,000 partisans and destroyed more than 150,000 lengths of rail. Both concentrated on the Germans' central front, and although they fell short of Soviet expectations, had significant material effect on their rail transport. Also, with the Red Army on the advance, partisan efforts in the countryside switched from destroying crops and livestock (to deny them to the Germans) to saving them for use by the liberators. They helped secure crossing sites over the Dnepr, Desna and Pripiat rivers. Partisans provided intelligence on the Germans, interdicted supplies and reinforcements and even contributed directly in Red Army attacks.

By the winter of 1943–44 most Russian territory had been liberated, so the Soviets disbanded the Central Staff on 13 January. Partisan staffs of the individual republics, Belorussia and Ukraine, took over. That spring even larger organizations emerged, such as the 1st Ukrainian Partisan Division. As the Red Army advanced it absorbed partisan units into its own structure, some 93,000 fighters by mid-August. This did not always sit well with the semi-autonomous and regional or nationalistic insurgents. For their part, Soviet authorities began to scrutinize partisan units and individuals for doctrinal or political reliability. The NKVD and its subordinate SMERSH investigated the detachments and brigades for 'doubtful elements' and anti-Soviet activities during the war. This created distrust between the partisans and the central government and party organs that continued well after the war. This trend was most marked in the Ukraine, where fighting between Soviet forces and Ukrainian elements continued at least until October 1945. Nearly 90,000 Ukrainian 'bandits' (the same word the Germans used to describe them) were killed.

During the last months of 1944, partisans contributed to the liberation of Belorussia and the Ukraine. They actively participated in Operation *Bagration*, fulfilling their usual roles of intelligence gathering and interdiction. They also launched long-range raids deep into the Germans' rear areas, often far into Poland, for example. Here they alternately co-operated with or fought against indigenous partisan groups. They came into conflict with non-communist, frequently Jewish, resistance movements that took on a doctrinal and internecine nature. Therefore partisans became just another weapon in Stalin's arsenal to consolidate Soviet communist power in post-war eastern and central Europe.

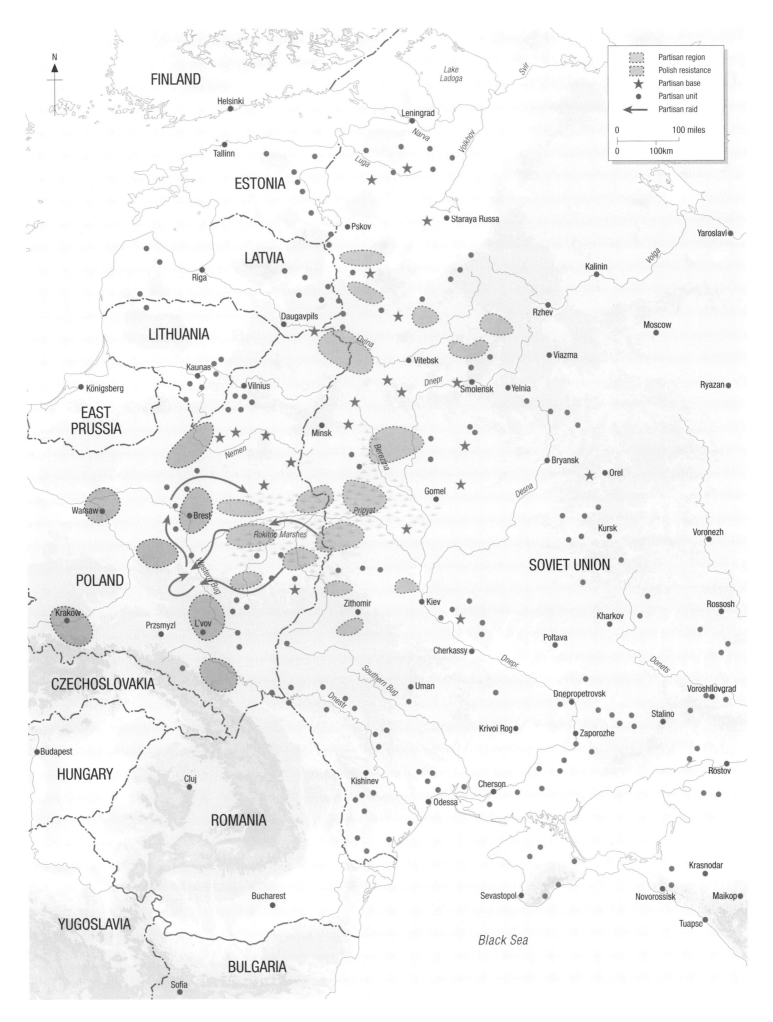

N

FINLAND

Helsinki

Leningrad

Tallinn

Narva

ESTONIA

Luga

Staraya Russa

Pskov

Lake Ladoga

Svir

Volkhov

Yaroslavl

LATVIA

Kalinin

Volga

Riga

Rzhev

Moscow

Dvina

Daugavpils

Vitebsk

Viazma

LITHUANIA

Ryazan

Kaunas

Dnepr

Smolensk

Yelnia

Königsberg

Vilnius

EAST
PRUSSIA

Nemen

Minsk

Berezina

Bryansk

Orel

Gomel

Desna

Warsaw

Brest

Pripyat

Kursk

Voronezh

Rokitno Marshes

SOVIET UNION

POLAND

Western Bug

Kiev

Zithomir

Kharkov

Rossosh

Kraków

L'vov

Przsmyzl

Poltava

Cherkassy

Dnepr

Donets

Voroshilovgrad

CZECHOSLOVAKIA

Stalino

Uman

Southern Bug

Dnepropetrovsk

Budapest

Dnestr

Krivoi Rog

Zaporozhe

HUNGARY

Cluj

Rostov

Kishinev

Cherson

ROMANIA

Odessa

Krasnodar

Bucharest

Sevastopol

Novorossisk

Maikop

YUGOSLAVIA

Tuapsc

Black Sea

BULGARIA

Sofia

	Partisan region
	Polish resistance
★	Partisan base
●	Partisan unit
←	Partisan raid

0 — 100 miles
0 — 100km

265

APPENDIX 7: BATTLE AND OPERATION MATRIX

Military practitioners and historians refer to three levels of warfare: strategic (wars), operational (campaigns) and tactical (battles and engagements). This provides a useful framework for conceptualizing and studying, although respective systems do not always correspond exactly across national lines. The accompanying matrix provides a side-by-side comparison of how postwar Germans (www.bundesarchiv.de/findbuecher/ma/...) and Soviets (Glantz, *When Titans Clashed*, Table B) have organized their 1941–45 war.

NORTH

GERMAN		SOVIET	
1941			
Border fight in Lithuania	22–29 Jun	Baltic Defence	22 Jun–7 Sep
Advance over the Dvina	27 Jun–12 Jul	Leningrad Defence	10 Jul–30 Sep
Conquest of Estonia	7 Jul–5 Sep	Tikhvin Defence	16 Oct–18 Nov
Advance into Russia, operations south of Lake Il'men	8 Jul–23 Sep	Tikhvin Offensive	10 Nov–31 Dec
Operations against Leningrad	13 Jul–25 Sep		
Conquest of Baltic Islands	8 Sep–15 Oct		
Defensive battles around Leningrad and Oranienbaum	26 Sep–30 Jun '42		
Defence between lakes Ladoga and Il'men	26 Sep–15 Oct		
Battles for Valdai Hills	26 Sep–7 Jan 42		
Advance to Tikhvin and Volkhov	16 Oct–7 Dec		
Defence of Tikhvin and Volkhov	8–27 Dec		
1942			
Defence south of Lake Il'men	8 Jan–30 Jun	Lyuban Offensive	7 Jan–30 Apr
Static warfare	1 Jul–31 Dec	Demyansk Offensive	7 Jan–20 May
		Lyuban Relief	13 May-10 Jul
		Siniavinsk Offensive	19 Aug–10 Oct
		Leningrad Offensive	Dec–Jan 43
1943			
Static warfare	1 Jan–31 Dec	Mga Offensive	22 Jul–22 Aug
1944			
Static warfare	1–13 Jan	Leningrad-Novgorod Offensive	14 Jan–1 Apr
Defence of northen Russia and Baltic States	14 Jan–23 Apr	Rezekne-Dvinsk Offensive	10–27 Jul
Static warfare	24 Apr–12 Jul	Pskov–Ostrov Offensive	11–31 Jul
Defence and retreat through Baltic States	13 Jul–4 Oct	Madona (Latvia) Offensive	1–28 Aug
Battles of Riga and Mitau (Jelgava)	5–26 Oct	Tartu Offensive	10 Aug–6 Sep
Kurland battles	27 Oct–31 Mar '45	Baltic Offensive	14 Sep–20 Oct
1945			
Static warfare in Kurland	1 Apr–10 May		

FINLAND–POLAR

GERMAN		SOVIET	
1941			
Attack to Liza River	29 Jun–5 Jul	Northern Defence	29 Jun–10 Oct
Battles around Salla, Nurmi, Uhtua	29 Jun–15 Sep		
Karelian Offensive	10 Jul–5 Dec		

Lappland Defence	16 Sep–14 Sep 44		
Karelian Defence	6 Dec–9 Jun 44		
1942			
Lappland Defence	1 Jan–31 Dec		
Karelian Defence	1 Jan–31 Dec		
1943			
Lappland Defence	1 Jan–31 Dec		
Karelian Defence	1 Jan–31 Dec		
1944			
Lappland Defence	1 Jan–14 Sep	Vyborg-Petrozavodsk Offensive	10–27 Jul
Karelian Defence	1 Jan–9 Jun	Petsamo–Kirkenes Offensive	7–29 Oct
Evacuation of northern Finland	15 Sep–30 Oct		
Defence of northern Norway	1 Sept–17 Dec		

CENTRE

GERMAN		SOVIET	
1941			
Battles of Bialystok and Minsk	22 Jun–10 Jul	Defence in Belorussia	22 Jun–7 Sep
Battle of the Dvina and Dnepr Rivers	2–15 Jul	Battle of Smolensk	10 Jul–10 Sep
Battle of Smolensk	8–31 Jul	Yelnia Offensive	30 Aug–8 Sep
Advance to and battles of Mogilev	12–28 Jul	Moscow Defensive	30 Sep–5 Dec
Battle of Roslavl	1–9 Aug	Moscow Offensive	5 Dec–7 Jan '42
Defense of Yelnia & Smolensk	10 Aug–1 Oct		
Defensive battles along Berezina and Dnepr Rivers	28 Jul–11 Aug		
Pursuit and battles of Gomel & Chernigov	12 Aug–8 Sep		
Battle of Kiev	21 Aug–27 Sep		
Battles of Viazma & Bryansk	2–13 Oct		
Advance to Moscow	14 Oct–3 Dec		
Advance toward Orel	21 Oct–18 Nov		
Defence of Kalinin	18 Nov–14 Dec		
Defence before Moscow	4 Dec–18 Apr '42		
Defence around Yelez and Kursk	5 Dec–4 Feb '42		
Defence around Tula and east of Orel	6 Dec–18 Apr '42		
1942			
Static warfare	19 Apr–4 Jul 43	Rzhev–Viazma Offensive	8 Jan–20 Apr
Eastern Offensive (Bläu)	28 Jun–18 Nov	Toropets–Kholm Offensive	9 Jan–6 Feb
Winter defensive battles	19 Nov-13 Feb 43	Rzhev–Sychevka Offensive	30 Jul–23 Aug
		Rzhev–Sychevka Offensive (Mars)	24 Nov–16 Dec
		Velikie-Luki Offensive	24 Nov–20 Jan '43
1943			
Static warfare	1 Jan–4 Jul	Rzhev–Viazma Offensive	Feb–31 Mar
Defensive operations, incl. Zitadelle	1 Jan–31 Dec	Kursk Defensive	May–23 Jul
Defensive battles in Belorussia, Rokitno Marshes	Dec–19 Apr 44	Orel Offensive	12 Jul–18 Aug
		Smolensk Offensive	7 Aug–2 Oct
		Bryansk Offensive	1 Sep–3 Oct
		Nevel–Gorodok Offensive	6 Oct–31 Dec
		Gomel–Rechitsa Offensive	10–30 Nov

1944			
Defensive battles in Belorussia & Rokitno Marshes	1 Jan–19 Apr	Kalinkovichi–Mozyr Offensive	8–30 Jan
Static warfare	20 Apr–21 Jun	Rogatchev–Zhlobin Offensive	21–26 Feb
Defence and retreat	22 Jun–10 Aug	Belorussian Offensive (Bagration)	22 Jun–29 Aug
Defence between Neman River and East Prussian border	13 Jul–10 Aug	Goldap Offensive	16–30 Oct
Battles along Vistula River and around Warsaw	27 Jul–16 Sep		
Static warfare on East Prussian border	10 Aug–15 Oct		
Attacks against Siauliai-Tukums	16–28 Aug		
Defence of Lithuania and Kurland	19 Aug-10 Oct		
Defence of Vistula River and Varka bridgehead	17 Sep–12 Jan 45		
Static warfare on Narev River and Pultsk bridgehead	17 Sep–13 Jan 45		
Battles for East Prussia, incl. Gumbinnen, Goldap	16 Oct–2 Nov		
Defence of East Prussia, incl. Memel	3 Nov–21 Jan 45		
1945			
Retreat between Vistula and Oder Rivers	13–31 Jan	Vistula–Oder Offensive	12 Jan–3 Feb
Retreat through East Prussia	13 Jan–8 Feb	East Prussia Offensive	13 Jan–25 Apr
Static warfare along Oder River	1 Feb–16 Apr	Lower Silesian Offensive	8–24 Feb
Defensive battles in East Prussia, incl. Königsberg & Samland	9 Feb–8 May	East Pomerania Offensive	10 Feb–4 Apr
Defence of Pomerania	22 Feb–23 Apr	Upper Silesian Offensive	
Battle for the Oder River, retreat towards Berlin	17 Apr–1 May	Berlin Offensive	16 Apr–8 May
Retreat through Western Pomerania & Mecklenburg	24 Apr–8 May		

SOUTH

GERMAN		SOVIET	
1941			
Frontier battles of Galicia and Vohynia	22 Jun–12 Jul	Defence in Ukraine	22 Jun–6 Jul
		Defence in Moldavia	1–26 Jul
Breakthrough to Kiev & Dnepr River	2–25 Jul	Kiev Defence	7 Jul–26 Sep
Liberation of Bessarabia	2–8 Jul	Odessa Defence	5 Aug–16 Oct
Penetration of Stalin Line	2–25 Jul	Donbas–Rostov Defence	29 Sep–16 Nov
Pursuit and attack over the Dnepr River, incl. Uman	25 Jul–5 Oct	Crimean Defence	18 Oct–16 Nov
Battle of Kiev	21 Aug–27 Sep	Rostov Offensive	17 Nov–2 Dec
Breakthrough to Perekop Isthmus	31 Aug–30 Sep	Sevastopol Defence	30 Oct–4 Jul '42
Battle of Sea of Azov	26 Sep–11 Oct	Kerch–Feodosia Offensive	25 Dec–2 Jan '42
Pursuit to the Donets River	1 Oct–21 Nov		
Battles for Crimea	18 Oct–16 Nov		
Battles on upper Donets and Don Rivers	26 Oct–29 Jun 42		
Defence of Donbas	22 Nov–21 Jul 42		
Retreat from Kerch Peninsula	28 Dec–18 Jan 42		
1942			
Defence of Donbas	18 Jan–7 Apr	Barvenkovo-Lozovaya Offensive	18–31 Jan
Reconquest of Kerch Peninsula	8–21 May	Kerch Defence	8-19 May
Spring battles around Kharkov	12 May–26 Jun	Kharkov Offensive	12–29 May
Barvenkovo Pocket	17–27 May	Voronezh Defence	28 Jun–24 Jul
Conquest of Sevatopol	2 Jun-4 Jul	Stalingrad Defence	17 Jul–18 Nov
Eastern Offensive (Bläu)	28 Jun–18 Nov	North Caucasus Defence	25 Jul–31 Dec
Pursuit to Kuban	27 Jul–13 Aug	Stalingrad Offensive	19 Nov–2 Feb 43

Conquest of Taman Peninsula, incl. Novorossisk	14 Aug–10 Sep		
Battles for western Caucasus Mountains	18 Aug–18 Nov		
Winter defensive battles, incl. Stalingrad	19 Nov–31 Mar '43		
Winter battles 1942-43	19 Nov–31 Mar '43		
Defence and retreat from Caucasus Mountains	19 Nov–11 Feb 43		
1943			
Defence of Kharkov area	9 Feb–4 Mar	North Caucasus Offensive	1 Jan–4 Feb
Defence of Kuban beachhead	12 Feb–14 Sep	Voronezh–Kharkov Offensive (Star)	13 Jan–3 Apr
Offensive in Kharkov area	5–31 Mar	Krasnodar Offensive (Gallup)	9 Feb–24 May
Positional warfare	1 Apr–3 Jul	Kharkov Defensive	Mid-Mar–3 Aug
Defensive battles on Mius River	4 Jul–2 Aug	Belgorod–Kharkov Offensive (Rumiantsev)	3–23 Aug
Defence and withdrawal to Dnepr	13 Jul–27 Sep	Donbas Offensive	13 Aug–22 Sep
Defence of Donbas	18 Aug–16 Sep	Chernigov–Poltava Offensive	26 Aug–30 Sep
Evacuation of Kuban beachhead	15 Sep–9 Oct	Novorossisk–Taman Offensive	10 Sep–9 Oct
Defence of southern Russia and withdrawal to Dnepr	17 Sep–3 Nov	Lower Dnepr Offensive	26 Sep–20 Dec
Defence of Dnepr River	28 Sep–31 Dec	Melitopol Offensive	26 Sep–5 Nov
Defence of Crimea	1 Nov–12 May '44	Zaporozhe Offensive	10–14 Oct
Defensive battles on lower Dnepr	4 Nov–31 Dec	Kerch–Eltigen Offensive	31 Oct–11 Dec
Defence of southern Ukraine, incl. west of Kiev	24 Dec–27 Apr '44	Kiev Offensive	mid-Sep–13 Nov
		Kiev Defensive	13 Nov–22 Dec
		Right Bank of Ukraine Offensive	24 Dec–17 Apr '44
		Zithomir–Berdichev Offensive	24 Dec–14 Jan '44
1944			
Defensive battles in southern Ukraine	1 Jan–12 May	Korosten–Shevchenkovsky Offensive	24 Jan–17 Feb
Defence of Crimea	1 Jan–12 May	Crimean Offensive	8 Apr–12 May
Evacuation of Sevastopol	17 Apr–12 May	L'vov–Sandomierz Offensive	13 Jul–29 Aug
Static warfare	13 May–19 Aug	Jiassy–Kishinev Offensive	20–19 Aug
Static warfare between Dniestr and Prut Rivers	7 Jun–20 Aug	East Carpathian Offensive	8 Sep–28 Oct
Battle of Brody, retreat to Carpathian Mountains, Bug and San Rivers	14–27 Jul	Belgrade Offensive	28 Sep–20 Oct
Defence of Galicia and San River	26 Jul–late Sep	Debrecen Offensive	6–28 Oct
Battles for Carpathian Mountain passes	28 Jul–early Oct	Budapest Offensive	29 Oct–13 Feb 45
Static warfare on Vistula River, incl. Baranov bridgehead	Early Aug–11 Jan '45		
Battle for Bessarabia	21–24 Aug		
Defence of Transylvania, retreat through Carpathian Mountains	25 Aug–27 Sep		
Battles for eastern Hungary	28 Sep–29 Oct		
Static warfare between Vistula and Carpathian Mountains	early Oct–14 Jan '45		
Static warfare in Slovakia	Mid-Oct–24 Dec		
Battles between Tisa (Thiess) and Danube Rivers	29 Oct–18 Dec		
Battles between Lake Balaton and Danube	19 Dec–5 Mar '45		
Battles for Slovakia, incl. Beskid Mountains	25 Dec–mid-Feb '45		
Battles on Gran River	25 Dec–early Apr '45		
1945			
Defence of Moravia	Mid-Feb–8 May	West Carpathian Offensive	12 Jan–18 Feb
Panzer battles in Hungarian plain	6–23 Mar	Balaton Defensive	6–15 Mar
Defence and retreat to eastern Alps	24 Mar–8 May	Moravia–Ostrava Offensive	10 Mar–5 May
		Vienna Offensive	16 Mar–15 Apr
		Bratislava–Brno Offensive	25 Mar–5 May
		Prague Offensive	6–11 May

BIBLIOGRAPHY

Allen, W. E. D. and Muratoff, Paul, *The Russian Campaigns of 1941–1943*, Penguin (1944)

Allen, W. E. D. and Muratoff, Paul, *The Russian Campaigns of 1944–45*, Penguin (1946)

Adair, Paul, *Hitler's Greatest Defeat*, Arms and Armour (1996)

Bergstrom, Christer, and Mikhailov, Andrey, *Black Cross, Red Star*, Pacifica Military History (2000)

Blakemore, Porter, 'Manstein in the Crimea', PhD. Dissertation, University of Georgia (1978)

Bock, Fedor von, *The War Diary*, Schiffer (1996)

Boog, Horst, et al., *Germany and the Second World War*, Vol. IV, *Attack on the Soviet Union*, Clarendon Press (1998)

Boog, Horst, et al., *Germany and the Second World War*, Vol. VI, *The Global War*, Oxford University (2001)

Barratt, Stephen, *Zithomir-Berdichev*, Helion (2012)

Beevor, Anthony, *Stalingrad*, Viking (1998)

Carell, Paul, *Hitler Moves East*, Ballantine (1966)

Carell, Paul, *Scorched Earth*, Ballantine (1971)

Chales de Beaulieu, Walter, *Der Vorstoss der Panzergruppe 4 auf Leningrad-1941*, Scharnhorst (1961)

Chales de Beaulieu, Walter, *Generaloberst Erich Hoepner*, Vowinckel (1969)

Chaney, Otto, *Zhukov's Memoirs*, University of Oklahoma (1971)

Chickering, Roger and Förster, Jürgen, eds., *Shadows of Total War*, German History Institute (2003)

Chuikov, Vasili, *The Fall of Berlin*, Ballantine (1969)

Clark, Alan, *Barbarossa*, William Morrow (1965)

Dallin, Alexander, *German Rule in Russia, 1941–1945*, Macmillan/St Martin's Press (1957)

Denschner, Gunther, 'Warsaw Rising' in *The Pan/Ballantine Illustrated History of World War II* (1972)

Dollinger, Hans, *The Decline and Fall of Nazi Germany and Imperial Japan*, Bonanza (1982)

Dunn, Walter, *Hitler's Nemesis*, Greenwood (1994)

Dunn, Walter, *Soviet Blitzkrieg, the Battle for White Russia, 1944*, Stackpole Books (2008)

Ellis, John, *Brute Force*, Viking (1990)

Erickson, John, and Dilks, David, eds., *Barbarossa*, Edinburgh University Press (1994)

Erickson, John, *The Road to Stalingrad*, Westview Press (1984)

Erickson, John, *The Road to Berlin*, Weidenfeld and Nicolson (1983)

Glantz, David, *Armageddon in Stalingrad*, University of Kansas (2009)

Glantz, David, *Barbarossa*, Tempus (2001)

Glantz, David, *Before Stalingrad*, Tempus (2003)

Glantz, David, *Colossus Reborn*, University of Kansas (2005)

Glantz, David, *From the Don to the Dnepr*, Frank Cass (1991)

Glantz, David, ed., *The Initial Period of the War on the East Front, 22 June–August 1941*, Frank Cass (1993)

Glantz, David, *Stumbling Colossus*, University of Kansas (1998)

Glantz, David, and House, Jonathan, *When Titans Clashed*, University of Kansas (1995)

Glantz, David, numerous self-published booklets and atlases

Hardesty, Von, *Red Phoenix Rising*, University Press of Kansas (2012)

Haupt, Werner, *Als die Rote Armee nach Deutschland kam*, Podzun (1981)

Haupt, Werner, *Heeresgruppe Mitte*, Schiffer (1997)

Haupt, Werner, *Heeresgruppe Nord*, Schiffer (1997)

Haupt, Werner, *Heeresgruppe Süd*, Schiffer (1998)

Haupt, Werner, *Das Ende in Osten*, Dörfler Verlag (2009)

Haupt, Werner, *Die Deutschen vor Moskau*, Podzun Verlag (1996)

Haupt, Werner, *Kiev*, Podzun Verlag (1964)

Haupt, Werner, *Krim, Stalingrad, Kaukasus*, Podzun Verlag (1977)

Haywood, Joel, *Stopped at Stalingrad*, University of Kansas (1998)

Hinze, Rolf, *Das Ostfront Drama*, Motorbuch Verlag (1987)

Hinze, Rolf, *Mit dem Mut der Verzweiflung*, Leonidas-Verlag (1993)

Hinze, Rolf, *Die Rückzugkämpfe in der Ukraine, 1943–44*, Rolf Hinze (1991)

Hinze, Rolf, *Der Zusammenbruch der Heeresgruppe Mitte im Osten, 1944*, Motorbuch Verlag (1980)

Hoth, Hermann, *Panzer Operationen*, Vowinkel (1956)

Jukes, Geoffrey, *Stalingrad: The Turning Point*, Ballantine History of WW II (1968)

Jukes, Geoffrey, *Kursk: The Clash of Armour*, Ballantine History of WW II (1969)

Kehrig, Manfred, *Stalingrad: Analyse und Dokumentation einer Schlacht*, Deutsche Verlags-Anstalt (1974)

Kirchubel, Robert, *Hitler's Panzer Armies on the Eastern Front*, Pen & Sword (2008)

Kirchubel, Robert, *Operation Barbarossa*, Osprey (2013)

Lehman, Rudolf, *Die Liebstandarte*, Vol III, Munin Verlag (1982)

Lüttichau, Charles von, unpublished manuscript, Ft McNair, Washington, DC, n.d.

Mackensen, Eberhard von, *Vom Bug zum Kaukasus*, Vowinkel (1967)

Magenheimer, Heinz, *Hitler's War*, Arms & Armour (1998)

Manstein, Erich von, *Lost Victories*, Presidio Press (1984)

Messe, Giovanni, *Der Krieg im Osten*, Thomas Verlag (1948)

Meyer, Georg, ed., *Generalfeldmarschall Wilhelm Ritter von Leeb*, Beitrage zur Militaer und Kriegsgeschichte (1976)

Müller, Rolf-Dieter, et al,, ed., *Germany and the Second World War*, Vol. V/2, *Organization and Mobilization in the German Sphere of Power, Wartime Administration, Economy, and Manpower Resources 1942–1944/5* , Oxford University (2003)

Muller, Richard, *German Air War in Russia*, Nautical and Aviation Publishers of America (1992)

Parotkin, I. V., *Into the Reich, History of the Second World War*, Part 78, Marshall Cavendish (1974)

Plocher, Hermann, *German Air Force versus Russia*, Arno Press (1968)

Raus, Erhard, *Panzer Operations*, DeCapo Press (2003)

Reinhardt, Klaus, *Moscow, The Turning Point*, Berg (1992)

Salisbury, Harrison, *The 900 Days: The Siege of Leningrad*, Harper & Row (1969)

Samsonov, Alexander, *Stalingrad: The Relief, History of the Second World War*, Part 44, Marshall Cavendish (1974)

Seaton, Albert, *The Russo-German War, 1941–45*, Arthur Barker (1971)

Seaton, Albert, *Stalin's War*, Combined Books (1998)

Showalter, Dennis, *Armor and Blood: The Battle of Kursk*, Random House (2013)

Shukman, Harold, ed., *Stalin's Generals*, Grove Press (1993)

Slepyan, Kenneth, *Stalin's Guerrillas*, University Press of Kansas (2006)

Spaeter, Helmuth, *The History of Panzer-Korps Grossdeutschland*, J. J. Fedorowicz (1995)

Stahel, David, *Kiev 1941*, Cambridge University (2012)

Stahel, David, *Operation Barbarossa and Hitler's Defeat in the East*, Cambridge University (2009)

Stahel, David, *Operation Typhoon*, Cambridge University (2012)

Sterrett, James, 'Southwest Front Operations, June–September 1941', MA Dissertation, University of Calgary (1994)

Streit, Christian, *Keine Kameraden,* Deutsche Verlags-Anstalt (1978)

Tooze, Adam, *The Wages of Destruction*, Viking (2007)

Topitsch, Ernst, *Stalin's War*, St Martin's (1985)

Ueberschär, Gerd, ed., *Unternehmen Barbarossa*, Schoeningh (1984)

Ungvsry, Krisztian, *The Siege of Budapest*, Yale University (2005)

Wagner, Ray (ed.), *The Soviet Air Force in World War II*, Doubleday (1973)

Weidinger, Otto, *Division Das Reich,* Vol III, Munin Verlag (1973)

Werth, Alexander, *Russia at War, 1941–45,* Pan Books (1964)

Willmott, H. P., *The Great Crusade*, Free Press (1989)

Zhukov, Georgi, *Marshal Zhukov's Greatest Battles,* Harper & Row (1969)

Zhukov, Georgi, 'The War Begins: The Battle of Moscow', in *Main Front*, Brassey's (1987)

Ziemke, Earl, and Bauer, Magda, *German Northern Theatre of Operations, 1940–45*, US Army (1959)

Ziemke, Earl, and Bauer, Magda, *Moscow to Stalingrad*, Military Heritage Press (1988)

Ziemke, Earl, *Stalingrad to Berlin,* Barnes & Noble (1996)

ABOUT THE AUTHOR

Robert Kirchubel is a retired US Army Armor Branch Lieutenant Colonel, and has had a keen lifelong interest in the Nazi-Soviet conflict in World War II. He teaches military history at Purdue University, where he is also a doctoral student, studying the planned *coups d'etat* of German Generals Erich Ludendorff, Kurt von Schleicher and Ludwig Beck. This, his definitive atlas of the battles and campaigns of the Nazi-Soviet War, is the product of several years' research and work.